E70
Title 2 vocs

4) 13

D1808952

Sri Lanka

The British Documents on
the End of Empire Project
gratefully acknowledges
the generous assistance of
the Leverhulme Trust.

The Project has
been undertaken
under the auspices
of the
British Academy.

BRITISH DOCUMENTS ON THE END OF EMPIRE

General Editor S R Ashton
Project Chairman A N Porter

Series B Volume 2

Sri Lanka

Editor
K M DE SILVA

Part I
THE SECOND WORLD WAR
AND THE SOULBURY COMMISSION
1939–1945

Published for the Institute of Commonwealth Studies
in the University of London

London : The Stationery Office

Applications for reproduction of government documents in this work should be addressed to the Copyright Officer, Public Record Office, Kew, Richmond, Surrey TW9 4DU

Applications for reproduction of any other part of this work should be addressed to the publisher:
The Stationery Office Ltd, Publications, St Crispins, Duke Street, Norwich NR3 1PD

The map on page xiv was originally published in the Sri Lanka volume of the World Bibliographical Series (Clio Press, 1987) and is reproduced by kind permission of ABC-Clio Ltd.

ISBN 0 11 290558 7

British Library Cataloguing in Publication Data
A CIP catalogue record for this book is available from the British Library

If you wish to receive future volumes from the British Documents on the End of Empire project, please write to The Stationery Office, Standing Order Department, PO Box 276, LONDON SW8 5DT, or telephone on 0171 873 8466, quoting classification reference number 040 30 017

Printed in the United Kingdom for the Stationery Office Ltd
Dd. 303014, 6/97, 2100, 29858

The Stationery Office

Published by The Stationery Office and available from:

The Publications Centre
(mail, telephone and fax orders only) PO Box 276, London SW8 5DT
General enquiries 0171 873 0011
Telephone orders 0171 873 9090
Fax orders 0171 873 8200

The Stationery Office Bookshops
49 High Holborn, London WC1V 6HB (counter and fax orders only) Fax 0171 831 1326
68–69 Bull Street, Birmingham, B4 6AD   0121 236 9696   Fax 0121 236 9699
33 Wine Street, Bristol BS1 2BQ   0117 9264306   Fax 0117 9294515
9–21 Princess Street, Manchester M60 8AS   0161 834 7201   Fax 0161 833 0634
16 Arthur Street, Belfast BT1 4GD   01232 238451   Fax 01232 235401
The Stationery Office Oriel Bookshop, The Friary, Cardiff CF1 4AA   01222 395548   Fax 01222 384347
71 Lothian Road, Edinburgh EH3 9AZ (counter service only)

Customers in Scotland may mail, telephone or fax their orders to:
Scottish Publications Sales, South Gyle Crescent, Edinburgh EH12 9EB
0131 479 3141   Fax 0131 479 3142

Accredited Agents
(see Yellow Pages)

and through good booksellers

Contents

Foreword

The main purpose of the British Documents on the End of Empire Project (BDEEP) is to publish documents from British official archives on the ending of colonial and associated rule and on the context in which this took place. In 1945, aside from the countries of present-day India, Pakistan, Bangladesh and Burma, Britain had over fifty formal dependencies; by the end of 1965 the total had been almost halved and by 1985 only a handful remained. The ending of Britain's position in these formal dependencies was paralleled by changes in relations with states in an informal empire. The end of empire in the period at least since 1945 involved a change also in the empire as something that was more than the sum of its parts and as such formed an integral part of Britain's domestic affairs and international relations. In publishing official British documents on the end of empire this project is, to a degree, the successor to the two earlier series of published documents concerning the end of British rule in India and Burma which were edited by Professors Mansergh and Tinker respectively.[1] The successful completion of *The transfer of power* and *The struggle for independence*, both of which were based on British records, emphasised the need for similar published collections of documents important to the history of the final stages of Britain's association with other dependencies in Africa, the Middle East, the Caribbean, South-East Asia and the Pacific. In their absence, scholars both from sovereign independent states which emerged from colonial rule, as well as from Britain itself, lack an important tool for understanding and teaching their respective histories. But BDEEP is also set in the much wider context of the efforts made by successive British governments to locate Britain's position in an international order. Here the empire, both in its formal and informal senses, is viewed as an instrument of the domestic, foreign and defence policies of successive British governments. The project is therefore concerned with the ending of colonial rule in individual territories as seen from the British side at one level, and the broader political, economic and strategic considerations involved in that at another.

BDEEP is a sequel, not only to the India and Burma series but also to the still earlier series of published Foreign Office documents which continues as Documents on British Policy Overseas (DBPO). The contemporary volumes in DBPO appear in two parallel series covering the years 1945 to 1955. In certain respects the documents published in the BDEEP volumes will complement those published in DBPO. On issues where there is, or is likely to be, direct overlap, BDEEP will not provide detailed coverage. The most notable examples concern the post-Second World War international settlements in the Far East and the Pacific, and the immediate events of the Suez crisis of 1956.

---

[1] Nicholas Mansergh *et al*, eds, *Constitutional relations between Britain and India: the transfer of power 1942–47*, 12 vols, (London, 1970–1983); Hugh Tinker, ed, *Constitutional relations between Britain and Burma: the struggle for independence 1944–1948*, 2 vols, (London, 1983–1984).

Despite the similarities, however, BDEEP differs in significant ways from its predecessors in terms both of presentation and content. The project is of greater magnitude than that undertaken by Professor Mansergh for India. Four major differences can be identified. First, the ending of colonial rule within a dependent empire took place over a much longer period of time, extending into the final years of the twentieth century, while having its roots in the Second World War and before. Secondly, the empire consisted of a large number of territories, varying in area, population, wealth and in many other ways, each with its own individual problems, but often with their futures linked to those of neighbouring territories and the growing complexity surrounding the colonial empire. Thirdly, while for India the documentary record for certain matters of high policy could be encapsulated within a relatively straightforward 'country' study, in the case of the colonial empire the documentary record is more diffuse because of the plethora of territories and their scattered location. Finally, the documents relating to the ending of colonial rule are not conveniently located within one leading department of state but rather are to be found in several of them. As the purpose of the project is to publish documents relating to the end of empire from the extensive range and quantity of official British records, private collections and other categories of non-official material are not regarded as principal documentary sources. In BDEEP, selections from non-official material will be used only in exceptional cases to fill gaps where they exist in the available official record.

In recognition of these differences, and also of the fact that the end of empire involves consideration of a range of issues which operated at a much wider level than that normally associated with the ending of colonial rule in a single country, BDEEP is structured in two main series along with a third support series. Series A represents the general volumes in which, for successive British governments, documents relating to the empire as a whole will be published. Series B represents the country or territory volumes and provides territorial studies of how, from a British government perspective, former colonies and dependencies achieved their independence, and countries which were part of an informal empire regained their autonomy. In addition to the two main documentary series, a third series – series C – will be published in the form of handbooks to the records of the former colonial empire which are deposited at the Public Record Office (PRO). The handbooks will be published in two volumes as an integral part of BDEEP and also as PRO guides to the records. They will enable scholars and others wishing to follow the record of the ending of colonial rule and empire to pursue their inquiries beyond the published record provided by the general studies in series A and the country studies in series B. Volume One of the handbooks, a revised and updated version of *The records of the Colonial and Dominions Offices* (by R B Pugh) which was first published in 1964, is entitled *Records of the Colonial Office, Dominions Office, Commonwealth Relations Office and Commonwealth Office*. It covers over two hundred years of activity down to 1968 when the Commonwealth Office merged with the Foreign Office to form the Foreign and Commonwealth Office. Volume Two, entitled *Cabinet, Foreign Office, Treasury and other records*, focuses more specifically on twentieth-century departmental records and also includes references to the records of inter-departmental committees, commissions of inquiry and international organisations. These two volumes have been prepared under the direction and supervision of Dr Anne Thurston, honorary research fellow at the Institute of Commonwealth Studies in the

University of London.

The criteria which have been used in selecting documents for inclusion in individual volumes will be explained in the introductions written by the specialist editors. These introductions are more substantial and contextual than those in previous series. Each volume will also list the PRO sources which have been searched. However, it may be helpful to outline the more general guiding principles which have been employed. BDEEP editors pursue several lines of inquiry. There is first the end of empire in a broad high policy sense, in which the empire is viewed in terms of Britain's position as a world power, and of the inter-relationship between what derives from this position and developments within the colonial dependencies. Here Britain's relations with the dependencies of the empire are set in the wider context of Britain's relations with the United States, with Europe, and with the Commonwealth and United Nations. The central themes are the political constraints, both domestic and international, to which British governments were subject, the economic requirements of the sterling area, the geopolitical and strategic questions associated with priorities in foreign policy and in defence planning, and the interaction between these various constraints and concerns and the imperatives imposed by developments in colonial territories. Secondly, there is investigation into colonial policy in its strict sense. Here the emphasis is on those areas which were specifically – but not exclusively – the concern of the leading department. In the period before the administrative amalgamations of the 1960s,[2] the leading department of the British government for most of the dependencies was the Colonial Office; for a minority it was either the Dominions Office and its successor, the Commonwealth Relations Office, or the Foreign Office. Colonial policy included questions of economic and social development, questions of governmental institutions and constitutional structures, and administrative questions concerning the future of the civil and public services and of the defence forces in a period of transition from European to indigenous control. Finally there is inquiry into the development of political and social forces within colonies, the response to these and the transfer of governmental authority and of legal sovereignty from Britain to its colonial dependencies as these processes were understood and interpreted by the British government. Here it should be emphasised that the purpose of BDEEP is not to document the history of colony politics or nationalist movements in any particular territory. Given the purpose of the project and the nature of much of the source material, the place of colony politics in BDEEP is conditioned by the extent to which an awareness of local political situations played an overt part in influencing major policy decisions made in Britain.

Although in varying degrees and from different perspectives, elements of these various lines of inquiry appear in both the general and the country series. The aim in both is to concentrate on the British record by selecting documents which illustrate those policy issues which were deemed important by ministers and officials at the time. General volumes do not normally treat in any detail of matters which will be fully documented in the country volumes, but some especially significant documents do appear in both series. The process of selection involves an inevitable degree of

---

[2] The Colonial Office merged with the Commonwealth Relations Office in 1966 to form the Commonwealth Office. The Commonwealth Office merged with the Foreign Office in 1968 to form the Foreign and Commonwealth Office.

sifting and subtraction. Issues which in retrospect appear to be of lesser significance
or to be ephemeral have been omitted. The main example concerns the extensive
quantity of material devoted to appointments and terms of service – salaries,
gradings, allowances, pension rights and compensation – within the colonial and
related services. It is equally important to stress certain negative aspects of the
official documentary record. Officials in London were sometimes not in a position to
address potentially significant issues because the information was not available.
Much in this respect depended on the extent of the documentation sent to London by
the different colonial administrations. Once the stage of internal self-government
had been reached, or where there was a dyarchy, the flow of detailed local
information to London began to diminish.

Selection policy has been influenced by one further factor, namely access to the
records at the PRO. Unlike the India and Burma series and DBPO, BDEEP is not an
official project. In practice this means that while editors have privileged access (in
the form of research facilities and requisitioning procedures) to the records at the
PRO, they do not have unrestricted access. For files which at the time a volume is in
preparation are either subject to extended closures beyond the statutory thirty years,
or retained in the originating department under section 3(4) of the Public Records
Act of 1958, editors are subject to the same restrictions as all other researchers.
Where necessary, volume editors will provide details of potentially significant files or
individual documents of which they are aware and which they have not been able to
consult.

A thematic arrangement of the documents has been adopted for the general
volumes in series A. The country volumes in series B follow a chronological
arrangement; in this respect they adopt the same approach as was used in the India
and Burma series. For each volume in both series A and B a summary list of the
documents included is provided. The headings to BDEEP documents, which have
been editorially standardised, present the essential information. Together with the
sequence number, the file reference (in the form of the PRO call-up number and any
internal pagination or numeration) and the date of the document appear on the first
line.[3] The second and subsequent lines record the subject of the document, the type
of document (letter, memorandum, telegram etc), the originator (person or persons,
committee, department) and the recipient (if any). In headings, a subject entry in
single quotation marks denotes the title of a document as it appears in the original.
An entry in square brackets denotes a subject indicator devised by the editor. This
latter device has been employed in cases where no title is given in the original or
where the original title is too unwieldly to reproduce in its entirety. Security
classifications and, in the case of telegrams, times of despatch and receipt, have
generally been omitted as confusing and needlessly complicating, and are retained
only where they are necessary to a full understanding. In the headings to documents
and the summary lists, ministers are identified by the name of the office-holder, not
the title of the office (ie, Mr Lyttelton, not secretary of state for the colonies).[4] In the
same contexts, officials are identified by their initials and surname. In general

---

[3] The PRO call-up number precedes the comma in the references cited. In the case of documents from FO
371, the major Foreign Office political class, the internal numeration refers to the jacket number of the
file.
[4] This is an editorial convention, following DBPO practice. Very few memoranda issued in their name were
actually written by ministers themselves, but normally drafted by officials.

volumes in series A, ambassadors, governors, high commissioners and other embassy or high commission staff are given in the form 'Sir E Baring (Kenya)'. Footnotes to documents appearing below the rule are editorial; those above the rule, or where no rule is printed, are part of the original document. Each part of a volume provides a select list of which principal offices were held by whom, with a separate series of biographical notes (at the end) for major figures who appear in the documents. Minor figures are identified in editorial footnotes on the occasion of first appearance. Link-notes, written by the volume editor and indented in square brackets between the heading and the beginning of a document, are sometimes used to explain the context of a document. Technical detail or extraneous material has been extracted from a number of documents. In such cases omission dots have been inserted in the text and the document is identified in the heading as an extract. Occasional omission dots have also been used to excise purely mechanical chain-of-command executive instructions, and some redundant internal referencing has been removed, though much of it remains in place, for the benefit of researchers. No substantive material relating to policy-making has been excised from the documents. In general the aim has been to reproduce documents in their entirety. The footnote reference 'not printed' has been used only in cases where a specified enclosure or an annex to a document has not been included. Unless a specific cross-reference or note of explanation is provided, however, it can be assumed that other documents referred to in the text of the documents included have not been reproduced. Each part of a volume has a list of abbreviations occurring in it. A consolidated index for the whole volume appears at the end of each part.

One radical innovation, compared with previous Foreign Office or India and Burma series, is that BDEEP will reproduce many more minutes by ministers and officials.

Crown copyright material is used by permission of the Public Record Office under licence from the Controller of Her Majesty's Stationery Office. All references and dates are given in the form recommended in PRO guidelines.

*   *   *   *

BDEEP has received assistance and support from many quarters. The project was first discussed at a one-day workshop attended by over thirty interested scholars which, supported by a small grant from the Smuts Memorial Fund, was held at Churchill College, Cambridge, in May 1985. At that stage the obstacles looked daunting. It seemed unlikely that public money would be made available along the lines provided for the India and Burma projects. The complexities of the task looked substantial, partly because there was more financial and economic data with which to deal, still more because there were so many more territories to cover. It was not at all clear, moreover, who could take institutional responsibility for the project as the India Office Records had for the earlier ones; and in view of the escalating price of the successive India and Burma volumes, it seemed unlikely that publication in book form would be feasible; for some while a choice was being discussed between microfilm, microfiche and facsimile.

A small group nevertheless undertook to explore matters further, and in a quite remarkable way found itself able to make substantial progress. The British Academy adopted BDEEP as one of its major projects, and thus provided critical support. The Institute of Commonwealth Studies served as a crucial institutional anchor in taking responsibility for the project. The Institute also made office space available, and negotiated an administrative nexus within the University of London. Dr Anne Thurston put at the disposal of the project her unique knowledge of the relevant archival sources; while the keeper of the Public Records undertook to provide all the support that he could. It then proved possible to appoint Professor Michael Crowder as project director on a part-time basis, and he approached the Leverhulme Trust, who made a munificent grant which was to make the whole project viable. Almost all those approached to be volume editors accepted and, after consultation with a number of publishers, Her Majesty's Stationery Office undertook to publish the project in book form. There can be few projects that after so faltering a start found itself quite so blessed.

Formally launched in 1987, BDEEP has been based since its inception at the Institute of Commonwealth Studies. The work of the project is supervised by a Project Committee chaired by Professor Andrew Porter, Rhodes professor of imperial history in the University of London. Professor Porter succeeded Professor Anthony Low, formerly Smuts professor of the history of the British Commonwealth in the University of Cambridge, who retired in November 1994. At the outset Professor Michael Crowder became general editor while holding a visiting professorship in the University of London and a part-time position at Amherst College, Massachusetts. Following his untimely death in 1988, Professor Crowder was replaced as general editor by Professor David Murray, pro vice-chancellor and professor of government at the Open University. Mrs Anita Burdett was appointed as project secretary and research assistant. She was succeeded in September 1989 by Dr Ashton who had previously worked with Professors Mansergh and Tinker during the final stages of the India and Burma series. Dr Ashton replaced Professor Murray as project director and general editor in 1993. When BDEEP was launched in 1987, eight volumes in series A and B were approved by the Project Committee and specialist scholars were commissioned to research and select documents for inclusion in each. Collectively, these eight volumes (three general and five country)[5] represent the first stage of the project which begins with an introductory general volume covering the years between 1925 and 1945 but which concentrates on the period from the Second World War to 1957 when Ghana and Malaya became independent.[6]

It is fitting that the present general editor should begin his acknowledgements with an appreciation of the contributions made by his predecessors. The late Professor Crowder supervised the launch of the project and planned the volumes included in stage one. The volumes already published bear lasting testimony to his resolve and dedication during the project's formative phase. Professor Murray played a no less crucial role in establishing a secure financial base for the project and in negotiating contracts with the volume editors and HMSO. His invaluable advice and

---

[5] Series A general volumes: vol 1 *Imperial policy and colonial practice 1925–1945* (published 1996); vol 2 *The Labour government and the end of empire 1945–1951* (published 1992); vol 3 *The Conservative government and the end of empire 1951–1957* (published 1994).

Series B country volumes: vol 1 *Ghana* (published 1992); vol 2 *Sri Lanka* (published 1997); vol 3 *Malaya* (published 1995); vol 4 *Egypt and the defence of the Middle East*; vol 5 *Sudan*.

[6] Research is currently in progress for a second stage covering the period 1957–1964.

expertise during the early stages of editing are acknowledged with particular gratitude.

The project benefited from an initial pump-priming grant from the British Academy. Thanks are due to the secretary and Board of the Academy for this grant and for the decision of the British Academy to adopt BDEEP as one of its major projects. The Academy made a further award in 1996 which enabled the project to employ a research assistant on a fixed-term contract. The principal funding for the project has been provided by the Leverhulme Trust and the volumes are a tribute to the support provided by the Trustees. A major debt of gratitude is owed to the Trustees. In addition to their generous grant to cover the costs of the first stage, the Trustees agreed to a subsequent request to extend the duration of the grant, and also provided a supplementary grant which enabled the project to secure Dr Ashton's appointment.

Members of the Project Committee, who meet annually at the Institute of Commonwealth Studies, have provided valuable advice and much needed encouragement. Professor Low, the first chairman of the Committee, made a singular contribution, initiating the first exploratory meeting at Cambridge in 1985 and presiding over subsequent developments in his customary constructive but unobtrusive manner. Professor Porter continues in a similar vein and his leadership and experience are much appreciated by the general editor. The director and staff of the Institute of Commonwealth Studies have provided administrative support and the congenial surroundings within which the general editor works. The editors of volumes in stage one have profited considerably from the researches undertaken by Dr Anne Thurston and her assistants during the preparation of the records handbooks. Although BDEEP is not an official project, the general editor wishes to acknowledge the support and co-operation received from the Historical Section of the Cabinet Office and the Records Department of the Foreign and Commonwealth Office. He wishes also to record his appreciation of the spirit of friendly co-operation emanating from the editors of DBPO. Dr Ronald Hyam, editor of the volume in series A on *The Labour government and the end of empire 1945–1951*, played an important role in the compilation of the house-style adopted by BDEEP and his contribution is acknowledged with gratitude. Thanks also are due to HMSO for assuming publishing responsibility and for their expert advice on matters of design and production. Last, but by no means least, the contribution of the keeper of the records and the staff, both curatorial and administrative, at the PRO must be emphasised. Without the facilities and privileges afforded to BDEEP editors at Kew, the project would not be viable.

S R Ashton
Institute of Commonwealth Studies
July 1996

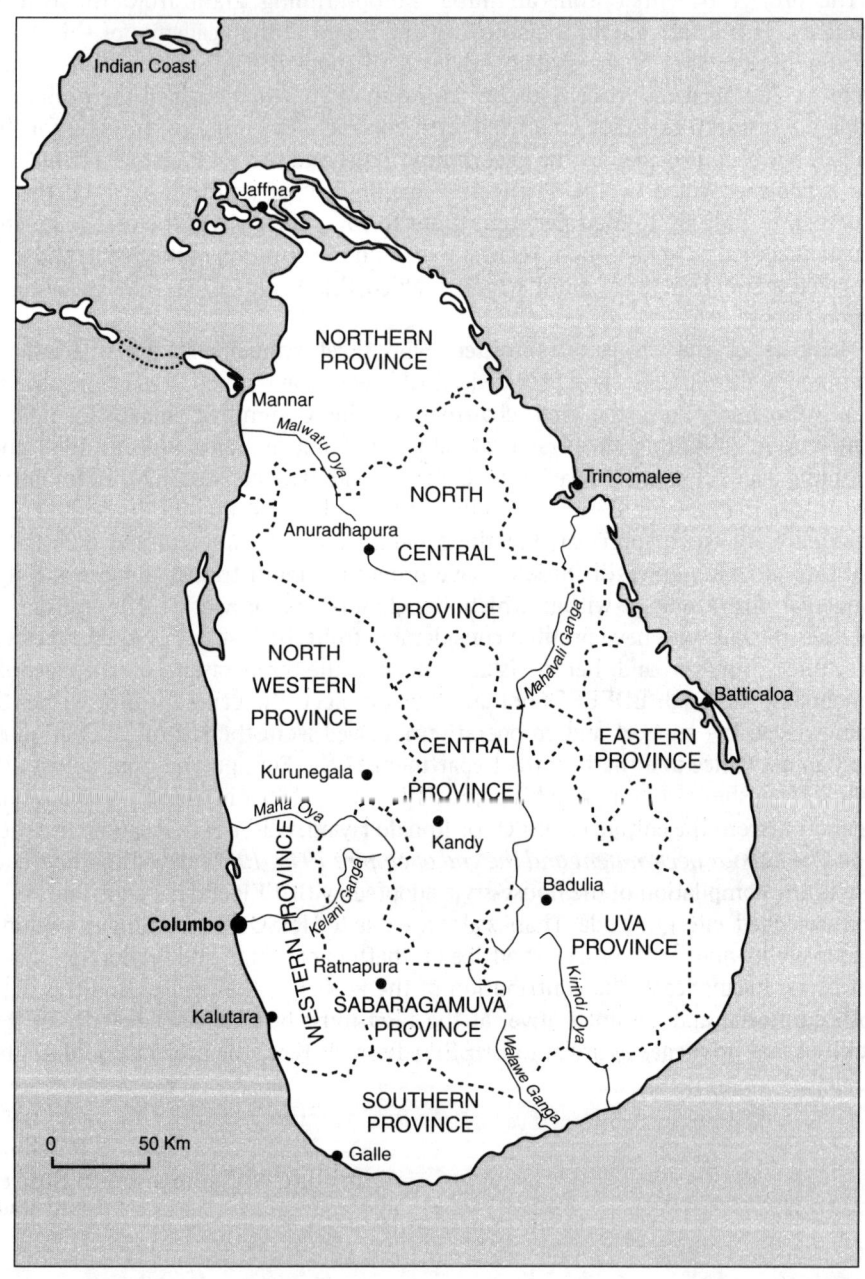

Sri Lanka: Provincial Divisions and Principal Towns

Sri Lanka

Schedule of Contents: Parts I–II

Abbreviations: Parts I–II

ACTC	All-Ceylon Tamil Congress
AFPFL	Anti-Fascist People's Freedom League (Burma)
ARP	air raid precaution
BSI	Burma: Struggle for Independence (Burma documents series)
CB	Companion of the Order of the Bath
CBE	Commander of the Order of the British Empire
CCS	Ceylon Civil Service
CD	coast defence
CDF	Ceylon Defence Force
CGA	Ceylon Garrison Artillery
c-in-c	commander-in-chief
CIC	Ceylon Indian Congress
CICLU	Ceylon Indian Congress Labour Union
CID	Criminal Investigation Department
cif	cost in freight
CIWF	Ceylon Indian Workers' Federation
CLI	Ceylon Light Infantry
CMG	Commander of the Order of St Michael and St George
CNC	Ceylon National Congress
CNVF	Ceylon Naval Volunteer Force
CO	Colonial Office; commanding officer
Con	Conservative Party (UK)
COS	Chiefs of Staff
COSSEA	Chiefs of Staff, South-East Asia
CPRC	Ceylon Planters Rifle Corps
CRO	Commonwealth Relations Office
corrupt gp	corrupt group (undeciphered word or words in telegram)

DFC	Distinguishing Flying Cross
DO	Dominions Office
DSC	Distinguished Service Cross
DSO	Companion of the Distinguished Service Order
EPT	excess profits tax
Ex Co	executive committee/committees
FAA	Fleet Air Arm
fob	free on board
GA	government agent
GB	Great Britain
GCMG	Knight Grand Cross of the Order of St Michael and St George
GOC	general officer commanding
GOI	Government of India
gov	government; governor
gov-gen	governor-general
HE	His Excellency
HM	His Majesty
HMG	His Majesty's Government
HQ	headquarters
ICS	Indian Civil Service
IGP	inspector general of police
ILO	International Labour Organisation
IO	India Office
IRRC	International Rubber Regulation Commission
KBE	Knight Commander Order of the British Empire
KC	King's Counsel
KCMG	Knight Commander of the Order of St Michael and St George
kt	Knight
Lab	Labour Party (UK)
LSSP	Lanka Sama Samaja Party
MC	Military Cross
MP	member of parliament

MSC	member of State Council
OAG	officer administering the government
OBE	Officer Order of the British Empire
PM	prime minister
PRO	Public Record Office
QMG	quarter master general
RAF	Royal Air Force
RN	Royal Navy
RNVR	Royal Naval Volunteer Reserve
RTC	round table conference
SAC	supreme allied commander
S of S	secretary of state
SACSEA	supreme allied commander, South-East Asia
SEAC	South-East Asia Command
SMS	Sinhala Maha Sabha
TOPI	Transfer of Power in India (India documents series)
UK	United Kingdom
UN(O)	United Nations (Organisation)
UNP	United National Party
VP	vital point

Principal Holders of Offices: Part I
Sept 1939–Apr 1945

UNITED KINGDOM

1. *Ministries*

(a) *National government (from June 1935) for the period 3 Sept 1939–10 May 1940*

Prime minister	Mr A N Chamberlain (28 May 1937)
S of S colonies	Mr M J MacDonald (16 May 1938)
S of S India and Burma	Marquess of Zetland (7 June 1935)

(b) *Wartime coalition 10 May 1940–23 May 1945*[1]

Prime minister and minister of defence	Mr W S Churchill (10 May 1940)
Lord president of the Council	Mr A N Chamberlain (11 May 1940) Sir John Anderson (Nat) (3 Oct 1940) Mr C R Attlee (Lab) (24 Sept 1943)
Lord privy seal	Mr C R Attlee (Lab) (11 May 1940) Sir Stafford Cripps (Lab) (19 Feb 1942) Viscount Cranborne (22 Nov 1942)
S of S foreign affairs	Viscount Halifax (11 May 1940) Mr A Eden (22 Dec 1940)
Chancellor of Exchequer	Sir Kingsley Wood (12 May 1940) Sir John Anderson (Nat) (24 Sept 1943)
President of Board of Trade	Sir A Duncan (12 May 1940) Mr O Lyttelton (3 Oct 1940) Sir A Duncan (29 June 1941) Mr J Llewellin (4 Feb 1942) Mr H Dalton (Lab) (22 Feb 1942)
S of S colonies	Lord Lloyd (13 May 1940) Lord Moyne (8 Feb 1941) Viscount Cranborne (22 Feb 1942) Mr O F G Stanley (22 Nov 1942)
S of S India and Burma	Mr L S Amery (13 May 1940)

[1] All Conservative unless otherwise indicated.

S of S dominion affairs	Viscount Caldecote (14 May 1940)
	Viscount Cranborne (3 Oct 1940)
	Mr C R Attlee (Lab) (19 Feb 1942)
	Viscount Cranborne (24 Sept 1943)

(c) *Colonial Office: junior ministers*

Parliamentary under-secretary of state	Marquess of Dufferin and Ava (28 May 1937)
	Mr G H Hall (Lab) (15 May 1940)
	Mr H M Macmillan (4 Feb 1942)
	Duke of Devonshire (1 Jan 1943)

3. *Civil servants*

(a) *Secretary to the Cabinet*

Sir Edward Bridges (1938–1947)

(b) *Colonial Office*

(i) Permanent under-secretary of state	Sir Cosmo Parkinson (1937–1940)
	Sir George Gater (Feb–May 1940)
	Sir Cosmo Parkinson (1940–1942)
	Sir George Gater (1942–1947)
(ii) Deputy under-secretary of state	Sir John Shuckburgh (1931–1942)
	Sir William Battershill (1942–1945)
	Sir Arthur Dawe (1945–1947)
(iii) Assistant under-secretary of state, responsible for the Eastern Department and, from Apr 1943, the Ceylon and Pacific Department	Sir Henry Moore (1938–1939)
	Sir Alan Burns (1940)
	W D Battershill (1941)
	G E J Gent (1942–1946)
(iv) Assistant secretary, head of the Eastern Department and, from Apr 1943, the Ceylon and Pacific Department	G E J Gent (1939–1941)
	K W Blaxter (1941, *acting*)
	J J Paskin (1942–1943)
	J B Sidebotham (1943–1948)

CEYLON

1. *Governors*	Sir Andrew Caldecott (16 Oct 1937–17 Oct 1944)
	Sir Henry Monck-Mason Moore (3 Dec 1944)
2. *Officers administering the government*	G S Wodeman (3–6 Dec 1940)
	(Sir) Robert Drayton (Kt 1944) (4–7 Feb 1943)
	Sir Robert Drayton (17 Oct–3 Dec 1944)

3. *Board of Ministers*

Chairman	The chief secretary (*ex-officio*)
Vice-chairman	Sir D B Jayatilaka (17 Mar 1936–30 Nov 1942)
	acting D S Senanayake (11 Jan–27 Mar 1936; 7 Dec 1936–12 Jan 1937; 14 Apr–4 July 1937; 14 Aug 1937–9 Oct 1942)
	D S Senanayake (2 Dec 1942)
Minister of home affairs	Sir D B Jayatilaka (17 Mar 1936–30 Nov 1942)
	A Mahadeva (2 Dec 1942)
Minister of agriculture and lands	D S Senanayake (17 Mar 1936)
Minister of local administration	S W R D Bandaranaike (17 Mar 1936)
Minister of health	W A de Silva (17 Mar 1936–18 Feb 1942)
	G E de Silva (25 Feb 1942)
Minister of labour, industry and commerce	G C S Corea (17 Mar 1936)
Minister of education	C W W Kannangara (17 Mar 1936)
Minister of communication and works	J L Kotelawala (17 Mar 1936)

6. *Officers of State*

(a) *Chief secretary*	G S Wodeman (22 Oct 1938–23 Nov 1939, *acting*)
	M M Wedderburn (23 Nov 1939–3 Feb 1940)
	G S Wodeman (3 Feb–4 Mar 1940, *acting*)
	M M Wedderburn (4 Mar–8 Apr 1940)
	G S Wodeman (8 Apr–30 May 1940, *acting*)
	G S Wodeman (30 May–3 Dec 1940)
	W L Murphy (3–6 Dec 1940, *acting*)
	G S Wodeman (6 Dec 1940–7 Apr 1942)
	R H Drayton (7 Apr–6 July 1942, *acting*)
	R H Drayton (6–24 July 1942)
	C H Collins (24 July–2 Aug 1942, *acting*)
	(Sir) Robert Drayton (2 Aug 1942–17 Oct 1944)
	C H Collins (17 Oct–3 Dec 1944, *acting*)
	Sir Robert Drayton (3 Dec 1944–13 May 1945)

(b) *Legal secretary*

J C Howard (1 Oct 1936–1 Dec 1939)
J W R Illangakoon (1 Dec 1939–10 Feb
   1940, *acting*)
R H Drayton (10 Feb 1940–9 Apr 1942)
J M Fonseka (9 Apr–23 June 1942, *acting*)
J H B Nihill (24 June–7 July 1942, *acting*)
J H B Nihill (7 July 1942–1 Sept 1943)
R H Drayton (1–22 Sept 1943)
J H B Nihill (22 Sept 1943–5 Apr 1945)
M W H de Silva (5 Apr–4 Oct 1945, *acting*)

(c) *Financial secretary*

H J Huxham (2 Oct 1937–22 Apr 1940)
C H Collins (22 Apr–6 Dec 1940, *acting*)
H J Huxham (6 Dec 1940–17 Nov 1942)
C E Jones (17 Nov 1942–23 Jan 1943,
   acting)
C H Collins (24 Jan–13 July 1943, *acting*)
H J Huxham (13 July 1943–30 Jan 1945)
C E Jones (30 Jan–1 May 1945, *acting*)

INDIA

Governors-general and Viceroys

Marquess of Linlithgow (18 Apr 1936)
Field Marshal Viscount Wavell (20 Oct
   1943)

Glossary: Parts I–II

conductor	a minor supervisory officer on a plantation
estate	plantation
government agent	administrative head of a province
Kachcheri	provincial or district secretariat
Kandyan	pertaining to the old Kandyan kingdom which occupied the central highlands and much of the north central and south eastern plains; Sinhalese from the Kandyan region
kanakapulle	a minor official in a plantation, generally with some responsibility over maintenance of accounts, especially those relating to wages of workers
kangany	organiser or head of a group or gang of workers on plantations; on the larger estates there were several kanganies of whom one or more would be given the title of head-kangany
Korale	administrative unit within a district
Perahera	a famous ritual ceremony associated with the Temple of the Tooth in Kandy. Generally for ten days in July or August there is a magnificent procession of elephants and dancers which attracts thousands of people to the town. The head of state is traditionally the guest of honour on the last day – hence the presence in British times of the governor
Pongal (also Thaipongal)	Hindu harvest festival, observed early in January
rupee	coin in use in Ceylon; worth about 1s 6d or 7½p (UK) or 30 cts (US) in the 1940s. Ceylon had and has a decimal currency of 100 cents to a rupee
sangam	a trade union on a plantation
suriya mal	*thespesa populnea*; marxist groups in Ceylon began selling this flower on memorial day as an anti-imperialist gesture, and in opposition to the sale of poppies
visiting agent	a senior planter, overseeing work of several plantations

Chronological Table of Principal Events: Parts I–II

1939

3 Sept	War declared between Great Britain and Germany
3 Oct	CO decides that constitutional reform in Ceylon should be postponed until after the war

1940

10 Jan	Police shooting of Indian plantation worker at Mool-oya, Hevaheta
27 Feb	Resignation of Board of Ministers on constitutional issues arising from Mool-oya incident
6 Mar	Ministers re-elected by executive committees
12 July	Arrest and detention of Lanka Sama Samaja Party leaders
4 Nov	Exploratory talks between delegations representing the governments of India and Ceylon in New Delhi
12 Nov	GOI reports failure of Indo–Ceylon talks

1941

11 Jan	A contingent of the Ceylon Garrison Artillery, the first batch of Ceylon servicemen sent for overseas service in Second World War, leaves the island
14 Mar	Major G StJ Orde Browne, CO labour adviser, arrives in Colombo to report on labour conditions in Ceylon
4 Sept	Indian delegates arrive in Colombo for Indo–Ceylon talks
21 Sept	Delegates at Indo–Ceylon talks conclude their sittings on reaching 'agreed conclusions' on all subjects
28 Oct	Governor Caldecott submits reform proposals to CO
17 Nov	Ceylon placed under the command of the c-in-c, India. Major General R D Inskip appointed general officer commanding troops in Ceylon
8 Dec	Declaration of war between Great Britain and Japan

1942

15 Feb	Singapore surrenders
25 Feb	Senanayake leaves for India to negotiate food supplies
5 Mar	Vice Admiral Layton appointed c-in-c, Ceylon
9 Mar	Dutch forces in Java surrender
23 Mar	Japanese occupy Andaman islands
24 Mar	War Council established in Ceylon
5 Apr	75 sea-borne Japanese aircraft attack Colombo in morning raid

8 Apr	Escape of Lanka Sama Samaja Party leaders from jail
9 Apr	American forces in Bataan, Philippines, surrender. Japanese raid on Trincomalee
6 May	Surrender on Corrigedor ends American resistance in Philippines
1 July	Establishment of University of Ceylon with Dr W Ivor Jennings as first vice chancellor
8 Aug	Indian National Congress adopts 'Quit India' resolution
9 Aug	Indian National Congress leaders arrested and interned
2 Dec	Senanayake chosen as leader of house and vice-chairman of Board of Ministers. A Mahadeva elected minister for home affairs in place of Sir D B Jayatilaka
18–20 Dec	Ceylon National Congress, in annual session at Kelaniya, adopts resolution that its objective is 'the attainment of Freedom for Ceylon'

1943

26 May	Official announcement from Whitehall on future constitution for Ceylon. Speaker reads message to State Council
8 June	Senanayake makes statement in State Council on ministers' response to declaration of 26 May; announces ministers' resolve to draft a constitution
6 July	M S Aney appointed agent for GOI in Ceylon
9 July	Clarification of policy statement of 26 May
25 Aug	Admiral Mountbatten appointed supreme allied commander, SEAC
6 Nov	Publication of report of special committee on education
21 Dec	Senanayake resigns from Ceylon National Congress

1944

3 Feb	Ministers' draft constitution despatched to London
15 Apr	Mountbatten arrives in Ceylon; headquarters of SEAC transferred from New Delhi to Kandy
6 June	Allied landings in Normandy (D-Day)
15 June	Whitehall announces decision to appoint a commission to visit Ceylon and report on constitutional reform
15 July	Appointment of commission to report on social services
25 Aug	Paris liberated
18 Sept	CO announces appointment of Sir Henry Moore as new governor of Ceylon
17 Oct	Caldecott relinquishes office and leaves island
29 Oct	All-Ceylon Tamil Congress established
19 Nov	Official announcement of appointment of commission on constitutional reform in Ceylon chaired by Lord Soulbury
4 Dec	Arrival of Sir Henry Moore in Colombo
22 Dec	Arrival of Soulbury commission

1945

8 Jan	Admiral Layton relinquishes post of c-in-c, Ceylon; succeeded by Lt-Gen E de R Wetherall

22 Jan	Soulbury Commission begins public sittings
13 Mar	Soulbury Commission concludes public sittings
10 Apr	Soulbury commissioners return to London
20 Apr	Sir Oliver Goonetilleke, civil defence and food commissioner, appointed financial secretary
23 Apr	Japanese evacuate Rangoon
9 May	End of hostilities in Europe
17 May	White paper on Burma published
23 May	Coalition government dissolved in Britain
11 July	Senanayake leaves for London for discussions at CO on constitutional reform
26 July	Labour Party victory in British general election
14 Aug	Japanese surrender
11 Sept	British Cabinet decides to accept Soulbury Report as basis of Ceylon's future constitution
12 Sept	Japanese forces in S E Asia surrender to Mountbatten in Singapore. Publication of Senanayake's note on Ceylon's claim for dominion status
1 Oct	Free education introduced in Ceylon from primary school up to university, with Sinhalese and Tamil as medium of instruction
9 Oct	Soulbury Report published
1 Nov	White paper on constitutional reform in Ceylon published
8 Nov	State Council accepts motion introduced by Senanayake on white paper proposals by 51 votes to 3

1946

25 Jan	J H B Nihill, legal secretary, leaves for London for consultations on drafting of new constitution
23 Mar	Cabinet Mission arrives in India
16 May	Cabinet Mission plan for India announced
17 May	Order-in-Council promulgating new Ceylon constitution published
18 July	Senanayake introduces 16th and last budget under the 1931 constitution
6 Sept	United National Party established

1947

6 Jan	R Aluvihare appointed first Ceylonese inspector-general of police
27 Jan	Attlee-Aung San agreement on Burma
20 Feb	British government announces intention to transfer power in India by a date not later than June 1948
12 June	Official statement on dominion status for Ceylon
1 July	Last meeting of State Council
15 Aug	Polling commences for election to new parliament of Ceylon. Indian independence (14 Aug for Pakistan)
20 Sept	Parliamentary elections concluded in Ceylon
24 Sept	Senanayake becomes Ceylon's first prime minister
8 Oct	First formal meeting of new Cabinet
14 Oct	First meeting of House of Representatives

11 Nov   White paper on new constitutional status of Ceylon published. Agreements on Ceylon independence signed in London and Colombo

12 Nov   First meeting of Senate

13 Nov   Ceylon Independence Bill introduced in House of Commons

25 Nov   Ceremonial opening of parliament

26 Nov   Senanayake moves independence motion in House of Representatives

1 Dec   First national budget presented in House of Representatives by J R Jayewardene, minister of finance

5 Dec   Independence motion passed in House of Representatives by 59 to 11

10 Dec   Ceylon Independence Bill receives Royal Assent. Sir H Moore appointed first governor-general

1948

4 Jan   Burma becomes independent republic

4 Feb   Ceylon Independence Day

Introduction

The issues and the nature of the official documentary record

The outbreak of the Second World War forms the starting point in selecting documents for the Sri Lanka volume in this series. There are three reasons for this. From 1931 Ceylon (the country was officially renamed Sri Lanka* in 1972) had one of the most advanced constitutions of the colonial empire – the Donoughmore constitution. The principal features of that constitution are discussed later in this introductory chapter. Almost from the time of its introduction agitation had begun for changes in that constitutional framework. By the middle of 1939, a consensus had been negotiated, over a two-year period commencing with the appointment of Sir Andrew Caldecott as governor of Ceylon in 1937, on the principles of an even more advanced constitution. The outbreak of war inevitably led to a postponement of any serious consideration by Whitehall of the proposals that formed the essence of this consensus. Nevertheless these proposals had an important influence on constitutional reform once the process was started afresh in 1943.

Secondly, the outbreak of the war also led the Colonial Office to encourage the conversion of the then Board of Ministers into a quasi-Cabinet. This decision was taken as early as October 1939 but there was no policy statement issued on it (2). Wartime conditions necessitated this change, and it was initiated informally and through usage and convention. The balance of power in the constitution shifted in favour of the ministers as against the executive committees which, as we shall see, formed the core of the novel system introduced in 1931, and the individual legislators. In initiating this change the CO was conceding one of the main demands in the 1930's agitation for constitutional reform.

Thirdly, wartime conditions led to the emergence of a genuine political partnership between the Board of Ministers and the governor. This relationship was not without tensions and disagreements – anyone reading these documents will see that there were a great many of these, especially in 1940 and 1941 – but there was a qualitative difference in the relationship between the governor and the Board of Ministers prior to 1939 and thereafter. Ceylon's entry into the war had been decided upon and announced by the metropolitan power but this did not lead to any opposition from the bulk of the country's politicians. Unlike their Indian and Burmese counterparts, the political leadership of the day actively supported the war effort. This association in the war effort from 1939, and direct participation in it, gave the Board of Ministers a far greater influence on the making of policy and decisions in regard to areas of authority which, before the war, had been the

---

* Although the volume carries the modern-day name of the island, the documents all refer to 'Ceylon', the name used by the island's Dutch rulers in the seventeenth and eighteenth centuries and continued by the British. Accordingly, the references in this introduction are likewise to Ceylon. However, as a number of the documents illustrate, the name 'Lanka' was in use among the Sinhalese even in British times. In Sinhala or Sinhalese, Sri Lanka means 'resplendent isle'.

exclusive responsibility of the governor and his three principal British officers, the officers of state. These included immigration policy and citizenship rights. The Sinhalese[1] political leadership in the Board of Ministers was permitted to take the lead, in regard to them, in negotiations with the Government of India.

Even a cursory glance at the CO archives and related Cabinet papers will show that, in regard to Ceylon, there was a concentration of attention, at both the Whitehall and Colombo ends, on constitutional reform. The selection of documents in this volume tends to reflect this. So many hopes had been raised by the prolonged discussions on constitutional reform between 1937 and 1939, and the consensus reached in 1939, that Whitehall's declared policy of postponing consideration of these issues until after the war did not succeed in lowering expectations or diverting attention from constitutional reform to the more urgent business of putting the country on a war footing. The priority given to constitutional reform and political issues was the result of sustained and, eventually, successful efforts on the part of the island's political leadership to keep alive their demand for the conventional constitutional system associated with semi-responsible status, preparatory to the attainment of dominion status. Moreover, as colony after colony in East and South-East Asia and the Pacific – British, French, Dutch and American – fell to the Japanese, Ceylon's strategic importance was underlined. In the early 1940's it served as a major base of operations in the allied campaign against Japan, and as a supply base for the dispatch of arms and equipment to the Soviet Union through the Persian Gulf. As we shall see, the Board of Ministers gave their unstinted support to the war effort but would not be diverted from the issue of constitutional reform. Their persistence in this dual track policy succeeded in keeping the issue alive throughout the early 1940's.

Thus, political issues and considerations of wartime strategy took precedence, and this is reflected in the CO documents at the Public Record Office. Above all the contrast – and one cannot emphasise this too strongly – between the Ceylonese political leadership and their Indian and Burmese counterparts in their attitude to the war effort and to the survival of the empire, evoked a very positive response from British officials in the island, civil and military, to the ministers' pressure for a reform of the constitution and very soon they were pressing Whitehall in support of the ministers to reopen the question of constitutional reform. They succeeded in doing so, and constitutional reform assumed a central place in governmental affairs after December 1942, and through 1943 and into 1944. The CO documents reflect this.

Under the constitutional structure introduced in 1931, responsibility over large and important areas of government activity was transferred to the Board of Ministers and the executive committees. As a result the flow of despatches from Colombo to the Colonial Office in regard to these began to dry up. With the outbreak of war this process was accelerated and indeed completed. Thus there is very little on social policy in the CO records of this period, although radical changes were being introduced in education and language policy, and Ceylon's embryo welfare state was in the process of construction and elaboration just at the time the final phase of the transfer of power was being negotiated.

But despite this emphasis on constitutional reform, economic issues form a significant part of the documentary record. After the fall of Singapore and the loss of Malaya in 1942, Ceylon's role as a supplier of essential war materials assumed crucial importance. The island's tea, copra and above all rubber were in great demand. Over rubber production in particular, Ceylon's support for the war effort could not conceal an underlying tension between the island's interests as a producer and those of the Treasury and supply departments in Britain as purchasers and distributors. This aspect of the wartime relationship is reflected in the documents reproduced here. So too, at the end of the war, are two further issues of economic significance, namely Ceylon's attempts to negotiate preferential trade agreements with Britain, and the exchanges between Whitehall and Colombo over the issue of Ceylon's sterling balances which, according to both the CO and the Treasury, had been run down to dangerously low levels on the eve of independence.

From 1939, when the documents in this volume begin, until April 1943, Ceylon's affairs were handled by the Eastern Department of the CO. Under a reorganisation in 1943, responsibility was transferred to a new Ceylon and Pacific Department, an arrangement in Ceylon's case which continued until independence in February 1948.

Throughout both parts of the volume, the overwhelming majority of documents have been selected from two CO series, one geographical, the other subject. The geographical class is CO 54, Ceylon: Original Correspondence. For the period from 1939 until the end of 1945, CO 54 contains the correspondence (despatches, letters and telegrams) on the main political and constitutional questions between Whitehall and Colombo, together with memoranda and minuting thereon by ministers and officials in the CO. The subject class is CO 537, Colonies General Supplementary ['Secret'] Correspondence, the depository from 1944 for the files of the CO secret registry. For the last two years before Ceylon's independence, all correspondence and internal CO minuting on the main political and constitutional issues which previously had been deposited in CO 54 are to be found in CO 537. In both cases the documents in CO 54 and CO 537 record in detail the views of the India Office and Government of India on the important issues of Indian immigration into Ceylon and the voting rights of Indians resident in the island.

In addition to these two series, two further CO series, both from the records of the subject departments, have provided valuable documentation. First, CO 852, the records of the Economic Department, contains extensive material on Ceylon's role as a source of wartime supply, especially of rubber. The documents selected from CO 852 have been chosen to illustrate, not only the views of the CO and the Ceylon government but also those of the other departments in Whitehall – the Treasury, Board of Trade and the Ministries of Production and Supply – which became involved. Secondly, CO 323, the records of the General Department, contains important material on the questions of nationality and citizenship and provides the background to Ceylon's participation at the British Commonwealth Conference on Nationality and Citizenship which was held in London in February 1947.

The records of the CO have been supplemented by those of the War Cabinet/ Cabinet and the papers of four Cabinet committees which dealt with questions relating to Ceylon: the War Cabinet Committee on the Ceylon Constitution which was appointed in 1943 to consider the terms of the British government's policy statement on Ceylon of the same year; the Cabinet Ceylon Committee, appointed in July 1945 on the eve of the general election in Britain to consider the report of the Soulbury Commission; the Cabinet Colonial Affairs Committee under the Labour government which resumed the discussion of the Soulbury Report and which continued to consider policy for Ceylon until June 1947 when, largely at the behest of Prime Minister Attlee, it was amalgamated with the India and Burma Committee under the title of the latter.

The Cabinet papers from 1945 also include reports from the Chiefs of Staff on the strategic aspects of ending British rule in Ceylon. Coverage of defence issues has been supplemented by documents selected from three further sources: ADM 116 (Admiralty and Security Cases) which provides key insights into Admiralty views on the defence aspects of constitutional reform in Ceylon; WO 32, the registered files (general series) of the War Office; and WO 203, the voluminous series containing nearly 6500 files which documents the activities and operations during the war of the South-East Asia Command. A little over seventy files from WO 203 deal with Ceylon. While the majority have not yielded material useful for inclusion in the volume, one of them – WO 203/5412 – records the important role played by Admiral Mountbatten, supreme allied commander, SEAC, in the appointment of the Soulbury Commission in 1944. Other files in the series contain the minutes of meetings of the Ceylon War Council from September 1942 to December 1945.

While it is gratifying to report that in selecting documents for inclusion in this volume the editor has not been faced with the problem of restrictions on access to the records, readers and future researchers should be aware that in two cases, both of which concern CO 537 for the year 1947, the documentary record for Ceylon is not complete. The main political file for 1947 – carrying the original CO reference 55541/47 – is not recorded in the PRO handlist for the CO 537 series. There is an entry for the file in the Ceylon register of correspondence in CO 337 which itemises the file's contents in the standard numerical sequence throughout the year. The register entry indicates that the file was removed in 1950 but does not make clear by whom or for what purpose. It was not returned and its absence was evidently not noted when the records relating to Ceylon for this period were transferred to the PRO. At the time of this volume going to press, a search for the file has not revealed its whereabouts or even if it still exists. Fortunately, however, and this applies for the entire period covered by this volume, duplicates of the correspondence on the main political and constitutional questions are to be found in the confidential print series for Ceylon in CO 882. Prints were made of the documents from file 55541/47 before it went missing. Although the print does not contain the internal CO minuting on the correspondence, it has been possible, using selections from the print, together with other documents from Cabinet papers and an important file from the records of the Prime Minister's Office (PREM 8/726), to assemble a selection of material illustrating the key political issues and considerations which led to the British government's statement of policy in June 1947 to the effect that Ceylon would achieve fully responsible status within the British Commonwealth of Nations. The documents to which this applies are all in part two: they are numbers 381–385, 387, 391–394, 398–403, 405–408, 417, 421–424. Also missing from CO 537 is file 55569/8/47 on the issue of nationality towards the end of 1947 and, in particular, on Ceylon's request that the British Nationality Bill be deferred to allow time for Ceylon to conduct negotiations over citizenship with India. This file has been destroyed under statute. Again, recourse has been made to the confidential print to cover the issue in question – see numbers 427, 429 and 434.

The publication of this volume completes a trilogy of documentary histories based on the official British record for the end of empire in South Asia in 1947–1948. Readers familiar with the earlier series on India and Burma edited by Professors

Mansergh and Tinker respectively will detect a similarity between all three publications in that most of the documents reproduced are in the form of exchanges of
telegrams. In Ceylon's case, from the time the Donoughmore constitution was
introduced in 1931, there had been more frequent resort than before to telegrams, to
and from London, as a means of communication. Despatches and memoranda from
the colony became less frequent. Again in Ceylon's case, and especially for the period
covered by this volume, one consequence of this preponderance of telegrams is that
many of the documents do not lend themselves to any great elegance of style. In
selecting documents for inclusion, therefore, although readability and quotability
were regarded as advantageous, they have not been the primary concerns; the
emphasis throughout has been on the importance and significance of the issues
under consideration. The Ceylon record differs, certainly from that relating to India,
in that it does not include an equivalent of the regular and at times highly colourful
personal correspondence which passed between the secretary of state for India and
the viceroy. But for a limited period, there is a similarity with the weekly personal
reports submitted by Mountbatten to the India Office when, as the last viceroy
between March and August 1947, he presided over the dissolution of the *raj*. From
September 1939 to August 1941 Governor Caldecott was in the habit of sending to
the CO rather long personal commentaries on the affairs of the colony in which he
indulged in some candid remarks on political issues and on the foibles of his
ministers. These commentaries are eminently readable and quotable. Caldecott
named them 'Things Ceylonese' and over the period in question he submitted fifteen
such reports in total. All are reproduced in part one of this volume. Whether they had
any great direct influence on policy making is difficult to judge but they are
important nevertheless in filling in the background to decisions as they were made.

The Ceylon papers provide little by way of dramas or crises. Indeed the processes of
transfer of power were singularly free of dramas and crises; they were too smooth to
be really credible to critics in Ceylon, especially the marxist left, who argued that
Ceylon's independence was a sham, a piece of make-believe in which Whitehall had
willing collaborators in the island's political establishment (437, 438). The 'dramas
and crises' came in tragic profusion after independence. But this said, it should not
be assumed that the cognate processes were entirely free of anxieties, for some of the
issues involved, especially those concerning the future and position of the Indian
community in the island, were extraordinarily complex. Commenting in January
1940 on what he had seen of Ceylon affairs over the last two and a half years, Sir
Cosmo Parkinson, the permanent under-secretary of state at the CO, observed that
he had formed the opinion that 'of all the Colonies, Ceylon was likely to present the
most difficult problem with which the Colonial Office would be dealing' (9). Even
allowing for the fact that Parkinson made this observation two years before the
collapse of the empire in the Far East and South-East Asia at the beginning of 1942,
the documents in this volume bear ample testimony to the validity of his assessment.

This introduction now continues in three sections. The first surveys the background to the issues involved in the reform of the Ceylon constitution from the
inauguration of the Donoughmore constitution in 1931 to the outbreak of war in
1939. The second and third sections introduce the documents reproduced in the
volume in parts one and two respectively.

The background
The Donoughmore Report

A reforms package based on the recommendations of the Donoughmore Commission was introduced in Ceylon in 1931 with the avowed object of breaking the mould of Ceylonese politics. Together they marked a deliberate crossing of one of the last barriers between colonial status and responsible government, in much the same way as the Durham Report, that path-breaking nineteenth century document on the Canadas, had accelerated the evolution of responsible government in the white dominions in the mid-nineteenth century and after. In both cases the changes introduced were seen to be of decisive importance, and in both a considerable period of transition was envisaged in reaching the goal of self-government which was defined in terms of control over internal affairs and the civil administration while Whitehall continued to have control over defence and external affairs. Writing in 1946 at a time when the Donoughmore constitution was on the verge of being superseded, Martin Wight described it as 'the most remarkable state paper of Colonial affairs of the twentieth century',[2] an assessment that has stood the test of time. In the acuity of its analysis of the constitutional problems of the colony, and its singular readiness to depart from convention and tradition in the solutions recommended, it is very much like the Durham Report with the significant difference that while the latter 'found the solution of the problems of the Canadas in the model of the British Constitution, [the former] was remarking that western parliamentary systems are irrelevant to non-western communities'.[3]

Like the Durham Report of its day, the Donoughmore Report found the basic issue to be the divorce of power from responsibility. While rejecting the demands of the principal political organisation, the Ceylon National Congress, for full responsible government, it nevertheless recommended a form of semi-responsible government and conceded a very substantial measure of responsibility to the colonial politicians with – and this is the significant point – commensurate power. The central feature of the constitutional structure recommended for the colony was the departure from what hitherto had been the mode of advance to semi-responsible government: instead of the conventional device of a Cabinet or quasi-Cabinet there was to be a system of executive committees modelled on those of the League of Nations and the London County Council. As a device in colonial constitutional practice, the executive committee system was at once novel and unusually complex. The members of the unicameral legislature, the State Council, were grouped into seven executive committees,[4] with the aim, quite explicitly, of giving them administrative experience and political education apart from political responsibility. The members of these executive committees elected one of their number as its chairman, the latter then becoming the minister in charge of the area or areas of responsibility allotted to the committee, and a member of the Board of Ministers.

This constitutional structure was fundamentally dyarchical as well. While it was intended that the elected members should have a large measure of responsibility for internal affairs, there were clearly marked limits to their power. Three of the most important executive departments were assigned to officers of state, senior British officials, with responsibility for these to the governor alone.[5] The principal officer of state, the chief secretary, was also chairman of the Board of Ministers. The vice-chairman was an elected minister who became leader of the State Council, a dual position which endowed him with greater political influence than the chairman of the board who did not play any overt political role. In the period covered by this volume the former position was held by two men, Sir D B Jayatilaka to the end of 1942, and from then on by D S Senanayake, the principal Sinhalese politician in the negotiations over the transfer of power in the years 1943 to 1947. Apart from the executive powers assigned to the officers of state, the governor also had his reserve powers. These had been a feature of the constitutions devised in 1920–1924, but now they were more precisely defined and strengthened. The governor had at his disposal a greater variety of courses of action in matters of paramount importance and in emergency situations.

The leadership of the Ceylon National Congress saw the Donoughmore scheme as an outsider's view of what was good for Ceylon and not as a natural stage in the political evolution of the country. They had envisaged the introduction of that salient feature of the government of colonies elevated to semi-responsible status, the orthodox Cabinet form of government, as the logical next step in the slow process of constitutional evolution that had begun in 1910, and they neither expected any deviation from the norm, nor showed any willingness to accept a new model which appeared, by reason of its very novelty, to be inferior in design and functionally inadequate for the purposes it was intended to serve.

Some of the most radical features of the Donoughmore recommendations, those relating to the franchise and electoral systems, left their intended beneficiaries more bewildered than elated. To avoid what they perceived as the transfer of power to a small oligarchy at the expense of the poor, the Donoughmore commissioners were quite unwilling to consider the conferment of semi-responsible status on the island without introducing at the same time a phenomenal widening of the franchise (under the constitution of 1923–1924 only four per cent of the population had the vote). None of the principal political organisations in the island and none of the important politicians envisaged any noteworthy widening of the franchise, much less advocated it in their evidence before the commission. They were taken aback when the Donoughmore commissioners recommended that all males over twenty-one and females over thirty should be eligible to vote. In implementing this recommendation in 1931, the CO went even further and brought the age limit for females down to twenty-one. The scale of the change assumes its true proportions when set against a regional and indeed an international perspective.[6] Ceylon was thus the first British colony in Asia – and indeed the first Asian country – to enjoy the benefits and face the challenges of universal franchise. Ceylon's first general election under universal franchise was held in 1931, twenty-one years before India's first such election, and only two years after Britain's own first general election under universal suffrage.

Just as radical in approach was the commissioners' attitude to the question of communal representation. Quite deliberately no provision was made for communal representation, although the minorities were almost unanimous in urging that it be retained. Unlike the Montagu-Chelmsford Report on Indian constitutional reform, the Donoughmore Report took rejection of 'communalism' to its logical conclusion by devising an electoral system which made no concession to communal interests. Thus the minorities were bitterly hostile to the report because of its forthright condemnation of communal representation.

The recommendation that the franchise be extended to the immigrant Indian minority resident in the island – in the main plantation workers – on the same terms as the indigenous population, that is to say, after five years' residence in the country, to all British subjects aged twenty-one in the case of males and thirty in the case of females, led to a prolonged and acrimonious political dispute in which all the important Sinhalese politicians, the Ceylon National Congress leadership no less than the more conservative leadership of the Kandyan Sinhalese,[7] found themselves ranged against the Donoughmore proposals. The immigrant Indians were eleven per cent of the population and their enfranchisement on the liberal terms outlined in the Donoughmore Report was seen as a potent political threat to the interests of the Sinhalese population in the plantation districts. The Indians were present in some districts in such large numbers that the Sinhalese political leadership and especially its Kandyan segment was thoroughly disturbed at the possibility of an Indian domination of the central highlands of the island if permanent citizenship rights were conferred on them on these generous terms. The Donoughmore commissioners saw the problem thus:

> The problem of the Indian immigrant labourers is a serious and difficult one and arises here in connection with communal representation of the Indian community. There are at present about 700,000 of these people in the island, most of them employed on the tea and rubber estates at the higher levels where Sinhalese have hitherto been unwilling to work in large numbers. Indian Tamils are also engaged as labourers on Government, Municipal, or other work in the towns, and are also to be found as traders and shopkeepers. The coolie section of the people are not very happily placed in their own country of Southern India. Many of them are of the depressed and outcast [sic] class and have lived in great poverty, and in many ways their lot in Ceylon is an improvement on that of their fellows in South India. At the same time, the conditions of the Indian labourer in Ceylon are still capable of improvement, and must be bettered before they can be described as satisfactory.[8]

Apart from the sheer size of the numbers to be enfranchised, there were other reasons why the recommendations on the franchise for the Indians in the island roused the Sinhalese politicians to such intense opposition. First, there was the perception among the Sinhalese that the bulk of these people were only temporary residents in the island with no permanent interests in it. Almost all of them maintained close ties with the villages in southern India whence they or their parents came. The frequency with which they visited their villages in southern India, and the regular remittances of money they made to them, were seen as evidence of the transient nature of their connection with Ceylon where they earned a livelihood and, despite their poverty, enjoyed a standard of living well above that of their kinsfolk in southern India. Sinhalese politicians firmly believed that the loyalties of these people were with India and not with Ceylon. Secondly, there was the ease with which impoverished unskilled labour moved to Ceylon from southern India through the traditional emigration routes to the plantation districts and elsewhere in search of work. The number of Indians entitled to citizenship after five years' residence would keep increasing through this immigration process.

In the Legislative Council, as the national legislature was called in pre-Donoughmore days, the Donoughmore proposals were adopted by the slimmest of margins – 19 to 17 (the vote being restricted by the then governor, Sir Herbert Stanley, to the unofficial members) – after a long and acrimonious debate. They were adopted at all only because the CO, at the instance of the Ceylon government, imposed restrictions on the franchise for Indians resident in Ceylon in modification of the Donoughmore proposals, restrictions which were enforced in the face of strong protests from the Indian government and representatives of Indian opinion in the island.[9]

This compromise saved the Donoughmore Report from defeat in the Legislative Council but the problems that arose from the implementation of the formula adopted kept the governments of Ceylon and India at loggerheads for much of the period covered by this volume. It led to controversies within the island between the Sinhalese political leadership and the representatives of the Indians – quite apart from disputes between the governor and the Board of Ministers, and between Ceylon and India. The CO and the India Office acted as intermediaries between the contending parties, the India Office sometimes advocating a parochial point of view.

All the minority representatives in the Legislative Council voted against the acceptance of the Donoughmore proposals, as did two Sinhalese but the reasons which caused the latter to vote against were totally different from those which guided the representatives of the minorities. The two Sinhalese dissidents voted against the Donoughmore proposals because they felt that these did not go far enough in the direction of self-government.

Pressure for reform of the constitution, 1935–1937
Although the leadership of the Ceylon National Congress and its allies had been apprehensive of the effect of universal suffrage on their political fortunes, they adjusted to the needs of the new situation with remarkable political skill and alacrity, and found to their pleasant surprise that the massive rural vote easily swamped the urban vote. Indeed the immediate effect of universal suffrage as demonstrated in the general election of 1931 was to help them consolidate their hold on power within the State Council, the new national legislature.

A E Goonesinha, the Labour leader and advocate of universal suffrage, entered the State Council with great hopes of establishing himself and his fledgling Labour Party as a powerful influence within the legislature but his role turned out to be altogether less prominent than what he – and his British Labour Party mentors – had in mind. To a large extent this was a reflection of the demographic profile of the country, with its small indigenous working class vote overshadowed by the Indians in the plantations and to lesser extent in the urban areas, but it also reflected a steady erosion of his power in the trade union field in the wake of the extensive unemployment that followed the depression. Besides, younger rivals, more doctrinaire in their radicalism, were in the process of replacing Goonesinha in the leadership of the trade union movement and the politics of the urban working class. These radical forces had as yet no base in the State Council. Moreover, because of the Jaffna boycott of elections,[10] the Tamils were under-represented in the State Council and until 1934, when G G Ponnambalam entered the legislature, they had no articulate spokesman.

The Ceylon National Congress leadership and their associates entered the State Council and secured election to a majority of places on the Board of Ministers, despite their reservations about the new apparatus of government and despite fighting the election as individuals and not as members of a political party. They were not intent on deliberately wrecking the system. Their objective, on the contrary, was to make the system work as well as possible. In doing so they were intent on demonstrating their fitness for a more advanced form of self-government than the complex and cumbersome Donoughmore structure with its built-in deficiencies. In their strong commitment to constitutional methods of agitation, these tactics and strategies had the same self-imposed restraints as those of their predecessors in the Legislative Council of the 1920's. Nevertheless they made no secret of their intention to agitate for the conventional form of government associated with semi-responsible government. Their agitation began from 1932.

There were three main demands in the 1930's agitation for constitutional reform. Of these the most important was pressure for the establishment of a Cabinet form of government on the Westminster model in place of the central feature of the Donoughmore system, the novel experiment of executive committees. The others were the abolition of the dyarchical aspects of the Donoughmore scheme by the elimination of the posts of officers of state and the transfer of their powers to elected ministers, and a substantial reduction of the governor's powers.

When these claims first emerged the CO took up the position that it was too early to consider changes of so far-reaching a character in a constitution that had taken nearly three years to devise. The Board of Ministers might have achieved greater success if they had won the support of the minorities for their proposals. This they did not have and it weakened their case substantially. The executive committee system had less support in the CO – and very soon in the colonial administration in the country – than other features of the new constitution, but any willingness there might have been to consider a change vanished in the face of persistent claims by the minorities that their position vis-à-vis the Sinhalese, weak as it was, could deteriorate still further should the executive committees be abolished. By now the minorities had the same strong faith in the executive committee system as a buttress of their inherently weak political position as they once had in communal (and weighted) representation. The executive committee system had enabled them to secure the election of two minority representatives as ministers. Hence the decision was taken in Whitehall to postpone any consideration of a reform of the constitution until after the general election of 1935–1936.

By the mid-1930's the political situation in the country was changing rapidly, one feature of which was the emergence of a marxist challenge to the established politicians, and to the urban trade union movement dominated so far by Goonesinha. Two marxists, Philip Gunawardena and Dr N M Perera, secured election to the State Council at the general election of 1936 as members of the Lanka Sama Samaja Party (LSSP),[11] a significant if numerically meagre reward for an intelligent and vigorously conducted campaign in which they had come out strongly against the policies, methods and objectives of the Ceylon National Congress and the Labour Party.

Apart from the marxist challenge to the political establishment in the State Council, there were two other noteworthy consequences of the impact of universal suffrage on the politics of the country. First, universal suffrage was among the main determining factors in the revival of a linkage between nationalism and a Buddhist resurgence and the cultural heritage associated with Buddhism. In the perspective of the island's long history, this was a more significant development than the entry of the marxists into national politics. The leadership in this was taken by S W R D Bandaranaike's Sinhala Maha Sabha, the progenitor of the Sri Lanka Freedom Party (SLFP) of today. This form of nationalism was inherently divisive in its impact on the politics of this period but no less democratic for that. It was kept in check by the duumvirate of Jayatilaka and Senanayake. Secondly, and on a different level, universal suffrage was largely responsible for a broad impulse towards social welfare in the Donoughmore era, especially in the period of the second State Council (1936–1947) when the political leadership became more responsive to the social and economic facets of the resurgence of nationalism.

When Congress politicians and their sympathisers retained control of the State Council at the January 1936 general election, they scarcely revealed any perception of a change in the political system. On the contrary their first act was significant in underlining their belief that nothing had changed. This was the election of a homogeneous Sinhalese Board of Ministers by the device of disposing their supporters in the various executive committees according to plan.[12] The 'Pan-Sinhalese' ministry established through these manoeuvres secured a show of unanimity for the demands of the Board of Ministers, but the immediate effect of this not too subtle move was to aggravate communal feelings in the island without the compensation of impressing on the CO the urgency of the need for a reform of the constitution. Nor was the CO persuaded that the new unanimity of views in the board was genuine.

The board treated its return to office as an endorsement of its demand for a further measure of constitutional reform, and soon set about the business of outlining its proposals. In a memorandum which it eventually submitted to the governor, Sir Edward Stubbs, in March 1937,[13] the board outlined its priorities on constitutional reform: the curtailment of the governor's reserve powers, abolition of the posts of officers of state, and the replacement of the executive committees by 'the ordinary form' of Cabinet government with a chief minister either invited by the governor to form a government or elected by the State Council itself. This memorandum was issued by the Board of Minsters without consulting the State Council. While there was general support for the proposals on the officers of state and the governor's powers, the minorities continued to express fears that the Cabinet system would make it more difficult for them to secure appointment as ministers except on terms laid down by the Sinhalese majority.

Although Stubbs himself felt constrained to agree that the Donoughmore constitution was now 'a proved failure', he was far from certain about what should take its place; he would not support the demand for a reduction of the governor's powers, at any rate not for a long time to come; nor would he agree to abolish the posts of officers of state, since he believed that it was too soon to transfer their functions to elected ministers. He suggested that the only practicable course of action would be to appoint a commission to take a fresh look at the island's problems and determine whether a more satisfactory constitution could be devised.[14]

The tempo of these exchanges on constitutional reform quickened with remarkable suddenness in the first quarter of 1937, the last months of Stubbs's governorship. Through what came to be known as the Bracegirdle incident, the change was precipitated by the intrusion of marxist agitation on an issue relating to the balance of power in the constitution. Mark Antony Bracegirdle, a young communist from Australia (and a recent immigrant there from Britain), had arrived in Ceylon in 1936 as an employee of a tea estate company. He outraged the planting community by taking an interest in trade union activity among the plantation workers, and even more by appearing on LSSP platforms in planting districts. He was dismissed from his post, and his deportation from Ceylon was arranged mainly between the inspector-general of police and the chief secretary on the basis of powers conferred on the government by an order-in-council of 1896.[15] The deportation order was served on Bracegirdle on 22 April 1937, but before it could be enforced he was successfully spirited away by the LSSP. In the meantime legal action was taken against the police through a writ of *habeas corpus*. The validity of the deportation order was challenged before the chief justice and the senior puisne justice, who held that Bracegirdle could not be deported for exercising his right of free speech, which in fact was all he had done.[16]

The Bracegirdle incident provoked a constitutional crisis of the first magnitude. The basic issue, in brief, was that of relations between ministers and heads of government departments within their ministries. More specifically, from the point of view of members of the State Council, ever suspicious of the officers of state, one of the latter – the chief secretary – was seen to be encroaching on the functions of an elected minister, the minister of home affairs, vice-chairman of the board of ministers and leader of the State Council, Sir D B Jayatilaka, no less. The uproar that ensued surprised Stubbs, and he saw it, quite correctly, as the direct result of the intervention of the LSSP, which had ensured that tempers would remain at fever heat for as long as possible by taking the issue to the wider public beyond the walls of the State Council, within which debates on such issues had been confined in the past. By so doing and securing the support on this issue of the Board of Ministers, of Goonesinha and the majority of members of the State Council, the LSSP demonstrated that constitutional negotiations conducted at the official level between Whitehall, the governor and the board were strangely remote from the new realities of the political situation in the island. Apart from bringing the LSSP into the limelight on a national scale and giving it substantial publicity and increased popularity, the Bracegirdle incident saw Stubbs receiving a decisive rebuff, and Jayatilaka's reputation considerably tarnished as a result of his maladroit handling of this issue.

Caldecott and constitutional reform, 1937–1939

The CO did not realise that the Board of Ministers was under attack in an altogether more systematic manner than before from a younger generation of radical politicians, for otherwise it would hardly have gone ahead as it did, in the aftermath of the Bracegirdle incident, with a constitutional amendment strengthening the governor's reserve powers. On 10 November 1937 the British Cabinet approved an order-in-council amending the Donoughmore constitution and bringing it, so far as the governor's reserve powers of legislation and control of the civil service were concerned, more in line with the Government of India Act of 1935. The order-in-council was introduced in the island in January 1938. The governor was now authorised to legislate independently of the State Council on all matters that concerned 'public faith, public order, and the essentials of good government', in a manner vitally different from the practice of the past in regard to the exercise of his limited powers of 'certification'. He could proclaim his ordinances direct and needed only to communicate them to the clerk of the State Council; the council's right to discuss or delay such measures was thus removed. The order-in-council caused considerable public agitation, and coming as it did in the wake of the Bracegirdle crisis, it was assumed that there was a connection between the two. But there was no such connection. Indeed senior officials at the CO were very critical of Stubbs's actions on the Bracegirdle issue, arguing that he had precipitated the crisis by acting without due regard to constitutional practice and plain good sense.

A constitutional amendment on these lines had been thought of as early as 1932 when there were fears (largely in the CO) of a potential breakdown of the constitution over a budgetary crisis. Such a breakdown had not occurred. Indeed by the end of 1933 the CO was satisfied that the constitution was working as smoothly as could have been expected in a period of acute economic crisis, and so the proposed amendment was shelved. By the middle of 1935, however, this proposal was revived. Not that there had been any constitutional crisis, much less a breakdown: there were a few occasions when it became necessary for the governor to use his reserve powers. Most, if not all, such instances related to salaries and leave privileges of members of the higher bureaucracy, about which Whitehall was especially sensitive. One of the disadvantages, as CO officials saw it, of the machinery devised under article 22 of the Donoughmore constitution for the use of the governor's reserve powers, was that it permitted a debate in the State Council on every occasion when these powers were used. As most such debates related to conditions of service of public officers, this procedure was regarded with increasing distaste for its presumed demoralising effect on the higher bureaucracy (especially the British element in it). The decision to proceed with the amendment to article 22 was hastened by the delaying tactics adopted by the State Council, with the connivance of the deputy speaker, in 1936-1937, over an increase in the salaries of police officers.

The experience of the years 1936–1937 would seem to indicate that while the ministerial group in the island – especially the representatives of the Sinhalese – believed in the inevitability of progress from semi-responsible status to self-government on the model of the white dominions, the permanent officials in Whitehall held a diametrically opposed view. For them there was no such inevitability in constitutional development. They could point to the example of Cyprus and, most recently and prominently, to that of Malta, where semi-responsible status had not led to responsible government but to political crisis, constitutional breakdown and a reversion, if only temporarily, to direct British rule.[17] The concurrent constitutional crisis in Malta must, no doubt, have weighed heavily with the permanent officials in the CO as they viewed the situation in Ceylon, and affected to notice signs of incipient crisis in the legislators' pique over the fringe benefits of the higher bureaucracy.

But the starting point of a clear understanding of events in the final phase of the transfer of power in Ceylon is a realisation of the breakthrough that came in 1937-1938 when two men of liberal instincts, Malcolm MacDonald as secretary of state and Caldecott as governor, brought fresh and unorthodox minds to bear on the problems of constitutional reform in the island. Within days of his arrival in the island, Caldecott had to cope with the political fall-out from the Bracegirdle incident, an unusually difficult if not inauspicious start. He found that the island's political establishment in the form of the Board of Ministers was intent on bringing the dispute to an end for two reasons. First, they realised that the only beneficiary of its prolongation would be the LSSP. But more important, there was the expectation that with the arrival of a new governor their campaign for constitutional reform could be resumed in more propitious circumstances than under his predecessor. The CO for its part was agreeable to this but the Board of Ministers was unaware of the price they were expected to pay for it – the amendment to article 22 of the Donoughmore constitution. Once the order-in-council embodying this amendment had been approved by the CO, a despatch was prepared informing the governor that the constitution of the colony would be modified in certain directions more acceptable to ministers after examination by the governor and possibly by a further commission of inquiry. This, it was maintained, would help reduce the level and range of criticism of the amendment that was to be introduced.

The despatch, dated 25 November 1937, made no reference to the appointment or sending of a commission, but asked Caldecott to review the constitutional problems of the island on his own by seeking the views of all sections of opinion in the island, and to make a report as soon as he had time to form his own conclusions. Caldecott himself was not in favour of a commission sent from Britain. He believed that the governor of the colony was in a much better position to conduct the preliminary negotiations on the reform of the constitution than a commission. The first six months of his stay in the island were spent in studying memoranda on reform of the constitution submitted in response to his request from the Board of Ministers, state councillors representing minority interests, and from numerous political and communal associations and interested individuals.

The initial response to the publication of the order-in-council on the change in the machinery of the governor's reserve powers had ranged from pained surprise on the part of the Board of Ministers to vigorous protests from the LSSP, but once the former decided to treat it as a peripheral issue that could be conceded without too much objection in the greater interest of a comprehensive reform of the constitution on which Caldecott was intent, the original tempo of the discussions initiated by him was sustained without any serious interruption. This order-in-council was regarded as a minor inconvenience rather than a serious setback by all except the LSSP.

The 'fifty-fifty' campaign

Between January and May 1938 Caldecott received eleven formal deputations which placed before him a bewildering array of views ranging from demands for a limitation of the franchise, the establishment of a second chamber, to the 'fifty-fifty demand' then being advanced by Ponnambalam, the principal leader of the Tamils, which envisaged an equal apportionment of seats in the State Council between the Sinhalese majority and the minorities collectively. The climax of the 'fifty-fifty' campaign[18] directed by Ponnambalam on behalf of the coalition of minorities he had organised came in later years.

The term 'fifty-fifty' was, in fact, no more than a slogan, a simplification of a rather complex set of proposals first devised by Ponnambalam in 1937. His scheme involved a complicated system of multiple weightages in a combination of territorial and communal representation supposed to ensure the reinstatement of the constitutional concept of 'balanced representation' by which was meant that no single ethnic group would be able to out-vote a combination of the others. It was, in brief, a return to the electoral system of the 1920's – the so-called Manning constitutions[19] – but modified to accommodate the principle of universal suffrage.

That Jayatilaka and Senanayake opposed this scheme was not a matter for surprise. Ponnambalam found that Caldecott was not more favourably disposed towards these claims than the two Sinhalese leaders. Very soon the governor became inflexibly opposed to the scheme in all its permutations. In June 1938 in a despatch which came to be known as his reforms despatch he informed the CO:

I have made known my opposition to what is called here the "fifty-fifty" demand. That is that seats in the State Council should be apportioned half to 'the majority community' i.e. the Sinhalese, and half to the 'minority communities'. I am similarly opposed to the 'sixty-forty demand' and to any other form of fractional representation on a race basis. The elected seats must in my opinion continue to be filled on a territorial franchise though (as will emerge later in this despatch) I would gladly see the electoral areas so constituted as to afford a chance of more seats for members of minority communities. . . . My reason for opposition to the 'fifty-fifty demand' or to any modification of it is that any concession to the principle of communal representation would perpetuate sectionalism (which I believe to be anathema to thinking people in Ceylon of all races) and preclude the emergence of the political issues. To ease the present position by affording a chance of more seats for minority candidates is one thing; to introduce the principle of representation of minorities on any mathematical formula is quite another. . . .

I am in favour of re-shaping, and adding to the number of electoral areas in order to afford more chances for minority candidates. Redelimitation is also necessary in the Kandyan areas in order that the Kandyan interest, which is that of an agricultural peasantry, may not be swamped by the Indian interest which is that of plantation labour. . . .[20]

Caldecott stated that he had a number of specific proposals for these purposes, but that he was not prepared to sponsor any of them until they were examined by a delimitation committee. He recommended the following terms of reference for that committee:

To consider the present electoral areas of the island and to advise what changes or additions could be reasonably made with a view to affording more chances for the return of candidates belonging to the minority communities and to securing adequate representation of the Kandyan rural interests.[21]

Caldecott's forthright rejection of what was popularly called the 'fifty-fifty' demand was an unexpected and insuperable setback to Ponnambalam and other advocates of it.

The rhetorical excesses of this campaign, and the political posturing associated with it, alienated large sections of Sinhalese opinion. Apart from conferring a greater political acceptability on communal organisations such as the Sinhala Maha Sabha, which was as committed to emphasising ethnic identity as the central motivating force in political organisation and activity as Ponnambalam himself, it eventually lost the support of other minority groups, especially the Muslims, who came to view the 'fifty-fifty' campaign as a self-destructive pursuit of excessive political demands. More important, memories of it lingered on long after the campaign itself had petered out in the mid-1940's. The result was to arouse Sinhalese suspicions about demands for a federal political structure which emerged in the late 1940's from Tamil politicians whose entry into national politics had been through the 'fifty-fifty' campaign.

The distinguishing feature of Caldecott's reforms despatch of June 1938 was his forthright but carefully considered rejection of the executive committee system. He recommended that it be replaced by a Cabinet form of government in which a member of the legislature, most likely to command the support of a majority there, would be chosen as chief minister by the governor. The officers of state would not be members of such a ministry. Many of their functions and responsibilities would be transferred to the appropriate ministries. Indeed Caldecott came to attach as much importance to the introduction of a Cabinet form of government as the Board of Ministers itself. The success of democracy in Ceylon, he argued, would depend greatly on the discipline and drive which party loyalties alone could infuse into a democratic political system. He seized upon one of the noticeable shortcomings of the country's evolving political structure, namely its underdeveloped if not inchoate party system, and argued that one of the great advantages of Cabinet government was that it would stimulate the development of a dynamic and competitive party system. One link in the reforms he advocated placed him at odds with most sections of opinion in the State Council. This was his insistence that the advance to responsible government would have to be accompanied, as a temporary measure, by an increase instead of a substantial reduction in the governor's reserve powers.

On 10 November 1938 MacDonald sent Caldecott a short formal reply to his reforms despatch and expressed general agreement with the principal recommendation it embodied, namely the replacement of the executive committee system by a Cabinet form of government. Caldecott was instructed to publish his reforms proposals and to submit them for discussion in the State Council. This he proceeded to do.

The debate which began on 9 May 1939 continued over the next two months and was concluded on 12 July 1939. With all restrictions on the length of speeches removed, the debate itself turned out to be the most exhaustive review of the constitutional structure of the country ever attempted up to that time by the national legislature. Caldecott's proposals were introduced in the form of a series of resolutions and these were dissected with a thoroughness that had seldom been seen before in discussions of constitutional reform. All the proposals were adopted after prolonged discussion and without substantial modification. These included a resolution supporting the appointment of a commission from Britain to review constitutional reform in Ceylon. The prime movers of this last recommendation were the minorities, including representatives of British commercial interests in the country. It was the only one on which Caldecott was lukewarm, not unsympathetic. Thus a consensus on constitutional reform had been successfully negotiated by Caldecott by mid-1939. A decisive breakthrough had been achieved and the stage was set for one more step in the country's constitutional evolution to responsible government.

The formulation of a constitution on the basis of the consensus that had emerged in support of Caldecott's proposals was bound to be a time-consuming affair. The CO was nothing if not slow and deliberate in these matters at the best of times. The Office had hardly begun the process of examining Caldecott's long despatch, reviewing the debate of March–July 1939, when war broke out in Europe. This had an immediate dampening effect on the CO mandarinate which was now not inclined to expend time and energy on any serious consideration of constitutional reform in Ceylon.

Part I: The Second World War and the Soulbury Commission

Although the island served as an important base of operations in the allied campaign against Japan and from which arms and equipment were dispatched to the allied forces in the Persian Gulf, the impact of the Second World War on Ceylon is one of the least researched aspects of its modern history. The neglect of this important theme can be explained by two factors. First, there was no invasion of the island and only the barest minimum of air attacks. Secondly, as a British colony, Ceylon's entry into the war was decided upon by the metropolitan power. The political leadership of the mainstream nationalist movement who shared power with the British colonial administration actively supported the war effort, unlike their Indian and Burmese counterparts. Thus association in the war effort, indeed active participation in it, did not lead to any notable political agitation and controversy and the war left few scars in the collective memory of the people of Ceylon.

After the Japanese conquest of the British, French and Dutch possessions in South-East Asia, Ceylon became the principal if not the sole supplier of rubber to the allied powers. In order to meet an insatiable wartime demand for this vitally important commodity, Ceylon's rubber plantations were tapped far beyond the generally accepted production norms – 'slaughter-tapping', the technical term used for this process, conveys the meaning most appropriately. The island was not threatened by invasion until the first quarter of 1942, after the attack on Pearl Harbor and the surrender of the British, French, Dutch and American colonies to the Japanese. In April 1942 there were two Japanese air-raids on the island, on Colombo and its suburbs and on Trincomalee. The damage inflicted was not severe, except on the morale of the civilian population. There was no Japanese follow-up to these raids and the threat receded in time. By 1943 the tide had begun to turn in favour of the allies in the war against Japan, and the decision taken at the Quebec conference to establish the South-East Asia Command was an important landmark in this. In mid-April 1944 the headquarters of SEAC were shifted to Ceylon and to the town of Kandy in particular (178).

Michael Tomlinson's *The Most Dangerous Moment*[22] deals in detail with the Japanese threat to Ceylon in early 1942. The author, an airman stationed in the island and personally involved in the events of that momentous year, regrets that historians have 'touched only briefly and generally obliquely on the Japanese Navy's only major offensive westwards'. History, according to Tomlinson, 'has almost forgotten' the April raids and the impact that they made. He points out that Churchill himself regarded 1942, when the Japanese fleet which had attacked Pearl Harbor was approaching Ceylon, 'as the most dangerous moment of the Second World War, and the moment which caused him the most alarm'. In assessing the significance of the events described in his book, Tomlinson asserts that the Japanese air-raids on Ceylon in April 1942 were 'the furthest incursions westwards that the Japanese were ever to make by land, sea or air, with all its trenchant and catastrophic possibilities'.[23] He concedes that 'the operation . . . neither much hastened defeat nor ultimate victory, nor led to irreparable losses or material gains to either side'. Nevertheless, 'it is only too easy to overlook the enormous importance which was attached to these events at the time or to underrate the consternation and gloom which prevailed in the British camp as the Japanese swept ever westwards and there seemed no holding them'.[24]

The postponement of constitutional reform
As early as the first week of October 1939 the CO had decided that constitutional reform in Ceylon should be postponed until after the war (2). The Office was strengthened in this decision by Ponnambalam's message sent on behalf of the minorities on 18 October 1939 that they had suspended all political activities on the reform of the constitution as it was felt that the country should not be distracted by any political controversy at this juncture (4). Minority representatives repeated this a month later in a statement which went on to say that they had suspended political agitation for the duration of the war (13). Thus the consensus reached though

prolonged debate in the State Council in March-July 1939 was being undermined by the minorities' decision to wait for more settled times.

The first inkling of a change in the CO attitude, if not policy, on constitutional reform in Ceylon reached Caldecott by the beginning of 1940. In a despatch of 26 January MacDonald, much to Caldecott's surprise, rejected the idea of a delimitation committee or commission which the latter had always treated as crucially important to his reforms proposals (9, 23). Instead three options were proposed, the first of which was a governor's conference at which the Board of Ministers would meet other leaders – presumably the leaders of the minority groups – to negotiate a settlement of existing differences between the Sinhalese and the minorities. The second was a constitutional conference in London (MacDonald himself admitted that this would be difficult in wartime) and the third was a round table conference, after the war, of all important groups. Above all it was suggested that the general election, the third under universal suffrage and scheduled for 1941, should be postponed. Thus the only option really available to Caldecott was the first and with regard to that neither he nor the ministers were very enthusiastic especially after the time and energy spent debating and writing on constitutional reform over the two previous years.

While MacDonald and his officials at the CO were reluctant to consider reform of the constitution because of the outbreak of war, they nevertheless encouraged a far-reaching change in the balance of power between the Board of Ministers and their executive committees. In a minute he wrote on 3 October 1939 MacDonald stated that he regretted that Ceylon did not have a Board of Ministers that really worked as a responsible Cabinet in all matters which came under its purview (2). His officials had come to the same conclusion. They encouraged the governor to permit the Board of Ministers to operate as a quasi-Cabinet. Thus while the executive committees continued to exist, they were reduced in all but name to the status of advisory standing committees, a trend which was strengthened by the operation of two other factors. First, wartime spending in Ceylon and a more buoyant economy placed greater resources than ever before at the disposal of the ministers and these they used to good effect in keeping members of executive committees busy and happy with projects in which they were interested. Later, in March 1942, a War Council was established and the Board of Ministers became members. All important decisions relating to the conduct of the war were taken in the War Council rather than by the board and the executive committees (124).

The Board of Ministers was unaware, until late in 1941, that Whitehall had decided that reform of the constitution would not be taken up during wartime. The ministers believed that the CO – despite the outbreak of war in Europe – would have these matters under active consideration on the data already available (14). Caldecott himself was not unsympathetic to this view and persisted in his campaign for constitutional reform despite the war in Europe (36, 40, 42, 44, 47, 51).

In the early months of 1940 Caldecott was under increasing pressure from British planting and commercial interests in the island, especially the former, to take firm action against trade unionists in plantation areas (12, 26). The LSSP had created considerable apprehension among the planters by sponsoring a series of strikes (accompanied by sporadic acts of violence) in some of the plantation districts. This was part of an attempt by the LSSP to break into the trade union monopoly in the plantations held by the traditional Indian leadership. Although they made little headway against the latter, they nevertheless succeeded in disturbing the planters to a greater degree than the Indian plantation trade union leadership because of the nature of their propaganda and techniques of agitation – their anti-British and anti-imperialist slogans, their advocacy of class conflict and violence and spectacular shows of strength. The planters and British officials – but not the governor – were perturbed and from the planters came insistent demands for pre-emptive punitive action against the LSSP before it could establish a bridgehead in the plantation districts.

The planting community, rattled and frightened, were increasingly hostile to all political activity in the island. British mercantile and planting communities were not without influence within the island itself. With the active support of the British-owned *Times of Ceylon* they sought to exploit the extraordinary situation caused by the outbreak of war to embarrass Caldecott by making out to Whitehall that he was not as vigilant as he ought to be about potential threats to civil order. Many of these were hysterical outbursts rather than sensible criticisms, but Caldecott would not be diverted from his own way of handling these matters and refused to take hasty action.

The *Times of Ceylon* began a political campaign designed to exploit minority grievances and fears and to thwart the reformers among whom was placed Caldecott himself. In a leading article on 16 March 1940, it set out the case for a Royal Commission on constitutional reform and this was taken up by the minorities. The ministers – and the governor himself – were wary of any such commission and were much more favourable to Caldecott's proposal for a delimitation commission. Yet another point of divergence between them and the minorities had emerged, and one that was to cloud the whole issue of constitutional reform in Ceylon. It gave strength to the arguments of those in the CO who believed that agitation for constitutional reform would inevitably exacerbate communal rivalries to the detriment of the island's war effort.

In the meantime an incident arising out of a strike on a plantation in Hevahata near Kandy – Mool-oya estate – in January 1940 triggered another political and constitutional crisis (21). The Mool-oya crisis[25] was the direct result of the LSSP's campaign of establishing itself as a plantation trade union. The LSSP moved in once more to seize the initiative in a bid to repeat its successful stage-managing of the Bracegirdle affair, but the Board of Ministers, with Senanayake assuming the leadership, handled the situation much more astutely than it had over the Bracegirdle affair.

The State Council appointed a commission of inquiry to report on these incidents, and the inspector-general of police was directed by the minister of home affairs (Jayatilaka) to instruct police officers not to actively oppose any applications for the postponement of cases concerning the Mool-oya incident filed in the magistrate's court of Kandy, until the commission had completed its investigations and had reported to the council. The inspector-general of police refused to carry out these instructions on the grounds that the minister's decisions had neither been authorised by the executive committee of home affairs nor ratified by the governor in accordance with article 45 of the order-in-council of 1931. When Caldecott upheld the action of the inspector-general of police, the Board of Ministers resigned on 27 February 1940. It was their contention that article 45 had never before been strictly observed in practice. This well-publicised resignation focused attention on the constitutional issues involved. The flurry of telegrams between Colombo and London, of which a few are reproduced here, captures some of the drama and excitement of this episode (27-32). But behind it all there was a reluctance on both sides – the governor no less than the Board of Ministers – to permit a breakdown in the governmental machinery, in the certain knowledge that it would only strengthen the LSSP even further. The governor's interpretation of the rules regarding the working of the executive committee system, made in the wake of the Mool-oya affair, greatly strengthened the position of the minister as chairman of the committee as against the committee itself, particularly in the vitally important sphere of initiating action in directing administrative policy. The ministers were happy with this. Caldecott, for his part, was keeping within the framework of policy of the strengthening the powers of the ministers *vis-à-vis* the executive committees which the CO was intent on implementing.

For the LSSP this episode made a big difference. Caldecott ordered their arrest and detention in July 1940, giving in at last to pressure from the planters and the CO (50, 52, 53, 55, 56, 60, 63).

Indo–Ceylon negotiations

Throughout the years 1939 to 1948 the voting rights of Indians resident in the island continued to be a highly sensitive political issue. This was – as we shall see – partly because the modifications of the Donoughmore proposals on the franchise of the Indians resident in the island did not prove to be as effective as Sinhalese politicians were assured, and believed, they would be. There was also, in 1937, a controversy over the franchise of Indian plantation workers in local government elections at the village level.

Under the provisions of Ordinance 13 of 1889, Europeans, Burghers[26] and Indian plantation workers had been excluded from the franchise in elections to village committees. The rationale for this denial of voting rights was that none of these groups paid taxes to such committees, or formed an integral part of the village community served by such committees and could not possibly benefit from the social objects these councils were designed to provide. When this ordinance was amended in 1924 the exclusion of these groups was retained. Representatives of Indian opinion in the island acquiesced in it on that occasion, and indeed raised no objections until 1937.

In 1937 a more comprehensive amendment of Ordinance 13 of 1889 was attempted and implemented on the initiative of Bandaranaike, the minister of local government. Plantations were included within the area of operations of such committees and, in addition to the existing commutation tax, provision was made for a land tax on an acreage basis as an alternative method of village taxation. But the more controversial amendment concerned the continued exclusion of Indian plantation workers from the franchise while Europeans and Burghers were now given the right to vote at village committee elections. Representatives of Indian opinion reversed their previous and long-established acceptance of the exclusion of Indian plantation workers from the franchise at village committee level, and protested against their exclusion under the terms of Bandaranaike's amending ordinance, charging that it was a clear case of ethnic discrimination.

More important still, Ponnambalam made a significant entry into this debate as a champion of the rights of the Indians. In the early 1930's, when, in modification of the recommendations of the Donoughmore scheme, the Ceylon (State Council Elections) Order-in-Council of 1931 had imposed restrictions on the voting rights of the Indians resident in Ceylon, Tamil politicians in Jaffna and elsewhere had paid little or no heed to the protests from the Indian Tamil leadership in the island. Ponnambalam, in a notable reversal of this attitude, came out in 1937 as a defender of the rights of the Indian Tamils. He was hoping thereby to enlarge the composition of the minorities coalition he led, and an advocacy of unrestricted voting rights for Indians in Ceylon became a staple element in his political campaigns in the late 1930's and early 1940's.

Ponnambalam's intervention strengthened the resolve of Sinhalese politicians to stand firm against the inclusion of plantation workers in yet another area of political activity. The numbers of such workers on the electoral roll in the country had increased far beyond the limits envisaged by the Sinhalese politicians when they had accepted the restrictions on the voting rights of Indians introduced through the 1931 order-in-council. As a result of the controversy that ensued, the bill passed by the State Council was not approved, in its intended form, by the CO. Instead, at the suggestion of the then secretary of state, the amending bill was itself amended by the exclusion from the village committee franchise of all plantation workers irrespective of ethnic identity. The vast majority of plantation workers were Indians, but by making the restriction general rather than specific, the amendment was made more acceptable to the colonial administration in the island if not to representatives of Indian opinion.[27]

Much of the opposition to the extension of the franchise in village committee elections to Indian plantation workers stemmed from dissatisfaction among Sinhalese politicians with the working of articles 7 and 9 of the order-in-council. Article 9 had been devised to provide enfranchisement of Indians who had difficulty in proving domicile of choice under article 7 where the requirement was five years' residence. Applicants for certificates of permanent settlement under article 9 were required, not merely to make a declaration that they were permanently settled in the island but also to renounce claims to rights and privileges which, under the existing laws of the land, were not common to all British subjects. Also registration under article 7 was found to be much easier than anticipated, partly at least, because British officials in charge of enforcing the law were inclined to be less exacting and demanding than the spirit if not letter of the law warranted, to say nothing of the assurances given on these matters to Sinhalese politicians in 1931. Registration through article 7 proved to be so uncomplicated that not many Indians resorted to article 9.

The number of Indians registered as voters stood at around 100,000 in 1931; it rose to 145,000 in 1936, at the time of the second general election to the State Council, and to 225,000 in 1939.[28] This steep increase led to strong protests from Sinhalese politicians against what they described as laxity in registration procedure. With a general election scheduled for early 1941 this pressure increased.

Caldecott responded by ordering a tightening of the rules and regulations on registration in 1940 (45, 49, 54). By 1943 the number of Indians on the electoral registers had dropped to 168,000. Even so only two per cent of Indian registrations were obtained through certificates of permanent settlement under article 9. Thus Sinhalese grievances against the registration procedure remained almost undiminished from what they had been before 1940, while Indian opinion was invariably hostile to the insistence on a stricter adherence to the requirements of the law in regard to the registration of Indians as voters (58).

With the depression of the late 1920's and early 1930's, working class Indians in the urban areas, especially in and around Colombo, were resented as competitors in a tight labour market. The plantation workers were seen – to a greater extent than in the past – as a privileged group, and trade union leaders like Goonesinha, who had earlier worked with their Indian counterparts in the island and championed the cause of the underprivileged workers, indigenous and Indian alike, turned against the latter.

Above all the depression focused jealous attention on a small but wealthy section of the Indian community in the island; on the Indian moneylenders foreclosing on mortgages on land and houses, and on Indian traders who controlled the wholesale distribution of textiles, rice and other food items and who held a commanding position in their retail distribution throughout the island. The prominence attained in their respective spheres by the moneylenders and traders attracted hostile criticism towards the Indian community as a whole. At a time of high unemployment, vocal sections of the Sinhalese, including influential politicians, feared that their economic and political interests were under threat from the Indian minority in the island.

The Board of Ministers, with J L Kotelawela, the minister of transport and works, in the lead, responded by imposing restrictions, in 1939, on the employment of Indians in government service. These restrictions affected skilled as well as unskilled workers employed on the railways, in road construction and in sanitation services among others. The Government of India retaliated by placing an embargo on the emigration to Ceylon of unskilled labour from India, which in turn inevitably produced an outcry from the planters who feared that the supply of Indian labour on which they were so dependent would be reduced as a result (6, 7, 8, 10). A partial ban on the emigration of unskilled labour from India had first been imposed in 1937 as a retaliatory measure during the controversy over votes for Indian plantation workers in village council elections. Over and above all this the voting rights of Indians in Ceylon became a matter of acute controversy in early 1940. K W Blaxter, a principal in the CO Eastern Department, provided a succinct summary of the issues involved:

On the existing register of voters a large number of Indians have been wrongly included owing to the lax interpretation of a memorandum by the Legal Secretary. The Board of Ministers are assuming that the election next January [ie January 1941] will duly take place and it is therefore necessary during the present year to carry out a further revision of the register. The Legal Secretary has recently issued a further memorandum impressing upon the registering authorities the procedure they must adopt for enrolling Indian voters. The strict observance of this memorandum will result in the removal of a large number of voters from the rolls. The Ministers have become thoroughly alarmed by the realization of what the position is and are not disposed to introduce in the State Council the necessary financial supplementary estimate for the money required to carry out the revision of the register until certain changes have been made in the Elections Order in Council relating to Indian voters. They wish the Order in Council to be amended so as to provide for the payment of a rupee fee and also to ensure that Indians who obtain the vote in Ceylon should renounce the special privileges which they had as Indians. They propose to move a resolution in the State Council on the 14 May to the effect that the serious condition of the Electoral Register demands that immediate steps be taken to give effect to paragraph 35 of Sir Herbert Stanley's despatch of the 2nd June 1929 and to paragraph 10 of Lord Passfield's despatch of the 10th October 1929.[29]

These conflicts showed little signs of abating, wartime conditions notwithstanding. Two integral units of the empire were bickering like two sovereign states over the protection of their respective interests, almost oblivious to the larger interests of an empire whose very existence was under severe threat from its enemies. Caldecott himself was aware of the dangers of the continuation of this conflict and endeavoured to cool tempers among Ceylon's politicians. He realised that the planters were apprehensive about the threat posed to the efficient running of their plantations from potential labour shortages as a result of the Indian ban on the emigration of unskilled labour. In addition there were hints, from India, of trade sanctions. The CO was anxious that these controversies should be brought to an end through a process of negotiation (17,19).

Attempts at resolving these issues had been made towards the end of 1939 but these failed almost at once. A terse communiqué issued by the Government of India on 5 January 1940 announced the failure of the talks (18). In the meantime the Government of Ceylon, under pressure from the Board of Ministers, proceeded with its plans to tighten the regulations on registering Indians resident in the island. The Indian government was perturbed and sought an opportunity to comment on the changes proposed. In early July 1940 moves were afoot to resume talks between the two governments (58, 59). The CO suggested on 15 July that the first discussions should be of an exploratory nature, a proposal that found acceptance both in Colombo and Delhi, the latter being chosen as the venue.

From the time the resumption of the talks was announced on 14 August 1940 the two governments as well as the CO found themselves involved in an attempt to discourage politicians in the Ceylon delegation from meeting their Indian counterparts (62, 64, 70). This was more difficult than usual because at the same time a delegation from the Ceylon National Congress was attending the annual session of the Indian National Congress; the delegation included some members of the Board of Ministers. On 22 October 1940 Caldecott sought to reassure the viceroy by stating that any conversation between Ceylon ministers and Indian political leaders would be strictly unofficial and informal (73).

Representatives of the two governments met to discuss outstanding issues at informal and preparatory talks in Delhi in November 1940. The four-member ministerial delegation from Ceylon was led by Senanayake and included G C S Corea, minister for labour, industry and commerce, Bandaranaike, and a British official, H J Huxham, the financial secretary. The talks soon produced a deadlock. In their official report the delegation from Colombo stated: 'As no agreement could be reached on the question of the status of Indian immigrants in Ceylon, the Indian delegation was unwilling to proceed to the consideration of other questions noted for discussion. The talks thus came to an end' (74, 75).

Struggling hard to control the damage to Indo-Ceylon relations that could have flowed from the abrupt failure of these preparatory talks, Caldecott successfully prevailed upon the Ceylon ministers in the official delegation not to publish, at once, their version of the breakdown. The governor feared that any hasty public official statement by the ministers could make things worse than they already were (76). He succeeded in this to the extent that no official statement was issued, but he could not prevent Senanayake from making a reference to the talks in the course of his address at the annual session of the Ceylon National Congress on 22 December 1940. Senanayake's strident explanation of why, in his opinion, the talks in Delhi had failed, was given wide coverage and great prominence to in the local newspapers (79; also 82, 83, 89).

Caldecott was now intent on patching up this quarrel between his ministers and the Indian government and decided to make a statement to the State Council on the undertakings which Ceylon had given to India on the treatment of Indians in Ceylon, and which were still valid obligations (84). He felt this course of action to be essential 'as being the only way of reassuring India of the bona fides of the Ceylon government, and of inducing the Ceylon politicians to adopt a realistic approach to the Indian question in the island'.[30]

The text of this statement was agreed upon between Colombo and the CO and was conveyed to the State Council on 5 February 1941. However, the governor's attempt at mediation succeeded only in aggravating the situation. The Board of Ministers strongly protested against the statement and proceeded with plans to introduce legislation to control immigration to the island, and for the registration of resident Indians (86, 88).

It was against this background that Caldecott persuaded the Board of Ministers to make another effort at reaching an agreement on outstanding issues with the Government of India. This second round of talks was held in Colombo in September 1941 between a delegation led by Sir G S Bajpai and a delegation of Ceylon ministers and officials.[31] Both sides were in a more conciliatory mood on this occasion, the Ceylonese more so than the Indians. The Ceylon delegation offered the status of permanent settlers – with the right to vote – to all Indians with a minimum of seven years residence in the island, with all those admitted to the country thereafter being treated as temporary residents. This was part of a six-point formula offered by the Ceylon delegation. An agreement was reached and initialled on this basis on this occasion, but significantly the Indian government, under pressure from the leadership of the Indians resident in Ceylon, failed to ratify it even though its terms were published.

Wartime conditions and the revival of pressure for constitutional reform
Britain's energies were now concentrated on the war in Europe and the constitutional problems of a small Asian colony took very low priority in this. With MacDonald's departure from the CO on 13 May 1940, there were three short tenures of the secretaryship of state for the colonies between that date and 24 November 1942 when Oliver Stanley took over and remained in office until August 1945. All the secretaries of state during this period – Lords Lloyd, Moyne and Cranborne – were coalition Conservatives, as was Stanley himself.

It came as no great surprise to Caldecott when, on 18 December 1940, Lloyd sent him a telegram stating the impracticability of further examining the constitutional problems of the island before the end of the war (78). This was not immediately divulged to the ministers, much less published. Instead Caldecott played for time in the hope that Whitehall could be persuaded to make a more generous response (81, 97). Even at this stage the ministers and other Sinhalese spokesmen felt that the CO was unnecessarily delaying a decision on a matter on which it possessed all the relevant data. The governor realised that there was no support for a constitutional conference or a commission from these sources in the colony. Instead he reverted to the proposals put forward in his despatch of October 1939 (9), with minor modifications (100). The governor's arguments made little impression on the CO, although some officials were prepared to acknowledge that it would be difficult for Britain to impose a solution (101–103). Eventually, an official announcement –

approved by the War Cabinet in August 1941, communicated to the Board of Ministers in September and placed before the State Council in late October – was made to the effect that constitutional reform was postponed until the war was over, and that the position would be examined afresh by a committee or conference thereafter (106). This declaration was tantamount to an indefinite postponement of constitutional reform. It was clearly a disappointment for the Board of Ministers but they reacted as was customary with a polite note of disagreement and continued to press for a more generous gesture from Britain (107, 109–112).

Caldecott now watched the consensus on constitutional reform which he had patiently put together in 1938-1939 dissolve in the face of world events and their impact on local politics. At the beginning of 1942 the moderate wing – by far the most influential – of the nationalist movement was no longer bound by the 1938–1939 consensus and had set out dominion status as its objective. Within a year a group of young men, with J R Jayewardene and Dudley Senanayake (Senanayake's elder son) among the most prominent of them, persuaded the Ceylon National Congress to spurn dominion status for the more emotionally satisfying and politically attractive concept of independence. It needed all Senanayake's personal prestige and tenacity of purpose to stand up against this current of opinion, and to insist that the goal of Ceylon's constitutional evolution should be dominion status, to be attained in association with, rather than in opposition, to Britain. At this stage, Caldecott was not enthusiastic about dominion status for Ceylon, arguing that 'it is obvious that the implications and obligations of Dominion Status are either not understood or are being deliberately ignored by people who should know better' (113).

Japan's entry into the war in 1941 and the string of spectacular successes she achieved initially had an immediate impact on the thinking both of Whitehall and the Board of Ministers. Caldecott reported, at the end of 1941, that these developments 'thrust every other consideration out of mind, and everybody [has] plenty to do in organizing services and preventing panic' (113). Ceylon was by now a frontline state in the war against Japan. Caldecott never had to worry about the political loyalties of the Board of Ministers. Whitehall, for its part, understood the new strategic significance of the island and the new secretary of state, Lord Cranborne, explained CO thinking on this to Caldecott in a telegram of 3 March 1942 (118). This was followed on 5 March by a directive from the Chiefs of Staff on the appointment of Vice Admiral Sir G Layton as commander-in-chief of the British forces in the island (119).

Layton's appointment was important on its own because of its regional military significance, for earlier, on 17 November 1941, the island had been placed under the commander-in-chief, India, and Major General R D Inskip had been appointed general officer commanding the troops in the island. Locally, Layton's appointment had an even wider significance because his authority was not restricted to the armed forces but extended to the civil government as well – he was authorised to use the governor's reserve powers under the constitution to any extent he thought fit. Indeed Layton's powers were so extensive that clashes with the civil government – the governor and the Board of Ministers – seemed inevitable, and there were fears that such clashes could lead to a constitutional breakdown. For Senanayake, manifestly now the most dynamic figure in the Board of Ministers and the obvious successor to the ageing Jayatilaka, the powers conferred on Layton and the establishment of a War

Council in the island on Layton's initiative and under his control (124), were new and unpredictable complications that confronted him and his allies in their campaign for constitutional reform. The War Council was thus constituted: Layton (as chairman), the governor (as a member), the three officers of state, the seven Sinhalese ministers, the service chiefs and the civil defence commissioner as well (from the last quarter of 1942). It met for the first time on 24 March 1942. Its main objective was the co-ordination of the war effort, but a reading of its minutes shows that, from the outset, it's writ extended well beyond that.

There were also fears that the island's strategic importance in the struggle against Japan would be a further constraint in pressing ahead for constitutional reform. What happened, however, was that Layton, by virtue of his regular meetings with the ministers, displayed a greater appreciation of the political problems they faced than might have been the case had he relied solely on the governor's views, or the views of the British officials, civil and military. More to the point, Senanayake soon established an amicable working relationship with Layton. He got on cordially enough with Caldecott, despite the latter's occasional fits of antipathy to him, of which we have evidence in the acerbic comments on Senanayake in some of the governor's 'Things Ceylonese' reports to the CO. But in the event they worked together with much less friction after Layton's arrival than before; a triangular relationship seemed more stable than the earlier one between the governor and Senanayake as aspirant to the *de jure* position of leader of the State Council, and vice chairman of the Board of Ministers. With this new situation and with the board continuing to give its unstinted support to the war effort, Senanayake found that the island's strategic importance actually strengthened his bargaining powers.

The fear of a Japanese invasion was very real. When the first Japanese air-raid occurred on 2 April 1942 with bombs being dropped on Colombo, to be followed soon after by another raid, this time on Trincomalee, there was panic. People fled the capital and the suburbs to towns and villages in the interior of the island; large numbers of Indian money-lenders, businessmen and traders fled to India. There were fears of a return of Indian workers to their villages in southern India but these proved to be exaggerated. Fortunately the threat from Japan receded quickly. The antici-pated invasion never came, nor did the Japanese air raids continue.

The dispatch of the Cripps Mission to India in March 1942 undermined the credibility of CO policy on constitutional reform in Ceylon. The Office, for its part, did not see it that way, even when there were requests from the Board of Ministers and the Ceylon National Congress that Cripps should visit Ceylon as well, or failing that receive a ministerial delegation from Ceylon in Delhi. On 1 April 1942 Cranborne informed Caldecott that the Cripps Mission was restricted to India (125). The same telegram renewed the CO pledge that discussions on constitutional reform would be resumed once victory was won, not a very reassuring prospect at a time when that victory seemed so far away. The minorities now proposed that a national government be formed during this emergency period, a proposal which neither Caldecott nor the CO were willing to consider, much less to support (125). April 1942 was not a good month for the colonial administration in the island. On 8 April the LSSP detainees staged a daring jail-break, escaping from the detention barracks in Kandy (127).

As the threat from Japan receded, other changes occurred in the last quarter of 1942, all of which strengthened the administration. In early September Caldecott reported that Senanayake would have a larger role in the distribution of food (138), an important matter at a time of threatened food scarcities and the introduction of a rationing system. O E (later Sir Oliver) Goonetilleke now emerged in a role that was to give him great prominence, as civil defence commissioner, in charge of the distribution of food. In this capacity he was invited to attend meetings of the War Council (138), thus strengthening his long association with Senanayake and beginning an equally important one with Layton and Caldecott who recognised his talents as a gifted administrator and general establishment figure *par excellence*.

By the end of September 1942, the old duumvirate of Jayatilaka and Senanayake was over with the former's retirement. On 2 December Senanayake was elected leader of the house, and took over as vice chairman of the Board of Ministers, a *de jure* recognition of what had been, for long, a *de facto* situation. Equally significant, he secured the election of a Tamil, A Mahadeva, as minister of home affairs, in place of Jayatilaka thus bringing to an end the experiment of an all-Sinhalese Board of Ministers.

In the meantime Caldecott and Layton between them took the initiative in reopening the question of constitutional reform for Ceylon by urging the CO to respond to the spirit of co-operation demonstrated by the Board of Ministers with a new declaration of policy that would meet the desires and aspirations of the more moderate elements in Ceylon (140, 141). Caldecott drove home the point in his telegrams that a more convincing and forthright statement on constitutional reform than that issued in 1941 was called for to retain the goodwill and co-operation of the Board of Ministers and to secure the whole-hearted co-operation of the Ceylonese in the war effort. The pressure from Caldecott and the cogency of his arguments had their effect and the War Cabinet considered it politic to issue a fresh declaration of policy on constitutional reform in the island (142, 143). The central feature of this pronouncement made in December 1942 was its definition of the objectives of constitutional evolution. These were stated to be the 'fullest possible development of self-governing institutions in Ceylon within the Commonwealth partnership having regard both to the single interest of the island and the larger interests of the Commonwealth on which the island's security and prosperity ultimately depend'.

But this declaration did not have the desired effect, and the Board of Ministers complained that it was couched in 'far too indefinite and conditional terms' (148). Senanayake, at an interview with Layton and Caldecott on 25 February 1943, emphasised the need for a very early response to the board's demand for dominion status (154). Caldecott would not support this claim, but he and Layton had already informed the CO that moderate opinion in the country demanded full responsible government and internal home rule (150). After some initial uncertainty (150, 152), Stanley and his officials appreciated the distinction made by Caldecott and Layton between dominion status on the one hand, and full responsible government and internal home rule on the other, and this helped to persuade them to look at the problem afresh.

On 17–18 February 1943, Caldecott and Layton sent the CO the draft of a declaration of policy on constitutional reform as a substitute for that made in December 1942 (153). The draft spelt out the limits on responsible government, especially in the areas of defence and external relations. Amendments were made by the CO (155), the Board of Trade commented on safeguards for British commerce (158) and Leopold Amery, secretary of state for India and Burma, drew attention to the analogy between Burma and Ceylon (159). The issue was placed before the War Cabinet in March 1943. Using arguments which were substantially those of Caldecott and Layton, Stanley produced four reasons in support of a new declaration. First, to prevent any serious deterioration in Ceylon's war effort. Secondly, to avoid giving the impression that more could be obtained from the British government by making trouble than by methods of co-operation; a contrast in this respect was drawn with the 'largely non-co-operative' attitude of the 'political element' in India. Thirdly, to persuade Sinhalese politicians to turn their minds to a settlement with the minorities and to a 'realistic appreciation' of their future relations with India. Finally, to retain the initiative and to avoid a situation in which, at the end of the war, the same offer would have to be made but in conditions where much goodwill would have been lost. Against these arguments the secretary of state accepted that the governor's proposals would involve 'very real difficulties'. The first was the crucial issue of minority rights, for which the only definite safeguard was the requirement that any new reform proposals would need the approval of three-quarters of the members of the State Council. Stanley admitted that he had feared that discussion of constitutional reform would run the risk of losing minority co-operation in the war effort but he had been assured by the governor that the minorities were 'just as keen to be released from Whitehall apron strings as the majority' (153). There were also concerns that a popular government would assume complete financial responsibility at precisely the time when the post-war financial and economic problems of Ceylon might be most acute, and that it would be difficult to devise adequate safeguards for British commercial interests. But weighing all the arguments, the secretary of state maintained that the balance of advantage lay in making an immediate declaration (161).

The War Cabinet was not immediately persuaded by Stanley's arguments and a Cabinet committee was appointed to examine the proposals further (161). The committee emphasised in particular the importance of protection for minority rights and British commerce and clarification on these issues was sought from the governor (163–166, 168). Eventually, and with the approval of the War Cabinet (169), a revised declaration was made on 26 May 1943.

A comparison of the two declarations – of December 1942 and May 1943 – is revealing. In both no hope is held out of any changes during the war. But the second definitely committed Britain to a far-reaching reform at the end of the war. Where the first declaration offered a vague promise of 'the fullest possible development of self-governing institutions within the Commonwealth partnership' (143), the second was more precise. It offered 'full responsibility for government under the Crown in all matters of civil administration'. The only matters to be reserved would be defence and external affairs. The 1943 proposals did not include the right of secession. But as Stanley had explained when he first took the issue to the War Cabinet in March 1943, constitutionally, while not attaining full dominion status, Ceylon would be 'very much in the position now occupied by Southern Rhodesia' (161).

In February 1943, at the beginning of the consultation which led to the May declaration, Caldecott and Layton had cautioned that although in their judgement 'all moderate political opinion' would be satisfied with the proposed declaration, this did not of course mean that there would not be 'such measure of expressed disappointment as is inseparable from any concessions less than what is asked for' (153). This assessment of the situation in the island was as sensible as it was accurate. Although the proposals outlined in May 1943 fell short of dominion status (which Senanayake had set out as the objective he aimed at), and far short of the goal of independence (which the Ceylon National Congress advocated), the Board of Ministers under Senanayake's leadership preferred to accept the offer as one further stage in the constitutional advancement of the country and as the basis for further negotiations.

The first task confronting Senanayake was to formulate a draft constitution on the basis of the conditions laid down in the May 1943 declaration and the clarification of this given on 9 July 1943 (170, 171, 173, 174). The requirement that such a draft constitution needed to obtain the approval of three-quarters of all members of the State Council practically ensured that it would have to be nothing less than a national consensus on constitutional reform, because a constitution so formulated and so approved would then face another and equally exacting test – rigorous examination by 'a suitable commission or conference' once victory over the axis powers had been achieved.

Ceylon and wartime supplies: the case of rubber production
Of the many arguments used in justification of the May 1943 declaration, perhaps the most significant was concern to avoid any disruption of Ceylon's war effort. Indeed Stanley had reminded the War Cabinet of Ceylon's 'vital importance' as a strategic base and source of essential raw materials, rubber in particular (161). However, as already observed at the beginning of this introduction, beneath Ceylon's co-operation on the question of materials there existed an underlying tension between the island's interests as a producer and those of the Treasury and the supply departments in Britain as purchasers and distributors. In the process, and with the CO playing the role of an intermediary, the issue was one which reactivated the former controversy with India over immigration and also threatened to further complicate Anglo-American wartime relations.

With the Japanese occupation of Burma in 1942, Ceylon became even more dependent on India for food supplies, especially of rice. By the end of 1942 Ceylon's rice stocks had fallen to dangerously low levels, not only from the standpoint of the island's defence but also from that of meeting Ceylon's production of rubber and other essential raw materials. There were already indications that the morale and efficiency of workers in the island were beginning to suffer from the food shortage (146).

But it was over the question of rubber production that the main difficulties arose. At the beginning of 1943, in his capacity as minister of agriculture, Senanayake launched a drive to increase rubber production over the year from 100,000 to 130,000 tons. His methods included extensive slaughter-tapping on plantations and the special, temporary recruitment from India of 20,000 workers who would be repatriated at the end of the war. The Indian government was prepared to release the labour but refused to accept the condition of compulsory repatriation; some officials in the CO believed that India was 'blackmailing Ceylon on a long-standing and deep-rooted political issue' (151). However, the CO also saw fit to remind Caldecott that an intransigent attitude on the part of Ceylon might influence the War Cabinet to consider less favourably the governor's proposals for a new reforms declaration. Caldecott responded angrily that neither the CO nor the Indian government appreciated the 'intensely bitter and suspicious feeling' that existed in Ceylon over immigration (156, 157). He reported in March 1943 that despite the evident difficulties, Senanayake was preparing to recruit the extra labour from local sources (160).

Friction with India was only one part of a complicated equation. Slaughter-tapping on the scale now contemplated threatened the ultimate destruction of thousands of trees. Compensation to growers was first considered but it proved impossible to reach agreement over the terms because of the different applications of taxes on excess profits for London—based and local concerns. The view of the Ceylon government was that whereas London companies should be dealt with on a compensation basis, their own growers should receive a straight increase of price. Anxious to maintain Ceylon's rubber production and to avoid 'another political complication from the American side if Ceylon production in fact falls short', the CO and the Ministries of Production and Supply were prepared to concede Ceylon's demands. The Treasury, however, refused, on the grounds that there was no guarantee that higher prices would be matched by increased rubber production. Ceylon, according to the Treasury, was 'virtually blackmailing us' (162, 167, 180).

In June 1943 Caldecott reported that rubber production was causing both himself and Layton 'grave anxiety'. The extra labour from local sources promised by Senanayake had so far failed to materialise and there was a real danger that Ceylon would not achieve its production targets. The governor's assessment now convinced the CO that the real issue at stake was not one of price but of labour (172) but negotiations over the recruitment of Indian workers were deadlocked and remained so until well into 1944.

It was at this juncture, and as feared by the CO and Ministries of Production and Supply, that American officials became involved. Ceylon provided about sixty per cent of the allies' natural rubber. The maintenance of Ceylon rubber production was said by the American consul in Colombo to be an 'A-1 priority'; the dispute between India and Ceylon was jeopardising allied operations (189, 192). By the autumn of 1944 the CO was considering asking Churchill to intervene personally in the labour dispute with India but no action was taken.[32] Putting pressure on Ceylon would only undermine other aspects of the island's war contribution (229).

Throughout this dispute the view from the economic departments in Whitehall was that while India had been at fault in stipulating conditions which were bound to revive old antagonisms over immigration, Ceylon itself had been unreasonably rigid and inflexible. On the price issue, Ceylon's argument that higher prices were needed as an inducement to persuade growers to produce more rubber ultimately antagonised the Treasury and the Ministries of Production and Supply. At the end of 1943, P Saravanamuttu, the Ceylon rubber commissioner, visited London for discussions over rubber prices. C Y Carstairs, an assistant secretary and head of a newly formed Production Department in the CO, minuted after a discussion with D E H Pierson of the Ministry of Supply:

Mr. Pierson gave me the interesting view that our path had been made very difficult by Mr. Saravanamuttu's presentation of the case. On enquiry, I elicited that this means that Mr. Saravanamuttu had been entirely too candid, not having attempted to represent that the present price was an unremunerative one for the great majority of the industry, but that a higher price would stimulate the Ceylon producers (large and small) to greater efforts than hitherto. This idea offends against the principles current here that increases in price are only justifiable on account of increases in costs of production, and that the profit motive is a bad one. All this is true enough, but of doubtful applicability to a territory such as Ceylon, and it ignores completely certain political and psychological factors, including the prices which Ceylon has to pay for imports from India, which we did our utmost to make clear to the Ministry of Supply and the Treasury.[33]

Others in the CO, most notably Sydney Caine, the financial adviser, took a less favourable view of Ceylon's case and began arguing in a manner which suggested that Ceylon was ignoring the sacrifices being made in Britain and by producers elsewhere in the colonial empire.[34] Such ideas resurfaced at the end of the war when Goonetilleke, in his new capacity as financial secretary, made an unsuccessful attempt to negotiate preferential trade agreements with Britain (368–372, 374).

The ministers' draft constitution

Following the clarification in July 1943 of the May declaration, the Board of Ministers set to work, almost immediately, on the process of drafting a new constitution. Much to Caldecott's annoyance and chagrin, Senanayake chose as his principal adviser on constitutional affairs Dr W Ivor Jennings, vice chancellor of the newly established University of Ceylon. Caldecott was upset that the principal legal advisors and officers of the government, the legal secretary and the attorney-general, were left out of the drafting process. For the outlines of the constitution Senanayake and his colleagues reverted to the policy framework that had emerged in the discussions that had taken place in the mid and late 1930's, and especially to the reforms debate of March to July 1939.

The key feature was a return to the Westminster model in the structure of government, with suitable modifications to accommodate the needs of the minorities in regard to the protection of their rights. One of the first questions that arose was whether or not a bill of rights should be introduced into the constitution. Senanayake was not unsympathetic to the view that a bill of rights would be a useful means of allaying the fears of minorities as to their position in an independent Ceylon, but he was dissuaded from supporting it by the arguments of Jennings, for whom the applicability of the Westminster constitutional model to the Ceylonese situation was an unalterable article of faith. Jennings would not give any serious consideration to the incorporation of a bill of rights in the constitution. On his advice it was rejected by the Board of Ministers and replaced by a provision based on section 5 of the Government of Ireland Act of 1920, prohibiting legislation infringing on religious freedom or discriminating against persons of any community or religion. The draft constitution prepared by the Board of Ministers in 1943–1944 contained a clause (clause 8) prohibiting parliament from enacting laws which discriminated against ethnic or religious groups, restricted or prohibited the free exercise of any religion, or conferred on 'persons of any community or religion privileges or advantages which are not conferred on persons of other communities or religions'. This was transferred, with only minor additions, to the constitution on which the transfer of power was effected in 1947–1948, the Soulbury constitution, as section 29(2). In retrospect it would seem that this was no substitute for a bill of rights, and the protection afforded to the minorities proved to be far from adequate. But at the time of the transfer of power the constitutional guarantees against discriminatory legislation in the new constitution, in combination with other provisions which were made to accommodate minority interests, seemed sufficient for that purpose.

'The representation clauses', as Jennings remarked all too accurately, 'were undoubtedly the most contentious . . . [and the] task of the Ministers was exceedingly difficult'.[35] Addressing itself to the thorny question of representation, the ministers' draft constitution devised a structure that found wide acceptability. One of its distinctive features was the incorporation of the principle of weightage in representation to allay the fears of the minorities and to provide greater electoral influence to the backward areas of the country. The province – there were nine provinces in British Ceylon at the time of the transfer of power – was the unit adopted for demarcation of constituencies, with a parliamentary constituency for each 75,000 persons, ascertained to the nearest 75,000, in a province. While this naturally favoured the more densely populated parts of the country, the population formula was combined with a provision that there would be, in addition, a constituency for every 1,000 square miles of territory. This area weightage varied from a minimum of one in the Western province, to four each in the Northern and Eastern provinces (in the first of which Tamils formed a clear majority, while the Muslims were a substantial minority especially in the Eastern province) and the North Central province. The area weightage in this last province was designed to benefit the Kandyans. The other comparatively backward Kandyan provinces, Uva and the North Western province, gained three seats each on the area rule.

The advantages of weightage in representation were several; its beneficiaries were also many. Sinhalese politicians welcomed it because of its avoidance of communal representation. By reducing the size of constituencies both in area and in population in those parts of the country where the minorities were the, or a, dominant element, comparatively homogeneous constituencies, which were not specifically communal, could be demarcated by a future delimitation commission. Equally, because the sparsely populated areas were also, coincidentally, the areas with larger concentrations of minorities, these latter would increase their representation, and this appealed to the minority groups such as the Muslims who were growing increasingly disenchanted with Ponnambalam's own campaign for balanced representation. The Kandyans were among the principal beneficiaries of weightage in representation, a point on which both Caldecott and the Sinhalese political leadership of the day were agreed; and there was an element of equity in that the sparsely populated areas (some of which were Kandyan) would have greater representation, and thus greater influence politically, than they might have had if population figures were the sole criterion in demarcating constituencies.

The draft constitution recognised that 'No system of representation would necessarily ensure that all sections of the community would be adequately represented'. Provision was therefore made for the nomination of up to six members by the head of state 'where he considers that any important interest was not adequately represented'. This was designed with the minorities, or rather the smaller minorities, in mind.

The preparation of a draft constitution that would meet the requirements of the Whitehall declaration of 1943 was a challenge to the statesmanship and political acumen of Senanayake and the Board of Ministers. They – and their advisers – worked with remarkable speed, and by the beginning of 1944 a draft – the minister's draft constitution as it came to be called – was ready for submission to Whitehall (181). On the whole it bore the stamp of Senanayake's political vision, in which concern for the interests of the minorities went beyond the formal need to conform to the letter and spirit of terms laid down by Whitehall. The speed with which they had completed their work was mainly because nobody outside the Board of Ministers, not even members of the State Council, had been invited to participate in the preparation of the draft constitution. While this was not contrary to the terms of the declaration of 1943, it was nevertheless one of the criticisms of the draft raised by the more vocal representatives of Tamil opinion and British business interests in the island (182, 188, 193, 194).

The Soulbury Commission
Under the terms of the declaration of May 1943, it was envisaged that the draft constitution would be examined by a 'suitable commission or conference' after victory over the axis powers had been achieved. Once the draft was ready – by February 1944 – Senanayake and the Board of Ministers pressed for an immediate consideration of their scheme. Senanayake argued that urgent local circumstances made an early decision on the constitution a matter of vital necessity (183). He had the backing in this of Caldecott and Layton, a powerful combination on their own. Both favoured the appointment of a commission. They emphasised that failure to meet Senanayake's wishes would deal a 'death blow' to the ideal of Ceylon becoming an internally self-governing unit of the Commonwealth and lead to 'a general demand for inclusion in a new federal India'. They also reminded the CO that the alternative to the appointment of a commission would be an election in Ceylon at the very time that SEAC was being established in the island (186, 190, 191, 196, 198). The governor and Layton strengthened their bargaining powers in Whitehall when they sought and received the active support of Admiral Mountbatten, supreme allied commander of SEAC, whose headquarters were transferred from New Delhi to Kandy in April 1944 (199).[36] Having been consulted by the Chiefs of Staff in London, Mountbatten warned that SEAC operations might be disrupted if an election were held in Ceylon (200). His intervention helped greatly in overcoming the original reluctance of the CO and the War Cabinet to concede Senanayake's request (184, 187, 195, 197, 202). The decision might have gone against Senanayake had Mountbatten not intervened.

The official announcement on the appointment of a commission to visit the island was made on 5 July 1944, but far from being received with cordiality and a sense of satisfaction at the extraction of an important concession – for, after all, the war was not yet over – it was greeted in ministerial circles in Colombo with undisguised dismay (208). And not merely ministerial circles. The Ceylon National Congress, naturally enough, was even more forthright in criticism (207). The point at issue was what both ministers and Congress saw as a widening of the commission's terms of reference well beyond that set out in the declaration of May 1943, from merely an examination of the draft constitution prepared by the Board of Ministers, under the terms of that declaration, to include consultation with 'various interests, including the minority communities, concerned with the subject of constitutional reform in Ceylon'. Taking a rather narrow view, Senanayake and his colleagues in the Board of Ministers argued that this amounted to an abrogation of one of the terms of the 1943 declaration. They urged that the work of the commission should be restricted to the scope set out in the declaration which meant in effect that it should be limited to an examination of the ministers' draft constitution. The requirement that the constitution should be approved by at least three-quarters of members of the State Council was, according to the ministers, sufficient protection for minority interests. The ministers' protests were considered over a period of nearly two months but ultimately they were overruled and the terms of reference of the commission were left unchanged (209–221, 224–227).

Over the personnel of the commission, Caldecott was clear as to what the situation called for: a three man commission, one member of which should have British political experience; one, experience in the lower house of a dominion parliament; and the third, British Treasury experience. Three names were mentioned as the sort of persons who would fit the bill. Among them was a former Conservative MP and minister, Lord Soulbury. Dons and constitutional theorists, he urged, should be studiously avoided (a reflection perhaps of his antipathy to Jennings who was both a don and a constitutional theorist) and none of them, he added, should have had any previous association with Ceylon or with other colonial administrations, or with India (186).

Caldecott did not make any suggestions for the position of chairman of the commission, but the CO did not look beyond Soulbury – who was suggested by the governor only for nomination as a member – as chairman. His name was submitted on 8 August to the prime minister as the CO nominee for the chairmanship; the prime minister's approval was given on 21 August. Thereafter the search began, in consultation with Soulbury, for the two other members.

One was a nominee of the Labour Party or, to be more exact, of Ernest Bevin in particular. Trafford Smith of the CO, who was appointed secretary to the commission, minuted on 12 October 1944: 'Mr Bevin does not wish to recommend anyone other than Mr F. J. Burrows, President of the N[ational] U[nion] [of] R[ailwaymen] as a possible member of the Ceylon commission.'[37] When it became necessary to make the official announcement on the personnel of the Ceylon commission, the secretary noted somewhat testily that Burrows was not in *Who's Who* and 'that neither I nor anyone else here knows anything about him beyond the fact that he is the retiring President of the National Union of Railwaymen'.[38] The nomination for the third position proved to be more difficult. On 25 October J B Sidebotham, assistant secretary and head of the Ceylon and Pacific Department, argued that Caldecott's views on keeping out dons and constitutional theorists should be disregarded. 'I have always felt myself', he stated 'that somebody with some knowledge of constitutional law problems would be of great assistance to this particular commission'.[39] At this stage Sir James Colquhoun, principal and vice chancellor of St Andrews University, had been approached to serve on the commission. He declined and the CO turned instead to Professor J F Rees, vice-chancellor of the University of Wales and principal of the University College of South Wales and Monmouthshire. Rees eventually accepted the invitation but in case he did not, the CO had prepared a short list of dons and constitutional theorists whom it wished to invite to serve.[40]

On 19 November 1944 the names of the personnel of the commission were officially announced. Caldecott had already relinquished office on 17 October, the date on which he left the island. His successor, Sir Henry Moore, arrived in Colombo on 4 December.[41] The commission travelled to Colombo by air and its first public sessions were on 22 January 1945. It was the last of three important commissions sent from Britain to report on the affairs of the island, the first being the Colebrooke-Cameron Commission of 1828–1831, and the second, a century later, the Donoughmore Commission. The distinguishing feature of the Soulbury Commission was that its terms of reference were the narrowest of the three.

To demonstrate their disapproval at the widening of its terms of reference, Senanayake and the Board of Ministers resolved on an official boycott of the commission. The Ceylon National Congress acted likewise and at a special session came out in support of an all-party conference on constitutional reform. So far as the ministers were concerned the boycott meant, in practice, merely that they did not appear before the commission at its public sittings. Intermediaries, the most notable of whom was Goonetilleke, conveyed their views to the commissioners and Senanayake and the ministers met them informally, especially at receptions. Above all, although the ministers did not present their draft constitution before the commission, the latter regarded the examination of that document as its main task during its stay in the island. The Congress leadership, however, were more committed to the decision to boycott the commission. Senanayake, for his part, had already resigned from Congress, a move designed to emphasise that he had distanced himself from an organisation which had not succeeded in winning the confidence of the minorities.

Up to the appointment of the Soulbury Commission, events had gone Senanayake's way. He had succeeded in keeping the process of drafting the constitution under his control, and had also guided it so astutely that he had been able to win the backing of the Board of Ministers for the final document. Now, however, doubts were cast about his ability to produce results. Unhappy at being left out of the drafting process, and anxious to make their own views on the constitution known and their influence felt, Senanayake's critics – of whom there were more than a few within the State Council and Congress – sensed the possibility of exploiting the weakening of his position. Not that Senanayake entirely minded, for the situation had the advantage – such as it was – of giving Whitehall and the Soulbury commissioners a sobering comparative perspective in which Senanayake's moderation came through with greater clarity than it might have done through his own efforts.

It was against this background that a resolution was moved in the State Council calling upon the Board of Ministers to draft another constitution of the 'recognized Dominion type' appropriate for a 'Free Lanka'. This initiative was immediately successful. An amendment pledging support to the Whitehall declaration of 1943 was beaten soundly by twenty-six votes to four. The board was bound by the provisions of the Donoughmore constitution to implement a resolution adopted by the State Council, and a bill making provision for such a constitution was introduced at the next session of council by Bandaranaike.

A Free Lanka Bill was prepared between November 1944 and the beginning of February 1945. That a further draft constitution could be produced with such speed was made possible because it was based on the ministers' original draft. Apart from certain minor dissimilarities incidental to the variance in intentions of the two drafts, the Free Lanka Bill diverged from the ministers' scheme only in regard to the provisions dealing with the powers of the governor-general. These powers were, of necessity, much more limited in the former because it deliberately placed control over defence and external affairs with the Cabinet and not with the governor-general as envisaged in the Whitehall declaration of May 1943. The Soulbury Commission was in the island and engaged in its task of examining witnesses and documents when the State Council debated the Free Lanka Bill. British officials in the island and in Whitehall recognised this debate for what it was, a piece of political theatre, set in an atmosphere of unreality and therefore not to be taken too seriously, an opinion Senanayake himself shared with them (236).

Part II: Towards independence
Senanayake at the Colonial Office

In the meantime Senanayake had decided on his own course of action. Once the Soulbury commissioners left the island he was anxious to be in London for the publication of their report. Before he departed he had to deal with two issues. First, he needed a statement on the CO's attitude to the Free Lanka Bill; secondly, he had to determine who would deputise for him as leader of the house and vice chairman of the Board of Ministers during his absence, a period which might extend over several weeks (247).

It was as clear to Senanayake as it was to the other members of the Board of Ministers that the Free Lanka Bill would not secure the royal assent. It was, however, important that the CO's refusal to approve it should be notified officially to the board before he left for London. The reason was clear. Nobody could then undermine his position on the board and in the country by accusing him of participating in discussions at the CO about the rejection of the bill. The CO readily responded; officials and the secretary of state were alert to the need to support Senanayake (256). On the grounds that it had neither secured a three-quarters majority in the State Council, nor adhered to the limits on external sovereignty imposed by the 1943 declaration, the rejection of the bill was officially conveyed to Moore on 19 June.

On the question of Senanayake's deputy, Moore seemed more concerned about this than Senanayake himself. But there too, by a combination of shrewd man-oeuvering and luck, the matter was speedily resolved. The governor reported that Senanayake preferred Bandaranaike to J L Kotelawala for the acting position (253). Given Bandaranaike's unconcealed desire to set himself up as Senanayake's successor, this seemed, at first sight, a strange decision. But it was a shrewd one. Bandaranaike was almost certain to cause difficulties for Kotelawala who also saw himself as a strong candidate in any struggle for the succession to Senanayake. Kotelawala, for his part, would tolerate Bandaranaike's temporary tenure of Senanayake's position because he had no desire to embarrass Senanayake politically or upset his plans in London. Fortunately the manner of Bandaranaike's selection for the acting position worked very much to Senanayake's advantage, for he was not the unanimous choice of the Board of Ministers. Three members of the board were contenders – Bandaranaike, Kotelawala and G C S Corea – and since none of them had a clear majority, lots were drawn to settle the issue. Bandaranaike won, and apparently that too on the third draw. In these circumstances Bandaranaike's position for the eventual succession to Senanayake was not as secure as it might have been had he been unchallenged for the temporary vacancy during Senanayake's absence in London. At Bandaranaike's insistence, the refusal to grant the royal assent to the Free Lanka Bill came up for discussion in the Board of Ministers, but here Senanayake and his associates were strong enough to thwart Bandaranaike's attempts to exploit the situation to his political advantage. The latter, however, had a more amenable arena for publicity, the State Council, and there, at a hastily summoned meeting, a motion protesting against the rejection of the bill was easily carried (255). Bandaranaike himself was one of the principal speakers on the occasion. There was, nevertheless, for all his polished indignation, a perceptible note of restraint in his speech as befitted a minister and a challenger to the leadership, which was absent from the contributions made by other speakers. Bandaranaike did not confine his criticisms to the State Council. He had access to the resources of the Sinhala Maha Sabha which he controlled, and he used these now to prolong the controversy. But once again there was an element of restraint if not caution in his use of that organisation's resources. A telegram of protest was sent on its behalf to the CO. The new leadership of the Ceylon National Congress was much more in earnest. They began a concerted protest campaign, in all parts of the country, in association with the communists – who had recently secured membership of that body – in support of independence and secession from the Commonwealth. The campaign was conducted over several months.

Once the Soulbury commissioners left for London to prepare their report, Stanley extended an invitation to Senanayake to visit London for talks. Ponnambalam felt that he was entitled to equal treatment with Senanayake (249), and sought CO agreement for him to be present at any interview that Senanayake had with officials. This was firmly resisted by Moore and the CO, and Senanayake for his part rejected the suggestion out of hand (250, 252). Nevertheless Ponnambalam proceeded to London to lobby support for his views, and was soon joined in this enterprise by representatives of the Indian minority in the island, including Indians with some official standing in India. All of them secured interviews with ministers and officials at the CO. Senanayake had decided on his own line of action. If the Soulbury Report was favourable he would ask for more, for dominion status, but if it was unsatisfactory he would repudiate it and refuse any longer to be bound by the declaration of 1943 which, in his opinion, the British government had itself disregarded by widening the commission's terms of reference. He arrived in London in mid-July 1945 to find that events were moving with disconcerting rapidity. His first interview was with Stanley on 30 July but by this time the secretary of state was on the verge of vacating office as a result of the landslide victory secured by the Labour Party at the general election.

This meant, inevitably, that no immediate response was likely from the new Labour government to the Soulbury proposals. By the time Senanayake first met George Hall the new secretary of state, on 9 August, he had already been given a copy of the Soulbury Report. To his great relief and satisfaction he found that the Soulbury commissioners had, in fact, endorsed the main principles of the ministers' draft constitution. There were adjustments, modifications and additions, but none of any real substance save the recommendation for the establishment of a second chamber. More important still, the minorities' political campaign orchestrated by Ponnambalam and his Tamil Congress had little impact on the commission's thinking and recommendations.

Simultaneously, on the international scene, the war in the east was over with dramatic suddenness and the defeat of Japan now influenced Senanayake's attitude to the Soulbury proposals. Had circumstances been different – that is to say had the war with Japan not come to so sudden an end – he would have been elated to find that the Soulbury commissioners had endorsed the main principles of the ministers' draft constitution. But the war was over and there was no reason for accepting anything that fell short of the ultimate goal of dominion status. Moreover, account had now to be taken of the British government's intentions with regard to India and Burma. In September 1945 Lord Wavell, the viceroy, announced that after elections had been held to the Indian central and provincial legislatures in the coming cold weather, it was the government's intention to hold discussions as a preliminary step to the convening of a constitution-making body and then to proceed with the institution of an Executive Council having the support of the main Indian political parties.[42] With regard to Burma, the government's white paper of May 1945 envisaged a three-year period of direct British rule, followed by elections and an invitation to the new legislators to draw up a constitution for full self-government.[43]

Apart from a small group of officials he took with him, Senanayake had the advantage of Jennings's presence in London. Jennings's hand was clearly seen in the long letter – it was more a memorandum than a letter – dated 16 August which Senanayake submitted to the CO as a prelude to his discussions (266, 268). The letter began by explaining why and how opinion in the island had shifted since the early months of 1944. It pointed out that Burma had been promised full self-government and stated that there was nothing in the social and economic conditions, or the recent history, of the two countries to justify the placing of Ceylon in an inferior position. Senanayake outlined his case for dominion status for Ceylon and maintained that the existence of communal divisions could not be regarded as an argument against, as such divisions had not prevented the offer of the same status to India where, in fact, they were more pronounced.

To most of the recommendations of the Soulbury Report, Senanayake had no objections. The one proposal over which he had serious reservations was the establishment of a second chamber. He believed that a bicameral legislature would be controversial in the island. Above all, he concentrated on the procedures for defence and external affairs set out in the report; the mechanisms recommended would, in his view, be unworkable in practice because of their complexity. Both the Soulbury commissioners and the ministers themselves in their 1944 draft constitution had accepted the limits on Ceylon's external sovereignty laid down in the 1943 declaration. In the report and the ministers' draft, bills relating to defence and external affairs fell into the category which the governor-general was empowered to 'reserve' for approval by Whitehall, to ensure that 'only legislation conforming with the policy of the imperial Defence Authorities may be enacted by the Parliament of Ceylon'. The governor-general's powers in regard to defence were not limited to the control of legislation. Where legislation was required for the implementation of long-range imperial defence policy, or for other reasons, it was envisaged that the governor-general would explain what was required to the prime minister who would then obtain his Cabinet's consent to the introduction of such legislation. But if for political or other reasons the Cabinet declined, the governor-general was empowered to implement a governor-general's ordinance.

The Soulbury commissioners endorsed this procedure, but went beyond it in situations 'which may not be capable of being dealt with by normal constitutional methods or by a Governor-General's ordinance'. They referred to 'the emergency of war or a grave national emergency in which the normal constitutional machinery has either broken down or become ineffective'. The Soulbury Report argued that in 'order to deal with either of these emergencies it may be necessary for His Majesty in Council to legislate by order-in-council',[44] and proceeded to recommend that an express provision to this effect be inserted in the constitution. The practical difficulties of implementing the defence proposals outlined in the Soulbury Report became one of the main arguments in Senanayake's case for the immediate grant of dominion status, without the intermediate stage which the report envisaged. He suggested that this transition could be effected through an order-in-council, and offered to sign agreements with Britain on defence and external affairs for the mutual benefit of the two countries in the immediate post-war situation.

On 29 August 1945, Arthur Greenwood, chairman of the Colonial Affairs Committee, placed before the Cabinet the committee's views on the Soulbury Report. The committee had considered at length the arguments for and against abandoning the stipulation in the 1943 declaration that the new constitution had to be approved by three-quarters of the State Council. It recommended on balance that Hall should be authorised to explain to Senanayake, if the latter raised the question, that the government would not necessarily insist on a three–quarters majority; instead the largest possible majority, preferably including a substantial element of minority support, would suffice (270). The Cabinet considered the committee's report on 30 August but wanted more time to consider (271). In the meantime, Hall informed Moore that in his discussions with Senanayake he would adhere to the conditions laid down in the 1943 declaration; there would be no consideration of Senanayake's claim for dominion status. Assessing the changing situation in Ceylon, the governor responded that Senanayake ought not to linger in London, 'unless he's going to bring back Dominion Status or something very like it' (272). The Cabinet met again on 3 September. Hall was authorised to begin discussions with Senanayake on the understanding that the government was not committed to the proposals in the Soulbury Report and that after the discussions the secretary of state would report back. The decision on waiving the three-quarters majority was confirmed. It was also decided that Wavell should be acquainted with the position and the action now contemplated by the government (273).

Senanayake had four formal discussions at the CO between 4 and 17 September. At the first he reiterated the points made in his letter of 16 August and proceeded to argue his case for full dominion status (274). Referring to the declaration of policy on Burma in the white paper of May 1945, he asserted that his country deserved equally generous treatment and that Britain should show to Ceylon the same consideration that she had shown to former enemies whose constitutional rehabilitation she was assisting. Much of the discussion was based on the second part of Senanayake's letter with its detailed responses to and criticisms of the Soulbury proposals. Again he expressed reservations on the second chamber but ultimately he accepted it. At meetings on 7 and 10 September the Soulbury recommendations were discussed in detail. Senanayake handed in drafts he had prepared (or rather had prepared for him by Jennings and others) of a proposed section of the new constitution dealing with the reservation of bills amending the constitution, and outlined a definition of external affairs. The position of public officers under the new dispensation was aired; Senanayake also spoke at some length on the Indian franchise in Ceylon and the difficulties involved in resolving the issue as well as its political implications (279, 282).

While Senanayake's discussions with Hall and his officials were proceeding apace, Ponnambalam was interviewed at the CO (284), and representatives of the Indian community in the island – working in tandem with Ponnambalam – renewed their demand for the enfranchisement of thousands of Indians, together with the granting of full civic rights to those regarded as entitled to citizenship. They received a polite hearing but not much more (288, 291, 299).

Prior to his final round of discussions with Senanayake, Hall submitted a memorandum to the Cabinet on 10 September explaining that Senanayake had made it plain that he had come to England to request the grant of dominion status and that he had offered to sign agreements on defence and external affairs (280). The secretary of state's view was that the time was not ripe for any constitutional advance beyond that adumbrated in the 1943 declaration, and he indicated that he would leave Senanayake in no doubt on this key point. At a meeting the following day, the Cabinet agreed and recommended that Hall should not make any statement on dominion status in the course of any further discussion with Senanayake. It was also agreed that there would be simultaneous publication of the Soulbury Report in Britain, Ceylon and India (283).

Hall's last discussion with Senanayake, on 17 September, revolved round the final communiqué (292). Senanayake expressed regret that the government's policy was not to be announced simultaneously with publication of the Soulbury Report. Hall explained that this was the inevitable consequence of the change of government and the end of the Japanese war. Senanayake asserted that he now regarded himself as having complete freedom of action upon his return to Ceylon; the secretary of state responded that he hoped this did not mean that Senanayake had given up all intention of co-operating with Britain.

Senanayake returned home in the last week of September, in a much better mood than Hall had reason to expect. Moore sensed this after a brief discussion with him, and on 25 September he informed the CO that Senanayake would accept a constitution on the lines of the Soulbury Report, plus agreements on defence and external affairs (295). Moore added that there was, at this point and by the exercise of a little courage, a golden opportunity of making a generous and spontaneous offer to Ceylon, and one that in the long run would pay a handsome dividend. Lord Soulbury, with whom Senanayake had stayed for a weekend during his visit to London, was of the same opinion. He wrote to Hall on 5 October expressing general support for the views outlined in Senanayake's letter of 16 August. Soulbury stated his own view that the government should now go considerably further in the direction of self-government than had been recommended by his commission (300). He added that so long as the commission's recommendations on safeguards for the minorities were embodied in any new constitution, nothing more was required from the government for that purpose. He regarded the three-quarters majority as indispensable for the protection of minorities. Soulbury was unaware that the Cabinet itself had decided to release Senanayake from this latter obligation.

The negotiating team
Very little has been written on the decisive phase of the transfer of power in Ceylon that was soon to begin. In 1949, Ivor Jennings published his book on *The Constitution of Ceylon* and promised, in his preface, that he would some day 'explain in print how much Ceylon owes to Mr. Senanayake and Sir Oliver Goonetilleke'. 'But for them', Jennings asserted, 'Ceylon would still be a colony'. From about the middle of 1943 Jennings had become the principal, though unofficial, adviser to Senanayake (and Goonetilleke) in the negotiations with the CO on the transfer of power, a position he retained until the process reached a successful completion in early 1948. He thus had unusual access to a great deal of confidential information and he used it to good purpose in drafting the book on the transfer of power that he had in mind.

The book was ready by the early 1950's. Entitled *Donoughmore to independence*, it carried the subtitle *A contribution to the constitutional history of Ceylon, 1931 to 1948*, but he died prematurely before he could polish the draft to meet the exacting demands of his publishers, and before the thirty-year rule was introduced releasing a flood of CO documents for the last phase of British administration in Ceylon.

This draft now forms part of the Jennings papers in the library of the Institute of Commonwealth Studies in the University of London. Together with chapter xi of his unpublished autobiography and other documents in that collection, it is indispensable for any serious study of the transfer of power in Ceylon. Jennings was aware that the future historian would have to examine the CO records to gain an understanding of the negotiations about which he provided so much information and in such rich detail: 'We shall not know the whole truth until the official documents are made available'.[45] But he added a caveat about a dimension missing from the official record. 'History drawn from documents', he asserted, 'is apt to mislead because the importance of personal influences is rarely placed on record and indeed such influences are difficult to assess'.[46]

In his unpublished autobiography Jennings described his own role as that of 'the draftsman'; 'the real work', he claimed, 'was done by Mr. Senanayake and Sir Oliver Goonetilleke'.[47] In playing down his own role, Jennings was being uncharacteristically modest, for he knew more than anyone else that Senanayake and Goonetilleke could not have negotiated so successfully with the CO mandarinate and British politicians, to say nothing of the governor and the officers of state in Colombo, without the expertise on constitutional matters which only he could have provided. That rich expertise he placed at the disposal of Senanayake and Goonetilleke with a dedication and generosity unmatched by any expatriate adviser on constitutional affairs in any other colony seeking independence from Britain. It would also be true that few constitutional advisers, indigenous or expatriate, had as great an influence in determining the shape of the post-independence constitutional framework of a colony as Jennings had in the case of Ceylon. Governor Caldecott (and to a lesser extent his successor) and the officers of state were distinctly unhappy about the extent of Jennings's influence in the negotiations on the transfer of power. In giving guarded but occasionally pointed expression to their feelings in this regard they reveal a facet of the negotiations on the transfer of power not generally noticeable in the CO records published in this volume – the extraordinary role of Jennings as Senanayake's unofficial constitutional adviser.

In his unpublished study of the transfer of power in Ceylon, Jennings sought to justify the role he played as Senanayake's adviser:

I was . . . in sympathy with Mr. Senanayake's aim to secure Dominion Status at the earliest possible moment, though my reasons differed from his. It had to be Dominion Status, for Ceylon was neither large enough nor rich enough to dispense with such help as the Commonwealth could give by agreement. Had I not been in sympathy, however, I should have given the assistance; and indeed I was not in agreement with every sentiment that I put into the documents over the next four and a half years. The University tradition in these matters is very clear. Universities are public corporations containing experts on most branches of knowledge who regard themselves as holding that knowledge in trust for the community. If, therefore, the government of the country, or indeed any country, requires assistance it is the duty of the university to provide it. My knowledge would have been at Mr. Senanayake's disposal even if I had not agreed with his objective, though no doubt the association was the more fruitful because I agreed.
The association . . . continued throughout the four and a half years between the

declaration of May 1943 and the end of December 1947. It was modified when one of us was out of the country, and after the general election of August 1947 and the establishment of the Senanayake government with Sir Oliver Goonetilleke as Minister of Home Affairs I became a mere consultant, called in when questions of some difficulty arose. Until then the three of us could have been described as the nucleus of a Reforms Ministry, with Mr. Senanayake as Minister, Sir Oliver as Permanent Secretary, and myself as the Constitutional Adviser on tap.[48]

Had Jennings's two books, presently in draft form, been published, a substantial amount of new information on the Ceylonese side of the story of the transfer of power would now be available, even if provided by an unusual Englishman. As it is considerably more information exists on British policies and initiatives – although the information is admittedly rather slight in comparison with that which is available for the cognate process in India and Burma – than material illustrating the independence movement in the island from the Ceylonese viewpoint. By far the most significant gap for the study of the transfer of power in Ceylon is the lack of a comprehensive biography of D S Senanayake.[49]

One of the most striking features on the Ceylonese side of the transfer of power is the dominance of Senanayake in the negotiating process. In insisting that dominion status should be the primary objective, and that this could be attained in association with the Britain rather than in opposition, Senanayake stood against the prevailing current of opinion in the island. By 1942 even the moderate Ceylon National Congress had committed itself to independence in preference to dominion status in emulation of the Indian National Congress. Senanayake's model was not India but the old settlement colonies of the empire whose development to dominion status had been one of constitutional advance by measured stages. His tactics and strategy reflected his own political convictions, with their emphasis on moderation and pragmatism, as well as the political traditions of the mainstream of nationalist politics in Ceylon with its well-known proclivity for peaceful constitutional agitation. Above all he was a realist who saw nothing dishonorable in an acceptance of constitutional reform in instalments. Jennings explained that Senanayake

> had the good politician's unconcern with detail. In consultation with Sir Oliver – and the relationship was so close that it was rarely possible to say whether an idea came from the one or the other – he had worked out the grand strategy. The aim was Dominion Status. Any proposal which seemed to be a step in that direction should be accepted, though an effort should first be made to make it go a little further. In working out the details, the proposal should be pressed to its limits and just a little beyond. Having gone some way towards Dominion Status, a suitable opportunity should be sought for presenting a demand for the next step, and if it proved impossible then to secure Dominion Status, any offer which nevertheless went further should be accepted and pressed its utmost limits.[50]

One important theme which Jennings emphasised in *Donoughmore to independence*, as well as in his unpublished autobiography, was the 'personal influence which Mr. Senanayake gained in London' during his visits to the CO in July–August 1945.[51] Jennings described it as 'a triumph of personality rather than of organization'. Though he had no reason to believe that Senanayake was not adequately briefed, and was quite sure that the administrative arrangements for which Senanayake's aides were responsible were up to the CO standard, 'it was obvious that Mr. Senanayake himself created a great impression'. It was evident from the 'casual remarks' thrown out by senior officials that Senanayake had 'surprised them by the strength of his character and the sincerity of his purpose'. 'It was perhaps an advantage', Jennings added, that Senanayake

> had not the facility of language of the English-trained Ceylonese graduate or slick self-assurance of the professional advocate. A Ceylonese prototype of the English official would not have made such an impression because the Colonial Office was familiar with it. It had never met Mr. Senanayake's type before. . . . Mr. Senanayake completely captured the Colonial Office and the Secretary of State. If he had been able to meet the Cabinet I am sure that he would have obtained independence in 1945.[52]

'The result of all this', Jennings added in his unpublished autobiography

> was that an entirely different relationship was established between Mr. Senanayake and the Colonial Office, a relationship which made the last step towards Dominion Status supremely easy. The Colonial Office was on Mr. Senanayake's side from 1945 onwards, and the problem was only to choose a suitable moment for persuading the Cabinet.[53]

In these assessments Jennings seems to have carried his assessments too far. While clearly Senanayake made a favourable impression on officials and had the CO on his side from 1945, there were still significant hurdles to overcome and the final persuasion of the Cabinet proved no easy matter.

The Soulbury Report, Tamil protests and the white paper

Following the publication of the Soulbury Report on 9 October 1945, the CO was inundated with telegrams and letters of protest from the Tamil Congress and representatives of the Indian community in the island expressing their deep disappointment with its recommendations (309, 323, 327). They were joined in this by the European Association of Ceylon (314). The CO also received a long and wide-ranging document from Ponnambalam, complaining that the proposals for representation of minorities fell far short of what had been hoped for, and arguing that the commission's recommendations would not give the minorities anything approaching an adequate share in the government of the country (322). Nobody was more disappointed or more alarmed by the report than the representatives of the Indians. Wavell sent a message to the India Office protesting against the Soulbury Commission's recommendations on the Indian franchise (310).

By the middle of October the Cabinet in London was in the process of spelling out its policy on constitutional reform in Ceylon. Hall put before the Colonial Affairs Committee a recommendation that a constitution based on the Soulbury proposals should be reviewed after six years. Some of his colleagues on the committee expressed the view that it would be unwise to commit the government to a fixed period for review; others raised questions relating to the island's minority problem (304). When Moore was sent the draft of a policy statement on 16 October he responded immediately that while on the whole it would be acceptable to Senanayake, any reference to a review after six years might jeopardise acceptance of the Soulbury Report and the statement itself. He suggested instead something on the lines of the statement of policy contained in the white paper on Burma (306, 308).

Simultaneously Lord Soulbury, in discussion with Trafford Smith, expressed concern over delays in the introduction of the new constitution (311). He explained that his two colleagues on the commission endorsed the views outlined in Senanayake's letter of 16 August (266). Soulbury, in fact, felt keenly about

Senanayake's difficulties and indicated that he might even publish his own letter of 5 October to Hall (300); if the government's decisions were not to his satisfaction, he would speak out against them in the House of Lords.

The impact of Soulbury's intervention remains unclear. On 26 October the Cabinet considered a report from the Colonial Affairs Committee which retained the provision for a constitutional review after six years (312). Ministers raised objections and they were also uncertain about the wording of that part of the policy statement which dealt with the issue of the three-quarters majority (316). These questions were referred to a small group of ministers chaired by Clement Attlee, the prime minister, which revised the draft statement. At Attlee's suggestion a reference to the evolutionary character of constitutional development was substituted for a review after a six years (317). Soulbury was shown the text of the new statement at a meeting with Hall on 30 October (318). His reaction was reported to have been generally good, and he felt that the statement would help Senanayake. The statement was announced on 31 October, followed by a white paper embodying the decisions of the British government.[54] Moore reported in early November that although the white paper did not meet all of Senanayake's *desiderata*, he was prepared to accept it and place it before the State Council for approval (320).

The Indian problem, post-war reconstruction and the communist challenge

On 23 October 1944, after the appointment of the Soulbury Commission was announced, the Indian government sought to reopen negotiations on the rights and status of Indians in the island. This was rebuffed by the Board of Ministers. The board did not think that any agreed basis existed for the resumption of negotiations, and pointed out that the general question of the rights and status of Indians in the island was, in substance, a different matter from the particular problems of constitutional reform which were the subject of inquiry by the commission. Above all ministers insisted that they did not want the case for the Indian community in Ceylon to be presented or openly sponsored before the commission by the Government of India (230; also 233, 234, 243, 251).

The unresolved issues relating to the position of the Indians in the Ceylonese polity, and the conflicting grievances involved in these, were ventilated afresh when the Soulbury Commission began its sittings. Spokesmen for the Indian community argued that Indians resident in the island had been clearly discriminated against in regard to the franchise, and urged that this subject as well as immigration should be among those reserved under the terms of the 1943 declaration.

The Soulbury Commission, which devoted two chapters of its report to the issues of the franchise and immigration,[55] came down on the side of the Board of Ministers in declaring that the policies pursued by the latter on the franchise 'did not seem to His Majesty's Government to involve any racial discrimination against Indians, whereas some of the Indians protests amounted in effect to a claim to a position of privilege rather than of equality'.[56] Paragraph 242 of the report recommended that:

(i) Any Bill relating solely to the prohibition or restriction of immigration into Ceylon shall not be regarded as coming within the category of Bills which the Governor General is instructed to reserve for the signification of His Majesty's pleasure . . .;
(ii) Any Bill relating solely to the franchise shall not be regarded as coming within the category of Bills which the Governor-General is instructed to reserve for the signification of His Majesty's pleasure.

The Indian leadership in the island regarded these comments and recommendations as a grievous setback to their cause and, as we have been, began a campaign of opposition to the franchise recommendations embodied in the report, but to no avail. When the government's policy statement was under consideration in October 1945, Moore was informed by the CO that no concession had been made to the Government of India's representations on any main issue (313).

The publication of the Soulbury Report and the white paper had one major political consequence: it guaranteed Senanayake's triumph over his critics in the Board of Ministers and the State Council. Senanayake's motion for the acceptance of the Soulbury proposals was seconded by none other than Bandaranaike himself. When George E de Silva gave the blessing of the Ceylon National Congress to the proposals in a long speech (prepared by J R Jayewardene),[57] Senanayake's triumph was complete. Thanks to a concerted campaign of persuasion, all waverers in the ranks of the minorities were won over, and when the debate began on 8 November the tide turned so strongly in Senanayake's favour that only one vote – that of W Dahanayake, a Sinhalese radical who wanted nothing short of independence – eluded him. At the vote taken on 9 November two others joined Dahanayake in opposition to Senanayake's motion, which was approved by 51 members (326). Two Indian representatives voted against the resolution. They themselves had been inclined to vote in favour even though the *quid pro quo* they asked for was not forthcoming, but M S Aney, the agent for the Government of India,[58] seated in the gallery of the house, sent down a note asking them to vote against the motion. It was, as Moore observed, 'a stupid and improper piece of interference' on the part of the representative of the Indian government (325).

Senanayake was elated at the majority he had won but Aney's indiscretion did not pass unnoticed. If nothing else it confirmed fears of undue Indian influence in the affairs of Ceylon through the Indian minority once both India and Ceylon had won their independence. Indeed relations between Senanayake and his associates on the one hand, and the leadership of the Indian community in the island on the other, remained strained throughout the year 1946–1947.

In just over six months after the debate in the State Council on the white paper, the order-in-council embodying the new constitution was enacted.[59] Almost all the work was undertaken in Colombo. Senanayake was anxious to hasten the process. As early as November 1945 he informed the CO that he would like to send J H B Nihill, the legal secretary, to London with a draft of the constitution. Although the CO urged that the drafting of the constitution be left to a legal draftsman sent from the Whitehall (330), Senanayake's views – which were supported by Moore – prevailed and the drafting was left in the hands mainly of Nihill, B P Pieris of the legal draftsman's office in Colombo and, of course, Jennings.

The Tamil Congress persisted with its campaign against the Soulbury Report and the white paper (339, 347) but there was stronger pressure from other sources, and on other issues: the defence clauses and the question of the Indian franchise.

In July 1945 Layton, now returned to Britain as commander-in-chief, Portsmouth, expressed concern to the Admiralty about the defence implications of the proposed reforms. Adumbrating a much wider interpretation of defence requirements than bases, ports and airports, he argued that some control over the island's internal communications, roads and railways was essential for defence purposes. He also revealed himself to be suspicious of CO motives over Ceylon (263, 315). When the

Admiralty sought to reassure him on this (335), Layton responded by emphasising the need for unceasing vigilance in matters of the island's defence (337). Senanayake insisted that the definition of the term defence must be in the form adopted in the 1943 declaration and on this he had the support of the CO. In March 1946 the CO persuaded the Chiefs of Staff Committee to accept Senanayake's position (348).

The pressure for a revision of policy on the Indian franchise was stronger, more persistent, and came from powerful political sources as well: the viceroy's executive, the secretary of state for India and the British Cabinet Mission to India in 1946. While Indian leaders in the island sent telegrams of protest to the CO calling upon the latter to intervene directly in the matter of the Indian franchise (331), the most influential advocate of the Indian case was Sir Ramaswami Mudaliar, member for supply on the viceroy's executive and formerly Indian representative on the War Cabinet in London. At an interview with Hall in December 1945, Mudaliar suggested that the Soulbury recommendations on the Indian franchise be modified if not changed (336). He repeated this request in February 1946 (342) and received the backing of the secretary of state for India, Lord Pethick-Lawrence (343).

Senanayake had returned home from London with the belief that the obstacle to the immediate grant of dominion status was not the minority problems of Ceylon but the complex issues of the transfer of power in the Indian empire. This gave him an entirely new and much more satisfactory perspective to the problems with which he was now confronted. Dominion status, he believed, was now in the offing. Also, his reading of the Soulbury Report – and no doubt the assessment of his advisors – had led him to conclude that questions relating to the franchise and citizenship would be treated as falling within the ambit of the powers of the Ceylon government under the new constitution. Thus, when requests came for a revival of talks with India, he adopted the position that questions relating to the Indian population in Ceylon should be left to the new parliament to decide (338). He insisted that talks could take place only after the new constitution was in force (340).

The policy of the CO on such matters was clear; it would support Senanayake. This was conveyed to Mudaliar in February 1946 (346) and to the India Office, reiterating the CO's commitment to the Soulbury recommendations on the franchise. Although occasionally the CO itself was not entirely happy with Senanayake's interpretations of the franchise clauses in the Soulbury Report (349), the Office supported him against the Indian protests, arguing that these had been made in good faith, based on the opinion of the legal secretary. Senanayake, for his part, responded to this pressure by asserting that he would not accept any changes in the franchise and immigration clauses at this late stage (352).

On 11 April 1946 the Cabinet Colonial Affairs Committee met to discuss definitions of defence and external affairs and the conflicting interpretations of powers relating to the reservation of bills on franchise matters (357). In regard to both the committee felt it necessary to support Senanayake. These decisions were conveyed to Pethick-Lawrence who was now in India as a member of the Cabinet Mission. The secretary of state for India requested clarification of the safeguards for the Indian population which would be written into the constitution. He expressed himself satisfied with the answers he received (358–360). From the CO, Sir Charles Jeffries assured Moore that difficulties with India over the franchise and immigration had been satisfactorily overcome.[60] Labour issues, however, were still in dispute (361, 362, 364, 366).

The Ceylon (Constitution) Order in Council was enacted on 15 May 1946. The subjects expressly reserved to the imperial government were defence and external affairs. Despite Pethick-Lawrence's acceptance of the minority safeguards, the Commonwealth Relations Department of the Indian government expressed regret that no opportunity had been given to comment on the draft order-in-council before it was published.[61]

Once the constitution had been settled, Goonetilleke, in his capacity as financial secretary, turned his attention to the question of post-war reconstruction. In September 1946, he submitted to the CO a comprehensive report in which he proposed an extension of the wartime bulk purchasing agreements for Ceylon's principal commodities of tea, copra and rubber. Underpinning Goonetilleke's main economic argument that Ceylon was entitled to preferential treatment because of the island's contribution to the war effort, lay a thinly-veiled political threat that if his proposals were not considered favourably, the consequence might be a break with the imperial connection and Ceylon's gravitation towards India (368). During his discussions in London he was said by the CO to have staked his personal reputation on a successful outcome. The CO Economic Department, however, together with the Ministries of Food and Supply, remained unimpressed. Arguing for the former, Sydney Caine challenged Goonetilleke's analysis of how Ceylon's contribution to the war had worked to the island's detriment and maintained that there were no grounds, commercial or political, upon which Ceylon could expect favourable treatment (371). In the middle of his negotiations in London, Goonetilleke travelled with a British delegation to Washington to discuss the implications of a recent rapid increase of rubber production in Malaya for rubber prices generally. He received no more encouragement from American officials than he did from those in London (369, 370). The trade agreements which he was offered when he returned to Ceylon from Britain in October 1946 were much less than he had hoped for. CO officials described his attitude as 'repressed and gloomy' (372, 374).

Over the last two years before independence, Senanayake and the Board of Ministers faced a serious political challenge from a revived left wing. Recruitment to the forces and to the civilian staff of the military bases of SEAC had provided a short-term solution to the unemployment problem in the island. With the closing down of these bases, and the demobilisation of Ceylonese from the British armed services, unemployment increased but not to the extent of causing severe problems for the government on its own. The social discontent that manifested itself stemmed from severe inflation arising mainly from the increase in the money supply from the massive defence expenditure of the years 1943 to 1945. The inevitable consequence of this inflationary pressure was discontent among the working class and white collar workers over the fall in value of their wages. The Defence Regulations and the Avoidance of Strikes and Lockout Act were designed to curb strike action by trade unions during wartime, but even so there were strikes in Colombo in 1944 and 1945. The communists had replaced the banned LSSP as the chief influence on the working class in Colombo and its suburbs, but although they helped organise trade unions they were not inclined to encourage or support strike action. The strikes broke out despite them. Now, with the ban on the LSSP lifted, strikes became more frequent and among the most militant of the trade unionists were those in the clerical grades of the public service.

The LSSP turned, almost at once, to activity in the industrial sectors to regain the primacy they had lost to the communists and organised a series of major strikes between 1945 and 1947, culminating in the general strike of 1947. These strikes were as much political demonstrations as they were trade disputes – one of the demands was the rejection of the new constitution – and the Board of Ministers was inclined to treat them, particularly the general strikes of 1946 and 1947, as a serious bid for political power by the marxists.[62]

Senanayake was perturbed by the violence that often erupted during these strikes and the demonstrations that accompanied them. At a meeting of the Board of Ministers in October 1946 he stated that he had lost faith in the administrative services generally and in the ability of the police to provide protection to law-abiding citizens against acts of lawlessness (373). His lack of faith in the police (375) had reached the point where he recommended in November 1946 that a Battalion of Army Volunteers be established and kept permanently mobilised. Such a unit, he argued, could well be the nucleus of a Ceylonese army (376). There were sharp differences between him and some of the officers of state in their attitude to the police, and to trade unionism in the government services (378, 379).

India, Burma and Ceylon

While Senanayake was preparing for the forthcoming general election, scheduled for the middle of 1947, and had established his own political party – the United National Party (UNP) – to face the formidable challenge he anticipated from the marxist parties (in the form of the LSSP and the communists) and Ponnambalam's communalist Tamil Congress, events were moving with remarkable rapidity in India and Burma. Policy pronouncements made in Britain on the political future of the *raj* and of Burma, and the responses to these from Indian and Burmese political leaders, had an immediate impact on the affairs of Ceylon.

The documents in the second part of this volume reveal an unusual sensitivity on the part of officials at the CO to Senanayake's predicament in the face of the rapidly changing situation in India and Burma. In a minute dated 16 December 1946, J B Sidebotham referred to the recent demand made by the Anti-Fascist People's Freedom League (AFPFL) in Burma for complete independence within a year. Any decision on Burma's independence, he warned, could undermine Senanayake's position in Ceylon. If the British government decided to concede Burma's demands before the new Ceylon constitution came into force, Sidebotham argued that it should be prepared to make a further declaration on the grant of dominion status to Ceylon and undertake to reopen discussions for that purpose, if necessary, as soon as the new constitution became fully operational. He returned to this theme two days later with the comment that it would be unfair, because of potentially 'disastrous political consequences', to allow a promise of independence for Burma to be sprung upon Senanayake at the outset of his election campaign, without due warning and without giving him firm assurances of progress, in the near future, beyond the new constitution. Jeffries agreed and stated that if it were decided to make any such promise to Burma, it would be essential, at the same time, or before, to make a further offer to Ceylon (377).

On 27 January 1947, after a series of talks in London between a Burmese delegation and members of the Cabinet, Aung San (the leader of the AFPFL) and Attlee signed an agreement on the methods by which Burma would achieve its independence, either within or without the Commonwealth, 'as soon as possible'.[63]

Just under a month later, on 20 February, the government made its historic announcement that Britain intended to transfer power to responsible Indian hands by a date not later than June 1948.[64] Senanayake responded on 28 February in a letter to Arthur Creech Jones, Hall's successor at the CO. In it he stated that Ceylon could not accept a lower political status than India or Burma (381). He had explained his position at considerable length and with great candour to Moore and had spoken of his fear and distrust of India, and his profound concern for Ceylon's regional security. The stark choice the country faced, he asserted, was survival as a small but independent partner of the Commonwealth or absorption by an independent India. Indeed Senanayake feared that Nehru's ambition was to make independent India the dominant power in this part of the world. Nehru's great interest in Ceylon, Senanayake believed, was solely because of its strategic importance through its naval base at Trincomalee and air bases in other parts of the island.

Moore sent to the CO his own appreciation of the political situation. Senanayake's current difficulties were said by the governor to be the result of his acceptance of the Soulbury proposals. Many of Senanayake's supporters felt that if he had rejected the Soulbury constitution, Ceylon would have received the same offer now made to Burma. Political pledges to India and Burma were seen as evidence that the speed with which independence was attained was governed, not so much by the merits of the case as the nuisance value of the applicants. Moore himself felt that this conclusion was inescapable in the circumstances, and he went on to argue that if Ceylon was to be retained as a loyal and willing member of the Commonwealth, the most serious and urgent consideration should be given to Senanayake's arguments. Goonetilleke had been deputed by Senanayake to discuss matters further with the secretary of state (382).

From the time Senanayake's and Moore's letters were received in the CO, Creech Jones took the initiative to seeking to persuade the Cabinet that the island's progress to dominion status should be accelerated. On 29 April 1947 he submitted a memorandum to the Colonial Affairs Committee which explained that Goonetilleke, now in Britain, had emphasised the importance to Ceylon of Britain's decision to withdraw from India and the anxieties which this raised in relation to Ceylon's future. Particular concern had been expressed that the British government would not be willing to face a major clash with India in order to protect Ceylon's interests. If independence was granted to Ceylon, there would be no pressure brought on Senanayake to leave the Commonwealth. The latter had urged that full independence within the Commonwealth should be granted as soon as possible after the elections in Ceylon. Creech Jones added that Senanayake was willing, if the government so desired, to negotiate agreements in respect of imperial defence and external affairs. These could be drafted in consultation with the governor who would, in turn, consult his ministers. Goonetilleke had pressed for the use of the word 'independence' rather than dominion status in any statement on Ceylon's constitutional advancement, since, up to this point, the latter had not been used in the case of India and Burma.

The secretary of state emphasised the urgency of a decision. He appreciated that the government was facing accusations at home of 'scuttle' and of 'squandering the empire' but felt that if the matter were handled correctly, Britain would have an excellent opportunity, not only of keeping Ceylon within the Commonwealth and securing vital defence interests in the Indian Ocean, but also of demonstrating to the world that Britain's policy towards colonial peoples was not an 'empty boast'. Subject to the views of the Chiefs of Staff and the dominion governments, the Colonial Affairs Committee supported Creech Jones's recommendations (388).

The chiefs of staff were more cautious than the CO. They expressed concern that an unconditional grant of independence to Ceylon was a gamble and that it should be accompanied by assurances that the defence requirements of the Commonwealth would not be jeopardised in any way (389, 396).

Creech Jones found himself isolated when the Cabinet debated the issue on 6 May 1947. Cabinet decided that it would be unwise to reach a hurried decision on a question of such major importance. Ministers asked whether it was not premature to agree to any further measure of constitutional reform in Ceylon. They were still not satisfied on the issue of safeguards for the minorities. They were also anxious to avoid giving an impression of weakness or of encouraging demands for similar concessions in Malaya and elsewhere. Ministers were equally emphatic that they could not subscribe to Senanayake's assumption that the British government would not be prepared to risk a clash with India over Ceylon. Creech Jones and his officials at the CO were left with the unenviable task of drafting a new policy statement in the light of the Cabinet's discussion (390).

There followed a month of intense correspondence between Whitehall and Colombo over the wording of the statement (392–394). On 1 June Creech Jones submitted a draft to Cabinet, together with a draft of an accompanying letter of explanation to Senanayake. Prompted by T L Rowan, his principal private secretary, Attlee dismissed the draft of the statement out of hand, describing it as one of the worst examples of 'turgid jargon' that he had ever seen and ordering that it should be rewritten. Cabinet was equally critical when it considered the drafts on 3 June (395).

Revised drafts of a statement and letter to Senanayake were agreed on 6 June. The statement made no definite pledge of immediate dominion status; negotiations on this would would proceed once elections had been held in Ceylon and a new government was fully functioning (398, 399). Senanayake, however, refused to accept the text which he described as 'retrograde' (400). His view was influenced, not only by the strike situation in Ceylon and the imminence of the election, but also by the decision to grant dominion status to India and Pakistan almost immediately under the 3 June plan negotiated between Mountbatten and the Indian leaders. Further intense correspondence followed (401–403) before a new statement, pledging, for the first time, that 'immediate steps' would be taken to confer upon Ceylon 'fully responsible status within the British Commonwealth of Nations', was made on 12 June (405). Attlee was clearly dissatisfied with the manner in which the whole affair had been handled by the Colonial Affairs Committee. His concern prompted a review in the Cabinet Office of the Cabinet committee arrangements for dealing with constitutional and other problems arising in various parts of the Commonwealth, including the colonial territories (404).

There was one final complication over the new statement and this arose out of the use of the term dominion status in the transfer of power arrangement in India. Having previously pressed for the use of the word 'independence', Senanayake was now unhappy with 'fully responsible status within the British Commonwealth of Nations' in the Ceylon statement. Although rejected by the Burmese leaders, India's acceptance of dominion status had given the expression a new political credibility in South Asia and its absence in the statement on Ceylon appeared to raise doubts about the nature of the independence that was being offered. Senanayake therefore suggested alternative expressions for use in the Ceylon statement, although Moore informed the CO that he would agree to accept the existing text if his suggestions were deemed inappropriate (406). Goonetilleke sent a message that it was too late to change the wording and Senanayake accepted Creech Jones's assurance that it meant the same as dominion status, no more and no less (407). The statement was announced by Creech Jones in the House of Commons on 18 June 1947, and by Senanayake in the State Council on the same date.

The defence agreement, sterling balances and citizenship

With agreement in principle on Ceylon's independence now reached, it remained to finalise the details. Goonetilleke was deputed by Senanayake to negotiate on his behalf in London where he was joined in July by Moore. There were three agreements to be negotiated: on defence, external affairs and the rights of British civil servants. Of these the most politically sensitive related to defence.

Senanayake had no objection to British insistence that Ceylon's independence should not impair the defence requirements of the Commonwealth. For him no less than for Whitehall, the defence agreement was part of a process of adjusting to the uncertainties of a new pattern of international politics in South Asia where India was an independent state. If defence was important to the Chiefs of Staff because of Britain's interest in the Indian Ocean, especially for securing links with Australia and New Zealand, for Senanayake it served a different but no less important purpose. The Ceylonese negotiators believed that a defence agreement offered them security against possible threats from India to Ceylon's independence.

In the drafting of their defence requirements, the Chiefs of Staff considered a number of models. One was South Africa and the Simonstown base but they considered that the defence agreement negotiated by the United States with the Philippines prior to the grant of independence to that country in 1946 to be more appropriate for the Ceylon situation (396). The sensitivity surrounding the defence question covered such issues as whether the agreement should identify the base facilities and military establishments which Britain would occupy, the extent to which Britain would retain responsibility after independence for the maintenance of internal security in Ceylon, the control of British forces in the island, and, as a matter of special concern, not only to the Chiefs of Staff in London but also to the government of Australia, whether the agreement should be subject to a time-limit (412, 415, 416, 418, 419, 420, 428). On all such matters the agreement eventually concluded was either silent or cast in very general terms (436).

Throughout the discussions, Goonetilleke's assignment was not confined to negotiations on the formal agreements: it ranged over the whole question of ensuring that Ceylon's independence conformed to the traditional pattern of dominion status (410). This included recognition of Ceylon's right to secede (411). There was also some discussion of whether it would be necessary or desirable to have agreements safeguarding the rights of minorities and covering the treatment of foreign nationals, companies and shipping. In all cases it was decided against, Senanayake being adamantly opposed to any attempt to reopen the minority question (409, 413, 415, 419).

On other outstanding questions the CO and the War Office attempted, unsuccessfully, to obtain an increase in Ceylon's defence contribution (296, 445). The CO and the Treasury also voiced anxiety over what both departments viewed as serious depletion of Ceylon's sterling balances. With the Treasury arguing that Ceylon was 'just about broke', an effort was made in November 1947 to impose a ceiling on Ceylon's sterling withdrawals. This was resisted (435, 442, 444).

Dominion governments were kept informed of Ceylon's impending independence (416). There were no comments, much less objections, from three of them. Only Australia had objections, of a sort, to make. Insisting that there should be no time-limit placed on the defence agreement, the Australian government suggested that a Commonwealth conference be held in London to discuss Ceylon's new status prior to the grant of dominion status (418). In the face of Australian persistence, Moore, on behalf of Senanayake, advised that the proposal for a Commonwealth conference should be politely but firmly rejected (422–424).

The six months prior to independence were not without incident. The Ceylon government was anxious to introduce emergency legislation to cope with the threat to public order that had emerged from the militancy and politicisation of the trade union movement under the direction of the LSSP. This legislation was welcomed by the Colonial Office and a Public Security Act was approved by the State Council on 11 June 1947 as one of its final acts before it was dissolved. The emergency powers order-in-council which had been prepared earlier was not proceeded with once this bill had been approved (397).

The general election of August–September 1947, at which Senanayake's UNP did not fare as well as the Colonial Office had expected, caused some worries in the initial stages. But the UNP was easily the largest party in the new parliament and Senanayake was able to form a government with a comfortable majority (425). In the aftermath of the election, and indeed almost from the time nominations were called, it was rumoured that ministers and others elected to the House of Representatives, or elected or appointed to the Senate, might be disqualified on the grounds that at the time of their election or appointment they were, technically, public servants within the meaning of the law. Moore informed the CO in October 1947 that there were difficulties in filling the Senate because of this ambiguity in the law. The CO was not keen to amend the Ceylon (Constitution) Order-in-Council to meet this difficulty and indeed felt that such an amendment would be open to the objection that it had been introduced for the benefit of the governing party. With Moore's clarification sent in November 1947 that further amendment was required merely to plug a loophole, the CO eventually agreed, much to the relief of Moore and the ministers.[65]

On 29 October 1947 the Ceylon Cabinet approved the three agreements which had been negotiated in London (431) and decided further that the bill to give effect to independence be titled 'The Ceylon Independence Bill', following the Indian precedent. This was agreed, although at the outset the parliamentary timetable in London gave cause for concern (432, 433). The text of the white paper containing the proposals for conferring on Ceylon fully responsible status within the British Commonwealth of Nations was published simultaneously in London and Colombo on 11 November 1947. The three agreements were signed on the same day in London and Colombo (436). The second reading of the independence bill was debated in the House of Commons on 21 November 1947, and in the House of Lords on 4 December 1947. There was unanimous support for the bill in both houses, but the debate in the Commons was notable for the anxieties expressed by some members of the Conservative opposition about imperial defence in the light of the political and constitutional changes on South Asia then being introduced, and in particular the independence now envisaged for Ceylon.[66] Senanayake, in the meantime, had fixed 4 February 1948 as independence day (440). Moore, the last governor, of the colony was invited to accept appointment as the first governor-general of the new dominion to whose creation he had contributed a great deal on his own, and through the support he gave Senanayake.

There remained questions relating to citizenship for the Indian minority in Ceylon, Senanayake's hand in this respect had been strengthened considerably in January 1947 when, overturning its own previous advice, the CO recommended that Ceylon should be included in the countries to be represented at the British Commonwealth Conference on Nationality and Citizenship which was held in London in February 1947. Participation in the conference carried with it an acknowledgement that henceforth Ceylon would be entitled to enact legislation to determine its own local citizenship. The decision to allow Ceylon to participate in the conference was not made without misgivings; officials at the CO recognised that the Ceylon government might use citizenship legislation to discriminate against Indians. However, in the political circumstances then prevailing, the CO felt that the risk was one that had to be taken (380).

It was reported in October 1947 that Senanayake had arranged negotiations with India over citizenship (427, 429). As a consequence of the London conference, Senanayake was aware that a British Nationality Bill was under consideration. He was concerned that British legislation might affect his negotiations with Nehru and he suggested that the British bill should be deferred until his discussions with India were over. He clarified his views further in November 1947 explaining that a definition of Ceylon citizenship was being prepared but that he would not proceed with it until the conclusion of his talks with India which were scheduled for December 1947 (434).

The substance of the offer Senanayake made to Nehru on this occasion was the grant of citizenship to all Indians who had lived in the island for a 'prescribed number of years'. He defined the prescribed period as seven years' continuous residence for married persons and ten for single persons, with 31 December 1945 as the operative date. This, in fact, was a much more generous offer than the one made in 1941, but it did not satisfy Nehru who held out for a qualification of eight years for all persons, married or single, with January 1948 as the qualifying date.[67] Sena-nayake, with memories of what had happened at the negotiations in 1941 very much in mind, refused to give in to Nehru's demands. The talks collapsed. Hugh Tinker, the historian of the Indian communities settled in British colonies, blames Nehru for the failure of these talks. He points out that, as a result of Nehru's rigidity and his refusal to bargain or compromise on what he thought were matters of principle, a unilateral settlement was imposed by Senanayake's independent government in 1948–1949.[68]

One of the first political initiatives of Senanayake's government after independence was the definition of Ceylonese citizenship. The Ceylon Citizenship Act, No 18 of 1948, restricted the status of a national of Ceylon to those who could claim it by descent or registration. The application of these conditions to Indians in Ceylon was defined in the Indian and Pakistani Residents (Citizenship) Act, No 3 of 1949. The requirements were much the same that Senanayake had offered Nehru in 1947. A third piece of legislation, the Ceylon (Parliamentary Elections) Amendment Act, No

48 of 1949, removed the voters of Indian origin from the electoral rolls. Under the second of these acts applicants were required to produce documentary evidence in support of their claims to Ceylonese citizenship. Such evidence was hard to come by, but the difficulties involved in this were compounded by the initial refusal of the Ceylon Indian Congress (later the Ceylon Workers Congress) to co-operate in the implementation of this legislation. By the time they changed their minds, it was too late for most potential applicants for Ceylonese citizenship to stake their claims.

Epilogue

Ceylon had few of the difficulties of transition that caused so much concern in regard to the process of ending empire in Africa and other parts of the colonial world. The island had a well-developed education system which was being purposefully expanded and improved in the 1940's. University College, Colombo, established in 1921, was converted to the University of Ceylon in 1942 with Jennings as vice chancellor. The colony had an excellent administrative system, a smaller version of the steel framework of the *raj*. Most of these officials in the higher bureaucracy were Ceylonese; the recruitment of civil service cadets from the UK and British colonies came to end in the late 1930's. The judiciary was largely if not entirely Ceylonese at all levels. The chief justice was an Englishman, as were one or two puisne justices, but the great majority of judges of the supreme court and the legal profession generally were Ceylonese. The same applied in the cases of the technical and medical services, especially the latter.

There was no significant deviation from this pattern in regard to the police and the armed services. The top positions in the police were still held by British officers, and even lower down the scale officers from the Metropolitan Police Service had been recruited but, by and large, there was a strong and growing Ceylonese element in the higher echelons of the service. By 1945–1946 the pressure was on for the replacement of British officers by Ceylonese. The problem with the police, as the political leadership in Ceylon saw it, was that it seemed incapable of maintaining law and order in the city of Colombo and its suburbs during periods of labour unrest. Hence, as we have seen, Senanayake favoured the creation of a small detachment of soldiers to help the police maintain order in times of crisis (375, 376). The island had no standing army worth speaking of, no navy, and no air force. There were, of course, volunteer regiments, manned by young Ceylonese who had served in the British forces. Significantly enough, when a small army was built at independence or shortly thereafter, its nucleus consisted of demobilised officers and men, and with volunteer regiments in support. Its first commanding officer was seconded from the British army.

The manner in which power was transferred to Ceylon proved to be controversial, and the agreements over defence and external affairs were at the heart of the problem (437, 438). They seemed to suggest a qualitative difference in the nature of the independence that was won by Ceylon through a process of orderly negotiation – in comparison with the cognate process in India, Pakistan and Burma. Once Senanayake had set his sights on dominion status and membership of the Commonwealth, the manner of its attainment seemed to him less important than the fact of its achievement. But his most vocal critics on the left of Ceylon's spectrum, who had no faith either in dominion status or in the Commonwealth, denied that the island was really independent, and pointed to the defence agreements as evidence of this. As for Whitehall, it sought to justify Ceylon's passage to self-government in 1948 on the basis that it was not merely a special case but an unusual one as well because of the strength of its civil society, the political maturity and sophistication of its leaders and, above all, the fact that it had had adult suffrage for nearly two decades.

The emphasis at that time – it must be noted – was also on the characteristic British belief that there was something unique in each of territory of the empire. The uniqueness of India, for instance, was regarded as so self-evident that it offered no precedent for the countries of the colonial empire, save possibly Ceylon. The constitutional future of the island could hardly be separated from the momentous decisions on India then being taken.

The general significance of Ceylon's advance from colonial to dominion status was thought to be far-reaching. 'This is the first occasion in our history,' Lord Addison, the lord privy seal and former dominions secretary, said in introducing the second reading of the Ceylon Independence Bill in the House of Lords on 4 December 1947, 'upon which a colony, developing this system of self-government of its own accord, had deliberately sought to become a Dominion state in our Commonwealth, but we hope and expect it will not be the last'.[69] Much later, in 1960, Sir Charles Jeffries justified the decision to concede Ceylon's case for dominion status because 'of its size, its economic strength, its advanced state of social organization. Since 1931 it had in fact had a form of political constitution which placed the main responsibility for the conduct of its affairs on an elected State Council and on Ministers answerable to that [body]'. Ceylon in brief, was a special case. Jeffries added that 'no other colony seemed to be in sight of fulfilling these conditions. If Ceylon was the forerunner, it had a long start'.[70]

Nicholas Mansergh, the historian of the Commonwealth, viewed Ceylon's independence in much the same terms:

> Ardent nationalists from other and less peaceful lands might allude in tones of condescension to Ceylon's fight for freedom but the gentlemanly pressure for independence exerted by its conservative nationalist leaders upon Whitehall made up in good sense what it lacked in political passion. As a result Ceylon acquired the status of a Dominion of the British Commonwealth without bitterness, by orderly constitutional advance which made the matter of its attainment a source of unfailing satisfaction to British constitutional historians and its status in the academic world that of the model Dominion.[71]

Ceylon, then, was at the head of the queue and it was not expected that others would follow too soon along the same path. But by the 1960's others had followed this path – in Africa and Asia, no less than in the Caribbean. And as colony after colony reached independence, men like Jeffries and the historian Duncan Hall saw the transfer of power in Ceylon as a historic event. Thus Hall argued:

> Historically, Ceylon had almost as much right as India to be regarded as an original member of the Commonwealth. It was not only the first of the 'colonies' (the dependent areas administered by the Colonial Office) to achieve full membership of the Commonwealth. It was also the first to envisage, to look forward to, and to prepare for that goal. And it pursued that goal steadily, without ambivalence, patiently and without violence.[72]

Jeffries was just as enthusiastic about Ceylon's special claims:

> Ceylon provides the classic example of how with good sense and good will, two peoples

can carry through the extremely difficult and delicate transition from a ruler-subject relationship to an equal partnership.

Ceylon has been the prototype and model for the new Commonwealth of the latter part of the twentieth century. In Ceylon the British learnt, by trial and error, the art of colonial administration; but they learnt, also, the wisdom of relinquishing control when it was no longer tolerable by a people willing and able to maintain itself as an independent state.[73]

Jeffries, one feels, was claiming more than he was entitled to do in arguing that the rapid progress in ending empire in the 1960's was the result of the steady application of a policy initiated by those who participated in the late 1940's in the making of policy on Ceylon's future. A reading of the papers in this volume would not support such a claim; rather one sees a whole series of *ad hoc* decisions taken to deal with each problem as it arose. The most that could be claimed is that these *ad hoc* measures eventually provided a rough pattern of action for the future. On every occasion a pragmatic acceptance of political realities was more important than any careful application of principles.

*   *   *   *

The work on this volume would have been more time consuming and much more difficult but for the facilities available to me at the International Centre for Ethnic Studies (ICES) by way of secretarial and other assistance. The introduction was word processed by Ms Sepali Liyanamana of the ICES. Several drafts were prepared by her with her usual cheerful efficiency. Mrs Kanthi Gamage, librarian/documentalist at the ICES, helped in the laborious process of proof reading and in the preparation of the index. This was work done more as a labour of love than as part of her duties at the ICES. Iranga Athukorale word processed the index. In addition Rajeewa S Jayasinghe (BA, Sri Lanka) served as a very efficient and conscientious research assistant to me on this project, helping to check references, to locate material at the Sri Lanka National Archives in Colombo and with data for the biographical entries and the chronology of principal events. I am very grateful to all of them for their assistance so generously given to me.

K M de Silva

Notes to Introduction

1   Sinhalese refers to the majority community; Ceylonese (the expression today is Sri Lankans) refers to the whole people of the island.

2   M Wight, *The development of the legislative council, 1606–1945* (London, 1946) p 94.

3   *ibid*, p 95.

4   The seven executive committees into which members of the State Council were divided were: agriculture and lands; communications and works; education; home affairs; health; labour, industry and commerce; and local administration.

5   The three officers of state were the chief secretary, who was also chairman of the Board of Ministers; the financial secretary; and the legal secretary. They were directly responsible to the governor. The Public Service Commission was composed of the three officers of state.

6   See K M de Silva, 'The introduction of universal suffrage', and 'The Minorities and universal suffrage' in K M de Silva, *Universal franchise, 1931–1981 – the Sri Lanka experience* (Colombo, 1981) pp 47–62 & 75–92 respectively.

7   Generally, the Sinhalese population of the territories of the Kandyan kingdom, the last independent Sinhalese kingdom before British rule. This was ceded to Britain in 1815. The territories are in the central hills, the north central and north western plains and part of the Eastern and Southern Provinces.

8   *Ceylon: Report of the Special Commission on the Constitution* (Cmd 3131, 1928) p 95.

9   Sessional Paper (hereafter SP) XXXIV, 1929, despatch from Sir H Stanley to Lord Passfield, 2 June 1929, and Passfield's reply, 10 Oct 1929.

10   On the Jaffna boycott, see J Russell, 'The dance of the turkey-cock – the Jaffna boycott of 1931' in the *Ceylon Journal of Historical and Social Studies* vol VIII(I) (1978) pp 47–67.

11   On the formation of the LSSP, see G L Lerski, *Origins of trotskyism in Ceylon* (Stanford, 1968).

12   Ironically this plan for the capture of all seats in the Board of Ministers by Sinhalese was devised by Professor C Suntheralingam of the then University College, Colombo. Suntheralingam was a Tamil and one of Senanayake's many advisers.

13   SP XI, 1937.

14   *ibid*.

15   These powers should have lapsed with the termination of hostilities in 1918 but they were renewed in 1924 (CO 54/872, despatch from Amery to Manning, 10 Nov 1924).

16   On the Bracegirdle question, see SP XVIII, 1938 and CO 54/948/13–14.

17   On the suspension of constitutional government in Cyprus and Malta in 1931 and 1934 respectively and the contrast drawn by CO officials between Cyprus and Ceylon, see BDEEP series A, vol 1, S R Ashton & S E Stockwell, eds, *Imperial policy and colonial practice 1925–1945* part I, 45 & 53.

18   The best study of the 'fifty-fifty' campaign is in J Russell, *Communal politics under the Donoughmore constitution, 1931–1947* (Colombo, 1982).

19   Named after Sir W Manning, governor of Ceylon, 1918–1925.

20   SP XXVIII, 1938, p 4.

21   *ibid*.

22   M Tomlinson, *The most dangerous moment* (London, 1976).

23   *ibid*, pp 16–17.

24   *ibid*.

25   There is no study, as yet, of the Mool-oya incident, apart from occasional references to it in books relating to this period of Sri Lankan history. SP XV, 1940, contains much useful material.

26   Burghers are descendants of the Dutch and Portuguese settlers and rulers of the country. They are generally resident in urban areas.

27   This restriction, devised in 1938, survived until the end of 1977 when, at last, it was removed from the statute book by the UNP government which came to power in that year.

28   *Ceylon: Report of the Commission on Constitutional Reform* (Soulbury Report) (Cmd 6677, 1945) paras 210 & 213.

29   CO 54/978/7, minute by Blaxter, 13 May 1940.

30   CO 54/982/1/1, no 2, tel from Caldecott to Lloyd, 23 Jan 1941.

31   *ibid*, no 66.

32   CO 852/605/9, minute by Gent, 4 Aug 1944.

33   CO 852/514/14, minute by Carstairs, 3 Jan 1944.

34 *ibid*, minute by Caine, 4 Jan 1944.

35 W I Jennings, *The constitution of Ceylon* (New Delhi, 1949) p 33.

36 On Mountbatten's brief stay in Kandy, see P Ziegler, *Mountbatten* (New York, 1985) pp 278–280 and P Ziegler, ed, *The personal diary of Admiral Lord Louis Mountbatten, 1943–1946* (London, 1988) pp 96–166.

37 CO 54/986/14, minute by Trafford Smith, 12 Oct 1944.

38 *ibid*, minute by Trafford Smith, 19 Nov 1944.

39 *ibid*, minute by Sidebotham, 25 Oct 1944.

40 This was an exceptionally distinguished group. It included: Dr E C S Wade, fellow and tutor of Gonville and Caius, Cambridge; Professor W K Hancock, Chiclele professor of economic history and fellow of All Souls, Oxford; Professor K C Wheare, Gladstone professor of government and public administration and fellow of All Souls, Oxford; and Professor L Keir, University of Belfast.

41 If the wartime prime minister Winston Churchill had had his way, the Duke of Windsor might have succeeded Caldecott as governor of Ceylon. P Ziegler, *King Edward VIII* (London, 1990) p 493.

42 P N S Mansergh *et al*, eds, *Constitutional relations between Britain and India: the transfer of power 1942–7* (hereafter TOPI) vol VI, 116.

43 H Tinker, ed, *Constitutional relations between Britain and Burma: the struggle for independence 1944–1948* (hereafter BSI) vol I, 153.

44 Soulbury Report, *op cit*, para 351.

45 Jennings, *Donoughmore to independence* (unpublished typescript) in Jennings Mss (Institute of Commonwealth Studies, University of London) p 29.

46 *ibid*, p 27.

47 Jennings, *Autobiography* (unpublished typescript) in Jennings Mss, p 140.

48 Jennings, *Donoughmore to independence*, *op cit*, pp 23–24.

49 H A J Hulugalle, *The life and times of Don Stephen Senanayake* (Colombo, 1975) is quite inadequate.

50 Jennings, *Donoughmore to independence*, *op cit*, p 24.

51 *ibid*, p 28.

52 *ibid*, pp 28–28(a).

53 Jennings, unpublished *Autobiography*, *op cit*, p 139(a). Like Senanayake, Oliver Goonetilleke made a favourable impression on the CO, although there were disagreements, as demonstrated in 1946 when Goonetilleke attempted, unsuccessfully, to negotiate preferential trade agreements. He had the unusual distinction of having Sir Charles Jeffries, joint deputy under-secretary of state at the CO at the time of the transfer of power, as his biographer – Sir Charles Jeffries, *O.E.G.: a biography of Oliver Ernest Goonetilleke* (London, 1969). Jeffries included a chapter on Ceylon in his book on the *Transfer of power* (London, 1960) and he also produced another book specific to the problems of Ceylon – *Ceylon: the path to independence* (London, 1962).

54 *Ceylon: Statement of Policy on Constitutional Reform* (Cmd 6690, 1945).

55 Soulbury Report, *op cit*, chapters X and XI.

56 *ibid*, para 209.

57 K M de Silva & H Wriggins, *J R Jayewardene of Sri Lanka: a political biography* vol 1 (London, 1988) pp 181–182. For G E de Silva's speech, see *Hansard* (State Council), 8 Nov 1945, cols 6932–6942.

58 Dr Madhao Shrihari Aney, member for Indians Overseas on the Indian Executive Council, 1941–1943, was appointed agent in Ceylon of the Government of India in July 1943. In the 1920's the Indian government had insisted on the appointment of an agent (usually an Indian official) to British colonies admitting Indians for labour either on plantations or in other areas of economic activity. On the role of

these agents, see H Tinker, *Separate and unequal: India and Indians in the British Commonwealth, 1920–1950* (London, 1976). Among the first countries to which such agents were sent were Ceylon and Malaya. They were expected to supervise 'the proper working of labour legislation, and to negotiate regarding pay and conditions with estate employers' (*ibid*, p 80).

59   Ceylon Constitution Order-in-Council, 17 May 1946, published in the *Ceylon Government Gazette Extraordinary* of the same date.

60   CO 537/1675, no 8, letter from Jeffries to Moore, 30 Apr 1946.

61   CO 537/1672, no 22, tel no 4858, Government of India, Commonwealth Relations Dept, to India Office, 29 May 1946.

62   Hence the decision of the Ceylon government to refuse to lift a ban on Dr S A Wickremasinghe, leader of the Ceylon Communist Party, and their resort to emergency powers to disqualify him from standing as a candidate at the 1947 general election. See correspondence in CO 54/992/1.

63   BSI, *op cit*, vol II, 258.

64   TOPI, *op cit*, vol 1X, 438.

65   For correspondence and CO minuting on this issue, see CO 537/2212.

66   *H of C Debs*, vol 444, cols 1477–1524.

67   H Tinker, *The banyan tree: overseas emigrants from India, Pakistan and Bangladesh* (Oxford, 1977) pp 38–40 & *Separate and unequal, op cit*, pp 198–199.

68   H Tinker, *The banyan tree, op cit*, p 42.

69   *H of L Debs*, vol 152, col 1205.

70   Sir Charles Jeffries, *The transfer of power, op cit*, p 62.

71   P N S Mansergh, *Survey of British Commonwealth affairs: problems of wartime co-operation and post-war change, 1939–1952* (Oxford, 1958) p 246.

72   H Duncan Hall, *Commonwealth: a history of the British Commonwealth of nations* (London, 1971) p 801.

73   Sir Charles Jeffries, *Ceylon: the path to independence, op cit*, preface.

Summary of Documents: Part I

Chapter 1
The war and postponement of constitutional reform;
Indo–Ceylon relations, Sept 1939–Apr 1941

NUMBER			SUBJECT	PAGE
		1939		
1	Sir A Caldecott for CO	7 Sept	'Things Ceylonese', 1st periodical report	1
2	Mr MacDonald	3 Oct	Minute on 1	4
3	Sir A Caldecott for CO	4 Oct	'Things Ceylonese', 2nd periodical report, + *Minutes* by G E J Gent & Sir H Moore	4
4	G G Ponnambalam to Sir A Caldecott	18 Oct	Letter explaining views of minorities on reforms	7
5	Mr MacDonald to Lord Zetland (India Office)	19 Oct	Letter on labour relations between India & Ceylon	8
6	Sir A Caldecott for CO	21 Oct	'Things Ceylonese', 3rd periodical report	9
7	Sir A Caldecott to Mr MacDonald	23 Oct	Tel on forthcoming Indo–Ceylon conference in Delhi on trade negotiations & labour relations	11
8	Mr MacDonald to Sir A Caldecott	26 Oct	Tel (reply to 7) on labour relations	12
9	Sir A Caldecott to Mr MacDonald	28 Oct	Despatch on reforms debate in State Council; minority representation & proposal to appoint a re-delimitation committee [Extract] + *Minutes* by G E J Gent, Sir C Parkinson, Mr MacDonald & Lord Dufferin	12
10	Sir A Caldecott to Mr MacDonald	31 Oct	Tel (reply to 8)	19
11	G G Ponnambalam to Sir N Stewart Sandeman (Con MP)	3 Nov	Letter explaining views of minorities on reforms	20

Chapter 3

The ministers' draft constitution and the Soulbury Commission; Ceylon and wartime supplies: the case of rubber production (2), Sept 1943–Apr 1945

1   CO 54/971/11, no 1   7 Sept 1939
'Things Ceylonese': first periodical report by Sir A Caldecott for CO

[This informal review on the affairs of Ceylon was the first of fifteen such commentaries
Caldecott sent to the CO between 7 Sept 1939 and 24 Aug 1941. All of them are
reproduced here (see 1, 3, 6, 16, 21, 24, 32, 34, 46, 57, 64, 72, 89, 96 and 105). These
commentaries varied in length and the quality of analysis and value of information
provided, but all of them had insights on the changing political scene in the island and
personal rivalries among its politicians which the official documents do not provide.
Because they were not official despatches they were more relaxed in tone, and Caldecott
often gave vent to his personal views, fears and expectations, not to mention prejudices,
without the restraints that one saw in his official correspondence. The governor was not
above retailing gossip about his ministers' personal affairs. But flaws and all, these
commentaries are a unique source of information on the island's affairs at this time.]

I. Intercommunal relations in Ceylon prior to outbreak of war

1. It would be wrong to deny that the publication and debate of my Reform
Proposals caused considerable interracial feeling between politicians. The only item
of the proposals that aroused fierce interest was that dealing with more seats for the
minorities. Mr. G.G. Ponnambalam put forward exorbitant demands on behalf of the
Jaffna Tamils, and the Moors and Indians followed his lead in respect of their own
people. At a speech at Nawalapitiya Ponnambalam resorted to aspersions on
Sinhalese ancestry and his own was quickly associated with Timbuctoo and with a
Simian prelude by Mr. Bandaranaike (Minister for Local Administration) and Mr.
Goonesinha (Labour Party).

2. This irrelevant mud-slinging weakened Ponnambalam's position in Jaffna and
Goonesinha did little good for himself by too obviously endeavouring to stage a
come-back for his party (i.e. himself) on a national Sinhalese slogan quite
incompatible with his labour tenets. The result is that while he has been indulging in
squibs and crackers his real (red) fire has been stolen by the Sama Samajists
(Communists) and added to their own.

3. It is generally recognised now by all parties that constitutional reforms are
unlikely to mature during the war; Ponnambalam has therefore made an eloquent
appeal for unity and Goonesinha has ceased organising anti-Jaffna boycotts which he
started after Ponambalam's speech at Nawalapitiya.

4. I consider it true therefore to state that the intercommunal bickering which
arose in the political (it never extended to the social) sphere as a result of the
Reforms Proposals has passed away, and that it will not re-emerge until constitutional reform is again on the tapis.

5. The recent bitterness of feeling between Sinhalese and Indians was much more
serious in as much as it percolated through the political and permeated the whole
social sphere. It flared up immediately on the publication (unauthorized) in the Press
of a Memorandum by Major Kotelawala (Minister of Communications and Works) in
which he proposed the dismissal of all daily-paid Indian employees of Government
and their replacement by Ceylonese. Although the Kotelawala mountain has brought
forth only a mouse of notices given to Indians engaged since 1934 (when
employment of Ceylonese was made obligatory) this mouse has borne in Indian eyes
all the objectionable features of the mountain, and has thus caused India to make
absolute its ban on the emigration of unskilled labour to this Island. On the Ceylon
side the egregious Goonesinha published a lot of inflammatory articles in broad-

sheets and mushroom newspapers and engineered boycotts of Indian boutiques.

6. This was of course a game at which two could play; Indian labourers boycotted Sinhalese boutiques and Indian propagandists drew level with Goonesinha in the publication of lampoons and canards.

7. A fortnight ago the position caused me some uneasiness: there were in fact two outbreaks of disturbance, with both of which the Police dealt promptly and summarily. Since then however prosecutions have put the brake on mischievous propaganda and Goonesinha nowadays ends all his speeches with a fervent doxology to law and order. His latest service to the Sinhalese masses is to encourage the opening of Sinhalese barber shops in competition with Indian by undergoing as an inaugural ceremony on such premises a public shave. So far, I understand, he has not lost much face.

8. The situation therefore is satisfactory for the present and, if India will only accede to Ceylon's renewed request for a conference at which to discuss outstanding questions and differences between us, there would appear no impediment to its permanent liquidation.

II. Crisis psychology

9. The populace, the politicians and the press all behaved with patience and philosophy during "the war of nerves". The huge crowds assembled for the Kandy Perahera were restrained and orderly to a degree of perfection, on which fact I duly felicitated the Kandyan Chiefs in the course of a short speech at the Government Agent's reception of them after the final Day Perahera.

10. Defence measures were pressed to finality during the days of crisis, and all was ready when war was declared.

11. There is no doubt whatever that the people of Ceylon of all races are behind us in this war. The local Astrologers, in unison with some European Theosophists, proclaimed that there would be no war; but the general verdict was that it was daily becoming inevitable and that peace could be no longer had with honour.

III. Reactions to war

12. The first general reaction to the declaration of war was a sense of relief from long suspense and of duty at last begun. This was manifested in the speed with which mobilization of local forces was effected and in the cooperation of the public in observing the coastal black-out etc.

13. The second reaction was a wave of unfortunate memories of the riots of 1915,[1] resulting in suspicion and criticism of Defence measures already taken and of

---

[1] The riots of 1915 occurred during the cententary commemorations of the Kandyan Convention which marked the cession of the Kingdom of Kandy to British rule. National Day celebrations which were observed for the first time over the whole island in Apr 1915 were followed in May and June by the outbreak of communal disturbances. The riots were directed specifically against the Coast Moors, a section of the Muslim community who were mainly recent immigrants from the Malabar coast in south India. Active in the retail trade, the Coast Moors were said to be more willing than their competitors to extend credit. They also sold at higher prices, thus incurring the hostility of the people at large and their competitors among the Sinhalese traders who were an influential group within the Buddhist movement. Having initially treated the riots as communal disturbances, the British came to regard them as part of an organised conspiracy by the Sinhalese against the imperial government. Retribution was severe and enacted by the military operating under the protection of an Act of Indemnity which placed them beyond

those thought likely to be taken. In view of the fact that four of my seven Ministers, the Deputy Speaker and the Proprietor of the Daily News group of newspapers were all arrested, imprisoned and in fear of having to face a firing squad in 1915 this second reaction, however regrettable, need cause neither surprise nor undue concern.

14.   At first I was both annoyed and disappointed that Mr. Senanayake should have vented his suspicions in open Council without ever having given me a hint or inkling of them. On second thoughts I now recognise that it was best that the balloon should have thus gone up, because it gave us the opportunity to puncture it publicly. This I did by addressing State Council on 5th September: A Press cutting of my speech is attached.[2] From Editorial comment and from private information from Sinhalese, European, Tamil and Muslim sources I gather that for the time being at any rate confidence and cooperation is restored.

15.   The "1915 Complex" is nevertheless a hydra-headed bogy and may require periodical exorcism.

16.   My speech was followed (after my departure from the Council Chamber) by the passing of a resolution of loyalty to His Majesty and of cooperation in waging the war. This resolution was not 'suggested' by myself or other Britisher; it was spontaneously initiated by the Ministers. There were three abstentions from voting: that of the two Muscovy Ducks (Sama Samajists) was expected, but nobody expected Senanayake's son Dudley (Member for Dedigama) to make such a sorry exhibition of himself. These abstentions should not be taken seriously but given a Pickwickian interpretation.

IV. The constitution in wartime

17.   It was the intention of my advisers and myself to use the ordinary machinery of Government so far as possible for war purposes. The first failure of this policy occurred yesterday when the State Council amended the Control of Exports Bill by providing for appeals to the Executive Committee and making other quite unacceptable amendments. I shall therefore refuse Assent to the Ordinance when it is submitted to me, and am having the necessary Regulations prepared under the Emergency Powers (Defence) Act.

18.   The truth is that the Executive Committee just won't allow the Ministers to be Ministers, but want all the power in their own hands. Too many cooks cannot be allowed to spoil the war broth, and it will therefore be necessary to deal with nearly all Defence measures under the Emergency Powers Act, including legislation regarding Trading with the Enemy. I shall of course work in close liaison with the Ministers and the result will be a makeshift approximation to Cabinet Government.

19.   It is a real tragedy that Sir Baron Jayatilaka, the nearest approach to a Statesman among them all, has lost all leadership and nearly all influence since the Bracegirdle Affair.[3] Senanayake is now often openly disloyal to him and at a conference of Ministers which I held on Saturday they squabbled and both made a

---

the reach of the law. Sinhalese Buddhist leaders and trades union activists in the railway workshops in Colombo were amongst those arrested. A Riots Damage Ordinance imposed collective fines on all Sinhalese residents of specified districts, irrespective of whether or not they were implicated in the riots.
[2] Not printed.
[3] For the Bracegirdle incident, see the introduction to this volume, pp xli–xlii.

pretence of threatening to resign. Among the remainder there is no cohesion and Mr. Bandaranaike likes to pose as a sort of Opposition within the Ministry.

20. In any other country such an Administration would be unpromising, but in Ceylon it not unfaithfully represents in miniature the psychology and sociality of the majority of its inhabitants. It may therefore prove to be the best, even in war.

2   CO 54/971/11, no 2   3 Oct 1939
[Things Ceylonese]: minute by Mr MacDonald on Sir A Caldecott's first periodical report

> [Having read and commented on the governor's report (see 1), MacDonald minuted on 4 Oct: 'I should rather like my remarks on this to go to the Governor. Perhaps a note from me to him saying that I welcome his intention to send this Report periodically, and saying that the following is a minute that I wrote on reading his first Report . . . would be a good idea' (CO/54/971/11).]

Yes, I would like to read these always. We must watch Things Ceylonese carefully; opinion in a colony like Ceylon may be profoundly changed during this war, and we must keep control of it. We can do this by constant contact with it, and by taking responsible Ceylonese as much as possible into our confidence, and by making them feel that they are real, active partners of ours in the war. But I do not regard all the members of all the Executive Committees as being "responsible Ceylonese"! The present constitution therefore does not fill the Bill in war-time. It is a pity that we have not got already in Ceylon a Board of Ministers which really is, in the matters which fall to it, a responsible Cabinet. Something on that line is wanted, and I therefore welcome the Governor's statement at 'A'[1] that he will "work in close liaison with the Ministers and the result will be a makeshift approximation to Cabinet Government". He will have to be careful not to lose the confidence of the committee members, though. I agree that all question of constitutional reform should be shelved for the time being; the Governors' reasons against reviving controversy are sound in present circumstances. But it may be desirable later in the war to introduce progressive reforms which make a more efficient machine of government. At the same time we must keep something back to "give" to the Ceylonese in the way of a further extension of liberties or self-government after the war.

---

[1] 'A' refers to the last sentence of para 18 of Caldecott's report.

3   CO 54/971/11, no 4   4 Oct 1939
'Things Ceylonese': second periodical report by Sir A Caldecott for CO. *Minutes* by G E J Gent and Sir H Moore

I. Internal security schemes

1. In my last Report[1] I stated that the "1915 Complex" was a hydra-headed bogey and that Sir Baron Jayatilaka had lost all leadership. The main event of the past three

---

[1] See 1.

weeks, i.e. the Internal Security Scheme Controversy, had its roots in these two facts.

2. In the early days of my Governorship I added the Vice-Chairman of the Board of Ministers (i.e. Sir Baron Jayatilaka, Home Minister) to the Local Defence Committee in order to get effective liaison between that Committee, the Board of Ministers and the Home Ministry. Unfortunately, owing to ill health and the strain which he underwent during the Bracegirdle inquiry, Sir Baron has for a considerable time past been resting on his oars. His Executive Committee have found him dilatory and somnolent, and as liaison member of the Defence Committee he has just failed to function. As a result he subscribed to an internal security chapter in the Defence Scheme without consulting either his ministerial colleagues or his Executive Committee. Nor was he awake to the fact that the chapter incorporated certain features that had been unfavourably criticized by a 1928 Committee whose members included Sir Herbert Dowbiggin, Sir Forrest Garvin and Mr. D.S. Senanayake.

3. A Sinhalese proverb has it that an elephant never forgets and Mr. Senanayake shares with the elephant this formidable quality in addition to that of charging headlong through obstructions. He remembered both the events of 1915 and the advice tendered by his 1928 Committee for the alteration of certain police arrangements that dated from 1915. With trumpetings and bellowings in Council he demanded of the dazed Jayatilaka what was the internal security scheme to which he had subscribed. A demand was thereupon made for the chapter of the Defence Scheme to be 'tabled', which I promptly and persistently refused – not because there was anything particularly secret about the chapter, but because once a Secret document were released on popular demand Colonial Regulation 145(4) would cease to be our citadel of secrecy.

4. The discomfited Sir Baron came to me at this stage, and at his request I granted his Executive Committee an interview. While I would not give the Committee the relevant chapter of the Defence Scheme I gladly produced for them in proof form a draft Internal Security Scheme (recently compiled by the Police) about which there need be no secrecy and which in fact forms the basis of the Civil items in the Defence Scheme Chapter. The Committee has bitten onto this draft and will doubtless in due course produce what they consider a better one.

5. Mr. Senanayake was however determined to get onto the table of Council not the mere draft of a Scheme but something to which his already launched epithet of "diabolical" could conceivably be applied. Notwithstanding the fact that the previous (1923) scheme, commonly known as "the red folder", had long since been withdrawn Sir Baron allowed a copy of it to be dug out and 'tabled' for this sacrificial purpose. It was reprinted in the newspapers and duly anathematized all round; but, to quote the Hunting of the Snark,[2]

> "The sentence will not have the slightest effect
>   as the pig has been dead for some years".

6. What Mr. Senanayake really dislikes about our Internal Security Schemes, new as well as old, is that they leave local emergencies to be dealt with to too great an

---

[2] Lewis Carroll, *The hunting of the snark* (1876). Lewis Carroll was the pseudonym of Charles Lutwidge Dodgson (1832–1898), an English mathematician and logician, who became celebrated as the author of stories for children. His most famous works were *Alice's adventures in wonderland* (1865) and *Through the looking-glass* (1871).

extent by European planters either as Unofficial Police Magistrates or as Special Police Officers. There is in my opinion a ponderable element of truth in this contention but it is a pity that it was not enunciated more sanely and less wildly.

7. I am not yet clear in my mind as to whether Senanayake is deliberately trying to unseat Jayatilaka from the Council Leadership or not. The rift between them appears very wide at times and Sir Baron went so far as to threaten to resign on this matter at a Conference which I had with the Ministers. Senanayake thereupon promptly followed suit; but I pointed out to them that the Conference had more important matters to occupy it than unnecessary talk about resignations.

II. Relations with India

8. India is being very dilatory about answering our request for a round-table Conference on trade, immigration and other outstanding matters. She has not however banged the door this time so far. In the mean time Sinhalese–Indian feeling has so improved throughout the Island that the Police are no longer sending special reports on it. Things are normal again.

III. Volunteer pay on mobilisation

9. There has been a big muddle over Volunteer pay on active service, concerning which there is bound to be a lot more talk in Council. In 1935 the Treasury approved certain rates without reference to the Board of Ministers or the Governor, who is the statutory authority. The rates included Colonial Allowances for European Volunteers (not paid during the last war) and Separation Allowances on different scales for Ceylonese and Europeans. The scale for the latter was unduly generous. Although these rates were never properly authorized they were published in regimental orders more than once, and I therefore gave orders (with which the Ministers agree) that Government must keep faith and pay them for September. Most of the European Volunteers were demobilized on the 30th September, so that they will not be affected by the new rates which will come into force as from the 1st October.

10. The new rates, though prescribed by the Governor, will in reality be determined by the law which provides that the Governor may apply (or not apply) regular army rates but does not give him power to vary them. The 1935 rates were not merely unauthorized but illegal!

IV. State Council

11. The Council, having after all its alarums and excursions passed the Budget, is in recess until the 17th October so that Ministers and Officers of State have time now to get on with their jobs. The Agenda of Executive Committees however seem to me to be getting more and more overloaded.

12. Mr. Dean, recently General Manager Designate of the Ceylon Railway, has telegraphed an eleventh hour refusal of the appointment. His recorded reasons are his failure to get satisfactory pension and leave terms out of India or an extension of his offered agreement (from 4 to 5 years) from us. He may quite likely also have read the State Council debate on the March resolution authorizing his appointment, and have reached the conclusion that his position here might prove precarious. If that be so one cannot blame him.

Minutes on 3

Para 5. Mr. Senanayake, the Minister for Agriculture & Lands, is a genuine representative of the political Sinhalese in being a 100% racialist.[3]

That, after all & amidst the other & lesser political issues in Ceylon, is the fundamental rallying ground of the various elements in the Island, & not excluding the European.

Sir A. Caldecott has in the past been criticised for an alleged excessive faith in Mr. Senanayake's advice and abilities. Sir Andrew himself is free of racial prejudice, and has gone out of his way in local social life to make this clear. If he loses faith in Mr. Senanayake, by far the biggest political force in the Ministry & the Council, on this score, the trouble will be that there is no other Sinhalese leader whom he can usefully take to his bosom instead.

In those circumstances it is essential that, for the time being & until the situation in the matter of a reformed constitution can be effectively re-surveyed, he shd. have continued and clear assurance of H.M.G's support in his personal discretion – equally in his firmness towards Executive Committees and their several Chairmen, the "Ministers", as in his concessions to them.

C.E.J.G.
18.10.39

I am afraid Sir A. Caldecott is in for a difficult time. The war, while it lasts, may temporarily lessen communal frictions, but if at the end of it India gets Dominion Status we may expect a revival of Sinhalese nationalist sentiment in Ceylon.

H.M.
18.10.39

---

[3] Gent added in the margin against the first para of his minute: 'Sir B. Jayatilaka is equally a racialist but in the main anti-Indian. Mr. Senanayake is in the main anti-European. I think that this is a fair representation.'

4   CO 54/964/3, no 36   18 Oct 1939
[Reforms]: letter from G G Ponnambalam to Sir A Caldecott on the views of the minorities

I have the honour to inquire, in view of the conditions created by the outbreak of war, what action Your Excellency proposes to take in the matter of the Reform of the Ceylon Constitution. All agitation by the minority communities has been suspended as it is rightly felt that the country should not be distracted by any political controversy at this juncture.

As there is no consensus of opinion among the representatives of the various communities in the Island and as there are strong differences of opinion between the majority community and the minority communities with regard to further constitutional changes, we feel that a Parliamentary Commission should investigate the whole question before any action is taken.

In the event of Your Excellency proposing to recommend changes in these circumstances, any action on the part of the Secretary of State conceding the substance of the demands of the Sinhalese Ministers is bound to be viewed with extreme disfavour by the Tamils and other minorities and give rise to acute dissatisfaction at a time when we feel that all communities should stand united behind Britain for the successful prosecution and speedy termination of the war.

As I am writing this letter at the instance of a number of representatives of the minority communities, I shall be obliged if Your Excellency will be pleased to communicate its contents to the Secretary of State at as early a date as possible.[1]

---

[1] Caldecott forwarded Ponnambalam's letter to MacDonald in despatch no 699 (19 Oct) which explained that, owing to the pressure of war work, his despatch on constitutional reform was not ready for transmission to the CO.

5   CO 54/966/1/2, no 98   19 Oct 1939

[Indo–Ceylon relations]: letter from Mr MacDonald to Lord Zetland on labour relations between India and Ceylon

You will remember our correspondence regarding current difficulties in the relations between the Governments of India and Ceylon, in the course of which the Government of India have placed an embargo on the movement of Indian labourers from India to Ceylon. We had hoped that a settlement of the difficulties could be reached by an early arrangement between the two Governments for discussion of the outstanding points at issue, but my most recent information is that the Government of India have so far made no response to the approach which, partly on my pressure exercised through the Governor, the Ceylon Board of Ministers made a month ago to Delhi. I think you will agree that this is disappointing. I don't know whether you can see your way to suggest to the Viceroy the harmfulness of delay in present circumstances, but the particular matter which I want to bring to your notice is set out in the enclosed letter[1] received in the Colonial Office from the Ceylon Association in London in the matter of the rigid ban on the return of Indians to Ceylon who have had occasion to go to India on a visit and are now unable to get back to their work. Apart from the difficulties which such action causes to the estate managements in Ceylon and the discontent it creates amongst the estate population it does seem to me extremely unfair on individuals that the Government of Madras should persecute them in this way. If you can take any steps to induce the Department concerned in the Madras Government to take a more reasonable attitude, I am sure it would be greatly appreciated by those affected.

Please let me have back Mr. Baynham's letter and enclosure.

---

[1] Not printed.

6   CO 54/971/11, no 6   21 Oct 1939
'Things Ceylonese': third periodical report by Sir A Caldecott for CO

Myself
1. This first paragraph will be in explanation of my present temporary address; which is Government House, Madras. As long back as March last my recently de-tonsilled throat showed signs of further streptococcal infection. The trouble spread forward at the side of the tongue, and until last week I had not had an undisturbed night or been without pain since April. My wife was taken ill with a severe neurosis in August, when my son arrived from Eton for the holidays and was marooned here by the cancellation of return sailings. There also arrived the Admiral's wife and daughter, only to find the Admiral "somewhere at sea" and their houses at Trincomalee and Diyatalawa commandeered for barracks and offices. In spite of my wife's condition they had therefore to be quartered at Queen's House. In these conditions and under stress of war work my throat deteriorated rapidly so that (by the time my wife was removed to a Nursing Home and beginning to convalesce, the Admiral back in Colombo and provided with a house, and my son booked back to England by the "Viceroy of India") the doctors pronounced deep-ray therapy the only cure. There being no apparatus for it yet at Colombo I left for Madras on the 28th October, since when I have enjoyed the hospitality of Lord and Lady Marjorie Erskine[1] and the professional attention of Dr. Rama Rao.
2. The treatment has been in all respects satisfactory and I return to Colombo tomorrow night. I have already received the good news of my wife's recovery.

Import and export control
3. The Secretary of State's reply to my telegraphed request for permission to show Secret documents concerning economic warfare to the Executive Committee for Labour, Industry and Commerce being in the expected negative I at once so informed the Board of Ministers. Thereupon Mr. Senanayake and Mr. Corea (an unusual combination) asked what would be the position if the Executive Committee delegated all its powers and functions in regard to this subject to the Minister (Corea). I replied that the position in that case would be perfectly simple and that it was precisely because the Ministers had assured me that the Executive Committee would do no such thing that I had, at their request, sent my telegram to the Secretary of State. A few days later the Executive Committee actually passed a motion of unlimited delegation, and the position is now regarded as 'constitutional'. Corea is always tactful but I attribute the Committee's unusual exercise of common sense to pressure brought to bear by Senanayake through his son, who is on the Committee. It is unfortunate that Senanayake's influence is not always so commendably directed.

Administrative difficulties
4. The position of the Governor under the Committee system becomes increasingly difficult in times of stress or crisis. During the first weeks of the war (with which the budget debated coincided) meetings of the Executive and Standing

---
[1] Lord Erskine, governor of Madras, 1934–1940.

Committees, of Council, of the Board of Ministers and of Sub-Committees were so numerous and continuous that I found it almost impossible to maintain liaison with any Minister or Officer of State. They were always and at all hours engaged. My meetings with them were nearly all arranged at their telephonic request when points of difficulty had arisen. While it is perhaps gratifying that they should wish to bring their difficulties to me, it would be far more satisfactory if they were to discuss with me their plans and policies before difficulties arise. That however is unfortunately not the Ministerial conception of constitutional procedure.

Indo–Ceylon relations

5. The Ministers came to see me on this subject because I had refused to approve the draft of a telegram that would have wrecked the chances of the desired conference. I had prepared another draft which agreed to hold in abeyance the retirement-cum-bonus scheme and to postpone for a month any question of further retrenchments of Indian personnel. This met with immediate opposition from Senanayake, who said over 3,000 Sinhalese labourers were under notice in the Survey Department alone (see, however, paragraph 7 infra) and in these circumstances to give even temporary immunity from retrenchment to Indians would be to provoke the certainty of riots. At this stage Bandaranaike said that if a telegram was to be sent in the sense I desired he proposed to regularize it by introducing a confirmatory resolution in State Council next day. Such a motion would of course have aroused bitter communal altercation and was certain of defeat. I therefore drafted a far more conciliatory telegram than that which I had refused to approve, which left it to India to press their demands further. A few days later in an interview with the Indian Agent I agreed to a compromise put forward by him in regard to the retirement-cum-bonus scheme; i.e. that applicants to retire under it should be allowed to take the bonus now and go if they wanted to, but should be told that the scheme was under discussion with India and that, if they preferred their applications under it could be held in temporary abeyance. I heard from Mr. Wedderburn last week that there had been a subsequent interchange of telegrams; that the Conference was unlikely to materialize this month, but that he did not apprehend anything more serious than a postponement.

6. Through friends here in Madras my fears have been confirmed that the anti-Indian speeches of irresponsible Sinhalese politicians have aroused real irritation and annoyance. The prevailing opinion is that hard cases under the Indian emigration ban (of separated families) are unlikely to receive humane consideration so long as feeling runs as high as it does now. The inoffensive cooly too often pays the price of political blunders.

Financial position and salary level proposal

7. At another meeting with the Ministers I refused to support their proposal for a salary levy. It had been mooted at a previous meeting, but on that occasion I stated my inability even to consider such a proposition until I had before me the Ministers' general financial policy. At this second meeting the view was expressed by Mr. Senanayake that one 'could not in justice dismiss thousands of labourers without demanding some sacrifice from permanent employees. Otherwise the full brunt of war-time economy would fall exclusively upon the poorest. I thereupon asked who were these thousands of labourers doomed to dismissal and learned to my surprise

that (following apparently a precedent set in 1915–18) it was proposed to stop all survey and settlement of lands during the war and so to retrench all survey coolies. Ceylon already suffers acutely from arrears in land settlement, and I requested the Ministers carefully to reconsider what appeared to me a proposal of very false economy. Moreover it would form an extremely bad example for Government, which should be a model employer, to dismiss the labour force engaged on a perennial service; unless indeed conditions of bankruptcy necessitated it. At this stage in our discussion it transpired that the Ministers had not understood the Financial Secretary's exposition of the financial situation, and the question was reserved for their further consultation with him.

8. The proposal for a salary levy is the second barrel fired by the Ministers at the public service, the first being the request (already communicated to the Colonial Office) for a Commission to consider the question of reducing the salaries paid to "non-new entrants", to use the local Treasury jargon. The following appear to me the reasons for Ministerial objection to the present scales of remuneration:–

(a) the Donoughmore Commission's remarks about salaries. There is a good deal, I think, in Sir Drummond Shiel's contention that failure to send out a Salary Commission as recommended by them was an omission which will long affect the attitude of Ministers and State Council towards the Service;
(b) the fact that in Ceylon, owing to the overcrowded condition of the legal and medical services and the small salaries given on Coconut estates, Government service affords the most lucrative career for the young man; indeed the superiority of his prospects is notoriously reflected in the size of the dowry which he can expect with his bride;
(c) an inferiority complex which excites unintelligent Councillors when they find a high average of intelligence in the public service;
(d) the control of personnel by the Secretary of State and Governor and not by the Ministers or Council; and
(e) the fact that a Civil Service rooted in the bureaucratic tradition is not uncritical of the imperfections of infantile democracy.

9. I cull the following from a personal letter from Senanayake, just received:–

"Nothing useful is likely to come out of these talks with India,; it is best for both Ceylon and India to decide to look after their own affairs independently of each other".

Senanayake's scope of vision is no less limited than his power of expression. If Jayatilaka fails, negatively, to lead Senanayake would, positively, mislead.

7   CO 54/966/1/2, no 99   23 Oct 1939
[Indo–Ceylon relations]: inward telegram no 293 from Sir A Caldecott
to Mr MacDonald on the forthcoming conference in Delhi on trade
negotiations and labour relations

Your telegram, No. 165, Confidential. Ceylon has now accepted invitation from the Government of India to Conference in Delhi about the third week in November for the purpose of trade negotiations contemplated in Article XIII of Indo-British Trade Agreement and for discussion on the question of emigration and immigration and other outstanding questions of common interest. Ministers would not agree to Indian proposal to hold in abeyance scheme for voluntary retirements of non-Ceylonese on the ground that those who have applied for them and wish to go would consider it a breach of faith on our part, which is of course true. They have also refused to extend undertaking to treat non-Ceylonese with 10 years' service or over on the same footing as Ceylonese for the purpose of retrenchment to cover persons with less than 10 years' service. In view of the fact that owing to the curtailment of services due to the war thousands of Ceylonese labourers are being retrenched any extension of undertaking given to non-Ceylonese would certainly cause dangerous recrudescence of anti-Indian feeling both in the State Council and outside. I much hope, therefore, that the Government of India will appreciate the realities of the situation and that the Conference will take place without further impediment.

8   CO 54/966/1/2, no 100   26 Oct 1939
[Indo–Ceylon relations]: outward telegram (reply) no 265 from Mr MacDonald to Sir A Caldecott on labour relations

Your telegram No. 293.[1] I do not understand why, if necessary, suspension of scheme of voluntary inducement to non-Ceylonese to anticipate risk of retrenchment should not be conceded in respect of those who have not yet taken advantage of it. No breach of faith could reasonably be said to be involved.

Should be glad to know briefly what are the existing services which have been curtailed owing to the war with consequent retrenchment of thousands of Ceylonese labourers.

Advantage of successful negotiations with India are of such importance as to warrant substantial effort on part of Ceylon even at risk of criticism in State Council to reach mutually acceptable basis.

---

[1] See 7.

9   CO 54/964/2, nos 22 & 24A   28 Oct 1939
[Reforms]: despatch from Sir A Caldecott to Mr MacDonald on the reforms debate in the State Council, the question of minority representation and a proposal to appoint a re-delimitation committee
[Extract]
Minutes by G E J Gent, Sir C Parkinson, Mr MacDonald and Lord Dufferin

I have the honour to report to you on the recent Reforms Debate in the State Council of Ceylon, six encased copies of the Hansard of which are being despatched to you by Ocean Mail.[1]

---

[1] Enclosures not printed.

2. With this despatch itself I enclose

(1) A report by the Legal Secretary, who moved the resolutions, in two volumes;
(2) a note on the proposed Reforms handed to me at Kandy by the Agent of the Government of India on the 23rd June; and
(3) a Memorandum submitted by the Ceylon National Congress dated the 28th July.

3. I have already forwarded, as they came to hand from week to week, a number of representations addressed to you from various quarters; a large number of additional letters and memoranda have been addressed to, and carefully perused by, myself.

4. The form which the Debate took (of one general and thirty-one particular motions) has already been accounted for in my despatch No. 322 of the 5th May. It was not of my own choosing.

5. In this despatch I propose (rather than to heap Pelion on Ossa by meeting argument with counter-argument) to summarize seriatim my own reactions to each item of the Debate. Under certain heads it will be found that I have revised a previous opinion, although my general view remains much the same as before.

6. Before proceeding to consider its parts it is necessary to face the fact that the Debate as a whole reflects cleavage rather than concord and that my proposals have not received (to quote Mr. Ormsby Gore's[2] (now Lord Harlech) despatch No. 763/1937) "the general consent of all important interests in Ceylon". I am convinced that nearly all our political fissures radiate from the vexed question of minority representation, and it has been a great disappointment to me that various efforts that were being made some months ago by representatives of different communities to get together on a basis of some agreed variation of paragraph 6 of my Reforms despatch[3] should have proved entirely infructuous. I realize however that in a country where there are no parties or political loyalties and indeed nothing to bind anybody to anybody else's word, agreement to-day might well have spelt disagreement tomorrow. . . .

34. The preceding paragraphs of this despatch cover all the resolutions moved by the Legal Secretary on the basis of my Reforms Despatch; but the curtain was rung down on the Debate by the Member for Point Pedro's motion for the immediate appointment of a Royal Commission. Later, in his letter of the 18th October forwarded with my despatch No. 699 of the 19th October,[4] Mr. Ponnambalam has spoken of a Parliamentary Commission as eventually necessary, but has deprecated any further distraction of the Island by political controversy at this juncture of war. The position however is that if the whole question of constitutional Reform is shelved for the duration of the war, political agitation in the ranks of the majority community will be just as inevitable as agitation by minority spokesmen if the question is not shelved. This is a dilemma from which there is no escape.

35. The Legal Secretary has on pages 64 and 65 of his Report, Volume II, put forward three possible courses. The first (preparation of a new Order in Council forthwith) I am unable to regard as compatible with the position as I have summarized it in paragraph 6 of this despatch, quite apart from the difficulties and dangers foreseen by the Legal Secretary. The second (appointment of a Royal

---

[2] S of S for the colonies, 1936–1938.   [3] SP XXVIII, 1938.   [4] See 4.

Commission) is not in my view advisable at any rate for the present. If one arrived in the immediate future the result would inevitably be that expressed in Carroll's lines:–

> "And when he asked them to explain
> They simply said it all again."[5]

The third course considered possible by the Legal Secretary is the making of a further effort to settle the question of the representation. The proper method of doing this would, it seems to me, be to appoint the [Re-delimitation] Committee envisaged in paragraph 6 of my Reforms Despatch and in No. 11 of the State Council Resolutions. . . . The personnel of the Committee might be five gentlemen selected respectively from among the Lowland Sinhalese, Kandyan, Jaffna-Tamil, Moorish and Indian communities under the presidency of the Legal Secretary.

36. If the appointment of such a Committee commends itself to you there is one contingency that must be carefully guarded against. This is that some members of the Minority Communities might represent it as an opportunity for increasing their representation under the present Constitution. It should be made quite clear that there can be no piece-work tinkering of this kind; the Committee's recommendations will be relevant only to an overhaul of the whole Constitution.

37. Owing to the medical necessity of my proceeding to Madras this week I find myself constrained to send this despatch with very little alteration of my original skeleton draft, which I had intended considerably to amplify and supplement. On reading it through, however, I am satisfied that it contains all that I feel it essential to report at this stage; nor do I wish to delay my report in view of a practical consideration that has just arisen. Some Rs.50,000 is spent annually on revision of the Register of Voters. The Board of Ministers would like to cut out the work in 1940 and save this sum if there is not to be a General Election in 1941. If indeed there is to be constitutional reform in the near future it would be reasonable to provide by an Order in Council for an extension of the life of the present Council until an election can be held under the amended Constitution. The Ministers would be prepared to support such an extension provided only that you were prepared to pursue the question of reforms and that their consideration were not deferred for an indefinite period such as the duration of the War.

38. My opinion of the present system of administration being what it is I find it impossible to look forward to another general election under it with any degree of satisfaction or complacence. I should nevertheless unhesitatingly press for a postponement of the constitutional issue if I thought that its abeyance would have any chance of achieving even temporary political tranquillity; but, as I have already indicated, I entertain no such illusion. The Sinhalese will not let matters rest.

39. In all the circumstances I feel that appointment of the proposed Re-delimitation Committee should be the next step. Believing as I do in the sincerity of the numerous assurances, which still reach me daily from every quarter of the Island, of Ceylon's determination to help win the war I am bold to hope that the work of the Committee may be facilitated by a realization on the part of all communities that one of the most effectual ways of assisting His Majesty's Government in the months immediately ahead will be for Ceylonese to bring to their own constitutional problem a maximum of compromise and conciliation and a minimum of sectional animus and obduracy.

---

[5] Quotation from Lewis Carroll, see 3, note 2.

Minutes on 9

In paragraph 12 of his memorandum to the Cabinet in November, 1938, (No.7 on 55541/5/38 secret below) the Secretary of State summarised as follows the procedure which he recommended in pursuance of the Governor's proposals for constitutional reform, set out in his despatch at No.18 on 55541/38:–

"I propose now to authorise the Governor to publish his proposals, and to arrange that they shall be debated in the State Council. On the result of that debate will depend the nature of our further action. If it should show, as I hope it will, a general opinion in favour of the principles of the Governor's recommendations, I should proceed without further delay to the drafting of the necessary amending Order in Council; and in this task I should hope to avail myself of the experience of the India Office in the working of the Indian constitution. If, on the other hand, the Governor's proposals should be inadequately supported, or should be received with irreconcilable hostility by any important section of the population, I should have to consider whether any amendment of the constitution could be effected without a further full enquiry by a Parliamentary Commission".

The Cabinet agreed "that the Secretary of State for the Colonies should have authority to instruct the Governor to publish the proposals . . . for the reform of the constitution of Ceylon, and that, if general opinion was in favour of the principles of the Governor's recommendations, he should proceed without delay to draft the necessary amending Order in Council".

The Governor, in his despatch at No.22 herein, sends his conclusions and recommendations on the result of the State Council debate, the proceedings of which are recorded in the Hansards which are available with me. The Governor admits, in paragraph 6 of his despatch, that "the debate as a whole reflects cleavage rather than concord and that my proposals have not received the general consent of all important interests in Ceylon". A perusal of the Legal Secretary's report on the debate, which forms enclosure 1 to No.22, shows that this is indeed the case. Motions 10, 11 and 12, relating to the numerical representation to be granted to minority communities and the method of effecting it, gave rise to a number of amendments, and voting followed communal lines. Furthermore, the very important motions 15–18, relating to the abolition of Executive Committees and Officers of State and the substitution of a Cabinet system of government, were strongly opposed by the Tamil, Moslem and Indian representatives, and motion 25 concerning the appointment of Deputy Ministers, which the Governor considers to be an essential part of his scheme, was rejected by the Council altogether.

At pages 64–65 of his Report (enclosure 1 to No.22) the Legal Secretary suggests that three alternative courses of action are now open to us. These are as follows:–

(1) That the Secretary of State should now proceed on the basis of the State Council debate and the Governor's recommendations, to frame an Order in Council revising the Constitution.

As stated above, the Cabinet agreed that the Secretary of State should proceed to draft an amending Order in Council if general opinion was in favour of the proposals. As the debate has revealed no such general agreement, it seems that course (1) must be definitely ruled out.

(2) That a Royal Commission should be sent to Ceylon immediately to examine afresh the question of reforms.

The Governor points out (paragraph 34 of No. 22) that the only effect of a Royal Commission appointed to visit Ceylon at this juncture would be a repetition of all the arguments recently aired at such length in the State Council debate. Moreover, the State Council rejected, by 29 votes to 12, Mr. Ponnambalam's motion that a Royal Commission should be sent out to examine the Donoughmore constitution – (see page 61 of the Legal Secretary's report). It is therefore apparent that the Sinhalese majority would be strongly opposed to the appointment of a Royal Commission at this juncture, and communal differences would be accentuated at a time when a welcome truce between rival political factions has been brought about by the outbreak of war. Course (2) therefore seems to be out of the question.

(3) That a Committee should be appointed now to consider the re-delimitation of electoral areas – [see motion 11, pages 6–8 of the Legal Secretary's report) – in the hope that such a Committee will be able to find a solution of the representation problem which will be acceptable to all parties and thus remove the principal obstacle to the introduction of a new constitution without the preliminary of a Royal Commission.

This is the course favoured by the Governor – see paragraphs 35, 36 and 39 of No. 22. But there appears to be this fundamental objection. Although the appointment of a local Re-Delimitation Committee is intended as a step towards securing more satisfactory representation for the minority communities, the voting on motion 11 shows that the representatives of those communities voted against it – (Hansard Vol. 49, page 2339). The minorities wanted the terms of reference to be more favourably defined and they wanted a Commission appointed by His Majesty's Government instead of a local Committee. It therefore seems improbable that a local committee, constituted as suggested by the Governor in paragraph 35 of No. 22, would be successful or that it could carry out its task without arousing communal ill-feeling afresh. The Legal Secretary admits that, unless the Committee were completely successful, it would probably have to be followed by a Royal Commission, and this would be most undesirable, particularly in war time, for the reasons stated above. Taking these factors into consideration, course (3) seems to be no less open to objection than courses (1) and (2).

It therefore seems necessary to search for any other courses of procedure which will:–

(1) not give the impression that the question of reforms is abandoned sine die;
(2) not revive active communal feeling at this juncture;
(3) not encourage the leading interests to stump the island canvassing support.

I have come to the conclusion that the best hope may lie in asking the Governor to consider the plan of an announcement by the Secretary of State to the following effect: that he considers that the debate has shown that there is not a sufficient basis of agreement in Ceylon to justify proceeding with the reform of the Constitution on the lines proposed without further exploration of the interests of all concerned; that in the present war all our efforts must be directed towards the immediate object of achieving victory and that no distraction must be allowed to interfere with that supreme aim. A full further exploration of the constitutional problem would therefore be taken up on the successful conclusion of the war, when a Round Table

Conference *in London* will be called with the object of arriving at a solution of the problem in consultation with the leaders of the political and other interests affected.

The considerations which prompt me to recommend this course of action are as follows: the Governor's despatch at No. 24 and paragraph 34 of his despatch at No. 22 make it clear that the Ministers and the Sinhalese majority would not rest content with a mere neglect to formulate any new proposal for the constitutional issue until the war is over, and it is for this reason that the Governor has not recommended such a course. But I cannot help feeling that the promise of a Round Table Conference in London would make an appeal to the Sinhalese and the rest for the reasons – (1) of the adoption of that procedure formerly with India and Burma, (2) that it will avoid the hazard of such another report as the Donoughmore Report, (3) that it will avoid the need for actively resuscitating communal issues by political agitation in the Island at the present juncture. I feel not only that the immediate essential is to avoid the exhibition of communal feeling in Ceylon during the war, and that the knowledge that the problem would be threshed out *in London*, between representatives of all parties, would remove any incentive on the part of the rival factions to continue their communal crusades *in Ceylon* in the meantime, but also that a Conference in London will encourage leaders in Ceylon to explain their essential interests in conference in the least extravagant fashion and will enable those politically concerned in this country to obtain a better idea of the points and personalities at issue.

If this course of action is considered worth pursuing it should in the first place be confidentially proposed to the Governor for his consideration and advice. And it will involve the consideration of certain questions of intermediate procedure. A new general election to the State Council will be necessary in the normal course (under the provisions of the Order in Council) in January 1941. The Governor and the Ministers feel, and I think it would be generally agreed here, that it would not be desirable to extend the life of the present Council indefinitely until the war is over. The Ministers have said that they would be prepared to support an extension of the life of the present Council for one year, but only on the understanding that the question of reforms would be pursued and would not be deferred for an indefinite period (paragraph 37 of No. 22 and No. 24). The Governor has said that he finds it impossible to look forward to another general election under the present Constitution with any degree of satisfaction or complacency (paragraph 38 of No.22). If the war were to last 3 years and a Conference in London met in the fourth year, it would be the fifth year at least before a new Constitution could be put into operation. This would be too long an extension of the life of the present Council. I doubt whether the risk of local disturbances in Ceylon in the course of a wartime general election need be apprehended if it were realised locally that the members were being elected for a sort of "Rump" Parliament which would be replaced by a Council elected under such new Constitution as might follow the holding of a Round Table Conference. Whether the elections, if held, should take place in 1941 or should be postponed for one year seems to me to be a question on which we should take the Governor's advice.

I should make it clear that my proposal is that we should defer during the war *all* questions connected with the proposed reform of the constitution, including any possible amendment of Article 38[6] on the lines which were suggested in paragraph

---

[6] Which dealt with premature retirement of government officers on proportionate pension.

31 of the Governor's first Reforms despatch at No.18 on 55541/38. We have had representations on this and kindred subjects from the Ceylon Public Service Association – (see No.34 on 55531/1/39). My idea is that, when the Round Table Conference takes place, our sole concern should be to safeguard (1) the necessary powers of the Governor, (2) the essential rights of the minorities (including European capital interests), (3) the essential rights of the Public Service. It would be for the Ceylonese themselves to agree upon a satisfactory solution for the remainder of the problem.

G.E.J.G.
20.12.39

Secretary of State
Judging from what I have seen of Ceylon affairs during the last two and a half years, I had formed the opinion that, of all the Colonies, Ceylon was likely to present the most difficult problem with which the Colonial Office would be dealing. That opinion is certainly not weakened by the developments set out in the Governor's despatch (No.22).

I agree with Mr. Gent's criticisms of the three possible courses of action discussed in the first part of his memorandum: none of those would be satisfactory. And I think that Mr. Gent has made an admirable suggestion, i.e. that on the successful conclusion of the war the Ceylon constitutional problem will be further explored by means of a round-table conference in London at which leaders of the political and other interests affected would be brought into consultation. I believe that a conference of that kind held in London would be more effective and certainly safer than anything in the nature of a commission sent to Ceylon. And in view of the India and Burma precedent it should appeal strongly to the Ceylonese.

? Consult the Governor by confidential despatch as proposed in Mr. Gent's memorandum.

A.C.C.P.
1.1.40

There are strong points to be made in favour of a Round Table Conference immediately after the war. But there are also arguments for making progress during the war, if that is feasible. The main one is that the various communities may be more willing to compromise during the war than in the safe days of peace; so agreement between them may be easier now than it will be after the Empire has emerged victorious. I wonder whether a Governor's Conference a little later on might not work. If the Singhalese [sic] majority want to make progress with a new constitution, they may be ready to make bigger concessions to the minorities than has yet been indicated. Let us discuss in the first instance; then despatch putting alternatives to Gov.

(I would not even rule out a Parliamentary Commission later on – as an alternative to a Governor's Conference – though the opposition of the Singhalese majority is a formidable obstacle to that.)

M.M.
3.1.40

? Discuss. My first inclination wld. be to have a small R.T.C. over here fairly soon.

There are obvious objections, though I think they cld. be overcome. The promise of a R.T.C. after war is over seems to me too vague to help us very much if the position is going to be difficult to hold, and unnecessary if it is not.

D & A.
8.1.40

I agree with X[7] and this prompted me to suggest a Governor's Conference in Ceylon at an early date. I think it would be difficult to have a R.T.C. here during the war, and embarrassing. But perhaps the difficulties could be overcome. However, the Governor's knowledge of these people and problems is so good that it would be a pity to leave him out of it, as would be the case if the conference were over here. But discuss tomorrow.

M.M.
10.1.40

This was discussed last week by the S of S, & I have drafted a despatch putting to the Gov for his consideration & comment the various suggestions which the S of S wd like him to think over.[8]

C.E.J.G.
16.1.40

---

[7] X refers to the last sentence of Dufferin's minute of 8 Jan.
[8] See 23 for the despatch which was sent.

10   CO 54/966/1/2, no 103   31 Oct 1939
[Indo–Ceylon relations]: inward telegram (reply) no 323 from Sir A Caldecott to Mr MacDonald on labour relations

Your telegram No. 265, Confidential.[1] On 31st of May notice was issued to every non-Ceylonese daily paid employee of the Government with over five years' service offering bonus calculated on length of service and free transport if he chose to return to his home abroad in preference to risking retrenchment in 1940. Offer was stated to remain open until 31st of December only. During the past six weeks forms have been sent to several thousand employees reminding them of the offer stating the amount of the bonus and requesting decision. Replies accepting or rejecting being received daily. About 250 acceptances to date. Considered impossible to break faith with employees of this Government by withdrawing the offer, but have instructed Department(s) concerned to stop the issuing of further forms containing renewed offer pending reply from India to my telegram accepting the invitation to the Conference.

Budget 1939–1940 recently passed does not curtail social services but provides greatly reduced works programme. Further cuts necessary if expenditure to be kept within revenue even with additional taxation. Consequent reduction in wages payable at least 1½ million rupees representing wages of about 4,000 workmen.

---

[1] See 8.

11   CO 54/964/3, no 40   3 Nov 1939
[Reforms]: letter from G G Ponnambalam to Sir N Stewart Sandeman explaining the views of the minorities

[Sandeman, a Conservative MP representing the Middleton and Prestwich Division of Lancashire from 1923, forwarded Ponnabalam's letter to MacDonald. The secretary of state acknowledged it and returned it to Sandeman who then wrote a further letter to the CO as follows: 'As you know, I am taking almost as much interest in Ceylon as I did on the question of the India Bill. My sole aim in doing so is my feeling that the minorities have to be protected, and very actively protected, more in the East even than in Europe. I also have the feeling that a western form of government is not the most suitable for Eastern mentalities, who for centuries have had something else engrained in them. I am perfectly certain that you are taking every measure which is possible to see that so far as it can be done under the proposed constitution, the rights of the minorities will be guarded. I should very much like to know whether you are going to issue a White Paper on the Governor's Report. I have the feeling that the Sinhalese may try to exploit the fact that there is a war on, in the same way as [the Indian National] Congress is undoubtedly doing, in order to gain their own ends' (CO 54/964/3, no 42, Sandeman to MacDonald, 14 Dec 1939).]

I do hope you won't mind my writing to you at a time like this. In reply to your last letter I wrote to you in Kenlygreen, St. Andrews, Scotland. I do hope you received that letter. Since then I did not wish to worry you as Parliament had adjourned and as I realised only too well how tremendously worried you must have been with the serious developments on [?in] the International situation. I would not worry you even now with a letter as I realise only too well that things are no better and, if anything, worse for those like you who have to shoulder the Nation's and the Empire's burden, but I am forced to write to you as I find that there are certain sinister moves being made by our Sinhalese friends just now. The position is this. On the declaration of war the representatives of the minority communities ceased all political agitation and publicly called a truce in order that the country might unitedly co-operate towards the successful prosecution and speedy termination of the war. In the meantime we find that the Governor has forwarded his despatch on the Reforms debate in council with his recommendations thereon.[1] As there was no measure of agreement at all between the majority community and the minority communities on the Reform proposals we demanded a Royal Commission. Now there seems to be a move afoot on the part of the Pan Sinhalese Board of Ministers to wrest all the Reforms they possibly could have when we have ceased agitation here and England is engaged in war, without a comprehensive examination of the constitutional position by a Royal Commission. This attempt of theirs must be strongly resisted.

The actual position is that, if anything, the minorities are anxious for an amendment on the constitution in order that the balance might be restored, but we, not wanting to embarass England at this stage, are content to leave everything in abeyance till the termination of the war. The Sinhalese on the other hand having all the power they have under the constitution want a further accession of power and hope to obtain it by joining forces with the extremists of India and Burma. This in short is the situation here, and I do sincerely hope that in the midst of all your cares and worries you and your party will be able to afford a little time to prevent the

---

[1] See 9.

Secretary of State from being stampeded into taking hasty action along the path of least resistance.

We in our little way have placed unreservedly our persons and resources in the cause of England and the Empire, and in this moment of stress we whole-heartedly join with you in striving for the final triumph of freedom and justice.

Kindest regards to Lady Sandeman and your good self.

12 CO 54/973/14 13 Nov 1939
[European unofficials in Ceylon]: minute by Sir C Parkinson to Mr MacDonald

[Parkinson's minute was prompted by a private letter written by Ralph Skrine to Sir H Moore at the CO. Skrine, of Bosanquet & Skrine Ltd which was based in Colombo, described himself as a businessman with thirty-nine years' experience in Ceylon. He began by asserting that events in Ceylon were 'drifting badly' and that the Donoughmore constitution, the root he suggested of the island's problems, had been framed by individuals with no 'first-hand knowledge of the people whose evidence they were taking'. Assessing the subsequent working of the constitution, Skrine was especially critical of Caldecott: 'I have no personal animus against Caldecott whatever as an individual. I have had glowing accounts of him from a man I know at Home who knew him well in the Straits, and at the start I was disinclined to believe that he was weak. He works like a black, and its not ability he lacks but a certain firmness which *must* go hand in hand with conciliation, if justice is to be done to all parties. His reputation as a good mixer is true enough so far as the Native population goes, but I think he has overdone it most unwisely in attending endless Dinners and functions which for health reasons he would have been wise to curtail after the first few weeks. I believe him to be a very "shuck" man and much worried, and Lady Caldecott is in the same condition. He no doubt is doing what he believes to be right, but he does not appear to have grasped the fact that "familiarity breeds contempt", and that the people he is trying to conciliate will give him no help whatever if his actions do not accord with their wishes. From all accounts I receive he is very much under the thumb of Senanayake, who knows just exactly what he wants and will stick at nothing to get it, viz: Complete Self-Government *in the hands of his own Party*.' Skrine also suggested that the CO was at fault in that it had failed to give clear guidance or instructions to the governor: 'If you discuss this point with any British Official here or men of my own business Community, you will invariably get the answer: "Well, of course, the Governor's hands are tied and the Colonial Office are far too busy with Palestine and the other Colonial responsibilities to worry about a little Island like Ceylon" . . . I imagine that the position with Caldecott at any rate is that he has been told, "We have got enough trouble on our hands already, so for God's sake keep the place quiet!!".' He concluded that the 'Senanayake crowd' were 'much like children, and "human nature is human nature" all the world over. You cannot run a School, a Regiment, a Business Concern or anything else without a firm hand to direct it, and that is what is so badly lacking here' (CO 54/973/14, no 2, Skrine to Moore, 29 Oct 1939).]

Secretary of State
You will be interested to see this letter from a Ceylon unofficial. I do not know the writer myself, but it is always interesting and often useful to get views of this kind from unofficials in a Colony. But I think that when you have read Mr. Skrine's letter you will feel able to discount what he says about Sir Andrew Caldecott. Mr. Skrine does not, I suspect, realise that things cannot remain static: it would indeed be a dreadful thing if they were to. And yet it is quite understandable that he and many other people should prefer efficient government to government which, for the time being at any rate, sacrifices a certain amount of efficiency to what we should regard as progress. Very few people, I imagine, would maintain now that the Donoughmore

Commission produced an entirely satisfactory constitution for Ceylon. But we have got to work towards self-government in the Colonies and we have got to face up to many difficulties in the process. Dr. (now Sir) Drummond Shiels[1] used to say to me when he was Parliamentary Under Secretary of State that the way of democracy is not easy, but the goal is worth while. The days when the Governor of Ceylon can administer the Island as a benevolent autocrat are gone. It does not follow from this that there is not room for revision of constitutional arrangements in Ceylon, and I hope we may be able to effect something useful.

It is not necessary to comment at length upon Mr. Skrine's letter, but you will notice on page 7 two passages which show how utterly people who are not in the Service can, and often do, misconceive things. Of course, nobody has said to Sir Andrew Caldecott anything to the effect that he must keep Ceylon quiet because the Colonial Office has other worries: nor, of course, is it true that because you have been overburdened with Palestinian affairs, no time has been given to Ceylon or other Colonies—in any case the Eastern Department does not cease to function in the Colonial Office because the Middle East Department is working at high pressure on its own subject.

---

[1] Parliamentary under secretary of state for the colonies, 1929–1931, who was a member of the Donoughmore Commission.

13   CO 54/964/3, no 37   18 Nov 1939

[Reforms]: despatch from M M Wedderburn to Mr MacDonald forwarding a message addressed to the secretary of state on behalf of representatives of the minority communities

With reference to Sir Andrew Caldecott's Confidential despatch of the 28th of October on the subject of the Reform of the Ceylon Constitution,[1] I have the honour to forward at the request of Mr. G.G. Ponnambalam, Member of the State Council, a copy of a message addressed to you on behalf of Representatives of Minority Communities whose names appear at the end of the message.

The message was submitted for transmission to you by telegraph, but in view of the expense Mr. Ponnambalam subsequently requested that it be sent by Air Mail.

Message with 13

Secretary of State for the Colonies, London.

Minorities have suspended political agitation during pendency of war. Owing to lack of agreement with majority community, minorities are anxious that further opportunity be given for discussion of your proposals before decisions are reached.

S. Dharmaratnam	M.S.C.	C.G.C. Kerr	M.S.C.
T.B. Jayah	"	S. Natesan	"
S. Kanagasabai	"	R. Sri Pathmanathan	"

---

[1] See 9.

I.X. Pereira	M.S.C.	S. Vytilingam	M.S.C.
G.G. Ponnambalan	"	G.A. Wille	"
A.R.A. Razik	"		

14   CO 54/964/2, no 24   27 Nov 1939

[Reforms]: despatch from Sir A Caldecott to Mr MacDonald conveying the views of the Board of Ministers

At the request of the Board of Ministers I have the honour to address you on the position created by the War in relation to the question of the Constitutional Reforms which have during the past year been the subject of debate in the State Council. By virtue of Article 19 of the Ceylon (State Council) Order in Council, 1931, as amended by the Amendment Order in Council, 1935, it is incumbent on me as Governor to dissolve the present State Council upon a date that shall enable the polling of votes at the ensuing General Election to take place in or about the month of January, 1941. The Board is of opinion that the indefinite continuation of the present Constitution is undesirable and harmful to the best interests of the country and therefore feels that the next General Election should be held under the reformed Constitution. The Board, however, realises the fact that it may not be possible for the question of Reforms to be settled so as to allow of a General Election by this date. The Ministers, therefore, request that steps may be taken without delay with the object of introducing a reformed Constitution. In this event, they are prepared to recommend to the State Council an extension of the life of the present Council for such reasonable period as may be necessary for this purpose. This may be effected by an Order in Council extending the life of the present State Council for one year.

2.   In connection with the holding of the next General Election there is one other matter that has received the attention of Ministers. Under Part IV of the Ceylon (State Council Elections) Order in Council, 1931, it is provided that the registers of voters should be revised annually. The Board of Ministers consider that such annual revision is unnecessary and the expense thereby involved amounting as it does to approximately Rs.50,000 should not be incurred in the present state of the Island's finances. If, therefore, the Order in Council is amended to extend the duration of the life of the present Council, such amendment shall be accompanied by a modification of the provisions of the State Council Elections Order in Council so as to obviate the necessity for the revision of the registers of voters in the year 1940.

3.   You will doubtless consider the Ministers' request when you review the recent debate of the State Council on Reforms: in connection with which I have already addressed you (vide my Confidential despatch of the 28th October 1939).[1]

---

[1] See 9.

15   CO 54/966/1/2, no 114   30 Nov 1939

[Indo–Ceylon relations]: outward unnumbered telegram from Mr MacDonald to Sir A Caldecott on the deadlock over labour relations

Your confidential telegram, No. 418. I much regret to learn of deadlock with Government of India, and I am sure you will continue to use all your influence to resolve it.

I note that Government of India contemplate public statement. Both Secretary of State for India and I are anxious that anything in the nature of public recrimination should be avoided, especially at a time when it is most important not to publish matter which will be useful for enemy propaganda. It may be taken as certain that anything suggesting dissension within the Empire will be seized upon by the enemy and made the most of.

Secretary of State for India is also telegraphing privately to Viceroy to whom it is being suggested that it would be very desirable if he were to find it possible to consult with you as to terms of any public statement proposed by Government of India.

Similarly, if Government of Ceylon intend to make public statement, great care should be taken as to its terms about which I should like you to consult Viceroy personally, if that should be possible, and I should also wish to be consulted.

16   CO 54/971/11, no 7   28 Dec 1939

'Things Ceylonese': fourth periodical report by Sir A Caldecott for CO

1939–1940

1.   The passing of an old year and the beginning of a new is the time-honoured occasion for a review of the past and a forecast of the future. None of our important Ceylon happenings in 1939 can however be written off as belonging to the past; there is a carry-over into 1940 under each head, and in every case it is a carry-over of worry and anxiety.

Startup affair

2.   The "Startup Affair"[1] is likely to fizzle out as soon as the debate on the subject has been concluded next month. It has however wrecked whatever faith I had left in the present Ministry. The Ministers were perfectly well aware that, failing other attempts to instal Startup in his professorate, I should enact a Governor's Ordinance. They made no remonstrance to me and based their inability to introduce a ministerial measure to the same purpose not on any disagreement as to the necessity of placing Startup in his job without further delay, but on the consideration that Council, in view of its previous resolution condemning the appointment, would throw their bill out. I felt certain that opposition to my Governor's Ordinance would come from any other quarter but the ministerial bench. Until 2 p.m. on the day of the debate the Ministers felt themselves, I understand, similarly certain. At that hour

---

[1] On 12 Dec 1939 Caldecott used his reserve powers to appoint Dr C W Startup as professor of physiology at University College, Colombo and registrar of the Ceylon Medical College despite the general disapproval of the appointment both in academic circles and among politicians.

however they learned that the protest motion of which notice had been already given by Mr. Samarakoddy[2] was going to be made the vehicle of some anti-ministerial criticism and that the Governor was not to be the sole butt of the debate. Thereupon they hurriedly drafted their ministerial resolution of protest and had not even the decency to let me know about it until it came to my notice in supplementary agenda of Council two hours after its introduction. I have not hesitated to tell the two Ministers whom I have happened to meet on other business since the introduction of the motion exactly what I think. I do not however flatter myself that what I think, or what any responsible person thinks, will weigh in the least with Ministers and Councillors whose attentions are even at this early date exclusively focussed on the polling booths of 1941.

Salary levy

3. I understand that Mr. Senanayake has expressed indignation at my refusal to support any proposal for a salary levy, the idea of which I characterized as a recourse to bankruptcy. I am informed that he has since given utterance to the remark that ministerial policy must now therefore aim at producing a degree of bankruptcy sufficient to justify a levy on salaries of Government servants. In my last Notes[3] I tried to analyse this hatred of the public services. I omitted however from that analysis the consideration that to many modern Ceylonese minds the system of Government through administrative heads of provinces and districts is unpalatable as being undemocratic and anomalous under the new Constitution. If in future the only public servants required for district administration were to be clerks of Provincial or District Councils then of course men with lesser qualifications could be had for smaller remuneration. The country is however far from ripe for such accelerated democratisation, and the replacement that is being gradually effected of Headmen by (horrible title) Extra Assistant Divisional Revenue Officers does not in fact represent an abolition of the traditional Headman system but a reform and modernization of it.

Salary revision

4. I have written at length in a Confidential despatch regarding the Select Committee recently appointed by State Council to report on public salaries, present and future. Although the appointment of this Committee was against ministerial wishes there is no doubt in my mind that any objectionable features in its report will nevertheless fail to receive ministerial denunciation, and that it will be left to the Governor as usual to hold the fort for the public service.

Volunteers' family relief

5. I am meeting the Ministers on the 7th January to discuss a point of disagreement between us that may eventually lead to my having to provide for local Defence expenditure by Governor's Ordinance. New rates of pay and allowances for mobilized Volunteers have been duly agreed with the Ministers and promulgated, as foreshadowed in paragraph 10 of the second issue of these Secret Notes of mine.[4] These rates are, as I there explained, really determined by law and so outside the

---

[2] The reference is to Siripala Samarakkody, member of the State Council.
[3] See 6.   [4] See 3.

bounds of disputation: although within the (unmobilized) Ceylon Planters' Rifle Corps there has, I believe, been some disgruntlement concerning them. The present controversy concerns the relief for his family that a mobilized volunteer is entitled to claim under Cap.258 Section 15. The law makes the Governor the arbitrator and in order to systematize awards I have ordered that the amount paid in relief must not

(a) exceed Rs 5 for a wife or Rs 4 for a child (with a maximum of three) per diem;
(b) bring the applicant's post-mobilization income to more than his pre-mobilization income; or to more than
(c) Rs 1,000 a month for an officer or Rs 800 a month for other ranks.

6. The Ministers, I understand, want a maximum of Rs 300 a month to cover pay, allowances and family relief. I shall point out to them that the law will not admit of such an arbitrary maximum, even if it could be justified by any argument outside the law; which of course it cannot. Mobilized volunteers are inevitably more expensive than regular troops; the economics of the Volunteer system accrue in peace time when the Force is unmobilized, and this the Ministers appear to forget.

7. Although the Ceylon Planters' Rifle Corps was demobilized at the end of September and there is no apparent likelihood of its remobilization I believe the Ministers' attitude in this matter to be due to Mr. Senanayake's dislike of this strictly European regiment. If he openly took the line that the money spent on it should be devoted to a new regular Ceylon Regiment; that in modern warfare the young European's place was either on his job, or in a mixed Volunteer Force, or in the British Army; one could appreciate a measure of reason in his argument and respect his attitude. But indirect hitting at it is not straight politics and I sincerely hope that I shall be able to guide the Ministers to this conclusion.

Reactions to the war

8. The preceding paragraphs bring me to a consideration of Ceylon's reaction to the War. I have heard people say that the State Council's resolution of loyalty and cooperation (followed by similar motions by other public bodies) was nothing but eyewash and that the local politicians are out to embarrass us as much as they can while we are pre-occupied with war. It is not to be disputed that Ceylon politicians like fishing in troubled waters; that is nothing new. They make the most of our own disavowals of imperialism and of the attitude of the Indian Congress. I do not think that any of them are out to be helpful, but that is partly because they don't think us in need of their help. Ceylon is out of the zone of hostilities and in a life that goes on much as usual they are behaving no better and perhaps a little worse than usual. They do not question the certainty of our victory and the big future event for them is the next general election for the State Council. Outside the ranks of politicians a considerable general interest in the war is evidenced by an enormous increase in the circulation of vernacular newspapers. The great majority of these emanate from Lake House (the home of the Ceylon Daily News) and are sane, sound and loyal. If anybody ever anticipated that with the outbreak of war all hatchets would be buried, all agitations smothered, and all nationalistic aspirations abated he is already proved wrong – but it would have been a most unintelligent anticipation. If Ceylon's reaction to the war is nothing to enthuse about it is in my opinion nothing unduly to groan about. It may be summed up in the phrase "Pinpricks as usual". They should not be taken too seriously.

Labour unrest

9. Last week I received a deputation of representative Planters and Visiting Agents and heard their views on labour unrest. There have been some twenty five strikes on estates during the past six weeks of which some five are still unsettled. Immediately after my return from India I had discussed the position with the Controller of Labour and had also impressed on the Minister of Labour (Mr. Corea) the day after his return from Burma the seriousness of labour unrest. An additional officer of the Labour Department has already been stationed at Hatton. The causes of unrest are agreed on all sides; it has nothing to do with conditions of employment but is fermented by persons whom the planters call 'agitators' and whom the Labour Department more correctly term 'politicians'. As the period of the present State Council approaches expiry the vote-catching propaganda of its members increases. The subtle and clever Brahmin, Natesa Aiyer, Member for Hatton, creator of the Ceylon Federation of Workers, finds it necessary not merely to stir up his supporters but to detach them from any tendency to exchange his Federation for the newly formed Ceylon Indian National Congress which, since Nehru's visit, has been started as an offshoot of Congress in India. The latter body is trying to form branch associations among labourers on each estate, and Natesa Aiyer is similarly forming cells of his Federation. There may be serious clashes in some places as a result; but the probability in my opinion is that some compromise will soon or later be reached between the contestant parties. In the mean time there is a spate of oratory and an avalanche of pamphlets; all very carefully kept within the law. What the planters want me to do is to use the Governor's powers "to arrest and repatriate the agitators". I told their representatives straight that I would do nothing so silly or so fatal to their own and everybody's interests. The labourers, or most of them, now have the vote and any attempt to prevent Council Members or candidates from addressing their constituents would raise a whirlwind not only here but in India. Political awakening was inevitable under the present Constitution and things would never again be so easy for the employer as they were "in the good old days". The deputation then suggested that the Ceylon Government should indent on the Colonial Office for a "Trades Union expert" to come out and organize "proper and satisfactory" unions on the estates instead of the present "Kuttus" or "Sangams" organized by the Federation of Workers or Ceylon Indian Congress. I pointed out to them that the only result would be that those two organizations (possessing one thing in common – Indian Nationalism) would jointly and successfully promote a boycott of the expert. The representatives of the Planting Industry who saw me were all elderly, and obviously "had the wind up". The view of Sir Thomas Villiers[5] and of a young planter with whom I have discussed the situation is that the present phase will pass without any Island-wide downing of tools. The position is however serious and requires the constant and careful watching which the Labour Department is giving it.

Looking ahead

10. It will be gathered from the preceding paragraphs that the political weather forecast for 1940 is definitely "stormy". Mr. Corea's election to the presidency of the Ceylon National Congress is unlikely in my opinion to convert that amorphous body

---

[5] Planter and merchant in Ceylon; member of Legislative Council, 1924–1931, and of State Council, 1931–1932.

into any resemblance of a responsible political party: which is a pity as Corea (a Christian and the husband of a Tamil lady) might if he could only develop the personality and the leadership have a very salutary influence on Ceylon politics. He is not however the stuff that leaders are made of, and I cannot among our present politicians detect anyone approaching that category. Jayatilaka is played out, and Senanayake is too often off side to captain any team. The longer one serves in this beautiful Island the more one appreciates the political insight of Bishop Heber.[6]

---

[6] Reginald Heber (1783–1826), bishop of Calcutta and author of *Journey through India from Calcutta to Bombay, with notes upon Ceylon, and a Journey to Madras and the Southern Provinces* (1828).

17 CO 54/966/1/2, no 129   29 Dec 1939
[Indo–Ceylon relations]: despatch from Mr MacDonald to Sir A Caldecott on the implications for Ceylon of the failure of labour negotiations

I have the honour to refer to your confidential despatch of the 23rd of October, and to subsequent telegrams which have reported the failure of the Governments of Ceylon and India to arrive at a satisfactory basis for the opening of negotiations on outstanding trade and other matters in need of settlement. I regret that the promise of negotiations has not been followed by the opportunity for personal discussion between representatives of the two Governments which would have been afforded and which might have led to mutual understanding and accommodation; in these circumstances there appears unhappily to be no immediate prospect of that détente which must be maintained as the chief aim of all concerned. In the present situation therefore my attention is particularly directed to the effect in Ceylon of the prohibition by the Government of India against the emigration from India to Ceylon of unskilled labourers, and I have been considering again the memorandum by the Controller of Labour, a copy of which was enclosed in your despatch No. 565 of the 18th of August.

2. You have reported to me, and I have received representations from other sources also, to the effect that the embargo has been strictly applied by the authorities in Madras, and evidence is forthcoming to show that the restriction is having an unsettling effect on the minds of Indian labourers employed on up-country estates in the Island. I understand from Mr. Gimson's memorandum that in particular the effect was expected to be felt on such estates and in certain important industries in Colombo itself.

3. At this juncture of war, it would be a matter of serious concern if the situation were to deteriorate in a manner subversive to the economic well-being of Ceylon and her plantation and other industries and to the maintenance of public order. It appears to me that in present circumstances it is necessary to consider what steps, if any, can usefully be taken to protect the vital interests of the Island, so long as the Government of India's attitude remains unchanged. I have, of course, no intention of suggesting that it would be right or wise to contemplate any policy of reprisals or counter action in any way damaging to the interests either of the Government of India or of Indians in Ceylon.

4. I request, therefore, that you will consider what steps are open to you with a view to achieving a modification of the prohibition imposed by the Government of India (e.g., its mitigation in respect of Indians and their families who are already in employment in the Island) or if that is not considered practicable, what steps can be taken by the Government of Ceylon to meet in the Island the difficulties which may result from its maintenance.

5. I shall be grateful if you will report to me as soon as possible upon the situation in these respects and furnish me with any recommendations which you may have to make.

18   CO 54/974/6, no 2   5 Jan 1940
[Indo–Ceylon relations]: letter from Lord Zetland to Mr MacDonald conveying the views of the Government of India on the failure of the labour negotiations. *Enclosure*

I have now received the Viceroy's observations regarding the hardship caused in individual cases by the rigid enforcement of the Government of India's ban on emigration to Ceylon to which you drew my attention in the latter part of your letter of the 19th October.[1]

The Viceroy prefaces his remarks by saying that the policy of the Government of India appears to be both logical and inescapable until the Government of Ceylon modify their attitude, for not only has the Ceylon Government's policy of discriminatory retrenchment created a state of uncertainty as to the future employment of Indians in the Colony, but there is a large section of public opinion in India, especially in Madras, that lends support to the view that Ceylon should not be allowed the benefits of estate labour from India while the Ceylon Government persist in the replacement by Ceylonese of Indians engaged in other forms of labour. As you are aware, the Government of India have since issued their proposed public statement announcing the breakdown of negotiations, and I enclose herewith for your information the text of their communiqué which was issued on the 13th December. I can only add a word of regret that our joint efforts have failed to bring the two parties together.

I fear that cases of individual hardship are an inevitable consequence of the ban on emigration, but Linlithgow assures me that exemptions are being granted when special circumstances justify them. Dependants in India are freely granted permits to rejoin labourers in Ceylon, and the Madras Government have been authorised to use their discretion in exempting persons in permanent employment of the Ceylon Government who have a guarantee of employment on their return to that country. Incidentally, the Viceroy draws attention to the fact that in this matter of emigration restriction, the Madras Government merely act as agents of the Government of India who are ultimately responsible for the policy pursued, and he adds that in carrying out this policy the Madras Government have not gone beyond the general instructions issued to them.

Linlithgow has also referred to another Ceylon question, namely, the proposals for

---

[1] See 5.

the amendment of the Constitution which were contained in the White Paper (Command 5910) published towards the close of last year. Since then the proposals have been debated in the Ceylon State Council and it is understood that Caldecott is likely to send his comments shortly if he has not already done so.

You will recall that the Government of India asked for an opportunity of considering any part of the proposed scheme that might affect Indian interests. This request was conveyed to the Colonial Office in an official letter of the 8th October, 1938, No. P. & J. 4624/38, to which Parkinson replied in a personal letter to Stewart to the effect that there would be ample time for the Government of India to express their views. The Government of India are naturally anxious that their views should be given due weight and consideration before any decision is reached. May I assure the Viceroy that this will be done when their views are received? (He says that they have delayed sending them owing to the uncertain position created by the war.) I am not sure what the position may be in regard to the constitutional changes, and whether there is a possibility of the whole question being postponed until after the war. I shall be very grateful to hear from you what the probabilities are.

Enclosure to 128: communiqué issued by the Government of India on the 13th December, 1939

In September last, the Ceylon Government suggested to the Government of India that a conference should be held to discuss the former's proposal to restrict immigration into Ceylon and that the opportunity should be taken to enter into trade negotiations and to discuss other outstanding matters of common interest. The Government of India saw no objection and expressed their readiness to receive a delegation from Ceylon in India, provided the Ceylon Government's scheme for retrenchment of non-Ceylonese daily-paid employees, which had proved the stumbling block to an earlier inception of trade negotiations, could be discussed at the conference and its operation held in abeyance.

It will be recalled that the Government of India had based their objections to the scheme on two main grounds. First, the scheme as originally announced gave preference so far as retrenchment was concerned to all Ceylonese, however short their service, over all Indians. Second, it placed indirect pressure upon Indian labourers by requiring all those with less than 10 years' service to decide before 31st December, 1939, whether they would give up their employment in consideration of receiving a bonus and free ticket to their home, the alternative being to continue in employment at the risk of retrenchment in 1940, without any bonus or other consideration.

The negotiations between the two Governments on this question have, it is regretted, not been successful. The Government of Ceylon have found themselves unable either to hold the scheme in abeyance or to modify it, except to the extent already announced in the Assembly on 12th September, that Indians with more than 10 years' service would be treated in respect of retrenchment on the same footing as Ceylonese. The Government of India have come to the conclusion that this does not offer a sufficient basis for entering the conference proposed by the Government of Ceylon and have informed the Government accordingly.

19　CO 54/974/8, no 3A　　　　　　　　　　　　　　　　[Jan 1940]

[Indo–Ceylon relations]: CO note on the history of the labour dispute in preparation for a meeting with a deputation from the Ceylon Association

A deputation from the Ceylon Association in London will wait on the Secretary of State at 4 p.m. on Thursday, 18th January, to make representations regarding the ban on emigration of Indian labour to Ceylon, its bearing on the prevailing labour unrest on the tea and rubber estates, and its probable adverse effect at a later stage on the supply of labour for the estates. The nature of the representations which the deputation will make may be seen from the letter enclosed with No. 2 on this file.

It may be worth while recapitulating the history of the events leading up to the Govt. of India's ban on emigration of labour. In April 1939 it became known that the Ceylon Ministers had under consideration a scheme, put forward by the Minister of Communications and Works, for replacing non-Ceylonese employees of the Government by Ceylonese. The scheme found its way to the press and the Government of India sent a protest. After the Ministers had considered the scheme, they decided upon a course of action far less severe than that recommended by the Minister of Communications and Works. Their scheme amounted to:—

(1) The immediate discontinuance of non-Ceylonese daily paid Government employees who had been engaged since 1934 in defiance of a resolution adopted at that date to the effect that no non-Ceylonese should be engaged where suitable Ceylonese were available;

(2) An offer of special repatriation terms to other non-Ceylonese daily paid employees who wished to retire in anticipation of extensive retrenchment measures which the Government proposed to put into effect later in the year: it was made clear that in such retrenchment preference would be given to Ceylonese over non-Ceylonese, and it was pointed out that it would, therefore, be to the advantage of non-Ceylonese employees who were in danger of retrenchment to opt for voluntary retirement under the special repatriation terms: the offer was to be open until 31st December, 1939.

At this time proposals were already on foot for a trade conference between India and Ceylon, but no time or date had been fixed. As Ceylon refused to abandon its scheme regarding non-Ceylonese employees in deference to the Government of India's protest, the Government of India threatened to cut off the supply of Indian labour to Ceylon and hinted that the projected trade negotiations might have to be cancelled. Ceylon made no definite move, and Pandit Nehru visited Ceylon and discussed the question with the Ministers. Partly as the result of these discussions, the Ministers gave way so far as to modify their scheme to the following extent: notices of dismissal were withdrawn in the cases of employees who were:—

(a) registered as married to a Ceylonese wife,
(b) registered as the father of children by a Ceylonese mother,
(c) married to a non-Ceylonese spouse who was being continued in Government employment.

The Ministers also undertook to give due consideration to cases of hardship and conceded that, when retrenchment took place, the preference accorded to Ceylonese over non-Ceylonese would be confined to the case of employees of not more than 10 years' standing, and that in other cases equal treatment would be given. The Government of India, however, was not satisfied with these concessions, and imposed a ban on the emigration of Indian labour to Ceylon on 1st August.

Telegrams continued to be exchanged between the two Governments, and every effort was made by the Secretary of State, the Viceroy, and the Governor to bring the parties to terms. Ceylon eventually suggested that the shortest way out of the impasse was to call a conference at which the two Governments could discuss their differences over emigrant labour as well as other outstanding questions, including trade relations. The Government of India accepted this suggestion on the condition that the scheme offering voluntary retirement terms to non-Ceylonese employed before 1934 was held in abeyance pending the discussions. The Government of India actually went so far as to suggest a place and date for the conference—(Delhi, third week in November). Ceylon replied, welcoming the suggestion as to the time and place for the conference, but saying that they would not be able to hold the voluntary retirement scheme in abeyance as it would constitute a breach of faith to those who had already opted for it. The position then deteriorated again, the Government of India holding out for suspension of the voluntary retirement scheme, and the treatment of all employees on an equal basis, when retrenchment began, and Ceylon offering only an extension of the time limit for voluntary retirement, and refusing the suggestion of equal treatment in retrenchment, which was already imminent. The Government of India finally issued a communication to the press on December 13th,[1] explaining the nature of the differences between the two Governments, and their reasons for deciding that the proposed negotiations could not now take place. The ban on emigration of labour from India remained, and still remains, in force.

Turning to the question of labour unrest on the Ceylon plantations, the decision taken in April to dismiss non-Ceylonese employees seems to have given rise to an accentuation of inter-communal feeling between the Sinhalese and Indian elements in Ceylon. It gave Mr. Ponnambulam [sic] an opening for some more than usually abusive remarks on the subject of discriminatory action by the Ministers. Mr. Goonesina [sic] (Labour Party) took up the cudgels on the other side, and feeling got fiercer throughout the summer. The vernacular press on both sides conducted a fierce campaign by means of pamphlets and lampoons which had a wide circulation among estate labourers. Boycotts were organized, and rival politicians seized the occasion to advertise their claims to public favour by thumping the tub more loudly than usual. The situation deteriorated after the introduction of the ban on the emigration of Indian labour on 1st August, and towards the end of August there were two affrays between Tamil and Sinhalese elements in one of the tea areas.

In September the Governor reported (paragraph 1 in 8 in enclosure to 1 on 56104/39) that the outbreak of war had brought about an improvement in the situation. Inter-communal feeling had eased and the rival politicians had, temporarily at any rate, buried the hatchet. The Governor felt that, if only the projected conference with India could be brought about, local differences might be permanently liquidated. As stated above, however, the arrangements for the conference broke down, and there has been intermittent trouble on the estates ever since. Some

---

[1] See 18, enclosure.

account of these troubles up to the end of September is given in the police report enclosed in No. 5 on 55569/1/39, and the Ceylon Association have from time to time sent us letters from planters describing local disturbances. Sir Cosmo Parkinson recently received from Mr. Bowman a copy of a letter from "an English lady resident in Ceylon" (enclosure to 13 on 55569/1/39) giving a vivid account of the situation as it appeared to her; and a most gloomy forecast of the future. The most recent official report is contained in paragraph 9 of the enclosure to 7 on 56104/39, the Governor's fourth report on "Things Ceylonese".[2] It will be seen that in that report the Governor attributes the troubles to the efforts of two rival trades union organisations which are competing to gain the favour of Tamil labour, particularly in the Hatton District.* The Governor has also stated, in his despatch in 1 on 55569/40, that the ban on emigration of labour from India has contributed to the unrest.

More recent information still comes from the Chairman of the Mooloya estates (1 on 55569/1/40). A strike began on the estate on the 5th January, and on the 10th January it developed into an attack by Indian strikers on Sinhalese labour. The police had to fire to restore order.

As to what is being done to improve matters, on the planters side we know that an admirable circular has been sent to all estate managers stating the attitude which they should adopt when strike action is taken or threatened by their labourers (enclosure to 12 on 55569/1/39). On the official side, we know that the Labour Department is doing its best to prevent the trouble from becoming widespread (enclosure 2 to No. 5 on 55569/1/39). But their task is made more difficult by the fact that labourers apparently have no real grievance against the estates to put forward. It seems to be generally accepted that if free migration of labour could be restored between India and Ceylon, the principal source of irritation would be removed. We have no evidence, however, that the Ceylon Government is taking any steps to this end, and indeed responsible Ministers seem to hold the view that Ceylon can get on very well without help from India (see paragraph 9 of No. 6 on 56104/39). The only thing we can boast of is a letter just received from the Secretary of State for India (No. 2 on 55569/40)[3] stating that, although individual cases of hardship are inevitable while the ban on emigration lasts, exemptions are being granted when special circumstances justify them. Dependants in India are now permitted to rejoin labourers in Ceylon, and the Madras Government have been authorised to exempt from the ban, at their discretion, persons in the permanent employment of the Ceylon Government who have a guarantee of employment on their return to Ceylon.

On the 29th of December the Secretary of State wrote a despatch to the Governor (No. 129 on 55569/39)[4] expressing his serious concern over the prospect as affecting vital economic interests in the Island, and asking for his early recommendations as to the steps which were open to him to take in mitigation of the effects in Ceylon of a continued interruption of the free movement of labour between India and the Island.

* *Hatton District.* One of the most important high-country tea areas in Ceylon. Represented in the State Council by Natesa Ayer, the Indian leader in the Council, who depends for his seat on the suffrage of the Indian labourers on the estates in the constituency. His position is being compromised by a new Indian labour organisation formed as a result of the visit to Ceylon last summer of Nehru, the Congress leader in India, which under the name of the Ceylon Indian Congress, is in active opposition both to the Ceylon Labour Party and the Ceylon Communist Party (Sama Samaj) and is instigating an extreme anti-Sinhalese feeling amongst Indian estate labourers. Mr. Natesa Ayer's policy is less extreme.

---

[2] See 16.   [3] See 18.   [4] See 17.

20   CO 54/973/14, no 5   20 Jan 1940

[Reforms]: despatch from Sir A Caldecott to Mr MacDonald transmitting a resolution of the Ceylon National Congress

With reference to my Confidential despatch of the 28th October 1939,[1] on the subject of the Reform of the Constitution, I have the honour to transmit a copy of a letter dated the 15th January 1940, from a Joint Honorary Secretary[2] of the Ceylon National Congress embodying a Resolution which the Congress requests may be forwarded to you.

2.   The demands for constitutional reform made by the Congress at its Session on the 4th March 1939 are contained in the memorandum which formed Enclosure 3 to my Confidential despatch of the 28th October 1939.

Letter with 20

I am directed by the Ceylon National Congress to request Your Excellency to be good enough to forward to the Right Hon. the Secretary of State for the Colonies the following resolution unanimously adopted at the 20th Annual Sessions of the Ceylon National Congress held at Dharmarajah College, Kandy, on the 27th of December 1939.

Resolution referred to:—

"That the Ceylon National Congress asks that the Minimum demands for constitutional reform by the Congress made at its Special Session held on the 4th March 1939, should be granted before the next General Election of the State Council, and such election should not be postponed beyond the period now provided for by the Constitution, unless it be necessary for the purpose of inaugurating a Constitution which satisfies our demands."

---

[1] See 9.   [2] J R Jayewardene.

21   CO 54/977/7, no 1   22 Jan 1940

'Things Ceylonese': fifth periodical report by Sir A Caldecott for CO.
Minute by G E J Gent

Labour unrest

1.   Since my last instalment of these Notes[1] the Police have had to fire on strikers on Mooloya Estate and one striker has died from loss of blood caused by gun-shot. The shooting was justified, the Sergeant having been forced to give the order by the strikers' assault on a police convoy of non-strikers. The latter were mostly Sinhalese engaged to replace striking Tamils and the "Times of Ceylon", with its lamentable bent for mischief and misrepresentation at once plastered Colombo with posters announcing a "communal clash". The Manager of the estate has since written to the

---

[1] See 16.

Ceylon Daily News pointing out that there was nothing communal about the clash at all; it was just a normal one of strikers v. non-strikers. What has been disclosed by the strike however is something almost as ominous: while it had nothing to do with communalism it did have something to do with communism. Mr. Gunawardena, Sama-Samajist member for Avissawella, and other members of the Sama-Samajist party were found by the Police on their way to the estate, which is in the Nuwara Eliya constituency whose member promptly telegraphed for measures to be taken against the Sama Samajist movement. In my last Notes I mentioned as the sources of unrest rival estate trade unions or "Sangams" promoted by (a) the newly formed "Ceylon Indian National Congress" and (b) Natesa Aiyer's "Federation of Workers". To these must now be added (c), the Sama-Samajist "All-Ceylon Estate Workers' Union", which I understand to have enrolled some eight thousand members.

2. At my meeting with Ministers at Nuwara Eliya on January 7th we had discussed Labour Unrest at length. The Home Minister was in full touch with the Police and they on their part were ready for any emergency. The Mooloya incident on the 10th therefore caught nobody unawares. The Home Minister was away in Batticaloa when it occurred but immediately returned to Colombo, and on the 12th I had a conference with the Legal Secretary, the Ministers for Home Affairs and Labour, and the Inspector General of Police at which certain small amendments of the Defence Regulations were agreed to which will facilitate prosecution of pamphleteers. Certain inflammatory pamphlets have, I understand, been definitely traced down to the Sama-Samajist Press in Colombo. On January 15th the Indian Agent came to discuss the situation with me and later I saw the Controller of Labour. I wish that the former would co-operate rather than try to compete with the latter but my past experience in Malaya prevents my expecting any fulfilment of the wish. Mr. Vittal Pai represented that planters would not avail themselves of his services as an arbitrator in labour disputes and that they were often rude to his Assistant. As far as my information goes his attempts at arbitration (which of course are outside his Agency functions) have invariably failed; and if I were a planter myself I should not call him in because, although a nice fellow, he has neither the necessary authority nor the personality for successful mediation.

3. On Elgin Estate a big strike still continues and I understand the Manager to have refused a chance of settlement recommended by the Minister for Labour and the Labour Department. This is a pity as it is bound to weaken Governmental authority.

4. After writing the preceding paragraphs I had to lay these Notes by in the press of other business. I am glad that I did so as the Controller of Labour was able to report to me yesterday evening that to the best of his knowledge not a single labourer in the Island would be out on strike this morning. This marks a great improvement in the situation, and means that the Elgin Estate Manager has at the eleventh hour shown a more conciliatory attitude. Mr. Vittal Pai has also seen me again; his main concern now seems to be for his own reputation as Indian Agent. Labourers who have joined one or other of the three bodies mentioned in paragraph 1 look to their Union for leadership and advice, and Mr. Vittal Pai feels himself left out in the cold when for all other parties things are uncomfortably warm. The inconsiderate manner in which the Government of India has operated their emigration ban, leading to separation of families etc., has also naturally diminished their Agent's reputation among the coolies as a 'protector'.

5. A recent report from the Ceylon Emigration Commissioner in India justifies the hope that hard cases under the ban may at last be going to receive more consideration from the Indian authorities than hitherto. Apart from these hard cases and from its interference with the voluntary efflux and influx of labourers on holiday or on private business the ban is doing Ceylon no harm. One cause of labour unrest is undoubtedly the fact that the Island at the moment has more estate labour than it requires, with the result that one hears of employment for four days only in the week being provided by a number of estates.

6. On the advice of the Minister for Home Affairs I have ordered a Commission of Inquiry into the Mooloya shooting (although the Coroner's finding leaves us in no doubt that it was justified) because the Garvin–Dowbiggin–Senanayake Committee on Police Questions, which reported some years ago, recommended that this should always be done. If it were not done the State Council would inevitably appoint a Committee of its own, and the wisdom of the recommendation is therefore beyond question. I understand that two Minority Members (Messrs Ponnambalam and Jayah) have already visited Mooloya Estate and interrogated the dead man's relations.

Ceylon and India

7. Although Messrs Corea and Senanayake during their recent absences in India posed as doves of peace they neither bore with them nor brought back tangible sprigs of olive. They told me however at Nuwara Eliya that they hoped to evolve some compromise on the so-called bonus repatriation scheme, and I still await further news. In the meantime I was lucky to notice in a number of documents appended to the Agenda of a Board of Ministers meeting another memorandum on the subject of non-Ceylonese labour by Major Kotalawala in which he said that the Government of India was using the discharge of non-Ceylonese as a pretext for avoiding trade negotiations. I at once issued orders for the Memorandum to be made Confidential; otherwise it might have got into the Press like the former one and have still worsened our relations with India. Apparently the gallant Major is incapable of learning a lesson.

8. In a few days' time the Ministers are coming to see me concerning the addition to the election registers during the past year of some eighty thousand Indian voters. As far as I understand the position instructions given by the Legal Secretary have been ignored through lack of supervision and Ceylon domicile taken for granted. The worst feature of the case, as I so far understand it, is that the Legal Secretary approved with Treasury concurrence the payment of a clerical fee to estate clerks of three cents per cooly registered. This has induced the estate clerks to register as many names as possible. It is almost unbelievable that such a situation should have arisen in the department of an Officer of State, and I fear that the Sinhalese Ministers will make much political capital out of it.

Volunteers' family relief

9. I am glad to report that at my Nuwara Eliya meeting with Ministers they accepted the position explained in paragraph 5 of my last Notes. The European Association may however possibly address you on the subject, as apparently a number of its members object to the principle of claims under Cap. 258, Section 15, as "savouring of the dole". I fancy however that when the Committee which the Association has appointed to look into the matter finds that the law is being faithfully

followed in regard both to pay and allowances and to claims for relief the projected Memorial to you may not eventuate. What has really riled a large number of Europeans are irresponsible and opprobrious remarks in State Council about the Ceylon Planters' Rifle Corps. As I pointed out in my last Notes no part of this Corps is now mobilized or likely to be mobilized, and this question of Family Relief is a live one only for members, mostly Ceylonese, of other units of the Ceylon Defence Force.

Startup affair

10.   It is hardly credible that the Ministers, the debate on whose protest motion will be resumed in State Council tomorrow, should have chosen this of all junctures to introduce a Bill to deprive the Medical College Council of its powers of appointment; it is however a fact, and is being widely criticized! Their motion is now of course out of time as any protest under Article 23(2) has to be made within seven days of the Governor's Message enacting an Ordinance. I suppose, however, that it will be passed with some saving amendment or other. The danger of legal proceedings to test the validity of the Ordinance seems to be finally dissipated by the redoubtable Mr. R.L. Pereira,[2] K.C's Chairmanship of a Protest Meeting of Citizens on Saturday; all that seems contemplated is yet another protest to the Secretary of State. I expect that Mr. Pereira must have drawn quite a fat fee for his presidency over what was largely a gathering of Medical Students; in return for it he dealt out liberal doses of his usual Buzfuzz stuff. I, for instance, in the newspaper account of it, was headlined as having (in my first speech here 2½ years ago!) indulged in "psychological claptrap". Parturiunt montes.

Minute on 21

This memorandum of the Governor's is more than usually interesting on the labour problem. We have heard from another source that at long last the Government of India is contemplating a relaxation of the Emigration Ban to the extent of allowing those labourers, who happened to be in India at the time the ban was introduced (August 1st), to go back to Ceylon in cases where there is personal or family hardship involved. This is, of course, an elementary point which ought to have been conceded by the Government of India from the very first. There is no other indication yet of any concession to the labourers themselves but we understand that the dependants of labourers in Ceylon, in cases of proved hardship, are to be allowed to return there from India.

It is interesting to read the Governor's remark that one cause of the present labour unrest is genuine unemployment on estates at present, but I do not think that it would be right to suppose that there is a surplus of Indian labour on Ceylon estates at present, having regard to the sustained high output of rubber and tea and the likelihood of a drift back to India if the Emigration Ban is maintained, and particularly a drift back in the near future, in accordance with the customary seasonal movement of labourers to their motherland in March and April.

The Governor is, no doubt, wise to order a Commission of Inquiry into the fracas on the Mooloya Estate.

---

[2] R L Pereira was the country's leading lawyer.

The information in paragraph 7 that the two chief Ceylonese Ministers concerned (apart from the Minister of Communications and Works—Major Kotalawala, whose recurring stupidities make him a factor to be reckoned with in this problem) are giving their minds to evolving some compromise on the Ceylon policy which has irritated the Government of India. One interesting and important aspect of the problem, which may have an increasing influence on the situation, is that the Congress Party and ex-Ministers in India have a stake in the game not only on the Indian side but also vis à vis the Ceylon Ministers. The ban in India which was imposed before the Congress Party deserted office is being maintained by a stop-gap authority in India which may feel a particular difficulty in compromising with the Government of Ceylon over a decision imposed while Congress was still in power & in a matter which is one particularly of political prestige in the Indian mind. The Ceylon Ministers themselves may be feeling (following upon Mr. Nehru's visit to them in July last year) that they too would see political advantages in forcing the hands of the present Government of India by means of reaching an agreement direct with the Congress Ex-Ministers. There was evidence last summer that Nehru's personal visit to Ceylon was a matter of suspicion to the Government of India, who regarded, with some apprehension, any appearance of the dispute at that time being settled down between the Ceylonese ministers and Congress leaders behind the back, so to speak, of the Government of India; i.e. there was a little jealousy in India itself which was suspected of accounting for the over-quick and drastic action which the Government of India took against Ceylon. The new Ceylon Congress Labour Union which was established amongst the labourers on the estates following upon Nehru's visit, appears to be making good headway as would only be natural, in competition with the various estates and other union organisations of local origin, some of which are reputable and others less so. It may well, therefore, appear both to the Planters' Association, to the labourers themselves, and to the Ceylonese Ministers, that the most promising line of effective relief is to come to terms with Congress and to rely on the latter's influence in India to have the ban removed by the Government of India.

The Governor's comments on Mr. Vittal Pai, the Agent of the Government of India and Ceylon, are interesting. I sought him out a year ago in Ceylon to have a long conversation; and though a pleasant and agreeable person, he did not strike me as a very impressive figure. (I should be glad to have this file back after it has been seen).

G.E.J.G.
7.2.40

22   CO 54/974/6, no 4   23 Jan 1940

[Indo–Ceylon relations]: letter (reply) from Mr MacDonald to Lord Zetland on proposals to resolve the labour dispute and constitutional reform in Ceylon

I have delayed answering your letter of the 5th January[1] about the Government of India's ban on the emigration of unskilled labour to Ceylon until I had received a

---

[1] See 18.

deputation from the Ceylon Association in London which came to see me on the 18th of January to represent to me, on behalf of tea and rubber estates in the Island, the difficulties which were being already experienced, and were to a greater degree to be apprehended, as a result of the labour unrest for which the Government of India's action has been mainly responsible.

The disturbance of the rubber and tea industries at the present juncture is, of course, extremely undesirable, and no less so is any avoidable stimulation of racial feeling in Ceylon. I think you will agree that the Ministers in Ceylon, heavy-footed and tactless as they were in the early stages of this controversy, have gone some way, although not far enough for the Government of India, in modifying their original scheme in the matter of retrenchment of daily-paid non-Ceylonese labour in public employment. On the other side of the picture it seems to me that it might not unfairly be said that the Government of India were unduly hasty and drastic in imposing the ban on the 1st August, and though I do indeed welcome the assurance in your letter that permits are now being freely granted in India to dependents to rejoin labourers in Ceylon, there remains for the tea and rubber producing interests which employ Indian labour in the Island the principal difficulty that the ban is still kept against the free movement of labourers themselves.

I feel that the time has come when we must take the view that both Governments have got into a position in which it is difficult for them to initiate further steps likely to lead to a solution of the present difficulty, and that it would be as well if a joint discussion could be arranged between representatives of the India Office and the Colonial Office who are immediately concerned with the problem in order to explore the lines of any suggestion which could be made here for a settlement which the two Governments might be persuaded to accept. At the end of December I sent a despatch[2] to the Governor reiterating the serious view which I took of the matter both from the Ceylon and a wider point of view, and I urged him to make a fresh effort to think out steps which might be contemplated with a view to a solution of the present impasse. I shall presumably have the Governor's reply towards the end of this month, but I don't think that the Departmental discussions which I propose need be delayed for it. If you are inclined to agree perhaps a message from your Private Secretary would be sufficient to get an inter-Departmental discussion started.

You refer also in your letter to the matter of constitutional reforms in Ceylon. It has always been my intention that the Government of India should have the fullest opportunity to express their views before any decisions were taken as to either the manner or substance of Constitutional changes in Ceylon. The Governor's proposals in the White Paper (Command 5910), to which you refer, were debated in the summer in the Ceylon State Council with a result which I can only regard as insufficient to justify any immediate action on the lines of those proposals, and in consultation with the Governor I have latterly been considering how best to proceed. On the outbreak of war a political truce set in, but I am advised that it might not be acceptable to the Board of Ministers if all further consideration of the problem were deferred until the end of the war, even though any actual amendment of the constitution might be so deferred if it were made plain that prompt action would then be taken and that in the meantime a satisfactory measure of agreement on the lines of procedure had been thought out. I am accordingly now contemplating the

---

[2] See 17.

advisability of sending a despatch to the Governor to ask for his views on possible courses of action for obtaining such agreement; for instance, by means of a Governors' Conference locally to which it might be thought desirable to attach one or two constitutional experts from here, or some form of Conference in London, either during or after the war. But I attach importance to securing, if possible, the consent and co-operation not only of the Board of Ministers but of other representative political leaders in Ceylon on any procedure which we may settle upon. It is my full intention that the Government of India should have their opportunity to let their views be known in any such discussions, and any contribution which they may be able to make will I feel sure be more effective if an early *détente* can be reached in the present difficulties over the labour and emigration question.

23   CO 54/964/2, no 25   26 Jan 1940
[Reforms]: despatch (reply) from Mr MacDonald to Sir A Caldecott suggesting three possible courses of action

I have the honour to acknowledge the receipt of your confidential despatch of the 28th October, 1939,[1] in which you reported upon the recent Reforms Debate in the State Council and enclosed a report by the Legal Secretary, a note by the Agent in Ceylon of the Government of India, and a memorandum submitted by the Ceylon National Congress.

2. As you are aware, I had hoped that the course of the Debate might have disclosed a general opinion in the State Council in favour of the recommendations which you have yourself formulated in your confidential despatch of the 13th June, 1938, and that it would then have been possible to proceed without further delay with the drafting of the necessary amending Order in Council.

3. An examination of the report of the Debate, facilitated as it has been by Mr. Howard's detailed appreciation of the sense of the speeches and the significance of the voting on the several resolutions, forces me to the conclusion that important sections of the State Council were not able to give their support to many of the substantial motions which were debated and passed. I much regret, therefore, that I am not able to conclude that the way is now clear for me to advise the issue of an Order by His Majesty in Council to amend the present constitution on the lines contemplated, and it becomes necessary to consider what policy should be adopted with a view to obtaining a satisfactory measure of agreement on the future constitution of Ceylon.

4. The problem has been materially affected by the outbreak of war since the Debate took place, and the magnitude of the effort which must be contributed in every part of the Empire to ensure the prosecution of the war to a successful conclusion may be such that any further steps towards the revision of the constitution of Ceylon likely to have the effect of disturbing the unity of effort in the Island should be deferred until peace is attained. His Majesty's Government are aware of the determination of the Board of Ministers and other political leaders in Ceylon that the Island should make its maximum contribution to the war effort, and they

---

[1] See 9.

fully appreciate this attitude. It has, however, been shown that the present constitution has defects which must to some extent cause continuing difficulty and doubt in the political life of the Island and I should be disappointed if further consideration of the problem were deferred for the duration of the war. I should prefer that a suitable procedure for examining further the possibility of reaching agreement on the constitutional question should be devised and put in motion at an early date, even though the actual steps for introducing reforms may have to be deferred at this juncture in face of the critical struggle in which all democratic principles and free institutions are now involved.

5.   In Mr. Howard's report, three possible courses are suggested. As to the first, I have already set out my agreement with your view that it is not practicable to proceed with the preparation of an amending Order in Council in view of the present failure to secure any substantial agreement in Ceylon. The objection to the second course suggested, viz. the appointment now of a Royal Commission to visit Ceylon to examine the question afresh, presents difficulties as well as objections, and I am not satisfied that at this juncture it would lead to the achievement of satisfactory results. The third course suggested by Mr. Howard is that a further effort should be made to settle certain questions of representation in the State Council. I recognize it to be possible that useful, although limited, results of a kind generally acceptable in the Island might be achieved by this means, but I cannot see that it could serve as a substitute in any measurable degree for a plan to make headway with the general problem of constitutional reform.

6.   I therefore find myself considering whether any other courses remain to be explored, and I base myself on the expectation to which you yourself refer in the final paragraph of your despatch, with particular reference to the work of a Redelimitation Commission, namely, that there is a realization on the part of all communities in Ceylon that one of the most effectual ways of assisting His Majesty's Government in the months immediately ahead will be for Ceylonese to bring to their own constitutional problem a maximum of compromise and conciliation and a minimum of sectional animus and obduracy. The Debate in the State Council, which was held before the outbreak of war, appears to me to have had the effect of giving special prominence to sectional differences of view; and it may be that in the emergency of war the more fundamental claims of the points of unity and mutual interest shared by all communities in Ceylon, in association with the other parts of the British Empire, will secure special observance and induce a beneficial compromise on outstanding differences of view. This spirit of compromise may be dissipated if all further discussion and progress is postponed until after the war.

7.   It seems to me desirable therefore to search the possibilities of fresh lines of early progress. First, I shall be glad if you will carefully consider the advantage of convening a Governor's Conference of the Board of Ministers and other leaders representative of the chief interests in the Island with a view to discussing the best means of achieving agreement. These discussions, under your guidance, might take place formally in regular gatherings of those whom you chose to call into counsel, or informally by your conducting, in the first place, a series of conversations with individuals or groups. If this procedure seemed hopeful, it might be possible to lead the Conference on to an investigation by committee or otherwise of the main heads of reforms to be agreed upon. I should be ready, if you so advised, to invite one or two constitutional experts to proceed to Ceylon to assist you in such a Conference, as it is

my experience that consultants closely acquainted with such work are able to contribute substantially towards the removal of difficulties and disagreements which arise in the course of settlement of constitutional problems. It may be that you will see in this proposal the risk of reviving in Ceylon a sectional agitation of a character harmful to the unity of front which the prosecution of the war demands. If so, that consideration must be weighed against the risk that important groups in the political life of Ceylon may not be willing to have all further investigation of constitutional reform deferred for an indefinite period.

8.   Secondly, it has been suggested to me that a conference might be convened in London forthwith which would be equally representative of the various interests in the Island. But, in present circumstances, I see great difficulties in this course. Apart from the risks of enemy action on the voyage, it would appear to me undesirable to ask that the principal political personages should at this juncture all absent themselves from Ceylon. Moreover, the effects of a failure to reach agreement would be exaggerated to an undesirable extent in the stress of war-time.

9.   Thirdly, it might be contemplated that a decision should be reached now, if it were acceptable in Ceylon, that a Ceylon Round Table Conference should be convened in London on the successful conclusion of the war. Such a Conference would comprise representatives of all important groups in the Island which are interested in the problem of Constitutional Reform; the representatives would be nominated by the Governor, as in the case of the Burma and India Conferences, upon such advice as he deemed it appropriate to seek, and, as in the case of the Burma Conference, it would be desirable that the Government of India should have the opportunity to nominate a representative to attend the meetings.

To this course the objection can be raised that it means that not only actual reforms, but even the intensive consideration of proposals for reform, will be deferred until after the conclusion of the war. This may be too disappointing to important political opinion in Ceylon. It also has the disadvantage that, as I have suggested already, the present disposition towards compromise between the various sections may disappear when the stress of war has been removed. Nevertheless, the proposal has certain advantages, and you may think that it is not an unattractive course, that it may equally appeal to opinion in Ceylon, and that if there is a need for some special measures of administrative association of political leaders in the Island with the wartime problems of government, it may be met by some extra-constitutional arrangement for the purpose.

10.   I shall be grateful if you will give your careful consideration to these suggestions and communicate to me your views on them and on any other lines of action which may occur or be suggested to you. There remain the matters of the General Election which the Order in Council requires to be held not later than next year, and the revision of the Voters' Register, which are the subject of your confidential despatch of the 27th November 1939. There appear to me to be advantages in deferring a General Election in wartime, if you are satisfied that such a decision would be generally acceptable in Ceylon; but it would seem to be a matter largely affected by any agreement on the procedure for further action in the problem of constitutional reform, and if time permits, I hope that decisions can first be reached on the latter.

24   CO 54/977/7, no 3   18 Feb 1940
'Things Ceylonese': sixth periodical report by Sir A Caldecott for CO

Storms and rocks ahead
1. I am afraid that my Notes this month will consist of a number of typhoon warnings, though whether the ship of state will suffer any very great blowing and tossing cannot at present be predicted with any certainty.

Jayatilaka versus Banks: 2nd round
2. The most serious development has been a row between Jayatilaka and Banks in which the former has been wrong and the latter rude. It has culminated in a minute addressed to me by Sir Baron on the 13th February accusing the Inspector-General of insubordination and indiscipline. A copy of this minute and of my reply thereto are annexed [as Enclosures 'A' and 'B')[1] to these Notes; I feel that these two documents not only explain the circumstances and the manner of their arising but also illustrate the extraordinarily invidious position in which the Governor too often finds himself placed by Ministers and high officials. Neither refer to him until, between them, they have made a nasty mess of things and then he is expected to clear the mess up. The likelihood of the present mess developing into a political crisis is caused by the Communist Dr. Perera's having filed in State Council a motion of censure on the Home Minister for having failed to implement the Council's Resolution quoted in paragraph 6 of 'B'. Council refused at its last session to suspend standing orders and give the motion priority but Jayatilaka in the short statement to which he alludes in paragraph 9 of 'A' has promised a full statement later on, and everything depends on what that statement will be. Left to himself the old man might perhaps manage to parry Dr. Perera's thrust without involving himself and others in a general mêlée. On the other hand if he should listen to Senanayake—well, I fancy, that nothing would give Senanayake greater satisfaction than to help push Jayatilaka off the ministerial raft with one hand and to throw dung at Banks with the other. And in case I may be thought to be doing Senanayake an injustice by this fancy I am bound to say that I agree with his view that Sir Baron is now too senile, too casual, too lazy and too flabby to lead the Council or even his Executive Committee. He allows himself to drift into crises because he no longer has steerage way to keep a straight course and so avoid them. And yet (this is the tragedy) he is the nearest, if rather remote, approximation to a statesman that Ceylon has yet produced.

Senanayake tonans
3. I very nearly allowed myself to be stampeded into hasty and foolish action by Senanayake last month. The third annex [Enclosure 'C'][2] to these Notes is an unsent despatch, the enclosure to which will show what it was that so rattled me. It's fifth paragraph is indeed abominable, coming from a Minister who has sworn to be faithful and to bear true allegiance to the King, and my first reaction was to draft a forwarding despatch in order that the Secretary of State might gauge for himself the

---

[1] The three enclosures with this report are not printed. Enclosures 'A' and 'B' dealt with the conflict between Jayatilaka and P N Banks (inspector-general of police) over the issue of prosecutions arising from the shooting incident on the Mool-oya estate.
[2] For Caldecott's difficulties with Senanayake which he reported in Enclosure 'C', see 32, paras 1–4.

measure of that fidelity and allegiance. Before the despatch came up for signature however I had thought again and more wisely. The letter had of course no constitutional significance, since it had not been shown to or approved by the Executive Committee, and it was after all an effusion thoroughly typical of a Sinhalese village bully, whose characteristics (like the spots on a black panther) occasionally show through the ministerial veneer of "Jungle John". I therefore asked him to come round and told him that, if I had sent his letter to the Secretary of State, I considered that he would have had in decency to resign his Ministry. To this he did not demur. I then went on to say that I should in common courtesy forward no representation to the Secretary of State until we had received his promised despatch, and that I presumed that he (the Minister) would address me when the despatch had been duly considered. The despatch has since arrived and was sent to the Minister on the 9th February; I await his comments with interest. I trust that the tone of them will be less objectionable than the first ebullition of his wrath though I expect something pretty loud and harsh. As the Customary Law of Negri Sembilan[3] has it (I still find the Custom a great aid to ethical philosophy) "it is the language of the mud-buffalo to snort and to bellow".

Welcome reinforcement

4. I am too busy to add much to these Notes before the next mail goes, but I feel that I must append a brief expression of my great pleasure at meeting our new Legal Secretary.[4] He has been staying with us at Queen's House since his arrival, and will continue to do so for another three days; after which he takes up residence at the Galle Face Hotel. He gives me great confidence and I feel his arrival at this juncture of possible political tempest as a most welcome reinforcement. To-morrow I meet the Board of Ministers again on the subject of the improper registration of Indian voters (Things Ceylonese No.5 paragraph 8)[5] and they may incidentally ask me about reforms. Whether I consult them then about the chances, if any, of round-table agreement will depend upon the atmosphere prevailing.

C.P.R.C. grievances

5. With reference to paragraph 9 of my last Notes I had a talk with the chief Volunteer Officers on February 3rd and visited the headquarters and mess on the 15th. Unless the European Association or the "Times of Ceylon" decide to go on dragging this puddle for political live-bait I don't think that we shall hear much more of this matter.

---

[3] One of four Federated Malay States.   [4] R H Drayton.   [5] See 21.

25 CO 54/978/7, no 1   23 Feb 1940

[Reforms]: despatch from Sir A Caldecott to Mr MacDonald on the registration of Indian voters. *Enclosures 1–4*

I feel it my regrettable duty to report, without waiting for the Hansard report of the State Council debate of the 21st February, a position serious in itself but still more serious in regard to speeches which it has evoked, that has arisen in connection with the registration of Indians as voters.

2. You will remember that in paragraph 3 of my Reforms despatch, dated the 13th June, 1938, I expressed myself as against any proposal to alter the regulations governing the Indian franchise. I added however that the question of tightening up procedure would receive my careful attention. I accordingly asked the Legal Secretary to look into the matter and on the 24th June, 1938, the position was discussed by the Board of Ministers. On the 9th August, 1938, the Legal Secretary issued his Circular No. 56 of which a copy is the first enclosure to this despatch.

3. In paragraph 7 of my Confidential despatch dated the 28th October, 1939. I adhered to my recommendation that no alteration of the regulations should be made and described the present position as follows:—

"Under the Ceylon (State Council Elections) Order in Council, 1931, an Indian can be enfranchised by

Article 7 (a) proving Ceylonese domicile of origin,

(b) proving, if he has been resident for five years or more, Ceylonese domicile of choice;

Article 8 (c) proving that he possesses the prescribed literacy and property qualifications, or

Article 9 (d) proving that he has been continuously resident in Ceylon for five years and declaring that he intends to settle here permanently.

Proof of domicile of choice (b) is notoriously difficult and (d) was provided to make enfranchisement easier for the intending settler. What actually happened was that registering officers allowed people to be registered under Article 7 without proof of domicile of choice, and therefore without even the declaration required by Article 9. This loose procedure is now being tightened up and in my opinion nothing further is necessary."

When I wrote that last sentence I had in mind the Circular issued by the Legal Secretary and had no reason to apprehend that Registering Officers would have failed to implement it.

4. On the 17th January, 1940, however I received from the Acting Legal Secretary a request that I should grant the Board of Ministers an interview at which to discuss a position that had arisen out of a contravention of Mr. Howard's Circular in the important planting districts of the Central, Sabaragamuwa and Uva Provinces. The extent and gravity of the contravention may be gauged by the second enclosure to this despatch which is a copy of a Circular issued by the Government Agent of the Central Province, the penultimate sentence of paragraph 4 of which completely negatived Mr. Howard's instructions. In Uva, I understand the Government Agent substituted on his own initiative ten years' residence in the Island for any domiciliary qualification. The result of the failure to carry out instructions has been the addition last year of perhaps 100,000 Indian voters to the electoral rolls of ten constituencies for which figures are already available.

5. I met the Board of Ministers on the 24th January and the question of invalidating the 1939 registers by an Order-in-Council was raised by certain Ministers. I expressed the view that the first thing to do was to ascertain whether the Elections Order-in-Council did not provide for rectification in a normal way by revision. It was agreed that the Acting Legal Secretary should give a written opinion. His opinion (Enclosure 3) was considered at a further interview which I gave the Board on the 7th February. As doubts as to its correctness were expressed I suggested

that the new Legal Secretary's arrival should be awaited and a second opinion be obtained from him. This was agreed to.

6. Mr. Drayton's opinion is contained in my fourth enclosure and was accepted at a third Conference with the Board of Ministers on the 19th February. It was then decided that the Legal Secretary should prepare (a) the draft of a new Circular to Registering Officers for the avoidance of future error and (b) an estimate of the staff required for the coming revision of registers which must be put in train by the 1st April.

7. On the 21st February the State Council continued its debate on Sessional Paper XIV, 1938, a copy of which is my fifth enclosure.[1] I enclose a report of this debate taken from the *Ceylon Daily News* of the 22nd February. The speech of the Minister for Local Administration, if it has been correctly reported, contains a passage (which I have underlined in red) calculated to cause a further deterioration in Indo-Ceylonese relations. My sixth enclosure, a cutting from this morning's paper, purports to reproduce a declaration by the Hon. Mr. D.S. Senanayake at a public meeting which, if the reported words were actually spoken, would be difficult to associate with the utterance of a responsible Minister.

Enclosure 1 to 25: letter from J C Howard to J R V Ferdinand,[2] 9 Aug 1938

I have the honour to inform you that at a meeting of the Board of Ministers held on the 24th June, 1938, the present method of registering immigrant labourers was discussed and it was agreed that I should send out a circular to all Registering Officers pointing out what other qualifications are required of those voters who claim to be registered on the ground of domicile other than domicile of origin under Article 7 of the Ceylon (State Council Elections) Order-in-Council.

2. Article 7 of the Order in Council contemplates

(a) a domicile of origin which is determined at the time of birth: and
(b) a domicile of choice which is a domicile a person can acquire.

In the case of Ceylonese there is a presumption in favour of a Ceylon domicile but in the case of non-Ceylonese domicile shall not be deemed to have been acquired for the purpose of registration as a voter unless he has also resided in Ceylon for a total period of or exceeding five years.

3. The definition or "domicile" involves legal questions of much difficulty and complexity but it is quite clear that a total period of or exceeding five years' residence in Ceylon cannot in itself give an immigrant labourer a domiciliary qualification under Article 7. "Domicile" is not synonymous with "residence" and mere "residence" by itself cannot constitute "domicile." The law allows a person not under disability to acquire for himself a domicile of choice by the fact of residing in a country other than his domicile of origin with the intention of continuing to reside there indefinitely; in other words the physical fact of residence must be accompanied by the required state of mind to make the country in which the person resides his sole and permanent home.

---

[1] Enclosures five and six not printed.
[2] Principal assistant, Registrar-General's Dept.

It follows therefore that Registering Officers are not justified in permitting the registration of "immigrant labourers" under Article 7 unless they are reasonably satisfied that such labourers

(i) have resided in Ceylon for a total period of or exceeding five years; and
(ii) have determined to make Ceylon their sole and permanent home.

4. I appreciate the difficulties that confront Registering Officers but I trust that they will make every endeavour to see that the requirements of the law are satisfied before they permit the registration of immigrant labourers under Article 7 of the Order-in-Council.

Enclosure 2 to 25: letter from E T Dyson[3] to estate owners on the revision of registers of voters, 1939, Kandy district, 20–30 July 1939

I have the honour to request that you will be so good as to assist me again this year in the preparation of the lists of labourers on your Estate who are qualified for inclusion in the register of voters on the ground that they possess Ceylon domicile.

2. I enclose, for your information, a list of persons whose names appear under the address of your Estate as revised in 1938, and would request you to be good enough to return this list to me before the 31st August, 1939, after striking off those who have died or who are no longer under you, making the necessary comments against the names. In the case of those who have left the Estate, I would be glad if you would state wherever possible the address to which they have gone. In cases in which the exact address to which they have gone is not known, any information as to their present whereabouts would be most useful, i.e., India, Uva, Gampola, et cetera.

3. Please furnish a separate list of persons who do not appear in the list now sent by me but who are qualified for registration on the grounds set out in paragraph 4 below and who are not disqualified for any of the following reasons:—

(1) No person shall be qualified to have his name entered in any register of voters for this year if such person—

(a) Is not a British subject;
(b) is less than 21 years of age on the 1st day of August, 1939;
(c) has not for a continuous period of six months in the eighteen months immediately prior to the 1st day of August, 1939, resided in the Electoral District to which the Register relates;
(d) is serving a sentence of penal servitude or imprisonment imposed by any Court in any part of His Majesty's dominions or in any country under His Majesty's protection or in respect of which a mandate is being exercised by His Majesty or by Government of any part of His Majesty's dominions, for an offence punishable with hard labour or rigorous imprisonment for a term exceeding twelve months or is under sentence of death imposed by any such court or is serving any term of imprisonment awarded in lieu of execution of such sentence;
(e) has been adjuged by a competent Court to be of unsound mind; or
(f) is incapable of being registered as a voter by reason of his conviction of a

---

[3] Government agent, Central Province.

corrupt or illegal practice, or by reason of a report of an Election Judge, in accordance with the Order-in-Council.

4. Any person not otherwise disqualified is qualified to have his name entered in the register if he is domiciled in Ceylon; but except in the case of persons possessing Ceylon domicile of origin, domicile shall not be deemed to have been acquired by any person who has not resided in Ceylon for a total period of or exceeding 5 years. Domicile further implies the intention of making Ceylon a permanent place of residence but since it would be unduly laborious to prove such intention in the case of every individual, I think it would suffice if you omit the names of any who clearly have no such intention. I should further be grateful if separate lists could be prepared for males and females.

5. I am authorised to pay at the rate of cents –/03 per name as remuneration to your staff for this information.

6. I regret having to trouble you in this manner, but I can see no other means of maintaining the accuracy of my Electoral Registers.

7. A franked addressed envelope is enclosed for the return of the list of voters.

Enclosure 3 to 25: memorandum by J W R Ilangakoon[4]

At the interview Your Excellency granted to the Board of Ministers on the 24th January Your Excellency requested me to consider further and advise Your Excellency on the question whether a Registering Officer in revising a register of voters for any electoral district in any year can expunge from the register the name of any person who, in his opinion, is not at the time of such revision qualified in accordance with the Ceylon (State Council Elections) Order-in-Council, 1931, to have his name entered in the revised register of voters.

2. The qualifications of a voter are prescribed in Articles 6, 7, 8 and 9. Every voter must possess all the qualifications mentioned in Article 6, which are put in a negative form, and, in addition, the domicile qualification under Article 7, or the literacy and property qualification under Article 8, or the certificate of permanent settlement qualification under Article 9.

Clauses (1) and (4) of Article 15 confer on the Registering Officer a general power to revise the register of voters. Clause (2) of Article 15 provides that in revising the register the Registering Officer—

(1) shall expunge the name of any person who is dead or has become disqualified or no longer resides in the electoral district to which the register relates;

(2) shall insert therein the name of every person who not being already registered nor otherwise disqualified has a literacy and property qualification under Article 8 or a certificate of permanent settlement qualification under Article 9 and has made application to have his name entered in the register on such qualification;

(3) to correct any mistake in the register;

(4) to supply any omission which has been made in the register.

3. It appears to me that the particular powers conferred by Clause (2) of Article 15

---

[4] Acting legal secretary.

are not exhaustive but merely explanatory of the general powers of the Registering Officer in his task of revision. I am, therefore, of opinion that it is competent for a Registering Officer in revising a register of voters in any year to expunge from the register the name of any voter who, in his opinion, is not qualified in accordance with the provisions of the Order-in-Council to have his name in the register at the time of such revision.

Enclosure 4 to 25: minute by R H Drayton to Sir A Caldecott, 16 Feb 1940

I confirm the views expressed by the Acting Legal Secretary in paragraph 3 of his confidential memorandum dated 31st January, 1940. It will perhaps be convenient if I give further reasons in amplification of those already given.

2. It seems to me that, in order to determine the powers of the Registering Officer to review the register of voters, it is, in the first place, necessary to form an opinion as to the exact force and effect of the register.

Articles 7, 8 and 9 of the Ceylon (State Council Elections) Order-in-Council set out the qualifications entitling a person to be entered upon the register. A person possessing any of those qualifications is not entitled to exercise his right to vote unless he is on the register which is in force at the time at which the right to vote arises. Article 35 states that "the register of voters in operation . . . at the time of any election . . . shall be conclusive evidence for the purpose of determining whether a person is or is not entitled to vote at such election."

The two characteristics of the register which I think are important are—

(a) that it has an evidential value only, and
(b) that it is in operation for a period of one year only.

In my view therefore the right to exercise the franchise must at all times depend primarily on the voter being qualified to vote. The register is conclusive evidence at a particular election that a particular person is entitled to exercise the franchise even though his name may have been wrongly inserted in the register, but it seems to me to be a wholly fallacious argument that, when once a person has had his name wrongly entered for the first time in any register, he thereby becomes qualified to have his name retained on the register until he dies or becomes disqualified under Article 6. Such an argument involves the assumption that the register is something more than evidence of the right to exercise the franchise at a particular election and ignores the limitation of the period during which a particular register remains in operation.

3. The opinion expressed in the preceding paragraph strengthens the view of the Acting Legal Secretary as stated in paragraph 3 of his memorandum of the 31st January. A close examination of Article 15 of the Order-in-Council further strengthens this view.

Clause (1) of that Article imposes in each registering officer an obligation to revise the register. The clause is quite general in its terms and it seems to me to be clear that the obligation is an obligation to ensure that every person entitled is registered and that no person is registered who is disentitled or, if entitled, is registered incorrectly.

Clause (2) imposes on the Registering Officer an obligation to expunge from the register certain entries therein if the circumstances set out in the first four lines are proved to exist. This is an obligation—not merely a power. Line 18 of Clause (2) contains a power as distinct from an obligation to "correct any mistake or supply any omission which appears to have been made in the register." This power is subject to the limitation expressed in the clause but that limitation does not relate to the point that is being dealt with in this memorandum. It seems that this power to correct a mistake is not limited to the correction of clerical errors, but comprises also the power to expunge from the register the name of a person who is not qualified at the time of the revision to have his name entered on the register. Unless the Registering Officer has this power it seems to me that the whole purpose of the register and the revision thereof will be defeated: for example, a person who is 18 years of age on the first day of August in 1939 may have been wrongly entered in the register; at the time of the revision in 1940 it is not correct to say that this person "has become disqualified" (see lines 2 and 3 of clause (2): he has at no time been qualified: therefore he cannot "have become disqualified." Is his name to remain on the register because it was inserted in error in the year 1939? If the argument that the power to expunge arises only from the express duty to expunge which is contained in clause (2) is correct, then the answer is, yes. If, on the other hand, the argument that the power to correct mistakes enables the Registering Officer to expunge the name is correct, then the answer is, no. I have no doubt that the whole purpose of the Order-in-Council would be defeated unless the second argument prevails.

4. If a Registering Officer acts in accordance with the view expressed in this memorandum, it seems to me that he must give notice to the person whose name he has expunged from the register notwithstanding that his is not specifically required to do so by any provision in the Order-in-Council.

5. If the person to whom such notice is given claims to have his name re-inserted in the register he becomes, in my view, a claimant within the meaning of Article 17 and therefore has the right of appeal referred to in Article 18 if the Registering Officer refuses to re-insert his name. It seems that the Revising Officer will be entitled to decide whether the action of the Registering Officer was correct. By Article 18 his decision is made final and conclusive. In these circumstances I doubt whether the person whose name was expunged would have any remedy by way of prerogative writ.

6. I understand that names have been inserted on the register of persons who have resided in Ceylon for a period exceeding 5 years with little proof of such residence and with no proof that such persons have acquired a domicile of choice in Ceylon.

Registering Officers will have a task of considerable magnitude and difficulty if they are to revise the register so as to correct errors falling within this category. Their task will include—

(a) an interpretation of the expression "resided in Ceylon for a total period of, or exceeding, 5 years"; and

(b) a decision as to the proof required in order to establish a domicile of choice.

The expression "total period of or exceeding 5 years" is one which unfortunately is not as clear as it might be. To establish a domicile of choice, residence as well as intention to remain are necessary. The object of the proviso to Article 7 of the Order-in-Council is solely to prevent any person being allowed to claim a domicile of choice for the purposes of the Order-in-Council unless he has resided in Ceylon for a total period of or exceeding 5 years. Does "total period" mean a continuous period or the aggregate of a number of interrupted periods? And must residence with intention to remain still be continuing when an entry is made in the register or the register is revised? It may be that a number of cases will be disposed of because it will not be possible to establish an intention to remain but, if an intention to remain can be established, Registering Officers will have to decide the questions in regard to the meaning of the phrase "total period" which are raised in this paragraph.

I should like to consider further the question of the interpretation of the expression "total period." I have said nothing in this memorandum in regard to the proof necessary to establish a domicile of choice and I am sure that there is no need for me to emphasise the difficulty of deciding whether a domicile of choice has been established in a particular case. I however mention both these points now because I feel that the interpretation which I have placed on the Order-in-Council in this memorandum imposes on Registering and Revising Officers a task of considerable magnitude and difficulty.

26   CO 54/973/14, no 9   28 Feb 1940
[Situation in Ceylon]: letter from Sir A Knox, MP,[1] to Mr MacDonald on the views of a constituent with an interest in tea planting in Ceylon

I have received a sheaf of papers about Ceylon from a Constituent, who is interested in tea planting in the Island.

The position he paints is very pessimistic.

My Constituent's informant, in a covering letter agrees that the present Constitution cannot be allowed to go on in its present form—as to any advance towards self-government, he feels that it would be disastrous. He thinks the Governor is to blame as he has disregarded warnings from the Police and the European Community. He imagines that, owing to instructions from the Colonial Office, his hands are tied, and that he feels he must delegate responsibility to his Cinghalese [sic] Ministers. The latter squabble over every petty detail, oppose expenditure on the defence of the Island, and squander money on anything that concerns themselves. They have no loyalty to the Empire, and would regard further concessions as weakness. If we surrender further power all big contracts will go to the Germans or the Japanese, and trade with Ceylon will be lost, as that with China has already gone, and the vast British capital invested by the British, who have given the Island any prosperity it possesses, would be wiped out.

The writer encloses a Memorandum on Labour unrest prepared by three well-known planters. This complains of the increasing frequency of strikes, not one of which has been initiated by demands of higher wages or better conditions, but which have been worked up over trivial grievances by Political Agitators, and are partly caused by discontent due to the cruel discriminatory legislation against Indian workers by the Cinghalese majority in the State Council.

It is complained that while the Governor has reserve powers to safeguard the

---

[1] Conservative MP for the Wycombe division of Buckinghamshire, 1924–1945.

internal security of the Colony and its people, and to deal with all matters which tend to cause strife and unrest, the recent arbitrary retrenchment of Indians in Government Service at the behest of Cinghalese politicians, shows that he is not prepared to use such powers till such time as may be too late to be of any use to the tea and rubber industries.

My Constituent's informant says that the Governor is entirely under the thumb of Senanayake. The majority of the Tamils, all the Burghers, Malays, Moors and the bulk of the Cinghalese know that the only chance of a fair deal for every Community lies in the British Rule, backed by adequate safeguards in the hands of the Governor. The present Constitution can only be continued if the powers of the Governor are amplified and a first class man of the MacCallum or Ridgway[2] type, with a good staff, be appointed.

Just before dictating this letter I note in the press that the Governor has at last used his reserve powers, and in consequence the Cinghalese Ministers have resigned. I do hope the Governor will be backed up and some attempt made to stem the rot that has set in since the unfortunate Donoughmore Commission, and so save some of our trade with the Island.

---

[2] Sir H E McCallum, governor of Ceylon, 1907–1913; Sir J West Ridgway, governor of Ceylon, 1896–1903.

27   CO 54/978/3, no 13   4 Mar 1940

[Ministerial resignations]: outward telegram no 150 from Mr Mac-Donald to Sir A Caldecott requesting clarification of the circumstances which led to the resignations

Your memorandum, No. 6,[1] "Things Ceylonese," just received and has given me essential elements of background of Ministers resignation. Am I right in deducing that if request of Minister for Home Affairs to I.G.P. regarding postponement of Court proceedings had been submitted for your ratification as a direction to Head of Police Department from Executive Committee you would have declined to ratify this or any other instructions which went beyond what you agreed to on 1st February. I shall be grateful if you will inform me by telegram what were your reasons for this conclusion. Were there particular reasons for resignation of Minister of Agriculture preceding remainder?

I shall also be grateful for very early summary by telegraph of developments between 16th February date of your minute to Minister for Home Affairs and 27th February date of resignation of Minister with special reference to any action taken by yourself.

---

[1] See 24.

28   CO 54/978/3, no 15   5 Mar 1940

[Ministerial resignations]: inward telegram no 230 from Sir A Caldecott to Mr MacDonald transmitting a message from the governor to the State Council

Regret to learn that my despatch, No. 94, of 24th February, forwarding copies of all correspondence laid by the Minister for Home Affairs on the Council Table and newspaper accounts of debate on 22nd February, may have been lost in the wreck of the mail plane Hannibal. Following message which after full consideration with the Legal Secretary I have sent to-day to the State Council shows clearly the points on which Ministerial resignations have risen. Message from the Governor to the State Council of Ceylon.

1. It has caused me great distress that my Ministers should have tendered their recent resignations without affording me an opportunity of examining with them the reasons for, or likely consequences of, such a course.

2. At the meeting which I had with them on 26th February, called at the shortest notice, my decision on a particular reference to me was discussed. The paper laid on the Table of the State Council at its last session by the Minister for Home Affairs contains both reference and decision.

3. My refusal to take disciplinary action against Mr. P. N. Banks was in the exercise of the responsibility vested in me by Article 86 of Ceylon (State Council) Order in Council, 1931. I informed the Ministers of my inability to vary this decision but offered to transmit to the Secretary of State any representation that they might wish to make thereon.

4. I confirmed that my decision based on three grounds: (1) that the Home Minister's communication to Mr. Banks was a request and not an instruction; (2) that if it had been an instruction it would have been unconstitutional in the minor sense that the Home Minister had not placed it before his Executive Committee and in the major that it concerned the conduct of proceedings before a Court of Law; and (3) that there had been no failure on the part of Mr. Banks to give effect to the formula which was reached at the conference between the Home Minister, the Acting Legal Secretary himself, and myself on 1st February.

5. The conversation then veered to paragraph 7 of my minute to the Minister for Home Affairs, dated 16th February. In that paragraph I set out my views of what would have been the correct constitutional procedure if Minister had (though he actually had not) referred any proposed instructions in this matter to his Executive Committee. I stated that the Committee could not justifiably have treated the matter either as so unimportant or as so urgent as not to require reference to me of any instruction to be issued.

6. At this point I understand one Minister to represent that Article 45 (2) left the criterion of importance or urgency entirely to the opinion of the Executive Committee, so that whatever they opined would be justifiable.

7. To this I replied that if, on a proper construction of Article 45 (2) Executive Committee were to decide that an instruction affecting the proceedings before a Court of Law should not require prior reference to me I should feel it my duty to see that such a decision was made impossible in the future; and to secure that any instructions affecting the administration of justice, or carrying out by public officers

of duties and responsibilities imposed upon them by the law of the land, must be referred to the Governor before any instruction was issued.

8. Article 45 (3) of Ceylon (State Council) Order in Council provides the machinery for defining what instructions should and what should not require the approval of the Governor as explicitly contemplated by Donoughmore Commission on page 48 of its report.

9. In view of the present unhappy situation that has arisen I now feel that we should consider forthwith what class of decision by an Executive Committee should always require prior reference to the Governor before effect can be given to them. In drafting such a schedule I should, of course, take my Ministers into full consultation and endeavour to correlate any schedule made by me with any schedule made by the State Council under the same article. I have already asked the Secretary of State for information as to any limitation observed in the issue of Ministerial instructions to the police in England, and would similarly refer to him any other proposed items in the schedule.

10. I have not contemplated, and do not contemplate, any other action in regard to the powers of Executive Committees under Article 45.

11. I do not desire or counsel any interference with the practice whereby a Minister directly communicates to a Head of Department his wishes in any matter. If the Head should consider that compliance with any request so communicated would not be in the public interest it is his loyal duty to his Minister to point out any objections or impediments. If a Minister has occasion to substitute an order for a request his procedure must necessarily conform with the provisions of Article 45 which it is in nobody's power to abrogate. If paragraph 41 (b) of my reform despatch is represented as such abrogation, my reply is that the phrase "Minister's directions" in that paragraph must, so long as we have our present constitution, connote directions issued conformable with the constitution and general law of the land.

12. The reason for this message is that I understand that notices have been given of a resolution for non-co-operation by the Council in working the constitution, on the grounds that I have gravely infringed constitutional rights. I trust that I have made it clear in the preceding paragraphs that my steadfast purpose has been, and is, carefully to guard and conserve those rights for all concerned, to the best of my ability and understanding. Before committing themselves and thereby our whole island to a course of action which can be contemplated with satisfaction or even equanimity only by enemies of our commonwealth and of democracy I earnestly appeal to the State Councillors that they will subject the situation to calm, wise and dispassionate review in order that nothing inimical to the country's interests may be done as a result of misapprehension or precipitancy.

29   CO 54/978/3, no 16   5 Mar 1940
[Ministerial resignations]: inward unnumbered telegram (reply) from Sir A Caldecott to Mr MacDonald

Your telegram No. 150[1] your deduction is correct, and reason for my conclusion was given in a subsequent minute to Minister for Home Affairs as follows:— "I cannot

---

[1] See 27.

agree that formula approved by me on 1st February constituted an approval of the action already taken by the Ministry. The formula carefully guarded essential points in the administration of Justice that action of the Ministry appeared to me to have left unguarded or insufficiently guarded, i.e. (a) the principle that the Police must press criminal proceedings to finality as expeditiously as possible; and (b) The right Court to hear conscientious and independent opinion of a Police Officer who has laid an information before it."

Please see also paragraph 7 of my minute, dated 16th February. Legal Secretary informs me that my conclusion was legally and constitutionally correct in every way and I am certain that if the principle at stake were not jealousy [sic] guarded interference with the prosecutions by Ministers, Committees and Council would in our local condition and absence of tradition become frequent. Home Committee has control of the Police only in respect of their executive duties and in the opinion of the Legal Secretary with which I agree though we have not advanced it such control as can be exercised over the Police in the administration of Criminal Justice vests in him.

Resignation of Minister of Agriculture was undoubtedly due to loss of temper because I had resisted strong(ly) argument and statement put forward by him at my meeting with Ministers on 26th February. Summary of developments from 16th February to 27th February as far as I am aware of them is as follows:— 21st February, Minister for Home Affairs sent me further minute in reply to mine of 16th February which ended by saying he considered it his duty to table all papers relating to incident before a State Council. 22nd February.—After consulting Legal Secretary I sent reply dealing with specific points and maintaining my previous attitude. In the afternoon Minister laid all papers on Council, and on Motion of Minister of Agriculture. Council adjourned without doing further business till 5th March in order to consider the statement of the Minister and papers laid. 26th February, Ministers met me at their request in the afternoon and I with Legal Secretary present stood by my position as already explained in my minute. Meeting ended after spirited discussion in agreement that Ministers should confer with Legal Secretary next morning. At 9.30 p.m. I received first intimation by private letter from ?Sen(glu)yak to send (?group omitted, ?notice) of his resignation.

27th February, remaining Ministers met the Legal Secretary in the morning and in the afternoon sent me an omnibus resignation signed by them all.[2]

---

[2] Acknowledging receipt of Caldecott's two tels of 5 Mar (see 28 and 29), MacDonald replied on 6 Mar: 'In absence of definite request from you no action has been taken so far in respect of Amending Order in Council, but draft is ready in case you need it. I should be glad to be kept informed daily of developments particularly as to likelihood of policy on non-co-operation' (CO 54/978/3, no 17).

30   CO 54/978/3, no 18   6 Mar 1940
[Ministerial resignations]: inward unnumbered telegram from Sir A Caldecott to Mr MacDonald on the re-election of the ministers

Ex-Ministers were all re-elected by Executive Committees this morning and through medium of Speaker have asked for informal meeting with me before they decide to refuse or accept ministerial office. I have replied suggesting tomorrow morning. *Lake House* newspaper while laying all blame for crisis on me and *Times of Ceylon* while laying all blame on ex-Ministers are alike in strongly opposing non-co-operation and general opinion of all classes throughout the Island except Communists seems thoroughly against it. I am credibly informed that ex-Ministers have for the past four days been anxious for conciliation but were awaiting re-election. My message to the Council yesterday appears to have had pacific effect and return of normality now seems probable. If so crisis should have had useful effect of preventing precipitate resignations in future.

31   CO 54/978/3, no 28   13 Mar 1940
[Ministerial resignations]: inward telegram no 265 from Sir A Caldecott to Mr MacDonald on the resolution of the crisis

With reference to my telegram No. 230 of 5th March[1] following will be laid on the table of State Council by Legal Secretary this afternoon. *Begins:*—

Memorandum by the Governor on the point discussed with ex-Ministers at their recent meetings with His Excellency.

1. (i) The ex-Ministers represented to me that paragraphs 10 and 11 of my message to the State Council dated 5th March might be interpreted as a desire or intention on my part to terminate, or in future to prevent any reasonable "adjustment of relations between an Executive Committee, the Ministers and heads of a department" along the lines of paragraph 43 of Sir Herbert Stanley's despatch of 2nd June, 1929, reprinted in sessional papers No. 34–1929. I informed the ex-Ministers that I had never had, and had not now, any such desire or intention.

(ii) The following is relevant passage from Sir Herbert Stanley's[2] despatch:—
"The adjustment of relations between the Committee, the Ministers and Heads of Departments respectively need not in practice present a problem much greater than the complexity thus far presented in the affairs of a public company by adjustment of relations between the Directors, the Chairman and General Manager. I do not conceive that a Committee would expect—at any rate for long to be consulted by the Minister on every point and at every stage of every matter with which he had occasion to deal, before he took any action. That would involve almost daily meetings of the Committee throughout the year, an obvious impossibility as a permanent arrangement. The Minister, having been selected by the Committee as its Chairman and exercising ministerial functions in virtue of that chairmanship, would be entitled to presume that members of the Committee, or at least the majority of them, would repose some confidence in his judgment and discretion, and he would soon acquire the kind of instinct which would enable him to foresee what matters the Committee would wish to discuss orally, what matters it would desire to have submitted by circulation of papers, and what matters it would be prepared to leave to him for disposal with the Heads of Departments in reliance upon its subsequent confirmation of his action if such confirmation should be necessary. Some Committees, no doubt, would be more exacting than others, but I postulate for all of them an allowance of reasonableness not less than would be requisite for the working of any system dependent on mutual accommodation."

---

[1] See 28.   [2] Governor of Ceylon, 1927–1931.

(iii) In answering despatch of 10th October, 1929, Lord Passfield[3] stated that the devolution of duties between Ministers, executive committees and Heads of Departments was one of the questions which the special commission recommended should be worked out and embodied in General Orders. In the actual event the matter seems neither to have been worked out nor embodied in General Orders. The statement of administrative procedure prescribed by the Gazette Notification 7,858 of 5th June, 1931, did no more than to repeat the provisions as to general control over departments contained in Article 39. Unless therefore there can be reasonable adjustment envisaged by Sir Herbert Stanley almost daily meetings of the Committee, which he described as "an obvious impossibility as a permanent arrangement," become unavoidable.

2. (i) As regards paragraphs 8 and 9 of my message to the Council I suggested to ex-Ministers that the State Council might appoint a select committee to advise what class of decision should (a) be made the subject of requirement by the Governor or the Council under Article 45 (3) or (b) be made the subject of authorisation under Article 45 (4).

(ii) I feel certain that the recommendations of the Committee, if appointed, will include the necessity for reference to the State Council and the Governor in respect of all decisions or instructions of an executive committee (a) which, if carried out, might affect the administration of criminal justice; or (b) which purports to relieve a public officer from executing any duty or obligation specifically imposed upon him by any Ordinance or Rule or Regulation thereunder.

(iii) It may prove possible for select committee to define in greater detail decisions and instructions or classes of decisions and instructions which fall within sub-clause (ii), but that needs more care and time than present circumstances permit. For example, so far as instructions to the Police are concerned information regarding English practice with which I have already requested the Secretary of State to furnish me may help to more precise definition.

(iv) The recommendations of the Select Committee and of the State Council thereon would be considered by me in consultation with my Ministers and referred to the Secretary of State with any addition or amendment that I might, after such consultation, consider necessary.

3. In the meantime I do not desire to interfere with the *status quo ante* but I should rely on the Ministers concerned to consult me regarding any decisions or instructions of an executive committee which in his opinion might fall within the category mentioned in sub-clause (ii) of preceding paragraph before it is carried into effect.

4. It is not of course, and never has been, my intention to detract from the powers of general control over their respective departments vested in executive committees by Article 39 or to interfere with practices that fall within the principle set out in the passage of Sir Herbert Stanley's despatch quoted in paragraph 1 (ii) of this memorandum.

5. I informed ex-Ministers that my decision not to take disciplinary action against Mr. Banks had been in the exercise of my responsibility under Article 86 and that I was not prepared to alter it. I confirmed the view which I expressed in paragraph 4 (i) and (ii) of my message to the State Council in regard to the Home Minister's

---

[3] Secretary of state for the colonies, 1929–1931.

communication to Mr. Banks. I repeated my willingness to consider and to forward to the Secretary of State for his orders any statement of protest or of appeal or of disagreement with my views that might be tendered. *Ends*.

32   CO 54/977/7, no 4   21 Mar 1940
'Things Ceylonese': seventh periodical report by Sir A Caldecott for CO

The ministerial crisis

1. It is over a month since last I wrote an instalment of these Notes.[1] The 'crisis' has in fact kept me too busy to do more than get through my papers and keep pre-arranged engagements. My telegrams have provided a day to day commentary on the crisis but I will try to add something to them now in the nature of calm retrospect.

2. The "Times of Ceylon" of March 18th quotes Mr. Corea as having stated at a public meeting as follows:—

> "Explaining why Mr. Senanayake had resigned before the others Mr. Corea said that there had been a heated discussion between the Governor and Mr. Senanayake when the Board of Ministers met the Governor at Queen's House. During the discussion the Governor, Mr. Corea alleged, *had told Mr. Senanayake that he was lying and asked him to prove what he was saying*. It was that incident that had led Mr. Senanayake to resign earlier without informing his colleagues."

Knowing the mischievous inaccuracy of the "Times of Ceylon" reporters I do not suppose that Mr. Corea ever employed these words. If however for the [italised] words were substituted

> "protested that Mr. Senanayake was misrepresenting what he (the Governor) had written, and that he (the Governor) considered the words that he had employed plain enough proof of what he had meant."

I think that the genesis of the crisis would have been described with substantial correctness, though I cannot of course remember at this distance of time the exact words of the conversation. Mr. Senanayake was arguing that paragraph 7 of my minute of the 16th February[2] was aimed at depriving Ministers and Executive Committees of all discretion and so at knocking the basis out of Ceylonese democracy. Quod erat absurdum.

3. Although Senanayake was in his most argumentative mood there was no indication at the meeting of his being about to run seriously amok; in fact when we shook hands at its conclusion the agreed programme was that the Ministers should confer with the Legal Secretary next morning and see me again later when the legal and constitutional points had been fully explained to them. At 9.30 the same evening I received Senanayake's private and personal notice of resignation. It ran as follows:—

---

[1] See 24.   [2] See 28, para 5.

"Your Excellency

The attitude adopted by Your Excellency at today's Conference makes it difficult for me to continue as a Minister. I shall thank you to accept my resignation.

Yours sincerely,
D.S. Senanayake"

To this I replied next morning:—

"Dear Senanayake,

I received your letter last night with much regret. That the attitude adopted by me at yesterday's Conference (i.e. my usual attitude of frank speech and straight discussion at all consultations with Ministers) should afford you ground for resignation has caused me not only sorrow but surprise. As I cannot reconcile it with my duty to depart from, or to modify, that attitude (which, your letter says, makes it difficult for you to continue as a Minister) I should feel that there was no alternative course to my acceptance of your resignation, with most real and personal regret, if it were formally tendered by you in an official communication.

Yours sincerely,
A. Caldecott"

4.   I have no doubt whatever that the 'attitude' on my part on which Senanayake based his resignation in his personal letter was (as Corea and others have since stated) my refusal to listen to arguments based on misrepresentation of my words and intentions. In his official notice of resignation, however, Senanayake shifted his grounds and gave the resignation a wider political basis:—

"The attitude of Your Excellency as disclosed in the correspondence tabled by the Minister for Home Affairs and confirmed by Your Excellency at the interview granted to the Ministers yesterday is, in my opinion, a complete negation of the democratic basis of the constitution accepted by this country."

If on receipt of Senanayake's private letter I had begged him not to resign I think that I might have avoided, or at any rate shelved for the time being, a crisis; but recent developments (e.g. those adumbrated in paragraph 3 of my Things Ceylonese No.6, paragraph 3 of No.4, paragraph 9 of No.3 and paragraph 3 of No.2)[3] made it plain to me that the time had come for Mr. Senanayake to be allowed the discipline of the consequences of his hectoring and precipitancy.

5.   However worrying the crisis has been for me it has been an even more anxious time for the Ministers. Some were even degraded to the depth of seeking a place on Sama-Samajist platforms in order to make sure of their reelection as Chairmen of Committee. One, I believe, was shame-facedly present when the Sama-Samajists burnt an effigy of me (unfortunately not Mudaliyar Amarasekera's portrait of me in oils recently exhibited at the Royal Empire Society) on Galle Face Green. Once re-elected they of course turned round and repudiated their recent strange bedfellows. In Council and in the Press they have had an awkward time, and I am

---

[3] See 24, 16, 6 and 3.

informed that the mass meetings organized by them failed to hold the crowds, which kept moving on and treated the platform as a mere side-show. Bandaranaike has added to his notoriety as a slinger of dirt and abuse but his, I believe, is the only Ministerial reputation to be enhanced, and that in wrong direction.

6. Out of all the turmoil emerges the strange fact, for which I have not yet had time sufficiently to account even to myself, that I have felt really glad to welcome Senanayake back. In spite of his lack of education, hedgelawry, and tiresome blustering he is big and vital and a man. Of the rest it may be said (except of Jayatilaka whose increasing senility is a public danger) that they are as good a team as the State Council with its present personnel can put up.

Reforms

7. On the 19th February I confidentially conveyed to Ministers the sense of the Secretary of State's despatch (Confidential No. (2)) of the 26th January[4] with a view to ascertaining whether the Board would take part in a "Governor's Conference" as suggested in paragraph 7 of that despatch. Mr. Senanayake replied that this would depend on what reforms I myself was prepared to support in the light of the State Council's criticisms of my original proposals. I said that I would confer with the Ministers later on this basis; that I had indeed no desire to keep my views from them, but that my recommendations on any point must in no way be regarded as indicative of what may be finally approved or as in any degree prejudicing a full and proper consideration by the Secretary of State of quite opposite views. The Ministerial crisis has of course prevented the further conference taking place. At the moment the Ministers are busy overtaking arrears of work and that they are not at unity among themselves is disclosed by the newspaper report that Sir Baron Jayatilaka has not yet been re-elected by them as Leader of Council but has been asked by four of them (Bandaranaike, Kannangara, Corea and Kotelawala) to stand down, a request to which he will give his answer on 1st April. In such circumstances, and until the full political consequences of the recent crisis become apparent, it is clearly impossible for me to proceed further in the matter.

8. The "Times of Ceylon" has meanwhile been busy with mischievous machinations. On the 20th February their Political Correspondent 'understood' that I had received a despatch and went on to invent its contents, the main feature in which was represented as mistrust in the Secretary of State's mind of the Sinhala Maha Sabha, Mr. Bandaranaike's party. On the 21st February this was followed by a second article purporting to be derived "from unassailable political sources in England." On March 16th this paper's leading article (of which a copy is annexed)[5] announced that "the Secretary of State had also noticed that the significance of the Sinhala Maha Sabha movement had not apparently received a satisfactory explanation from the Governor" and ended by declaring that "despite the other anxieties of the War the Secretary of State should regard Ceylon as a War problem and send a Royal Commission before it is too late."

9. With Mr. Bandaranaike's irresponsible anti-Indian and anti-Banks utterances on the one side, and the "Times of Ceylon's" unscrupulous intrigues on the other, the chance of evolving any measure of agreement on the question of reforms seems slender indeed. Nor has the lightning Strike of Ministers helped matters. It would

---

[4] See 23.   [5] Enclosures not printed.

however be a mistake in Ceylon to take sayings or events at their face value, and for the present I propose just to sit on the bank of the political pond and watch where the rises come.

10. I am glad to say that Mr. Ponnambalam, in the course of an interview which he sought from me on the non-cooperation issue, apologised for (and tried to explain) certain misrepresentations in his speech on the Reforms debate. The chief of these was his "solemn statement" that I had promised a deputation led by him "that 40% of the elected seats should go to the Minorities." I accepted his apology. He is the best speaker in the Council and the cleverest in debate, but he requires most careful watching.

Labour unrest

11. On the 15th March I had to make my annual address to the Planters Association at their General Meeting. This takes place at 3 p.m. in the afternoon, is attended not only by planters but by their wives, and is followed by a Garden Party. The atmosphere always reminds me of the Primrose League meetings to which I was dragged willy-nilly in extreme youth at Eridge Green in Sussex. Although I was 'born a little conservative' I leave the Planters' meetings, as I did the Primrose ones, suffering from Pink-Eye. I annex a newspaper cutting (Ceylon Observer of 16th March) of my remarks, because my allusion to "outside forces" was greeted by a "thunderous applause" which considerably disconcerted me. It showed that most of those present (and this was confirmed in the Chairman's vote of thanks) look to some marvellous "round up of the reds" as the way out of their difficulties. My warning was of course meant for the Sama Samajists whose "Estate Workers' Union of Ceylon" has been sailing perilously near to sedition, and on which the eyes of the Police are being sedulously kept. The more important part of my message was that concerning the "new consciousness of the employer", which has pervaded by no means all of our Ceylon estate managers. It is indeed instructive to find that most of the present unrest is centred in a District where planters are notoriously "die-hard".

12. That the "new consciousness of the employer" is nevertheless beginning to leaven the whole lump is indicated by today's good news of the decision of the Planters' Association to grant a Cash Bonus to Estate Labourers to help meet the increased cost of living. My third annex to these Notes is the "Ceylon Daily News" leader on the subject, which strikes me as containing sound sense.

Postscript

13. With reference to paragraph 2 of these Notes I am glad to add that Mr. Corea has by letter to the "Times of Ceylon" point-blank denied the words ascribed to him in that newspaper's report. He goes on to say that "there was no doubt whatsoever that the real reason for Mr. Senanayake's resignation was the opinion he held, which was shared by his colleagues, that the Governor's interpretation of Article 45 made it impossible to work the Constitution and that the rights hitherto enjoyed by the Ministers and the Executive Committees were seriously infringed." I do not however feel it in the interest of accuracy to modify what I have written on this subject in paragraphs 2, 3 and 4 supra.

33   CO 54/987/7, no 1   21 Mar 1940
[Indo-Ceylon relations]: letter from Sir G S Bajpai[1] to India Office commenting on Mr Bandaranaike's anti-Indian speech

I am directed to enclose[2] a summary of the speech delivered in the Ceylon State Council by Mr S.W.R.D. Bandaranaike, ex-Minister for Local Administration, on Election Law and Procedure, in which he is reported to have said that nothing would please him more than to see the last Indian leave the shores of Ceylon and that "then he would die a happy man". The Secretary of State will appreciate that statements of this nature made in public by Ceylonese Ministers cause both resentment and alarm amongst Indians in Ceylon as well as in India and do not facilitate the Government of India's task in seeking a friendly solution of the differences between the two countries. I am to request that, if the Secretary of State sees no objection their difficulty in this respect may be brought to the notice of the Secretary of State for the Colonies.

---

[1] Secretary to the Government of India, Dept of Education, Health and Lands.
[2] Not printed. Bandaranaike's speech in the State Council was reported in the *Ceylon Daily News*, 22 Feb 1940.

34   CO 54/977/3, no 5   11 Apr 1940
'Things Ceylonese': eighth periodical report by Sir A Caldecott for CO

Crisis aftermath
   1. Paragraph 7 of my last Notes[1] reported a split in the "Homogeneous" Ministry in regard to the election of a Vice-President of the Board of Ministers and, as the result, a leaderless State Council. Bandaranaike, Kannangara, Corea and Kotelawala had asked Jayatilaka to stand down or (later) to give an undertaking to resign within a year if he were reelected to the leadership. Sir Baron had refused both requests and they had given him till April 1st to reconsider his refusal.
   2. Subsequently the State Council Agenda displayed a Motion to be moved by the well-intentioned but bumble-brained, Gandi-capped [sic], Member for Matale (Mr. Bernard Aluwihare) in the following words:—

> "That this House considers that Sir Baron Jayatilaka having jeopardised the safety of the people of this country by proposing the Internal Security Scheme whilst withholding the fact that the Police repudiated his authority; having with the Inspector General of Police consented to a formula which defeated the resolution of the House that the Mooloya prosecutions be postponed pending the inquiry by the Governor's Commission; and having asked the Governor for rulings which diminished the authority of the Ministers, has lost the confidence of the State Council and is unfit to be the Chairman of the Committee for Home Affairs or the Vice-Chairman of a Board of Ministers."

   3. On March 27th Mr. Senanayake asked to see me about Reforms (of which later)

---

[1] See 32.

but I very soon realized that the main purpose of his visit was to find out whether I thought that Sir Baron should resign. He told me of Aluwihare's motion and said that he and others had done their best to get Aluwihare to withdraw it. It would certainly be passed and Sir Baron had told the other Ministers that, if it was, he would expect them to resign with him. He considered that that would not be in the country's interest. He still felt a debt of loyalty to his old Chief, but considered that his powers were failing and that he was no longer capable of leadership. I replied that in my opinion Aluwihare's motion was a mischievous one and likely to cause further waste of the Council's time on subjects exhaustively discussed during the Crisis Debate; further that it made retirement with honour impossible for Sir Baron; and lastly that, whatever the Council's voting on a division might be, the Country would certainly not approve a forced and opprobrious end to his distinguished political career.

4. On March 29th Senanayake, by arrangement, again saw me on Reforms and this time brought with him Bandaranaike who had also asked to see me on that subject. Once again the conversation turned onto Aluwihare's motion and I received the impression that the two of them had come to some agreement as regards the leadership in the event of Sir Baron being unseated. I fancy that the agreement must have been for Senanayake to succeed but with a promise of non-opposition to the Sinhala Maha Sabha. They both expressed certainty that Aluwihare's motion would be passed but uneasiness as to whether Jayatilaka would resign on it. I told them that my view remained as expressed in the last sentence of paragraph 27 of my Reforms Despatch and that to expect a Minister to resign on an issue arising out of gubernatorial action or which he disapproved was most illogical.

5. On April 1st the Ministers once more failed to elect a Vice-President and on April 2nd the Council again met without a Leader. Standing Orders were suspended for Aluwihare to introduce his motion which (after speeches by himself, Mr. George de Silva, Dr A.P. de Zoysa and a fighting reply from Sir Baron) was negatived by 24 votes to 8 with 16 abstentions. The same evening the Ministers unanimously reelected Sir Baron and so events have revolved full circle to where they stood before the 'crisis'!

6. The "Times of Ceylon" cartoon yesterday pictured Singho (representing the average Ceylonese) standing on the Ship of State and shouting "Come aboard, Sir" to Sir Baron, who is hailing the ship from the pilot's launch. The cartoon is entitled "Picking up the Pilot", and I devoutly wish that it really were so. If however we are to indulge in maritime metaphors I attach greater verisimilitude to that which I employed in "Things Ceylonese No.6",[2] where I wrote of Sir Baron that "he allows himself to drift into crises because he no longer has steerage way to keep a straight course and so avoid them." Of his crew it is now certain that among his colleagues only old de Silva (Minister for Health) is loyal to him and among the State Councillors only twenty-four. The "Ceylon Daily News" moreover raises the storm against him whenever possible, and I fear that I cannot in these circumstances pretend to any degree of confidence in his future pilotage.

Reforms
7. I stated in my last Notes that I was sitting on the banks of the political pond

---

[2] See 24.

waiting for rises. The ministerial fish have since risen, and the Board of Ministers will confer with me here at Nuwara Eliya on the 18th April to consider the suggestion of a Round Table Conference under my presidency. That was the earliest date to which they would agree, for they appear to think that their recent strike has earned them a holiday. They probably do require a rest, for they have had a hard time reaping what they sowed.

Indophobia

8. Both Senanayake and Bandaranaike, when I saw them on March 29th, were suffering violently from Indophobia. They assured me that at the next election, unless the electoral rolls were purged of a large number of Indian voters as a result of the coming revision (reported and explained by me in a recent despatch)[3] Indian representatives would be returned not only for Hatton and Talawakele (which are already so represented) but for Kandy, Dumbara, Galagedera, Gampola, Matale, Bandarawela, Badulla, Balangoda and Ratnapura. I thereupon asked for figures of voters in each area by race, but they could not produce them. It is so much easier for politicians to deal in assertions than in ascertained facts; I am trying however to get the figures for myself. I reminded them of my anticipation that the majority of Indian voters disqualified under Article 7 of the electoral Order in Council would qualify themselves under Article 9, and I added that the revision of the registers would make all Indian labourers vote-conscious and probably result in many others qualifying themselves under Article 9. The Indian ban on Emigration would also have a marked effect on any election held during its continuance, because it has resulted in anchoring in this Island perhaps as many as a lakh of labourers who would otherwise be paying their periodical visits to India but dare not now do so with the impossibility of return.

9. It is important in relation to reforms, to the present problem of labour unrest, and indeed to nearly all current problems to realize the extent to which Indophobia has gripped the Islanders. I say "the Islanders" and not only "the Sinhalese" because Jaffna Tamils have complained to me before now that only one Jaffnese business house remains in Jaffna town; all the rest having been bought up by Indians. It is a matter of history that when the British first took over the maritime provinces of Ceylon from the Dutch a number of minor officials were introduced from Madras whose rapacity and unpopularity later necessitated their recall. Dislike and fear of the Indian however has its roots deeper in the past even than that, and the collapse of the ancient Sinhalese civilization is associated in the modern Sinhalese mind (more than is probably historically justifiable) with the periodic Indian invastions and incursions. During the past century the Sinhalese trader has been largely squeezed out of urban trade by the shrewder, harder-working Indian with his lower standard of living; the Ceylonese peasant has fallen into the clutches of the South Indian chetti and in many cases dispossessed of his land while the Ceylonese petty official finds himself similarly in the grasp of the 'Afghan' money-lender; the highlands of the Island are now in many districts almost exclusively populated by the immigrant labourers of the tea estates, and sufficient land has not been conserved for the expansion of Kandyan villages.

10. This is the picture, the outlines of which are mainly true, which the Sinhalese

---

[3] See 25.

patriot paints of the past. In the present he sees a huge number of immigrants breeding in the Island, whose children must be considered Ceylonese though they speak a different language, practise a different religion and exhibit a different culture (or lack of it) from the language, religion and culture of the people in whose midst they are living. To this must be added that (as a result of centuries of pressure of population in India) they accept and may be said to flourish under a lower standard of living than the Sinhalese. To these immigrants, if they decide to settle after five years experience of this (to them) Eldorado, has been given complete political equality with the people of the Island. Moreover they have recently been roused to a sense of their political power by no less a person than Nehru, who preaches an early end of the British Empire and the inclusion of Ceylon in an independent Greater India. The fecundity of the immigrants has been illustrated in Fiji where they now outnumber the Fijians. For these reasons says the Sinhalese politician (and he finds a ready and sympathetic audience) bitter fear of India is come on Ceylon.

11.   This sort of representation is of course by no means new to me, being very reminiscent of past conversations with the Rulers of Malaya on the subject of Chinese and Indian infiltration of their States. In Ceylon however there has been no brake on the process such as that imposed by the Malay Reservations legislation in most of the Malay States and by the Customary Land Tenure of Negri Sembilan and Malacca. While the Sinhalese are prone to exaggeration and overstatement there is nevertheless room, and need, for a sympathetic understanding of their point of view.

Labour unrest

12.   The position still affords ground for anxiety and need for constant attention. A strike broke out at Rangbodde Estate (on the Kandy—Nuwara Eliya Pass) last week in which the labourers, although they did not proceed to violence, carried staves and truncheons of heavy Kitul wood. This is the first instance of such 'arms' being found. Thirteen labourers so armed are, I understand, being charged with unlawful assembly. The strikers, some 600 strong, are members of the Estate Workers Union of Ceylon (the Sama-Samajist trade union) and are demanding the dismissal of the Head Kangani who is supported by some 200 labourers who belong to the Ceylon Indian National Congress party. The latter are still at work and so also are some 50 Sinhalese.

13.   The item in the news of this strike that worries me most is the allegation (so far uncontroverted) that the labour force is in debt to the Head Kangany to an aggregate amount of Rs 16,000. I am told that the majority of estates in Ceylon still work on the antediluvian system wherunder the Head Kangany is paid by the Estate 'pence-money' for every cooly who turns out to work per diem, and is also allowed (and indeed expected) to finance the labourers' weddings, funerals etc. which he does by lending them money at interest. The Sama-Samajist Union is concentrating its attention on this weak spot in Ceylon estate administration and so, I believe, is Mr. Natesa Iyer's Federation of Workers. The demand put forward is that the labourers should be "put on estate account", i.e. that "pence-money" should no longer be paid to anybody in respect of a labourer's work, but that the amount should be paid to him as a bonus for good attendance. Where, as at Rangbodde, labourers have got seriously into debt to a Head Kangany, the desire to be rid of a perpetually dunning creditor who is also taskmaster is inevitably a potent stimulus to discontent and unrest. The Head Kangani System is in my opinion doomed and without any present or future

justification. Those Managers who have already abolished it on their estates (unfortunately a smallish minority) are being proved to have been prudent and wise.

14.   Another matter that causes me the gravest concern is the neurotic condition of many planters and their panicky reaction to the present troubles. Three things must be remembered in this connection:—

(a) that there has never before been in Ceylon serious trouble among Indian estate labourers; the planters have been taken aback by it.

(b) When the Donoughmore Constitution was introduced the planters anticipated that their labourers would vote for some popular estate Manager. The negation of this forecast induced in most of them resentment and a contemptuous blind eye towards local politics; only a few recognized the necessity of accommodating themselves to a new order under which their employees would be citizen-voters instead of, as heretofore, immigrant protégés.

(c) The altitude of many tea estates affects the nerves of employer and employee alike. One has only to stay some time in Nuwara Eliya to find this out for oneself.

15.   Although I have no comfortable words for the planters in the sense that they desire, I am particular to give them a sympathetic hearing whenever they wish to see me. On the 27th March I gave an interview to the Chairman of the Dimbula Planters' Association (Mr. K. Morford) and Mr. J. Forbes (Manager of Thornfield, Chairman of the Tea Research Institute and, incidentally, brother of the Commander-in-Chief, Home Fleet) at which Mr. Gimson, Controller of Labour, was present. This was, I think, a useful conference although many of their suggestions were impracticable. An interview with a Deputation from the European Association on the 2nd April, 1940, was on the other hand entirely infructuous except that it gave the members of the delegation an opportunity to blow off steam. Their "Practical" proposals were (a) Suppression of the Sama-Samajist Party by Governor's Ordinance; (b) abrogation of the present constitution; (c) proclamation of Martial Law; and (d) summoning of a British Regiment from India. My Secretary who was taking notes, has reported my reply to these proposals as follows:—

"His Excellency pointed out that all these suggestions were completely impracticable and would not receive support. They would cause most serious and widespread unrest, martyrize the agitators and be exploited by the enemy in this time of war. The Defence of the Realm Regulations had in fact been modified in the United Kingdom and any action to be taken here must be in accordance with Democratic traditions. His Excellency suggested that the European Association might put their views in the form of a Memorandum that could be forwarded to the Secretary of State in order that he might be au fait with their outlook."

I doubt the eventuation of such a Memorandum.

16.   On the 9th April I conferred at length with the Minister (Mr. Corea) and the Controller (Mr. Gimson) on the whole problem. It was agreed:—

(a) to introduce as a measure of urgency legislation on the Mauritian model for conciliation in disputes with compulsory arbitration as the 'sanction' if conciliation fails or is not agreed to.

(b) that the Minister should invite deputations from the Planters' Association and

Estates Proprietary Association to meet and discuss the position with him, and extend a similar invitation (for another day) to the leaders of the Labour Unions.

It is hoped that the way may thus be paved for regular conciliatory procedure. At present it is largely irregular and hampered by refusals of the parties to meet each other and also by repudiation of settlements agreed to.

Senanayake tonans
17.   With reference to paragraph 3 of No.6 of these Notes Senanayake, just before the 'crisis', sent me a memorandum on the Debt Conciliation Bill which contained all the passages to which I had objected in his original memorandum. The new Memorandum has not yet been returned to me by the Legal Secretary, to whom I referred it: but somehow or other (probably through the agency of a member of Senanayake's Executive Committee) it has appeared in both the leading newspapers. The amusing thing is that publication has evoked from the "Ceylon Daily News" another leading article *against* the Bill! Cuttings are annexed.[4]

18.   Senanayake has also sent me a letter in which (in effect) he seems to state that the Board of Ministers will not cooperate with me in a Round-Table Reforms Conference unless I consent to recommend a limitation of the Indian Franchise. I am not prepared to depart from my former recommendation for a continuation of the present regulations and it therefore remains to be seen what happens at my Conference with the Ministers on the 18th April. I gathered however from Corea that Senanayake did not consult the other Ministers about this letter. I am afraid that, having seen the other Ministers resign merely because they funked carrying on without him, he may feel himself safe in arrogating to himself the position of de facto Leader.[5]

---

[4] Not printed.

[5] K W Blaxter minuted (1 May 1940) on this report: 'This is again an interesting, but, at the same time, I must confess, disquieting report. The Governor gives a valuable historical analysis of the antipathy between the Sinhalese and the Indians, & at the present there seems to be no doubt that this antipathy is growing, & it is growing at a time when, in the midst of war, we can ill-afford to have serious friction in Ceylon & between Ceylon and India. The decision whether an election is to be held in Ceylon before long depends upon the Governor's reply on the subject of reforms. On present showing, there might well be serious clashes between Ceylonese & Indians if an election is held & (as wd. almost certainly be the case) passions became inflamed.

Sir A. Caldecott's analysis of the Ceylonese-Indian position almost reminds one of the Palestine question. I remember that, about a year ago, either in the State Council or in a letter, Mr. Ponnambalam observed that, if H.M.G. were not careful, Ceylon wd. become a second Palestine. This was no doubt said for debating purposes, & at the time not much attention was paid to it, but Sir A. Caldecott's paragraph 10 might, in parts, have been written about the Palestine problem' (CO 54/977/7).

35   CO 54/978/4, no 8   22 Apr 1940
[Ministerial crisis]: despatch from Mr MacDonald to Sir A Caldecott proposing amendments to the Ceylon (State Council) Order-in-Council of 1931. *Enclosure*

I have the honour to refer to your secret telegram No. 209, of the 29th of February regarding the recent ministerial crisis, and to transmit to you for your information a draft Order in Council which has been prepared for the purpose of combining the two draft Orders enclosed with my secret despatch of the 30th of July, 1938. It is not, of course, intended that the Order should be submitted to His Majesty in Council unless and until a further emergency may so require.

2.   Attention has been drawn to the fact that events necessitating the passing of any of these Orders in Council might also create difficulties under Articles 56 to 70 of the Ceylon (State Council) Order in Council, 1931. A note dealing with this question is enclosed, and I should be obliged if you would furnish me with your observations thereon.

Enclosure to 35

Secret. If non-co-operation were to last very long difficulties might arise under the financial clauses, i.e., Articles 56 to 70. Their terms are quite unworkable if there are no Ministers or the State Council is not meeting. There should not be any immediate difficulties because the Governor would have almost unrestricted legislative power, and under Article 61 the Financial Secretary is authorised to make payments authorised by law other than the annual appropriation law so that if necessary the Governor could apparently enact an Ordinance even to cover expenditure which would normally require a requisition from a Minister under Article 64. (But of the wording of Articles 62 and 64).

It would not be difficult to adapt the articles in question to such a situation by transferring powers as to the preparation of estimates and appropriation bills, the sanctioning of expenditure, etc., from the State Council and the Ministers to the Governor and Heads of Department. In some cases it would suffice to provide that an article shall have effect as if, say, reference to the Governor were substituted for a reference to the Board of Ministers. Some articles, however, would probably need some recasting while others could be left alone.

For this purpose something on the following lines could be added to the new Article 49A:—

> "and may, in like manner, make provision for the performance by himself or by any other person or body of persons of any functions of the Board of Ministers or of any Minister or of any Executive Committee or of the State Council, other than the power to make laws under this Order."

Note that this would cover not only the financial clauses but the whole Order. There is a somewhat similar provision in the Government of India Act, 1935 (26 George V., Cap. 2, Sections 45 and 93) part of which might be adapted.

An alternative would be to add an entirely new provision to the effect that in the event of failure of the State Council, etc., to perform their functions, Articles 56 to 70 (or perhaps some of them) should cease to have effect, and make some short general provision in lieu.

36   CO 54/973/13, no 6   23 Apr 1940

[Reforms]: despatch (reply) from Sir A Caldecott to Mr MacDonald reporting the refusal by the Board of Ministers to take part in a governor's conference

With reference to your Confidential No. (2) despatch of the 26th January, 1940,[1] I have the honour to inform you that I asked the Board of Ministers at a special conference convened on the 18th April whether they would be prepared to take part in a Governor's Conference of themselves and other leaders representative of the chief interests in the Island as adumbrated in paragraph 7 of your despatch. I regret to say that the answer of the Ministers has been in the negative.

2.   This negative answer was reached by them after long, careful and friendly discussion, and appeared to me based on the following main considerations. The Ministers had read paragraph 6 of my Reforms Despatch (in which I wrote that I anticipated that a Redelimitation Committee would, with the limitation of purpose inherent in my proposed terms of reference, find itself in a position to recommend not more than ten additional seat(s) as imposing a maximum limit of ten on any additional seats. In paragraph 9 of my Confidential Despatch dated the 28th October, 1939,[2] I have pointed out that such had not been my intention, but I have no hesitation in accepting the Ministers' word that they voted for Motion No. 11 (which reproduced paragraph 6 of my Reforms Despatch) on the definite understanding that not more than ten extra seats would be permitted under my scheme. They had, they informed me, incurred a great deal of criticism in Sinhalese quarters for assenting to ten extra seats; and such criticism would be magnified into non-confidence and revolt against their leadership if they now took part in a Conference which, they thought I would agree, would stand no chance whatever of achieving consensus of opinion on any important point unless potential new seats in excess of ten were used as bargaining counters. The Jaffna Tamils and Muslims at their political meetings were still sticking to claims which they (the Ministers) considered ridiculous and so long as that spirit was abroad they certainly could not, as representatives of the Sinhalese, go any distance beyond their recent more generous than reasonable acquiescence in the future creation of as many as ten extra seats.

3.   The Ministers went on to say that even if a more reasonable and compromising spirit were to pervade the minority communities, of which there was at present no sign, they would nevertheless not feel themselves in a position even to consider further sacrifices of political principle beyond their already given assent to a proposal for ten extra seats unless they knew precisely what any such sacrifice would achieve. At present all that they were really cognisant of were my recommendations as to reform and their own demands; these failed to coincide on important points and no idea had been given them of what the Imperial Government was prepared to concede if intercommunal agreement here could be arrived at. They had already gone as far towards compromise as ordinary reason and political principle would allow, and if they were to proceed any further it must not be blindfold but with definite and assured consequences in view.

4.   As regards the immediate future the Ministers could see no alternative, in view

---

[1] See 23.   [2] See 9.

of your inability to approve any revision of the Constitution on the representations at present before you to a general election next spring. They did not expect any unusual disorder or other disadvantageous result from the election.

5. Although it is impossible for me to conceal my personal feelings of disappointment and frustration in this matter of reform (for I am convinced that truly responsible government can never be evolved out of the Executive Committee System and that its ill effects on administration will become progressively pronounced) I realize that the attitude of the European Community, in particular the demand of its leading Associations for a Royal Commission which was stated by them in the enclosure to my Confidential despatch dated the 12th February, and the stand taken up by those among the minorities who are championed by the redoubtable and intransigent Mr. Ponnambalam render it impossible to make any progress towards constitutional revision at this juncture. If delay should afford the opportunity for the formation and development of a sound moderate opinion (I hear that a number of Sinhalese moderates are now exploring the idea of an unpaid Second Chamber of leading citizens and elder statesmen) it will not perhaps have been without its compensations.

37 CO 54/973/13, no 7   23 Apr 1940
[Reforms and Indo–Ceylon relations]: letter from Sir A Caldecott to Mr MacDonald

I am afraid that you must have thought me very remiss and ungrateful for not having replied before to your kind letter of the 21st March. You will however see from the enclosed envelope that it was posted by ocean mail (instead of coming by Air Mail in the C.O. Bag) and it reached me only this morning. Thank you so much for your encouragement and appreciation which I find most heartening in these most difficult days.

I find it hard to assess the results of the "crisis". It has certainly not weakened my position, rather the reverse: but it has terribly weakened the Ministers' position, and poor old Jayatilaka (in spite of his quite fine fighting speech on the recent censure motion against him) has emerged completely discredited. He hasn't even yet compiled his memorandum of appeal to you, of which he has talked so much. I doubt indeed whether it will ever eventuate. All this I find most dispiriting, because the Island is becoming more leaderless than ever and its politics more irresponsible. During the crisis and after I have been conscious of having a large measure of moderate opinion behind me, but that opinion is seldom vocal and the part which it plays in present-day Ceylon politics is inactive and therefore negligible.

As regards reforms I am sending you a despatch this week to report the Ministers' refusal to join in a Governor's Round Table Conference. I feel that I could have got agreement but for young Bandaranaike. Senanayake however, though he did not oppose a conference, said bluntly "whether there is a conference or not there will never be real or even more than momentarily apparent agreement: the Secretary of State will find that there is only one way to deal with reforms in Ceylon, i.e. he must say I am prepared to give you this and this but not that or that: take it or leave it." I feel that there is a good deal in this remark of his and am thinking things over carefully in the light of it.

The Indian ban on emigration is a serious and worrying business but its effects are being grossly exaggerated. I have insisted on getting exact figures which are now to hand. It is persistently represented that families are being separated by the refusal of the Indian authorities to permit the return of wife, husband, child etc. The figures show that 2091 applications for permits to return were made; 1876 permits have been issued, 184 are awaited *and 31 only have been refused*. Similarly I was recently told that 100,000 or more of Indian labourers were unable to take leave in India because of the ban preventing their return. The figures show that the number of estate labourers going back to India from 1st August 1939 to 14th March 1940 was 15,000 less than in the previous corresponding period; a considerable figure but a very different matter from 100,000. I have suggested to Corea a possible line of re-approach to India, which he is considering: but it is important meanwhile to clear the ground of exaggerations and inaccuracies, and this I am trying to do.

Drayton was staying up here with us last week for my conference with the Ministers, and I hope he will shortly be with us again as he has got a return of the phlebitis which he contracted in Tanganyika, and this garden is a better place for him to sit in the cool and rest his leg than is his Hotel in Colombo. He is a tower of strength to me.

38   CO 54/974/6, no 13   30 Apr 1940
[Indo–Ceylon relations]: letter (reply) from Lord Zetland to Mr MacDonald transmitting the viceroy's response to a proposal for inter-departmental discussions between the CO and the India Office

You wrote to me on the 23rd January[1] suggesting that a joint discussion might be arranged between representatives of the India Office and the Colonial Office who are immediately concerned with the problem in order to explore the lines of any sugestion which could be made here for a settlement which the Governments of India and Ceylon might be persuaded to accept. As I told you at the time, I referred your letter to Linlithgow. I asked him whether he would like us here to discuss matters with the Colonial Office as you suggested (without commitment), or whether as an alternative we should have here a purely preliminary discussion with you to explore any suggestions for ending the immediate deadlock and making a conference in India possible.

The Viceroy's reply has been somewhat delayed by the resignation of the Ceylon Ministers, but that difficulty being out of the way he has now sent me an answer in the following terms:—

> "I am glad to say that we now find ourselves able to agree with MacDonald's suggestion that interdepartmental discussions should take place between the India Office and the Colonial Office for the purpose of discovering some basis for negotiations between India and Ceylon. We should, however, make one

---

[1] See 22.

point clear, namely, that in any negotiations between the two Governments which might ensue, we should probably raise the question of finding employment in Ceylon for those Indian labourers who left it, voluntarily or otherwise, under that Government's scheme, but have not returned to India. We should find it difficult, after all that has happened, to enter into negotiations on any other basis. I should be grateful if you would let me know how discussions proceed. I know that, at this end, we would welcome a *rapprochement* between ourselves and Ceylon, but you will agree that this must be on terms which will not expose us to legitimate public criticism in India."

Will you let me know if you think this message offers a basis upon which negotiations between the two Governments can be re-opened?

39 CO 54/974/6, no 14   6 May 1940
[Indo–Ceylon relations]: letter (reply) from Mr MacDonald to Lord Zetland

I am much obliged to you for your letter of 30th April[1] about the possibility of discussions between our two Departments to see whether any useful suggestions could be made to the Governments of India and Ceylon for a settlement of their present difficulties.

I note what the Viceroy says about a condition which the Government of India would probably see fit to insist upon in any inter-governmental negotiations; I don't know whether he means to refer both (1) to daily paid Government employees in Ceylon who were discharged as having been engaged by Ceylon Departments in disregard of the policy which the State Council approved in 1934, and also (2) to those others who accepted before the end of 1939 the inducement of free repatriation and a bonus in anticipation of possible retrenchment. The latter have presumably left Ceylon in order to obtain the financial benefit of their decision. As regards the former I should expect the Ceylon Government (who are, of course, like the Government of India, exposed to legitimate local public criticism) to find great difficulty, at a time of retrenchment and unemployment amongst Ceylonese, in reabsorbing under pressure from India those who were discharged from daily paid Government employment last year. But I am telegraphing personally to the Governor for his views and for information of the approximate number involved. When I get his answer possibly a preliminary talk could be arranged to see what the prospects are.

---

[1] See 38.

40 CO 54/973/13 7 May 1940

[General situation in Ceylon]: minute by G E J Gent on the main issues and Mr MacDonald's view that the governor should return to the UK for consultation

The Secretary of State discussed the present general situation in Ceylon yesterday evening with special reference to the following matters.

1. The Ministers rejection of the Governor's invitation to take part in a Round Table Conference with him in Ceylon for the purpose of further discussion of the Reforms problem.
2. The deterioration in the labour situation amongst the Indian workers on the tea estates.
3. The impasse existing in the relations between the Government of India and the Government of Ceylon.
4. The question of an amendment of the State Council Order-in-Council for the purpose of deferring the General Election to the State Council which would otherwise have to take place by the beginning of 1941.

The Secretary of State had formed the impression that the labour situation might sooner rather than later have serious developments unless the various political questions, which were the main root of the unrest according to our available information, were decisively tackled without delay. He came to the conclusion that Sir Andrew Caldecott should be asked to come home for early consultation. It was possible that Sir Andrew's state of health would justify his taking short leave to England for medical consultation, but in the personal telegram which he directed should be sent to inform Sir Andrew Caldecott of the Secretary of State's desire that he should come home preferably by air for consultation as soon as possible, the Governor's advice should be asked for as to what reason should be published for his journey to London. I submit a draft personal telegram for consideration and approval.

41 CO 54/975/1, no 29 9 May 1940

[Labour situation]: despatch no 206 from Sir A Caldecott to Mr MacDonald. *Enclosure*: report by Mr Corea, 3–6 May 1940

With reference to paragraph 2 of my despatch No.197 of the 4th May current I have the honour to enclose for your information a report by the Minister for Labour, Industry and Commerce, of his conferences with representatives of the Planting Industry and of the Labour Organizations. As soon as I receive a report of the further joint conference mentioned in his tenth paragraph I will transmit a copy to you.

Enclosure to 41

Your Excellency
I conferred with representatives of the Workers' Federation, the Estate Workers'

Union and the Indian Congress on the 22nd April 1940, and with the Emergency Committee of the Ceylon Planters' Association, representing the Planters' Association of Ceylon, the Ceylon Estates Proprietary Association, and the Ceylon Association in London on the 23rd April 1940, on the present state of labour unrest in estates.

2. The Workers' Federation and the Workers' Union stated that the main causes for the unrest were:—

(i)   the inadequacy of wages;
(ii) the opposition by Superintendents of Estates to the formation of Labour Unions, and their refusal to treat with such Unions;
(iii) the existence of the kangany system.

In their view much of the present unrest would disappear if the labourers were permitted to form their own unions and if they are recognised by Superintendents of estates. The Ceylon Indian Congress supported this view. They were, however, opposed to the abolition of the kangany system. They also urged the immediate consideration of the question of wages.

3. The Emergency Committee of the Planters' Association agreed that labourers should be permitted to form their own unions, and that estate Superintendents should deal with such bodies if they were Trade Unions duly registered. They, however, expressed the view that they should be permitted to decide whether they would deal with all such registered Trade Unions. They had in mind the Sama Samajist's Trade Union called the Estate Workers' Union which they were unwilling to recognise. They urged as a serious difficulty the existence of several unions within one estate owing allegiance to different organisations, and suggested that Government should take steps to form an amalgamation of all these bodies.

I discussed the question of amalgamation with the Ceylon Indian Congress and the other two bodies. There seems very little hope of securing such an amalgamation as both the Workers' Federation and the Indian Congress are determined to oppose each other.

4. There is considerable force in the argument of the Planters' Association but I do not see any possibility of compelling by law either the amalgamation of these groups, or compelling labourers to join a specified organisation, but the difficulty could to some extent be solved by the suggestion discussed later with regard to the establishment of Conciliation Authorities. I am, however, considering further whether steps could not be taken to recognise only one labour organisation within each estate. I am also definitely of opinion that in spite of the difficulty referred to above, much of the prevailing unrest and tension will disappear if labourers are permitted to join any registered Trade Union, and if such Trade Union is recognised by Estate Superintendents as a body authorised to negotiate on behalf of the labourers in the event of any disputes. It gave me, therefore, great satisfaction to find that the Planters' Association was prepared to accept that view. I only regretted that they should have qualified it by refusing to recognise every Trade Union duly registered. Difficulties are sure to arise if a duly registered Trade Union is to be refused recognition merely by reason of the fact that members of the Sama Samajist party happen to be members of such Trade Union also.

5. The Planters' Association are opposed to an immediate consideration of the question of wages on the ground that they had granted, voluntarily, a war bonus, and

that the material which the Labour Department was collecting on the question of wages is not yet ready. I myself do not accept this view as I am satisfied that the cost of living has definitely increased. Whether it has increased above the figure that prevailed at the time of the Renganathan Budget is, I think, immaterial. The industry can very well stand a rise in the wages, and it would be far more desirable and conducive to settlement if instead of the voluntary war bonus a suitable wage increase could be given effect to.

6. The Planters' Association has not definitely made up its mind on the question of the abolition of the kangany system. They are inclined to favour its gradual disappearance, but they informed me that that matter was down for discussion at the next meeting of the Planters' Association towards the end of this month, after which their definite views would be communicated to me. While there are, no doubt, practical difficulties in the way of the immediate abolition of the system, I feel that as the definite advantage that will accrue from such action more than counter-balances any immediate difficulties that may exist, such as the question of settlement of debts, etc., steps should be taken to abolish the system.

There is ample evidence which, in my opinion, discloses the existence of great dissatisfaction on the part of the labourers with regard to the kangany system. Apart from its intrinsic defects, as a system, there appears to be no doubt that in practice the kangany is now looked upon as an exploiter of labour and is viewed almost with enmity by many labourers.

6. [sic] The question of surplus labour was also fully discussed. The Planters' Association represented that they were collecting figures and would be in a position to state definitely whether there was such surplus or not. They do not agree that there is any surplus. It was the opinion of the other three bodies that there was a definite surplus. The view of the Labour Department and of myself is definitely that there is a surplus. The question is whether the existence of this surplus leads to unrest: I am of the opinion that it does, because in most estates it is difficult to obtain a full week's work nor is it possible for labourers to move from one estate to another. I feel, therefore, that it is necessary to make an offer of voluntary repatriation. In view of the prevailing ban on immigration I am satisfied that there will not be a large exodus.

7. I then discussed the proposal for the establishment of Conciliation and Arbitration Boards. None of the bodies I conferred with on the 22nd and the 23rd April, 1940, are in favour of the establishment of Arbitration Boards.

8. The Planters' Association requested that lightning strikes should be prevented. I am in accord with this proposal and propose to provide in the new Industrial Disputes Bill that before labourers strike disputes should be referred to a Conciliation Board.

Although I am aware of the difficulties in the way of Arbitration Boards, and also of the fact that they have after trial not been favoured in other parts of the world, I feel very strongly that in the present state of Trade Union development in this country, properly established Arbitration Boards which really is the sanction behind attempts at conciliation, are essential. It apparently is the same view which was taken in Mauritius after the recent labour troubles there. I therefore propose to place this point of view before my Executive Committee.

9. The Planters' Association requested that steps should be taken to declare tea and rubber as essential commodities. I declined to do so and explained my reasons.

10. As there appeared to me the possibility of a general agreement between these various groups on measures necessary for putting an end to the present unrest, I propose to summon a Conference on May 9th, at which representatives of all the bodies with whom I have already conferred would be present. I shall submit a further report to Your Excellency after that Conference has taken place, and I would therefore desire that Your Excellency agree to discuss the matter with me.

11. I omitted to mention that Mr. Parfitt pressed on my attention the urgent need for the early introduction of the new Sedition Bill. I explained that the law as it stood at present was perhaps better than the proposed draft of the new Sedition Bill, but agreed that I would support the introduction of a Bill which would definitely prevent incitement to violence.

12. Finally, I feel that a good deal of the present unrest could be satisfactorily removed if Trade Unions are formed and are accepted by Superintendents of estates as the media for the settlement of labour disputes.

42   CO 54/973/13, no 9   9 May 1940

[Constitutional reform]: inward unnumbered telegram from Sir A Caldecott to Mr MacDonald recommending the appointment of a constitutional commission and the postponement of the general election and explaining why it would be inadvisable for him to return home. *Minutes* by Sir G Gater and Mr MacDonald

Your Secret and personal telegram of 7th of May has arrived just as I was about to draft a despatch to convey distasteful but (?group omitted) conclusion that I have reached in view of the attitude and psychology displayed by Minister(s) on the 18th April and 4th May that sending out by you of a commission to investigate and report on political and general situation under the present consitution has become imperative and that general election should be postponed by Orders in Council until you have had time to consider its report. If I come home by air to see you I shall certainly find it necessary to make this recommendation which however I strongly urge should be acted upon now forthwith in order to allay growing unrest and uncertainty, all round. This being so I am most doubtful as to wisdom of my leaving the Island at present juncture for following main reasons first I am informed that SENANNAYAKE [sic] has spoken of non-cooperation in connexion with forthcoming resolution in Council reported by my telegram No.438. Although I doubt whether such a development is immediately probable I cannot in view of the precipitancy of the recent crisis ignore the warning. Secondly Commissioner of Enquiry on MOOLOYA shooting whose report I alone have so far seen has reported that the shooting was not justified in law. Although this finding is vitiated in my opinion by bad law and bad logic (with which no doubt the law officers are likely to agree) publication of the report which cannot I think be avoided will inevitably cause situation that will need firm but delicate handling. Thirdly I feel that any action or policy on which you might decide after conference with me in gratitude would be criticized here as having been due to pressure by me. My views on reforms have met with general acceptance in no quarters and I feel all parties desire some sort of court appeal. There is absolutely no chance that I can see of constitutional reform or of amelioration of SINHALESE attitude towards Indian question by agreement or on my advice. Fourthly I am nervous that my absence from Island in present conditions might be taken advantage of by forcing issues which an officer administering the Government would not be in a position to deal with as in the case of STARTUP affair while I was in Madras and the Brace Girdle [sic] business during INTERREGNUM after sanctioned departure. My health is better now than since 1933 and if I fly home I consider the true reason should not be concealed i.e. that you wish to confer with me. I am however apprehensive as to what might be inferred or result from such announcement and before making arrangements regarding passages I should be grateful for your definite instructions in the light of this telegram. In any case I hope that announcement of a Commission and of a postponement of general elections may receive your immediate consideration. I am very conscious that this course must be one of great difficulty in war time and I would not propose it unless I was convinced that it is the only method of coping with a situation which will otherwise deteriorate.

Minutes on 42

Four main points arise on the Governor's telegram and Mr. Gent's draft reply:—

1. The question whether the Governor should leave Ceylon to come here for consultation. I agree with Mr. Gent that it would be wiser for him not to leave Ceylon in present circumstances.
2. The postponement of the general election. On this we must reach a final decision in the light of the Governor's views, but my first reaction is that the election should be postponed, if possible, for the period of the war.
3. The appointment of a Commission. The difficulties of sending a Commission to Ceylon at the present time are obvious and I don't think that a decision in favour of the proposal can be reached without very careful consideration. I should personally like to reflect further on it before reaching a conclusion.
4. The desirability of making certain that the Governor is equipped with sufficient powers (a) to meet the challenge of non-co-operation; (b) to maintain law and order, to carry out any measures necessary for the effective prosecution of the war and to secure a satisfactory settlement with the Government of India. . . .

G.H.G.
10.5.40

This matter is so important that I do not think it should be dealt with by me in view of the possibility that there will be a new Secretary of State in the course of a day or two. He should be free to reach his own decisions. In the meantime the telegram which I suggested on my copy of the Governor's most recent telegram should go off for immediate answer by him.[1]

M.M.
10.5.40

---

[1] cf 40.

43 CO 54/978/4, no 9   10 May 1940
[State Council Order-in-Council]: inward telegram (reply) no 445
from Sir A Caldecott to Mr MacDonald

Your secret despatch of the 22nd April.[1] Draft Order in Council. After consultation
with the Financial Secretary, Legal Secretary recommends that Article 49A should be
amended by the insertion after the words "this Order"—in the second and ninth
lines—of the words "or in any other written law" and "or by any other written law"
respectively, and by the addition of the following words at the end of the Article: "and
may, by Order, make provision for the performance by himself or by any other person
or body of persons of any functions vested by this Order or by any other Law in the
Board of Ministers or any Minister of the Executive Committee or the State Council,
other than the power to make laws under this Order."
    Objects and reasons for these amendments are:—

(a) To provide for possible non-co-operation in respect of powers and duties
created by Statute and not by the State Council Order in Council.
(b) To make it clear that, although the original suspension of the Constitution
requires your approval and is effected by Proclamation, the Administrative
arrangements do not require your approval but can be made by the Governor by
Order. A large number of Administrative arrangements will have to be made
quickly and the requirement of your prior approval in each case would be
embarrassing;
(c) To make clear that the functions of Ministers, Executive Committees, etc.,
created by written laws other than State Council Order in Council, of which there
are many under recent legislation, can be transferred by order of the Governor.

I agree with the above proposed amendments and in view of possible early need of
power of suspension of the Constitution I shall be grateful for early consideration and
telegraphic reply.

---

[1] See 35.

44 CO 54/973/13, no 10   11 May 1940
[Reforms]: outward unnumbered telegram (reply) from Mr Mac-
Donald to Sir A Caldecott

Your telegram 9th May.[1] I agree that in the circumstances which you report it would
be better that you should not leave island for the present. Your recommendations
regarding appointment of commission and postponement of General Election are
receiving active consideration, but please telegraph your advice on following
points:—

(1) is it likely that latest war news from Europe will have any moderating
influence on Ministers and their attitude and on tension which you report in
Ceylon political and labour problems.

---

[1] See 42.

(2) Are your views as expressed in telegram under reference modified in any way by intensification of war situation.

(3) If it turned out to be impracticable or undesirable for a Royal Commission to visit Ceylon at an early date or at any time during war, would you still advocate postponement of General Election, and if so should it be postponed indefinitely until end of war?

45 CO 54/978/7, no 10 17 May 1940
[Reforms]: despatch from Sir A Caldecott to Lord Lloyd on the election law and Indian voters. *Enclosure*: note of a meeting between the governor and ministers

With reference to correspondence on the subject of Ceylon Election Law and Indian Voters, which rests at present with my Confidential telegram, No. 438, dated the 8th May. I have the honour to enclose copy of a Note of the meeting which I had with the Ministers on the 4th May. Although the substance of the greater part of this Note was in a condensed form contained in my telegram the important bearing of paragraphs I and III on the general question of Constitutional reform was not touched upon therein.

2. It will be seen from Mr. Bandaranaike's statement, recorded at the end of paragraph III, that his speeches and votings in the State Council debate on reforms are no longer regarded by him as binding; and I have little doubt that the same holds of the opinions of some other Ministers.

3. The position that I took up in my Reform Proposals is explained in paragraph I, and I have no doubt whatever that it was thoroughly understood by everybody at the time. The debate which is at the moment still proceeding in the State Council (and which looks like causing a definite split in the Sinhalese ranks) will be fully reported upon by me in a subsequent despatch. The object of this present communication is to bring it to your attention that views previously expressed on questions of reform are essentially affected by present developments and that any measure of agreement that may have been apparent hitherto should not be counted upon.

Enclosure to 45: note of a meeting at Queen's Cottage, Nuwara Eliya, 4 May 1940[1]

I. His Excellency stated that he first wished to make clear that when he recommended in his Reforms despatch that there should be no change in the franchise he referred solely and entirely to the franchise as defined in the existing Order in Council. At the time of that recommendation he had not read the 1928 and 1929 papers and debates, nor had he seen the Secretary of State's telegram of 10th June, 1930 (S.P. XVI-1930). As there was no reference in the existing law to the

---

[1] Present: Caldecott, R H Drayton (legal secretary), Sir D B Jayatilaka (home affairs), C W W Kannangara (education), Senanayake (agriculture and lands), Bandaranaike (local administration), Corea (labour, industry and commerce), E R Sudbury (secretary to Caldecott). W A de Silva (health) and Major J L Kotalwala (communications and works) were unable to attend.

imposition of a Rupee fee for Certificates of Permanent Settlement, the consideration of that point had not risen, though if in fact such a fee was being imposed His Excellency would not have objected to its continuance in a reformed Constitution. The Hon. Mr. S. W. R. D. Bandaranaike and a delegation of the Sinhala Maha Sabha had indeed, prior to the Reforms despatch, suggested the imposition of a substantial fee on the analogy of Naturalisation fees, but His Excellency had informed them that he could not support such a proposition.

When His Excellency had expressed his proposal to "tighten up the electoral procedure" he had in mind the prevention of registration under Article 7 of persons who were entitled only under the procedure laid down in Article 9. Under the past improper procedure applications on the ground of domicile of choice had been automatically accepted by Registering Officers, but in the future it was intended that proof of such domicile should be insisted upon.

II. The *History* of the present franchise was then discussed at length. The Donoughmore Commission had recommended five years' residence as the basis for a universal adult suffrage, but the Sinhalese had insisted on a more restrictive franchise for Indians. The result was the formula which was drawn up at Mr. D. S. Senanayake's house by the then Governor and incorporated in paragraph 35 of Sir Herbert Stanley's despatch of 2nd June, 1929. According to the understanding of the Legislative Council of the time the proposals contained in that formula were approved *in toto* by paragraph 10 of Lord Passfield's despatch of 10th October, 1929, and it was on that understanding that the Sinhalese had accepted the present Constitution. The Ministers considered the imposition of a Rupee fee for Certificates of Permanent Settlement and the renunciation of rights as essential elements in the restriction of the Indians' franchise, and they could not agree to any interpretation of Lord Passfield's despatch which modified this restriction.

His Excellency referred to the explanation of the limited effect of any "renunciation of rights" given by the Colonial Secretary in his speech of 11th December, 1929, following that of Mr. T. L. Villiers (Hansard 1929—p. 1777); and to the view expressed by the Hon. Mr. C. W. W. Kannangara in the Reforms Debate on 11th May, 1939, that the Rupee fee was immaterial (Hansard, 1939—p. 1486). His Excellency also pointed out that Sir Herbert Stanley's proposal in regard to the fee was that it should be "nominal" and not exceed Rs. 1/-. His Excellency could not agree that a "nominal" fee was intended to be "restrictive." In reply to a question by His Excellency as to why the imposition of the Rs. 1/- fee was not raised in the Select Committee's Report on Election Law and Procedure in 1938 (S.P. XIV—1938), the Hon. Mr. S. W. R. D. Bandaranaike (the Chairman of that Committee) stated that the Committee felt that the "renunciation of rights" was sufficient to impose the required restriction.

As to the "renunciation" of rights His Excellency read out a list of such rights prepared by the present Legal Secretary, and pointed out that, while the holder of a Certificate of Permanent Settlement could not himself claim such rights, in practically all cases there were corresponding obligations which were enforceable by the Controller of Labour under criminal law. The Legal Secretary went further and stated that it was arguable that inasmuch as any citizen had the right to lay information on a criminal charge, the holder of a Certificate of Permanent Settlement could not be regarded as having lost the right to bring an action in such cases.

In this connection His Excellency requested the Legal Secretary to review his list of "rights peculiar to Indians" in conjunction with the list detailed by the Hon. Mr. C. W. W. Kannangara in the Legislative Council on 9th November, 1928 (Hansard, 1928—p. 1813).

The Ministers then referred (1) to the Colonial Office letter (of which they had only just became [sic] aware), dated 18th June, 1930 to Mr. I. X. Pereira, the then Indian Member of the Legislative Council, in which it was stated that the proposal to levy a fee on Certificates of Permanent Settlement had been dropped, and (2) to the Secretary of State's telegram of 10th June, 1930 (S.P. XVI—1930), in which he had stated that His Majesty's Government would not feel justified in agreeing to any substantial modification of the essential proposals for Constitutional Reforms which had been accepted by the Legislative Council. The result which had in fact emerged was that after the Council had accepted the Constitution two vital restrictions on the Indians' franchise had been removed without the cognizance or consent of the Sinhalese: *viz.* (1) the Rupee fee was not imposed, and (2) by the interpretation placed upon paragraph 3 of the Secretary of State's telegram of 10th June, 1930, the renunciation of rights by the holders of Certificates of Permanent Settlement had become purely illusory and unreal.

His Excellency pointed out that the implementation of the recent Labour Conventions, to which Ceylon had acceded, would remove all racial discrimination between manual workers, so that special Indian rights would in any case disappear.

III.   The Ministers said that the Sinhalese had accepted the Constitution on the basis of certain real restrictions of the Indian franchise, and they considered that the agreements made with the Indian Government in regard to the franchise of Indians after their acceptance of the Constitution were a breach of faith. When the new Labour legislation is passed the position will have reverted in effect to the Donoughmore Commission's recommendation of a five years' residence qualification, which had been rejected by the country. The Ministers asserted therefore that they could not support any Reforms unless they included a satisfactory solution of the Indian question and they claimed that legislative provision should be made forthwith for (1) the imposition of the Rs. 1/- fee on Certificates of Permanent Settlement, and (2) the real renunciation of special rights by Indians. The Hon. Mr. S. W. R. D. Bandaranaike further stated that until this was done he must withdraw his agreement with other proposals in His Excellency's Reforms despatch for which he had voted in the State Council. The other Ministers said that they would also wish to consider whether they should adopt the same attitude as Mr. Bandaranaike.

His Excellency said that he could support neither the imposition in the Order in Council of a Rupee fee (as being a retrograde and undemocratic step) nor the denial to Indians of rights which he considered should be enjoyed by all labourers. He would, however, as requested by the Ministers, telegraph their demands to the Secretary of State for his consideration, and a draft would be placed before the Board of Ministers at its next meeting on 7th May.

IV.   The Legal Secretary asked the Ministers to consider the question of the 1940 Revision of the Electoral Registers before the next meeting of the Board of Ministers. The Ministers, however, proposed to await the Secretary of State's reply before making any decision regarding the proposed revision.

46   CO 54/977/7, no 6   **20 May 1940**

'Things Ceylonese': ninth periodical report by Sir A Caldecott for CO. *Minutes* by G E J Gent and Lord Lloyd

The ministry and current politics

1.   Over a month has passed since my last instalment of these Notes.[1] I have been waiting for the position to show signs of stabilisation, but I have now reached the conclusion that there is going to be no stabilisation so long as the shadow of a coming general election falls across the political stage. One might have hoped that the world events of the past fortnight would give our politicians some sense of perspective and responsibility. Save for Jayatilaka (who, I hear and believe, contemplates retirement from ministerial if not from political life when the present State Council is dissolved) and Corea the Ministers do not however appear in the least worried about the Empire's ordeal. I have noticed no worthy response from them to any appeal for War Charities, they have left it to a private member (George de Silve) [sic] to give notice of a private motion for a vote of money towards the war (when they will put it down for debate I have no idea), and their present political philosophy seems to be founded on three considerations:—

(1) The British Navy and Mercantile Marine are invincible, and Ceylon has therefore no need to envisage any change of her world-status arising out of the war;

(2) This being so her politicians can go on with, nay intensify, their usual game of pinpricks (see "Things Ceylonese" No.4[2] paragraph 8) and with impunity blame Britain for everything that Ceylon has got and for everything she hasn't;

(3) The great goal, that looms dominatingly across the whole political horizon and blots out all other vision, is re-election to State Council and thereby a further provision of livelihood from State Funds. As there is no opposition party (and because an election cannot be staged in Ceylon without slogans of abuse against somebody) Whitehall, Queen's House, the fictitious "Governor's Government" of the three Officers of State, the domination of the Capitalist Planter and the Indian invasion of estate labourers are all being paraded with the usual turgid oratory and no less usual disregard for accuracy and truth in order that Councillors may be floated back to Council and Ministers back to office on a muddy flood of Sinhalese nationalism.

2.   The preceding paragraph does not mean that anybody wants an election. Far from it. The present State Councillors would, I have no doubt, welcome a respite from the necessity of having to incur election expenditure; and no thinking person contemplates with complacency another election under the present Constitution. All communities have however manoeuvred themselves into positions from which there can be no give and take in the matter of reforms, and so (unless action is taken over their heads) they must drift willy nilly into an extension of the existing system of Government and a general election. Wijewardene[3] (proprietor of the Ceylon Daily News, Observer and the Vernacular Press) told me two days ago in conversation that

---

[1] See 34.   [2] See 16.
[3] Mr D R Wijewardene, who owned the influential Lake House group of newspapers.

a further five-year dose of administration by Executive Committees would in his opinion spell the impossibility of any development during our lifetime of responsibility, cohesion or consistency among Ceylonese politicians.

3. That the position is deteriorating is patent to everybody. When I arrived here 2½ years ago the seven Ministers (self-styled a homogeneous Ministry) did in fact stick together. Jayatilaka's failure to resign after the Bracegirdle report started the rot. The three members of the Sinhala Maha Sabha (Bandaranaike, Kotelawala and Kannangara) wanted him to go and said so: Senanayake wanted to take his place as Leader but daren't say so; Corea and de Silva stood by him as a moderating influence. The recent row between Jayatilaka and Banks, which was followed by the Ministerial crisis, was considered by all Jayatilaka's colleagues except de Silva (who doesn't count) a piece of bad blundering on his part. At my recent conference with Ministers on 16th May it was uncomfortably clear that all his colleagues (including now Corea) were in rebellion against his leadership. The Conference was immediately followed by a particularly dirty attempt (even for Ceylon) to unseat the old man. The attempt is worth describing and explaining, as it may be followed by others:—

(a) At the beginning of the war, when Defence Regulations were being considered by the Board of Ministers and Executive Committees, it was decided not to enact regulations on matters already provided for by local law;

(b) One of these matters was the prohibition of public meetings, which has hitherto been satisfactorily dealt with under sections 114 of the Criminal Procedure Code and 185 of the Penal Code;

(c) On 12th May an order under the former not to hold a meeting was disobeyed by Dr. Perera, the Sama Samajist leader; but case law in India has established that if no disorder or injury results from such breach no prosecution lies. Dr. Perera undoubtedly found this out before his disobedience;

(d) On my return to Colombo from up-country on 14th May I saw Jayatilaka and discussed this defect in the law, which his Executive Committee desired to be amended by Statute. I thereupon invited the Board of Ministers to meet me on 16th May to consider whether a Defence Regulation should not be passed in anticipation of amendment of the law, because the mills of State Council grind even more slowly than those under Divine management;

(e) At this Conference there was some reasonable argument (especially by Corea) and there are certainly cons as well as pros, e.g. we do not want to jeopardize at this juncture the success of Corea's scheme of conciliation in labour disputes.[4] The question is still under my consideration. But the attitude of the majority of his colleagues towards Jayatilaka was one of abuse rather than argument, and I had to call them to order on his behalf;

(f) My meetings with Ministers are always by my invitation or at their request and are entirely confidential and informal. No communiqué or proceedings is ever issued;

(g) Next morning however I was amazed to see in the usually circumspect "Daily News" what purported to be an account of the meeting under the headline "Home Minister asks Governor to use Emergency Powers". As Jayatilaka has of course been a protagonist for the curtailment of gubernatorial powers, and as the use of

---

[4] cf 41.

them in this case was entirely my own and not Sir Baron's idea, I at once scented intrigue;

(h) Soon after breakfast Jayatilaka was in my office asking me to publish a démenti. I never issue démentis; if I did, lies would be published merely for the nailing. I gave him a minute however, which he was quick to publish. Nor too soon: he was questioned in Council that very afternoon. Newspaper cuttings of the original article and of my Minute are attached.[5] Wijewardene, the proprietor of the newspaper and no friend of Jayatilaka, was (I believe) quite innocent in this instance. Senanayake has this paper's support and Bandaranaike the reverse. Therefore I have concluded, with regret, that the dirty work has been Senanayake's, probably through his son Dudley.

4. The State Council has transacted no real business for over three months. In February–March the 'crisis' monopolized its attention; then came the Easter recess, and on reassembly last week it set aside standing orders and proceeded to the debate of Bandaranaike's motion on the Indian Franchise. This motion has not fared as its mover or seconder (Senanayake) intended. The Legal Secretary tells me that if a division has [sic] been taken on Thursday it might even have been defeated. The Sinhalese have disclosed a serious split in their ranks and the motion's failure to arouse deep nationalist feeling was evidenced by lack of a quorum at two points in the debate. On Friday, in the middle of the mover's reply and with 1½ hours of normal sitting-time still to go, the debate was adjourned till May 28th. The object of the adjournment was probably twofold:—

(a) to whip up Kandyan feeling at a public meeting at Kandy, whose member (George de Silva) had spoken against the motion;

(b) to delay the question of revising the registers until it is impossible to revise them for a general election next year and thereby to provide a basis on which to request a postponement of the general election.

5. Whatever the eventual voting on the motion may be I do not now anticipate that Bandranaike [sic] or Senanayake (even if both or either ever really had the intention) will be able to make it a platform for non-cooperation. I think that they realize that a country asking for a further measure of democratic self-Government hardly improves its case by demanding that Indian labourers to which it grants the franchise should be ipso facto deprived of the rights which labourers enjoy throughout the world by virtue of international conventions to which Ceylon is a party. But then the charge of deception against Whitehall (a 'deception' which has been plain to everybody ever since the new constitution came in) was too good a piece of nationalist propaganda for either of the two demagogues to let the other get away with. So we have their duet, with the other Ministers in a faint unenthusiastic chorus.

Senanayake tonans

6. With reference to paragraph 17 of No.8 of these Notes Senanayake has sent in yet another Memorandum on Debt Conciliation, challenging certain opinions of the Legal Secretary to whom reference has therefore again had to be made. That

---

[5] Enclosures not printed.

Senanayake's interest in this subject is not solely ministerial is indicated by the second annex to these notes.

Labour unrest

7. I have sent several despatches on this subject. Corea has worked hard and well on his conciliation programme. At the moment (so far as information goes; flood damage has cut Colombo off from many districts by mail, telegraph and telephone and from nearly all by road and rail) labourers are 'out' on only one estate. But the unrest is still there and if (on the one hand) the Sama Samajist Estate Workers' Union should fail within the next fortnight to confirm their undertakings given at Corea's Conference or (on the other hand) the Planters' Association should go back on the recognition of trade unions promised by its representatives at that Conference then, in either of these eventualities, there will be renewed and worse trouble.

Communists

8. The Sama Samajists are by their political antagonists, most newspapers and all Planters called Communists. They include one man who was in Moscow for several years, Comrade Gunawardene, and he is probably pukka scarlet. He is also, I understand, a nasty piece of work of the village bully type. The Samaj Samajist Members of Council boycott Queen's House so that I shall never have any personal knowledge of them. Dr. N.M. Perera, M.S.C, and Dr. Colvin de Silva (who largely finances the party) are, I understand, conscientious and intellectual socialists of a pronounced shade of red. In the middle and lower ranks of the party there is more opportunism than principle and vote-catching than policy. What the "Times of Ceylon" is agitating for is the proscription of the party, the prohibition of its meetings and the detention of its leaders. The Editor frequently cites anti-Communist measures taken in India and the Straits Settlements. Action could not be taken to suppress the Samaj Samajist party here without a breakdown of the Constitution and immediate non-cooperation, because the Ministers and State Council certainly will not take it; it could only be done under the special powers of the Governor. None of the Ministers like the Samaj Samajists, but their view is (1) that the party's principles although equalitarian are not communistic; (2) that, although they talk occasionally of revolution, anti-Imperialism and anti-Capitalism, they have in fact fastened their practical politics on to abuses and imperfections that have to be admitted; and (3) that the movement, if driven underground, will be far more dangerous and gain force more rapidly. My present personal opinion of the Samaj Samajists may be set out as follows:—

(a) There is no proof or even indication of current support from Moscow in the way of funds or tracts. That Comrade Gunawardene has correspondence with Russia I do not doubt. The "Pravda", I believe, made much in its columns of our "Ministerial Crisis";

(b) The Brigadier Commanding the Troops is satisfied that the Party is making no attempt to tamper with the loyalty of the Local Forces or to unpopularize recruitment for them;

(c) The Party is a growing political force which in my opinion the Ministers underrate. I think that in the next elections they will win many more than the two seats they now hold;

(d) the Party at present embraces within its fold all shades of red from pink to scarlet; suppression would suit the extreme leftists, and I agree with the Ministers that it would be a mistake to drive the movement underground even if suppression could be accomplished without non-cooperation and suspension of the Constitution;

(e) The Party needs most careful watching. It will derive advantage both from the anti-Trade-Union attitude of die-hard planters and from the anti-Indian spoutings of the Sinhalese nationalists. The leaders of the Party are arch-intriguers and their tactics are to set everybody else against each other;

(f) Their two papers (of which the Sinhalese edition has a circulation of 7500 and the Tamil edition one of 8000) frequently contain attacks on, and defamations of, the Police Department. So far these have been cleverly half-footed in fact and prosecution would have been a mistake. As soon however as the Editors provide an occasion legal proceedings should be taken. Their columns are being assiduously watched.

Minutes on 46

As the Secretary of State has at the moment under his consideration a draft personal telegram to the Governor of Ceylon in response to the latter's recommendation that a General Election should be postponed for the limited period of one year, it would be very desirable that he should see now this latest memorandum in the Governor's most secret and personal series on "Things Ceylonese." The memorandum, which I received this morning and which is dated the 20th May, reflects the Governor's deepening impression that political affairs in the island are deteriorating and that the Ministry (save perhaps Mr. Corea, the Minister of Labour) have no interest or inclination to take a grip of things.

I draw particular attention to the following statements in this memorandum:—

Page 1 "There is going to be no stabilisation so long as the shadow of a coming general election falls across the political stage."

Page 2 "No thinking person contemplates with complacency another election under the present Constitution. All communities have, however, manoeuvred themselves into positions from which there can be no give and take in the matter of reforms."

[In para 8] the Governor gives us a useful analysis of the Sama Samaj Party (or "Communists") which is the chief bugbear of the European plantation industry and of the Ceylon Association whose deputation, if the Secretary of State consents to receive it, will certainly refer to the desirability of strong action against this Party's leaders. Its activities amongst the Indian workers on the tea estates may be assumed to be wholly mischievous. But the Governor has stood his ground against the local demand of the planters' organisations for the suppression of the Sama Samajists as a seditious organisation, and he explains here that action could not be taken for the purpose without a breakdown of the Constitution and immediate non-co-operation because the Ministers and the State Council certainly would not take it themselves, and it could only be done under the special powers possessed by the Governor. The Governor himself believes that the Party is a growing political force which the

Sinhalese Ministers underrate. But there is no evidence to show that it is financed or instructed by Moscow or that its agents attempt to tamper with the efficiency of the local forces. He intends that legal proceedings should be taken against the two Sama Samaj newspapers, as soon as they provide an opportunity for their defamatory articles about the Police.

G.E.J.G.
28.5.40

I am not much impressed by the Governor's Memo. It reads like a District Magistrate's report during Satyagraha in India and he appears completely immersed in a mass of detail. All this is only [symptomatic] of radical trouble in the Constitution.

L.
3.6.40

47 CO 54/973/13, no 13   22 May 1940
[Reforms]: inward unnumbered telegram from Sir A Caldecott to Lord Lloyd recommending the appointment of a one-man informal mission. *Minute* by Sir C Parkinson

In continuation of my secret and personal telegram dated 12th May. Debate of Indian franchise, having wasted time of State Council for the whole of the session last week, has been adjourned until its reassembly on 28th May. Debate has disclosed some cleavage of opinion among Singalese and I do not anticipate non-co-operation on this issue. Legal Secretary suspects that adjournment, which was made quite unnecessarily during reply of mover and two hours before ordinary closing time, was intended to make sure that revision of registers cannot be completed this year and thereby to provide basis of which necessity for postponement of general election can later be argued. Yesterday Ponnambalam sought interview with me at which he made the following representations:—

> "If there is no possibility of general question of constitutional reform being decided upon in the immediate future then purely domestic question of re-delimitation of electoral boundaries with a view to giving enhanced representation to Minorities should be put in hand at once in order that at the next general election minorities shall be assured of greater representation."

My fully considered views are as follows:—(1) Any long continuation of the constitution in its present form is inconceivable. (2) A general election under it cannot therefore be justified. (3) Re-delimitation to enhance the representation of minorities cannot be entertained separately from other measures of reform. (4) Local politics are bound to deteriorate as the election approaches. (5) Upsetting of a general election during critical period of the war should be avoided. (6) Nevertheless postponement should be for a fixed and not indefinite period such as the duration of the war, though further extensions might later become necessary. I suggest the advisability of early announcement to the effect that you must have time yourself personally to examine the important question of constitutional reform in the light of very many representations that have been put forward from all quarters; that this examination cannot possibly be hurried and that it is therefore proposed to take steps to enable postponement of general election for a year. In view of recent events and present political atmosphere I consider it most desirable that independent examination of position on your behalf should be conducted on the spot. If this were entrusted to a commission, personnel would, of course, need to be most carefully selected and suitable persons might not be found available in wartime. I therefore suggest the possibility of a one-man informal mission such as that of Wilson to Malaya in 1932. There is no need to give opportunity for further representations as arguments of every community are on record and have already been repeated *ad nauseam*. I feel therefore that special one-man mission might be more suited to the circumstances of the case than fully fledged commission.

Minute on 47

Secretary of State
(through Mr. Hall)
It is difficult to see any satisfactory solution to the constitutional and political troubles in Ceylon. I entirely agree with Mr. Gent that there is no point in sending out a "missioner" as suggested by the Governor. There are, as I see it, only two practical courses:—

1. A strong Royal Commission in which presumably all parties in the House of Commons would be represented.
2. A round table conference in London.

Neither of these is practicable in the present circumstances, and for my part I should definitely advocate the second, i.e. the round table conference in London after the war. I need not elaborate the arguments, as no doubt you would like to discuss this matter with Mr. Hall and the Department. I agree with Mr. Gent's draft telegram which, as you will see, revives the suggestion for a round table conference after the war, together with postponement of the general election which is due next year.

A.C.C.P.
29.5.40

48   CO 54/975/90, no 5   25 May 1940
[State Council Powers and Privileges Bill]: letter from G E J Gent to Sir A Caldecott

[The State Council Powers and Privileges Bill had caused some controversy within the national legislature. A few members had expressed doubts about the need for immunities granted to members for speeches within the precincts of the legislature whether for legislative sessions of the whole house or meetings of executive committees. Some of the officers of state were also hostile to sections of the bill. The governor had been advised to use his powers of reservation until CO advice and His Majesty's approval were obtained. Gent's letter to Caldecott was in favour of granting approval provisionally. The memo by Campion (clerk to the House of Commons, 1937–1948) and the note by the assistant clerk, both of which supported that decision, are not printed here.]

It is a considerable time since you submitted to us in your confidential despatch of the 3rd October, 1939, copies of the State Council Powers and Privileges Bill for the signification of His Majesty's pleasures.

The Bill was passed to the Clerk to the House of Commons for his consideration and advice, and, owing to pressure of work there, it is only recently that we have received his observations on the subject.

I now enclose a copy of Sir Gilbert Campion's memorandum, and also a copy of a note prepared by the Assistant Clerk to the House of Commons regarding the Standing Orders of the State Council.

Our provisional view is that assent should be given to the Bill as passed by the State Council. Having regard to what is said in the memorandum, we doubt whether exception can be taken to the privileges being applicable to Executive Committees; and, since the Board of Ministers meet in secret, we are doubtful whether any attempt should be made to exclude them from the privileges conferred by the Bill. At the same time, however, we have certainly not overlooked the point that you made in paragraph 5 of your despatch where you observed that it was almost a certainty that State Council Committees would be appointed to enquire into matters of discipline within the public service, and that you thought that the present Ordinance should implement the Ceylon (State Council) Order-in-Council by expressly excluding from its scope the subjects vested in the Governor by Article 86 of that Order-in-Council.

Before reaching a final conclusion, we should be glad to know what further views you form in the light of Sir Gilbert Campion's memorandum, and also in the light of any further advice which Drayton may be able to give you both upon the Bill and upon the memorandum.

As regards the note by the Assistant Clerk, we send it to you for your information and consideration at leisure.

49   CO 54/977/7, no 7   27 May 1940
[Indian labour]: letter from Sir A Caldecott to G E J Gent. *Minute* by Gent

I have before now remarked on the great difficulty one experiences here in getting reliable figures for anything. In a personal letter which I wrote to MacDonald on the 23rd April[1] I gave figures for the separation of Indian families under the Indian Emigration Ban which had been supplied by our Emigration Commissioner in India. These were:—

Number of applications made for permits to return	2091
Permits issued	1876
Permits refused	31
Permits awaited	184

It now transpires that these figures were in respect of the following cases of separation only:—

(a) wives
(b) minor children   } of male workers now working in Ceylon.
(c) dependent non-working parents

---

[1] See 36.

Labour unrest can of course be aggravated by other separations (e.g. brother and brother, brother and sister, father and grown-up son etc.) and the following figures, now to hand, are inclusive of all separations and present a fuller picture:—

(1) Number of families in which there has been separation under the ban   3568

(2) Number of families in which separation has been remedied by return permits granted by India   1240

(3) Number of families in whose case permits have been refused   39

(4) Applications under reference to Indian Government   2289

2. Although these figures are more impressive than the former ones it will be remembered that the Indian estate population is more than 600,000; and I have been informed by planters of long standing that the unrest is most pronounced among the Ceylon-born labourers, who have had the benefit (?) of education in estate schools and not amongst the immigrant labourers who are nearly all illiterate. I consider in fact that the separation of families is a minor, if not negligible, cause of labour unrest: any ponderable effect of the ban on the labour situation has lain in the anchoring here of coolies who would (if the ban did not prevent their subsequent return here) go on holiday to India. This, I believe, (there are no available figures) resulted in a considerable surplus of labour over requirements during the first four months of the year, and is likely to have the same result again even if it does not (I myself apprehend that it does) at the moment persist.

3. The causation of Labour Unrest in Ceylon is complex and composite; I believe the following to be chief factors:—

(1) The "new consciousness of labour" which is world-wide but which has been accelerated among our Indian labourers by:—

(a) *the recent visit of Nehru*, whose appeal to labourers flattered their rising sense of self-importance. He told them to realize their collective power for bargaining with their employers and always to remember their Indian nationhood. To anybody who has heard the Indians clap whenever Gandhi or Nehru figures in the News reels at the Nuwara Eliya cinema the importance of Nehru's visit requires no further proof or argument;

(b) *the growing infusion of young literates* from the estate schools into the labour forces. These read such papers as the Sama Samajist 'Samathanam' to the illiterates and the cooly can now be 'got at' by the printed word. In some estate schools night classes in English have been held; the products of these are bound to present a tiresome problem, and in a few cases are already doing so.

(2) *The Indian labourer's vote* has not only become a bone of Indo–Ceylon contention, thereby raising nationalistic feelings; but the vote is being unscrupulously canvassed by three separate factions (i) Natesa Aiyer, (ii) the Sama Samajists and (iii) the Ceylon Indian Congress, each of whom has its own labour union. Whether Corea's effort to make these unions responsible machines of representation and conciliation will meet with any success remains to be seen. I will say no more at this stage, except that he and Gimson are doing their best.

(3) *Anachronisms in estate management*, especially the survival of the head kangany system on most estates. The Planters are now furiously considering this and other questions (such as revision of wages) but very much at the eleventh hour.

(4) *Nerves*. The Planters have never experienced labour troubles before and are panicky. The coolies have never been fussed over by politicians before nor have they previously dabbled in unions and strikes; they are effervescent. The war has upset everybody's nerves, and it is significant that labour unrest has so far been confined to the up-country where altitude has a very marked effect on people's psychology. It was a bit of a shock to my wife and myself to find a planter's wife who stayed with us recently at Queen's Cottage expressing definitely pro-Nazi views. We dealt with her kindly but, I think, effectively. Finally, Ceylon politics are not a sedative to the nerves of anybody!

4. I am keeping a copy of this letter in my "Things Ceylonese" file and you may care to do the same.

Minute on 49

The revised figures are interesting, but the actual numbers in the several categories, except possibly category 1, are probably not very important. The disturbing effect is produced by the uncertainty and delay rather than by the actual proportion of refusals of permits. In the rest of Sir Andrew Caldecott's letter it is odd to my mind that he nowhere includes as a cause of the unrest of Indian labour the pronounced policy of the Board of Ministers in the last few years against the immigration and employment of Indians in the Island. The new "consciousness of labour" is not a phenomenon of the last year or two as is the epidemic of strikes amongst Indian labour on Ceylon estates. The recent visit of Nehru, which admittedly had the effect of giving practical form to the unrest, was due to the anti-Indian policy of the Ceylon Ministers, and the Indian labourers' vote has acquired a particular value because the Ministers' policy could best be fought by political methods. Neither "anachronisms in estate management" nor the "panicky nerves" of estate managers can be properly included in a list of causes of the labour unrest. The Ceylon Ministers have reasons of their own no doubt for advising the Governor that this is so, but the panicky nerves at any rate can only be regarded, and regarded sympathetically in the rather isolated circumstances of many estates, as being an unfortunate result of the unrest.

The 1937 Annual Report of Ceylon draws attention to the first and partial ban on emigration from India which the Government of India imposed against Ceylon as a retaliation for political grievances against Ceylon, which that report described as being unrelated to the matter of emigration or of workers' conditions. The further and complete ban which the Government of India imposed last year was similarly a retaliation against the policy of the Ceylon Ministers, and as long as that policy persists it must bear the onus of being the primary cause of the disturbance of Indian labour. The fact that the leading role is played by the educated (generally Ceylon-born) worker is a natural one, and is a further pointer to the fact that the basis of the trouble is to be found in Ceylon politics and not in anachronisms in estate management.

G.E.J.G.
18.6.40

50   CO 54/975/2, no 50   4 June 1940

[Labour unrest on tea plantations]: letter from G F Bolster[1] to Mr A Lennox-Boyd[2]

I am writing this letter to you in the hope that you will be able to put in a word in high places on behalf of the Planting Community in Ceylon in their efforts to save the Tea Industry of the Island. There is serious unrest amongst our labour which has been stirred up by agitators and Fifth Columnists who are guilty of serious sedition. Our difficulty is that the Governor, Sir Andrew Caldecott, refuses to use his powers to stop the activities of these rascals. In the meantime matters are going from bad to worse.

The position is very complicated but roughly has developed as follows:— On the outbreak of war the Planters in the Dimbula and Uva Districts were mobilised for a month's training. While they were away agitators entered their estates, mostly at night, and began to stir up the coolies to strike and riot. The first District affected was Dimbula. The Planters returned to find their authority undermined and frequent strikes broke out. Up to the end of August there had been no trouble in any district.

The Planters Association for a considerable time have recognised that a properly led Trade Union for the Tamil estate labourers was most desirable. However, seemingly over-night, large numbers of Unions had started and a state of chaos was reigning due to the rivalry between them. The scramble to encourage membership frequently resulted in fights between factions on the new estate. This new ramp offered most lucrative rewards in monthly subscriptions from the coolies of 25 cents each. It was no wonder many half educated rascals were not slow to grasp this new way of earning an easy living, and set to with a will to create trouble in every way they could. The result was dozens of strikes in nearly every case over no real legal grievance. The general method adopted was for Union coolies on an estate to cause trouble then follow it up with a strike making wide and sweeping demands dictated by the outside agitator. He then comes into the open as the representative of the coolies and tries to negotiate favourable terms with the Superintendent. Naturally some of these rascals soon skipped with their takings. There are five main Unions, two of which deserve attention.

1. The Ceylon Workers Federation under Naki Tyer.[3]
2. The All-Ceylon Workers Union whose main leaders are Dr. M.N. [sic] Perera and P.M. Velachamy (who was responsible for the serious Mooloya Estate riot near Kandy). This Union is really the Ceylon Communist Party or Sana Sancajists [sic], whose leaders include D.P. Gunawardene (member of State Council like M.N. Perera), Dr. Colvin de Silva, Dr. S.A. Wichremsingha, Leslie Gunwardene, Edmond Samarakkoddy and W.A.P. Jayatilaka. All these men are notorious rascals and most of them are jail birds. Jayatilaka, for instance, has done a term for rape

---

[1] Bolster was a tea planter of the Napier Division, Rookatenne Group, Hali-Ela.

[2] MP (Con) from 1931; parliamentary secretary, Ministry of Labour, 1938–1939, Ministry of Home Security, 1939, Ministry of Food, 1939–1940, Ministry of Aircraft Production, 1943–1945; minister of state for colonies, 1951–1952; minister of transport and civil aviation, 1952–1954; S of S for the colonies, 1954–1959.

[3] A reference to K Natesa Iyer.

committed on Lunugala Estate, Madulsima. Such are the leaders of labour!

Having entered the arena rather late the Sana Sancajists did their best to exploit the situation in Dimbula. They then turned their eyes on the Uva District centring round Badulla. Up to March the Uva District was quite unaffected by the goings on in Dimbula. However nearly at once after the opening of the Union Office in Badulla trouble started. The Sana Samaj were first in the field and started to organise calls on some of the most important estates in the area. Their first try on was on Attempettia Estate. After a three day strike for no real reason their effort failed. Seeing that peaceful methods did not succeed they changed their tactics for the next four estates where they were engineering trouble.

1. *Unugalla Group*. This took the form of a show down strike which thanks to the capable handling of the Superintendents was settled without any real trouble and a few reasonable requests were granted. The main point in this case is that there was no justification for a strike as the coolies could easily have obtained the requests that were granted by asking the Manager in a constitutional way. This did not suit the Union leaders, who included a number of the most impossible demands that could be imagined, quite regardless of the regulations laid down in the Labour Ordinances.

2. *Oodoowerre Estate*. This is a private estate company owned by Mr. D.E. Hamilton. As this estate is next door to me I was indirectly concerned in the trouble. I can assure you that Hamilton pays his coolies high rates of wages and that his estate is run on model lines. The coolies had no justifiable complaint. The Sana [sic] Samajists however bore Hamilton a grudge as he stood for the Tala-wakellie Seat in the State Council in the last election. Though he failed to get in he was very close to it. They therefore organised trouble in the Upper Division of the estate and a small incident was made the excuse for a strike. A police armed guard was required to escort the estate lorry to the factory. Hamilton's bungalow and the factory were threatened with burning. This creditable [?sic] behaviour was of course followed up by a letter from the Union making eight demands on behalf of the strikers. I saw this letter and it was obvious that they were not "bona fide" as they showed a complete lack of knowledge concerning the organisation of the estate. It was obvious that the demands were made up by the Same [sic] Samaj leaders in their Badulla Office.

The above two cases show the complete folly of the present situation. These Unions are registered without any regard to their objects and intentions. The result is they have a free hand to cause great mischief. The serious side of the matter is that the All-Ceylon Workers Union is not a Union, in actual fact, it is a Political Party.

3. *Demodera Group*. This is the largest group in the Ceylon tea industry, and the labour were always well paid and contented until the arrival of Velachamy. He held a meeting however at Demodera Railway Station and as a direct result of this there was a riot on the Wevelhena Division of the Group between Unionists and others whom they were trying to intimidate into joining the Union.

This riot had a sequel in the Badulla Court when the Magistrate issued Notices banning the Sama Samajists from holding and addressing meetings.

On Sunday May 12th the Same Samajists held a meeting (in spite of the ban) in

Badulla (Report Cutting No.3 enclosed).[4] At this meeting the speakers referred to the police and magistrate as dogs. Dr. M.N. Perera further addressed another meeting at Demodera which again was the cause of a riot this time over 35 coolies were seriously hurt and many others suffered minor injuries.

These speeches are of particular interest as they are always insulting to the Empire and openly seditious. There is a sample of the tripe which is being allowed. They usually are on these lines. "My children of India, Awake! Awake and open your eyes to the world. You are slaves. Why? Because you allow the English rascal to abuse your rights and liberty. You must fight to the death for these rights. The police dogs can do nothing as the Governor pig is afraid because the British Raj is being beaten by the Germans. The white pigs and their King are all running away. This is your chance now while their backs are turned. Arise now and seize your rights. If the dogs resist kill them". It is on these lines that the Sama Samajists address the coolies and is it any wonder that some of the least intelligent of them lose their heads and cause trouble.

Now Boyd what I wish you to understand is this; the Governor attended the General Meeting of the Planters Association held in March at the Queen's Hotel, Kandy. At this Meeting he got up and said, before hundreds of witnesses, that the illegal activities of agitators would be stopped by the strong arm of the law. At last, we thought, after over four months of lawlessness, something would be done. Since then the Governor has done absolutely nothing and now the position is very serious indeed. He has been approached on three occasions by deputations of Europeans asking him to act. The last occasion was last Friday, May 31st. On each occasion Caldecott refused to do anything to prevent the activities of these agitators in spite of his promise.

I heard a verbatim report from Mr. Percy Will who was one of this last deputation from the Uva District Branch of the Planters Association. His remarks were amazing. One is only left with the impression that the Governor is either a Red himself or an incredibly incompetent fool. This is the unanimous opinion of every Planter in this District.

I hope the Censor will permit the following information to get to you as if you can do something for us you will do a great service. Now with Italy joining in this war, or at least it seems remarkably like it, the position of Ceylon requires careful consideration as raids on the Island become probable from Italian cruisers. Very frankly the native Sinhale troops of the Defence Force can not be trusted. Thus we will require every European that can carry a rifle. These agitators know this well and are doing the Naziz [sic] a great service by causing this unrest. For as long as this unrest continues ⅓rd of the Ceylon Planters Rifle Corps cannot be mobilised. If we were mobilised suddenly, Perera, Gunawardene and others would be up here as soon as our backs were turned. I shudder to think of the consequences. The place would be shambles. The only way to prevent this is to arrest the whole gang. This is what we have asked the Governor to do. It has been done in India and everywhere else in the Empire. Why not here, particularly after Caldecott's promise in March.

We all consider the tea to be a vital food for the Home and Fighting Fronts. Most estates are under contract to the Tea Controller to supply a vast quantity of tea. Is it right that under these circumstances agitators and other seditionists, in foreign pay,

---

[4] Enclosures not printed.

should be tolerated when they are doing everything in their power to upset the whole trade of the Island. I put it to you. Is it right?

4. Having digressed I will now return to the *Wewesse Estate* trouble. These are dealt with in Cuttings No.1 and No.2. I know Mr. Mayow, the Superintendent of this Estate, and can confirm that, until Velachamy began holding meetings on the Patna close to this estate, the labour force were quite contented. They surrounded the Bungalow and threatened to kill both Mayow and his wife and even dug graves close by. The police at the time were helpless so Mayow had to leave the estate.

Now I come to cutting No.4. This is taken from a report published in the Times of Ceylon of the State Council Meeting on Tuesday, May 28th. Please read it carefully. This is sedition with a capital S. Then why in the name of Job is the Governor allowing these rascals to carry on in this manner. Ceylon is at war. Can such talk be tolerated? There is no Regular Army Battalion of Infantry in Ceylon so if there is serious rioting as a result of this sedition we Europeans will have to roll up our sleeves and put a stop to it. If the Governor acts it may well be that it may save this happening, but as we will have to do the dirty work, our lives and those of our women and children, are at stake, we think it only right to demand that action be taken at once.

I do most earnestly appeal to you to put a word in the right place on our behalf.

P.S. My father is Dr. F. Bolster of Biggleswade.

51   CO 54/973/13, no 16   5 June 1940
[Reforms]: outward unnumbered telegram (reply) from Lord Lloyd to Sir A Caldecott advocating postponement of the general election until the end of the war

Much appreciate full statement of your advice in your personal and most secret telegram of 22nd May.[1] Position as I see it is as follows:

(1) We should avoid general election under existing constitution and especially the disturbance it would be likely to cause in local circumstances of Indian problem and general circumstances of war.

(2) Postponement for one year on ground that I must have time to consider matter personally would seem to imply that I was going to dictate reforms from here. This could not be expected to satisfy Ceylonese aspirations.

(3) For two reasons I do not favour your suggestion of one man commission to visit Ceylon as impartial investigator on my behalf. In the first place I do not think he could avoid giving all communities the chance to present their demands afresh, since they would assume critical moment had arrived for influencing my decision through agency of his report. Secondly, and more important, I obviously regard you yourself as fully informed and fully impartial and I should not like to give any other impression locally.

---

[1] See 47.

(4) Postponement of election for only one year would scarcely be long enough to prevent disturbing effect of active preparation for election campaign.

(5) In paragraph 9 of my predecessor's confidential (2) despatch of 26th January,[2] suggestion was made for round table conference in London after the war. I am not myself much in favour of such conference, and I hope that you will avoid any promise or commitment that reforms will not be decided upon until one has been held.

(6) Dictation of reforms may eventually be forced on us, but I would much rather we did not have to do it during the war.

(7) My present inclination is therefore to take the line that in view of general dissatisfaction with present constitution and desirability of avoiding unnecessary disturbance of community, general election should be postponed until victory has been achieved, when reform of Constitution can be considered afresh after such further consultation as may then seem profitable and desirable with leading interests in the island.

(8) Risk of consequences of postponement for indefinite period as explained in your telegram No. 495 may be offset by possible inclination of parties in Ceylon to restrain themselves in the interval in order to show their capacity for self-government.

Please take into your confidence any one you consider necessary on my provisional views as set out above and telegraph what your conclusions are.

---

[2] See 23.

52   CO 54/974/8, no 11A   13 June 1940
[Ceylon Association]: note by G E J Gent for Lord Lloyd's meeting with a deputation representing plantation interests

The deputation from the Ceylon Association to see the Secretary of State tomorrow at 4 o'clock will consist of the President Mr. Horner, the Vice President Mr. P.T. Edwards, Mr. Matthew, Mr. Masefield, Mr. Ferguson, and the Secretary, Mr. Baynham. All these represent plantation interests. The deputation will concentrate on the danger of the present labour unrest amongst Indian labour on the estates.

A few weeks ago the Governor sent home for the Secretary of State a copy of a memorandum from the two chief European Plantation Associations in Ceylon which made two comprehensive requests:—

(a) that tea and rubber be proclaimed to be "essential industries" (under the Defence Regulations) which they consider would undoubtedly prove to be a severe check on seditious agitators.

(b) that the Governments of India and Ceylon should be persuaded that the imposition of the ban on emigration from India is extremely detrimental to Ceylon's major industries and causes great hardship on Indian estate labourers who have been accustomed to passing freely between India and Ceylon.

A few weeks ago too at the Annual General Meeting of the Ceylon Association in London, a resolution was passed and sent to the Secretary of State as follows:—

"This Association deplores the present lack of concord between the Governments of Ceylon and India which is due not only to the discriminatory action of the Government of Ceylon towards many of its Indian employees but to the severe ban on emigration of Indian unskilled labourers to Ceylon instituted by the Government of India, and regrets the consequent adverse effect on the general and industrial welfare of Ceylon. This Association expresses its earnest wish that endeavours will be successful whereby the contention between the two Governments will be terminated and decides that a copy of this resolution be transmitted to the Secretary of State for the Colonies."

The problem of the political relations between the Governments of India and Ceylon cannot usefully be discussed in a short note. We all deplore the present bad relations which derive from the respective nationalist feelings in the Parliamentary Institutions in India and Ceylon. In India the affairs of Indians overseas are notoriously a matter of 'face' to the Government of India. In Ceylon the ruling principle is 'Ceylon for the Ceylonese'—in both a political and economic sense. We have lost no opportunity of urging the Government of Ceylon to bear in mind that the basis of the Island's economic well-being—not merely the European tea industry but also the Ceylonese coconut industry—depends on the maintenance of good relations with India. The Secretary of State has at present under consideration the question of a personal conference with Mr. Amery to see if a détente can be arranged and the Indian ban on emigration to Ceylon removed.

But the Ceylon Association's deputation will be urgently concerned with the present labour unrest which is undoubtedly extending to new areas where Indian labour is employed on the tea estates, and in which there are signs of the unrest being marked by petty violence and ill-humour. On many of the estates a war of nerves is going on amongst the European managing staffs who are often very isolated from contact with other Europeans. Moreover, the current opinion in planting circles is that in the absence of troops the Police Force is insufficient to control any dangerous situation which might develop. The chief European military volunteer force is the Ceylon Planters' Rifle Corps and the planters are of course apprehensive that estates would be denuded of European managing staff if this force had to be called out for action in a particular locality. They are also apprehensive that the attractions of coming home to join up in the Army may draw away from estate staffs some of the European assistants who are indispensable on the estates in present circumstances.

In this situation the Ceylonese Minister for Labour, Mr. Corea, urged by the Governor and the Secretary of State, has been holding conferences both with representatives of the planters and representatives of the rival Indian Trade Unions in Ceylon for the purpose of promoting arbitration and conciliation, and for reaching agreement between the representatives of employers and employed on the removal of certain features of estate employment to which the workers claim to take exception; particularly this includes the 'Head Kangany' system. It is not necessary probably to go into this as the planters are in general agreeable to the abolition of this system which briefly is that the working contacts between the management and the Indian workers are carried on through the medium of an Indian agent, the 'Head Kangany', on the estate. No doubt many of the Kanganys misuse their opportunities to enrich themselves at the expense of the labourers, and a particular Head Kangany can abuse his authority for oppression and victimisation of workers who are not fully amenable to him.

These conferences under the aegis of the Minister are achieving considerable promise. New legislation is before the Board of Ministers for local Boards of Conciliation and the matter of compulsory arbitration (to which the planters have objected) is also under the Minister's consideration. There appears also to be a growing appreciation by both employers and workers of the value of the Labour Department of the Ceylon Government although the Controller of Labour has stressed the difficulty which he has experienced in getting the employers, in particular, to notify the Department in good time of the labour difficulty on the estates. Only too often no request is made to the Department by an estate manager until the trouble has developed to a serious stage. There has also been a lack of readiness on both sides to accept any compromise towards a settlement. For this reason the adoption of compulsion may be a necessary incentive to a more ready acceptance of conciliation.

The deputation, in common with the general view, is likely to concentrate on the nefarious activities of one of the rival workers' organisations *viz*. the Sama Samaj, or 'Communist', Party. It is true that most of the exhibitions of violence can be traced to the hand of this organisation. The Sama Samaj Union is not a registered union and the planters' representatives have declined to meet it in conference. They regard it as deplorable that the Ceylon Government have failed to proscribe it and to suppress it. The Governor has told us that he does not believe that such action would remedy the situation; it is of a nature which would flourish underground.[1] Moreover, the Ministers would not consent to such a course. He says that investigations have not shown the Sama Samaj to derive any funds from the Communist International, nor have its agents been guilty of seditious activities with the troops or with recruitment for the forces. Nevertheless, to our knowledge, the two Sama Samaj members of the State Council have delivered themselves of such outrageous anti-British statements that the mischief of the Party's activities & policy ('anti-Imperialist' and 'anti-capitalist' nominally) in present circumstances in Ceylon seems to be beyond doubt, and any reliable evidence that the deputation may be able to produce on the Sama Samaj question should, I suggest, be welcomed by the Secretary of State. We could hope to solve straightforward economic difficulties in Ceylon and even politico-economic difficulties, but it will be made infinitely more difficult if a merely wrecking organisation is permited to 'rock the boat' in present circumstances without restriction.

Finally, the Secretary of State will no doubt like to inform the deputation in confidence of the announcement to defer the General Election for two years which will appear on the following day, Saturday. It is the general belief that the postponement of the Election will ease the present tension amongst Indian labour in Ceylon since the urgency of their voting support for rival candidates representing the various Union Organisations will be removed.

---

[1] See 46, para 8.

53 CO 54/978/10   14 June 1940

[Sama Samajists]: minutes by K W Blaxter and Sir G Bushe on the grounds upon which N M Perera and D P R Gunawardene might be arrested and detained

[In these minutes Blaxter and Bushe (legal adviser, CO) are contemplating recommending pre-emptive action against the Lanka Sama Samaja Party (LSSP), a Trotskyist group, whose two members in the State Council were using their privileged position there to oppose the war effort (cf 46, para 8 and 48). After his initial reluctance to take the action contemplated by the CO (see 55 and 56), Caldecott did authorise the arrest and detention of the Sama Samaja leaders, including their two members of the State Council (see 60).]

It is suggested that a telegram might be sent to the Governor on the following lines:—

The S. of S.'s attention has been called to the remarks made by Mr. Perera and Mr. D.P.R. Gunawardene in the State Council on the 29th May during the Debate on a Supplementary Estimate for Rs. 100,000 to meet the cost of the acquisition of land for an air base for the R.A.F.;[1] that the S. of S. regards the remarks made by these two members to be of such a nature as cannot be tolerated in the present circumstances; the S. of S. presumes that as the Powers and Privileges Bill has not yet received His Majesty's assent, there is at present no right of free speech in the Council; but that in any case it would appear likely that there exists at the private houses of these two members if they are searched literature and correspondence of such a kind as would justify their arrest; ask the Governor to consider at once what steps can be taken for the arrest of these two members.

It might be well to ask the Governor to report to us how he proposes to proceed before any action is actually taken. It is perhaps unlikely that a mistake such as was made in the case of Mr. Bracegirdle should be made again, but we don't want there to be any risk of such an occurrence, and it would probably be safest that we should be informed how the Governor proposes to act before anything is actually done.

K.W.B.
14.6.40

On thinking this over again, I do not think that the right of free speech really comes into it. Defence Regulation 18, which I presume the Governor has enacted, provides that the Governor may detain a person if he is satisfied that it is necessary so to do with a view to preventing him acting in any manner prejudicial to public safety or defence. Upon that I think the Governor is quite entitled to be satisfied that a person

---

[1] During the debate in the State Council on 29 May, Perera commented: 'At a time of intense suffering in Ceylon when every cent should be made available to the poor people of this country, when thousands were tendered homeless, it was criminal folly to vote money for the purpose which only consolidated their position as slaves.' Gunawardena made the observation that the British 'are a declining and decrepit empire' and continued: 'In view of the police terrorism that is going on such as the beating of labourers and labourers being charged falsely, it is criminal folly on the part of the country to vote money for the Royal Air Force who are not going to fight for them but to bomb defenceless men and women in this country. We are not going to be party to spending a single cent.' These, and other speeches during the debate, are reproduced in W S Muthiah & S Wanasinghe, *Britain, World War 2 and the Sama Samajists* (Colombo, 1996) pp 83–84.

who makes such speeches in the Legislature ought to be detained to prevent him acting in a manner prejudicial, etc. Of course, if they could get further evidence it is all to the good. We might say, therefore, that it is not clear what is the immunity enjoyed by members of the State Council in regard to speeches made there, but for the reasons given above that does not seem to us to come into the picture.

H.G.B.
14.6.40

54   CO 54/978/7, no 19   14 June 1940

[Reforms]: despatch from Sir A Caldecott to Lord Lloyd on the registration of Indian voters. *Enclosure* 2: extract from the minutes of a meeting of the Board of Ministers, 4 June 1940

With reference to my Confidential despatches of the 23rd February[1] and 17th May[2] on the subject of the registration of Indian Voters I have the honour to forward at the request of the Ministers the Hansard reports[3] of the debate begun in State Council on 14th May, continued on the 15th, 16th and 17th May, and concluded on the 28th May, on the following resolution moved by the Honourable Mr. S.W.R.D. Bandaranaike:—

> "That in view of the serious situation that has arisen in connection with the registration of non-Ceylonese voters for State Council elections, this Council demands that immediate steps be taken to give effect to the proposals contained in paragraph 35 of Governor Stanley's despatch, dated 2nd June, 1929, and approved by the Secretary of State in paragraph 10 of his despatch, dated 10th October, 1929.

The resolution was passed by 30 votes to 17. There was one abstention and certain other members who had spoken against the motion were absent at the division.

2. An abstract from the Minutes of the Meeting of the Board of Ministers, held on the 4th June, is enclosed: this extract contains a summary of the views of the Ministers in regard to the matters raised in the debate and describes the "immediate steps" which the Ministers desire should be taken.

3. The extract also contains a statement made by the Legal Secretary in regard to the revision of the electoral registers which should take place this year and the decision by the Board of Ministers that further action in regard to the supplementary estimate should be deferred until a reply has been received to this despatch.

4. As a result of the Council Debate I have received from the Indian Agent in the course of an interview a repetition of the representation made by him in June last year that

> "Indian opinion both in India and Ceylon is unanimous that the only logical and fair solution of the problem is a reversion to the simple test of residence of five years in Ceylon as recommended by the Donoughmore Commission.

---

[1] See 26.   [2] See 45.   [3] Not printed.

The Government of India agrees with this view and strongly recommends its adoption."

If any change is made in the present system of Indian representation we are, as you are aware, under obligation to consult the Government of India.

5. In order to make clear my own position *vis-à-vis* the Ministerial attitude on the one hand and Indian opinion on the other, I can only reiterate what I have already twice written on this subject in previous despatches. As I read the Ceylon (State Council Elections) Order in Council, 1931, an Indian can be enfranchised by

Article 7 (a) proving Ceylonese domicile of origin;
           (b) proving, if he has been resident for five years or more, Ceylonese domicile of choice.
Article 8 (c) proving that he possesses the prescribed literacy and property qualifications, or
Article 9 (d) proving that he has been continuously resident in Ceylon for five years and declaring that he intends to settle here permanently.

Proof of domicile of choice (b) is notoriously difficult and (d) was provided to make enfranchisement easier for the intending settler. The past mistake of registering officers has been to register people under Article 7 without positive proof of domicile of choice. The more recent failure of three Government Agents to implement the Legal Secretary's Circular of August, 1938, was reported in my despatch of the 23rd February. A revision of the registers still appears to me all that is necessary to remedy these mistakes and failures. The Legal Secretary, however, holds the view that difficulties will persist so long as domicile remains the basis of franchise.

6. I was unaware, when I formed (in connection with my reform proposals) the opinion expressed in the preceding paragraph, that the omission to prescribe in the Electoral Order in Council a fee of one rupee or less on a certificate of permanent settlement (as distinct from the stamp duty on an applicant's declaration, which is expressly waived by Article 9 (2)) was intentional; but this now appears plain from Lord Passfield's despatch No. 323, of the 20th June, 1930, which has since been brought to my notice. I was also then unaware that there is no general Fees Ordinance in Ceylon under which such a fee could be imposed. I had, however, before being informed on these two points, impressed on the Ministers my conviction that the proposed revision of the registers would not reduce the number of Indian voters but merely result in persons disqualified under Article 7 being re-registered under Article 9. It appears to me strangely inconsistent that those who so recently felt it necessary to debar Indian labourers from the Village Franchise (the grant of which would have involved the voter in an *annual* capitation of tax of Re. 1) should now think that the prescription of one single none-recurrent payment of Re. 1 would deter the labourer from registering under Article 9. In any case the Re. 1 was not intended to be a deterrent (Sir Herbert Stanley explicitly recommended it as "only a nominal fee") and I am unable to support (*vide* paragraph 5 of enclosure (2)) the prescription of any payment that has a restrictive purpose. I am also advised that it would involve an amendment of the Order in Council.

7. I am further unable to support any proposal (*vide* paragraph 4 of enclosure (2)) that the grant of the franchise to an Indian labourer should be made conditional on his deprivation of treatment or amenities to which a manual worker is entitled by local labour law and international convention.

8. As regards paragraph 3 of enclosure (2) I agree that domicile of choice must, for the purposes of Article 7, be proved positively. The purpose of the proposed revision of the registers was to delete registrations under Article 7 in respect of which domicile of choice had not been proved but merely assumed.

9. In regard to paragraph 2 of enclosure (2) there is no objection to the Legal Secretary reporting to the Board of Ministers what in his opinion are adequate methods of proving five years' residence. Whatever his opinion is, it must stand; as he is the authority in whom control over elections to the State Council is vested by the Constitution. There can be no question of his taking directions from the Board of Ministers in the matter, and any report furnished by him on this subject would be for their information only.

10. Paragraph 1 of enclosure (2) raises vexed questions of history and interpretation. Of the genuineness of the Sinhalese view that the present Constitution was accepted by them on the understanding that the recommendations contained in paragraph 35 of Sir Herbert Stanley's despatch of the 2nd June, 1929, would be implemented to the letter and *in toto* there can be no question. Mr. Wikramanayake undoubtedly spoke for his community when he said (Hansard, 12th December, 1929, page 1807):—

> "With regard to the fear of the vote being given to the immigrant cooly, that too has been removed because the test to be applied is such that we need have no fears."

On the other hand in a previous speech in the same debate (Hansard 1929, page 1777) the Colonial Secretary had drawn the attention of the House to the fact that "the renouncement of the claim to a right does not necessarily mean that the right actually disappears." In the same speech he said that "there are many questions of detail which will have to be worked out in the later development of the scheme." The contention of those who voted for Mr. Bandaranaike's motion is that in the development of the scheme details were not worked out but principles dropped out.

11. I have found that local records of correspondence that intervened between the Council Debate of December, 1929, and Lord Passfield's telegram of the 10th June, 1930 (published here as Sessional Paper XXXIV/1929), confused and incomplete. That telegram, however, should have made it clear to any who read it with care that any deprivation of rights inherent in the grant of a certificate of permanent settlement would not extend to the abrogation of any obligations imposed by Statute on an employer towards his employees, and that therefore the jettison of privileges previously envisaged (e.g., in Mr. C. W. W. Kannangara's speech reported on pages 1813 and 1814 of the 1928 Hansard) would not in fact eventuate.

12. Any idea of now going back on Lord Passfield's telegram after the passage of ten years appears to me quite outside practical politics, inconsonant with Ceylon's obligations under international conventions, and incompatible with such a development of responsible democratic tradition as alone could form the basis of any future constitutional advancement in this Island.

Enclosure 2 to 54

. . . 24. The Board considered a memorandum, dated 25th April, 1940, submitted by the Legal Secretary on the question of the revision of the Electoral Registers.

A Supplementary Estimate for Rs. 248,500 for the purpose was also placed before the Board.

Before considering these items the Ministers summarised their views in regard to the matters raised in the recent debate as follows:—

(1) The Order in Council does not appear, on the face of it, to conflict with the assurances resulting from the combined effect of paragraph 35 of Sir Herbert Stanley's despatch and paragraph 10 of Lord Passfield's despatch: hitherto it has been read as giving effect to those assurances: it is only recently that it has been realised that, by administrative methods and interpretation, those assurances have been defeated.

(2) Instead of the Committee proposed by Sir Herbert Stanley in paragraph 35 of his despatch the Board of Ministers would be agreeable to the Legal Secretary reporting to them what, in his view, were adequate methods of proving five years' residence for the purposes of Articles 7 and 9 of the Order in Council and the other matters contemplated by Sir Herbert Stanley in his despatch as being within the purview of this Committee.

(3) Persons claiming the franchise on the ground of domicile of choice must prove positively that they have acquired such a domicile.

(4) The holder of a certificate of permanent settlement must be, in law and in fact, deprived of special rights, privileges, etc. In so far as such rights, etc., depend on statutory obligations of employers, the employers must be relieved of those obligations in respect of holders of certificates of permanent settlement.

(5) A fee must be charged for a certificate of permanent settlement (under the 1930 Order in Council a declaration was not exempt from stamp duty, but the duty was not collected). Under the 1931 Order in Council the declaration was specifically exempted from stamp duty. Contention is that, if stamp duty cannot be charged on the certificate without amending the Stamp Duty Ordinance, the Governor could prescribe a fee for the issue of the certificate without amending the Order in Council or any other legislation.

The discussion was adjourned and resumed again at 2.30 p.m. All members were present except the Minister of Health.

The Legal Secretary then explained that the revision of the electoral registers was divided into three parts:—

(a) expunging the names of persons who had become disqualified under Article 6; this work was small and required little or no extra staff or expenditure;

(b) entering new names on the register: this work was small so far as persons claiming literacy and property qualification were concerned, but it was difficult so far as persons claiming a domicile of choice under Article 7 were concerned;

(c) revising the qualifications of persons already on the register; if anything substantial was to be accomplished within the time available, considerable staff and money would be required.

There were two limitations on the amount of work that could be accomplished under head (c), namely, the time table prescribed by the Order in Council which necessitated all the inquiries being completed by the 1st of August and the limited number of suitable staff available.

The scheme which he had prepared seven weeks ago contemplated the employment of 200 officers of Civil List status for a period of two months. With this staff the maximum number of persons on the register whose qualifications could be tested would have been 400,000, i.e., less than 14 per cent. to 15 per cent. of the total number of electors; only one month was now available and the staff could not be increased. Indeed it might be doubtful whether 200 officers of the status required could ever be made available, and if they could, it would only be at the cost of very considerable dislocation in public business. With only one month available the quantity of the revision which could be accomplished under head (c) would be less than 8 per cent. of the total number of electors.

The Board decided that, in view of the fact that any revision of the registers which could be undertaken in the time available would be inadequate, a supplementary estimate for the amount asked for by the Legal Secretary should not now be presented. Further action should be deferred until a reply had been received from the Secretary of State to the proposed despatch which is to report the recent debate on the State Council electoral registers.

55   CO 54/974/8, no 12   15 June 1940
[Sama Samajists]: outward unnumbered telegram from Lord Lloyd to Sir A Caldecott on the need for firm and effective action

I am continually receiving warnings from various sources both representative of European commercial interests and others of serious deterioration of public order in Ceylon and failure to take effective action against Sama Samajists is particularly and widely emphasised. I have just received deputation from Ceylon Association which stated *inter alia* that you had stated:—

(1) you were not prepared to use special powers to prevent intimidation and threats of violence by agitators because such action would not be supported by Secretary of State and because it would require a regiment from India;
(2) Ministers would not agree to tightening up existing law relating to sedition;
(3) you would only take action against Communist movement in Ceylon if evidence was forthcoming that it was financed from outside.

I do not know whether there is any substance in above statement, but I can assure you that I shall give you all possible support in regard to any measures you may have to recommend for ensuring firm and effective action against all and any disturbers of law and order or persons whose activities are likely to be prejudicial to efficient prosecution of war. I regard such firmness as paramount duty of Government in present emergency, regardless of opposition by Ministers or non-co-operation by State Council which must now be a subordinate consideration. I have not had any suggestion from you that police and other forces of order at your disposal would be inadequate to suppress disorder in the Island, but if you have any doubts on that point I request that you will consult your military and police authorities and let me have your views as soon as possible.

56   CO 54/974/8, no 13   18 June 1940
[Sama Samajists]: inward unnumbered telegraph (reply) from Sir A Caldecott to Lord Lloyd

Your Secret and Personal telegram of 15th June.[1] Deterioration of public order in Ceylon has been greatly exaggerated and with suppression of troubles on Wewessa estate position throughout the island is again normal, though, of course, possibility of further outbreaks of labour unrest is being continuously watched. I have throughout been in constant touch with Labour Police and military authorities and neither of the latter has any doubt of the ability to make arrangements for disorder in the island should it ever arise. I have already reported by my telegram No. 569 Secret that we can spare 50 men of the Rifle Corps for active service. I have always regarded firmness my paramount duty in matters affecting security and the prosecution of the war, and would not hesitate to request enactment of recently drafted Order in Council enabling me to take over Government if events should require and justify such a course. At the same time I have considered it essential to refrain from precipitate action at the dictation of the Times of Ceylon or on representations from other (? group omitted) which are only half informed and put forward in ignorance or disregard of their full implications. Of the representations quoted in your telegrams I can only conjecture that (1) may be a strange distortion of conversation reported in paragraph 15 of Government Ceylonese No. 8. As regards item (2) Legal Secretary informs me that proposed legislation was dropped on his advice that it would make conviction more difficult than under existing law. Item (3) may possibly reflect *obiter dictum* of mine that if Samajist party were ever found receiving money or literature from Moscow I should take immediate action under Defence Act.

A present difficulty is that the tone of recent articles and correspondence in the Times of Ceylon is stirring up feeling and friction between educated Ceylonese and local European community. Such articles and letters make it clear that its management would not be receptive of advice from myself or other authority and I apprehend that Minister may press for consorship of the press as only effective form of restraint, a course to which I am opposed if it can possibly be avoided. I am most grateful for your assurance of support, and I hope action reported to-day in my telegram No. 579 Secret which has been taken after continuous watching of Samajist [sic] activities and establishment of data may have a reassuring effect on Ceylon interests in London and elsewhere.[2]

---

[1] See 55.

[2] Lloyd replied on 24 June that he was 'glad to have your assurance, and I am confident that in association with authorities responsible for law and order you will continue to watch local opinion and advise me if and when you consider any special measures are necessary' (CO 54/974/8, no 13). The secretary of state, however, remained concerned over anti-British agitation in Ceylon (see 63).

57 CO 54/977/7, no 9   29 June 1940

'Things Ceylonese': tenth periodical report by Sir A Caldecott for CO.
Minutes by Lord Lloyd and K W Blaxter

General situation in the island

1. These Notes will not be placed under headings as usual, being in the nature of a general review.

2. At this critical period of the war, when France has collapsed and capitulated, I think that it would be correct to regard the people of this Island as divided into several political strata in relation to their local and Empire citizenship:—

(a) *Left-wing Samajists* [sic], who in these dark days have come out definitely anti-British. Five of their leaders are under detention or awaiting arrest, and other members are being prosecuted for offences under the Defence Regulations. This stratum does not comprise more than ½% of the population. They are under constant watch by the Police.

(b) *The non-English speaking classes* which may be roughly divided into (i) urban, (ii) agricultural and (iii) labour. There is no inherent antipathy to British Rule in any of these three categories. Members of all of them however, whether Sinhalese or Tamil, are impressionable and excitable fellows. They are an easy prey to politicians, and will respond to nationalistic and socialistic speeches. The postponement of the next elections gives them a respite from much such oratory. The Lake House vernacular newspapers (a great increase in whose circulation shows that real interest is being taken in the war by this stratum) are a thoroughly loyal and healthy influence.

(c) *The clerical classes*. These are all English-speaking and are predominantly pro-British. They contain, inevitably, individuals who have been dismissed from former jobs for misconduct and others who have not achieved the promotion they hoped for. Malcontents of this kind sometimes relieve their feelings in the trains and buses that bring them daily to Colombo by expressing satisfaction with unfavourable war news. Such persons are neither important nor entirely negligible: they need watching but not hunting.

(d) *The upper native classes*. Members of these fall into two categories (i) The *first* comprises those who dislike the new constitution as having involved them in a loss of political or administrative status. It includes the majority of those aristocratic families which once furnished Executive and Legislative Councillors in the days of Crown Colony Government and of the Karawa Christian families which (with the advantage of missionary education) tended of old to become a monopolistic element in the structure of the clerical and subordinate services of Government. People born into such families consider modern politics and elections a dirty game, talk of the good old days when the country was run by English Gentlemen, and are generally reactionary. The influence of such families is waning fast but, such as it may be, it is definitely pro-British. (ii) The *second* category consists of the *novi homines*[1] under the present constitution. They are not pro-British but pro-Ceylonese. They consider Ceylon's proper niche in the world scheme to be that

---

[1] In a side note to his report Caldecott defined them as 'The new nationalists'.

of a Dominion in the British Commonwealth of Nations. They are not therefore *anti*-British (the Union flag is very much in evidence at all celebrations in village or town) but they resent criticism by the local Britisher of the present administration and are very jealous and resentful of the British share in the development of the Island. They are techy, tiresome and unable to get beyond the shadow of the parish pump. Now that the pump's shadow has fallen within and become eclipsed by the dark shade of the French collapse and Italian belligerency there is a more realistic response to the Empire's cause. The Ministers and nearly all the State Councillors and politicians belong to this stratum.

(e) The *European community* is also in two strata. (i) The *reactionaries* may be considered first. Nearly all the older planters and some 25% of the business men in Colombo belong to this group. They consider that Britain made no greater mistake than when she gave a large dose of self-Government to Ceylon; they loathe the present administration and its politics; they resent the rising consciousness of labour and the emergence of Trade Unions; they will join the minority communities in any tirade against the Sinhalese Ministry but otherwise they have no truck with them or any other 'native politicians'. They want a speedy end made of the present constitution and "the Ministers to be shown where they get off". They are against any reforms that will not represent an effective diminution of self-Government. The older Planters are psychologically, educationally and politically of the type that was common in Malaya in the first fifteen years of the century: many of the Malayan pioneers in fact hailed from Ceylon. That type in Malaya began fading out over twenty five years ago under the ministrations of the Labour Department (N.B. Ceylon has never had an adequate Labour Department) and suffered final extinction under the castigations of Mr. Ormsby Gore in 1928. It is impossible not to feel sympathy for the Rip van Winkles of Ceylon; but there is no doubt that plantation interests will be better served both technically and politically by the younger men now coming on, many of whom express impatience with their bosses' anachronisms. (ii) The second European stratum may be labelled "the Moderates". They are less vocal than the reactionaries but possess the brains that most of the latter lack. They consider that the grant of a considerable measure of self-Government to Ceylon was justified; that universal suffrage was a blunder of the first magnitude; that the experiment of the Executive Committee system is one that should never have been tried out on an infantile democracy; that considering these handicaps the present constitution might have worked worse (though perhaps not much worse) than it has done; that the lot of the Britisher, official or unofficial, becomes yearly more individious as nationalism grows (but does not broaden); that there is no putting back the hands of the political clock at this late hour, however bad the time it is keeping; and that, in short, we must do our best by reforms and in everyday politics to make the best of a bad job. Nearly all European officials belong to this stratum. It is a philosophy of sanity but not of enthusiasm. Nevertheless there are many, both official and unofficial, who conscientiously and with little thanks work hard to oil the wheels and keep the country going with as little friction as possible. So long as they continue in this effort there is no cause for excessive despondency or apprehension. They deserve every encouragement and I repose my faith in them.

Stabilization

3. In "Things Ceylonese No.9"[2] I remarked that there had been no stabilisation of the local political position. The past five weeks have however brought with them developments that have had a marked stabilizing effect. These developments may be summarized as follows:—

(i)   the Planters' Association have agreed to recognize properly registered Trade Unions, under persuasion from the Minister and Controller of Labour.

(ii)   the Planters' Association (though there has been, I believe, some subsequent dissension) decided to appoint a Commission of their own to probe the causes of labour unrest. This is a notable advance from the attitude that the sole cause was political agitation by Sama Samajists and others.

(iii)   On a number of estates Managers of the new school of thought have begun putting their houses in order. More Scout Troops have been started on estates and the first Soccer match between the employees of one estate and those of another has been played at Nuwara Eliya. It was fully reported in the press and the level of play was good. Volley ball is being introduced on more and more estates.

(iv)   prosecutions for rioting and disorder during the recent unrest have in the law's own time (which is ever slow) led to many convictions and suitable sentences.

(v)   The Ceylon Estate Workers' Union has 'lost face' among labourers because of its failure to supply strikers on the Rangbodde Estate with rice and also as a result of the prosecutions of rioters some of whom have, in their defence, blamed the Union;

(vi)   Encouraged by the bad news from Flanders the Samajist Members became openly seditious in State Council on the 28th May. The Ceylon Daily News refused to publish a report of their speeches but the Times of Ceylon did. The Executive Committee of Home Affairs approved my taking extra powers under the Defence Regulations for the issue of detention orders, prohibition of meetings and prescription of flags. New regulations were promulgated on 3rd June.

(vii)   The Hansard issued on 12th June (based on proofs corrected by members themselves) confirmed substantially the newspaper report of the seditious Council speeches, though there had been rumours of inaccuracy. On the 14th June two Samajist vernacular newspapers (Sinhalese and Tamil) published flagrantly subversive matter. On Sunday the 16th (the Home Minister being away) I conferred with the Chief and Legal Secretaries and the Inspector and Deputy Inspector Generals of Police. After full examination of the data we agreed that we could not strike without fear of driving influential liberals like Bernard Aluwihare into the Samajist Camp and without endowing the Samajists with any public sympathy.

(viii) On the 17th, after consultation with the Home Minister and the Chief Secretary (with the Legal Secretary and Inspector General of Police present) I issued detention orders against Dr. Colvin de Silva (President of the Party), Dr. N.M. Perera and Mr. D.P.H. Gunawardana (State Councillors), Mr. Samarakoddy (leading member of the Party and a proctor) and Mr. Leslie Gunawardene, who largely finances the party. The last-named is still eluding arrest.[3]

(ix)   On the 21st June I was informed by the Legal Secretary that young

---

[2] See 46.   [3] See 60.

Bandaranaike had been all blood and thunder at a Ministers' meeting and that trouble might be expected in Council next week. I received however a request from the Ministers to meet me in discussion on the 24th, at which meeting Senanayake said that at this time of peril to the Empire they were all behind me and Bandaranaike remarked that, having visited the Samajists in jail and having heard what they had to say, he thought that they were properly detained.

(x)   On the 25th of June the Home Minister made a short statement about the detentions which was accepted without challenge. The Lake House press has calmly and sensibly supported the detentions from the first.

(xi)   On the 26th June the State Council voted a first contribution of Rs 5 million towards war expenditure.

Difficulties surmounted and endured

4.   The position of the Ministers, and preeminently of the Governor, has been rendered most difficult throughout the process of stabilization by the political tactics of the European reactionaries (see paragraph 1 (e) (i) of these Notes) which have received also support from a number of the Ceylonese "old gang" (paragraph 1 (d) (i)) and of disgruntled anti-Government clerks (paragraph 1 (c)). The "Times of Ceylon" by lending its columns to the campaign of vilification against the Ministers and myself has undoubtedly increased its circulation, but at the same time it is now banned from the houses of many thinking Europeans and most leading Sinhalese. I have of course resisted all Ministerial suggestions for a repression or suppression of the paper under the Defence Act. Nothing would have been more stupid or fatal to European-Ceylonese co-operation. On the 26th June the Minister for Home Affairs did the right thing by summoning the Manager of the paper and asking him to stop articles likely to cause friction. From subsequent editions it appears that the Minister's homily and appeal have not been in vain.

Aftermath

5.   I understand that signatures are still being obtained by a "Times of Ceylon" anonymous correspondent "J.B.K." for affixation to a Memorial for direct transmission to Whitehall. As the signatories are not being allowed to see the memorial their signatures must be rather "in the air". "J.B.K." is, I understand, a Mrs. Ashton with whom I have had quite a lot to do in connection with the Overseas League and Royal Empire Society. She struck me then as a nice and well-intentioned woman, but somewhat ill-balanced and oratorical. Another memorial is being fostered by a Mr. Aitken, who resigned the Police before reaching pensionable status many years ago owing to some disagreement with Dowbiggin. He has got himself into trouble with the Comrades of the Great War Association, by trying to identify the Association with the Memorial, and with the Police by alleging that they have not been backed up by the authorities. Both the Comrades and the Police have, I am told, written repudiatory letters to Aitken; who has however already committed himself to his statements by sending an advance copy of the memorial by hand to Field Marshal Lord Birdwood "in order to ensure its safe delivery to Lord Lloyd". I am of course well trained by past experience to endure and ignore anti-gubernatorial machinations, having had the privilege of serving under Sir Laurence Guillemard and Sir Cecil Clementi. Thank goodness, however, I have not to contend with the disloyalty of any

colleagues in the service (as had the former) or with the extreme but unprincipled cleverness of a Ward-Jackson, as had the latter.

Thankfulness

6. I cannot end these notes without an expression of my thankfulness that, whatever the future may have in store, the very tricky and critical period of the immediate past has been successfully steered through. At this time of Britain's ordeal there promises indeed to be greater mutual restraint and collaboration between the public, the Council, the Ministers and myself than at any time hitherto. The postponement for two years of the General Election has undoubtedly helped tremendously in achieving the stabilisation reported in these Notes; indeed I consider it the biggest single factor in the general improvement of the local situation.

Minutes on 57

The governor seems unable to draw the moral from his own actions. An unimpressive report. I should like to know more about the Governor's record. P.S. please tell me.

L.
[nd]

This report differs from the previous ones and is a general review of the position in Ceylon as on June 29th, that is, when the defeat of France was complete and the effects of it were becoming known. It is more encouraging than previous reports in that it seems to show what we hope is the case, viz., that the worst of the trouble in the Island may be over. The defeat of France and its possible consequences have clearly had a sobering effect on all classes and communities in Ceylon save the Left Wing Samajists who have by these events been encouraged to become openly anti-British. They are only a very small section of the population and, as the Governor shows, their actions in early June were such as to enable him to order the detention of the five leaders without much criticism of his action being shown in any quarter. I cannot get the file at the moment, but my recollection is that the information given here on page 1 that other Samajists are being prosecuted for offences under the Defence Regulations is the first we have heard that others besides the five leaders are being proceeded against. Also Sir Andrew Caldecott states on page 7 that Mr. Leslie Gunawardene is still eluding arrest. This is, I think, our first information on this point and he may of course have been arrested by now.

2. The Governor speaks of the improvement which has resulted from the postponement of the general election for two years. The two decisions (1) to postpone the election and (2) to detain the Samajist leaders have clearly had a sobering effect in many directions. In addition to this, there is now the hope that an informal conference between representatives of the Government of Ceylon and the Government of India will be held shortly to discuss means of improving relations between the two countries. All these facts, together with the realization throughout Ceylon of the critical days through which the Empire is passing lead one to hope that there may be a general improvement in Ceylon affairs in the near future.

3. The Secretary of State has already seen this report—see his minute at the end of the report. Mr. Eastwood has already spoken to him with regard to Sir Andrew Caldecott.

4. The Governor's position is a difficult one. He cannot have at his disposal the close collaboration and advice of senior officials which is available to the Governors of most of the Colonies. Under the Ceylon Constitution, the three Officers of State, the Chief Secretary, the Legal Secretary and the Financial Secretary, are Members of the State Council and are treated as Ministers in charge of Departments and are in many respects in the same position as the Ceylonese Ministers. The Governor has therefore to play a lone hand and at time has not available to him the channels of information which are open to Governors elsewhere. Also he has to be guided at all times by the Royal Instructions as to his relations with Ministers and to the promotion of self-government in the Island.

K.W.B.
9.8.40

58 CO 54/974/6, no 17   3 July 1940
[Indo-Ceylon relations]: outward unnumbered telegram from Lord Lloyd to Sir A Caldecott conveying the views of Lord Linlithgow

Your private and confidential telegram of 11th May. Viceroy in personal telegram to Secretary of State for India states as follows. *Begins*.—Our forbearance toward Ceylon appears to be repaid by anti-Indian ministerial pronouncements in Ceylon and projects of anti-Indian character, such as immigration restriction, limitation of Indian franchise, further restrictions on employment of non-Ceylonese on Government contracts, prohibitions of sale of private land to non-Ceylonese. Confidential information suggests more rigorous retrenchment of non-Ceylonese daily-paid labour than we anticipated. *Ends*. Viceroy goes on to report increasing embarrassment to Government of India from pressure of public opinion to take further retaliatory action against Ceylon and particularly advises that measures to safeguard copra industry in India are becoming increasingly necessary quite apart from question of retaliation against Ceylon. I am sure that you appreciate that measures suggested in India against Ceylon trade would have very serious effect on island's economic position as well as being extremely undesirable from point of view of Imperial unity in fact of present crisis. It is to my mind imperative that Ministers should clearly understand extent of economic threat to Ceylon which is likely to result from their intransigeance [sic] *vis-a-vis* Indians, and while I have no information on certain of reported matters of Ministers' policy mentioned above, I could not pretend to be surprised if Viceroy's report were well founded. Possibly new symptoms of realistic appreciation of present emergency by Ministers and their supporters of which recent gift to His Majesty's Government is evidence may promise hope of Ministers being convinced of urgency of need to come to terms with India by direct negotiations in which it would be essential for them to make substantial and real modifications of their present policy in return for securing modification of Indian ban on emigration and preserving as much as possible of copra market in India. I suggest you should have very early discussion with Board of Ministers with a view to communication being sent to Government of India to reopen question of inter-governmental discussion at earliest date on basis of *modus vivendi* at least for period of war.

59   CO 54/974/6, no 18   5 July 1940
[Indo-Ceylon relations]: inward unnumbered telegram (reply) from Sir A Caldecott to Lord Lloyd

Your telegram of 3rd July,[1] secret and personal, reached me simultaneously with communication from Chief Secretary to the effect that Minister[s] at Board meeting on 2nd July had pressed that their proposal for legislation to control immigration should be sent direct by him to the Indian Government for its observations instead of through you to the India Office in accordance with the Colonial Office circular despatch of 24th June, 1925. This is the first time that the Ministers' proposals have been finalised and referred to me and they follow substantially the confidential memorandum which I sent with my personal letter to Gent, dated 30th May, except for one very important and unacceptable alteration, i.e., the delation of Clause 14 which left existing machinery for immigration of estate labourers undisturbed. Receipt of these proposals would anyhow have necessitated my summoning Ministers to Conference and I now propose to tackle them on broader basis of your telegram. I have so often repeated to Ministers my strictures on anti-Indian tactics and utterances, and so frequently emphasised the importance of rapprochement that I would like your permission to reinforce my arguments by quoting in my conversation with them (which will be of a secret and personal nature round my table) following passages from your telegram under reply—first from words "Viceroy in personal telegram" down to "economic threat to Ceylon," and, secondly, from words "suggest you have very early discussion" to end of the telegram. If my powers of persuasion should be successful as to which I am not too sanguine though I shall strive my hardest, care will need to be taken that the first conversations with India are exploratory and that any measure of agreement reached is subject also to your agreement and that of Secretary of State for India. Ministers' present attitude towards the Indian ban on emigration is that it is salutary because there is at the moment a surplus of Indian labour on estates and because the disturbing separation of families could easily be avoided if Indian Government carried out its obligation to ensure the welfare of its nationals by issuing special permits to enable their reunion. They so far fail to appreciate that the ban if it becomes permanent will result in a dilemma most dangerous to the economic welfare of the island, i.e., either disgusted by their inability to take their usual holiday in India and moved by growing sense of Indian nationalism labourers may start a general exodus from Ceylon and cause immediate shortage of labour; or in determination not to lose their livelihood they may completely sever their connection with India and in succeeding generations present an increasingly serious racial and economic problem. Now that General Election has been postponed question of limitation of Indian Franchise referred to by the Viceroy is no longer at all pressing problem but can be considered in connection

---

[1] See 58.

with reforms and in full consultation with India. Prohibition of sale of land refers presumably to the recent consideration by the Executive Committee of Lands of legislation on the lines of the Malay Reservations Enactment of the Federated Malay States. As regards restrictions on contract of labour and alleged more vigorous retrenchment of non-Ceylonese employees I will discuss the position with Ministers but as far as I am at present informed I doubt whether either item has much in it.

60   CO 54/978/10, no 13   12 July 1940
[Sama Samajists]: despatch from Sir A Caldecott to Lord Lloyd on the arrest and detention of the Sama Samajist leaders

I have the honour to report, in accordance with paragraph 1 of your Secret (3) despatch of 22nd December 1939, that on the 18th June 1940, I issued detention orders under regulation 1 of the Defence (Miscellaneous No.3) Regulations (a copy of which I attach)[1] in respect of the following persons:—

(a) Dr. Colvin R. de Silva, President of the Lanka Sama Samaja party;
(b) Dr. N.M. Perera, Member of the State Council and Treasurer of the same party;
(c) Mr. D.P.R. Gunawardana, Member of the State Council and a member of the Committee of the same party;
(d) Mr. Edmund Samarakkody, a member of the Committee of the same party;
(e) Mr. Leslie Goonewardene, a member of the Committee of the same party.

2.   The first three persons named were taken into custody on the 18th June. Mr. E. Samarakkody was taken into custody on the 19th June, but Mr. Leslie Goonewardene has so far successfully evaded detention.

3.   The persons detained have been informed or their right to make representations to me in writing and to object to the Advisory Committee which I have appointed. The Committee consists of Mr. Justice Moseley, Mr. A.C.G. Wijeyekoon and Haji Sir Macan Markar.

4.   The reasons for their detention are set out in the document dated 24th June of which a copy is enclosed: this document was communicated to the persons detained on the 25th June, in order that they might make representations to me if they desire to do so.

I have not yet received any such representations but the Chairman of the Advisory Committee informed me on the 9th July that he had received a communication, which appears to express a wish to make objections, from each of the four persons detained.

5.   The grounds of detention rest primarily on publications of the party, both oral and printed, which are prejudicial to public safety and the defence of the Island and not on the activities of the party in relation to labour disputes.

These publications reached their climax in the speeches of Dr. N.M. Perera and Mr. D.P.R. Gunawardana in the State Council which appear on pages 1008–1010 in the enclosed copy of Hansard and in the issue of the Samadharmam dated the 14th June of which a summary is enclosed. The latter publication was issued after the regulations were made.

---

[1] Enclosures not printed.

6. The extent to which the Minister for Home Affairs and his Executive Committee co-operated in the making of the regulations and of the detention orders is indicated in the enclosed statement which the Minister laid upon the table of the State Council on the 25th June 1940.

7. The persons detained are at present accommodated in Welikada Prison and are receiving the same treatment as civil prisoners. This prison is the only prison in the Island with accommodation for special class prisoners but segregation is impossible in this, or in any other prison, in the Island. In order to prevent any possibility of undesirable association with regular prisoners steps are being considered for the removal of the persons detained to a special place of detention.

61   CO 54/974/1, no 1   19 July 1940

[European civil servants]: despatch from Lord Lloyd to Sir A Caldecott on the conditions of employment for European officers

I have the honour to refer to your confidential (2) despatch of the 26th of March, and my reply confidential (3) of the 21st of May, regarding the appointment of Mr. H. H. Jansen, as Deputy Chief Engineer and Manager, Electrical Undertakings.

2. I felt considerable misgivings regarding your proposal to appoint Mr. Jansen, even on probation, to this post, but in view of the very full consideration which you had given to all the factors involved, I decided that I should not be justified in withholding my sanction.

3. I think it well, however, to bring to your notice the views which I formed on this matter. In the first place, I took great exception to the action by the Minister for Communications and Works in making his support for a personal allowance for Major Brazel dependent upon the acceptance of the proposed arrangement regarding Mr. Jansen and on Major Brazel's giving Mr. Jansen what the Minister and his Executive Committee consider to be a fair chance. If there is a case on merits for a personal allowance, it certainly should be granted without conditions of this kind. If there is no such case on merits, the appointment of Mr. Jansen does not make such a case, unless it is conceded that Mr. Jansen comes so seriously short of filling the post satisfactorily that the Director's responsibilities are materially increased.

4. Furthermore, I felt some reluctance in giving my approval to this proposal, in view of the importance of maintaining the efficiency of the Department of Electrical Undertakings. It is clearly important that the deputy to the Chief Engineer and Manager should be a person who is thoroughly competent to fill the post. If the person appointed to the post were to turn out not to be fully competent, there would be a risk of serious financial loss to the public funds of Ceylon apart from the deterioration of an important public utility service.

5. An additional disquieting feature of the position is the well justified fear which is being created that, if a candidate from outside the Colony is selected for a Ceylon appointment, his position may be made unpleasant and possibly even intolerable for him. I know that you are fully aware of these factors in the general situation, but there is no doubt that such apprehensions very much restrict the number of applicants who are likely to come forward for any post which the Ceylon Government may wish to be filled by recruitment from overseas.

6. Finally, I cannot overlook the fact that it appears to be increasingly difficult to stand fast against recommendations for appointments submitted by the Ceylon Government which, if no political factors were involved, would not receive approval.

Article 88 of the Ceylon (State Council) Order in Council, 1931, provides that the appointment, promotion, transfer, dismissal, and disciplinary control of public officers shall be vested in the Governor, and I do not think that a situation ought to be allowed to grow up where the provisions of that article are subordinated to purely political expediency.

7. I do not wish you to think that I am necessarily advocating any drastic change of policy in dealing with cases of this kind, and I appreciate fully the difficult position in which you are placed in this important matter. I none the less thought it right to put my misgivings clearly before you, and I shall be glad to receive any observations you may have to offer in the light of my comments.

62   CO 54/974/6, no 24   23 July 1940
[Indo-Ceylon relations]: inward unnumbered telegram from Sir A Caldecott to Lord Lloyd on a proposed mission to India by a deputation of Ceylon ministers

Secret and personal. 23rd July. Your telegram of 15th July, secret and personal. I had conference with the Board of Ministers yesterday at which all were present except Silva and Bandaranaike from whom notice of inability to attend was received at last moment though six days' notice had been given. I had not for fear of leakage, communicated beforehand the subject for discussion, so that it can have had nothing to do with either of two absences. That the meeting was not unpropitious will be seen from the following personal telegram that I have sent to the Viceroy.

Begins.—Following telegram is being sent to-day by Chief Secretary to the Secretary to the Government of India's External Affairs Department. *Begins*.—Board of Ministers in conference with Governor yesterday expressed the desire to send to India as soon as possible a mission consisting of probably three Ministers and one Officer of State in order to (1) review and discuss in the course of informal conversations with Indian authorities all questions that require full understanding and adjustment between India and Ceylon; (2) clear up any misapprehension that may be found to exist on either side; (3) explore the possibility, and pave the way, for later formal conference and negotiations; and (4) generally promote mutual understanding and goodwill. Owing to the presentation of the Budget to the State Council, proposed mission could not leave here before the end of the first week in September but in order that preparations can be put in train betimes this Government would be grateful for early information by telegraph as to whether your Government will be willing to receive such an exploratory mission. *Ends*. I should be most grateful if you could see your way to exert your influence to secure a welcome for the proposed exploratory mission and without any pre-conditions because I feel that such a mission may be able to remove some of the obstacles that have so far stood in the way of formal negotiations. I am strengthened in this feeling by the fact that I myself have invariably found personal contact with my Ministers the best method of overcoming domestic difficulties. My hopes of the beneficial outcomes of the mission are encouraged by the generally more realistic attitude of the Ministers since the present phase of the war began and by the lull in the local politics that has followed the postponement of our General Election for two years. At the same time there is considerable anti-ministerial criticism which would receive immediate impetus if it could be represented that the mission was being sent to India under any form of pre-condition. Another reason for anticipating good results from the proposed mission lies in the opportunity which it will afford for the correction and explanation of the mis-statements, misrepresentations and distortions that have obtained currency in the newspapers or in gossip, e.g., that proposed legislation will prohibit the sale of private land to non-Ceylonese whereas it contemplates only the reservation of defined areas for indigenous agriculturists on the Malayan model. I therefore very much hope that proposed mission may be permitted to materialise and for my part, I will do all I can to foster a spirit of *rapprochement* and consideration. *Ends*.

Paragraph 2 of your telegram. Ministers desire control of immigrants to be included in the list of subjects to be discussed by the proposed mission with the Indian authorities.

Your paragraph 3. Ministers themselves anticipate that employment of Indians discharged or resigned is likely to be raised in the discussion with the mission which would not of course fail to listen to any representations put forward, though there is little or no likelihood of accommodation in this particular matter.[1]

---

[1] The Government of India accepted the proposal for informal exploratory discussions and on 22 Aug Lloyd sent a congratulatory message to Caldecott and the Board of Ministers (CO 54/974/6, nos 28–29 and 32).

63   CO 54/978/12, no 12   16 Aug 1940
[Situation in Ceylon]: minute by G E J Gent on Lord Lloyd's concern over anti-British agitation in Ceylon

The Secretary of State spoke to me yesterday about affairs in Ceylon. He is continuing to receive from various sources substantial complaints of anti-British agitation, subversive pamphlets distributed in the estate areas and inflamatory [sic] speeches by communist agents etc. Many of those which I have seen relate to the period before 18th June when the Governor issued detention orders under the Defence Regulations against five leading members of the Sama Samaj ("Communist") Party including the two State Council members of the Party. I told the Secretary of State that my impression of affairs in Ceylon was that in the last two months there had been a distinct improvement in the general attitude of the Ceylon Ministers towards the war effort and also in the general morale of the Island and a lessening of the tension on estates. This could be attributed to the decision to postpone the General Election for two years and the action taken against the Sama Samaj Party leaders as well as a realisation of the war position. This improvement was marked by:—

(1) the successful renewal of the approach to the Government of India for Indo-Ceylon discussions on the various differences which have been disturbing their relations;

(2) the vote of a handsome sum of money by the State Council to H.M.G. as a war contribution and the subsequent impressive and continuous stream of official and unofficial contributions for the same purpose;

(3) the absence in recent weeks of evidence reaching the Ceylon Association from European interests in Ceylon of disturbances, strikes etc.

The Secretary of State wishes the Governor to be reassured as to the importance which he attaches to a watchful and vigorous policy being maintained by the Ceylon authorities against any subversive anti-British activities locally whether Sama Samaj or other, and secondly, he wishes the Governor to be asked to send home translations of pamphlets, vernacular press extracts and so on obviously of an anti-British character which may be detected in Ceylon. Lastly he proposes to send personally to the Viceroy a telegram to express his grateful thanks and his earnest hopes in the matter of the informal preparatory discussions which have now been agreed upon by the Governments of India and Ceylon to be held early in November for a free discussion of all the various differences which have been poisoning the relations between the two territories. I submit three telegrams for this purpose, two personal and one official.

64 CO 54/977/7, no 10   20 Aug 1940
'Things Ceylonese': eleventh periodical report by Sir A Caldecott for CO. *Minute* by Lord Lloyd

Better times; club support for wartime effort

1. Nearly two months have passed since my last instalment of these Notes.[1] The saying that no news is good news is applicable to this period. The postponement of the General Election enabled local politicians to stop talking and the collapse of France started them thinking. The result has been a greatly enhanced effort for war funds which is reflected in the figures of remittances to England. The organisation of Social and Sports Clubs into collecting media under a central working Committee has done much to get people of different communities together and to induce a healthy rivalry in the amounts subscribed. The prime movers in this direction have been L. Nicholls, Director of the Bacteriological Institute and present President of the Royal Colombo Golf Club, and O.E. Goonetilleke, Auditor General. Senanayake has also done his bit in boosting the movement.

Newspaper help

2. Whatever criticisms I may have to pass from time to time on the "Times of Ceylon" for irresponsibility in politics, the zeal of this newspaper in canvassing subscriptions for the Gloucester and local Sailors' Funds and in organizing and assiduously running it's "Send a Plane" fund is most praiseworthy and successful. Their fifth plane has just been subscribed. The Ceylon Daily News and the Ceylon Observer are also affording great assistance, by propaganda and reports of progress, to the Ceylon War Purposes, St. Dunstan's and King George's (Sailors) funds.

---

[1] See 57.

Exit Peter Batten

3. I hear that the Times of Ceylon have sacked Peter Batten (the Australian journalist whose pen has literally filled half their columns for them during the past three years) and that he leaves for Australia to-day. He had his points; but on the balance the Island will be well rid of him. I am informed that he was responsible for a number of mischievous paragraphs, e.g. the statement (which has since been published in the London Times) that a wireless transmitter was found on the premises previously occupied by one of our internees, for which there was no basis outside his imagination; and an article querying the internment since the outset of the war of a German Buddhist priest (known to have Nazi opinions) on the ground that Italian Roman Catholic Bishops and priests (all of them under constant surveillance by the Police) have not since been interned.

Swing of the "Times" pendulum

4. I have in recent instalments of these Notes criticized the Times of Ceylon for unnecessarily antagonising the Sinhalese. In paragraph 4 of No.10 I mentioned that Jayatilaka had sent for the Manager of the paper and given him a talking to. The Times now appears to me to have gone unwisely far in the opposite direction by its leader of the 14th August entitled "Dominion Status for Ceylon", of which a copy is attached.[2] I know Sir Baron quite well by now, and am quite certain that he was *not* "inspired by the statesmanlike pronouncements made recently by the Secretary of State for India and the Viceroy" and that he never expected a declaration of post-war Dominion Status at this or at any early juncture. All that Sir Baron meant to say (and indeed he said no more) was that the request for reforms would not be pressed during the war, but that his countrymen expected them to be taken in hand as soon as victory was achieved, and that in the mean while the Secretary of State and the Governor might get agreed changes in train for early implementation when the war ends. His allusion to Ceylon's "rightful position among the free nations of the British Commonwealth" was a quite usual expression of the well-known and long standing policy of the Ceylon National Congress to aim at Dominion Status as an ultimate goal.

Follow my 'leader'

5. The Times has hitherto constantly and emphatically demanded a retention of the Governor's present reserve powers, and I rather doubt whether its editorial staff realize that such retention would be inconsonant with Dominion Status. The publication of a leading article of this nature by a journal associated in the Sinhalese mind with conservative or even reactionary European opinion in this Island is bound to accelerate the tempo of demands for reform. Thus the very next day after its appearance Mr. A. Ratnayake gave notice in State Council of the following motion:—

> "That this Council invites His Excellency the Governor to make an immediate declaration to the effect that Ceylon will be granted Dominion Status upon conclusion of the war".

I have no idea yet when the motion will come up for debate; at present the Council is fully occupied with the budget.

---

[2] Not printed.

Indo-Ceylon relations: official mission

6. It was fortunate perhaps that Bandaranaike was not present (though his excusing himself at the eleventh hour after receiving long notice was impolite) at my meeting with Ministers when I proposed an exploratory "good will mission" to India. I have commented before now on his self-appointed role of "opposition Minister" at all my conferences. His inclusion in the Mission (together with Corea, Senanayake and Huxham) is however very necessary and has been since arranged. It is he who has made the nastiest and stupidest utterances about Indians and his inclusion will enable the Indian authorities to take their measure of him and at the same time prevent him from upsetting the results of the Mission on its return to Ceylon.

Congress to meet Congress

7. From what I read in the papers the official Exploratory Mission may not be the only Ceylon approach to India. The Ceylon Congress apparently intends to send a deputation to the Indian Congress; and if Corea, this year's President of the former, finds himself a member of both missions he will need to be warned of the difficulties and potential improprieties of dual status.

Possible developments

8. I am not a prophet; but, as these Notes are intended to be a faithful portrayal of what passes through my mind from month to month, I do not refrain from expressing ideas for fear that they may be proved wrong by the event. I should not be surprised if, as a result of the get-together act the staging of which has now been successfully arranged, there emerged an entente between Indian and Ceylon politicians additional to and distinct from the desired agreement between the two Governments. The discharge of Indian daily-paid employees by the Ceylon Govern-ment was magnified out of its proper perspective on both sides of the Palk Strait for the purposes of local politics. That episode is now past and dead and I do not anticipate that either side will find much difficulty in composing the corpse for decent mutual burial. On general questions lying outside this particular issue my impression was that Nehru and the Ceylon Ministers found themselves last year far more often in consensus than at variance with each other's point of view. Of course the official mission will not *as such* meet Nehru or any other Indian Congress Leader; but there are bound to be many opportunities for unofficial contact and conversation between the Ceylonese Ministers and Indian Congressmen. On the immigration–emigration issue I fancy that Indians and Ceylonese will be at one in pressing for a rigid restrictive control and it is very necessary that the Controller of Labour (Gimson) should accompany and advise Corea in the interest of Ceylon employers and employees. His attendance has been arranged.

Changed ministerial attitude towards India

9. Nehru, I understand, lost no opportunity during his visit to Ceylon of laying emphasis upon Ceylon's geographic and economic identity with India. In their context (i.e. his protest against the discharge of Indian employees) his remarks annoyed and antagonized our Ministers. One of them is said to have retorted that British Imperialism was better than Indian Imperialism. I have been under a continuous necessity during the last two years of impressing on Ministers the need for keeping on good and neighbourly terms with India: but when I recently (having

previously obtained permission) read to them the Viceroy's telegram to the India Office criticising Ceylon's recent attitude I noted a receptivity never met with before. This I attribute neither to the Viceroy's criticism nor to my exhortations. It is no doubt partly due to the present grim crisis of the war and a desire to promote Empire unity (it is now fully realized by the Ministers and the Island's intelligentsia that in the event of our defeat Ceylon would lose not British bonds but British freedom) but equally due, I think, to the reflection that India is sure shortly to obtain Dominion or similar status, and thereby the ability to bring pressure to bear on Ceylon without effective restraint from Whitehall.

Relation of Ceylon to a federal India
10. It should not be forgotten that young Bandaranaike in his earlier political career definitely advocated the inclusion of Ceylon in a Federal India. A resurrection of this idea as a result of the forthcoming Mission to India is not therefore outside the bounds of possibility. I doubt if Jayatilaka or Senanayake could be wheedled by Nehru or anybody else into supporting it, but to younger politicians it may well appear a short-cut to Dominion status and the ethnic, geographical and economic arguments in favour of it are difficult to counter. I consider it advisable that the possibility of this development should be borne in mind.

Minute on 64

The two or three instalments of 'Things Ceylonese' which I have seen do not impress me. The Governor confesses he writes of things as they "pass through my mind". They do rather read so. He avoids speaking of so many things that really matter in Government—Law and Order; the welfare of the people; their content or discontent; the press and so on—I wonder if he is like his writing.

L.
27.10.40

65 CO 54/977/7, no 11   23 Aug 1940
[Indian labour]: letter from Sir A Caldecott to G E J Gent

1. I am most grateful for your secret and personal letter of the 3rd July concerning the aetiology of our labour unrest and for the opportunity thus given for expressing my dissent from the view that the *primary* cause of the disturbance of Indian labour on estates is the anti-Indian policy and utterances of the Ministers and State Council.[1]
2. The Censor has just sent for my perusal a telegram containing a report on current local conditions sent by the local branch of Harrisons Crosfield's to their London headquarters. It contains the following passage:—"Exercise of emergency powers for arrest (allusion is of course to detention of Samajist leaders) has assisted labour situation but there is still undercurrent of agitation *notably confined to European estates*." The [italics are] mine. If the Sinhalese attitude towards India is

[1] cf 49.

the primary cause of labour unrest, how do you explain the fact that the big estate-owning Sinhalese employers of Indian labour have throughout experienced practically no trouble at all? Would they not be the first on whom Indian coolies would visit the anti-Indian sins of Sinhalese Ministers and State Councillors?

3. Again why is it, if the primary cause be as stated by you, that in all the records taken of agitators' or politicians' speeches to coolies references to Government's discharge of Indian labourers or the ban on emigration from India have occupied only an infinitesimal space?

4. On receipt of your letter under reply I re-read paragraph 3 of mine of the 27th May after a three month's interval, and it still seems to me as accurate a summing up of the causes of labour unrest as any such short summary can be. I only wish indeed that I could accept your diagnosis of a primary cause; because I foresee rapprochement with India as a result of the November conversations and, if your theory is correct, this should spell an end to our labour unrest—whereas my aetiology provides no such promise of respite. In dealing with Asiatic psychology it is sometimes helpful to see a position through Asiatic eyes. I quote therefore the following passages from the July diary of young Rajendra, Deputy Controller of Labour, Hatton:—

> *1st July.* So far nearly a thousand labourers have applied for repatriation from the planting districts of Dimbula, Dickoya and Nuwara Eliya . . . Most of these labourers have convinced themselves that the conditions of employment which they found tolerable during the past 100 years are unendurable now. Many of them have admitted to me that they will face starvation in India: but they prefer starvation to continuing on the estates. This is a remarkable state of mind; for it must be admitted that conditions on estates though not ideal are better today than ever before.

> *3rd July.* I was long under the impression that the factions are due to rivalry between Congress and the Federation. Further experience shows that they arise out of there being on nearly all estates labourers who are satisfied with the status quo and others who are dissatisfied. The latter become suspicious when the former do not join in agitation against the Management. It is also my experience that high-caste labourers are generally supporters of the status quo. The Trade Union movement finds its largest support among the lower castes.

> *25th July.* There is a remarkable difference between the attitude of the Dimbula and the Dikoya planters towards the problem of labour unrest. Dimbula and Dikoya are adjoining districts but they are tackling their problems in very different ways. Dikoya believes in "moderation and toleration," as the Chairman of its Planting Association said at their last meeting. The result is comparative peace in nearly all the estates. Sangam leaders who led strikes in November and December are now useful members of the labour force, and in a number of cases are helping the Management in maintaining discipline. Not a single labourer has been repatriated from this district. Dimbula believes in repression and stern measures. . . . The demand for large scale repatriation is spreading. There is tension on most estates. I wonder when Dimbula will learn that no progressive movement has ever been stamped out by purely repressive action."

5. I still have no doubt whatever that, in Aristotelian phraseology, the new consciousness of labour is the "Material Cause" of our unrest and that "Efficient Causes" have been Nehru's visit and the attention paid to labourers by politicians when they thought there would be a General Election next Spring. So long as the Material Cause persists a succession of efficient causes are bound to arise and to give us trouble. I fear from your letter that you may think me unsympathetic towards planters. That however is not so; I am most sorry for them having to suffer a sudden eruption of unrest after a longer period of peace than has been enjoyed by employers elsewhere and which doubtless seemed to them permanent. For the "Dikoya School" of planters (i.e. those who are tackling the material cause of the problem) I have not only sympathy but admiration. As for the Dimbula Die-Hards I regret that it is impossible for me to conceal my disagreement with their tactics or my apprehension for their future.

P.S. Just as this letter is being typed the following telegram from Robertson Company to Robertson Bois, London, has come in from the Censor. "Consider emergency powers have been effective and labour troubles generally better with possible exception of Dimbula where tardy appreciation of Trade Union movement has tended to hamper better feeling and improvement and has involved appreciable demand for repatriation."

66   CO 54/974/10, no 9   31 Aug 1940
[Police]: letter from Lord Lloyd to Sir A Caldecott on the circumstances under which an investigation should be conducted into the shootings on the Mool-oya estate

I sent you officially in a despatch of the 1st June a memorandum prepared in the Home Office giving a statement of the practice and policy in the United Kingdom regarding the issue of instructions by the Home Secretary to the police in matters coming within their statutory obligations.

I noticed, in connection with the Mooloya Estate riot, that, after consultation with the Legal Secretary, you agreed that an inquiry was desirable "in view of the 1928 Committee's report." I gather that this refers to paragraph 4 of that report, where the following passage occurs:—

> "Where an act of shooting results in a proceeding in which the question of the culpability of the officer concerned is the subject of inquiry in a court of law the facts and circumstances are fully investigated in public. But in cases in which no such judicial investigation has taken place the position cannot be regarded as satisfactory from the point of view of the public or of the Police. The knowledge that every case in which any member of the public has been shot at by a member of the Police Force will be investigated by some authorized person other than an officer of the Police Force—preferably a senior judicial officer—will reassure the public while at the same time acting as a check upon any tendency to shoot without careful consideration and we recommend the adoption of this suggestion."

I should like you to know that in my view the report goes much too far in suggesting that every case in which any member of the public has been shot at by a member of the police force will be investigated by some authorized person other than an officer of the police force. Each case must, I think, be determined on its merits, and I certainly would not subscribe to a general rule of the kind suggested. So far as United Kingdom practice is concerned, you will see from the memorandum in my despatch that frequently when riots have taken place it has been alleged that the police acted in an unwise or provocative manner, and there are demands for an inquiry into the conduct of the police, but there has been no recent case in which such an inquiry has been granted. In India we generally set our faces against such inquiries. On the slightest provocation Congress would demand inquiries into the action of the police, but there is a real danger of weakening the authority and intiative of the police in times of emergency, if they feel that they will have to face public inquiry into their actions. I am not saying that an inquiry may not at times be necessary, for example, when the Governor on a careful review of the circumstances considers it desirable, or when there is a demand in Parliament here based on reasonable grounds. As you know, Parliament was taking before the war, and will no doubt continue to take when conditions are again normal, an increasing interest in Colonial affairs; so we may expect to have demands for inquiries when the police have had to take strong action against rioters, involving shooting. But the point I want to make is that in my view such inquiry should not be granted as a matter of course; and I thought it right to let you know this, as apparently you were guided by the 1928 Committee's suggestion when considering the Mooloya Estate case, and I did not wish you to assume that I accept their view.

67 CO 54/973/14, no 21   3 Sept 1940

[Reforms]: despatch from Sir A Caldecott to Lord Lloyd on a resolution passed by the Sinhala Maha Sabha demanding dominion status. *Minutes* by K W Blaxter and G E J Gent

In compliance with a request by Mr. S.W.R.D. Bandaranaike as President of the Sinhala Maha Sabha I have the honour to forward copies of a Resolution[1] passed at the Annual Session of that body held on the 24th August, 1940, demanding Dominion Status for Ceylon and requesting an assurance that this demand will be met at the next revision of the Constitution.

2. The Sinhala Maha Sabha has figured in previous correspondence on constitutional issues and all that I need say of it here is that membership of the Sabha is confined to the Sinhalese and that its representatives in the Ministry are Messrs Bandaranaike, Kannangara and Kotalawala. I understand that a recent movement to affiliate it to, or elsewise link it with, the Ceylon National Congress has been without result.

3. From an article which appeared in the "Ceylon Observer" on the 26th August I gather that the Executive Committee of the Ceylon National Congress is considering the following draft resolution:—

---

[1] Not printed.

"that the Secretary of State be requested to make a declaration with regard to political reforms in Ceylon before the expiry of the statutory period of the State Council."

The ultimate aim of the Congress has long been known and declared to be attainment of Dominion Status. Whether therefore, in face of the Sabha's resolution now forwarded the draft Congress motion will be allowed to survive in its present less adventurous form remains to be seen.

4. The issue of constitutional reform rests at present with Your Lordship's announcement of the 15th June that, in view of general dissatisfaction with the present Constitution and of questions that have arisen regarding cognate problems of franchise and delimitation of constituencies, the general election has been postponed; because such postponement is necessary in present circumstances if careful decisions are to be reached on these questions before new elections are held.

5. An acknowledgement by Your Lordship of the receipt of the Sabha's resolution appears to me all that is necessary or advisable.

Minutes on 67

The Sinhala Maha Sabha is the extreme Nationalist organisation, the leading spirit being Mr. Bandaranaike, who is such a bitter opponent of Indian immigration into Ceylon. It is to be expected that this body would come out for Dominion status, & I don't think that the resolution need be taken too seriously, though the number of supporters of demands for Dominion status is likely to increase steadily. The Ceylon National Congress is the more moderate body with a bigger following.

A letter has recently been sent to Sir A. Caldecott inviting his views on the next step which should be taken in consideration of constitutional reform. There has not yet been time for him to reply.

? reply requesting Gov. to inform the President of the Sabha that S. of S. has received their resolution.

K.W.B.
18.10.40

The Sinhala Maha Sabha is a comparatively recent creation of Mr. Bandaranaike, the Minister for Local Administration in Ceylon, and has much the same extreme Sinhalese nationalist colour as the Hindu nationalism of the Hindu Maha Sabha in India. The Ceylon National Congress claims to have a wider basis with some representatives of the minority communities in its membership. The latter is certainly the more important political association in the island, and is sending an unofficial delegation from Ceylon to discuss Indo–Ceylonese problems with Congress in India.

The Governor suggests that the draft resolution of the National Congress which he mentions in paragraph 3 of this despatch may be put into stronger terms under the influence of the Sinhala Maha Sabha; but any alteration of Congress policy in the direction of a demand for Dominion status, unless the minorities obtain assurances from the Sinhalese that their claims will be safeguarded, is a most unlikely development.

The problem of procedure in the matter of making headway with the constitutional position is being discussed on other papers but there is no need to be rushed on the score of this resolution by the Sinhala Maha Sabha. Simply ask that the president of the Sabha may be informed that the resolution has been received by the Secretary of State.

G.E.J.G.
22.10.40

68   CO 54/978/7, no 20   17 Sept 1940
[Reforms]: outward telegram no 558 from Lord Lloyd to Sir A Caldecott on the registration of Indian voters

Your Confidential despatch, 14th June.[1] Indian franchise. I feel sure that Board of Ministers will understand that the resolution adopted by the majority in the State Council on the 28th May advocating the amendment of the Ceylon Constitution for the purpose of restricting opportunities of non-Ceylonese immigrants to achieve enfranchisement in Ceylon would need to be considered by His Majesty's Government with full regard to views of all concerned.

Indian view, both official and unofficial, is not in doubt, and it must be expected that the successful outcome of projected conversations between Ceylon and Indian representatives would be seriously and perhaps fatally prejudiced by action of the kind advocated in the State Council Resolution opposed as it was in the State Council itself by representatives of minority communities in the Island. I recognise importance attached by Board of Ministers to restriction of privilege of franchise as present Constitution provides to immigrants who are genuinely making their permanent homes in Ceylon, but for their part I hope the Board will on further reflection agree that those who thus genuinely choose to adopt status of Ceylonese should not suffer special disabilities as compared with other labourers in Ceylon. Such discrimination would appear to me difficult to contemplate.

The question of Indian franchise must be considered in association with other problems of constitutional reform, but at this juncture especially it would be undesirable to disregard Indian susceptibilities. It must be assumed that Indian representatives at forthcoming Conference will seek full discussion on policy of Board of Ministers and State Council Resolution. I propose, therefore, to suspend my consideration of the Resolution pending the outcome of that Conference. In the meantime I hope that the Board will decide to proceed with revision of registers.

---

[1] See 54.

69   CO 54/974/1, no 2   17 Sept 1940
[European civil servants]: despatch (reply) from Sir A Caldecott to Lord Lloyd on the conditions of employment for European officers

I have the honour to acknowledge receipt of Your Lordship's Secret despatch of the

19th July, 1940,[1] on the subject of the appointment of Deputy Chief Engineer and Manager, Electrical Undertakings and the probationary promotion thereto of Mr. H. H. Jansen.

2. I desire to associate myself entirely with the exception taken by Your Lordship to the Minister's action in this matter; with Your Lordship's reluctance to approve recommendations that are not based primarily on considerations of administrative efficiency; with the disquiet, doubt and apprehension that have long been felt by many as to the tolerability of the conditions under which European officers now serve in this Island; and with Your Lordship's expression of the danger and improbity of subordinating correct principles of appointment to arguments of political expediency. I am indeed grateful for the opportunity given me of offering in a single despatch my general observations on a situation which causes me misgiving no less than it does Your Lordship.

3. Article 86 of the Ceylon (State Council) Order in Council, 1931, on the face of it vests in the Governor complete control of the Public Service. By recourse to Article 22 this control can in fact be rendered final and absolute in its application to any particular case. What is beyond gubernatorial control is the political atmosphere in which officers will have to serve. This point needs emphasis because the average public officer cannot feel, or do, his best in an uncongenial and antipathetic environment.

4. I have no hesitation or doubt in stating that quite 95 per cent of the present European employees of this Government have long found their environment uncongenial and difficult, if not positively hostile. The older of them are restrained from retirement under Article 88 only by considerations of domestic finance or by a sense of obligation to stick to their jobs for the duration of the war. Of the younger men, to whom Article 88 does not apply, not a few express regret at ever having come here and dissatisfaction that our local conditions should not have been realistically explained to them in England before they accepted appointment.

5. I can also state without doubt or hesitation that social and political opinion in this Island among all non-European communities is predominantly and progressively nationalistic and thereby in effect, if not in essence, anti-British. The great majority of Sinhalese and Tamils want to see as many Britishers out of the Island as possible, and as few of them as possible into it. It is true that among the educated and propertied classes there are many who realise that for a number of posts recruitment from Britain will for some years to come be necessary. But when it comes to an actual indent these very persons will be found joining in the protestations against it; for the reason that they have sons, nephews or other relatives whose chances of public employment they do not wish to prejudice. There is undoubtedly unemployment in the upper classes, even amongst youths who have been educated in Europe.

6. For protest and opposition against European recruitment every facility seems to have been provided. First, under Public Service Regulation 13 an Executive Committee will have its say; then the State Council will debate a "March Resolution"; next the Budget Debate will provide the opportunity to delete financial provision for any appointment which the Governor fills uncomfortably with the wishes of the Executive Committee and State Council. Finally there will ensue all the pother, Press publicity and recrimination inseparable from the enactment of a Governor's

---

[1] See 61.

Ordinance to restore the deleted provision. All this will be very enjoyable for the politician; for the Public Service (and in particular for the appointee or promotee concerned) it can only be detestable.

7. Fuel for awkward argument is often taken from published correspondence. At the moment of writing I am having a tussle with the Ministers over European recruitment for the Port Police. The Home Minister quoted to me in conversation the passage in paragraph 5 of Lord Swinton's despatch No.620 of the 14th November, 1932 (Ceylon Sessional Paper XXIII/1933) which anticipates that "the recruitment of European Officers will be confined to the filling of a limited number of posts for which special experience or qualifications are required." What special qualifications or experience, the Minister enquired, will a European recruit for the Port Police possess that a local Burgher candidate would lack. I replied that he would be British and that in dealing with Europeans, Australians and New Zealanders (including Troops) passing through our pivotal Port I considered an adequate proportion of British Inspectors in the Port Police essential. That reply was of course sound sense; but, if it were given to a similar query in State Council, the Governor would at once be accused of improperly attaching a racial significance to Lord Swinton's words and a debate of a nature most injurious to the morale of the Port Police would inevitably ensue.

8. I have heard it said here that the lot of our European officers would have been less unpleasant, and contentions as to their recruitment or retention fewer, if control of the public service had not been vested in the Governor and a Public Services Commission composed entirely of European Officers of State. Possibly; but the Services would not in my opinion have stood for any other arrangement and retirements under Article 88 would have been wholesale. The fundamental error in my view was that of bringing Executive Committees (which are nothing better than haphazard agglomerations of political busybodies) into every question of recruitment or promotion and on the ground floor. This is the effect of Public Service Regulation 13, which was the outcome of pages 140–41 of the Donoughmore Report. If any body, other than the Public Services Commission, had to be consulted it should have been the Board of Ministers, as being less irresponsible than an Executive Committee and in personal contact, whenever necessary, with the Governor. As things are, should the Board of Ministers agree to introduce a "March Resolution" for outside recruitment against the advice of an Executive Committee the motion is likely to meet with opposition from a majority of the Councillors who will side with their unportfolioed colleagues on the Executive Committee.

9. My recommendations for the reform of the Constitution contained an emphatic request for the cancellation, whatever happens, of Public Service Regulation 13 and suggestions for a recomposition of the Public Services Commission. Although implementation of these proposals might improve the position, we have now reached a stage at which it is necessary to realize that, whatever is done, opposition to European employment has become a political stalking-horse which will be trotted out on every possible occasion. Members of the State Council, if deprived of their powers of interference as members of Executive Committees, will carry on their attacks from the citadel of the "March Resolution." It might perhaps have been possible at their inception in March, 1933, to refuse to take cognizance of such resolutions even as advisory motions. The full correspondence concerning them will be found in Sessional Paper XXIII/1933. To have done so, however, would have

meant merely the transference of opposition and protests to the Budget Debate or to special *ad hoc* motions. Even if the salaries of officials had been made non-votable by Order-in-Council, the antagonistic atmosphere that surrounds the European Officer would not have been dissipated; on the contrary it would in my opinion have been intensified.

10. It is true that some Ministers (notably Mr. Senanayake) are in favour of recruiting highly qualified Europeans for key posts on high salaries for a term of years. Their aversion is not so much to the employment of Britishers as to their emplacement on the permanent and pensionable staff. Even so such temporary, highly-qualified and highly-paid experts cannot hope to escape the antipathy and mistrust that surrounds the permanent European official. I recommend that your Personal Branch should obtain, by interview or otherwise, from Professor L. P. Abercombie (who recently visited Ceylon to advise on the siting and planning of the Kandy University) his impressions and memories of how a leading British authority can be treated by Ceylon Ministries.

11. The Ceylonese antipathy towards British officers is of course nothing new. I remember the late Mr. J. Strachan when he returned to Malaya as General Manager for Railways, relating insults and indignities to which he had been subjected by members of the Finance Committee of the old Legislative Council during his directorate of Public Works in this Island, which could not probably be matched to-day. The trouble is that the long duration of this antipathy has generated among many European Officials a reciprocal antipathy towards the Ceylonese. The atmosphere may not be actually deteriorating, but its inimicality is persistent and its effect on those who live in it is accumulative. Moreover the anti-European complex is no longer confined to politicians, but is to be found in some strata of the public service itself. In considering therefore a European recruitment there has to be set against the advantages of superior qualifications and ability in the candidate the disadvantages of imperfect collaboration and continual fractious criticism of his work after appointment. There is also the consideration that, as the nature of our local conditions becomes more and more widely known, fewer and fewer good European candidates will be attracted.

12. I deem it right that I should at this point confess the increasing difficulty that I personally experience, after not quite three years in the Island, in fighting against the reciprocal antipathy mentioned in the preceding paragraph. There is an Eastern proverb to the effect that many small pricks make one big sore. If a friend of mine were to ask, on behalf of himself or of a person in whom he was interested, for my personal advice as to acceptance of a Ceylon appointment I could not with a good conscience advise him in the affirmative.

13. In the recent cases of Mr. Strong (Conservator of Forests) and Mr. Bradby (Principal of Royal College) I have succeeded by personal suasion and influence in obtaining a more or less willing request for European recruitment and a decent reception of the person appointed. I trust that the same will soon be predicable of Mr. Ivor Jennings, the Principal designate of University College; although I have just read in the newspaper that a portrait in oils of Professor Marrs (than whom young Ceylon could not have had a wiser, more patient or kinder mentor) has been slashed into ribbons by some disgruntled student. If persuasion should fail in the case of a recruitment or appointment that I consider essential, I shall not hesitate to ask your permission for the exercise of my powers under Article 22. It must however be

realized that every time resort is had to these powers stimulus and impetus will be given to the insularity and nationalism of our politicians, and the hostility of the atmosphere in which European officials have to work will be thereby enhanced.

14. I am painfully aware that the wholly unsatisfactory position reported in this despatch represents but a single facet of a general political situation that is equally unsatisfactory. Ceylon's loyalty to the Empire during this war, which I assess at over 99 per cent, should not be mistaken for something that it is not. It is due to two things, first, the realization that Nazi victory would set an end to Ceylonese nationalism; second, a high sentimental regard for the King's Person and Throne. The general election has been postponed and Sama-Samajist leaders are under detention. We are thus enjoying a lull, but not a calm. So soon as a victorious end to the war is in sight agitation will again be rampant for constitutional reform, for Dominion status, even for Swaraj. The pivot of my own Reforms Proposals, now two years old, was the anticipation that true political parties might emerge from the introduction of a Cabinet system. My experience over the last two years has belied that hope. The foundations of political parties could only be laid by the present Ministers and the two, or at most three other politicians to whom the word "Statesman" could conceivably be applied even in a restricted local sense. Unfortunately the Ministers have played so long and with such finesse in the dual rôle of Ministers on the one hand and creature-Chairmen of Executive Committees on the other that whatever may be left of the Dr. Jekyll in them can never be strong or courageous enough to shake off the Mr. Hyde. They are opportunists, not creators of policy; trimmers, not leaders; puppets, not agents. The appointment of a Commission to examine and report on the whole problem of Ceylon will in the opinion of all my advisers prove inevitable.

70   CO 54/973/17, no 1   10 Oct 1940
[Indo–Ceylon relations]: inward telegram no 2098-S from Lord Linlithgow to Mr Amery on the visit to India by a deputation of Ceylon ministers

Arrangements have as you know been made for a Ceylon deputation containing two Ministers (Messrs. Corea and Senanayake) for informal official discussions on matters of common interest early in November. Announcement has now been made by Executive Committee of the Ceylon National Congress that these two gentlemen will thereafter, with certain others, constitute a delegation to discuss with Indian National Congress the question of present and future relations between India and Ceylon regarding all matters of mutual interest.

2. We cannot of course predict at this stage what the relations of Government of India with Congress may be early in November. But I cannot help feeling that it is somewhat improper that Ministers on an official visit to this country (? should) (2 corrupt groups) after official visit, discuss with Congress matters which, at least so long as Government of India are a Government, can only be regulated by that Government. It may be of course that they have no appreciation of the possible embarrassment to us of their treating the Indian National Congress as a kind of

parallel Government: but I think that you will agree that we are (? justified in) taking some exception to this move. I shall be glad if you would mention to the Colonial Office. If the Colonial Office feel that they cannot or should not intervene to dissuade ministers from their intention, I agree that there will be nothing for it but to acquiesce.

71   CO 54/973/16, no 16   15 Oct 1940
'Note on the postponement of the election': joint note by G E J Gent and K W Blaxter

Under the provisions of the Ceylon Constitution Order in Council as they stood last year the Governor had to dissolve the State Council after it had been in being for five years if it had not been dissolved sooner.

For some time past it has been clear that in certain ways the Ceylon Constitution has not been working well; and when Sir Andrew Caldecott went to Ceylon as Governor in 1937 he was instructed to examine the constitutional position and to submit recommendations. These recommendations were duly received, and it was decided as a next step that they should be laid before the State Council for their consideration. The debate in the State Council showed lack of agreement between the Sinhalese and the minorities on most of the important questions. (e.g., the retention of the Executive Committees, "weightage" in the representation of the minority communities, communal franchise). Mr. MacDonald then suggested various methods of procedure for further pursuit of a solution. At this stage, the Spring of 1940, we received from Ceylon reports of increasing unrest amongst the Indian labourers in the Island. This unrest was due, partly to the growing consciousness of labour in Ceylon, under the fostering guidance of Pandit Nehru who paid a personal visit to Ceylon, and partly to suspicions aroused amongst the labourers of an anti-Indian policy of the Ceylon Ministers and the retaliatory ban placed by the Government of India on the immigration of "unskilled" labourers from India; this ban was imposed owing to the Government of India's dissatisfaction with the policy followed by the Ceylon Government in the treatment of Indians in the Island, and this quarrel between the two Governments over the rights of Indians in the matter of the franchise and employment, and the terms on which they may enter or reside in the Island, is still unresolved.

A General Election to the State Council was due to be held not later than January 1941 and certain politicians in Ceylon—both Sinhalese and Indian—were using the occasion of the coming election to stir up communal feeling and unrest amongst Indian labour.

It was necessary to take action to "stop the rot" and it was decided:—

(1) to detain under the Defence Regulations certain leaders of the Sama Samaj (Communist) party who were particularly active in stirring up trouble and whose representatives in the State Council had just indulged in some inexcusable defamation of the British defence forces; and

(2) to pass an Order in Council to enable the elections to be postponed for two years. These measures were taken last summer and have certainly resulted both in a relaxation of the political tension and a lessening of labour unrest.

The actual words of the official announcement of postponement of the election was as follows:—

> "In view of the general dissatisfaction with the present Constitution and of the questions that have arisen regarding cognate problems of franchise and delimitation of constituencies, an Order-in-Council will be enacted to enable the postponement for two years of the election which is due not later than next January under Article 19. This postponement is necessary in present circumtances if careful decisions are to be reached on these questions before new elections are held."

The Election of a new State Council is, under the present Constitution, immediately followed by the Councillors distributing themselves by vote to form the seven Executive Committees of the Council. Each Committee then elects its Chairman, and the resulting seven Chairmen are appointed by the Governor to be his Ministers; and they then have a rather indefinite corporate existence as the Board of Ministers (which also includes the three Officers of State—Chief Secretary, Legal Secretary, Financial Secretary). The suspension of the General Election means that the election of new Executive Committees (and Chairmen) is also suspended; and the Jaffna (Tamil) Association's present desire is that a special arrangement should be made to permit new Executive Committees (and Chairmen) to be elected, despite the suspension of the General Elections, in the hope that their community may snatch up one of the chairmanships and so have a Tamil on the Board of Ministers.

72   CO 54/977/7, no 12   18 Oct 1940
'Things Ceylonese': twelfth periodical report by Sir A Caldecott for CO

The budget
1. The State Council has wasted more time and paper than ever over the budget; and, as a result of insertions and additions, the last state of the estimated deficit is worse than the first. The Leader of the House introduced the Supply Bill with an assurance that after its passage a Reservations Committee would, similarly to last year, be immediately appointed for the purpose of reducing provision wherever possible. The State Council however showed itself more interested in increasing than in decreasing expenditure, and at a Board Meeting held immediately after the close of the Budget Session the Ministers with apparent weakness decided not to appoint the promised Reservations Committee but to review the financial position in three months' time.

Qualified assent thereto
2. The Acting Financial Secretary had at my request previously impressed on the Ministers the very serious view which I take of the financial situation, and they had appeared to him to take the warning to heart. I am indeed inclined to the view that their failure to appoint a Reservations Committee now is due to the consideration that three of them (Senanayake, Corea and Bandaranaike) are about to leave on our Exploratory Mission to India and fear that, if a Committee were to get busy during their absence, the expenditure of their three Ministries might be pruned more than

that of departments under the remaining Ministers. In assenting to the Supply Ordinance I have informed the Board of Ministers in writing that my assent is conditional on the promised Reservations Committee being appointed immediately on the Mission's return from India, i.e. in about six weeks' time. This short postponement will enable us to gauge the prospects of Indo–Ceylon agreement on questions of trade and tariff and to watch the trend of International developments in the Far East.

New loan money

3. It will be necessary in the near future to raise locally more money under our Loan Ordinance for loan works already in hand. The Ministers, I understand, are in favour of a prospectus to the effect that any money so raised and not found to be required for immediate disbursement will be applied to war purposes. I have told the Acting Financial Secretary that I am opposed to any idea of baiting a loan for local uses with a problematical and probably unrealizable relevancy to war purposes. The two things must be kept distinct. Here the matter rests for the moment.

The financial secretary

4. Mr. Huxham who has been on furlough in Kashmir will join our delegates to the Delhi War Supplies Conference towards the end of this month, and will also take part in the exploratory Conference on Indo–Ceylon relations. In his absence I have enjoyed working with Mr. C.H. Collins as Acting Financial Secretary. He combines tact with firmness, and enjoys the confidence and friendship of the Ministers and of many of the State Councillors in a marked degree. I have heard from European as well as Sinhalese sources that both he and Mr. Wodeman have carried more weight in Council Debates than has been associated with Officers of State for a long time.

The secretariat

5. On Mr. Huxham's return to Ceylon Mr. Collins will take up his new appointment of Deputy Chief Secretary. Under Mr. Wodeman and him the Secretariat will be strongly captained. The transfer of Mr. Hartwell to Palestine has meant loss of the Secretariat officer responsible for War and Defence files; but he has been replaced by Mr. Renison, my knowledge of whose work as Private Secretary in 1937–38 gives me confidence that the efficiency of the Defence work will not suffer.

The Bandaranaike Ratwatte wedding

6. I attended the wedding of "Young Banda" to Miss Ratwatte (daughter of Dissawa Barnes Ratwatte and niece of the late Sir Cudah) at Balangoda and, a week later, their ceremonial home-coming to Sir Solomon Bandaranaike's residence near Veyangoda. This marriage is of great sociological and political importance. Whatever opinion one may hold of young Bandaranaike as Minister for Local Administration, or as founder and leader of the Sinhala Maha Sabha, or as a pervert for political purposes from Christianity to Buddhism, or as a master of nationalistic rhetoric, one is bound to admit that he has taken to himself a wife who appears thoroughly nice, placid and sensible and that this union between a first-rank family of the lowlands with a first-rank family of the Kandyan highlands represents an accretion of considerable political influence to the Sinhala Maha Sabha. This is already noticeable in the parental attitude towards the happy pair. When I first met Sir Solomon (three

years ago) and Barnes Ratwatte Dissawa (two years ago) both were extreme examples of "the old gang", and their first topic of conversation was the rottenness of the State Council and of Ceylon politics in general. *Ils ont changé tout cela.* Both were purring, sometimes audibly, as the Sinhala Maha Sabha address of loyalty and flattery to the bridegroom was read out and when young Banda in his reply passionately referred with his usual irredentism to the renascence of Lanka. As he spoke in Sinhalese, which I cannot understand, Sir Solomon volunteered to interpret and muttered the choicer morsels of his son's oratory into my ear; and with obvious gusto. It was nice indeed to behold the old man (who has served us so well) such a proud parent. Three years ago the relations between father and son appeared to me as bordering on estrangement.

7. The rising tide of nationalism can of course no more be checked here or in India than could the waves which wetted Canute. The immersion therein of the two old conservative families of Dias-Bandaranaike and Ratwatte was only a question of time, and its acceleration by this wedding need not be unduly deplored. On the other hand a good wife and the discipline of married life may help to provide young Banda with the ballast that hitherto he has so sadly lacked.

Indo–Ceylon relations

8. Mr. Corea (Labour, Industry & Commerce) has been the first Minister to leave for India. He will be a member of our delegation to the Delhi War Supplies Conference as well as of the exploratory 'goodwill' mission. He has left early for two reasons. The first is to get into touch with coconut interests (and officials concerned with them) in Travancore, and the second is that foretold in paragraph 7 of my last Notes, i.e. as President of the Ceylon National Congress he is to pay a visit to the headquarters of the Indian Congress. In bidding me goodbye he told me that this visit would take only a day, and that there was no programme for discussions. I warned him that he was a Minister as well as President of Congress, and he gave me the impression that he sufficiently understood the niceties and dangers of this dual role.

9. I hear that the Planters' Association are sending two representatives to be in Delhi during the informal discussions, in order that the Ministers may be able to keep in touch with planting interests. The Ministers have apparently agreed to this arrangement, and the Association's choice of representatives (Messrs Temple and Newton) is a happy one. Mr. Temple has asked to see me before he goes. The Ceylon Indian Congress is also sending an emissary to watch developments at Delhi, but I do not know his name. As far as I am aware the Ministers have taken no cognizance of this arrangement, and the emissary is likely to possess only a nuisance, if any, value.

War funds

10. Ceylon's pecuniary contributions to War Funds and War Charities stood on October 10th as follows;—

1. *Send a Plane Fund		640,249
2. Jaffna Plane Fund		39,898
3. Ceylon Government War Purposes Fund		738,897
4. *Gloucester Fund (Red Cross & St. John's)		406,783
5. King George's Fund for Sailors		35,254
6. *Local Sailors' Fund		35,869

7. St. Dunstan's Fund		30,825
8. Hospital Supply Association (for cost of materials which the Association makes up)		22,294
9. *Air Raid Distress Fund		29,379
10. Government contribution		5,000,000
11. Colombo Municipal contribution		200,000
	TOTAL	Rs 7,179,448

The items prefixed by an asterisk are being run by the "Times of Ceylon"; Nos. 1 and 9 were initiated by that newspaper and Nos. 4 and 6 taken over by it shortly after initiation. The Local Sailors' Fund, which is for the entertainment of men of H.M. Ships visiting Colombo, has enabled the equipment of a "Fleet Club" which challenges comparison with any other club of its kind in the world. There can be no port in the Empire where men of the Royal Navy are more welcomed or better cared for. Colombo has not always had this reputation.

Times of Ceylon

11.   I had a long interview a fortnight ago with the Managing Director of the Times of Ceylon, Mr. P.J. Matthews, on the subject of War Funds. From that subject the conversation drifted to generalities and Matthews remarked that rumour had it that I disapproved of his paper. To this I replied that I considered that (a) some of its criticisms of the administration during the second quarter of the year had been unwise and hysterical and (b) that its more recent "Dominion Status for Ceylon" leader had been premature and injudicious. He replied that as regards (a) many people had thought that we should not get through the summer with its problems of labour unrest, Sama-Samajism etc without a constitutional bust-up and had felt that the sooner the bust-up was induced the better. Events had proved that that feeling had been erroneous, and the handling of the situation by the administration had been justified by its results; of which he and everybody else was very glad and appreciative. His paper had however all along faithfully reflected what was honest, if wrong, public opinion among many strata of the community. As to (b) he agreed that his leader-writer had dived too soon and too deep; but that was the worst of these leader-writers! After a long and interesting conversation, in which points of agreement largely outnumbered points of disagreement, he expressed the hope that if at any time I felt any doubt or concern about his paper I would invite him to talk things over. This was a very different termination of an interview from that in which, in November 1937, I asked the Acting Editor (Mr. Peter Batten whose departure I reported in my last Notes)[1] to refrain from falsely inventing agenda and proceedings of my conferences with Ministers at Queen's House. To this request Mr. Batten retorted that invention was the mother of journalism and that if an Editor couldn't get fact it was his business and vocation to substitute "intelligent imagination".

Our policy of de-imperialization

12.   I am a member of the Overseas League and have been responsible for others joining. I must confess however to grave doubt as to the wisdom of the League's latest stunt in propaganda, i.e. the broadcast dissemination (as a supplement to their

---

[1] See 63, para 3.

magazine) of Sir Norman Angell's[2] pamphlet "What is the British Empire?" *We have done our best to unconquer our conquests; disannex our annexations; turn what was originally an empire into a group of sovereign and independent nations; indeed the empire, so far as most of it is concerned, long since came to an end . . . "If valueless"* (argued an American) *"why not give up the empire?"* To which the answer is that we are giving it up to people who live there. To which the Ceylon nationalist retorts "Sez you?" There is a way and a time to say things. In this matter and in so far as Ceylon is concerned I do not consider that now was the time or Sir Norman Angell's the way. However the pamphlets are now all over the Island and the wind has been sown.

Tea coupons

13.   I have often commented on the extreme difficulty of the Governor's job here. He is outside the Governmental machine until something goes wrong and then he is called in without any previous inkling to set things right. Last week Mr. Senanayake suddenly demanded an interview at which to inform me that the price of tea coupons was so high that many might fail on their contracts under the Tea Supply Scheme. Thereafter at consecutive conferences with him, the Tea Controller, and the Legal Secretary or his representative I satisfied myself at least on one point, which is that neither the Minister nor the Controller know (nor under the present law possess the means of ascertaining) who holds the coupons, how many are being held against contracts and how many are in the hands of speculators. The Minister will introduce a bill to give the Controller the necessary powers of control over coupons as soon as Council reassembles in mid-November, and in the mean time Emergency Regulations have been framed to the same end under the Defence Act in the hope of safeguarding the contracted supply to Britain and the Forces. I am not however at all satisfied myself of the possibility of dealing satisfactorily with the post-contractual position in the first quarter of 1941. If the figures given to me at the conferences are correct there will (including 33 millions to be issued in November) be 98 million coupons extant to cover all tea exports between now and March 31st next. Fifty million pounds are still to be supplied to the Ministry of Supply on the present 1940 contract, and if a similar amount were needed for the first quarter of 1941 coupons would be insufficient by two million even if there were no contracted exports for America, Australia, etc. The difficulty has of course arisen from the 5% cut in the international quota; the coupon market prices having risen in unison with those of the commodity market. A free coupon market is in fact irreconcilable with a contractual scheme for tea supply to Britain at a fixed price so long as the prices offering in American and Australian markets are not fixed but rising. It is a pity that this was not foreseen by the Ministry.

A new acting minister

14.   Mr. Rajah Hewavitarne's election to be Chairman of Mr. Corea's Executive Committee during the latter's absence in India is a happy one and I had pleasure in swearing him in as Acting Minister. Mr. Sri Pathmanathan who acted for Mr. Corea last year made persistent but unsuccesful efforts to get me temporarily to release the

---

[2] Author and lecturer; correspondent of a number of American newspapers; Labour MP for Bradford North, 1929–1931; Nobel Peace Prize, 1933.

two Communist members of the Committee out of their Place of Detention at Kandy for the purpose of voting for him. Mr. Sri Pathmanathan's recent speeches and tactics have not been such as to qualify him for any ministerial portfolio.[3]

---

[3] Lloyd minuted (9 Nov 1940) on this report: 'Very interesting. No. 12 is much better than its predecessor.'

---

73 CO 54/973/17, no 6   22 Oct 1940

[Indo–Ceylon relations]: inward unnumbered telegram from Sir A Caldecott to Lord Lloyd on the visit to India by a deputation of Ceylon ministers

With reference to your secret and personal telegram of 19th October.[1] I interviewed Ministers yesterday and at their request have sent confidential telegram to the Viceroy which is repeated to you by my telegram No.931.[2] Ceylon National Congress is hopelessly unsystematic and I understand decision to send representatives to make contact with the Indian Congress was the decision of the Working Committee only and not of the Congress so that it is doubtful what, if any, standing such representatives possess. I further understand that two out of five representatives will probably not go in which case there will be only Corea who is President of Congress, Senanayake and George Silva, Member for Kandy. Last named is notoriously irresponsible and in my opinion, it is well that the two former (who thoroughly realise that they must do or say nothing that would embarrass the Government of India or in any way affect official conversations) will be there to restrain him. I am informed that delegation to the Indian Congress has also been sent by Ceylon Indian Congress and I do not anticipate much constructive result from this triangular contact.

---

[1] cf 70.

[2] Tel 931 read: 'Board of ministers desire me clear that members of forthcoming ministerial mission to the Government of India have no intention of treating with the Indian National Congress on any question of Indo–Ceylon relations. Any conversations which any of them may have with political leaders in India will be strictly unofficial and informal.

2. Ministers have undertaken to meet the Indian Congress Leaders on behalf of Ceylon National Congress but not in their Ministerial capacity and their discussions will be on the subject of the influence of the Indian National Congress upon the Ceylon Indian Congress and other Indian bodies in Ceylon. Please give any publicity that you may think desirable to this communication' (CO 54/973/17, no 5).

---

74 CO 54/975/4, no 13   29 Oct 1940

[Indo–Ceylon relations]: letter from T W Davies to S Caine on the visit by Ceylon ministers to India

[A principal at the CO and a member of the UK trade delegation to the USA in 1938, Davies acted as an observer for the CO at the Eastern Group Conference, Delhi, in 1940. He also acted as an observer at the Indo–Ceylon ministerial talks and visited Ceylon. His correspondence with Caine (assistant secretary, head of the Economics Dept within the General Division of the CO) was sent c/o the private secretary to the viceroy.]

You would have seen the telegram from Ceylon to the Secretary of State No. 919 of the 15th October about my proposed visit to that colony. You will have noticed from it that preliminary conversations regarding India and Ceylon relations are to take place next month. Actually they are to start on the 4th November, and I cannot conceive that they will not be over before the Eastern Group Conference is over. In fact, I think it is very unlikely that they will last more than a week. Their existence, therefore, should not mean any delay in my departure for Ceylon.

2. On the part of Ceylon, three Ministers are going to take part in these discussions—Corea, and two others who are expected to arrive almost immediately. On the side of India, I understand that Sir Girja Shankar Bajpai will be in charge. These discussions are to be entirely political, I understand. They will relate only to the immigration question. If that is settled, there should of course be no difficulty whatsoever in coming to an economic agreement. I lunched with Corea and the Ceylon Delegation (with the exception of Huxham who was out) to-day, and I understand from them that the crux of the matter is the question whether (a) birth in Ceylon and the absence of evidence of choice of Indian domicile, or (b) a period of years in Ceylon (which must not be unduly long), coupled with a declaration of permanent settlement, must be accepted as constituting domicile and conferring full citizenship rights.

3. I think Corea appreciates how highly undesirable it would be to let these political talks create a deadlock with a resulting Tariff War. He also, I am sure, appreciates the fact that if it comes to Tariff War, the trump cards are in the hands of India, since the loss of Ceylon's Indian market for copra would be a severe blow to her. Corea tells me that the two Ministers about to arrive here are by no means such reasonable men as he is himself. As you will know, I have up to the present been ignorant of Ceylon politics. I hope to meet the Ministers in a day or two. One of them, I believe, (I cannot remember his name for the moment) was Secretary of the Oxford Union when I was up.

4. Apparently these impending political discussions (of which the purpose is to prepare the way for the economic discussions) were Corea's idea. He went on to say that he believed that he made a mistake in making the proposal since, if they come to nothing, India may fulfil the threat she has previously made to denounce the interim trade agreement which, in the absence of such political discussions, she might perhaps allow to continue in being even for the duration of the war. If this is so, I think Corea certainly did make a mistake. It seems to me obvious that if the trade agreement could be extended for the duration of the war, Ceylon ought to be very much more than satisfied.

75   CO 54/975/4, no 19   16 Nov 1940

[Indo–Ceylon relations]: letter from T W Davies to S Caine on the breakdown of the ministerial talks

I hardly know whether it is worth while or not continuing my previous letter No. 9 of 6th November about the Ceylon "Goodwill" talks. Before you read this letter, you will probably have received an official report from the Government of Ceylon. But the perhaps erroneous views which have been formed by an innocent observer may nevertheless be of interest. They are based principally on Gimson, Controller of Immigration in Ceylon who was present at the talks, and upon persons concerned from the Government of India side, with just a little Huxham thrown in. I have not since I last wrote to you been in other than brief social contact with the Ceylon Ministers, Messrs. Bandaranaike and Senanayake, partly accounted for by the fact that they were often out of Delhi on off days.

2.   The point upon which the Goodwill talks turned was simply the question of the terms upon which an Indian immigrant into Ceylon should obtain the rights of citizenship. There is no point in my setting out in detail exactly what the position is in Ceylon now, what the Indian side wanted, and what the Ceylon side would offer. It is apparent that on this elastic and technical matter there was every opportunity to take stand upon any one of myriad planks if necessary, and there ought to have been abundant grounds for a compromise. The way that the thing was actually worked was most peculiar. As I indicated in my earlier letter, the talks were given out as being preliminary and exploratory. I had an account of them from Gimson from day to day as they proceeded, and he never quite gave up hope. Corea and Huxham sometimes said they were hopeful, sometimes hopeless. Gimson said that he was amazed at the patience of Bajpai and his fellow representatives of the Government of India. They were everlastingly forbearing even though Bandaranaike was rude to them on one occasion. There came a time when Gimson drew up some compromise proposals which he thought might possibly be the basis of an agreement, and he gave them to Corea who said that he agreed with them and would show them to his fellow-Ministers. When the next meeting came, Corea had these proposals before him on the table, but they were turned face downwards so that his brother-Ministers should not see them; and at that meeting Senanayake and Bandaranaike were so uncompromising that the talks could not go forward. Gimson asked the Secretary of the Goodwill Delegation a little later what Bandaranaike and Senanayake had thought of his proposals, and the Secretary replied that they had never seen them!

3.   The same day the Ceylon and Indian representatives came to draw up a Press Communiqué. The Indians wanted to say that the talks had been "adjourned", the Ceylonese insisted on substituting the words "broken down". Surely, the Indian side suggested, it would be as well for the Ministers to telegraph back to Ceylon? but no, they said it was not worth doing more than informing the Governor by telegram and the Communiqué had better be issued tomorrow.

4.   The Communiqué was accordingly issued the next day, and the next thing that the Government of India knew was that they received a telegram from the Governor of Ceylon to the Viceroy saying that the Ministers had no authority to come to any conclusions and, therefore, had no authority to let the talks break down without prior reference to him. This, of course, was after the Communiqué had appeared in the Press.

5.   The whole thing is to me, with my absence of background knowledge of Ceylon politics, obscure. It seems also to be obscure to Gimson. I think one can understand the attitude of Bandaranaike who just wants everything to break down. This will gain him votes in Ceylon, and things have gone just as he would have wished. Senanayake has possibly trailed along in his footsteps. What about Corea and Huxham? Corea is a more sensible man than the other two Ministers, and furthermore he is personally interested in copra since he owns plantations. The breakdown of the Goodwill negotiations therefore, if it is followed by a tariff war on the part of Indian authorities

(which may not be the case), may have adverse effects on his pocket. These are the reasons why I should have thought that he would at least have shown Gimson's compromise draft to the other two Ministers.

6. I said before that certain people in India contemplate with tranquility, or even with pleasure, the possibility of breaking Ceylon economically; and with equal tranquility people like Huxham have mentioned the possibility of a trade war between the two countries, Ceylon, for instance, prohibiting the imports of India. All this time the Eastern Group Conference is rolling along, busy considering, amongst other things, how Ceylon should in future increase its imports from India, and how it will be getting from India a number of things which it has hitherto been getting from the United Kingdom.

76   CO 54/975/4, no 5   25 Nov 1940
[Indo–Ceylon relations]: outward telegram no 698 from Lord Lloyd to Sir A Caldecott on the breakdown of the ministerial talks and a suggested compromise

Your telegram No. 974. Your telegram No. 976.

1. I very much regret to hear that informal preliminary negotiations with Government of India have broken down before opportunity appears to have been given for discussion of trade problems of immediate urgency to Ceylon.

2. Status of resident Indians in Ceylon and restrictions on Indian immigration appear to me to be problems incapable of agreement with India if Ceylonese proposals are persisted in, and failure on this account to make headway with *rapprochement* with India has such threatening prospects for Ceylon that I find it difficult to leave matters to take their course in view of my responsibility to His Majesty's Government and Parliament for good order and government of the island.

3. Subject to your advice as soon as you receive Minister's report, which I should like to have with least possible delay, it may even be necessary for me to consider proposing to the Secretary of State for India that he should suggest to Government of India a *modus vivendi* on following lines pending more permanent settlement between Governments of India and Ceylon, viz.:—

(a) no change in the present immigration law in Ceylon;
(b) no change in the present Order in Council provisions for franchise which would however be more strictly operated;
(c) assurance that I shall not approve discrimination against resident Indians in matter of public employment including daily paid employment.

On last point (on which Government of India would no doubt expect satisfaction) I should like your advice as to effective powers of His Majesty's Government under present Order in Council.

4. In return we should secure from Government of India (a) assurance of no change in present trade advantages in India for Ceylon produce, (b) relaxation of present ban on emigration of Indian workers to Ceylon at least to extent of workers and their families returning to island from temporary visit to India.

5. I fear that I should have to expect that undertakings in paragraph 3 on behalf

of Ceylon would not be acceptable to Ceylonese Ministers, and that negotiations on that basis with Government of India would have to be undertaken by this Department in London and might result in resignation of Ministers and possibly non co-operation by majority of State Council.

6. Even so, it may be necessary to consider that course as alternative to drifting into such further difficulties with Government of India as might bring widespread distress and demoralisation in Ceylon at a crucial stage in the war. It seems to me deplorable that while Board of Ministers have shown admirable appreciation of need of united front in war effort and have been discussing at Delhi co-operation in war production with representatives of India and other Empire countries this impasse in Indo–Ceylon relations should be prolonged in present critical time.[1]

---

[1] Caldecott responded in tel 1002 of 27 Nov: 'Present position is that short-hand proceedings of Conference are being printed and should be ready by the time Huxham and Corea return from War Supply Conference next week when they will collaborate with Senanayake and Bandaranaike who have already returned in preparation of formal report for submission to Board of Ministers and myself. I have impressed on Ministers absolute necessity of silence on this subject until the Board and myself have had time fully to consider the report and resultant situation. Report should be read[y] for consultation by the time I return from India on or about 18th December, after which I will report fully to you' (CO 54/975/4, no 8).

77   CO 54/975/4, no 9   27 Nov 1940
[Indo–Ceylon relations]: inward unnumbered telegram from Sir A Caldecott to Lord Lloyd on the breakdown of the ministerial talks and the question of trade retaliation

My telegram No. 1002.[1] Following is excerpt from private letter to me from James, member of Indian Legislative Assembly and of Standing Emigration Committee. *Begins*:—"Nobody here wants to take up the question of trade retaliation. Both countries can play at that game. Moreover everybody wants to avoid open quarrel on trade matters between two countries in the Empire. So the situation may be allowed to rest for the time being in the hope that better counsels may prevail in Ceylon and that the British Government may assist in persuading Ceylon Ministers to face the necessity for reasonable compromise." Following corroboration of above comes from Huxham:—

> "I am hopeful that India will maintain the *status quo* so long as no fresh step is taken to the detriment of Indians in Ceylon. All reports so far reaching me ascribe the breakdown of the Conference to the antics of Bandaranaike and it is in my view preferable that he should have done his mischief during the negotiations rather than torpedo the Agreement in the State Council after it had been reached by the Mission, which he would certainly have done if he had not been a member of the Mission. After interview with Senanayake this morning I am not certain that the breakdown of discussions may not have been due to his inability to make himself plain in English as well as to the interruptions of Bandaranaike and I propose while in Madras to discuss the whole position with Rutherford who was member of the Indian delegation. As

---

[1] See 76, note 1.

I understand the position India is not insisting on undertaking suggested in paragraph 3(c) of your telegram No. 698,[2] and I do not altogether despair of reaching a settlement that will not involve non-co-operation here even though it may have to be imposed by you from without. Although therefore I realise the necessity to remove the present impasse without delay I feel it advisable thoroughly to examine and digest the proceedings of the recent Conference before taking any further action.

[2] See 76.

78 CO 54/973/13, no 24   18 Dec 1940
[Reforms]: despatch from Lord Lloyd to Sir A Caldecott on the postponement of reform until the end of the war

I have the honour to refer to Sir Andrew Caldecott's confidential despatch of the 23rd of April[1] on the subject of constitutional reform in Ceylon.

2. I have had this question under my consideration in the light of the comments which you make in that despatch and in subsequent correspondence, and the announcement which was made on the 15th of June to the effect that an Order in Council would be enacted to enable the postponement for two years of the general election which was due to take place not later than January, 1941. As there stated, this postponement was considered to be necessary in the circumstances then existing, if careful decisions were to be reached on constitutional reform and certain cognate problems before new elections were held.

3. At the time when this announcement was made it seemed likely that it would be possible to proceed with the active consideration of constitutional reform during the period of the war, but new circumstances have arisen which make me regard it as impracticable to contemplate the further examination of this question until the war is over. Since the collapse of France the war has entered a critical phase which is likely to continue for many months to come, and I feel sure that you, the Board of Ministers, and responsible opinion generally in Ceylon will agree that it is essential that all our energies should be bent during the coming days on the prosecution of the war to a victorious conclusion, when careful decisions can be taken in an atmosphere freed from the threat which overclouds the institutions of representative government at the present time. I feel that the right course will be to make a public announcement to this effect at an early date.

4. When victory has been won, it is the full intention of His Majesty's Government to proceed to a reform of the constitution. The announcement should make this abundantly clear, and should state also that when the time comes, His Majesty's Government will, before reaching their conclusions, take into full consultation the representatives of the interests substantially concerned. The manner in which this consultation should be carried out cannot now be determined. If the war continues for a considerable time, a contingency for which we must be and are prepared, it may be necessary to advise His Majesty to enact a fresh Order in Council

[1] See 37.

enabling a further postponement of the general election in Ceylon. This would be done when the right moment came, and in taking that course His Majesty's Government would be applying in Ceylon the same procedure which operates in this country, since, as you know, the intention is that no general election shall be held in the United Kingdom while the war effort demands all our energies.

5. I shall be glad to receive at an early date any observations which you wish to make upon the views expressed in the previous paragraphs of this despatch. Subject thereto I shall be obliged if you will transmit to me the draft of a suitable announcement for the consideration of His Majesty's Government. When the terms of the draft announcement have thus been in general agreed upon, I should desire that the Board of Ministers should have the opportunity of being consulted in confidence before it is published, and I should hope that it would be possible to satisfy any wishes they might express for the amendment of the form or of the terms of the announcement provided that the draft were not substantially altered. I should also consider it to be a courtesy to the State Council if it were arranged for the announcement to be made in Council simultaneously with its general publication here and in Ceylon, and I should be glad to have your advice as to procedure for that purpose.

79   CO 54/982/1/1, no 32   23 Dec 1940
'Why Indo–Ceylon talks failed: Mr Senanayake's review of events': press report from Ceylon Daily News   [Extract]

The proceedings of the 22nd Ceylon National Congress commenced at Mirigama at 5 p.m. on Saturday amid enthusiastic scenes and in the presence of a very large gathering of Congressmen, visitors and a teeming crowd of villagers.

The President, Mr. E. A. P. Wijeyeratne, arrived on the Congress grounds conducted in a mile-long procession, with over a dozen elephants from the Mirigama Resthouse. On arrival at the grounds, a party of youths formed a historical pageant depicting Parakrama-Bahu the Great after his second coronation as Lord of Lanka.

Mr. D. S. Senanayake, the Chairman of the Reception Committee, then delivered his address.

He warmly welcomed the delegates and referred to the many problems affecting the social and economic life of the people, with whom he had come into close personal touch in his ten years' work as Minister of Agriculture.

Among the present evils, he mentioned the limited scope given to the activities of local bodies and the evils of the system of undivided ownerships of land.

Status of Indians
Mr. Senanayake then went on to give an account of what had happened at the Indo–Ceylon Exploratory Conference last month.

He said that the Conference commenced with the question of the status of Indians now in Ceylon.

"We placed before the Conference", said Mr. Senanayake, "certain tentative proposals laying down the conditions under which the status of Indians should be determined.

"They were as follows:—

(1) "Persons of Indian descent who possess a Ceylon domicile of origin, i.e. those born in Ceylon of a father having a Ceylon domicile of origin or of choice, will be considered Ceylonese and will be entitled to all rights and privileges of Ceylonese.
(2) "Other persons of Indian descent now resident in Ceylon. These will be entitled to the rights and privileges accorded to British subjects. Within this class those who possess a Ceylon domicile of choice (which must include 5 years' residence) will be entitled to State Council franchise but will not be entitled to certain privileges reserved for Ceylonese, e.g. under the Land Development Ordinance and the Fisheries Ordinance; and to apply for posts under the Ceylon Government. The whole of this class, i.e. other persons of Indian descent now resident in Ceylon, will be entitled on application to certificates of residence, subject to such conditions as may be set out in the certificate."

Three classes
"On our proposals Indians now in Ceylon may be divided into three classes:—

"(i)   The second generation of Indians who have made Ceylon their permanent home. To those we give full rights of citizenship and treat them as Ceylonese for all purposes.
"(ii)   Those Indians now in Ceylon who have made Ceylon their permanent home irrespective of who their parents were, and have resided at least five years. To those we not only give the right to reside and earn their living but also they will be entitled to the franchise. But they will not be entitled to certain special benefits, e.g. obtaining Crown land under Government schemes, etc.
"(iii) Those Indians now in Ceylon who have not settled permanently here but continue to have connections with India. These will be entitled to obtain certificates to enable them to continue to reside and earn their living, but they will not have any other rights such as the franchise."

Counter-proposals
"The representatives of the Government of India rejected these proposals and made the following counter-proposals:—

"(1) Our category (i), giving full rights of citizenship to the second generation of Indians permanently settled in Ceylon, to remain.
"(2) Full rights of citizenship, with the exceptions stated below, to be conferred on all Indians who can furnish proof
   "(a) of five years' residence, and
   "(b) of permanent interest in the Island.

"The fact that a married person lives in Ceylon with his wife and children should suffice to raise the presumption of permanent interests. Similar test to be adopted for unmarried persons. The only exceptions from the full rights of citizenship applicable to this class are:—

"(1) They may not claim the right to appointment in the Ceylon Government Services but their descendants are to be entitled to it.
"(2) They may not claim grants of Crown land already set apart for the Ceylonese, but they are to have equality of rights to all other Crown land.
"(3) Other Indians not coming under the above classes to be entitled to engage in

any lawful vocation or calling which they now exercise, without discrimination. These Indians now in Ceylon may however qualify in the future to come within category (2)."

"Impossible to agree"

Continuing, Mr. Senanayake added that the difference between the proposals made by the Ceylon delegation of Ministers and by the representatives of the Government of India, was as follows:—

"We proposed that the franchise should be given to all Indians now in Ceylon who have permanently settled down here, and that full rights of citizenship should be given only to the second generation of such Indians. Their proposal is that full rights of citizenship with very minor restrictions should be given to all Indians who have lived five years in Ceylon and have their families here.

"Their proposals would practically amount to our having to confer full rights of citizenship on the entire 900,000 Indians now in Ceylon irrespective of the fact that their real home is India and not Ceylon, except to those who choose to leave Ceylon.

"We found it impossible to agree to these proposals and so the Conference had to end in this unsatisfactory manner. We suggested that the proposed Indo–Ceylon trade talks be taken up, but the representatives of the Government of India said that as no mutual goodwill had been established they were not prepared to discuss questions of trade between the two countries."

Restrictions in India

Mr. Senanayake next referred to what India herself does in regard to British subjects from other parts of the Empire who reside in India.

He said: "Under the Foreigners' Act of 1939 of Madras the following definition of 'Foreigner' appears. I understand that this is taken from the Government of India Act.

'Foreigners' includes [sic] every person other than:—

'(1) a British subject domiciled in the United Kingdom;
'(2) a British Indian subject;
'(3) a Ruler or a subject of an Indian State, and
'(4) a Consul General, Vice Consul or a person appointed by a foreign Government to exercise diplomatic functions'.

"So that, if the law of India prevailed in Ceylon, all the Indians living in Ceylon would be classed as 'foreigners' and not entitled to any rights of citizenship. Our proposals are to give those who have made Ceylon their home certain definite rights, and we are told that this is discrimination. . . ."

Betrayal of the people

Mr. Senanayake next spoke of the assurances given to Ceylon by Sir Herbert Stanley in 1929 and by Lord Passfield, the then Secretary of State for the Colonies. Though, according to that assurance, the requirements for Indians were proof of permanent settlement in Ceylon and at least five years' residence, what actually happened was that all estate labourers were registered wholesale, without any enquiry regarding permanent settlement.

"This is how the British carried out this undertaking to the people of this country", said Mr. Senanayake. "This betrayal of the people, of the Kandyan people, is one of the darkest blots of British Administration in Ceylon."

He next referred to the present economic state of the Kandyans, who were in a miserable plight in territory nominally theirs but actually in the hands of British capitalists and peopled by Indian labourers.

The same conditions existed in other parts of the country.

"No one but a man who is absolutely blind or dishonest can fail to see that within the last few decades the Indians in Ceylon have made enormous strides in ousting our people out of their business and property. Compared to their own country, Ceylon has been a veritable paradise to them, said Mr. Senanayake.

Imaginary grievances
Continuing he said:—

"When those are the facts, it is a most depressing thought that some among them whose parents have made fortunes in Ceylon and who today are living in comfort and luxury only because of the hospitality of the people of Ceylon, should betray this country by carrying to India lying tales of imaginary ill-treatment and imaginary grievances. All this is for their own selfish political ends.

"I make bold to say that the chief reason why our Conference with the representatives of the Indian Government failed was because of the poisonous atmosphere already created by these so-called Indian leaders from Ceylon, who are betraying this country.

"The Indian delegates broke off the Conference because mutual goodwill had not been established. What chance was there for mutual goodwill when the air had already been poisoned?"

In other countries
Mr. Senanayake mentioned that the Indian problem existed not only in South Africa and Ceylon, but in many other countries.

Self-governing countries like South Africa had passed stringent regulations. In French Indo–China stern measures had been adopted to prevent property passing into the hands of Indian money-lenders as a result of the recent economic depression.

In Siam (Thailand) there were very stringent regulations against the entry into that country of Indians and Chinese who have hitherto exploited the country.

"We in this country have been so far looking to the British for protection of our interests, and I have shown you how grievously the British officials in Ceylon have disappointed us", said Mr. Senanayake. "But I have every confidence that if the true position, the real plight of our people is placed before the British public and the British Parliament we shall have the protection which we need."

In concluding Mr. Senanayake said:—

"I appeal to you with all the earnestness at my command to realise that unless we stem the tide of this growing domination of Indians in Ceylon in our economic and political life, our extinction as a Ceylonese nation is inevitable."

80 CO 54/977/7, no 13   30 Dec 1940
[Things Ceylonese]: letter from Sir A Caldecott to G E J Gent on the governor's proposal to discontinue his periodical reports. *Minute* by K W Blaxter

My last instalment of "Things Ceylonese" was dated the 18th October[1] and, when I left for India for treatment at the beginning of December, I left in my safe a number of notes for incorporation in the next instalment. On my return I found these quite out of date; and have reached the conclusion that, whereas these Personal Jottings were calculated to be of some value in the Colonial Office when I started them in September 1939, and the Air Mail would deliver them to you a week after they were written, the present time lag of a month or more between despatch and delivery renders a considerable proportion of their subject matter anachronistic and even potentially misleading by the time of their receipt. Moreover nearly all Ceylon's important problems are by now the subject of regular despatches (in many cases of telegraphic despatches) and the arrival of month-old personal impressions may tend to obscure and confuse particular issues rather than to elucidate and clarify them. I have therefore decided to discontinue the series, but I shall not of course hesitate to write personally about local problems and difficulties whenever it may appear useful or helpful to do so.

Minute on 80

I am sorry that Sir A. Caldecott has discontinued these notes. Actually the time lag may be more than a month. Some mails take considerably longer than a month to reach us, & of course the comments, particularly on the political situation, or say, labour unrest, are out of date on receipt. Even so the notes had news in them which was interesting, even if rather late in arriving, & we could make allowance for the delay in appraising the Governor's comments. For example, there were interesting comments in No. 12 on Mr. Banderanaike's [sic] marriage to Miss Ratwatte.[2] We shd. not have got this information from any other source. This is only one instance.

I suggest that we shd. ask Sir A. Caldecott whether he cannot continue the series, saying that the notes have much interesting information in them & and that we will make full allowance for the delay.[3]

K.W.B.
20.2.41

---

[1] See 72.   [2] See 72, para 6.
[3] After an appeal by the CO, Caldecott resumed his reports, see 89.

81 CO 54/973/13, no 25 30 Dec 1940

[Reforms]: letter from Sir A Caldecott to G E J Gent urging the
appointment of a constitutional commission. *Minutes* by K W Blaxter,
G E J Gent and Sir G Bushe

I find that I have never answered your letter No.55569/6/1940 of the 21st September,
1940, which (having gone all the way by sea) did not arrive until just before I left for
ray treatment in India. In the third paragraph you speak of "implementing the
understanding that within the next two years a procedure for further considering the
Reforms question should be thought out and agreed". The understanding, however,
as viewed here is that a new Constitution will be *ready* for the next General Election
in two years time; nor can I see how the present Constitution, Council or Ministers
could be expected to function for more than two years. The present ship of state
though still afloat is leaking at every plank, and Nationalist demands become inflated
with our every step towards victory in the war. At its recent rally at Mirigama the
Ceylon Congress has copied from the Indian Congress demands for independence (as
distinct from Dominion Status) and for the right of Ceylon to determine her own
Constitution. I am more than ever convinced that a Commission must visit Ceylon
and make its report before there can be any constitutional reform, and I am strongly
of the opinion that the appointment of one should not await termination of the war.
This, I believe, is the view of all informed opinion in Ceylon.

Minutes on 81

Sir Andrew Caldecott's letter of the 30th December has crossed our official despatch
to him of the 18th December.[1] What he favours in his letter is the opposite to what
we have proposed in our despatch.

The reasons which led us to send our despatch are given in my minute of the 10th
December. These reasons certainly still hold good. The critical period of the war, to
which we referred in our despatch, is likely to last for some time. Also there seem to
me to be two further possible objections to considering this matter during the war,
which have not been mentioned previously:—(1) if we attempt a revision of the
Ceylon Constitution before the war ends, it might be more difficult for H.M.G. to
maintain their present policy of postponing further consideration of the constitutions in India and Burma until the war is over. The three questions do not necessarily
hang together, but it might be said that if we can carry through a revision of the
Ceylon Constitution in wartime, it should be possible to do the same with India and
Burma. If we are to proceed with the revision of the Ceylon Constitution at once, I
think we ought to make sure that the India Office and Burma Office have no
objections to raise. (2) It is not possible to say now what will be the policy of H.M.G.
with regard to Colonial affairs generally when the war is over. The whole question of
Colonial Administration is bound to come up at the Peace Conference, and it does
not seem a very suitable plan that we should start a revision of the Ceylon
Constitution now, which may not conform with the policy decided upon for the
period following the war.

---

[1] See 78.

None the less, I do not think it can be said that it will be impossible to send a commission to Ceylon at once if that course is thought to be essential. I think, however, that we must await the Governor's reply to our despatch of the 18th December before the matter can be formally considered further.

K.W.B.
24.2.41

The actual announcement of the postponement of the Elections is in 17A in this file. The new latest date for the General Elections was then postponed to January 1943.

The objection to proceeding with any Constitutional Award in war-time in Ceylon was due to the belief that its chief effect would be to rouse to a pitch of tension the sharp communal differences which interfered with the war effort, and particularly with tea and rubber production in Ceylon, in which a large element of Indian labour is employed. That consideration to my mind is no less important now than it was last summer.

The fact that "nationalist demands" have become inflated with our every step towards victory and have now attained to a demand for independence as distinct from Dominion status is not surprising having regard to the pace which has been set by Congress in India.

In his letter to Mr. MacDonald, No. 7 in this file,[2] Sir Andrew Caldecott attached some value to the opinion of Mr. Senanayake, the de facto leader of Ministerial policy in Ceylon, to the effect that the Secretary of State would find that there was only one way to deal with reforms in Ceylon, viz. that he must say "I am prepared to give you this and this but not that or that: take it or leave it". It must be assumed that substantial claims by Mr. Senanayake and his fellow Sinhalese Ministers in their list of Reforms could not be conceded by H.M.G. without the strongest protests not only from British interests in the island, but also from the Government of India; and whether an impasse of that sort should be brought on while we are still engaged in the crisis of a war seems to me more than doubtful.

I believe that if necessary the State Council Elections should be postponed again if the war situation next year requires it, and that we should not envisage in Ceylon, any more than in Burma or India, further Constitutional concessions until the victory has been achieved. It may, however, be desirable that, on the occasion of any new Order-in-Council to postpone the Election date further, we should consider the advisability of providing at the same time for the State Council to re-elect the Executive Committees and each Executive Committee to re-elect its chairman, so that the Board of Ministers may be reconstituted with something of a new mandate from the State Council.

For the present I should be inclined to await the Governor's reply to the S. of S's despatch of the 18th December (No. 24 on this file).

G.E.J.G.
11.3.41

I agree. I still firmly hope that when the time comes there may be a Conference here and not a Commission to Ceylon.

H.G.B.
18.3.41

---

[2] See 37.

82   CO 54/975/4, no 20   31 Dec 1940
[Indo–Ceylon relations]: inward telegram no 1088 from Sir A
Caldecott to Lord Lloyd on the response of the Government of India to
Mr Senanayake's speech on the breakdown of the ministerial talks

Indo–Ceylon relations. Regret to report following developments since my telegram,
No. 1067. In spite of my warning and admonition to Ministers on 18th December and
understanding reached that in any public allusion to breakdown of recent Conference they would not (repeat not) go beyond general statement on lines of
communique issued in India, Senanayake at rally of Ceylon National Congress on
21st December made long speech[1] on lines of report of delegation, of which I have
refused publication before the 28th January. Indian Government telegraphed 25th
December that reports of this speech caused them much embarrassment and that
they wished to regard themselves as free to take public in India into complete
confidence as regards what passed at the Conference. I replied 27th December that
although I still felt in principle that any official statement in regard to joint
Conference by either Government should be previously notified by one to the other, I
nevertheless realised that speech of Senanayake, although completely unauthorised,
made it impossible for me to question freedom of Government of India in the
direction indicated. Speeches made at Village Committee's Conference, 29th December, by three Ministers for Local Administration, Communications and Works and
Education, are also calculated to cause offence in India. Leading articles in *Daily
News* to-day shows some Minister has already communicated to Editor my determination to veto any measure affecting Indians now in Ceylon that conflicts with our
undertakings, and that all Lake House newspapers, both English and vernacular, will
adopt violently anti-Indian line and lend Senanayake uncompromising support. In
reply to your telegram, no. 765, paragraphs 4 and 2. Telegram cited was published
here as Sessional Paper No. 16 of 1930 and was in the hands of our delegates to
Conference *vide* paragraphs 11 and 12 of my despatch of 14th June Confidential both
on subject of registration of Indian voters. This telegram and passage of prospectus
under Indian Immigration Rules, quoted in my telegram, No. 1069, are most
important among what I term "still current undertakings," which include also
elect(ed) (? Electoral) ? Reform Order in Council itself. Search for other possible
relevant documents is still being made.

---

[1] See 79.

83   CO 54/975/4, no 21   1 Jan 1941
[Indo-Ceylon relations]: inward unnumbered telegram from Sir A
Caldecott to Lord Lloyd on local reactions to the breakdown of the
ministerial talks

Developments reported in my telegram, No. 1088[1] show that the position must get

---

[1] See 82.

worse before it gets better. I have made it abundantly clear to Ministers ever since I insisted two years ago on amendment of Village Communities Bill that there can be no betrayal of our undertakings to India. Three of them are now out to assault this position by frontal attack and there can be no compromise. Following from *Daily News*, 30th December, is sort of article we must expect from Lake House Press; abbreviated quotation begins:—"If reserve powers are used to settle questions in manner inimical to the interests of the country and express wishes of its people we shall be faced with very grave situation indeed. Textile quotas were forced on Ceylon in spite of public opinion throughout the island. Present emergency? has a political background not unlike Swinton. But if he or his advisers here or in England believe the same process can be repeated with impunity they are gravely mistaken. Ceylon Delegation placed perfectly fair proposals before the Indian Government and any attempt to go further than those proposals will lead to grave consequences." Quotation ends. Senanayake might perhaps be said to have already afforded sufficient grounds for demanding his resignation but such action would only make him Nationalist martyr and excite anti-Indian passions among Sinhalese generally. Position is more likely to clear if I give time for politicians to blow off steam and for more moderate opinion to rally as it did last spring to my support. If, however, there should arise any indication of inter-racial disorder I shall take immediate steps to prevent it and the authorities concerned agree that I can rely entirely on the loyalty of the police, and also, if necessary, of the native units of Defence Force. Preceding sentence does not mean that I anticipate serious trouble but that I should not be unprepared for it if it came. I learned in India that Sir Girja Bajpai who presided over the abortive conference will shortly be on holiday in Madras Presidency and I have telegraphed 28th December suggesting that he might come on to Colombo on short private visit as my guest at the Queen's House so that we could talk the position over together. No reply yet received from the Viceroy.

84   CO 54/982/1/1, no 5   25 Jan 1941
[Indo-Ceylon relations]: inward telegram no 56 from Sir A Caldecott to Lord Lloyd on the undertakings given to the Government of India

Following is draft message from Governor which if you approve I propose to have read in State Council on the 11th February as indicated in my telegram, No. 47, Secret. Draft has been made with the assistance of the Legal Secretary. Circumstances render it undesirable that I should send draft to India for approval but perhaps you will see fit to communicate it to India Office. Up to the present there has been no breach of these undertakings but proceedings of Conference sent to you by air mail of 16th December show clearly, e.g., pages 28 and 55 that Ceylon Delegation intend future breaches in respect of Indians already in the island and on such basis Indians naturally refuse to negotiate. Message begins:—

Undertakings given to Government of India.

1. In connection with recent informal conference at Delhi between a Ministerial Mission from Ceylon and representatives of the Government of India it appears to me desirable to place on contemporary record in the easily accessible form of a message to the State Council, a schedule of certain matters in respect of which undertakings

have been given by the Government of Ceylon or by His Majesty's Government to the Government of India, together with references to latest statements made in relation to such undertakings.

2. Having regard to circumstances in which these undertakings were given I hold the Government of Ceylon bound by them to the Government of India in respect of all Indians now in the Island or on short and temporary absence from it, and I hold myself bound as Governor to withhold approval, ratification or assent in respect of any act, regulation or measure to which the Government of India has not agreed and of which effect would be to deprive any such Indians of benefits of undertakings.

3. The subject of State franchise and statements in regard to it are not included in schedule because it is a matter governed by order of His Majesty in Council and not by local Regulations or Ordinances requiring my approval, ratification or assent.

Here follows schedule in two columns headed (1) Subject Matter and (2) Statement:—

Subject Matter.	*Statement.*
Item 1.	
Restriction on immigration of Indians	Paragraph 112 of memorandum sent by the Governor to the Viceroy, 22nd August, 1921. Quotation begins:— *Any restriction by means of passport regulations or by law on immigration of other classes of Indians, e.g., traders, tourists, professional gentlemen, etc.*—There are no restrictions on immigration of classes mentioned or of any Indians as such. There are legal restrictions on immigration of destitutes, vicious persons and stowaways irrespective of nationality. Quotation ends. Footnote explains that phraseology "other classes" means Indians other than recruited labourers.
Item 2.	
Municipal Franchise.	Paragraph 16 of letter from the Colonial Secretary to the Government of India of the 27th July, 1922. Quotation begins: As regards municipal franchise members of the resident Indian community enjoy equally all privileges of indigenous population, and they are entitled if elected to hold seats on local municipal bodies. Quotation ends.
Item 3.	
Free repatriation in cases of sickness or of unemployment due to industrial depression.	Paragraph 4 of letter of the 28th October, 1922, from Colonial Secretary to the Secretary to the Government of India Departments of Revenue and Agriculture (Emigration) in reply to a request for an additional guarantee that Indian labourers would be free to return if unable to maintain themselves in times of industrial depression. Quotation begins: I am to state that this Government is ready to make provision to meet the cost of returning emigrants to India in the case of (a) sick men and (b) men thrown out of employment owing to retrenchment in times of industrial depression. Quotation ends.

Item 4.

Legal Rights.

Paragraph 23 of information relating to Ceylon for publication under rule 17 of Indian Emigration Rules sent to the Government of India for approval on 4th April, 1929. Quotation begins: Legal and social position. Indians in Ceylon have same legal rights as members of local population, and to-day can acquire and hold land. Quotation ends. Note the statement that information was approved by the Government of India on 1st July, 1930, and a Tamil or Telugu translation has since been furnished to every assisted immigrant before leaving India.

Item 5.

No intention of altering Ceylon Law to detriment of Indians.

Passage from Secretary of State's telegram No. 50 of the 10th June, 1929, published in Ceylon as Sessional Paper No. 16 of 1930. Quotation begins: His Majesty's Government wishes to make it clear that there is no intention of repealing or amending to the detriment of Indians any of the laws of Ceylon affecting their position or privileges. Quotation ends.

85   CO 54/984/10, no 1   27 Jan 1941

[Communism]: despatch from Sir A Caldecott to Lord Lloyd on the activities of communist bodies in Ceylon

With reference to Your Lordship's Secret telegram No.494 of the 18th August, 1940, and in continuation of my Secret despatch No. (2) of the 26th September, 1940, I have the honour to forward a further Report by the Deputy Inspector General of Police, Criminal Investigation Department, on the activities of Communist Bodies in Ceylon.[1] It will be seen from paragraph 6 of the present Report (to be read in conjunction with paragraph 17 of the last one) that these Bodies now number two, the Lanka Sama Samaja Party and a new 'Stalinistic' United Socialist Party. The first Resolution to be passed by the new party was one condemning the old for serving the capitalists and imperialists; the rift in the movement has gone deep.

2.   I have not considered it worth time or paper to have copies of the translations of four of the five documents mentioned in paragraph 1 of the Report type-written for transmission with this despatch. They consist of the usual voluminous tirades against Capitalists, Imperialists, the Ministries, the Police, the Ceylon Labour Party, the Stalinists, and in short everybody and everything that does not appertain to the Sama Samaja Party. A translation of the fifth document will however be found annexed to the Report. "Suriya Mal" is the Sinhalese name for the yellow tulip-like flower of a tree (Thespesia Populnea) very common in the coastal region of this Island. Its political symbolism is explained in the fourth paragraph of the translation. The fact, recorded in paragraph 1 of the Report, that for the first time in seven years

---

[1] Enclosures not printed.

no Suriya blossoms were sold or worn on November 11th (when the sale of poppies reached a record figure) is proof indeed of the eclipse of the Communists and of the true feeling of the people towards the War.

3. In conclusion I may add that, although I have not as yet received an official account of the All Ceylon Estate Workers' Union Meeting at Kandy mentioned in paragraph 4 of the Report, I have been credibly informed by an unofficial observer that it was a "complete frost". The only unsatisfactory feature of the present position is Mr. L.S. Goonewardene's continued evasion of the Police (paragraphs 3 and 5).

86 CO 54/981/14, no 10   31 Jan 1941
[Indo-Ceylon relations]: despatch from Sir A Caldecott to Lord Lloyd on ministerial proposals for the restriction of immigration into Ceylon

I have the honour to address Your Lordship in continuation of my Confidential (2) despatch of the 27th August, 1940, on the subject of ministerial proposals for restriction of immigration into Ceylon.

2. I caused Your Lordship's telegram No. 669 of the 15th November to be forthwith conveyed to the Board of Ministers, but I am still in the position of having received no communication from them on this subject. The Minutes of a Meeting of the Board held on the 21st January contain however the following item:—

> "The Board considered, at the request of the Minister of Local Administration, the need for immediate action to deal with the restriction of immigration and decided that legislation should be prepared immediately (if possible within a fortnight) by the Legal Secretary in accordance with the previous decisions arrived at by the Board on the subject, and that priority should be given to the drafting of this legislation."

3. The Chief Secretary has since submitted for my perusal a Memorandum by the Legal Secretary relative to the ministerial demand for the immediate drafting of legislation on the basis of the enclosure to my previous despatch. A copy of this Memorandum is enclosed.[1] I understand that the Legal Secretary's Memorandum will be considered at a Board meeting to be held on the 4th February, at which the Chief Secretary will at my request again draw the Ministers' attention to Your Lordship's suggestion that, for the avoidance of future difficulty, a copy of any proposed legislation should be sent in draft for your prior consideration before introduction.

4. I am further informed by the Chief Secretary that, at the request of the Minister for Agriculture and Lands, 12th February has been set aside for a debate in the State Council on "Indian immigration and franchise." I am in telegraphic correspondence with Your Lordship on the position arising out of the breakdown of the recent Indo-Ceylon talks; a breakdown which has in my opinion been caused by a failure of the Ceylon delegation to realize the sanctity of past undertakings. I mention this point in the present context only because the Legal Secretary has once more indicated to the Ministers the need to guard against a breach of faith in the penultimate clause of the last paragraph of his Memorandum.

---

[1] Not printed.

87   CO 54/980/4, no 16   14 Feb 1941
[Diary of stay in Ceylon]: report by T W Davies for CO

[Davies submitted with this diary separate notes (not printed here) on (1) the constitution, (2) Indo-Ceylon relations, (3) personal relations between the British and Ceylonese,
(4) the Ceylon Civil Service, (5) import control. He also appended an additional note on
colonial policy and minuted separately: 'It will be noted from the diary that Sir Baron
Jayatilaka and Mr. Bandaranaike both asked that what they said might be conveyed to the
Secretary of State.']

November 29th: the aerodrome
I arrived by air on the evening of Friday, November 29th. The landing ground at
Colombo compared very favourably with those at Madras and Trichinopoly both of
which were partially waterlogged. Apart from Colombo I believe there is only one
other landing ground in the whole of Ceylon.

Mr. Wodeman
I stayed with Mr. G.S. Wodeman, Chief Secretary and during most of my visit O.A.G.
Mr. Wodeman grows upon one. He is not showy, but in a few days one is impressed.
He is admirable in Ceylon. Where many are thrown into a state of high nervousness
by ministerial antics, he remains imperturbable. As he himself points out he has not
a white hair in his head. It is a pity I think that he should not be made a Governor
somewhere. My one criticism would be that he lacks dignity. When as O.A.G. he went
to the cinema, part of the audience pressed out in front of him.
   Incidentally the lack of outward respect shown for the O.A.G. was rather notable.
It seems to me a great pity that neither the Europeans nor the Asiatics in the streets
take off their hats when the King's representative goes by. Even some European
troops I saw on one occasion lounging about outside their quarters and not getting
up as the O.A.G. drove past.

November 30th: Lady Pieris
I attended a lunch given by Lady Pieris. Lady Pieris is a relic of the old luxurious days
when Ceylonese were proud to mix up with high European officials. Her son,
cultured and probably rather ineffective, was also present. I fear these people cut
little ice in 1940.

The Colombo municipal commissioner
I afterwards attended an A.R.P. demonstration by firemen (professional) and clerks
mostly employed by the Municipality. It seemed quite good. I sat next to Mr. [S P
Wickremasingha] the Municipal Commissioner, i.e. Town Clerk of Colombo. He is
said to be very efficient. The municipal elections were due in a week, and he cynically
though no doubt truly commented upon the corruption that would take place.
Certain English people say that the Mayor has been trying to engineer a strike in the
harbour in order to acquire votes.

Sir A. Caldecott
I dined with the Governor. No one else was present except his family and Private
Secretaries. Sir Andrew was due to go to Madras in a couple of days for medical
treatment.

I understood Sir Andrew to say that the United Kingdom Government (or probably it was the Governor of Ceylon – i.e. himself) was pledged to move forward not back, as a next step in regard to the constitution. If this is really his impression, it is surely a false one!

Sir A. Caldecott and ministers

I heard several criticisms of Sir Andrew on the ground that he tried to interfere with the Ministers constantly. He apparently summons them to meet him about once a week. Sir E. Stubbs,[1] it was said, seldom made himself felt by Ministers, but when he did it was like a ton of bricks! I am told the Ministers now hardly treat Sir Andrew with common politeness: for instance at a recent meeting Mr. Bandaranaike walked in very late without either apologising or taking his pipe out of his mouth.

And European officials

As a result of subsequent conversations with various people I got the impression that Sir Andrew does not sufficiently support European officials when they get into trouble with Ministers in cases where it is no fault of their own.

I understand that Sir Andrew recently stated that he thought it unfair to them to ask European cadets to come to Ceylon in future. I feel that this is essentially the view of an elderly man. Conditions of service in Ceylon are delightful. After speaking to junior members of the C.C.S. I am confirmed in my impression that I personally would be glad to enter the service. There are of course political worries that beset the civil servant here more than in Africa, but the senior civil servants make too much of them. They will not affect in the same way new recruits, who will breathe that atmosphere from the beginning. I am sure that the C.C.S. is still an admirable career to the young Englishman, and it will (a) shut off a pleasant career and (b) do irreparable harm to Ceylon if European recruitment is not started again.

The private secretaries

Sir Andrew has no A.D.C. but 2 Private Secretaries, Mr. O'Regan and Mr. Dobbs. Both these young men seemed to me very good: each has a striking personality and is exceedingly intelligent.

December 1st: rubber estate

This Sunday Mr. Wodeman took me to visit the rubber estate of his nephew, Mr. Notley. Naturally enough at a time like this no difficulties are being experienced over rubber. The Indian labour problem does not arise.

December 2nd: Mr. F.C. Gimson

I was taken to see the tea growing country by Mr. Gimson, Controller of Immigration. Mr. Gimson was exceptionally kind to me. He is a curious character— sometimes a little vague and dreamy, but very reasonable. He is a great enthusiast for the I.L.O. and a great admirer of Mr. Butler. He is a strong believer in the importance of encouraging economic trade unionism in Ceylon. By taking thought and planning for this he believes it may be possible to prevent an undesirable form of political trade unionism springing up spontaneously among the Tamil workers on the tea estates.

---

[1] Governor of Ceylon, 1933–1937.

Mr. Gimson

I understand that many planters regard Mr. Gimson and his ideas with a good deal of distrust.

We stayed the night at what Mr. Gimson regarded as one of the most progressive tea estates in Ceylon, and also the one which paid best. This was Mr. Irvine Stewart's Tiensin Estate at Bogowautalawa.

Mr. Irvine Stewart (tea planter)

Mr. Stewart is a prominent visiting agent. He is a most enthusiastic man who likes to regard himself (and seemingly justifiably) as the father of the labourers on his estate. The estate itself to a layman looks in perfect order and so does his factory. He pointed out with pride the lines on which his Tamil labourers lived. I confess they looked to me very poor and sordid. The hovel in which the ordinary Ceylonese villager lived would appear preferable. However the free maternity, medical and educational services which Mr. Strewart showed us seemed first class and there could be no doubt he is a most beneficent employer. His thesis is that his Indian labour force is his most valuable asset and it pays to be beneficent to it. This is borne out by his balance sheets.

Mr. Stewart is not liked by the Planters Association. According to Mr. Stewart some planters are wildly reactionary. Thus one recently broke the umbrella of a Ceylonese official who had been sent to see him holding it was impudent for a native to carry one in face of a European. Another young man who inherited an estate said with a sigh of relief after a year of it "At last I've broken the Tamil labourers of the habit of approaching me direct with their troubles". This last, according to Mr. Stewart, illustrates the tendency of the younger planters to breakaway from paternalism.

December 3rd

Mr. Gimson had arranged for me to meet members of the Planters Association at Kandy. Mr. Scott, the Chairman, was ill but I met Mr. Conway Davies (Deputy Chairman), Mr. Dalgety, Mr. Dulling, Mr. Gordon Pyper, and the Secretary.

Views of the Planters Association

Generally speaking they had no complaints. They expressed some alarm at the existence of communist propaganda. They thought there was a danger of Trade Unions becoming political rather than economic. They said labour troubles were to be expected in connexion with the 1942 elections, and that these would have repercussions in southern India. There are apparently at present two competing Trade Unions among the Tamil labourers.

Their chief worry was of course Indian immigration. They said their one concern was that movement should be free. The details of the citizenship did not concern them.

They thought that the export of papaine to Canada should have a future. I asked them what their views were on ministerial government. They said they had no objection to it: it had its uses. Ministers had done no harm to planters' interests except that they showed a tendency to fix wages in a totalitarian manner. I was very surprised at this attitude. Actually Mr. Barney Villiers, a more astute member of the Association who had heard what his colleagues had said, prayed me some days later not to take theirs as the official attitude of the planters as ministerial government was definitely inimical to their interests.

December 4th: Mr. Collins
I spent some time in the Financial Secretary's office. Mr. Collins was acting. Apparently there has been great competition between him and Mr. Murphy (who is very popular with all) for the post of Deputy Assistant Secretary and Mr. Collins has won. I thought he made a definitely good impression.

The influence of the financial secretary
I of course heard criticisms of Treasury control—e.g. that it was essential to build storage for 3 months supply of rice but that the Treasury would not allow it. On the whole however I think their influence is too little rather than too great. They are at least controlled by a European and have a sense of responsibility.

Mr. Tennison of the Financial Secretary's office seemed very good. I showed both Mr. Collins and Mr. Tennison the views of the Board of Trade on the export drive as set out in the telegram to Mr. Lococh at Delhi. This generally is a subject which has caused some bewilderment in Ceylon as elsewhere.

One particular enquiry that Mr. Collins made was why are chocolates still obtainable from the United Kingdom in unlimited quantities.

The Naval C. in C.
I lunched with Admiral and Mrs. Leathem. Admiral Leathem said that Colombo was not liked by Naval Officers—it is too cliquey. He obviously thought the Ceylon administration not much good. I later had some experience of the Navy Office and they were not perhaps very cooperative. They employ young women to do their most secret decyphering: I don't know if this is general practice in the Navy, but I would not have thought that the discretion of the girls employed for this purpose at Colombo could always be relied on.

During the day I had an interview with 5 out of the 7 Ministers, and I attended the State Council.

Sir B. Jayatillike [sic]
Sir Baron Jayatillike, Home Affairs, senior minister, asked that the following should be conveyed to the Secretary of State. He would like the Secretary of State to consider the question of amending the constitution at an early date so that the draft of a new constitution might be presented to the *present* State Council before the general elections. The Committee system should go. At present each minister acted independently of every other, and none was responsible. It was undesirable that the elections should be deferred beyond 1942.

Mr. Kannangara and Mr. W.A. de Silva
Mr. Kannangara, Minister of Education, and Mr. W.A. de Silva, Minister of Health, each gave a short talk on their respective Departments. Both seemed very enthusiastic. Mr. Kannangara was in Buddhist costume, and spoke very well. Mr. de Silva seemed rather past his best.

Colonal Kotalawala [sic]

Lieutenant-Colonel Kotalawala, Minister of Communications, was a man I was sorry not to see more of. At a very short interview he arranged a later meeting to make a point about the hydro-electric power scheme, but he never turned up. Colonel Kotalawala said he had now entered into contract for the whole of the hydro-electric scheme. He was getting the civil engineering part done first and the other part was held up. He is of the type of rich Asiatic who is always visiting Paris. He appears to be a playboy, very rich but able. (He and Mr. Senanayake are the principal owners of the plumbago mines where conditions of labour are said to be appalling—Europeans who go down the mines are sick). It was he who started a furore by dismissing the daily paid Indian labour employed by his Department. With Messrs. Senanayake and Bandaranaike, he is the most influential of the ministers.

The State Council

The State Council which I attended in the afternoon, was typically discussing a motion of censure on the Governor for appointing some European sub-police inspectors (which the Board of Ministers had advised him to do). The mover was Mr. George de Silva, an amusing buffoon. Mr. Senanayake spoke *for,* and voted *against*, the motion. His son, Mr. Douglas [sic: Dudley] Senanayake wanted to have the ministers included in the censure. The motion was carried by one vote. Among the majority—i.e. those who censured the Governor, seemed to be the Deputy Speaker, who was wearing the uniform of an officer of the R.N.V.R. and one European, Mr. Freeman, ex C.C.S. who did it on the ground that the sub-inspectors ought to be in the army.

    The Council was somewhat reminiscent of the House of Commons but still more so of the Oxford Union Society. As soon as the debate was over members rushed out, like schoolboys, to have their tea in a mood of complete irresponsibility. In the same spirit, the moment the Ceylon–Indian talks had failed Mr. Bandaranaike and Mr. Senanayake cried out to Mr. Gimson "Come on, come on, lets go and play bridge."

    I had tea with Sir Baron in the Council House and was introduced to the Speaker and a number of members.

Enquiries by the chief censor

Later on I saw the Chief Censor, Mr. Leech, and Lieutenant Commander Charasse who does economic warfare work at the Navy Office.

    Mr. Leech said that Colonial Office telegrams on censorship matters sometimes caused confusion by using technical words in a non-technical sense e.g. "in transit".

    He asked what Ministry of Economic Warfare's wishes were regarding *mails* addressed to and from persons on the Black List.

    It would be more convenient from the censorship point of view if the War Trade List went in countries (like the Statutory List) instead of alphabetically.

    Are Ministry of [Economic] Warfare fully satisfied with Ceylon censorship reports? Are they too long?

    Is French property to be put under the Custodian?

Mr. Corea

I dined with Mr. Corea and also had an interview with him during the day. Mr. Corea is credited with being the best of the Ministers. He is a Christian (alone of the Board) and married to a Tamil lady. He is quiet and shy. He probably himself realises, and the other Ministers also no doubt know, that he enjoys a good reputation with the English and this detracts from what little influence he might otherwise have with his colleagues. Mr. Corea is very likeable but his influence on import control at least cannot be regarded as satisfactory. He seems to be of the good weak category.

Mr. Corea introduced me to Sir Wilfred de Soysa, an owner of coconut estates, and fellow guests at dinner were Mr. and Mrs. Wirrawadena.[2] Mr. Wirrawadena is proprietor of the 2 principal Ceylon newspapers. Opinion in Ceylon seems to be that the local press is very good. It seems to me incredibly parochial, matters like the premature publication of some unimportant local examination papers receiving as much or more publicity than first rank war news. Ceylon papers are 16 pages long and contain very little. This wastage of newsprint cannot be stopped by the Administration "for political reasons".

December 5th: Mr. Leigh Clare and Mr. Jones
I paid the first of several visits to Mr. Leigh-Clare, Collector of Customs, and also to Mr. C.E. Jones, Controller of Imports Exports and Exchange and his staff.

Import control
So far as exchange and export control are concerned Mr. Jones works up to the Financial Secretary. So far as import control is concerned he works to Mr. Corea who merely has to refer to the Financial Secretary for advice. He does not always take that advice. As moreover that advice, even when tendered, is often already modified in the light of political circumstances the position is not wholly satisfactory. Cuts are not made which on exchange grounds ought to be made. Petrol is not rationed, nor is newsprint to any extent. American cars are still imported, and so on. The Minister threatens to give an open licence for steel imports from the United States up to the limits of pre-war trade.

Mr. Jones seemed to me very good, but he has no free hand. He reports the position fully from time to time to the Colonial Office. He is in the process of tightening up and I am certain that within the limits allowed him by Mr. Corea the Colonial Office may be satisfied that he is administering import control admirably. He is fully aware of all the factors.

Incidentally Mr. Corea sees all secret despatches about import control. His executive committee have delegated all their functions to him in the matter of import control, so they don't see them: but I think it most undesirable that even Mr. Corea should since they often touch on matters such as our future economic policy, vis a vis Japan which may be of the highest secrecy.

Mr. Jones said that he was granting import licences for aluminium from Shanghai. The importers in Shanghai must have paid dollars for it but they were prepared nevertheless to let it go to Ceylon for sterling.

Mr. Bandaranaike (minister for local government)
Mr. Bandaranaike gave me an interview. Mr. Bandaranaike who used to be a Christian recently turned Buddhist to gain political kudos. He usually wears Buddhist dress but today exceptionally was in European clothes. As always with me, he was friendly, affable and even amusing. He has a wild look in his eye: I understand

---

[2] This should read 'Wijewardene'.

there is madness in his family. He is quite irresponsible, shouts everyone else down when he is excited, is hated by European officials. Nevertheless I have a feeling that he would be susceptible to influence if some European really took pains with him and made of him a friend. It is typical that this wild, though not uncultured man, should be the son of the ultra conventional and 'honours' loving Sir Solomon Bandaranaike, who can hardly approve of his son's carryings on. He is very proud of the office he held in the Oxford Union. He is certainly susceptible to flattery and, as I said, I believe he would be to friendship.

Mr. Bandaranaike spoke in the following sense, requesting that the gist of it might be conveyed to the Secretary of State:—

Mr. Bandaranaike on the constitution

The Secretary of State having given it out as a reason for the suspension of the elections that he is going into the matter of the reform of the constitution, an early announcement of what he proposes to do is desirable. The appointment of a Commission to examine the subject should not be necessary: it would only create controversy and turmoil. The Secretary of State should have enough material before him by now to justify his taking a decision off his own bat.

The working of the Executive Committee system had disclosed faults and he (Mr. Bandaranaike) had acquiesced in the recommendation for a cabinet system. His personal view was that the existing system might be remodelled however (Mr. Bandaranaike at this point was probably thinking of the desirability of his getting votes from the minorities). The faults of the Committee system were (a) the impossibility of fixing responsibility or of calling anyone to account: and (b) lack of coordination: Ministers tended to support each other provided they got support for their pet projects in return. These defects, said Mr. Bandaranaike, might be rectified by so amending the constitution as to strengthen the powers of the Ministers with reference to the Executive Committee and the powers of the Board of Ministers with reference to each individual minister.

The Officers of State should be abolished.

The Public Service Commission should be reformed. Ministers must have the ultimate control of the civil service. Some public servants feel hostility towards Ministers. Mr. Senanayake had been particularly unfortunate with his officials. (In European circles Mr. Senanayake is credited with having driven at least 3 high British officials into premature retirement).

Mr. Bandaranaike on the Indian question

With regard to the Indian question and the failure of the recent "goodwill" talks, Mr. Bandaranaike hoped that the Secretary of State would wait till he received the full representations of the Ministers before he took any action. The situation was difficult: and the possibility of anti-Indian demonstrations in Ceylon could not be ignored.

I called on Mr. Samson, President of the Chamber of Commerce, and subsequently lunched in the company of Mr. Barney Villiers and Mr. Claude Bois, prominent business men. On the whole they had no complaints. The pre release of 5% of next year's tea quota was welcome news to them. Their chief worry was recent legislation that had altered the manner of dealing with tea coupons. They feared this might operate to their disadvantage, but it was only a 'might'.

In the afternoon I visited Mr. Hobday, Government Agent, Western province, and formerly Food Production Officer: and Mr. Coomaraswamy, Food Controller and Price Controller.

Sir Mohamed Macan Markar
I met Sir Mohamed Macan Markar jeweller, ex-Minister of Communications, and leader of the Moormen or Muslim minority. Sir Mahomed urged that if the Executive Committee system was abolished, some other method of protecting minorities should be devised in its place. Minorities should be better represented in the Council. Constituencies should be smaller.

Later in the evening I visited the Chief Justice, Mr. J.C. Howard: and at dinner I met Mr. Sudbury and Mr. Murphy.

December 6th: Mr. Balfour
Mr. Balfour, Director of Industrial Development, took me to see the Government Coir Factory. This works entirely for the internal market.

Mr. Balfour is a curious personality. Though educated in England, he is apparently a Tamil. It is commonly said that he has been very slow in getting promotion owing to an indiscretion he committed when acting as Public Trustee (or in some such office) some years ago, when he is alleged to have made some money by buying up part of the Ceylon estate of a deceased owner from some ignorant heirs living in Europe. Mr. Balfour is full of ideas, which is rare for a civil servant. Some of the ideas are wild, but few seem to be stupid. Mr. Balfour is an amateur chemist of some skill and a man of the greatest enthusiasm. He now occupies the very post for him and one he has long coveted. In spite of his defects, I think him probably a valuable man.

Mr. Senanayake
Mr. Senanayake gave me an interview today. It is a moot point whether he or Mr. Bandaranaike is more hated by European officials. Probably Mr. Senanayake takes the cake: he is said to have driven a number of Europeans into retirement. He is not so noisy as Mr. Bandaranaike but probably cleverer. Like all these people he is charming personally. He has also undeniably a real enthusiasm for agriculture. He has never got over being imprisoned in the 1915 riots.

Mr. Senanayake's chief points were the following. (1) The Public Service Commission should be reformed and the Civil Service brought under the disciplinary control of Ministers. (2) There should be coordination of ministerial authority. (3) The constitution has only worked because it has been ignored. (4) There are criticism and protracted delays over such things as the Estimates and public appointments.

Mr. Hoare and cotton piece goods
Mr. Hoare, former controller of restricted imports, took me to a wholesale seller of cotton and art-silk piecegoods to see the sort of article imported into Ceylon. Mr. Hoare said that the piece good quotas have *not* been abolished in Ceylon and are still announced. (This perhaps needs looking into).

I lunched with Mr. Murphy of the Secretariat and [the] head of the Criminal Investigation Department, who both agreed that the imprisonment of certain communists had done a world of good.

The greater part of the afternoon I spent in the Treasury and with Mr. C.E. Jones.

December 7th

Mr. Leigh-Clare[3] took me round the harbour, I was surprised at the absence of guards. Mr. Leigh-Clare would of course be well known but none challenged us at the gates at all.

Maldivian tribute

I attended the ceremony of the Maldivian Tribute. I hope the cowries which form part of the tribute are not currency in the Maldives. They are quite useless in Ceylon, though pretty. If they are currency in the Maldives, Greshams law must operate and prices rise after the annual tribute has been paid.

Mr. Drayton

I dined with Mr. Drayton, Legal Secretary. Mr. Drayton is a firm believer that, in spite of political discomforts, Ceylon is a far pleasanter place for a European to serve in than is Africa.

December 8th: Mr. Huxham

I called on Mr. Huxham, who had returned from India the previous day. Mr. Huxham is not liked by civil servants in Ceylon, probably because he did not come through the regular channels. He is undoubtedly a clever man. He is also a persistent man and he gets what he wants, a trait which on occasions such as the Eastern Group Conference, is as useful to Ceylon as it is irritating to others. But for all his ability Mr. Huxham is rather an enigma. He has possibly become rather orientalised: one feels with him that there may be an arrierè-pensées—that there are more reasons for Mr. Huxham's attitude than appears upon the surface. When he sets out to please Mr. Huxham has a charming smile which should go down well.

Mr. Huxham spoke of what Ceylon could do as a result of Delhi. He feared that Messrs. Corea and Balfour would over-enthusiastically embark on projects. Where an article is in short supply throughout the Eastern Group, there Ceylon can set about producing and count not the cost thereof. But where a product is already being produced elsewhere, there Ceylon should initiate production only if she can do so at a competitive cost.

Mr. Buxton

I had a talk with Mr. Buxton of Messrs. Vavasseurs about coconut products. One of his points was that it was a pity to reserve shipping space for coconut charcoal and not for desiccated coconut. According to him the charcoal is no longer needed in great quantities for gas masks whereas the desiccated product is very valuable if only as a sugar substitute in confectionery.

December 9th

This day was chiefly occupied by embarking on and subsequently disembarking from the S.S. Nyki which I found out might take a week to get to Penang.

Mr. Saravanamuttu

In the late afternoon I visited Mr. Saravanamuttu the Tea and Rubber Controller. It is

---

[3] Commissioner, Colombo port.

he who distributes the quotas. He has a high reputation among planters. He thought the coupon ordinance all right.

Mr. C. Bois
I also called on Mr. Claude Bois, a Colombo business man. He was somewhat alarmed at the taking of young men off the estates in Ceylon. He thought this process had gone quite far enough. One must guard against an emergency.

He thought that the franchise should be altered. Universal suffrage led to a lot of scallywags being elected to the State Council. Ceylonese of the better type would often not offer themselves for election because they did not wish to associate with men of the calibre of many of the present members.

December 10th: Mr. Sudbury
I had a talk with Mr. Sudbury, secretary to the Governor. Mr. Sudbury is palpably exhausted. Fortunately he is just going on leave. He said that so far as he knew no pledge had ever been given that the next constitutional step in Ceylon would be a forward one towards home rule, unless the various declarations of His Majesty's Government on 'trusteeship' could be so interpreted.

The railway workshops
I visited the Railway Workshops at Ratnapura. They impress a layman as being on a very big scale. It is here that Ceylon hopes to do her war-production—shell cases, and so on.

I boarded the S.S. Bloemfontein (Java Pacific Line) about 1 p.m. and we sailed an hour later.

88   CO 54/982/1/1, no 27   5 Mar 1941
[Indo-Ceylon relations]: letter from G E J Gent to Sir A Caldecott on the proposed immigration bill

In your telegram, No. 140, Secret, of the 24th of February about Indo-Ceylon relations, you asked for the Secretary of State's permission for the State Council to be informed of the purport of the Secretary of State's telegram, No. 669, Confidential, of the 15th of November, 1940. In that telegram, amongst other statements made, there was one that if certain proposals were included in the Immigration Bill as passed by the State Council the Secretary of State would feel bound on his present understanding of the proposals to advise His Majesty to refuse assent to the bill while these proposals formed part of it.

We are advised that constitutionally it would be improper for a statement to be made in the State Council as to the advice which the Secretary of State would give to the King in certain circumstances which have not yet arisen. If a statement to that effect were made in the State Council when the Bill was introduced, it would in effect be telling the State Council before the Bill is even debated or passed by the Council, that, if certain provisions are included in the bill, no matter what arguments may be adduced in favour of them and irrespective of what majority may be procured His Majesty will not assent to the bill as long as those provisions remain part of it. To do this might give rise to considerable trouble. The Secretary of State, and especially His Majesty, must not try to influence proceedings in the State Council by threats in advance as to what will be done if certain provisions are included in a bill.

We were proposing to reply to you on these lines when your telegram No. 152, Secret, of the 27th of February, arrived. The new position reported in that telegram seemed to show that in any case the statement would not now need to be made, and we therefore sent you our telegram No. 145, Secret, of the 28th of February. But you may like to know of the legal advice which was given to the Secretary of State on this particular point.

89   CO 54/984/4, no 1   29 Mar 1941
'Things Ceylonese': thirteenth periodical report by Sir A Caldecott for CO

Ceylon nationalism and the Indian question
1. The most important developments since my temporary discontinuance of these Notes have been the breakdown of the Indo-Ceylon Exploratory conversations and the Ceylon Nationalist reaction to that breakdown.
2. Ceylon Politics have become completely dominated by rivalry between the Ceylon National Congress and the Sinhala Maha Sabha. The former is represented in the Ministry by Senanayake, Corea and de Silva; the latter by Bandaranaike, Kannangara and Kotelawala. Jayatilaka belongs to the Congress, but his influence with the people of the Island is now personal and focussed on the past rather than political and relevant to the future. He is Leader of the State Council in name only.
3. There is no important difference in policy between the Congress and the Sabha. In fact it would be true to say that neither has any real or constant policy. The essential distinction between them is that most Congress people would like to see Senanayake Leader, and the Sabha members Bandaranaike.
4. In these circumstances rivalry between them takes the form of competing for Sinhalese adherents (the Sabha has no use for the Minorities, and the minorities have no use for either Sabha or Congress) by fostering and inflaming Sinhalese nationalism. This is the only political plank that either side possesses.
5. In this race to be the most nationalistic party the Ceylon Labour Party has recently become a third competitor. For all intents and purposes this is a one-man party, and its one man is Mr. Goonesinha who succeeded in being elected as Mayor of Colombo for last year. In the recent Municipal elections he managed with difficulty to retain his own seat of Maradana, but nearly all his nominees for other seats were rejected. His election tactics were characterized by rowdyism, racialism, and impersonation of voters; and the vigilance of the Police alone prevented rioting. Since his vacation of the Mayoral chair and the rebuff of his Party at the Municipal polls Goonesinha has thrown off the mantle of responsibility and respectability which (to his credit) he wore during his Mayoralty and has come out again in his true colours of a nationalistic demagogue and tub-thumper.
6. The political atmosphere described in the preceding paragraphs was not of course favourable to the New Delhi conversations. A delegation containing both Senanayake and Bandaranaike offered nevertheless the only if slender chance of

obtaining early agreement and understanding between the two Governments. If either of these two leaders had been omitted from the delegation any agreement reached would have been forthwith torpedoed in the State Council by the other. Even the present position is preferable to such a denouement.

7. The Financial Secretary's inclusion in the delegation was for the purpose of dealing with points of tariff and preference. Mr. Huxham was on furlough in India and went straight to the Conference from his leave. I had no opportunity therefore of seeing him before he joined the delegation. Although his subjects were never reached in the conversations Huxham appears from the shorthand proceedings to have joined without reserve in the discussions on questions of political status, immigration etc. and in a manner that has caused me great surprise. Such a bald and sweeping statement as "We do not accept the Jackson Report" (proceedings p. 47) came ill from an Officer of State, nor were other of his recorded remarks any more wisely conceived.

8. The Financial Secretary's contribution to the social side of the Mission was even less fortunate. On the day of his arrival he received, and accepted in writing, an invitation to dinner from Sir Girja Bajpai. All the other guests arrived but at 8.45 p.m. there was still no Huxham. The host's Private Secretary thereupon rang up the Hotel and was told by the absent guest that the dinner was not on his list of engagements and that he was not coming. In self-defence the Private Secretary thereupon produced to Sir Girja Bajpai Huxham's letter accepting the invitation; and with this unhappy incident the dinner of welcome to the Ceylon Delegates began. News of it reached me unofficially and I taxed Mr. Huxham with it on his return. His reply was that he was very sorry but that he just forgot; and that at 8.45 p.m. it was too late to get into dinner things.

9. The Sinhalese is no match for the Indian in intellect or in debate and his ostrich-like reluctance even to glance at inconvenient facts leaves him without sinews for defensive argument. I am now being accused of digging up in my Message to Council past undertakings in view of which, if I had represented them to my Ministers, they would have refused to approve the sending of any delegation. In actual fact the delegates took with them the files containing those undertakings, but as they did not suit their book they chose just to ignore them, with results necessarily fatal to the conversations.

10. Having had Sir Girja Bajpai to stay with me (a most entertaining guest whose visit we thoroughly enjoyed) I feel some sympathy with our delegates for having found themselves up against such an astute strategist. During his stay with me he suggested that the Agent to the Government of India would be better stationed in Colombo then in Kandy in order to be in more immediate touch with local politics. I replied that the Agent's concern was not with Ceylon politics but with the welfare of Indian labour, and that Kandy was obviously the best centre for the latter purpose. He then said that what was really wanted was a superior Indian Officer in Colombo possessing a status, similar to that of a Consul General, enabling him to watch the interests of Indian Nationals. I replied that I had understood that India was demanding full Ceylon citizenship for her emigrants after five years residence here (owing to the ban there are very few with less) and that if they became Ceylon citizens they would stand in no need of an Indian Consul General. Bajpai then shifted his ground and talked of "somebody more like a Trade Commissioner perhaps than a Consul General". At this stage our conversation was interrupted.

11. Although I have found it necessary in my Message to State Council to keep Ceylon reminded of her past undertakings, and am therefore being dubbed by some of our extreme nationalists a pro-Indian, nobody realizes more than I do that Indian claims often need discounting and her [sic] tactics very careful watching. Whether it be Nehru or Bajpai who speaks, the desire for Indian domination is clear; and I fear that the attitude of some Europeans in India towards the Colonial Empire is not unlike that of the public school boy towards the lower preparatory school. They suffer from a great Indian Peninsularity.

12. The Indian Government's application of their ban on emigration (which in regard to future immigrants no Ceylon interest, planting or otherwise, wants removed) to those estate workers already in the Island who would like to take a holiday in the old country is quite unconscionable. Even Ceylon politics would stop short of inflicting such hardship on Ceylon nationals. The wretched 'Palaiyal' or immigrant of long standing naturally wont take leave unless he can return to his job after it, so that the whole of that proportion of the estate population that used to be in annual flux between here and India is now 'frozen' in Ceylon and constitutes an unwanted surplus. The fluidity, of which the importance was stressed in the Jackson Report, no longer exists.

13. The quota and stock positions in the tea industry are such that the present year's production must be curtailed by some 25 million pounds. This will inevitably entail discharge of labour, and almost certainly repatriation of Indians as in 1933. That such an already difficult prospect should be worsened by India's 'freezing' of the palaiyals is indeed tragic. Any approach by this Government to the Indian Government on this question is opposed by the Ministers concerned on the grounds that (a) the imposition of the ban was unilateral action by India and can at any time be unilaterally modified by them in the interest of their own nationals; (b) that any recommendation from Ceylon might be interpreted as facilitating immigration or re-immigration of Indians, would therefore be contrary to Ministerial policy, and would further exacerbate anti-Indian feeling.

14. If the Agent of the Government of India (Mr. Rhagavan, I.C.S. has recently replaced Mr. Vittal Pai) were really protecting the interests of Indian labour in the Island he would long before now have urged his Government to enable the palaiyals to go to India on some form of 'exeat' enabling their return. I understand that the Planters may shortly ask him to place their views on this matter before his Government; they have of course every right to place such a request before him as the ban is the act of his Government and has been imposed without reference to Ceylon.

Labour problems

15. Major Orde-Brown's[1] visit has come at a most opportune juncture. There are complaints afoot on both sides that the Seven Point Agreement between the Planters and the Labour Unions is not being properly observed and questions of disputed interpretation have already arisen. Major Orde Browne has stayed with me here and at Kandy, and will pay a visit to Queen's Cottage, Nuwara Eliya, next month. His

---

[1] Major G StJ Orde Browne, labour adviser, CO, visited Ceylon, Mauritius and Malaya to report on labour conditions. The sections of his report dealing with Ceylon were published in Aug 1943 as SP XIX with the title *Report on Labour Conditions in Ceylon*. He had arrived in Ceylon on 14 Mar 1941.

influence will be most salutary in all quarters, as there has been talk by the Ceylon Indian Congress of a General Strike and the Planters' Association by a majority of (roughly) 160 to 100 has taken for its Chairman an Uva planter by name of Hamilton as "one who calls a spade a spade and will not funk a show-down". Having spoken with him after his election I doubt whether Hamilton will prove as impervious and intransigent as some of his critics fear. That, however, remains to be seen.

16.   There has been so much work on hand, so many interviews and engagements that the writing of the preceding paragraphs has been frequently interrupted and resumed at odd intervals. I hope however that they will afford a bird's eye view of the pressing problems to which they relate. As a mail goes out this afternoon and I have the rest of my morning scheduled I must close these Notes at this point and leave other matters over for my next instalment.

90   CO 54/980/15, no 3   3 Apr 1941

[Bandaranaike]: inward telegram no 250 from Sir A Caldecott to Lord Moyne on the proposed dismissal of Mr Bandaranaike. *Minutes* by G E J Gent and Sir G Bushe

In continuation of my telegram No.152 and my telegram No.203.

Both Bills have passed second reading and will come before Standing Committee next month after Easter recess. India has refused to comment on the Bills and maintains her refusal to consider questions of immigration apart from general settlement of all outstanding questions. Ministers have not yet made any further protest against my message and with one exception their attitude appears to be moderating. Exception is Bandaranaike to whom yesterday I addressed letter requiring him to explain how he can reconcile with his ministerial position (1) recent decision of his Executive Committee to withhold approval for contributions from Local authorities to the war funds under Ordinance No.32 of 1940 pending enactment of "satisfactory" legislation on the Indian question (2) series of alleged public utterances of his including a resolution of his party to boycott the Governor. If he is to retain office I shall of course demand immediate cancellation of (1) which has met with general condemnation. I will telegraph developments next week.

Minutes on 90

The two Bills were relatively harmless (1) an Immigration Bill of the ordinary type without the discriminatory provisions against "non-Ceylonese" which were at one time contemplated by the Board of Ministers. (2) a Registration Bill solely for compiling and maintaining a register of non-Ceylonese in the Island.

Mr. Bandaranaike, Minister for Local Administration, is the protagonist of the Sinhalese crusade against Indians (including Tamils) in the Island. His party is the extreme Sinhalese Nationalist Association known as the 'Sinhala Maha Sabha', of which he was the founder a few years ago and remains the principal figure. (1) in this telegram has been the subject of an enquiry from the Ministry of Information and I have sent Mr. Usill there a copy of this telegram for his information.

As regard the power of the Governor to get rid of a Minister I can find no provisions in the Order in Council for his doing so except on an address from the State Council (§37).

I suggest a telegram to the Governor as in draft herewith.[1] He would, I think, appreciate such an expression of support from the Secretary of State.

C.E.J.G.
5.4.41

I know of no provision in the Order in Council for the dismissal of a Minister other than Article 37, and I think that the existence of this article would be regarded as exhaustive of the Governor's powers. I have put forward therefore a new theory about which I am not prepared to say more at the moment than that it is worth thinking about; and no doubt the Governor will realise that we are not in any way committed to the view that there is an overriding power in the King to dismiss a Minister.

H.G.B.
7.4.41

---

[1] See 91.

91   CO 54/980/15, no 4   8 Apr 1941
[Bandaranaike]: outward unnumbered telegram (reply) from Lord Moyne to Sir A Caldecott

Your telegram No. 250.[1] I am sorry to hear of your difficulty with Bandaranaike whose behaviour seems to be intolerable. As regards (1) in your telegram my view is that such a decision by the Executive Committee for Local Administration purporting to bring pressure by such methods on other executive authorities of Government as well as Board of Ministers and Legislature is gross abuse of their powers in particular field of local administration. As regards point (2) in your telegram if Bandaranaike were associated with resolution or failed to dissociate himself from it his conduct is to my mind quite incompatible with his Ministerial Oath.

Are you advised (1) that apart from Article 37 of the Order in Council you have power to terminate a Minister's appointment or (2) that a Minister is a servant of His Majesty and that therefore he can be dismissed by the King as distinct from the Governor?

---

[1] See 90.

92   CO 54/980/15, no 5   13 Apr 1941
[Bandaranaike]: inward unnumbered telegram (reply) from Sir A Caldecott to Lord Moyne

Your telegram of the 9th April.[1] Personal. Present position is that Bandaranaike is

---

[1] See 91, where the date of Moyne's telegram is recorded as 8 Apr.

reported in the newspapers as having stated in public speeches that he has been misunderstood, that he wants England to win the war and that he has never advocated discourtesy towards the Governor. His reply to my demand for explanation is not yet in the form that I can accept and after consultation with the Legal Secretary I have sent further letter to him today. Reply to your question (1) is in the affirmative, vide opinion of Howard as Legal Secretary enclosed with my despatch of the 21st June 1938 Secret with which present Legal Secretary agrees. As regards (2) Legal Secretary feels that this is question which your advisers may be better able to answer but if reply is in affirmative he presumes that the power of His Majesty to dismiss will be in addition and not to the exclusion of the Governor's power of dismissal. There is no repeat, no deterioration in general position.

93   CO 54/980/15   18–21 Apr 1941
[Bandaranaike]: minutes by Sir S Abrahams[1] and Sir G Bushe on the governor's power to dismiss a minister

Sir G. Bushe
As a result of the discussion between yourself, Mr. Roberts-Wray and myself it would appear that we were all agreed that the Governor has no power to dismiss a Minister either (1) by importing the provisions of Section 9(c) of the Interpretation Ordinance, 1901, (Section 11(f) Revised Edition 1938) into the Order in Council, 1931, and adapting them for the purpose desired; or (2) by exercising the prerogative powers imputed to him in paragraph 7 of Mr. Howard's opinion of 15th June, 1938.

As to (1) it was our view that Article 37 of the Order in Council was exhaustive of the Governor's powers of dismissal of a Minister under that instrument since any attempt to effect dismissal by means of the Interpretation Ordinance would be, if inapt for no other reason, inconsistent with the pattern designed by the Order in Council for the working of that part of the constitution relating to the appointment and termination of appointment of a Minister.

As to (2) the power of the Governor to dismiss any servant of the Crown by virtue of the Royal prerogative is not something inherent in his authority as the King's representative but depends upon the constitutional instruments by which he is appointed and his functions are defined. The Governor of Ceylon therefore has no power as Governor to dismiss a Minister.

The prerogative power of the King to dismiss a Minister as a servant of the Crown holding office at the Royal pleasure is one which we found to be fraught with much difficulty and one which would obviously require careful unhurried consideration to decide. Presumably a communication should go to Ceylon stating that the views of the Legal Secretary as to the power of the Governor to dismiss are inacceptable, but that so far as the power of the King to dismiss is concerned the question is not free from difficulty and requires consideration.

S.S.A.
18.4.41

---

[1] Assistant legal adviser, CO.

There are two very learned persons in Ceylon taking the opposite view and therefore, both as a matter of courtesy and because if they have further arguments I should like to hear them, I think we should give some reasons. I suggest that we should insert after the first full stop in the telegram the following "Reasons shortly are (1) Article 37 is exhaustive of the Governor's powers to dismiss a Minister under the Order in Council and even if Interpretation Ordinance, apt to govern construction of a constitutional Order in Council provision referred to would be inconsistent with the pattern of the Order in Council in relation to the appointment and termination of appointment of a Minister; (2) the Governor has no general power to dismiss the King's servants, but only so much of the prerogative as is delegated to him by the constitutional instruments."

H.G.B.
21.4.41

94   CO 54/981/14, no 8   22 Apr 1941

[Indo–Ceylon relations]: inward telegram no 288 from Sir A Caldecott to Lord Moyne on the reservation of the immigration and registration bills

Your telegram No. 260. Grateful if Secretary of State for India might be asked to communicate to the Government of India your order that immigration and registration bills must be reserved. Reason for this request is that, although I made it quite clear by my message to State Council and subsequently in my reply to ministerial protest, that I shall reserve these bills, and although Clause 4 of the Royal Instructions makes reservation imperative, I have received unofficial but credible information that Government of India is waiting to see whether they are actually reserved or not, before it considers representations from Ceylon Planters' Association, made through Indian Government Agent here, for the relaxation of its immigration ban in respect of the return to Ceylon of estate labourers on holiday. Present position is that there is no provision whereby labourer can take accustomed periodical trip to India because his return is prevented by present method of working ban. Result is that large number of labourers are frozen here causing both discontent and surplus labour. Major Orde Browne who has given attention to the situation, authorises me to state that he is impressed by the seriousness of the problem of surplus labour on estates, although accurate figures are not available, and that he is satisfied as to its connexion with ban. If India once persist in refusal to provide holiday trips under ban it will not only perpetuate real hardships as regards nationals but will present Ceylon ministers with case for compulsory repatriation of surplus labour which is what they want. I should be glad if these considerations could be represented to Secretary of State for India, although owing to attitude at present taken up by my Ministers it is impossible for me to represent them direct to India as the views of this Government.

95   CO 54/980/15, no 6   23 Apr 1941

[Bandaranaike]: outward telegram no 278 from Lord Moyne to Sir A Caldecott on the governor's power to dismiss a minister

Your secret telegram No. 276.

I am glad to hear of your successful pressure on Bandaranaike. As regards your secret and personal telegram of 13th April[1] I am advised that Governor has no (repeat *no*) power to dismiss Minister either by (1) importing provisions of Interpretation Ordinance into State Council Order-in-Council 1931 and adapting them for purpose desired, or (2) by exercise of prerogative powers impute to him in Legal Secretary's opinion of 15th June, 1938.[2] Reasons shortly are (1) Article 37 is exhaustive of the Governor's powers to dismiss a Minister under the Order-in-Council and even if Interpretation Ordinance is apt to govern construction of a constitutional Order-in-Council provision referred to would be inconsistent with the pattern of the Order-in-Council in relation to the appointment and termination of appointment of a Minister; (2) the Governor has no general power to dismiss the King's servants, but only so much of the prerogative as is delegated to him by the constitutional instruments.

Question whether H.M. has power to dismiss Ceylon Ministers is not free from difficulty and requires consideration.

In these circumstances do you recommend that amendment of Order-in-Council should be prepared and held ready for enactment to meet any situation in which Governor might have to dismiss Minister in whom he had lost confidence? It would be necessary also to make it clear that Minister on dismissal would also cease to be Chairman of Executive Committee.

---

[1] See 92.   [2] See 93.

96   CO 54/984/4, no 2   1 May 1941

'Things Ceylonese': fourteenth periodical report by Sir A Caldecott for CO

Mr. S.W.R.D. Bandaranaike

1. In No.12 of these Notes[1] I reported the wedding of "Young Banda" to a lady of the Kandyan nobility and I expressed the hope that a good wife and the discipline of married life might provide him with the ballast that he had hitherto so sadly lacked. That hope has already been torpedoed by Bandaranaike's subsequent behaviour. On the domestic side an unpleasant altercation, in the course of which he denied his wife both board and bed, was overheard by fellow guests (European) in a Government Resthouse; while his public behaviour has necessitated my calling into question his retention of ministerial office.

2. People here always speak of "Young Banda", as if some allowance were permissible for youth and immaturity. It should be realized however that he is a man of forty, and has never yet shown any signs of acquiring principle or constancy. He

---

[1] See 72.

possesses eloquence, the power of quick and telling repartee, and agility in debate. If he were not indolent, he could also exercise a considerable mental capacity; but he finds it easier to peddle words than to deal in facts with the result that he never considers it worth his while to learn his brief or to match sound with sense. His recently deceased mother (a member of the aristocratic Obeyesekera family) was generally recognized as volatile and irresponsible so that her son may perhaps owe these traits to inheritance. Be that as it may I fear that in any estimate of Ceylon's political future he must be set down as an independable factor likely to upset the most careful calculations.

3. In the first annex[2] to these Notes are copies of the recent correspondence which has passed between me and Mr. Bandaranaike. In reference to the enclosure to my first letter of the 2nd April I should say that the reports of the Minister's statements were taken partly from Press shorthand and partly from Police longhand notes. There were numerous discrepancies between them and I was advised by the Legal Secretary that I could rely on neither source; nevertheless the tone of the Minister's speech in State Council (the proof of which he himself corrected for Hansard) leaves neither of us in doubt that, even if his other public statements have been misreported, they must have been of such a type as to render the words they wrote down credible at any rate to the reporters.

4. I have been reliably informed that the recipient's immediate reaction to both my letters was to seek out his colleagues and to try persuade them to join in a general walk out such as took place in February last year. They replied however that they disapproved of his action regarding contributions to the War Funds and also of his speeches, and that if he wanted to resign he could do so alone. The results have been his submission to my demand for a cancellation of the decision of his Executive Committee; a number of speeches in which he has said that he has been misunderstood and that he wants us to win the war; leading and other articles in all three English papers condemning him; and a momentary political eclipse. In Ceylon however political memory is short and consistency at a discount; it would be too sanguine therefore to expect any very long respite from Mr. Bandaranaike's vagaries. It is a tragedy that at this time of necessity for the utmost co-operation in war effort the most favourable thing that can be said for his possession of a portfolio is that he is more observable and more under restraint in the ministerial boat (and thereby less dangerous) than he would be outside it.

Indo–Ceylon relations

5. On April 21st Mr. Senanayake came to see me and began conversation by saying that he was most anxious to come to terms with India and wondered whether something could not be done to effect a settlement. He then proceeded to outline 'a possible basis' which, if he had put it forward in Delhi last November, would almost certainly have avoided the breakdown of conversations. I promised to base a

---

[2] Annexes not printed. They are filed separately on CO 54/982/2, no 8. They contain correspondence between Caldecott and Bandaranaike arising from a decision on 19 Mar 1941 by the Executive Committee on Local Administration to withhold its sanction to contributions to war funds by local bodies pending (a) a satisfactory settlement of the position on certain undertakings which the governor stated had been given by the Ceylon government to its Indian counterpart in regard to the Indian question (see 84), and (b) the passage into law in a satisfactory form of the bills relating to this question (see 90).

Memorandum on his suggestions and to let him see it. The next day I received a letter from Sir Baron Jayatilaka requesting an interview at which to discuss the Indo–Ceylon problem which, he wrote, "demanded urgent solution". I replied by telephone, telling him of Senanayake's visit to me and suggesting that they should see me together on April 25th. I finished my Memorandum in time to supply them with copies beforehand, and at our meeting a number of alterations in it were made by them but none of such a nature as to alter its general purport.

6. The question then arose as to how to get the Memorandum to India. They could not officially subscribe to it at the present stage because, if they did so and India turned it down, they would be criticised as having changed their views without achieving anything thereby. I therefore undertook to transmit the Memorandum secretly and personally to the Viceroy as a *ballon d'essai*. The second enclosure to these Notes is a copy of my letter to the Viceroy with its enclosure.

7. Mr. Gimson, Controller of Labour, who accompanied the Ceylon Delegation to India, tells me that in his opinion the Memorandum affords reasonable prospect of a settlement. However that may be, it represents a great advance towards reasonableness in Sinhalese opinion and I feel that we are nearer a solution than we were.

Labour unrest

8. Except on the Government Hydro-Electric Scheme Works at Norton Bridge (where employees have gone out against the orders of their Union and without waiting for the finding of a Conciliation Board) there is no Strike on at the moment, and the Controller of Labour reported to me verbally last week that things are better than they have been for a year.

Surprise (?) election result

9. The Colombo North seat in State Council fell vacant recently by the death by Mrs. Naysum Saravanamuttu. It was contested in the Ceylon National Congress interest by her husband, the present Mayor of Colombo, and in the Labour interest by Mr. M.J. de Silva. The latter won it by a majority of nearly three thousand. The Labour party will now have two members in Council; the other being its leader, Mr. Goonesinha.

10. The result has been a surprise to most people, but not to those who keep their eyes open for signs of the times. Universal suffrage might conceivably (?) have worked all right for Ceylon if registration as a voter had remained to be applied for. When in 1935 Government assumed the responsibility of registering every qualified person a mass of voters emerged to whom politics meant nothing, but a vote meant getting a free ride to the poll and (to avoid an uglier word) a douceur in some form or other. An immediate result was that most respectable people in Ceylon fought shy of standing for State Council because they knew that to fight clean for the support of such constituents was synonymous with losing the contest. This was the first stage in a development which has now reached its second and corollary stage; i.e. respectable people will not go to the polls at all, because of the vicious atmosphere of rowdyism and dirty play that surrounds them. In this latest election in Colombo North only half of the electors polled.

11. The police are certainly to be congratulated on having maintained order; but the Police cannot guarantee a clean fight, much less a reasonable exercise of the franchise. I have heard no 'election stories' about Colombo North yet, but a

European who heard an Electoral address by the ex-convict Batuwantudawe (recently returned for Kalutara on the death, and in the place, of his popular and pitied father) informed me that his most telling argument ran as follows:—"Why do I ask you to let me represent you? It is because I am just one of you; and nobody need be fearful of addressing me, not even the lowest; for who could be lower than I have been, serving time in a common prison for impersonation and cheating".

12. As the annexes to these Notes are of unusual interest I will not delay their transmission by adding any more paragraphs to this instalment.

97 CO 54/980/4, no 4   8 May 1941
[Reforms]: outward telegram no 307 from Lord Moyne to Sir A Caldecott on the statement to be made to Ceylon ministers

Your telegram 21st April. I assume that proposed statement is for use as reply to Ministers only and not for publication. I note your strong recommendation in favour of despatch of Commission to Ceylon, but you will appreciate that difficulties in wartime of securing adequate personnel are likely to be insuperable; moreover visit of Commission might be expected to bring to a head communal tension at time when this should be avoided. Nothing has occurred to suggest that claims of Sinhalese and of minorities could be reconciled by any recommendations which Commission could make. In these circumstances I think that conference in London after war may well be better procedure. I imagine Ceylonese representatives would be unlikely to be prepared to visit this country under present conditions, even if conference earlier were thought feasible.

If further postponement of election has later to be decided upon, possible method of meeting criticism that Ministers are clinging to office at all costs, would be to provide for Executive Committees to be re-elected, or alternatively Ministers could resign and submit themselves for re-election by Executive Committees.

I suggest that reply to Ministers could be shortened to read as follows:—"Urgency and importance of constitutional question is fully recognised by His Majesty's Government, and progress will be made as soon as circumstances permit of full consideration of present difficulties. Before taking decisions on a matter of such importance to well-being of Ceylon His Majesty's Government would desire that principal interests involved should be fully consulted by means of commission or conference. Ministers will appreciate that this is not possible to arrange under present war conditions."

You mention deterioration of position. While I know that Indian controversy is acute, I was not aware of deterioration in other respects which could be attributable to constitutional difficulties. Please inform me in what ways position has worsened and give me your further views generally in light of above remarks.

98   CO 54/981/14, no 13   15 May 1941
[Ceylon Indian Congress]: inward telegram no 250 from Sir A
Caldecott to Lord Moyne transmitting a message of protest from the
Ceylon Indian Congress over bills to regulate immigration and the
registration of voters

Following from Ceylon Indian Congress.
   Begins. Ceylon Indian Congress, representing Ceylon Indians with membership of
over 120,000, condemn and protest against the principles and provisions of two bills
now before the State Council, one for regulating and controlling entry of non-
Ceylonese into Ceylon, the other for registering persons in Ceylon not possessing
Ceylon domicile of origin, as absolutely unnecessary, vexatious, contrary to expressed and implied agreements undertaken between India and Ceylon governments, and
gravely threatening the fundamental rights, interests and honour of Indians; has
demonstrated by such unanimous condemnation protests of Ceylon Indians by over
35 crowded public meetings all over Ceylon, and pray that consent to the said bills be
refused. *Ends.*

99   CO 54/981/14, no 10   May 1941
'Indians in Ceylon': CO note

The history of Ceylon from time immemorial has reflected in its every chapter the
close relations between the island and the Indian Continent, and a large Tamil
population has long been settled in the Northern part of the Island.
   Indians, mostly from South India, have gone to Ceylon for employment as
labourers and traders, and since the birth of the tea and rubber industries Indian
workers have moved to and fro between India and Ceylon in great numbers in the
course of their work on the estates. In the past no particular difficulties have arisen
over this influx of Indians into the island, and with a minimum measure of control by
the Government of Ceylon and the Government of India, these workers have been
able to pass backwards and forwards freely between the two countries.
   It was soon after the 1914–1918 war that more carefully regulated arrangements
to control the immigration of Indians into Ceylon were made. In 1922 the
Government of India passed its Emigration Act, and much correspondence passed
between the two Governments as to the exact terms on which further immigration of
Indians into Ceylon should be allowed, the Government of India insisting upon
certain rules which were in their view required to safeguard the interests of Indians
overseas. At that date Ceylon agreed to the appointment of a resident Agent of the
Government of India in Ceylon. From this date, therefore, a more comprehensive
system was introduced for controlling the movement of Indians between the two
countries. Suitable regulations were made by the Government of India and
legislation was passed by the Government of Ceylon to regulate conditions of
employment on the estates, and in the constitution framed for Ceylon ten years ago
the political rights of all residents in the Island were given a new definition.
   The total population of Ceylon is about 5½ million of whom the most numerous

elements are the Sinhalese 3½ million and the Tamils 1½ million. Of the latter a substantial number have for generations past been settled in the Island and others come to and fro between the Island and India—in 1938, 180,000 Indians including 50,000 labourers were recorded in such migration.

Nationalistic feeling has increased in India and in Ceylon, and the economic problems which have affected the world so much since the 1914–1918 Great War have had their effect also upon the position of Indians in the island.

Of late, there has grown up a feeling in Ceylon, particularly among the Sinhalese, that there are too many Indians in the island, and that they are taking away work from the Sinhalese. The Government of India, in turn, have felt constrained to press for fuller recognition of the rights of Indians who have settled down in the island and have the intention of making it their home.

The conflict of views between the two Governments came to a head some two years ago when the Ceylon Government decided to reaffirm their policy of giving preference in Government employment to locally born Ceylonese, and to discharge a number of daily-paid Indians who had been recently taken into Government employment, and also to offer a scheme of voluntary repatriation to other "non-Ceylonese" in Government employment. This led the Government of India to place a retaliatory ban on the further emigration of Indian labourers to Ceylon which upset the normal free movement of such Indians between India and Ceylon.

There has also of late been a considerable growth in Ceylon of labour unrest, particularly on the estates, the causes of which reflect both the growing conscious-ness of labour as to its political and industrial rights and also the social disturbance created by the interruption of their free contacts with their homes and relatives in India.

In an attempt to solve round the table the differences between the two Governments arrangements were made for a delegation from the Ceylon Govern-ment to meet a delegation from the Government of India last November, but the negotiations broke down. The Ceylon Ministers then decided to introduce two Bills into the State Council to provide for the control of future immigration into Ceylon and for the registration of non-Ceylonese residing in the island. The Bills are considerably less drastic in form than at one time seemed likely, and they are at present before a Standing Committee of the State Council. The two Bills will be reserved for the signification of His Majesty's Pleasure before they can be placed on the Statute Book. In order that certain undertakings towards Indians in Ceylon by which the Ceylon Government is bound may be publicly appreciated in the Island the Governor has issued a message to the State Council which sets out the substance of those undertakings.

The following reports[1] are attached:—

(1) Report on Immigration into Ceylon by Sir Edward Jackson.
(2) Sessional Papers VIII, IX, AND X of 1941 which give the history of the Exploratory Conference in India.
(3) A copy of a message from the Governor regarding undertakings given to the Government of India.
(4) Sessional Paper XIV of 1941 which contains the Ceylon Ministers' protest in regard to the message, and the Governor's reply to that protest.

---

[1] Not printed.

100   CO 54/980/4, no 5   28 June 1941

[Reforms]: inward telegram (reply) no 495 from Sir A Caldecott to Lord Moyne on the governor's reform proposals

Your telegram No. 307. Secret.[1] Position is deteriorating in following major respects:—

(a) There is no longer any consensus of co-operation or even consultation between members of so-called Homogeneous Ministry except when Nationalist or Communist considerations dictate in any matter *ad hoc* combination.

(b) Executive Committees realise more and more the power and opportunities for interference.

(c) As a result of (a) and (b) defects enumerated in paragraph 13 of my 1938 reforms despatch are now much worse.

(d) Members of present State Council have become so stale and indolent that both in Council and Committee important measures are constantly held up for lack of quorum while only sensational items in the agenda, such as motions of censure or criticism are debated at length in full house.

(2) Any statement now to be made to Ministers must be in a form communicable by them to the public, political elements amongst which are growing restive and in particular Sinhala Sabha party has begun to raise outcry that three years after my reforms despatch, and nearly two since State Council debate thereon, there is still no indication of the extent to which His Majesty's Government would be prepared to consider reforms along the lines proposed. There is also general criticism of delay in view of decisions taken in war time in case of West Indies.[2] Demand is now for Dominion Status.

(3) It is recognised on all sides that no measure of agreement can ever be obtained by appointment of commission or by conferences however constituted held here or in England. Success of any reforms will lie not in pleasing all or any communities but in causing each to shed equal number of tears. My suggestion of commission was not based on any hope of agreement but on consideration explained in last sentence of paragraph (5) of my Secret and Personal telegram of 10th June last year.

(4) My recommendations for reforms remain as in my original despatch, as modified by my Confidential despatch of 28th October, 1939,[3] with the following exceptions:—

(a) Question of Indian franchise must now await resumption of conversations with India, my telegram No. 447. Secret.

(b) Insolvency and present or past conviction of crime should disqualify for membership of State Council; this is necessitated by recent return of ex-convict in by-election, and by public demand for enquiry into bribery and corruption of

---

[1] See 97.
[2] A reference especially to the proposed reform of the Jamaican constitution (see 101) which was subsequently enacted in 1944.
[3] See 9.

Councillors which State Council itself has recently supported by formal resolution.

(c) I revert to recommendation in paragraph 24 of original despatch for retention of Legal Secretary as Legal Adviser.

(d) Financial Secretary should be replaced by Financial Controller in purely advisory capacity as I first envisaged, *vide* second sentence of paragraph 26 of original despatch.

(e) Public Services Commission should consist of Principal Secretary to the Governor, Legal Adviser and three unofficials nominated by the Governor.

(5)   In view of impossibility of early commission or of ever achieving agreement by conference, Chief and Legal Secretaries agree with me that requirements of present situation would be best met by message from you to the effect that His Majesty's Government would be prepared to view favourably reform along general lines indicated in the preceding paragraph and suggest proposals should be crystallized here in the form of a draft new Order in Council for detailed consideration by His Majesty's Government. Preparation of such a draft will enable quick decisions on clear issues and avoid misunderstanding or obscurity. (? I urge moreover) Committee recommended in paragraph 6 of my original despatch should also be appointed so that its report may be considered by you at the same time as draft Order in Council.

(6)   Message from you in above sense would allay suspicion often expressed that war is being made the pretext for delaying consideration of reforms and there would I think ensue general agreement that the next general election should be postponed until after the war or until new Constitution is ready. It would also arrest the deterioration mentioned in paragraph (1) (d) above and re-animate the State Councillors.

101   CO 54/980/4   11–15 July 1941
[Reforms]: minutes by Sir G Bushe and Sir C Parkinson on the problem of an imposed solution

There are, as it seems to me, three possible things that one can do about the Ceylon constitution:—

(1)   Go backwards and govern the island and have no nonsense about it;

(2)   Go right forward into self-government on the Southern Rhodesia lines and throw your minorities to the mercy and good sense of the majority;

(3)   To have another compromise which protects or purports to protect the minorities, and which gives, or purports to give, reserve powers to the Governor.

I should have thought that the only one of these which could be dealt with without consultation and negotiation between the parties in Ceylon would be No. 1. I do not see how you can expect anything in the nature of a liberal constitution to work if it is imposed from here.

H.G.B.
11.7.41

Secretary of State (through Mr. Hall)
The fact that we can embark on an important measure of constitutional reform in Jamaica (not to mention Trinidad and British Guiana) during the war makes it difficult, at first sight, to refuse to undertake constitutional reform in Ceylon until the war is over. But (even apart from Mr. Gent's point about India and Burma) the answer is clear. In the case of Jamaica the proposed changes are not a matter for violent controversy; in Ceylon, with its racial majority and minority problems, the position is entirely different.

It is perhaps tempting to take the line that the Ceylonese will never agree among themselves: so let us introduce our own scheme of reform, and tell them that that is what we believe to be fair and that they will have to settle down and work the new constitution. But is that really wise? We may, of course, be driven to it if and when a conference fails, just as in the case of Palestine in 1939. But dictated settlements do not achieve finality and they almost certainly do achieve dissatisfaction and political unrest, and it is worth while struggling hard for an agreed scheme of reform even if in the end the attempt fails.

I agree that it would be well to telegraph as in draft.[1]

A.C.C.P.
15.7.41

---

[1] See 102.

102   CO 54/980/4, no 8   23 July 1941
[Reforms]: outward telegram (reply) no 496 from Lord Moyne to Sir A Caldecott

Your Secret telegram No. 495.[1] I am genuinely desirous of promoting beneficial reform of constitution as soon as possible without insisting on local agreement, but is it advisable to proceed with changes which in present conditions may create effects more damaging to Ceylon than mere indolence or slow motion on part of State Councillors? I quite understand what you mean in saying that touchstone of success of reforms would be equal shedding of tears by all communities, but is there any advantage in effecting that result in wartime unless and until it is necessary to relieve any intolerable distress which one or other of communities is suffering?

2. Your appreciation of position shows that principal defects of Committee system summarised in your despatch of 13th June, 1938, have tended to become more apparent and injurious to efficiency but at present we have something like political truce in Ceylon with emergency powers temporarily exercised by Government to ensure executive action in matters arising out of defence requirements. Before that is disturbed I should have to satisfy Parliament as well as Government of India that any changes to which substantial minority communities object are nevertheless urgently necessary in face of war conditions and in face of His Majesty's Government's policy towards constitutional changes in Burma and India. I do not think that principal measures in reforms scheme, *e.g.*, abolition of Executive Committees and Officers of State and institution of Cabinet system, would pass this

---

[1] See 100.

test in present circumstances and I believe you would agree that there would be no advantage in effecting merely a few relatively unimportant reforms now.

3. Subject to your further views I am still therefore inclined to think that statement to Ministers in terms of paragraph 3 of my Secret telegram No. 307[2] is most candid and practical course. It was intended for publication but if you consider its terms or form could be improved with that object I shall be very ready to reconsider.[3]

---

[2] See 97.

[3] Moyne sent a further tel on 23 July which read: 'I hope you will not be disappointed at the contents of my telegram No. 496. The facilities for inefficiency and obstruction offered by the present constitution must sometimes drive you almost to exasperation and you must often be tempted to think that anything would be better than the indefinite continuance of the present state of affairs. But I must confess that I am loath to stir up controversy on this most difficult subject during the war unless it is absolutely necessary to do so, for there is no obvious solution that we can feel clearly right in enforcing through thick and thin. I am sure that you will understand this point of view' (CO 54/980/4, no 9).

103   CO 54/980/4, no 11   15 Aug 1941

[Reforms]: inward telegram (reply) no 633 from Sir A Caldecott to Lord Moyne on the statement to be made to Ceylon ministers

Your telegram No. 496.[1] may I suggest slight variation of the statement proposed by your telegram No. 307[2] as follows:—

> "Urgency and importance of Constitutional Reform is fully recognised by His Majesty's Government and progress will be pressed for as soon as circumstances permit. Before taking decisions on the proposals, concerning which there has been so little unanimity but which are of such importance to the well-being of Ceylon, His Majesty's Government would desire that the position should be further examined and made the subject of further consultation by means of Commission or Conference. Ministers will appreciate that this is not possible to arrange under war conditions but the matter will be given immediate post war priority."

Statement along such lines will of course involve question of further postponement of general election. Leader of State Council speaking on the budget has stated the personal opinion that the Counsellors are stale and that the election should be held next year. I would wish however to await ministerial and general political reactions to the statement before submitting any recommendation.

---

[1] See 102.   [2] See 97.

104   CO 54/980/11, no 1   22 Aug 1941

[Reforms]: inward telegram no 651 from Sir A Caldecott to Lord Moyne transmitting the view of the Board of Ministers that HMG should apply the principles of the Atlantic Charter to Ceylon

My telegram No. 633.[1]

Board of Ministers have officially notified the view that further delay in making pronouncement on actual position regarding reforms is not in the public interest and have requested me so to represent to you by telegraph. Private member 19th August gave notice of motion containing following paragraph:—

> "This Council therefore requests H.M.G. to give effect to the eight-point Anglo–American declaration[2] by immediate assurance that proposals for full self-government will be granted to this country and requests the Board of Ministers to frame constitution for approval of this House and to take immediate steps to secure the assent of His Majesty to same".

---

[1] See 103.
[2] ie the Atlantic Charter, for coverage of which see BDEEP series A, vol 1, S R Ashton & S E Stockwell, eds, *Imperial policy and colonial practice 1925–1945*, part I, 26 & 27.

105   CO 54/984/4, no 3   23 Aug 1941

'Things Ceylonese': fifteenth periodical report by Sir A Caldecott for CO

The ministers

1.   Since my last instalment of these Notes[1] Mr. Bandaranaike has, I hear from the Legal Secretary, assumed the role of Governor's champion in the Board of Ministers. He has certainly been extremely affable and courteous to me: sed timeo Danaos.

2.   Mr. George de Silva, Member for Kandy, is acting as Minister for Health. 'Our George' is generally liked for his honesty of speech and action. In a character so volatile and undisciplined by restraints of rhyme or reason such honesty is somewhat hard to distinguish from irresponsibility. He is doing a lot of good however by rushing about the Island on hospital inspections which the substantive Minister, Mr. W.A. de Silva, has been too decrepit and senile to perform for a long time. The leave granted to the latter by the State Council followed the death of his wife, whose social service and philanthropy had endeared her to many, especially to her fellow enthusiasts in the Buddhistic religion. The old man is long past his period of usefulness and it is a great pity that he does not permanently lay down his portfolio.

The budget

3.   The Ministers' refusal to budget for the imposition of an all-round excess profits duty tax on the revenue side or for a full payment of Defence items on the expenditure side has elicited a large measure of criticism and condemnation from the

---

[1] See 96.

European community, nearly all of which is deserved. A case for debiting some of the Defence expenditure to loan account could be made out if profits arising out of the war were first adequately taxed for war purposes. This the Ministers refuse to do on the pleas that before the war the tea, rubber and plumbago industries were abnormally depressed and that a great proportion of the present improvement represents not war profits but reasonable adjustment of past deficits. The falseness of such a theory will in due course be proved by post-war economic history, and my impression is that the Ministers know this perfectly well and do not really believe in their own arguments.

4. Messrs Senanayake and Kotelawala both have extensive plantation and mining interests, and a profiteering mentality is often openly charged against both. There is probably something in this, but the general ministerial attitude towards public finance cannot in my view be explained so simply. I ascribe it to two main causes. The first is psychological and lies in their reactions to the character and manner of the Financial Secretary. The saying that a man is the creature of his career is not inapplicable to Mr. Huxham. His long service in the Board of Inland Revenue followed by his able initiation and primal administration of the Income tax organization here have inevitably evolved in him an efficiency and an outlook not unrestricted by specialism. He has neither statesmanship, administrative tact nor diplomacy and his idea of persuasion is to proclaim to the Ministers that if this thing is done, or if that thing is not done, the Secretary of State will need to advise refusal of the Royal Assent or order exercise by the Governor of his reserve powers. This of course is an inevitably unsuccessful method of approaching colleagues to whom a mere mention of Whitehall is as a red rag to a bull. The second main cause of the Ministers' imperviousness to sound financial considerations is not psychological but ratiocinative. They rather look forward to future bankruptcy than apprehend it. In their view it will provide the opportunity, nay the necessity, of raiding the roost of personal emoluments and of reducing the wealth and standard of living enjoyed by public servants to a local and non-European level.

Envious dislike of public servants

5. The dowry that a young Ceylonese Civil Servant can command in the local marriage market is the highest that the market attracts. The reasons for his desirability as a son-in-law include the following considerations. The average Ceylonese officer has his children well educated, but with remarkable cheapness, at the Government's Royal College or at one of the big State-aided schools in Colombo, Kandy, Galle and Jaffna. He has never to pay the expenses of two establishments or to provide holiday homes for his children. His womenfolk do not wear expensive European frocks but prefer the more beautiful but much less costly sarees of India. His domestic budget amounts therefore to much less than that of his European confrère though their emoluments (except in the case of recent appointees) are precisely the same. The result is that the Ceylonese holders of Government appointments (in the classes ordinarily recruited in other Colonies from Europe) form the best off and most securely placed sections of the population.

6. When to their comparative affluence is added their association with, and natural preference for, the ways of bureaucracy rather than those of democracy, their unpopularity with Ministers, State Councillors, politicians and nationalists needs no further explanation. If Ministers and State Councillors had not themselves accepted

remuneration at rates which nationalists represent as unnecessarily high for the requirements of a national life, criticism in State Council of the salaries enjoyed by the older Civil Servants would be even more frequent than it is. Successive revisions of scales of pay for new entrants to the Services have always had a lower level in view; but the provisions of Article 87 of the Order in Council, the recent refusal of the Secretary of State to approve consideration by a Commission of the pay of serving officers and my own refusal to entertain the idea of a salary levy have temporarily deterred the Ministers and Council from pressing any attempt to deprive present holders of Government appointments of the terms on which they hold them. The urge to do so is however always present in their minds.

7. It must be remembered also in this connection that the machinery of territorial administration in this Island remains of the Crown Colony form; that a Government Agent or Assistant Government Agent still regards himself as, and indeed still largely is, a 'Raja of Bhong'. This fact, and the public servant's consciousness of it, is most obnoxious to the 'democratic' politician. There already is talk abroad of substituting for the Government Agents and their Kachcheries a system of Provincial and District Councils. Their Chairmen would be "elected representatives of the people" and all that would be required of Civil Servants would be to carry out in a clerical or subordinate capacity the policies and dictates of the Councils.

8. Of the democratization of Ceylon it must be confessed that so far there are but few signs of the real thing. The aim of the self-styled 'democrats' is merely to push the public service out of the saddle and to hoist their own persons into it. It is certain, I fear, that Government Servants will more and more become subjected to attacks inspired by general jealousy of their position, the determination of dema-gogues to usurp their high places, and by the odium inseparable from the protection of Whitehall afforded to them by Articles 86 and 87 of the order in Council. It is a great pity that in the early days of Ceylonization of the Services a distinction was not made by means of an Overseas allowance or otherwise to adjust the salaries of local and overseas recruits to their respective economic circumstances. General accept-ance of the fact that Ceylonese officers are overpaid must naturally prejudice their popularity.

Labour unrest

9. The position is better than it has been for a long time, and at the moment of writing there is no strike that I know of anywhere. I have throughout our difficulties been impressed by the way in which Mr. Gimson, as Controller of Labour, and his two Deputy Controllers at Hatton and Badulla have kept their heads. The two Deputies are Ceylon–Tamil members of the Ceylon Civil Service, and the following excerpt from Mr. Rajendra's diary for June gives a retrospect of his eighteen months work at Hatton:—

> "*In Kandy: 14th June*. Assumed duties in Kandy. I have left Hatton after being there for exactly 18 months. The early months there were very trying. Labour Unrest was wide spread and there was absolutely no contact between the employers and the Trade Unions. My appearance on the scene as Deputy Controller was viewed with suspicion by both the Trade Unions and the employers. I was soon able to win the confidence of the Trade Unions because

my instructions were to encourage the growth of healthy and progressive Trade Unions. Winning the confidence of the employers was a slower process. At the outset they expected me to support them in their efforts to suppress Trade Union activities. When I explained that the policy of Government was to encourage healthy Trade Unionism, they resented my presence and often disapproved of the advice I tendered. With personal contact with individual employers the attitude changed first in Dickoya and later in Dimbula. Strangely enough my departure from Hatton is regretted more by the employers than by the Trade Unionists. After having gone all out to establish contact between the Trade Unionists and the employers, during the later part of my stay in Hatton, I had often to criticise the incompetent manner in which the Trade Unions were run. The Congress often took the criticism in good part but the Federation, which is more dishonestly run than incompetently, was inclined to resent any criticism. I am sure Mr. Natesa Iyer welcomes my transfer."

10. The other Deputy Controller at Badulla has recently started a movement in Uva Province for Social Service by the wives of Planters among women and children on their estates. It is meeting, I am glad to say, with response. The growth of the Boy Scout movement on the plantations continues to make excellent progress. As far as I see or hear of him Mr. Hamilton is proving a good and reasonable Chairman of the Planters' Association. He is not happy about things of course, and tells me that returns furnished by District Planters' Associations show that the number of instances in which estate employees have been reported to have resorted to restraint, intimidation, assault or violence against employers or their Agents since the seven point Agreement with the Labour Unions came into force thirteen months ago is over eighty. From his account of two cases of 'intimidation' I should have labelled both 'insult' or 'rudeness'. I have little doubt that few of the 80 reported cases can have been criminally actionable; though the number reflects the unpleasant atmosphere in which some unfortunate planters are living.

11. The recent Harbour Strike, the facts of which I have reported to the Colonial Office, needed to be nipped in the bud. As four Ministers were affected (Labour, Communications, Defence and Home Affairs) and as everybody's job tends to be nobody's I hurried down from Kandy, conferred with the Board of Ministers, and got the nippers applied with unanimity and prompt effectuality. The Port workers had legitimate grievances, but strike tactics had been stimulated by a few political agitators of Communist complexion.

Indo–Ceylon relations

12. The Conversations are to be resumed here on 1st September; the wording of a communiqué to this effect being still the subject of telegraphic correspondence between the two Governments. The personnel of the Indian delegation is not yet known but it will be led by Sir Girja Bajpai. The Ceylon delegation has been chosen by the Board of Ministers and will consist of Mr. Senanayake (Leader), Mr. Corea and Mr. Drayton. This means that our delegation will be identical with that which went to India last year except that Mr. Drayton takes the place of Mr. Bandaranaike who (being against the resumption of talks) voluntarily stepped out. I gather that the Board would have liked the inclusion of Sir Baron Jayatilaka, but that (a) Mr.

Senanayake made it clear that he himself must again lead the delegation and (b) Sir Baron was not going to be led. Mr. Huxham will not take part in any conversations until the stage of trade negotiation is reached. This cannot be until October as the Indian Trade Delegate is not yet available nor is India prepared to talk trade until agreement has been reached on other matters.

13. Indians in the Madras Presidency and in Ceylon are representing the recent Indo–Burman Agreement as a betrayal by India of her nationals in Burma. I fear that this political agitation, which is obviously causing the Indian Government embarrassment cannot be expected to contribute towards the much hoped for success of the renewed Indo–Ceylon conversations.

106   CO 54/980/11, no 2, WP(G)(41)82   27 Aug 1941
'Ceylon constitution': War Cabinet memorandum by Lord Moyne on the policy statement to be made to the Board of Ministers

In November 1938, Mr. MacDonald submitted recommendations to the Cabinet relating to the reform of the constitution of Ceylon. The Governor had made certain proposals for reform, and Mr. MacDonald sought the authority of the Cabinet for publishing these and arranging for them to be debated in the State Council of Ceylon. The intention was that, if general opinion was in favour of the principles of the proposals, an amending Order-in-Council should at once be drafted for putting them into effect. These recommendations were approved by the Cabinet.

2. The Governor's proposals were debated at length in the State Council, but resulted in a pronounced failure of the representatives of the Sinhalese majority community and those of the minority communities (Ceylon and Indian Tamils, Burghers, Moslems and Europeans) to reach any basis of agreement. Further examination of the problem was interrupted by the outbreak of war. There has followed a kind of informal political truce on this subject between the communities in Ceylon, and the local advocacy of communal claims has not been publicly pressed, though there is no reason to doubt that they would appear with no loss of virulence if opportunity were given. To avoid this, the life of the State Council, which should have expired not later than January 1941, was prolonged by Order in Council last year for a period up to two years—ostensibly to provide further time to consider the question of constitutional reform.

3. It has become increasingly clear that a settlement cannot be satisfactorily carried out until the war is over. In view of the opposition of the minorities to the recent proposals, I do not see how any substantial reforms can be brought into force until there has been a further examination of the whole position either by a commission sent to Ceylon, or by the summoning of a conference in Ceylon or, preferably, in London. Neither of these courses is feasible in present conditions. Moreover, it would be difficult during the war to carry into effect further substantial advances in the already advanced constitution of Ceylon, if in India and in Burma the lines of constitutional progress are not to be settled until the war is over. A decision by His Majesty's Government to reform the Ceylon constitution in any other direction than that of increased powers for the Ceylon Ministers and elected representatives would be in conflict with reasonable expectations and would confront us with very serious reactions in the Island.

4. The Governor reports that there is some deterioration in the local political position and that the present State Council is getting stale. Even so, I feel that there are greater objections to attempting to reform the constitution now than to allowing it to operate a little longer. At present communal feeling is not asserting itself in the political field, and the Governor has powers under Defence Regulations which he can and does exercise to ensure necessary executive action in matters arising out of defence requirements; whereas the knowledge that the reform of the constitution was under active examination would at once intensify public expressions of communal feeling, and might lead in present conditions to a difficult problem of law and order in the Island with some reactions even in political circles in India.

5. I propose therefore to instruct the Governor to issue to the Ministers in Ceylon the following statement which has been provisionally agreed with the Governor:—

> "His Majesty's Government have had under further consideration the question of constitutional reform in Ceylon. The urgency and importance of the reform of the constitution is fully recognised by His Majesty's Government, but before taking decisions upon the present proposals for reform, concerning which there has been so little unanimity, but which are of such importance to the well-being of Ceylon, His Majesty's Government would desire that the position should be further examined and made the subject of further consultation by means of a commission or conference. The Board of Ministers will appreciate that this cannot be arranged under war conditions, but the matter will be taken up with the least possible delay after the war."

This announcement would be intended for publication in the State Council by arrangement with the Ministers and would be published in this country at the same time. If the Board of Ministers wished to suggest any amendment of the form or terms of the statement before its publication, I should be ready to agree provided that it were not substantially altered.

6. As soon as the statement has been made public, it will be necessary to consider, in the light of the local expression of feelings, whether a further extension of the life of the present State Council should be arranged, or whether an election should be held in or before January, 1943.[1]

---

[1] The War Cabinet approved the statement on 28 Aug (WM 87(41)10) and the decision was conveyed by Moyne to Caldecott in tel 598 on 30 Aug (CO 54/980/4, no 15).

107   CO 54/980/4, no 18   1 Oct 1941
[Reforms]: inward telegram no 774 from Sir A Caldecott to Lord Moyne conveying the response of the Board of Ministers to HMG's statement

Your telegram No. 598.[1] My telegram No. 754. Ministers have asked me to telegraph the following expression of their views. *Begins*:—The Board of Ministers has carefully considered the letter of His Excellency The Governor of 1st September,

---

[1] See 106, note 1.

1931, conveying proposals of His Majesty's Government regarding reform of Ceylon constitution and are strongly opposed to such proposals for the following reasons:—

1. The proposals involve a delay in dealing with the question of constitutional reform for a period, which is both indefinite and may be protracted. Such delay is most undesirable because the present constitution was accepted as an experiment over ten years ago, during which period serious defects in the constitution have manifested themselves; an indefinite continuance of the constitution, in its present form, is detrimental to the best interests of the country. It must further be pointed out that the life of the present State Council has been extended for two years by the Secretary of State for specific purpose of dealing with the question of reform.

2. The appointment of a commission or holding of a conference for further investigation—(a) Is unnecessary because His Excellency The Governor, at the request of the Secretary of State, has fully examined the constitutional position, and, after consultation with all sections of opinion, has submitted his recommendations. These recommendations have also been carefully considered by the State Council, which has expressed its views thereon. (b) Is most undesirable, because, while such a commission or conference is not likely to produce any fresh material which would be helpful in dealing with the problem, it will undoubtedly create much bitterness and ill-will amongst the various sections of the people of the country. *Ends.*

My letter to which the Ministers have thus replied made it clear that you were prepared to consider only minor amendments to the draft statement not (repeat not) involving substantial alternations.

108   CO 54/980/4, no 19   1 Oct 1941
[Constitutional reform]: inward telegram no 775 from Sir A Caldecott to Lord Moyne conveying the views of representatives of the minorities

Four members of the State Council, Ponnambalam, Mahadeva, Pereira and Jayah interviewed me to-day on behalf of Ceylon Tamil Indians and Moslems of whom they are the representatives. They explained that, while they are most anxious not to embarrass the Imperial Government with the question of local constitutional reforms at this juncture, nevertheless they felt it their duty to emphasise that the continuance of the present inadequate representation of minority communities under the existing constitution is inimical to the minorities' interests. They urge therefore that if the Commission is unable to come out here before the termination of the war, Parliamentary Committee should, on the model of the Round Table Indian Conference, be appointed to meet delegates from all the Ceylon communities at any venue convenient to such Committee. They add that their present position has become intolerable and cannot be ameliorated by fresh election on the present electoral basis. Preceding representations, which I telegraph at their request, have been occasioned by the unauthorised newspaper statement reported by my telegram No 754.

109   CO 54/980/4, no 20   7 Oct 1941
[Reforms]: outward telegram (reply) no 701 from Lord Moyne to Sir A Caldecott

Your telegrams 774 and 775.[1] Please inform Board of Ministers that I have received and considered their views as expressed in telegram under reference, and that the course they advocate had been most carefully considered before His Majesty's Government had reluctantly reached their conclusion that, in face of wide measure of local disagreement, no substantial changes in existing Constitution could be introduced without further opportunity for examination of conflicting views of various interests concerned, which is impracticable in war conditions, but will be taken as soon as peace is won.

2. As regards your telegram No. 775, please inform four representatives concerned that I note and much appreciate their desire not to embarrass His Majesty's Government at this juncture: but that possibility of arranging adequate Commission in existing conditions was found to be quite impracticable if it were to be of required standard of representation and authority. It was precisely for reason that no decision for substantial changes in existing Constitution ought to be taken without most careful re-examination of views and interests of all concerned in Ceylon that conclusion was reluctantly reached that necessary consultation could not be carried through under war conditions.

---

[1] See 107 & 108.

110   CO 54/980/4, no 28   3 Nov 1941
[Reforms]: inward telegram (reply) no 863 from Sir A Caldecott to Lord Moyne

Your telegram No. 701.[1] Statement which was the subject of your telegram No. 598[2] was placed before the State Council on the 28th October. Ministers in Board meeting same day expressed (a) the view that:—

(i) Local circumstances are not materially different from when reforms were last discussed here.
(ii) Fullest representations on the subject are already before you.
(iii) No need therefore for further consultation by means of commission or conference or
(iv) For deferring question of reforms until after the war and

(b) Request that I should communicate their dissatisfaction to you by telegraph. I will inform them that I have done so.

---

[1] See 109.   [2] See 106, note 1.

111 CO 54/980/4, no 29   7 Nov 1941
[Reforms]: outward telegram (reply) no 773 from Lord Moyne to Sir A Caldecott

Your telegram No. 863.[1] Confidential. Please inform Board of Ministers that I have received their communiction, and that I hope that they will give their minds constantly to the question of how best the present conflict of views in Ceylon on the constitutional problem may be resolved and a general measure of agreement secured amongst all interests in Ceylon as to the reforms which are desirable. I cannot help doubting whether it is the case that Ceylon and her important general interests have been so untouched by the world events of the last two years that it can rightly be said that the local circumstances are not materially different now. Rather am I impressed with the urgent need for unity and concord to be sought by statesmen in Ceylon no less than in other parts of the Empire, and I hope that the Ministers and the leading members of all important interests in the island will lose no opportunity to work for agreement before decisions have to be taken which must affect Ceylon's orderly and peaceful welfare for years to come.

[1] See 110.

112 CO 54/980/4, no 30   10 Nov 1941
[Reforms]: inward unnumbered telegram (reply) from Sir A Caldecott to Lord Moyne

Much regret my omission to make clear in my telegram No. 863[1] my view that communication by me to you of Ministers' dissatisfaction was the only action required thereon and that no reply thereto was advisable. It is certain that communication to Ministers of your telegram No. 773[2] would cause immediate deterioration of political situation without any compensatory advantage. Newspaper to-day reports resolution of Ceylon Congress Committee to boycott any conference or committee appointed by you after the war; but both this resolution and Ministers' expression of dissatisfaction are merely face-saving reactions to recent statement of His Majesty's Government and will be best ignored. In these circumstances beg to request that your telegram No. 773 may be cancelled.

[1] See 110.   [2] See 111.

113 CO 54/980/5/1, no 1   23 Dec 1941
[Reforms]: letter from Sir A Caldecott to G E J Gent surveying the history of the reform proposals

I am most grateful for your letter 18330/12A/41 of the 15th November (in which you ask whether as regards reforms procedure we are now in complete suspense with no hope of any further constructive thinking on the problem by the several political sections in Ceylon) because it affords an excellent opportunity of removing any risk of our being at cross purposes in this tricky matter. The answer to your question is, I regret to say, undoubtedly in the negative.

2. In my Confidential despatch of 28th October, 1939,[1] I wrote (paragraph 6)

> "I am convinced that nearly all our political fissures radiate from the vexed question of minority representation"

and in paragraphs 35, 36 and 39 of that despatch I supported Howard's (third) proposal "to make a further effort to settle the question of the representation". To this end I suggested appointment of the Delimitation Committee recommended in paragraph 6 of my Reforms Despatch of 13th June, 1938, and agreed to by State Council in its eleventh Motion on Reforms. When Mr. MacDonald asked me to discuss with him certain points of my Reforms Despatch during my short trip to England in August and September 1938, I understood him to agree with me as to the fundamental necessity of appointing this Committee (whatever State Council might think about it) as a basis for reform; so that after Howard had on page 64 of his appreciation of the Reforms Debate (page 64, Vol.II of the first enclosure to my despatch of 28th October, 1939) given his opinion that

> "if the question of representation was settled and some of the other proposals slightly modified the Scheme of Reforms would be accepted".

it came as a shock to me to receive a direct rejection of our joint view in paragraph 5 of Mr. MacDonald's despatch of the 26th January, 1940:—

> "the third course suggested by Mr. Howard is that a further effort should be made to settle certain questions of representation in the State Council. I recognize it to be possible that useful, although limited, results of a kind generally acceptable in the Island might be achieved by this means, but I cannot see that it would serve as a substitute in any measurable degree for a plan to make headway with the general problem of constitutional reform".[2]

3. Events made it impossible to take immediate action on Mr. MacDonald's suggestion for "convening a Governor's Conference of the Board of Ministers and other leaders representative of the chief interests in the Island with a view to discussing the best means of achieving agreement". On the 19th February I confidentially conveyed to the Ministers the sense of the despatch, but before a Conference could be arranged the Ministers went on strike (February 28th, 1940) and remained 'out' till 17th March. On the 16th March the Times of Ceylon published a leading article entitled "Case for Royal Commission", which ended with the words "despite the other anxieties of the War the Secretary of State should regard Ceylon as a war problem and send a Royal Commission before it is too late". This rapidly became the shibboleth of all Minority politicians and when on the 18th April, 1940, I met the Board of Ministers at Nuwara Eliya the demand for a Commission had become exceedingly vocal. Nevertheless the Ministers, to their credit, did not pay undue attention to it and from my confidential despatch of 23rd April, 1940,[3] it will be seen their refusal to join in any Conference was due to (a) reluctance to bargain on the question of an increase of Minority representation by more than ten seats and (b)

---

[1] See 9.   [2] See 23.   [3] See 37.

lack of information as to what the Imperial Government would be prepared to concede in the event of intercommunal agreement being achieved.

4. The following months witnessed a marked deterioration in Ceylon politics. Labour unrest and the collapse of France affected local European psychology, which became impatient of Ceylonese democracy. I was told by leading articles in the "Times of Ceylon" newspaper to govern or get out, and there is no doubt that a majority of Europeans in the Island (which did not however include the best brains or wisest heads) wanted, and tried to manoeuvre, a 'show down'. At the outset of this unpleasant phase I sent my most Secret and personal telegram of the 9th May, 1940, asking for a Commission of Investigation and a postponement of the next General Election until its report had been considered. The Secretary of State's statement of 12th June, 1940, announced the postponement for two years of the general election in order that careful decisions might be reached on problems of constitutional reform, franchise and delimitation of constituencies. This was interpreted here as indicating that His Majesty's Government would have the matter under active consideration on the data already before it. There was nothing in the way of Commission, Committee or Conference for statesmen and reformers to bite on to. The abortive Indo–Ceylon Conference in the autumn of 1940 and its aftermath within the State Council and outside during the winter and spring kept our politicians busy. By the time however that Lord Lloyd's confidential despatch of 18th December, 1940,[4] (stating the impracticability of further examining our constitutional question until after the war) had reached me the Ministers were asking me to obtain by telegram a report on progress. In the following interchange of telegrams with the Colonial Office, having accepted the impracticability of an early Commission, I again (telegram of 28th June last) asked for permission to appoint the Redelimitation Committee recommended in paragraph 6 of my Reforms Despatch, and suggested the drafting of a new Order-in-Council along the lines of my despatches for detailed consideration by His Majesty's Government. Acceptance of either recommendation would have given local leaders something to bite onto. The approved announcement to State Council on 28th October, 1941 (that after the war the position will be further examined and made the subject of further consultation by means of a Commission or Conference) has unfortunately not provided this something to bite on; with the result that current reform talk has drifted right away from my Reforms Despatch and the Council Debate thereon and now revolves nebulously round the Atlantic Charter and Dominion Status. The latter has been recommended in successive issues of the hitherto reactionary "Times of Ceylon", and it is obvious that the implications and obligations of Dominion Status are either not understood or are being deliberately ignored by people who should know better.

5. The view of the Ministers and other Majority spokesmen is that the Colonial Office is unnecessarily delaying a decision in a matter on which it possesses full data. Such talk I of course invariably oppugn; but there is small use in my doing so as long as minority leaders make a boastful pretence of having staved off reforms by their memorials and protests. There is in such circumstances no chance whatever of a get-together between majority and minority leaders, and delivery to the Ministers of the message contained in the Secretary of State's telegram No.773 of 7th November

---

[4] See 78.

(implying that it was within their power to promote unity and concord) would have only antagonized them and elicited further remonstrance.

6. The Second Indo–Ceylon Conference (and the disagreement that has since arisen from the agreement reached by it!) has kept political minds and tongues fairly fully employed until recently. Now Japan's entry into the war and her initial successes have thrust every other consideration out of mind, and everybody has plenty to do in organizing emergency services and preventing panic. This state of affairs is quite likely to have an effect on the attitude, ministerial and public, towards the question of a further postponement of the next general election. The Ministers have, I understand, the question under consideration and I will make my recommendations as soon as I know their views.

7. The reason why my "Things Ceylonese" have petered out is that for some time past I have been so pressed by work that I have no time to write them. This week (owing to silly scares and panics) work is worse than ever and I cannot join my wife for Christmas at Nuwara Eliya.

Mark Young's[5] leadership at Hong Kong makes one proud to belong to the Colonial Service and Thomas[6] from all accounts is doing splendidly in Malaya. Our newly arrived G.O.C., Inskip,[7] is A 1: so is Arbuthnot,[8] the Naval Commander-in-Chief. So we are lucky.

Every good wish for the New Year, and may it bring victory!

---

[5] Sir M A Young, gov of Hong Kong, 1941; interned, 1941–1945; resumed duties, May 1946–May 1947.
[6] Sir S Thomas, gov of Straits Settlements and high commissioner for Malay states, 1934–1942.
[7] Maj-Gen R D Inskip, GOC, Ceylon, 1941–1942; retired Sept 1942, re-employed, Oct 1942–Feb 1946.
[8] Admiral Sir G S Arbuthnot, c-in-c, East Indies, 1941–1942.

114 CO 54/985/5, no 1   19 Feb 1942
[Fall of Singapore]: outward unnumbered telegram from Lord Moyne to Sir A Caldecott on the strengthening of Ceylon's defences

1. With the fall of Singapore and the enemy's penetration of Burma and the Netherlands East Indies, Ceylon has become a vital point in our Indian Ocean defence area, and particularly the security of the island as a naval and air base for our future operations against Japan is a matter of the very highest importance. Much planning is now concentrated on strengthening the defences of Ceylon.

2. I have addressed you in separate telegrams on various aspects of civil defence in the island in which immediate and thorough-going action is required by the Government of Ceylon to meet difficulties with labour which have already appeared in essential services, and to instil a sense of security and resolution in the general population.

3. You have, under the Constitution, powers in an emergency such as we are now faced with, to assume the direct administration of any Department of Government, and it will be essential that this power should be used without hesitation if in any matter such action will conduce to the strengthening of the island's capacity for defence and of its usefulness to the Allied war effort. I appreciate, of course, that if such action needs to be taken, it is likely to be at the expense of good relations with

the Board of Ministers and the State Council, but unfortunate as that may be, it must have no more weight than it is worth in the scales of Empire Defence. My impression is that hitherto Ministers have on the whole adapted themselves fairly well to war measures, and I hope that they will be found capable of the far more intense activity which is now demanded of them. But you have expressed opinions to me more than once as to their staleness and lack of vigour, and it may be that in such measures as special rations for Indian labour, and special measures of co-operation and accommodation with India, the effort may be too much for them. It is for that reason that I feel it necessary to impress upon you that the Government of Ceylon must not fail in the present crisis at any point, and that you must be prepared at any time to take up your emergency powers.

4. Against this possibility are you satisfied that you have available adequate staff of experienced and energetic officers to serve you in any field of administration which may be concerned? If you have any doubts I shall do my best to supply your needs, and I shall be grateful for your advice as to the best course to adopt to introduce them into Ceylon.

115　CO 54/985/5, no 3　　　　　　　　　　　　　24 Feb 1942
[Fall of Singapore]: inward unnumbered telegram (reply) from Sir A Caldecott to Lord Cranborne

Grateful for your telegram of 19th February.[1] Vital importance of defence of Ceylon fully recognised here and my replies on matters alluded to in your paragraph 2 will show that energetic action has been and is being taken. Constitutional question demands realistic approach. When the Far East war broke out there were three possible courses

(1) to attempt continuance of normal administration by Executive Committees. Necessity for speed and coordination made this impossible and the Committees themselves were persuaded to delegate their powers to the Ministers in all matters of defence. This made

(2) assimilation to Cabinet Government possible and State Council by passing block defence vote to be allocated by the Board of Ministers completed transfer of power and responsibilities in all war and defence matters from the Executive Committees to de facto Cabinet. If the Committees or the State Council had refused to effect such transfer resort might have been necessary to

(3) gubernatorial assumption or control under Article 49. Such assumption would have been inevitably followed by ?lack of cooperation, alienation of sympathy of great majority of the population which is now happily with us and consequently the outbreak of internal disorders. I therefore bent all my energies to achieving solution (2) and I am well satisfied with the result. Temporary reaction of the State Council after having parted with executive power in defence execution was inevitable and took the form of

(a) vote of non confidence in the Board of Ministers which was, after much effervescence, defeated by 37 votes to 5 and

---

[1] See 114.

(b) by subsequent adjournment of important war resolutions owing to lack of quorum.

I met (b) by immediate proclamation under Article No.17 reassembling Council and pointing out in an address that the Government of Ceylon is a trinity of the Governor, the Board of Ministers and the State Council in which each element must collaborate with the other two and that I relied on such collaboration to preclude the necessity for any revocation or ?replacement of my Royal instructions which results I should regard as defeat on our home front. State Council responded by forthwith putting through all urgent business required of it. This was before the receipt of your telegram. Present position in regard to ministerial cooperation and energy is good and far better than I dared to anticipate and it has been improved by the resignation on account of ill health of the Minister for Health who had become senile. Election of successor is on Wednesday and confirmation of acting Minister George de Silva is likely and desirable.

Concerning other points in your telegram, I am glad to report that racially discriminative ration for Indian labour has never been proposed here. As regards cooperation with India, Senanayake leaves for Delhi tomorrow by invitation of the Indian Government to discuss food supply. Relations between the people of the Island and Indian troops are generally satisfactory. Exodus of Indian labour alluded to in former telegrams unfortunately continues, but is due to nervousness about the Eastern War and has nothing to do with politics.

Your paragraph 4. If it became necessary to take over departments under Article No.49 senior Government Officers would, in my opinion, continue loyal to the Service, but I should expect serious deterioration in clerical and subordinate ranks, which would only be aggravated if senior officers were brought in from outside. As I have already said such action on my part would precipitate non cooperation and internal disorder, and I do not contemplate it except as a last resort to which I see no need why we should be brought.

116 CO 54/985/5, no 4   27 Feb 1942
[Fall of Singapore]: outward unnumbered telegram (reply) from Lord Cranborne to Sir A Caldecott

Your secret and personal telegram of 24th February.[1]

Your appreciation is most helpful to me, and I shall be grateful if you will continue to keep me closely informed of developments and prospects in the political situation. I note with approval the action you took in keeping the State Council up to its responsibilities in respect of 3(b) in your telegram.

The needs of the food position are being urgently pressed here, and I shall be grateful for information with least possible delay as to result of Senanayake's discussions in India.

As regards your last paragraph, situation I had in mind is that you might be forced to assume control of Departments if Ministers and State Council scattered under influence of enemy air action for instance. They might then, from their places of

---

[1] See 115.

refuge in the island, resent your assumption of control and obstruction and non-co-operation might be fomented. We must not let realism stop short of the point at which Government will have to be carried on in difficult and critical circumstances, and I must be sure that you as Governor have no risk of shortage of reliable officers to carry on essential tasks under your directions. Admittedly this would be last resort, and like you I hope it would not be reached, but if it is reached it would be essential that administration should be effective without any risk of failure.

## 117 CO 54/980/4, no 39	27 Feb 1942
[Elections]: outward telegram no 218 from Lord Cranborne to Sir A Caldecott on the postponement of the elections

My telegram No. 131 of the 7th February—postponement of elections. It is suggested that best method of amending Order-in-Council would be to provide that Article 19 shall have no effect until the Council last appointed and elected shall have been dissolved by virtue of Article 18 and a fresh Council shall have been appointed and elected. This is the form of instrument adopted in other Colonies. Order of 24th July, 1940, could be revoked without prejudice to things done by virtue thereof.

If, however, you consider that reference should be made to end of war it would be possible to add a proviso that the Governor shall dissolve the Council say not later than one year after date upon which the Emergency Powers (Defence) Act, 1939, expires.

In either case publication of order could be accompanied by an assurance that the Council would be dissolved as soon as practicable after the termination of hostilities.

I shall be glad to receive your observations on these suggestions.

## 118 CO 54/985/6, no 3	3 Mar 1942
[Impact of war]: outward unnumbered telegram from Lord Cranborne to Sir A Caldecott on the appointment of a commander-in-chief, Ceylon

War Cabinet have had under consideration position of Ceylon in light of developments in the war with Japan. Ceylon is now a key point for the concentration of forces and for defence of our communications in the Indian Ocean and War Cabinet have decided that Ceylon and its Dependencies should be temporarily placed as a "military area" under the supreme control of high service officer with title of "Commander-in-Chief Ceylon". All civil and military authorities in the area will be subject to his directions. On the civil side you will continue to carry out the civil functions of Governor subject to the Commander-in-Chief's overriding authority. I should have wished to give you time to explain the projected change to your Ministers but I fear that the military situation does not permit of the delay which that would occasion. I shall be telegraphing more fully but I wanted to let you know at once of the special arrangement which is to be made and to assure you that this exceptional appointment is entirely due to the absolute necessity of subordinating all other considerations in the present grave emergency to that of fighting efficiency.

119 CO 54/985/6, no 9 5 Mar 1942
[Commander-in-chief, Ceylon]: directive from the Chiefs of Staff to Vice Admiral Layton

Following from Chiefs of Staff.

You are appointed Commander-in-Chief, Ceylon. All naval, military, air and civil authorities in the area, including the Governor and the Civil Administration, will be subject to your direction.

2. Your immediate task is to ensure that all measures necessary for the defence of Ceylon are taken forthwith and that the military and civil measures are properly co-ordinated. The Governor has emergency powers under the Constitution, and the power of issuing Defence Regulations, which he can use to the extent you may require for any such measures.

3. You will convene and preside over any council or conference from time to time which you consider necessary for the effective co-operation of all services in Ceylon.

4. You will report as soon as possible whether, in order to carry out the tasks specified in paragraphs 2 and 3 above, it is necessary for you to assume supreme command of all the fighting services allotted to the defence of Ceylon, and what staff and other arrangements this would entail.

5. On all military matters your immediate superior will be the Commander-in-Chief, India. As to civil matters, the Governor of Ceylon will remain at his post and will exercise the civil functions of Governor subject to your overriding authority and direction.

6. You will communicate with higher authority as follows:—

(a) On military matters you will address Commander-in-Chief, India and repeat to the Admiralty for communication to the Chiefs of Staff.

(b) On civil matters you will address the Secretary of State for the Colonies and will ensure that the Governor is consulted and informed to the necessary extent. You will consult with the Governor as to the desirability of his continuing to communicate direct with the Secretary of State for the Colonies on civil affairs not touching upon defence issues.

7. In the exercise of your authority in civil affairs you will have regard to the importance and value of the maintenance of the services of the civil government as long as they can operate effectively in the prevailing conditions.

120 CO 54/985/6 9 Mar 1942
[Commander-in-chief, Ceylon]: minutes by G E J Gent and Sir C Parkinson on Vice Admiral Layton's appointment

Today the C.-in-C. Ceylon is telling the Ministers (who are all members of the War Council)—see No.10—the 'position' regarding his appointment.

There are recent telegrams from General Wavell[1] and from Admiral Layton which

---

[1] Commander-in-chief, India, 1941–1943; supreme commander, S W Pacific, Jan–Mar 1942, viceroy of India, 1943–1947.

seem to show some lack of definition as to the nature of the latter's present functions, and I feel that it is most desirable to have ready an approved form of official announcement against the inevitable leakage of information which will result from the explanation the C.-in-C. is to give to the War Council at Colombo today.

The form of a communiqué (from No.10 Downing Street) which we had proposed last week is as follows:—

> 'In the present emergency His Majesty's Government have decided that Ceylon should be placed under the supreme control of a Service Officer with the title of "Commander-in-Chief, Ceylon".
>
> Vice-Admiral Layton has been selected for this appointment and all naval, military, air and civil authorities in the area will be subject to his directions. He will be responsible for ensuring that all measures necessary for the defence of Ceylon are taken and that military and civil measures are fully co-ordinated.'

General Ismay[2] is reported to have preferred no announcement in order not to convey information to the enemy.

At present the enemy is talking of "feverish" preparations in Ceylon—see the attached German broadcast[3]—would it, on the balance, serve our cause best for British opinion here and in the East as well as the enemy to know that such feverish preparations were being directed and co-ordinated by a supreme defence Commander?

It seems to me that official silence will become an impossible course as well as an undesirable one in the very near future, and that we should have a form of words agreed here and telegraphed out at once to the C.-in-C. for concurrence and very early simultaneous publication here, in the East, and in the Dominions.

G.E.J.G.
9.3.42

Secretary of State (through Mr. Macmillan)
We discussed this at this morning's meeting when Mr. Macmillan was present. We may find difficulty still with the Chiefs of Staff owing to their own uncertainty as to what they want Vice-Admiral Layton to do, i.e. whether he is to be in executive command of all Ceylon forces or not. I agree with Mr. Gent that there should be a communiqué, which would have to be concurred in by the C.-in-C., Ceylon. The arguments for a communiqué may, I think, be summed up as follows:—

(1) Propaganda value in this country for the Government, as showing that they are taking the position in Ceylon very seriously.
(2) Correction of misunderstandings which may arise from "leakage" through Ministers in Ceylon as to the exact position.
(3) To clear the air for all concerned as to what the arrangement, as set forth in the first three paragraphs of No.6.

If you agree, the best plan might be for you to send an urgent minute to the Prime Minister enclosing the draft of a communiqué, which would be telegraphed to the

---

[2] Chief of staff to minister of defence (Mr Churchill).   [3] Not printed.

C.-in-C., Ceylon, for concurrence, and at the same time Mr. Thornley[4] might send a
copy of your minute to Colonel Hollis at the War Cabinet Offices.[5]

A.C.C.P.
9.3.42

---

[4] Private secretary to Lord Cranborne.   [5] See 123 for the communiqué as issued.

121   CO 54/981/15, no 5   14 Mar 1942

[Indo–Ceylon relations]: outward unnumbered telegram from Lord Cranborne to Sir A Caldecott on Indian immigration and food supplies

Government of India's telegram of 26th February to Chief Secretary regarding Indian
immigration. Viceroy has telegraphed 10th March to Secretary of State for India
personally to following effects. *Begins.*

(1) No reply yet received from Ceylon to Government of India's telegram 26th
February.
(2) Government of India would be ready to accord immediate exemption in
respect of labour requirements for Naval, Military and Air Force works provided
that

   (a) Ceylon Government makes request for such labour;
   (b) Ceylon declare that they will not proceed with draft immigration ordinance;
   (c) satisfactory guarantees are forthcoming regarding non discriminatory
   treatment, pay, compensation for injury or death and protection.

With regard to maintenance of ban in general Viceroy states that strict rice
rationing in Ceylon makes it difficult for Government of India to maintain an
impediment upon return to India of those who might find themselves short of food,
but that in any case Government of India must await Ceylon Government's final
reaction to proposals made regarding supplies of rice from India. *Summary of
Viceroy's telegram ends.*

As regards last point I should like to be kept promptly informed of developments in
Senanayake's conversations regarding food supply from India.

122   CO 54/981/15, no 6   16 Mar 1942

[Indo–Ceylon relations]: inward unnumbered telegram (reply) from Sir A Caldecott to Lord Cranborne

Your telegram of 14th March.[1]

Senanayake returned from India on 13th March having successfully achieved the
object of his mission, summary of results of which is as follows:—

Subject to certain conditions regarding methods of trade and distribution of food
grains, Government of India have agreed to consider Ceylon as within the economic

---

[1] See 121.

orbit of India concerning Ceylon's primary food requirements and to permit release of rice and food grains accordingly. Ceylon cannot however expect to be in better position than India herself if rationing necessitated in India owing to shortage, hence Ceylon expected to share deficiency. India will ascertain exportable quantities from various areas having regard to the varying conditions of supply in those areas. Government of India's policy is to restrict storage to minimum and request made not to build up stocks exceeding two months. Government of India have agreed to export of rice above the monthly average of next two months. Owing to transport difficulties export of rice preferred to paddy. Indian Government expressed definite preference to maintenance of purchase through trade channels and will assist in finding exporters shipping.

Reply has not yet been sent to the Government of India's telegram of 26th February but I will endeavour to expedite. There is of course no prospect of obtaining labour from India for defence works so long as the present nervousness among local Indians continues, of whom more than 30,000 have returned to India during the three months ending 5th March. Censorship Telegraphs Interception shows Hindustan Construction Company intended to recruit labour in India for military contracts at Trincomalee but failed to attract any recruits.

123 CO 54/981/15, no 7   18 Mar 1942
[Indo–Ceylon relations]: inward unnumbered telegram (reply) from Sir A Caldecott to Lord Cranborne

Your personal telegrams of 12th and 14th March.[1]

Following is text of reply sent today to telegram from the Government of India dated 26th February.

Begins. Ceylon Government agree that the present circumstances demand that further consideration of the Joint Report should be suspended until conditions favourable to its resumption recur. The Government also agrees to the continuation of the status quo on the understanding that the status quo includes the maintenance of your ban on the emigration of unskilled labour. Should circumstances arise in which the Ceylon Government might find it necessary and possible to recruit labour for the duration of the war for war purposes, this Government would ask for the relaxation of the ban for that purpose. *Ends.*

Insistance on the maintenance of the ban is essential, because it is the only check on the exodus to India reported in my previous telegram. We referred to India on 10th March a proposal to extend to adult males of every race including Indian labourers, the same prohibition of departure from the Island except under exit permit as that already applied to Europeans. There were operative difficulties locally inherent in this proposal, but the reply of India made it quite impracticable and we have told them that we will not proceed with it. Their demands included the fixation of the exact numbers of Indians to be retained in each of the essential services, various guarantees in respect of persons so retained and facilities for the return to India of persons not so retained. Fortunately the latest information is to the effect that the exodus is no longer affecting harbour labour.

---

[1] See 121.

124   CO 54/985/6, no 64   19 Mar 1942

[Commander-in-chief, Ceylon]: inward telegram no 293 from Sir A Caldecott to Lord Cranborne transmitting a message to the Board of Ministers on Vice Admiral Layton's appointment

Reference my telegram No. 1235/17.

Following is the text of message drafted by the Legal Secretary which the Governor will send to the State Council on 24th March. Board of Ministers have been shown it and will support the position indicated therein. *Message begins.*

There will to-day be tabled for the information of the Honourable Members the terms of appointment of His Excellency the Commander-in-Chief. It is desirable that I should at the earliest possible moment make clear to the Honourable Members certain matters relating to this appointment which are necessarily not apparent from the published documents.

On 10th March the Honourable Members were informed:—

In the present emergency H.M.G. have decided that Ceylon should be placed under the supreme control of a Service Officer with the title "Commander-in-Chief, Ceylon".

Admiral Layton has been selected for this appointment and all Naval, Military, Air and Civil authorities in the area will be subject to his directions. He will be responsible for ensuring that all measures necessary for the defence of Ceylon are taken and that the Military and Civil measures are fully co-ordinated.

On the same date they were also informed that His Excellency the Commander-in-Chief had made the following statement:—

> "I intend to leave the civil administration of the Government in the hands of the Governor, his Ministers and the State Council until such time as I might see fit to intervene, which I hope will be never; but if I do intervene it will be in the earnest and sure opinion that such interference is necessary in the best interests of our Empire".

The first point which I wish to make is that the sole reason for the appointment is the recent change in the war situation in the Far East, which has made it a matter of paramount necessity that there should be unity of command of the forces in Ceylon and that military and civil measures should be fully co-ordinated with all speed possible. It is for this reason, and not by reason of any past or anticipated incapacity or default on the part of the Board of Ministers or the State Council, that the appointment has been made.

In my last address to the State Council I described the Government as trinitarian to that partnership H.M.G. have added His Excellency the Commander-in-Chief and conferred upon him overriding powers, but His Excellency has stated that he intends to leave the civil administration of the Government in the hands of myself, my Ministers and State Council until such time as he might find it necessary to intervene. Attention in this connection is invited to paragraph 7 of the Commander-in-Chief's directive which reads as follows:—

> "In the exercise of your authority in civil affairs you will have regard to the importance and value of the maintenance of the services of the civil

Government as long as they can operate effectively in prevailing conditions".

Honourable members will wish to know what changes in their position are made by the appointment of His Excellency the Commander-in-Chief so long as he does not find it necessary to intervene. This question is best answered by considering what their position was immediately prior to this appointment.

At that time not only were all legislative or executive acts of Council subject to my assent or ratification, but it was also possible for the Council's powers of executive control to be taken out of their hands under Article No. 49 of the Order-in-Council. Furthermore the Governor possessed the power to legislate without the advice of the Council which is created by Article XXII of the Order-in-Council, and the power without the advice of the Council to legislate by Defence Regulation. It was also constitutionally possible for martial law to be declared.

It is of course apparent that the position to-day is not that of martial law although situation may arise in which it will be necessary to declare martial law. Until that time comes, which both His Excellency the Commander-in-Chief and myself hope will be never, the position is that the powers of executive control possessed by the State Council will be subject to no greater limitation than they were prior to the appointment of His Excellency the Commander-in-Chief, and that the only means by which local substantive legislative measures can be passed will be the same as they were prior to that appointment, namely, Ordinance, Governor's Ordinance, or Defence Regulation.

The Ministers remain my Ministers and His Excellency the Commander-in-Chief agrees that I should continue to communicate with the S. of S. on civil matters.

In order to secure prompt co-ordination of military and civil measures a War Council has been established which consists of His Excellency the Commander-in-Chief, myself, the members of the Board of Ministers and representatives of the Navy, Army and Air Force. The good results of this arrangement are already visible. Where defence and civil requirements conflict, the problem is investigated by a committee appointed by the War Council and such committees are already functioning in regard to the problems of co-ordinating civil and military food supplies, requisition of educational premises, priority of allocation of labour and materials between civil and military works, etc. Such committees consist of Ministers or other representatives of the civil authorities and representatives of the fighting services.

There is complete understanding between His Excellency the Commander-in-Chief and myself in regard to all our respective functions and I have no doubt that the existing arrangement is admirably adapted to the present emergency. I feel confident that it will have your loyal support and co-operation. *Message ends*.

125 CO 54/980/5/1, no 9   29 Mar 1942
[Constitutional reform]: outward telegram no 379 from Lord Cranborne to Sir A Caldecott transmitting a message to the president of the Ceylon National Congress

Your telegram No.244.

Please convey following message to President of Ceylon National Congress in reply to his message contained in your telegram under reference. *Begins*.

I have received and carefully considered your message telegraphed to me by Governor on the 7th March. His Majesty's Government have definitely undertaken to appoint a Commission or Conference on constitutional issues as soon as possible after the war. His Majesty's Government are in no doubt that the people of Ceylon realise that it is necessary to win the war before the continued existence of democratic principles can be assured to any state or nation. His Majesty's Government have also to bear in mind the lack of unanimity about constitutional reform manifested in the State Council during the Debates of 1939. This difficulty must be further examined before final decisions can be taken on matters of such importance to Ceylon. They feel that at the present time the effect of a declaration on the lines desired by the Ceylon National Congress could only evoke misunderstandings, doubts, questions and arguments and thereby turn thought and action from the war effort. His Majesty's Government do not therefore propose to make any anticipatory statement. They repeat their declaration that Ceylon's constitutional reform will receive earnest and early attention once the victory has been won. *Ends.*[1]

---

[1] Cranborne repeated the pledge made in the last sentence of this tel in a further message to the Board of Ministers which rejected a request made by the latter that Sir Stafford Cripps, then on a mission to examine constitutional issues in India, should visit Ceylon. The message explained that the Cripps Mission would be confined to the problems of India and that, as a member of the War Cabinet, Cripps would have to return to Britain immediately and would not have time to visit Ceylon (CO 54/980/5/1, no 12, outward tel no 389, Cranborne to Caldecott, 1 Apr 1942).

Later in the month four minority members of the State Council—Jayah, Natesan, Pereira and Ponnambalam—forwarded to the S of S through the governor a request that in furtherance of the war effort, it was imperative to set up immediately a national government in which minority representatives would have a voice. Cranborne replied reiterating the view that HMG would re-examine the issue of constitutional reform once victory had been won (CO 54/980/5/1, no 21, inward tel no 411, Caldecott to Cranborne, 20 Apr 1942, and no 23, outward tel no 490, Cranborne to Caldecott, 29 Apr 1942).

126   CO 54/985/4, no 11   3 Apr 1942
[War]: letter from K W Blaxter to War Office on the use of Ceylonese manpower in the military defence services of the island

I am directed by Viscount Cranborne to transmit, for the consideration of the Army Council, copies of telegrams exchanged with the Commander-in-Chief, Ceylon, regarding a debate on 24th March in the State Council of Ceylon on a motion for the adoption of compulsory military service for Ceylonese, and to draw their attention to the statement that all necessary recruits for the defence of the Island can be obtained by voluntary means.

2. In view of the experience in Malaya and of the criticism which has been continually expressed in Parliament and the Press that insufficient opportunities for military service were accorded in that territory to the local population and in view of the threat to Ceylon which has been created by the Japanese successes in the East, Lord Cranborne would like to be certain that the fullest possible use is made of Ceylonese man-power in the military defence services of the Island, apart from the engagement of large numbers of Ceylonese for civil defence services and in essential labour organisations.

3. Lord Cranborne will be grateful if the Army Council may be moved to give very

early consideration to this question with a view to timely instructions being sent to the General Officer Commanding in Ceylon.

127   CO 54/984/10, no 10   14 Apr 1942
[Sama Samajists]: inward telegram no 393 from Sir A Caldecott to Lord Cranborne on the escape of Sama Samajist prisoners

[This tel explained the circumstances under which four Sama Samajist prisoners—Dr N M Perera, D P R Gunawardene, Dr Colvin R de Silva and Edmund Samarakkody—who had detained under the Defence of the Realm Ordinance since June 1940, escaped from the detention barracks at Kandy early in the morning on 8 April.]

Your secret despatch (3) of 22nd December, 1939.

Warrants in force 8th April for detention of 22 members of Sama Samaja Party in following circumstances. Before dawn that morning all four detained persons mentioned in my secret despatch of 12th July 1940[1] escaped from Kandy Prison with the help of the gaol guard who absconded with them. Preliminary investigation indicated negligence inside and assistance outside the prison. With the approval of the C. in C. I therefore interdicted the gaoler and issued warrants against the second line Samajists. Position today, is that eleven have been arrested while the remainder, together with the four escaped prisoners and absconding guards, are in hiding. Power has been taken by Defence Regulations to attach the property of those evading detention. Person named in paragraph 2 of my despatch of 12th July 1940 has never yet been traced. No objection so far from persons arrested. Position under the constant attention of the C. in C. and myself.

---

[1] See 60.

128   CO 54/985/4   9–11 May 1942
[War]: minutes by K W Blaxter and Lt Col W L Rolleston[1] on compulsory military service in Ceylon

I thought that Col. White, the late Commandant of the Ceylon Defence Force, might be able to give some useful information on the question whether Ceylon's own resources of officer and N.C.O. material have or have not already been fully taken up. I asked him to come, and had a talk with him yesterday. It will be seen from Major Preston's minute of 6.5. that the War Office are quite agreeable to our having this discussion with Col. White.

It is hardly correct, I think, to say that Ceylon's own resources in this matter have been fully taken up, since it must be possible to take in to the Ceylon Defence Force further Ceylonese personnel of the type which could be turned into officers and N.C.O.s, but of course time would be required to get them trained up to a standard where they would be of real use. Some expansion of the Ceylon Defence Force has, of course, been proceeding for some time. The only way probably of organising further

---

[1] Head of military staff, CO.

units of the Force which would be of real value would be to have a certain number of British officers and N.C.O.s to give some strengthening to the Ceylonese personnel. This is the practice in the Indian Army, and there is, of course, some British personnel in some of the Ceylonese units. Here, however, we come up against a political difficulty. The Ceylonese Ministers strongly oppose the introduction of British officers and N.C.O.s into posts in Ceylon units which they argue could be filled by Ceylonese. There are, for example, a considerable number of Ceylonese N.C.O.s who have been members of the Force for a considerable number of years, and the Ceylonese Ministers argue that if further officers are required, they should be found from these N.C.O.s rather than by the introduction of British personnel. The natural place from which to obtain the British personnel, whether officers or N.C.O.s for the Ceylonese units is from the Ceylon Planters' Rifle Corps. That Corps has already been reduced to quite a small body of some 350 strong as a result of the departure of a certain number of members of the Corps either to the Middle East or India, and also by the non-calling up of a considerable number who are required to remain on the tea and rubber estates. Colonel White, during his period as Commandant, had actually made a move in the direction of using a few of the members of the Corps as officers of the Ceylon Light Infantry. But the opposition from the Ministers was so strong that the idea was dropped. The Ceylon Ministers have a deep-rooted dislike of the C.P.R.C. owing to past associations. Mr. Senanayake went so far as to say, in a heated moment, that he would rather have members of any nationality employed as officers of the Ceylon Light Infantry than members of the C.P.R.C.

The upshot is that even if it was thought desirable to reduce still further the cadre of this small Corps, it would be very difficult on political grounds to take members of the Corps and use them for supplying "strengthening" British personnel in the Ceylonese units.

Colonel White explained that there was no difficulty in obtaining Ceylonese officers for the Ceylonese units. There are a large number of young Ceylonese who have just left the schools and colleges in Ceylon who are without employment, and a number of these young men are anxious to become officers in the Defence Force, firstly because it provides them with employment, and secondly because it gives them a good social status. Actually, some of these young officers who have done courses in India have given quite a good account of themselves. But that does not mean that these young officers would necessarily have sufficient strength of character to be responsible for a whole Ceylonese unit without some British strengthening.

I do not really think that there is much more which can be done by way of expanding the Ceylon Defence Force than the developments which are already taking place, and the reasons given by the War Office . . . against attempting a further expansion of the Force at present seem to be convincing.

As to the question of conscription, I cannot believe that we should attempt to pursue this idea further at present. It does not seem to be much use organising large bodies of men on a military footing unless there is the necessary equipment available, and from the War Office letter this clearly is not the case, save by reducing India's supply. The introduction of such a measure would be bound to take considerable time, and many months would be bound to elapse before such a scheme could be brought into effective operation. The introduction of such a measure could hardly, therefore, be a means of assisting in repelling the immediate threat to Ceylon by the Japanese, although the knowledge that such a measure was being introduced might act as a stiffening to the morale of the Ceylonese.

The State Council rejected a motion for conscription in March, but from the account given in No. 10, the Council seem hardly to have been brought face to face with the square issue, and if the Council were asked now to approve conscription and the resolution was introduced as a Government measure with the full backing of the C.-in-C., I should say that it would have a fair chance of being accepted. (Conscription as discussed in this minute relates, of course, to the conscription of the Ceylonese population. There is already conscription for Europeans for service in the Ceylon Defence Force.) Even so, having regard to the difficulty that there would be of providing satisfactory officer and N.C.O. cadres within reasonable time for a Ceylonese Army, I should doubt whether we should press a proposal for the introduction of conscription upon the Ceylon Government at present.

K.W.B.
9.5.42

It is unfair to conscript people unless you give them arms, equipment, training and reasonable leaders. My recollection of a talk I had with Col. White (recorded elsewhere) is that he did *not* advise any further expansion of the C.D.F.

Have we asked C in C recently what he thinks about it? . . . C in C should be in a position to balance political and military requirements.

W.L.R.
11.5.42

129 CO 54/985/4, no 16   9 June 1942
[War]: inward telegram no 57 from Vice Admiral Layton to Lord Cranborne on the expansion of the local defence forces

Your telegram No.53. (re Formation of Home Guards).

Local military forces in Ceylon expanded since the outbreak of war as follows.

C.G.A. from 364 to 485.
C.L.I. from 1 battalion to 4.

Two battalions of auxiliary military pioneers recently raised and a third forming. Increase in Ceylon engineers from 264 to 3,585 authorized and taking place. Militarization *of pivotal railway* personnel in hand and similar scheme of posts and telegraphs under preparation. Scheme in hand for utilization of local personnel as guards for dispersed aircraft. In Colombo the town guard and reserve C.P.R.C. personnel have operational role in emergency. Arrangements already in hand to use suitable personnel on territorial basis for reporting enemy movements after invasion. Four battalions essential services labour corps enrolled. Excise personnel employed on organizing coast watching system to report shipping movements. G.O.C. reports that all the above stretch military resources to the utmost. Neither weapons nor organizing and training staffs are available for extending Home Guard into rural districts on British lines. No Ceylonese or British civilians with military background live in those districts except planters already much reduced by embodiment in C.P.R.C., and Home Guard training would reduce the output of essential commodities. To sum up, as suggested in paragraph 5 of the telegram under reference, most economical course is to concentrate on using suitable manpower for the expansion of local forces to the fullest extent. This is being done to capacity.

130   CO 54/981/15, no 8   14 June 1942
[Indo–Ceylon relations]: inward telegram no 4658 from the Government of India, Department of Indians Overseas, to Mr Amery on Indian labour in Ceylon

Reference my telegram No.1495 dated 26th February 1942. Regret attempts to secure compromise agreement with Ceylon Government have failed. In reply to our approach quoted in telegram referred to above Ceylon Government agreed to suspend consideration of joint report and further proceedings in regard to Immigration Ordinance provided we agreed to maintain our ban on emigration of unskilled labour. We in reply welcomed Ceylon Government's ready response but pointed out ban on emigration had been intended to prevent further flow of unskilled labour from India to Ceylon. War conditions render any such emigration highly improbable. Ban was in practice operating not to prevent such emigration but to obstruct return to India of Indian labour in Ceylon from fear that subsequent return to Ceylon would be prevented by reason of ban. We therefore proposed to relax ban so far as it applies to all Indians already in Ceylon. Ceylon Government have now finally refused to accept our proposal on the following two grounds:—

(1) That during negotiations preceding joint report it was recognised that ban operated as described by us and that consequently while ban was maintained there was no immediate need for Immigration Ordinance. They also urge that during negotiations Government of India delegates agreed to maintain ban until problem of political and economic position of Indians in Ceylon had been settled.
(2) That lifting of ban might encourage efflux from Ceylon of labour required in rubber and tea industries both of which are of vital importance in war effort.

2.   As regards first argument while it is true effect of ban upon Indian labour in Ceylon was clearly recognised by us, Ceylon Government do not appear to have appreciated first that war conditions themselves now render both ban and Immigration Ordinances in practice unnecessary and second that our proposal which still prohibits emigration of new labour to Ceylon is solely intended for war period after which whole problem must be re-examined. As regards second argument we have informed Ceylon Government that in our opinion control of labour for war purposes if necessary should be achieved by measures specifically designed to that end and not by indirect operation of measures designed for entirely different purpose.

3.   Position is now that Indian labour in Ceylon has for nearly 3 years been prevented on account of ban from paying normal visits to India for temporary domestic purposes. Result is very real hardship to large number of Indian labourers and their families. We feel strongly that our proposal to relax ban in favour of Indians now in Ceylon is urgently needed and cannot in effect be regarded as attempt to alter

situation in Ceylon in our favour while Ceylon agree to hold their hand over Immigration Ordinance. Moreover we understand Ceylon Government have already prepared an ordinance and regulations which will give them sufficient control over labour considered by them to be essential. We therefore propose at the end of this month to inform Ceylon Government that we regret they have not been able to accept our proposal but that we feel that it is necessary in the interest of Indian labour and must therefore relax ban as suggested by us. We shall greatly regret if Ceylon Government decide to proceed further with Immigration Ordinance especially as on Ceylon Government's own showing there is no surplus labour on estates and ordinance would therefore have the effect of excluding from Ceylon labour which they themselves admitted they need.

131   CO 54/981/15, no 9   19 June 1942

[Indo–Ceylon relations]: outward unnumbered telegram from Lord Cranborne to Sir A Caldecott on Indian labour in Ceylon

Your Secret and Personal telegram of 18th March.[1] Indian immigration. I have now seen further report by Government of India to Secretary of State on latest negotiations between Governments of India and Ceylon.[2] From this it appears that in reply to message quoted in your telegram under reference, the Government of India stated their intention to relax the ban on emigration as far as it applies to Indians already in Ceylon, on the ground that it was operating not to prohibit emigration, but to obstruct return to India of Indian labour in Ceylon. Government of India have reported that Ceylon Government finally refused to accept their proposal on grounds: (1) that in negotiations preceding Joint Report, it was recognised that ban operated in this manner, and that consequently while ban was maintained there was no immediate need for Immigration Ordinance; and that during negotiations Government of India delegates agreed to maintain ban until problem of political and economic position had been settled; and (2) that lifting of ban might encourage efflux from Ceylon of labour required for work in essential industries.

Understand that Government of India have replied to (1) that Ceylon Government do not appear to appreciate that war conditions render both ban and Immigration Ordinance in practice unnecessary, and that their proposal still prohibits emigration of new labour to Ceylon for war period, and that as regards (2) they have informed Ceylon Government that in their opinion control of labour for war purposes should be achieved by measures specifically designed to that end. They therefore propose at the end of this month to inform Ceylon Government that they feel it is necessary, in the interests of Indian labour, that their proposal should be accepted, and that they are, therefore, relaxing ban. They have expressed the hope that the Ceylon Government will not proceed further with the Immigration Ordinance especially as, on their own showing, there is no surplus labour on estates, and Ordinance would have effect of excluding from Ceylon labour which Ceylon Government has admitted it requires.

I should be grateful for your observations on the situation generally. It appears to

---

[1] See 123.   [2] See 130.

me that essential requirement is to prevent as far as possible further exodus of essential labour. This may require further consideration of exit permit system in respect of which Government of India have already stated that they see no necessity for their prior permission if measure is introduced by Commander-in-Chief for defence purposes. Have there been any further developments since the Commander-in-Chief's telegram, No. 33, of the 3rd May?

At the same time I trust that Government of Ceylon will not think it necessary to proceed with general Immigration Ordinance proposals, since that might lead to a deterioration of political relations at a time when defence needs including food supply demand in Ceylon's interest maintenance of intimate association.

132   CO 54/981/15, no 10   21 June 1942
[Indo–Ceylon relations]: inward unnumbered telegram (reply) from Sir A Caldecott to Lord Cranborne on Indian labour in Ceylon

Your secret and personal telegram of the 19th June.[1] Owing to pressure of work, and to the visit of H.R.H. the Duke of Gloucester it is difficult for me to reply adequately to your telegram under reference at once. Three points, however, stand out.

(1) That if India announces relaxation of ban as a *fait accompli* without notice, Indo–Ceylon relations, already strained, are bound to deteriorate;
(2) That if no notice is given, we shall not have been able to set up administrative machinery necessary to prevent embarrassing efflux, not only from plantations, but from other essential services;
(3) That India's conception of maintenance of *status quo* is that Indians leaving Ceylon now, for reasons of personal security, will have a right to return at any future time when the danger is past. This interminable right, the Minister cannot consistently, or within the bounds of political possibility, concede, and the unilateral raising of the ban would certainly be followed by legislation to deny such right, though such legislative action might not perhaps take the form of proceeding with the Immigration Bill. This arrangement has been made clear to India in the interchange of telegrams since the 18th March, copies of all of which are contained in my telegram No. 753 which follows. Whatever happens, it is essential that if the ban is to be lifted, I should be in a position to discuss the situation with the Minister as soon as possible, and that it should not (repeat not) be lifted until administrative machinery to secure the continuance of all essential services has been set up to the satisfaction of myself and the Commander-in-Chief.

Grateful if you will represent both these points to the Government of India.

---

[1] See 131.

133   CO 54/979/9, no 1   11 July 1942

[Kandyans]: despatch from Sir A Caldecott to Lord Cranborne on a memorial from the inhabitants of the Kandyan provinces. *Enclosures 1 & 2*

I have the honour to transmit a memorial addressed to me by the inhabitants of the Kandyan Provinces. The President of the Kandyan Youth League who submitted the memorial to me has requested that it be forwarded to Your Lordship and to His Majesty the King in Council. It is observed that while the petition relates almost entirely to Kandyan aspirations, more than 200 of the signatories (or over 10 per cent. of the total) bear distinctly non-Kandyan names.

2. I have given careful consideration to these and certain earlier representations recently made by the Kandyans, both lay and cleric, including representative Kandyan Chiefs and High Priests, and, after consultation with my Officers of State and the Minister for Home Affairs, I have approved a policy under which all recruitment of Divisional Revenue Officers for the Kandyan Provinces is reserved for the Kandyans, the term "Kandyan" being interpreted in a liberal sense to include:—

(a) any son of a Kandyan father; and
(b) any son of a Kandyan mother whose parents are permanent residents in a Kandyan district, whether the mother has been married according to Kandyan Marriages Ordinance or the general non-Kandyan law.

3. As regards educational facilities, there is ground for the argument that the inability of the Kandyans to keep pace with other communities in matters appertaining to general welfare and advancement is in large measure attributable to inadequate educational facilities. But the position is improving and it is my hope that this improvement will be steadily maintained in future. I enclose for Your Lordship's information a copy of a memorandum prepared by the Minister for Education in this connection.

4. The memorialists in basing their claims on the Convention of 1815 do not seem to appreciate that the system of administration of the Kandyan Provinces should not be regarded as fixed immutably by that convention, irrespective of any change which altered conditions may make inevitable in the interests of the efficient administration of the country. In the reply which I caused to be sent to the earlier representations referred to in paragraph 2, I subscribed to the confident hope expressed by the Donoughmore Commission (Report, page 107) that "Kandyan pride in their ancient Kingdom and historic institutions will form part of a larger national protagonism, and that Kandyan identity will best be preserved, and receive its noblest fulfilment, in the growth and final emergence of a strong and united Ceylonese nation."

5. With reference to the electoral and constitutional changes advocated on the last page of the memorial (preceding the appendices) the memorialists should, I suggest, be reminded that questions of political reform cannot be pursued during the present conditions of emergency but must be relegated to the thorough investigation which has already been promised after victory is won.

Enclosure 1 to 133

We the inhabitants of the Kandyan Provinces, beg respectfully to lay before Your Excellency their disabilities with the hope that Your Excellency will give them a fair hearing and such relief and redress as their case merits.

Your Excellency may not be quite familiar with the exact conditions of this country, yet we cannot, therefore, rest content to let Your Excellency be influenced in forming an opinion on vital matters affecting the well-being of our people, wholly to those outside our territory without running the risk of having our case prejudged. Therefore, the inhabitants of the Kandyan Provinces desire to state briefly their case themselves.

At the time the British Sovereign entered into a treaty with the people of the Kandyan Provinces, the Sinhalese were a sovereign power constitutionally, exercising political sway over the fairest, richest and the most extensive portion of territory in the Island.

By the clauses of that treaty Sinhalese Nationality was guaranteed its continuity under the British, and the several terms of the contract imposed a definite trust both impliedly and explicitly which the British voluntarily accepted.

At that time there were no people other than Sinhalese in this territory and none who did or could claim any political rights antagonistic to theirs or inimical to their advancement. All the land was theirs, owned either individually or communally, or nationally. All the Offices of the State were held by them.

Foreign interests, far from dominating theirs, did not exist at all. Although at the period political unrest was present economically their position was sound and unchallenged.

After 123 years of British rule it is true the country has been opened up with permanent plantations, producing for foreign markets, but a little consideration will show that these benefits have done little to improve the lot of the Sinhalese. Their economic condition has become deplorable. We say this not out of ill-will but as a statement of fact. We cannot exist and if the authority of the Government continues to be exercised to their detriment and for the purpose of supplanting them in their homeland by foreign elements, we are doomed to extinction.

To-day, they own the least extent of land individually as well as collectively, with not even the smallest share in the national ownership. They are, besides, the most backward from a want of better and more liberal educational facilities. In the last malaria epidemic over 125,000 Sinhalese in this territory perished, due largely to malnutrition and the consequent loss of vitality. If our interests continue to receive less and less recognition from the Government, we will not only cease to exist as a political unit but perish altogether. If non-Sinhalese interests are given predominance in every case as has been done hitherto, then they are being forced into national extinction.

This economic destruction and consequent human extinction is entirely due to the Government of the country which was totally alien and out of sympathy with the permanent population. The constitution formed under the Donoughmore report has intensified these difficulties and has doubled the problems.

During the first thirty years of British connection with these provinces, this economic destruction did not take place. During this time the language of Government was Sinhalese; all officials were Sinhalese; all the land was in their hands; the customary laws were maintained and protected; every village had its temple school; the Government, as promised, protected the religion and all the Buddhist institutions remained intact, and their temporalities well cared for and protected. Though there was trouble due to the so-called rebellions, the condition of the people remained sound and healthy. During this period the British connection with the Kandyan provinces was only by a Resident. The change of this well established form of Government against the wish of the people and of treaty obligations was the beginning of our destruction. Any form of Government which will not be able to remedy the mischief done will be of no use to us. The extent to which the economic and social life of the people have suffered should be realised before one can understand the peculiar problems that beset us. If it is necessary to know to what extent the economic and social life was destroyed by the unsympathetic form of Government, one must read the proceedings of the Parliamentary Committee appointed by Queen Victoria in 1849 on Ceylon affairs, the reports of the Temple Land Commissioners of 1856 to 1866 and the final reports of the Paddy Tax Commissioners. The number of our villages destroyed; the number of people killed and the temples broken up can be fully realised, if these reports are read. Then and then only will it be fully appreciated what form of Government alone will remedy these mistakes and re-establish a broken country.

The Sinhalese of this territory desire to co-operate with all, but, if such co-operation is interpreted to mean the total sacrifice of their national rights, with no guarantee of a proportionate share in the Government of their country, they can only stress their point of view as a distinct national entity.

The grant of universal suffrage without a clear definition of domicile of those who are not permanently resident in this country on a territorial basis meant a definite loss of representation to the Kandyan Sinhalese alone.

The introduction of an alien population as labourers, almost equal in numbers to the Sinhalese inhabitants, was economically an unkind and unsound act. That they be amalgamated on a territorial basis with us is an aggravation of the error. The labour population has an Indian Agent appointed by the Indian Raj and his sole business is to look after their interests. When anything goes wrong the local agent invokes the aid of the Raj to bring pressure on the Ceylon Government and not infrequently such pressure has been exerted on their behalf. With the exercise of the franchise they enjoy dual citizenship and double representation from within and without. This is a most disturbing political factor.

As a solution to this problem the Kandyan National Assembly urged before the Donoughmore Commission the division of the island into three states, one comprising of the Kandyan Provinces, the other the Tamil, and the third the Maritime provinces, each having a government of its own, but joined together by a Central Government of a federal basis. This suggestion was rejected and the present constitution was recommended. Though it has worked for nearly eight years, it has not solved our problems.

We are at one with the other communities in the desire for the development of · self-government in the Island. We feel very strongly that our special interests should not be sacrificed. Any form of Government which does not afford to us the share which is our due in the Government of the country, or adequate protection for their interests and exposes them to the domination of any other community or communities will be unacceptable to us.

The Kandyan Sinhalese have a special right to make this demand. When the Kandyan Country acknowledged suzerainty of the King of England by the Convention of 1815, a solemn promise was made that their interests would be protected by the British. Any form of Government, therefore, that fails to fulfil that obligation, would be a gross breach of faith with a people who trusted the plighted word of the British, and any reform of the constitution should be in so far as we are concerned, so adjusted as to implement that agreement.

The Donoughmore Commissioners who appreciated some of our problems expected to give us relief by the constitution they suggested. In dealing with this subject they stated: "with the extension of the franchise which we have already recommended . . . the political development of the Kandyans hitherto retarded will receive the stimulus which will enable the Kandyans to take their full share in the Government of the country and they will have small reason to fear the domination of the other communities. . . ." We equally believe that low-country Sinhalese will realise that the true policy for the country is one of comprehension and not domination and that the local patriotism will contribute to national contentment and progress.

We submit that the results of the elections of 1931 and 1936, far from realising this hope expressed by the Commissioners, have in fact weakened the position of the Kandyan Sinhalese and their fears of domination by other communities have come true.

Though 21 seats were allotted to the Kandyan provinces, which the Commissioners expected would be filled by Kandyan Sinhalese, what really has happened is that the majority of them have gone into the hands of others. As these facts are well-known we will not elaborate them here.

In these circumstances we submit that the least that might be done to give us our rightful share in the administration of the country, if no radical change in the constitution is contemplated at the moment, would be by the two following methods:—

1. The re-distribution of territorial electorates, such electorates being divided into Urban and Rural in order to give the town populations a chance of electing one of their own.

2. The exclusion of the Indian Immigrant Labourer from the Sinhalese territorial electorates, special representation being given to them by creating estate electorates. The Indian Labourer, as we have pointed out, has an Agent of the Raj to look after his interests. They do not form part of the permanent population. Their case, therefore, must be specially dealt with on the basis of Indian Immigrant Agricultural Labourer. Just now Indian interests, other than immigrant labour, are represented in the State Council by a nominated member.

The only form of Government that will satisfy us must be so constituted as to enable it to give our religion that protection as is contemplated in the 5th clause of the Convention of 1815; that will enable the re-establishing of our destroyed religious institutions; that will enable us to re-establish our broken peasantry and their village institutions; that will enable us to get more and cheaper education.

All these as contracted for in the Treaty. Any other constitution will never satisfy us. No form of Village Government wherein the controlling influence is in other hands will be acceptable to us.

The educational facilities in our territory has been so neglected that Your Excellency will be surprised to hear about them. A territory which had schools in every village and was well provided with educational facilities up to 1852, from that date onwards for a long period no education whatever existed. Even to-day we have only four secondary schools in all our five provinces; whereas in the North and West the country is studded with such schools. There are only about 700 Kandyans in the secondary schools of the Island, whereas there are about 13,000 in Jaffna and about 12,000 in the Maritime provinces. How can we be expected to compete with them and secure our legitimate share of offices in the public service. Though large sums are spent annually by Government for higher education in the North and West we get a very small amount for our provinces.

These are some of the matters to which we would like to draw Your Excellency's attention at this moment. We have made no extravagant or unreasonable demand, we have asked only what is our due as a people and as one of the contracting parties to the Convention of 1815. To these demands we pray that your Excellency give the consideration they deserve.

Enclosure 2 to 133: memorandum by the minister for education (Mr Kannangara)

This memorandum deals briefly with the question of educational facilities in the Kandyan Provinces. It is perhaps true that the Kandyans are under-represented in the Public Service of the Island, but it would not be correct to say that they are grossly under-represented. The cause of this under-representation in the opinion of the deputation that waited on His Excellency, is the inadequate educational facilities available to the Kandyans. Even if we assume that intelligence and aptitude for a particular vocation are evenly distributed among the various races—an assumption that may not be far wrong in its application to the few races or communities inhabiting the Island—social and economic conditions have a lot to do with this question. The mere provision of educational opportunities does not make a community efficient. These opportunities must be effectively utilised. However, in the past the inability of the Kandyans to keep abreast of the other communities in regard to general welfare and advancement was to a great extent due to inadequate educational facilities. But the figures for the various types of schools in existence in 1930 indicate an improved provision of such facilities. They are:—

Government Vernacular Schools	694
Assisted Vernacular and Bi-Lingual Schools	403
Assisted English Schools	59

The figures for the whole Island were 1,412, 2,168 and 264 respectively. The present position in respect of each district of the Kandyan Provinces appears from the following table:—

(a) Vernacular Schools.			(b) English.			
			Primary.	Junior.	Senior.	Collegiate.
Kandy District	242		6	16	11	5
Matale District	93		—	3	3	—
Nuwara Eliya District	68		—	4	1	—
Anuradhapura District	132		—	3	—	—
Badulla District	132		—	3	4	—

Ratnapura District	...	...	155	—	2	5	—
Kegalle District	...	...	227	—	—	2	—
Kurunegala District	...	...	285	=	4	2	=
			1,334	6	35	28	5
Total number of schools for the Island	...	...	3,795	27	140	114	15

These figures testify to further improvement at least in regard to quantity.

2. There are a sufficient number of Sinhalese schools in the Kandyan Provinces but in view of the nature of the country and difficulties of communication at least 150 more such schools have yet to be established in order to ensure that all the school-going children obtain at least an elementary education. The present-day Sinhalese schools are far from satisfactory as the content of education imparted there has so far not had much employment value, and it is proposed when the Special Committee on Education conclude their labours, to re-organize these schools so as to bring their curricula into closer relation with the needs of the country. The schools of the future will be established under the re-organized scheme. Altogether a little over 200 new schools are urgently needed all over the country, and the Executive Committee of Education has proposed to the Board of Ministers that these should be established within the next five years from funds raised on loan. Out of these 150 schools will be put up in Kandyan Provinces, mostly in the Kurunegala, Anuradhapura, Ratnapura and Badulla districts.

3. Teaching is perhaps the only white collared profession which a complete course in a Sinhalese or Tamil school has led to so far and the Kandyans have had equal opportunities with others of entering the teaching profession as certificated teachers. They have, however, not entered in sufficiently large numbers and there are not many among them who possess the teachers' certificate. A few years ago in view of the large number of certificated unemployed teachers the Executive Committee laid down a rule that no uncertificated teacher should be appointed to Government schools, an uncertificated teacher being one who has passed the Senior School Certificate examination and has not proceeded to obtain any professional qualification. As this rule was stated to cause hardship to Kandyans and Muslims desiring to enter the teaching profession the Executive Committee decided to make an exception in their case and uncertificated Kandyan teachers are being appointed. I should, however, mention in this connection that the Kandyans have had a long-standing grievance that adequate facilities had not been made available to them for getting themselves trained as teachers. Out of 18 Assisted Training Schools only one is in the Kandyan Provinces, i.e., at Kandy. The Executive Committee was not at all satisfied with this position and proposed about four or five years ago to open a Government Training School at Kandy. There have been inevitable delays and the proposal has materialised early this year. I am sure that the Executive Committee realizes that still greater facilities in this direction should be afforded to the Kandyans.

4. Under the present conditions the minimum educational equipment which would enable a student to enter the middle ranks of the Public Service is a good secondary education which can be had only in a Senior secondary or Collegiate school. Out of a total of 129 such schools in the whole Island, 33 of them are in the Kandyan provinces. Although the proportion may not be regarded as unsatisfactory the large majority of the Kandyan people have been denied the opportunity of

obtaining a secondary education by reason of the uneven distribution of these schools—there is none in the Anuradhapura District and there are two only in each of the districts of Kegalla and Kurunegala. It should also be borne in mind that not one of these English schools is conducted and controlled by the Government. They are all managed by various private agencies (Missionary Societies and others) on whose will and pleasure have hitherto depended the location of the schools, their accommodation, the facilities they afford and their standard of efficiency. Except in the town of Kandy the greater proportion of the more efficient secondary schools are situated in the non-Kandyan districts. This is a state of affairs over which the Government has so far had very little control. The Assisted school system has developed without any plan, and in deference to vested interests Government has so far been chary of taking powers to plan and carry out a school system based on the consideration of affording equal opportunities to everybody capable of profiting by them. The redress that Government can and should afford to the Kandyans is to establish some efficient State secondary schools in the Kandyan Provinces. I have no doubt that this question will be borne in mind in formulating the educational policy of the future.

5. The Executive Committee approved recently the establishment of Central schools in which English education for the most part will be free. Four such schools have already been established during the last financial year, one in each of the Kandy, Matale, Kegalla and Kurunegala districts, and it is proposed to establish some more this year in the Kandyan Provinces.

6. There is also a scheme of scholarships for bright children of the age of ten from Sinhalese, Tamil and Bilingual schools. These are distributed on the basis of electorates and Provinces—one for each electorate and one for each province, the Western Province getting two. The children of Kandyan Provinces do participate in these Scholarships.

7. Entry into the Civil Service and other higher ranks of the public Service demands the possession of a University education as a minimum qualification. In the matter of University education equal opportunities have all along been afforded to all, but certain able and competent students are unable to take advantage of the facilities afforded by reason of the economic status of their parents. To remedy this factor to some extent scholarships schemes have been in force. Yet the undesirable feature of most educational systems under which ability to pay determines largely the chance of higher education cannot be altogether removed. The number of Kandyans admitted to the University College during the past eight years is as follows:—

1934–35	...	...	...	5	1938–39	...	...	...	9
1935–36	...	...	...	10	1939–40	...	...	...	10
1936–37	...	...	...	4	1940–41	...	...	...	4
1937–38	...	...	...	6	1941–42	...	...	...	6

In 1939 the Executive Committee of Education approved of a "concession clause," to be of force for a period of years, to the effect that if a sufficient number of Kandyans and Muslims has not obtained admission in the normal way five further places should be filled by candidates belonging to each community from the list of those who have attained a minimum standard in the admission test. So far only one Kandyan candidate was admitted to the University College under this clause and that was at the commencement of this academic year. It must, of course, be admitted that compared to their population the number of Kandyans admitted to the University College has been rather poor. Perhaps economic causes may account for the small number of Kandyans seeking University education. Whatever the cause may be nobody who has the larger interests of the country at heart dare challenge the view that higher education should be restricted to those who can definitely profit by it whether rich or poor. So that the problem of Kandyan "backwardness" in education must be attacked at the beginning and middle of the educational ladder. Facilities should be made available at the very door of the Kandyans to enable them to obtain a good secondary education. This problem of securing an even distribution of educational facilities will receive the earnest consideration of the Executive Committee not only in respect of the needs of the Kandyans but also of those of all other communities or territorial groups occupying parts of the Island where educational facilities are at present insufficient. The recommendations of the Special Committee on Education on the question of a planned school system will be helpful and are awaited.

134   CO 54/981/15, no 18   17 July 1942

[Indo–Ceylon relations]: outward unnumbered telegram from Lord Cranborne to Sir A Caldecott conveying the views of Lord Linlithgow on Indian labour in Ceylon

My secret and personal telegram on 7th July.[1] Indian Immigration.

1. Secretary of State for India has now received personal reply from Viceroy, from which it is clear that Government of India feel that it now rests with Government of Ceylon to consider institution of any necessary measures for controlling exit of workers.

2. He points out particularly that necessary Ordinance and regulations to control employers and workers in any industry considered essential by Government of Ceylon are already in draft and suggests that these measures, which do not differ widely from similar measures in India, could be brought into effect in very little time.

3. Viceroy further (a) suggests that any efflux of Indian labourers to visit relatives in India could be controlled by issue of licences to leave to special number or percentage of labour force in particular industries at any given time; (b) states that Government of India have already promised to consider any application Ceylon Government might wish to make for recruitment of labour in India for war purposes.

4. I should be grateful to know whether Ceylon Government now considers time has come for enactment of regulations to control exit of workers, which would appear to be the right course—I hope that if so action in respective countries may be synchronised by arrangement between Governments of India and Ceylon.

---

[1] Cranborne sent a further tel on 29 July which read: 'Viceroy has now sent a personal message to the Secretary of State for India stating that his Government feel that they cannot postpone any longer their proposed modification of the ban on emigration to Ceylon and accordingly propose to give Ceylon Government about one (repeat one) week's notice that they shall take necessary action about middle of August. Viceroy has emphasized again that Government of India have most carefully considered possible reactions on Ceylon's war effort and that proposal is not intended as threat to Ceylon but simply as measure of justice to themselves and their nationals in Ceylon which cannot be longer delayed.

In the circumstances would be grateful for an early reply to paragraph 4 of my telegram under reference (CO 54/981/15, no 21).

135   CO 54/981/15, no 23   3 Aug 1942
[Indo–Ceylon relations]: inward unnumbered telegram from Sir A Caldecott to Lord Cranborne transmitting a telegram from the governor to Lord Linlithgow on Indian labour in Ceylon

Addressed to the Viceroy. Repeated to the Secretary of State.

1. I have received secret and personal telegram[1] from the Secretary of State for the Colonies stating that in personal message to the Secretary of State for India Your Excellency has represented inability of the Government of India to postpone any longer removal of ban on emigration from Ceylon and has stated that about one week's notice is likely to be given to this Government before announcement is made about the middle of August. The effect of such an announcement on our war effort must largely depend on its wording. If this were to admit of interpretation as an invite by your Government to our Indian labourers to seek sanctuary in India for so long as Ceylon is in danger of enemy attack and for so long as we are under the necessity of rationing food and substituting other diet for rice such an invite would inevitably undermine morale on plantations, create panic and at least in general efflux labour from estates. Any system of exit permits from the island would not in such circumstances serve to keep labourers on their place of employment once panic arose and we should attempt to deal with the situation by making Order under Defence Regulation No. 43B on the lines of draft communicated to your External Affairs Department by letter from the Secretary to the Commander-in-Chief, Ceylon, No. 5947/14 of 28th May. If, however, the announcement by your Government should result in mass urge for repatriation no machinery that we can devise or implement under Defence Regulations or otherwise could keep labourers contented or efficiently at work. So that conditions of general dislocation and disorder would thus inevitably arise such as might require strong and stern repressive measures in order to preserve internal security.

2. On the political side much will also depend on the wording of the announcement by your Government. Position of Ceylon Ministers remains as explained in my telegram No. 19, of 3rd June. If the announcement were to postulate the right of re-entry for persons who leave Ceylon after the ban is lifted and want to return after an absence of more than twelve months (vide part I, Section B, of paragraph 11 of Joint Report of Delegation from India and Ceylon) demand for retaliatory legislation here will be inevitable and the negotiations of last September will have been useless. If, on the other hand, the announcement were to disclaim demand for re-entry of persons after absence of more than twelve months and were to state as its object and reason the desire to provide opportunity for reasonable holidays to visit relatives in India and attend to family business, etc., demand for legislation here might possibly be avoided or resisted and the September negotiations be preserved as basis for future agreement.

3. For reasons given in the preceding paragraphs I shall be grateful if notice

---

[1] See 134, note 1.

about to be given to the Ceylon Government may contain actual text of proposed announcement by your Government and opportunity allowed to suggest any alterations conducive to present and future agreement between our two Governments which is our common aim.

136   CO 54/981/15, no 31   24 Aug 1942
[Indo–Ceylon relations]: inward telegram no 1142 from Sir A Caldecott to Lord Cranborne transmitting a telegram from the governor to Lord Linlithgow on Indian labour in Ceylon

Following for Governor-General, No. 64. Repeated to Secretary of State. *Begins.* Your telegram No. 2553-S. Lifting of the ban on emigration. *Ceylon Daily News* this morning publishes press telegram from New Delhi, dated 22nd August, stating that it is understood that provisional arrangements have been reached between the Indian and Ceylon Governments under which (1) Ban will be lifted 1st September. (2) Fresh Indo–Ceylon agreement will be negotiated after the war. (3) Ceylon will withdraw existing anti-Indian legislation, and undertake to refrain from new anti-Indian legislation. Until receipt of your telegram, No 2553-S, correspondence between the two Governments rested with my telegram No. 19, dated 3rd June, and decision of the Government of India to raise the ban on 1st September cannot be said to have been reached by agreement. With regard to (2) Ceylon Government has received no act of rejection by India, of the points of agreement reached in negotiations of last September. With regard to (3) there is no existing anti-Indian legislation in Ceylon, but on the contrary existing labour laws are preferential to Indians; nor has any undertaking been given by Ceylon Government in regard to future legislation. Above misstatements in New Delhi press telegram are bound to evoke criticism here, and demands for ministerial explanation, and I shall be grateful if the Government of India will secure early correction.

137   CO 54/981/15, no 33   24 Aug 1942
[Indo–Ceylon relations]: inward telegram no 2580-S from Lord Linlithgow to Mr Amery transmitting a press note on the lifting of the Government of India's ban on emigration

Following is text of press note referred to in my telegram No. 2553-S of 22nd August.[1] *Begins.* The Government of India have decided to (? relax) with effect from 1st September, 1942, their prohibition of the emigration of unskilled labourers to Ceylon so far as it affects labourers now in Ceylon. The effect of the ban on such labourers has been that, since its imposition three years ago, they have been prevented from paying their normal visits to India, for social and domestic purposes, for fear of not being allowed to return to their employer in Ceylon. The uncertainty about employment in Ceylon which was the reason for the ban being imposed cannot be considered to subsist in war time, when practically all Indian labour in Ceylon is employed on work essential to war effort. The Government of India are therefore of

---

[1] cf 136.

opinion that there is no justification for continuing to place any obstacle in the way of labourers wishing to pay their normal visits to India. The prohibition will continue to operate as heretofore in regard to labour not already in Ceylon.

Estate labourers who obtain leave to visit India should get their identity certificate endorsed with the date of their arrival by the Protector of Emigrants at Mandapam or Tuticorin. Non-estate labourers who obtain leave should obtain identity certificates from the Agent of the Government of India in Ceylon before leaving and get them similarly endorsed on arrival in India. *Ends.*

Addressed to Governor of Ceylon, repeated to Secretary of State.

138   CO 54/980/17, no 2   4 Sept 1942
[Food and price controls]: despatch from Sir A Caldecott to Lord Cranborne on new administrative arrangements and a proposal for a wartime national Cabinet

I have the honour to invite reference to my despatch No.239 in which I have reported the transfer of the following functions:—

"Food control in Emergencies"
"Control of Prices of Foodstuffs in emergencies or to prevent profiteering",

from the Ministry of Labour, Industry and Commerce to the Ministry of Agriculture and Lands.

2. I feel it necessary to inform Your Lordship as briefly as I can of the history and significance of this transfer.

3. Public discontent with Mr. G.C.S. Corea's administration of these subjects as Minister for Labour, Industry and Commerce culminated in the moving in the State Council on July 8th of the following resolution:—

"That in view of the very widespread discontent prevalent throughout the Island regarding the most unsatisfactory manner the food rationing and Control Schemes are operating particularly regarding curry stuffs and sugar, this Council has no confidence in the Hon. the Minister of Labour, Industry and Commerce, who has utterly failed to formulate and work the above Schemes satisfactorily."

The voting on the motion was Ayes 4, Noes 30; declined to vote 10. Ceylonese psychology, ever ready to criticize, always hesitates to condemn. Although the voting indicated confidence in Mr. Corea, the debate did not. Much less did the reaction thereto of the public and the press.

4. On the 20th July I summoned the Ministers to Queen's House and warned them that public discontent was still boiling and that although steam had been let off in the censure debate the danger of explosion remained imminent and that, if nothing were done, they would sooner or later be blown sky high by a vote of non-confidence in the whole Board. The Ministers requested a few days in which to think things over.

5. The result of their deliberations was a demand for Cabinet Government. Nothing was said of inviting non-Sinhalese to serve in a Cabinet (Sir Baron Jayatilaka alone made the suggestion in an obiter dictum) and I told them that I could not

entertain a mere proposal for Cabinet Government. After further consultation with them I appointed Mr. O.E. Goonetilleke, C.M.G., Acting Civil Defence Commissioner, to assume charge (in addition to his Civil Defence work, which is by now fully organized) of the purchase, pricing and distribution of food-stuffs under the Minister for Labour, Industry and Commerce. The Board of Ministers agreed to invite his attendance at all their meetings and the Commander-in-Chief gave him a seat on the War Council.

6. The public confidence which Mr. Goonetilleke has so notably inspired as Civil Defence Commissioner rendered this appointment a sufficient antidote to the more violent symptoms of dissatisfaction with Mr. Corea's administration of food questions. The epidemic of diffidence in him remained however uncured, and a private motion for the creation of a separate Food Ministry was moved in State Council and referred by Council to the Board of Ministers for solution "within the ambit of the present Constitution".

7. At this stage the idea of government by a special war-time national cabinet (to include the Officers of State, the present Ministers and two or more additional ones to cope with extra work occasioned by the war effort) was mooted both among the existing Ministers and among some minority members of Council. There were, I understand, certain conversations between these parties; but the project foundered on two rocks: on the ministerial side Mr. Bandaranaike refused to consider a Cabinet including Officers of State and on the side of the minorities an influential Member insisted on a quota of ministerial portfolios for the non-Sinhalese communities irrespective of qualifications.

8. In the result the Board of Ministers formulated the solution summarized in paragraph 1 of this despatch. To the extent that it harnesses together in the food waggon our ablest Minister (Mr. Senanayake) and our ablest executive officer (Mr. Goonetilleke) the solution is satisfactory. To the extent that it leaves certain Ministers still overburdened by unforeseen accretions of war work it is unsatisfactory; and the criticism that the Constitution should be broadened to our war effort rather than our war effort narrowed to the Constitution is heard in all quarters. It is possible therefore that the project mentioned in paragraph 7 of this despatch (which may or may not have been suggested by my Reforms despatch of the 13th June, 1938) may be revived at some future date.

139 CO 54/981/15, no 40   4 Sept 1942
[Indo–Ceylon relations]: despatch from R H Drayton to the Government of India, Department of Indians Overseas, conveying the views of the Board of Ministers on the lifting of the emigration ban

I have the honour to acknowledge the receipt of your letter No.F.35/42-O.S. dated the 20th August, 1942, and to state that your letter has been considered by the Board of Ministers who have asked me to reply as follows:—

The Board regret that the Government of India has not found it possible to meet the wishes of the Ceylon Government and has felt compelled to take unilateral action. The Board have already stated that, in their opinion, lifting the ban whether, wholly or partially, does change the status quo. Furthermore it may create economic and other problems in Ceylon which, in the interests of the war effort of Ceylon alone, apart from any other consideration, will have to be solved. The Board may therefore be compelled to take action which will change the status quo. They will keep the Government of India informed of any such action but they must reserve the right to deal with such problems if they arise notwithstanding that the solution of any such problem may cause further changes in the status quo and may not have the concurrence of the Government of India. The Board earnestly trust that no such action will become necessary.

140 CO 54/980/5/1, no 27   8 Oct 1942
[Reforms]: inward telegram no 1401 from Sir A Caldecott to Lord Cranborne transmitting a message from ministers renewing their demand for dominion status after the war

Ministers have requested me to telegraph to you the following message:—

Begins. There is growing concern in this country regarding our political status after the war. The State Council at its meeting on 26th March 1942 resolved that "this Council demands conferment of Dominions status on Ceylon after the war and requests that the British Government should give an assurance to that effect as has been done in the case of certain other British Possessions". The Ministers who are in entire accord with the resolution communicated it to you with the request that effect be given to it. In your reply dated 1st April 1942[1] you state that you renew on behalf of H.M.G. their pledge of immediate re-examination of Ceylon Constitutional reforms once victory is won. We are deeply disappointed and dissatisfied with this reply which takes no account of a demand made by the Council on behalf of the whole country for a status to which the people of Ceylon are justly entitled. Ceylon has always given the greatest possible measure of co-operation in prosecution of the war. It has been repeatedly affirmed by leaders of United Nations that they are fighting for the freedom of the peoples of the world and against tyranny and oppression. The enthusiastic co-operation in this war of a subject race like ourselves must be the natural result of expectations to share that freedom. Our demand is not only reasonable but will result in adding to the enthusiasm of the war effort. In these circumstances the assurance demanded by the State Council should be given without delay. *Ends.*

Purpose but not text of the message was published yesterday by the Times of Ceylon in article by their political correspondent.

---

[1] cf 125.

141 CO 54/980/5/1, no 29   15 Oct 1942
[Reforms]: inward telegram no 1445 from Sir A Caldecott to Lord Cranborne on the response to the ministers' demand

Reference my telegram No. 1402.[1]

When considering reply to Ministers, following points should be taken into account:—

(1) Acting Minister Home Affairs, who partook in message, was Tamil.

---

[1] cf 140.

(2) Only minority members who voted against council motion of 26th March were the British and Burgher.

(3) Times of Ceylon, newspaper which purports to reflect local British opinion, has for some time past supported the demand for Dominion status, and in leading article of 9th October states "Right of every country to govern itself can no longer be contested. War is being fought to vindicate principles not merely of self government, but of independence. Ceylon has as much right as any other country to govern itself."

(4) Co-operation of Ceylonese in war effort since entry of Japan has been admirable.

I consider therefore that reply to message should be that immediate re-examination of Ceylon constitutional reform after the war, to which H.M. Government stands pledged, will be directed towards the grant to Ceylon of rule within the British Commonwealth of Nations, to the maximum extent compatible with the security of the Island and of the Commonwealth.

In view of its failure to meet approval, I refer with diffidence to proposal submitted in paragraph 5 of my telegram No. 495 of 28th June, 1941;[2] which if accepted would have obviated subsequent progressive demands. Latter have rendered its exact terms out of date, but I am strongly of the opinion that if H.M. Government could see its way to invite constructive and formative work along given lines on problem of constitutional reform now, it will not only ensure the maintenance of the war effort, but will also prove of inestimable value in meeting the post-war situation. Present drift is away from all moorings.

Commander-in-Chief concurs in the above.

---

[2] See 100.

142   CO 54/980/5/1, no 32   3 Nov 1942
[Reforms]: outward telegram no 1251 from Lord Cranborne to Sir A Caldecott transmitting the draft of a reply to ministers

My secret personal telegram of 3rd November draft message:—

Begins. The re-examination of the reform of Ceylon's constitution after the war, to which H.M.G. stands pledged, will be directed towards the fullest possible development of self-governing institutions in Ceylon within the Commonwealth partnership. This development must obviously be conditioned by the extent to which Ceylon has the strength and unity to promote its own social and economic wellbeing, and it is, therefore, in the opinion of H.M.G., most important that the leaders of thought and affairs in Ceylon should carefully weigh the constitutional problems and their implications not only in the single interest of the island but in the larger interest of the Commonwealth on which the island's security and prosperity ultimately depend. The request that H.M.G. should now make a declaration on the lines advocated by the State Council as to the constitutional position in Ceylon after the war is to ask H.M.G. to pledge themselves to a course which might in the event be shown to provide neither a practicable solution for the Ceylonese themselves nor one which would contribute to the security of the Commonwealth. H.M.G. can however give an assurance that they will approach the question of a revision of the Constitution in the spirit and intention defined at the beginning of this telegram, and with the fullest appreciation of the effort and resolution which Ceylon and her people have shown in defence of the Island and in the cause of the Commonwealth. *Ends.*

143   CO 54/980/5/1, no 33   9 Nov 1942
[Reforms]: inward unnumbered telegram (reply) from Sir A Caldecott to Lord Cranborne on the draft reply to ministers

Your secret and personal telegram of 3rd November.[1]

I agree that debate on the Resolution of 14th ?January was absurdly unimpressive, but this must be attributed largely to the influence exerted by myself and colleagues through Ministers and others, to obliterate windy talk about political reformation, when all the available time and effort is needed for the prosecution of the war. Voting on the Resolution struck me as not less impressive than that on 12th December, 1929, when the present constitution was accepted by majority of two. Certainly no progress has been made towards reconciliation of majority and minority demands, but settlement can never be achieved by consultation or agreement between them, but only by decision of His Majesty's Government. Please refer in this connection to paragraph 5 of my personal letter to Gent dated 23rd December.[2] In these circumstances, I most strongly urge deletion of second sentence from draft message contained in your telegram 1251, that is to say, of all the words from "This development must be obviously" down to "prosperity ultimately depend". Sole but certain effect of this passage would be to resuscitate communal recriminations which would hinder the war effort, and fatally prejudice the chances of the election of Tamil Member, Mahadeva (who recently acted with success) as permanent Minister of Home Affairs, if Jayatilaka goes to India as our Representative. Realism dictates that we dismiss from the realm of (corrupt group) [?probability] all ideas of joint constructive deliberation between local communities, and remember that the whole of the Northern Province boycotted the present constitution and refused to return any Members to the State Council until 3 years after its inception. Ceylon Leopards have not changed their spots. C.-in-C. concurs in the above.[3]

---

[1] See 142.   [2] See 113.

[3] As a result of Caldecott's representations, the statement was revised as follows: 'The re-examination of the reform of Ceylon's constitution after the war, to which His Majesty's Government stands pledged, will be directed towards the fullest possible development of self-governing institutions in Ceylon within the Commonwealth partnership, having regard both to the single interest of the Island and to the larger interest of the Commonwealth on which the Island's security and prosperity ultimately depend. In their approach to the question of revision of the constitution in that spirit and intention, there will be on the part of His Majesty's Government the fullest appreciation of the effort and resolution which Ceylon and her people have shown in defence of the Island and in the cause of the Commonwealth' (CO 54/980/5/1, no 39, unnumbered tel, Cranborne to Caldecott, 11 Dec 1942).

144   CO 54/980/5/1, no 34   10 Nov 1942

[Constitutional reform]: inward telegram no 1586 from Sir A Caldecott to Lord Cranborne transmitting a message from minority representatives

Following message is sent at the request of the following six members of the State Council, Natesan,[1] Jayah,[2] Dharmaratnam,[3] Kaleel,[4] Pereira,[5] Ponnambalam[6]:—

Begins. On behalf of the minorities of the community of Ceylon, we respectfully reiterate that any declaration by H.M. Government on the future constitution of Ceylon must in fairness and justice provide for adequate and effective safeguard for the minorities in a balanced scheme of representation. Principles laid down by H.M. Government regarding the future Government of India and the rights of minorities therein are equally applicable to Ceylon. *Ends*.

[1] Indian Tamil (declined to vote on 26 March).
[2] Nominated member—Malay (not in house on 26 March).
[3] Tamil (voted for 26 March motion).
[4] Muslim (elected since 26 March).
[5] Nominated member—Indian (R.C.) (not in House on 26 March).
[6] Ceylon Tamil (declined to vote on 26 March).

145   CO 54/980/5/1, no 35   10 Nov 1942

[Reforms]: inward unnumbered telegram from Sir A Caldecott to Lord Cranborne on the message from minority representatives

Message contained in my telegram No. 1586[1] was received by me after the despatch of my secret and personal telegram of the 9th November[2] and is symptomatic of the communal intransigeance therein described. Its signatories however have no justification for the phrase "on behalf of the minority communities" as Mahadeva, member for Jaffna, subscribed to the message contained in my telegram no. 1401[3] as acting Minister of Home Affairs and there are other minority members also who do not follow the lead of Ponnambalam, who is the author of the present message. I do not therefore desire in any way to modify the recommendation contained in my previous telegram and if the reply to the Ministerial message is sent with the omission urged by me, answer to the present message would be that H.M. Government cannot at this juncture entertain schemes of representation, consideration of which must await the re-examination of the constitution after the war to which H.M. Government stand pledged.

[1] See 144.   [2] See 143.   [3] See 140.

146   CAB 65/28, WM 153(42)4   16 Nov 1942
'Ceylon: food supplies': War Cabinet conclusions on the supply of rice to Ceylon

The War Cabinet considered a Memorandum by the Secretary of State for the Colonies (W.P. (42) 522) regarding the supply of rice to Ceylon.

It was pointed out in the Memorandum that, in spite of the efforts made to obtain increased supplies from India since this question was discussed by the War Cabinet on the 14th September, the position remained unsatisfactory and a grave situation was now developing. Ceylon's minimum needs were 30,000 tons a month; and during October the Island had received only 1,250 tons from India, the only practicable source of supply. On the 20th October rice stocks in the Island amounted only to 23,000 tons, about a fortnight's supply.

It was therefore recommended:—

(a) That the Government of India should take exceptional measures to ensure Ceylon's essential rice supplies, to the extent of 30,000 tons a month.

(b) That, to supplement this supply of rice, shipments of wheat and flour from Australia should be assured at the rate of 15,000 tons a month.

(c) That, if rice supplies could not be maintained at the rate of 30,000 tons a month, the shipments of other cereals from Australia should be proportionately increased.

(d) That, if possible, additional quantities of rice, wheat and flour should be shipped to Ceylon for the purpose of building up a reserve stock of essential food.

The Secretary of State for the Colonies said that he was grateful to Sir Ramaswami Mudaliar[1] for the efforts which he had made to increase the supplies of rice sent from India to Ceylon. Since his memorandum was circulated, he had had a further letter from Sir Ramaswami indicating that the Government of India now hoped to send to Ceylon a total of 36,500 tons of rice during November and December. While this would be helpful, it would not avert the risk of grave shortage, for, even if actual shipments equalled the estimates—as they had not hitherto—the Island would be left at the end of December with no reserve stocks at all. This was most dangerous, not only from the standpoint of defence, but also from the point of view of maintaining Ceylon's production of rubber and other essential raw materials. There were indications that the morale and efficiency of workers in the Island were already beginning to suffer from the food shortage. He therefore suggested that the Government of India should be pressed to ship an additional 20,000 tons of rice during the next two months. Failing that, he asked for increased shipments of wheat from Australia—though it should be realised that the possibilities of substitution were limited, since the rice-eating population of the Island would not accept other cereals in place of rice.

Sir Ramaswami Mudaliar said that the Government of India were finding real difficulty in increasing these supplies. Though the total Indian crop was large, some of the small cultivators were withholding supplies, and Provincial Governments were finding great difficulty in getting supplies on to the market. There were also

---

[1] Representative of the Government of India on the War Cabinet.

difficulties of internal transport, for the areas nearest to Ceylon were those in which there was a deficiency. The Government of India had already exploited to the full the capacity of ordinary commercial agents to acquire supplies; it was only when these had failed that Provincial Governments had been asked to take exceptional measures to bring increased supplies forward.

The offer to ship 36,500 tons in November and December was without prejudice to the possibility of making fresh allotments during those months; and the Government of India were already considering what further supplies could be obtained. They were fully alive to the urgency of Ceylon's need, and he thought it undesirable that any pressure should be brought to bear on them by the War Cabinet.

The position should improve shortly, when the new crop would be available. Moreover, the Government of India had decided to establish a Central Secretariat to exercise co-ordinating powers over Food Supplies. This would enable the Central Government to exercise direct powers in this matter in the future.

In discussion, it was pointed out that the supplies required by Ceylon represented less than 1½ per cent. of the total Indian crop. In view of the strategic importance of Ceylon in connection with the defence of India, and the extent to which the Empire's war effort now depended on Ceylon's rubber production, it was felt that India should make strong efforts to provide the rice required to meet the Island's minimum needs.

The War Cabinet:—

Invited the Secretary of State for India and Sir Ramaswami Mudaliar to ensure that the Government of India were aware of the urgency of meeting Ceylon's minimum requirements for rice and the importance of building up reasonable reserve stocks. The Government of India should be urged to assure the delivery of 36,500 tons of rice during the months of November and December, and to make every possible effort to send increased quantities during that period. They should be asked, further, to arrange for larger shipments to be made after the beginning of the New Year.

147   CO 54/980/18, no 3   19 Dec 1942
[Reforms]: despatch from Sir A Caldecott to Mr Stanley on ministerial portfolios

I have the honour to acknowledge receipt of Lord Cranborne's Secret despatch dated the 11th November, 1942, and to confess my doubt as to whether I can have correctly understood His Lordship's assumption, in paragraph 3 thereof, that there must have been particular reasons why the question of Mr. Corea's resignation did not arise out of the defeat of the motion of non-confidence in him by thirty votes to four with ten abstentions.[1] This voting, as I ventured to point out, indicated confidence in Mr. Corea; and it is difficult to see how in view of it he could have been expected to consider, or anybody else to suggest, his resignation. Although I do not believe the voting in this matter to have represented the real feeling of many Members of Council in regard to confidence in Mr. Corea, it nevertheless showed very clearly that the great majority were definitely against any idea of a request for his removal under

---

[1] cf 138.

Article 37 of the Ceylon (State Council) Order in Council, 1931. No question of his resignation can therefore in my view be held to have arisen.

2. In regard to the fourth paragraph of Lord Cranborne's despatch I have always made it a point not, even vicariously, to question Ministers or Members about what goes on in the lobby of State Council. I am convinced of the wisdom of such abstention, though my intelligence in such matters is thereby limited to such information as may from time to time be volunteered. I regret therefore that I am unable to supplement paragraph 7 of my despatch of the 4th September[2] except to the extent of explaining that the 'influential member' was Mr. G.G. Ponnambalam, and that by "insistence on a quota of ministerial portfolios irrespective of qualifications" I meant to convey that (vide paragraph 18 of my Reforms Despatch of the 13th June, 1938) he insisted on a definite percentage of ministerial portfolios (what exact percentage I do not know) for non-Sinhalese members, whether or not there were in fact suitable non-Sinhalese for such appointment. My own profound disagreement with such a demand was expressed in my Reforms Despatch in the paragraph above cited.

3. The very strong support given by most Ministers to Mr. Mahadeva in connection with his recent election to succeed Sir D.B. Jayatilaka as Minister for Home Affairs confirms the view which I expressed in the first sentence of the same paragraph, i.e. that the Sinhalese Ministers would be quite ready to welcome non-Sinhalese colleagues in a Cabinet, provided that they were chosen for their personal qualifications and not under a system of racial percentages.

---

[2] See *ibid*.

---

148   CO 54/980/5/1, nos 49 & 50   11 Jan 1943
[Constitutional reform]: inward telegrams from Sir A Caldecott to Mr Stanley transmitting a further message from ministers and expressing the governor's view that a pledge of 'full responsible government and internal home rule within the British Commonwealth of Nations' after the war is now needed

No 49: telegram no 71
Your telegram No. 1411 and my telegram No. 1864.
    Ministers request me to telegraph the following submission:—

Begins. Although message[1] received in reply to our message telegraphed to you 8th October[2] concedes, for the first time, that the purpose of re-examination of our Constitution to which His Majesty's Government stands pledged, will be the fullest possible development of the self-governing Institutions in Ceylon within the Commonwealth partnership, we regret that your reply is in far too indefinite and conditional terms to allay the growing concern regarding our political status which we reported in our first telegram. It would indeed, if published, only magnify that concern inasmuch as it gives no promise of the full responsibility for government

---

[1] See 143, note 3.   [2] See 140.

asked for. We are gratified that His Majesty's Government fully appreciates the co-operation of Ceylon and her people in the war effort, but we are unable to reconcile such full appreciation with a denial to us of the promises which have been given to the great neighbouring country, whose leaders and people have not (repeat not) co-operated as we have. Publication of your message would certainly evoke the criticism that, in order to obtain promises, it is necessary to extort them by non-cooperation rather than earn them by co-operation. We and our people are in whole-hearted support of the ideals of national freedom, national development and international co-operation for which the Allied nations are fighting, and we are convinced that, if we are given our merited status within the British Commonwealth, we can apply those ideals both to our own advancement and to the advantage and security of all sister nations within the family partnership. We maintain that by our war effort and by our progress under the present admittedly difficult constitution, we have amply earned the grant of our request and that, should it be denied to us, the resolution of our people must seriously deteriorate owing to their disappointment of not being trusted or rewarded. We therefore most earnestly request an urgent and careful re-consideration of the reply to our former message. *Ends.*

No 50: unnumbered telegram
Message of Ministers contained in my telegram No. 71 has been substituted for the one which I asked them to reconsider owing to its peremptory and intransigent terms. I am confident that all moderate political opinion in the island now demands full responsible government and internal home rule within the British Commonwealth of Nations and that at this late hour no lesser assurance than this will meet the position. Commander-in-Chief requests me to convey his emphatic concurrence in the above view.

149   CO 54/980/5/1, no 52   21 Jan 1943
[Reforms]: outward unnumbered telegram (reply) from Mr Stanley to Sir A Caldecott requesting clarification of the views of the governor and Admiral Layton

Your secret and personal telegram of 11th January.[1]
   I note that you and the C.-in-C. advise that in order to meet the position no lesser assurance should be given now by His Majesty's Government than pledge of conferment of Dominion Status after the war.
   I find it difficult to reconcile full significance of Dominion Status for Ceylon in unforeseeable conditions of post-war world with Ceylon's obvious needs in matters of defence, commerce, and external relations generally. Further there are general Empire defence interests in the Indian Ocean which it must be the responsibility of H.M.G. to secure in their relations with Ceylon.
   Before I find it possible to carry further my consideration of Ministers' request I should greatly value your own and the C.-in-C.'s views:—

---

[1] See 148, tel no 50.

(1) as to what serious consequences you expect if His Majesty's Government find it impracticable to go beyond assurance already offered;

(2) what if any particular changes in the direction of responsible government (short of full Dominion Status) could safely be promised now for adoption after the war;

(3) what if any particular reservations, e.g. bases or other facilities for Empire defence, or political and economic rights of minority communities must in your view be maintained in any further promise at this moment as to post-war constitutional advancement.

(4) if the case of "certain other British possessions" mentioned in Ministers' message in your telegram No.1401[2] is intended to refer to India and Burma, have they overlooked the actual terms of the pronouncements in those cases (e.g. paragraph (d) of draft declaration for discussion with Indian leaders published 30th March, 1942:[3] and in the case of Burma statement by Governor in Burma Legislature on 26th August, 1940).

You will, I am sure, appreciate that advice in your telegram under reference goes considerably beyond view which you expressed with concurrence of C.-in-C. in your telegram No.1445[4] which postulated that self-governing powers must be restricted by overriding needs of local and Empire security. I should be grateful for a statement of the reasons for your change of view.

---

[2] See 140.

[3] Para (d) of the statement on India of 30 Mar 1942 referred to a constituent assembly which would be set up after provincial elections had been held at the end of the war. The entire membership of the lower houses of the provincial legislatures would form a single electoral college and proceed to elect a constituent assembly by means of proportional representation. The text of the declaration is reproduced in *TOPI*, vol I, 456.

[4] See 141.

---

150   CO 54/980/5/1, no 53   27 Jan 1943
[Reforms]: inward unnumbered telegram (reply) from Sir A Caldecott to Mr Stanley on the meaning of full responsible government and internal home rule within the British Commonwealth of Nations.
Minutes by G E J Gent and Sir G Gater

Your secret and personal telegram of 21st January.[1]

1. My secret and personal telegram of 11th January[2] did not (repeat not) recommend assurance of Dominion status, but of full *responsible* Government and internal Home Rule *within the British Commonwealth of Nations*.

2. Words [in italics] entail full reservation to H.M. Government, under any Constitution to be granted, of control of:—

(a) External relations.

(b) Provision for construction, maintenance, staffing, and manning of such Naval, Military, and Air defences as H.M. Government may from time to time pronounce

---

necessary to the security of the Commonwealth, including that of the Island. Allocation of expenses under (b) between the Imperial and Ceylon Governments should be settled between them and fixed by separate agreement and not by the constitution which should provide only for fixation by agreement.

3. View of the C. in C. and myself on the four points mentioned in your telegram are as follows:—

(1) We anticipate immediate and progressive loss of co-operation and decrease of war effort coupled with the deflection of the great bulk of now moderate opinion towards intransigent nationalism and demand for the right to secession.

(2) We can only repeat that any assurance, short of what we have recommended, will not meet the position, and that danger lies in promising too little rather than too much.

(3) There must be total reservation of control over defence, as stated in paragraph 2 above. No stipulation of safeguards for political rights for the minorities should be included in the assurance, but see paragraph (4) following, which will adequately serve this interest. As regards economic rights, there are none that belong to a minority community by virtue of being a minority community. Any denial or limitation of power under the new constitution to pass legislation affecting property or trade of *non*-Sinhalese (if this is what is meant) would inevitably evoke antagonism and hostility far more inimical to their interest than the absence of any such constitutional protection.

(4) Ministers and Members of the State Council referred to India and Burma, but unlikely that they looked up the pronouncements to which you refer, especially as that relating to Burma does not appear on record here.

As regards paragraph (d) of the draft of the Indian Declaration, any assurance to be given to Ceylon would necessarily, of course, include the statement that the present constitution must continue to operate until a new constitution has been approved by H.M. Government, in accordance with the terms of the assurance and until it has been accepted by a two-thirds majority of the State Council in accordance with the principle contained in Article No. 80 Ceylon *(State Council) Order-in-Council, 1931*. It should also be stated in the assurance that H.M. Government would be grateful for assistance of any committee that the Governor, after consultation with the Board of Ministers, might decide to appoint for preparation of a draft constitution along the lines of the assurance for consideration by H.M. Government.

Minutes on 150

This telegram gives us some light on the attitude of the Governor and of the C-in-C, but as the Ministers have come back with a reiterated demand for Dominion status (and it is now clear that the Governor's limits will be very definitely short of Dominion status) it is not obvious that they would be satisfied with the Governor's alternative words, especially as they probably know that the Governor intends his alternative to be something a good way short of Dominion status.

The expression "external relations" is quite an indefinite one. If there is to be full reservation to His Majesty's Government of control of "external relations" it must require a power of His Majesty's Government to interfere with internal legislation in Ceylon, for instance relating to Indians.

As regards defence, if the reservation to His Majesty's Government is to be full and real, there must be reserved powers to the Governor to veto legislation in Ceylon, or to take executive action in Ceylon, for security purposes, and to ensure that aerodromes for instance are not rendered useless by inappropriate development of surrounding lands.

As regards Minority Communities, there appears to be no safeguard in paragraph 3 (4) of the Governor's telegram since the Sinhalese have an assured majority of no less than two-thirds in a full House in the State Council. The "economic rights" of members of the Minority Communities are a very real bone of contention between Ceylon and India at present, and I can see no prospect of India, who must be consulted in any revision of the Ceylon Constitution, being convinced that there are no economic rights of Indians to be safeguarded in Ceylon as a condition of the grant of full responsible Government and internal home rule.

After Departmental discussion, we, therefore, suggest that a telegram should be sent to the Governor on the lines of the draft herewith.

G.E.J.G.
30.1.43

Secretary of State

1. I do not find it at all easy to make up my mind as to the best reply to make to Ceylon. I don't like Mr. Gent's draft. The first part of it puts a number of problems to the Governor, which he will be in no position to solve because they are ultimately dependent upon decisions of policy by H.M.G. in London. A preferable course would be for us to state what we think the answers to the problems should be and to ask the Governor for his observations on them. Paragraph 9 of the draft gives a further assurance which will certainly not satisfy the Ceylon Ministers, and will be unsatisfactory from our point of view in that it is not very clear what are its implications.

2. It is satisfactory to note from the Governor's last telegram that "dominion status" is not in question. What is asked for is full responsible government and internal home rule within the British Commonwealth of Nations. I assume that what is desired is a position similar to that occupied by Southern Rhodesia. We are asked to give an assurance that full responsible government and internal home rule within the British Commonwealth of Nations will be the objective in the discussions which will take place after the war.

3. The following courses of action seem open to us:—

(a) To stand on the previous declaration and to refuse to add to it.

(b) To accept the Government's proposals, subject to consultation with the other Departments concerned.

(c) To invite the Governor to return home for consultation.

(d) To invite representatives from Ceylon to come here to discuss the terms of the declaration with the Secretary of State.

4. Of the four alternatives mentioned above, I reject (a) on account of the considered view of the Commander-in-Chief and the Governor that the effect of refusal would be an immediate and progressive loss of co-operation and decrease of

war effort. (b) would involve lengthy discussions with other Departments which, under war conditions, it would not be easy to bring to an issue quickly. Even if we were able to reach agreement with other Departments it would not be very satisfactory to have to rely upon telegrams to obtain the Governor's views. (d) seems to me to be attended by great difficulties. It would be essential to represent the minority as well as the majority and the settlement of the composition of the delegation might well lead to very serious dissensions in Ceylon, which would be harmful to the war effort. Also the reception of a delegation here would have awkward repercussions elsewhere, e.g. Jamaica. I therefore reject (d). There remains (c), which I am inclined to think represents our best immediate move. Recent experience in the visits of Sir Harold MacMichael,[3] Sir Henry Moore[4] and Sir Arthur Richards[5] has shewn the immense advantage of being able to discuss outstanding problems with the Governor himself. I think I can say that in all these three cases difficulties have been overcome, and it has been possible to hammer out a policy in a way which would have been impossible by correspondence. The Governor may, of course, feel that it is difficult for him to leave Ceylon in present circumstances. I am inclined to think, however, that we ought to ask him whether, in his opinion, he can safely come home. We should also have to consult the Commander-in-Chief.

5. If it is decided that the Governor should return to confer with the Secretary of State, it will be essential that the whole question of constitutional reform in Ceylon should be explored by the Department, in consultation with other interested Departments.

G.H.G.

2.2.43

---

[3] High commissioner in Palestine, 1938–1944.
[4] Governor of Kenya, 1940–1944.
[5] Governor of Jamaica, 1938–1943; of Nigeria, 1943–1947.

151 CO 54/982/6, no 34   Jan 1943
'Ceylon labour for rubber production': CO note on a further dispute between the governments of India and Ceylon over a proposal to recruit Indian workers for the 1943 rubber drive. *Minute* by G E J Gent

The main driving personality in Ceylon to increase the Ceylon output of rubber this year from 100,000 to about 130,000 tons is the Minister of Agriculture, Mr. Senanayake. His measures include "slaughter" tapping[1] on part of each estate and the special temporary recruitment of 20,000 fresh workers from India who would be repatriated at the end of the war.

The matter of Indian immigration into Ceylon has for many years been a source of acute political controversy between the two countries. Ceylon has always feared the economic competition of Indians in petty trade and the displacement of Ceylonese from employment in the Island. They also fear the prospect of political power in the

---

[1] For an explanation of which, see 162.

self-governing Constitution of the Island being swamped by the votes of Indians in Ceylon who are not genuinely domiciled in the Island.

In 1941 representatives of the two Governments finally achieved agreement on the future of Indian immigration and Indians' status in Ceylon on the basis of an immigration law being passed in Ceylon which recognised the Ceylon Government's authority to control any new Indian immigration into the Island. Subsequently in view of war conditions affecting India and Ceylon, it was agreed not to proceed with the new immigration law but to maintain the status quo until the end of the war—this on the supposition that there would in the interval be no question of a resumption of Indian immigration.

On the new request for the special immigration of 20,000 Indian workers for this year's rubber drive, the Government of India have so far refused to consider it except on undertakings by Ceylon which completely destroy the basis of the 1941 Agreement, and which raise again the whole political aspect of Indian immigration.[2]

For His Majesty's Government to coerce Ceylon to accept India's terms would result in certain non-co-operation by the Ministers and the State Council, and not only in rubber production but in other respects would result in a net loss in Ceylon's present contribution to the war effort. Rather than this it would be better to abandon the attempt to increase the labour force.

The present drastic schemes for increasing the production of rubber estates are definitely being undertaken by Ceylon under the aegis of the Minister of Agriculture not in Ceylon's own long-term interests—far from it—but in the interests of the United Nations' war effort, and particularly in the interests of American production.

Therefore it may be possible to suggest that American influence should be brought to bear through the Raw Materials Board at Washington to persuade India to treat this request for extra labour at this time as a special war-time measure and not an occasion for blackmailing Ceylon on a long-standing and deep-rooted political issue.

That India are responsive to emigration for definite war work (as this can be represented to be) is shown by the fact that they have just agreed to allow the emigration of 3,000 labourers required by the Commander-in-Chief, Ceylon, for aerodrome construction work. They must be persuaded to take the same view of the importance of this year's rubber production.

The recent Private Member's resolution and vote in the State Council in Ceylon took place in a House less than half full, and the fact that it was a Private Member's motion shows that the Ministers gave no support to it.

Food cultivation schemes in Ceylon
Apart from the overriding importance of promoting food production the Sinhalese labour employed is not rubber estate labour nor is it suitable for estate work.

---

[2] The position adopted by the GOI in the 1943 labour dispute was that there were at the time in India in excess of 20,000 labourers who had previously worked in Ceylon but who were prevented from returning because of the GOI's ban on the emigration of unskilled labour. The GOI was prepared to allow up to a maximum of 20,000 to return to Ceylon on condition that there would be no compulsory repatriation at the end of the war. The Board of Ministers in Ceylon refused to accept the condition and would only accept the 20,000 labourers if it was agreed in advance that they would be repatriated at the end of the war (CO 54/982/6).

Minute on 151

We have added to the file the latest two telegrams from Ceylon and the whole situation has been discussed with the Ceylon Dept. and Sir Clifford Figg.[3]

We have reached the conclusion that in the impasse which has been reached in the negotiations between the Governments of India and Ceylon regarding the supply of Indian labour necessary to step-up rubber production in Ceylon by some 20 to 30,000 tons, there are four possible lines of action for His Majesty's Government to take.
These are:—

(a) To press Ceylon to accept the proposals put forward by the Government of India. This would mean that we should have to ask the Ceylonese politicians to swallow Indian demands which they have consistently in the past three years rejected and would be bound to lead to the gravest political discontent on the part both of Government and a large proportion of the people of Ceylon.

(b) That attempts should be made to find an alternative source of labour supply in the Indian Ocean area. There is not, however, much likelihood that such supply would be available. Labour in Mauritius is wholly taken up with keeping up sugar production both to meet the demands of the Middle East area and to supplement supplies for this country to replace West Indian shipments which have been diverted to the United States. There is no surplus labour in the Seychelles and East Africa has labour shortage troubles of its own. There remains Arabia and such labour as can be found there would be entirely unsuitable to plantation work in Ceylon.

(c) The scheme for increasing Ceylon's output can be abandoned altogether and reliance placed upon the continuance of existing arrangements to produce at most a slight increase in present output; in this connection it should be noted that the extra 20 to 30,000 tons which Ceylon was aiming at, could this additional labour be secured, is much more than the total output envisaged from East and West African sources on which so much labour and money has already been expended.

(d) The Government of India could be pressed to reconsider their views. It is suggested that the best means of doing this would be to approach the Government of India through Sir Ramaswami Mudalyar, the Government of India's representative on the War Cabinet. Any approach to him should be based primarily on an appeal from the standpoint of the war needs of the United Nations and the vital interest of the United States in the rubber output of the United Nations for this year, to which the output of Ceylon in particular will be the main contribution. If the Government of India are not responsive to appeals based on the general needs of war production they may well be moved to meet His Majesty's Government's request if they apprehend strong United States criticisms of their attitude.

From the Ceylon point of view the Secretary of State is aware of the long standing fear, on the part of the Sinhalese Ministers and people, of the economic competition in Ceylon of Indian traders and workers. The Indo–Ceylon Joint Report was a final, and apparently successful, effort of the two Governments to achieve some sort of

---

[3] Deputy chairman, Ceylon Chamber of Commerce, 1928–1930; deputy chairman, International Tea Committee, 1933–1947 (chairman, 1948); President, Ceylon Association in London, 1937; member, Imperial Economic Committee, 1937; unpaid business adviser to CO.

agreement on the extent to which Ceylon should be free to restrict this Indian competition in Ceylon by local measures to check the immigration and political power of the Indian community in the Island. It is this Agreement (never implemented in fact or officially approved by the Government of India) which the Indian proposals now would completely upset. Ceylon's fears of an unemployment problem in Ceylon after the war must make it even more impossible for the Board of Ministers now to agree to the proposed Indian conditions.

There is one further point which has been made in a recent telegram from the Ceylon Minister of Agriculture, viz:— that if the present food prospects cannot be improved in the Island then the addition of 20,000 Indian labourers would be an unpleasant problem from the food point of view, and it is only right to note that at a recent meeting of the War Cabinet Shipping Committee it was judged impossible to find tonnage to bring cereals from Australia within the next month or two at any rate. This is an additional complication; but I think it must be left to be used as an additional plank (if the 20,000 new labourers are taken into Ceylon) when we go again to the Shipping Committee for cereals from Australia.

G.E.J.G.

31.1.43

152 CO 54/980/5/1, no 54   4 Feb 1943

[Reforms]: outward unnumbered telegram (reply) from Mr Stanley to Sir A Caldecott requesting a further appreciation from the governor and Admiral Layton on the distinction between dominion status and constitutional reform

Your secret and personal telegram of the 27th January.[1]

I am grateful for fuller expression of your views and appreciate distinction you make between Dominion Status and constitutional reform which you recommend.

2. Ministers' request is for Dominion Status; your own advice to me is that general political opinion would be satisfied with the lesser assurance you have recommended.

3. You will of course understand that promise now of full responsible government on lines you propose could only be given with the approval of the War Cabinet, and they would need to be quite clear as to the significance of such promise in each of the several fields of interest for which His Majesty's Government have responsibilities. To do this with sufficient clarity would in fact seem to involve virtually the drafting of outlines of new constitution now in some detail and in spite of obvious great difficulties in attempting to do so. This would require consultation here with Service Departments and the India Office, and I cannot see how it would be possible to avoid some consultation or at any rate some disclosure to Ministers in Ceylon and to other interested official circles (including Government of India) with consequent provocation of political claims by all concerned in Ceylon and repercussions in India.

4. Resulting constitutional decision could not be expected to satisfy both Sinhalese and minority demands and I foresee risk of loss of co-operation in

---

[1] See 150.

important fields of war service and war industries by one section or another if this course were followed.

5. The choice is therefore between (a) adherence to present form of declaration, and (b) immediate preparation of proposals for new constitution as described in 3. Either course is considered likely to involve loss of co-operation and decrease of war effort. The balance of advantage between them therefore has to be assessed.

6. If you and Commander-in-Chief still feel on further consideration of my views that it is necessary to adopt course (b) it might be necessary for me to ask you to come home for consultation. A discussion with you would be of enormous advantage to me. Against this, however, your arrival here even if ostensibly for short leave, would be assumed to have significance relative to constitutional demands and, if so, might be most unfortunate if His Majesty's Government's decision were against any further promise now and gave you nothing satisfactory to take back to Ministers. But I should like to know in any case whether you and Commander-in-Chief think present political and economic situation in Ceylon would permit your coming home for short period for consultation if I desired it.

7. I want you to be in no doubt that I very fully appreciate and value great importance of contribution which Ceylon has made and is making to war effort and the co-operation which, under the leadership of Ministers and State Council, has made this contribution possible. The future reform of the constitution will be in no way compromised by absence of promise now in circumstances which make precision impossible and which without sufficient precision can only lead to misunderstanding and dispute to the detriment of all concerned in the prime task of concentrating on defeating the enemy.

8. I should have no objection at all to Ministers being so informed as in paragraph 7 with an assurance that message in my telegram 1411 is sincerely intended as promise without qualification and certainly with no feeling of distrust or lack of appreciation of Ceylon's participation in the war effort. But the structure of self-government must be worked out in detail and in negotiation, and it is not possible nor would it be right for His Majesty's Government now to promise results which can only be determined after the examination of the problem has been completed.

9. I shall value a further expression of the views of yourself and Commander-in-Chief on the opinions I have expressed above and particularly in paragraphs 3, 4, 5, 6, 7 and 8.

153   CO 54/980/5/1, no 57   17–18 Feb 1943
[Reforms]: inward unnumbered telegram (reply) in two parts from Sir A Caldecott to Mr Stanley, including a draft statement on reform

Part I: 17 February
Commander-in-Chief and I, in consultation with the Chief Secretary, have carefully considered all the points in your secret and personal telegram of 4th February.[1]

Your paragraph 2. Although in our judgment all moderate political opinion would,

---

[1] See 152.

in actuality, be satisfied with assurance on the lines which we propose this does not, of course, mean that there will not be such measure of expressed disappointment as is inseparable from any concession less than is asked for.

Your paragraph 3. We entirely realise that any statement on the lines proposed by us must receive the approval of the War Cabinet, but we see no reason why, if statement is drafted with due caution, it should involve virtually the drafting of the outlines of a new constitution. We strongly deprecate any consultation with the Government of India in this matter, beyond keeping the India Office informed of developments. Anticipation stated in my telegram of 31st March, that if the Cripps scheme eventuated Ceylon might seek admission to the Indian Union, has been completely negatived by the failure of his mission, and subsequent Indian events. The present position is that even a suspicion that any statement was made by permission of the Government of India, would preclude its acceptance in Ceylon. Our joint opinion, morever, is that, in view of the definite secessionist tendency in India, the security of Commonwealth communications and defence imperatively demand that Ceylon should not (repeat not) be subordinated to India, and that any possible future movement towards fusion should not (repeat not) be encouraged. Draft of statement such as we would propose follows in Part II of this telegram.

Your paragraph 4. We dissent from the view that there is a risk of losing minority co-operation in the war effort, if statement on the lines proposed by us is made. It must be realised that the minority communities are just as keen to be released from Whitehall apron strings as the majority, and that their disagreement with the latter is solely in regard to the allocation of Council seats, and share of Government appointments, etc., i.e., in regard to machinery and not the essential characteristics of the administration which all agree to keep national.

Your paragraph 5. It follows from the preceding paragraphs, that in our view no disadvantage will attach to course (b), whereas course (a) would indubitably induce progressive loss of co-operation, slacking of the war effort, and demand for secession.

Your paragraph 6. We do not regard the present juncture, when the food position and India–Ceylon relations besides other tricky political matters require daily attention, propitious for my going home. I would prefer indeed to be excused from personal consultation, because subsequent reply, if short of present demands, would render my position here most difficult. This is because, although recommendations made in my published despatch of 13th June, 1938, have been rendered inadequate by recent developments, my name is irrevocably associated with those recommendations, and I should be generally suspected of having opposed any more radical reform.

Your paragraph 7. Against your assurance that the absence of promise now would in no way compromise future reform of constitution, must be weighed the certainty that, without a promise now, reform will be undertaken in an atmosphere of disappointment, distrust and dislike, while in the interval, control will have progressively deteriorated as indicated in paragraph 3 (1) of my telegram of 27th January.[2]

Your paragraph 8. Any information given to the Board of Ministers on this subject would need to be communicated by them to the State Council, and we are convinced that intimation on the lines of your paragraph 7 would exacerbate, rather than

---

[2] See 150.

appease, both bodies. While agreeing that precision at present juncture is impossible, we see no reason why general statement of purpose and intention should lead to subsequent misunderstanding and detriment, if plainly and carefully worded. In that belief we commend for your consideration draft statement which follows in Part II. Recent election of member for Jaffna as Minister for Home Affairs means that there is now minority representation on the Board of Ministers. This fact, in conjunction with proposed stipulation that any constitutional change would require approval of three-quarters majority (not two-thirds as proposed in my telegram of 27th January) of the State Council, will compel the Ministers to take minor interests fully into account when evolving constructive proposals. We therefore advise that onus and method of constructive effort should be made to lie entirely on them rather than on the Governor in consultation with them, as suggested in paragraph 3 (4) of my telegram of 27th January. Governor would of course assist if invited by them.

Part II: 18 February
Second and last part of my secret and personal telegram of 17th February. Draft statement. *Begins.* The post-war re-examination of the reform of Ceylon's Constitution, to which His Majesty's Government stands pledged, will be directed towards the grant to Ceylon, by Order of His Majesty in Council, of full responsibility for Government under the Crown in all matters of internal civil administration, but with the retention by His Majesty's Government of control,

(a) over the Island's relations with foreign countries, and with other parts of the British Commonwealth of Nations, and
(b) over the provision, construction, maintenance, staffing and the manning of such naval, military and air defences, equipment and establishments, as His Majesty's Government may from time to time deem necessary for the security of the Commonwealth, including that of the Island, the cost thereof being shared between the two Governments in agreed proportions.

The framing of a constitution to implement this undertaking will require such an examination of detail, and such precision of definition, as cannot be brought to bear so long as the whole (? energies of the) Service and other Departments of His Majesty's Government must remain focussed on the successful prosecution of the war. His Majesty's Government will however, once victory is achieved, be ready to consider any draft instrument that Ministers may in the meantime have found themselves able to evolve, subject to the clear understanding that the adoption of it or of any other draft will depend

(a) upon acceptance by His Majesty's Government as being in full compliance with the first sentence of this statement, and
(b) upon its subsequent approval by three-fourths majority of all members of the State Council of Ceylon, excluding Officers of State, and Speaker or other presiding Member. *Ends.*

If statement on the above lines is approved, we suggest it should be accompanied by expression of appreciation of Ceylon war effort, as indicated in paragraph 7 of your telegram.

154   CO 54/980/5/1, no 59   26 Feb 1943
[Reforms]: inward unnumbered telegram from Sir A Caldecott to Mr Stanley on Mr Senanayake's request for the earliest possible reply to Ceylon's demand for dominion status

Senanayake requested urgent personal interviews with C.-in-C. and myself yesterday, whereat he emphasized the necessity for earliest possible reply to Ceylon demand for Dominion Status. He represented that delay was causing many moderate Ceylonese, who in reality desire Home Rule within the British Commonwealth of Nations, to abandon hope of progress along such lines, and to throw in their lot with India as alone offering a prospect of attaining their ambitions. This movement was being studiously fomented by the Ceylon Indian Congress, whose members were now applying for admission to the Ceylon National Congress at the rate of 500 a day. Ceylon Indian Congress was also bringing constant pressure to bear on all Members of the Council in whose constituencies the Indian vote might prove the decisive factor at the next elections. As a result, public meetings of protest against the incarceration of Gandhi had been presided over by such members, and motion demanding him to broadcast had been passed by the State Council on a Private Member's motion. He himself had resigned from the Executive Committee of the Ceylon National Congress rather than be associated with the demand of that body for Swaraj outside the British Commonwealth, and he had been gratified to hear that his following had caused reconsideration of Congress policy on that point.[1] Nevertheless his position as the champion of the British connection must progressively suffer, so long as there was no promise or prospect of the aspirations of his countrymen being realised within the Commonwealth, and Indian politicians would continue to poison and disrupt Ceylon politics, and undermine her loyalty. Without a flag to fly he could not lead moderate opinion, which he believed even yet to prevail among the majority, into battle against Separationists. Preceding representations were made with patent sincerity, and obvious apprehensions of the present dangerous trend of local politics, and we ourselves are more than ever convinced of the urgent necessity of stopping the rot by making a statement on the lines suggested in my telegram of 17th February[2] before it is too late.[3]

---

[1] On 2 Mar 1943 the joint secretaries of the Ceylon National Congress forwarded to Stanley a copy of a resolution passed at the 23rd session of the Congress held on 19 Dec 1942 at Kelaniya which read: 'The Ceylon National Congress is of opinion that Ceylon's association in a War said to be for democratic freedom, is manifestly contradictory and necessarily ineffective, without a guarantee of that very freedom to her. This Sessions [sic] therefore calls upon the United Nations to make forthwith a declaration, guaranteeing to Ceylon, freedom immediately after the war' (CO 54/980/11, no 29).

[2] See 153.

[3] Stanley replied to this tel on 27 Feb, asking Caldecott to assure Senanayake that while he appreciated the urgency of his representations which were being 'urgently and sincerely studied', ministers and other leaders of responsible opinion in Ceylon should realise that on a matter of such fundamental importance it would be 'neither right nor practicable to rush the War Cabinet on this important decision' (CO 54/980/5/1, no 60).

155 CO 54/980/5/1, no 61   2–3 March 1943

[Reforms]: outward unnumbered telegram (reply) in two parts from Mr Stanley to Sir A Caldecott, including a revised draft statement on reform for submission to the War Cabinet

Part I: 2 March

My secret and personal telegram of 27th February.[1]

I have now completed my examination of draft Declaration proposed in Part II of your secret and personal telegram of 17th February.[2] Having regard to the considerations which you and the Commander-in-Chief have urged so strongly, as well as to those stressed by Senanayake in your secret and personal telegram of 26th February.[3] I have decided to seek approval of War Cabinet for a further Declaration by His Majesty's Government of the nature which you suggest, with the object of giving greater precision to the assurance given to Ministers in 1941, and of removing any doubts regarding His Majesty's Government's intentions in this most important matter.

2. I should propose therefore to submit the Declaration, amended as in text which follows in Part II of this telegram, to War Cabinet at very early date with a view to obtaining their general concurrence in the making of a further declaration of the kind indicated on the understanding that the draft will be subsequently discussed with other interested Departments and submitted again to the Cabinet for final approval. You will realise that I cannot foresee what the War Cabinet's attitude will be, and this intimation of my next move is for you and Commander-in-Chief only (repeat only).

3. I fully appreciate point made in third paragraph of your secret and personal telegram of 17th February, Part I, but while there is no question of course of action being dependent on permission of Government of India it must be for the discretion of Secretary of State for India whether he consults authorities in India. The point you make however will be borne fully in mind.

4. As regards amendments to draft:—

(a) I have assumed that "under the Crown" in opening paragraph of your draft means "within the British Commonwealth," and that your proposal would preserve to the Governor (apart from the special powers relating to reserved subjects) only the normal veto powers of His Majesty's Representative in any self-governing territory.

(b) Reservation (a) in your draft is not in itself a restriction on full responsible government, and has therefore been included independently in the revised draft.

(c) The word "security" has been included after "maintenance" in your reservation (b) to prevent, e.g., the erection of a building on land adjoining an aerodrome which might affect its use for Royal Air Force purposes.

(d) The word "proposals" has been substituted for "instrument," since it might prove difficult for Ministers to evolve a satisfactory instrument, the drafting of which could probably best be undertaken here, once detailed proposals had been accepted by His Majesty's Government.

---

[1] See 154, note 3.   [2] See 153.   [3] See 154.

5. Please telegraph whether you agree draft Declaration which follows in Part II.

Part II: 3 March
Draft declaration begins:—

In August, 1941, the following assurance was given to the Board of Ministers in Ceylon:—

> "His Majesty's Government have had under further consideration the question of constitutional reform in Ceylon. The urgency and importance of the reform of the Constitution are fully recognized by His Majesty's Government, but before making decisions upon the present proposals for reform, concerning which there has been so little unanimity, but which are of such importance to the well-being of Ceylon, His Majesty's Government would desire that the position should be further examined and made the subject of further consultation by means of a Commission or Conference. This cannot be arranged under war conditions, but the matter will be taken up with the least possible delay after the war."

Following consultation with the Governor and the Board of Ministers, His Majesty's Government consider that it is in the general interest to give greater precision to the foregoing statement with the object of removing any doubts regarding His Majesty's Government's intention. Accordingly His Majesty's Government have asked the Governor to convey to the Board of Ministers the following message:—

> "The post-war re-examination of the reform of the Ceylon Constitution, to which His Majesty's Government stands pledged, will be directed towards the grant to Ceylon by Order of His Majesty in Council, of full responsibility for Government under the Crown in all matters of internal civil administration, but with the retention by His Majesty's Government of control over the provision, construction, maintenance, security, staffing and manning of such naval, military and air defences, equipment and establishments, as His Majesty's Government may from time to time deem necessary for the security of the Commonwealth, including that of the Islands, the cost thereof being shared between the two Governments in agreed proportions.
>
> "Ceylon's relations with foreign countries and with other parts of the British Commonwealth of Nations will be subject to the control and direction of His Majesty's Government.
>
> "The framing of such a Constitution to implement this undertaking will require such an examination of detail and such precision of definition as cannot be brought to bear so long as the whole energies of the Service and other Departments of His Majesty's Government must remain focussed on the successful prosecution of the war. His Majesty's Government, will, however, once victory is achieved, proceed to the examination, by a suitable Commission or Conference, of such detailed proposals as Ministers may in the meantime have been able to formulate, subject to the clear understanding that the acceptance by His Majesty's Government of these proposals will depend first upon His Majesty's Government being satisfied that they are in

full compliance with the preceding portion of this statement, and secondly, upon their subsequent approval by a three-fourths majority of all members of the State Council of Ceylon excluding officers of State and Speaker or other presiding member.[4]

"In their consideration of this problem His Majesty's Government have very fully appreciated and valued the contribution which Ceylon has made and is making to the war effort of the British Commonwealth and the United Nations, and the co-operation which, under the leadership of the Board of Ministers and the State Council, has made this contribution effective." *Ends.*

---

[4] On 13 Mar, in a further tel to Caldecott, Stanley explained what he meant by a three-fourths majority: 'I interpret "approval by a three-fourths majority" as meaning "approval by not less than three-fourths of the State Council (excluding Officers of State and Speaker or other presiding members)". Subject to your agreement on this interpretation I will substitute those words in proposed draft of declaration' (CO 54/980/5/2, no 66).

156   CO 54/980/5/2, no 74   16 Mar 1943

[Reforms]: outward unnumbered telegram from Mr Stanley to Sir A Caldecott on the labour dispute with India and the effect that the attitude of Ceylon might have on the War Cabinet's reception of the reforms declaration

In my immediately following secret and personal telegram I have explained my feeling as to course of action you have proposed in your secret and personal telegram of 12th March.[1] In this separate telegram (which will have no repeat no distribution at this end) I want to draw your particular attention to the likely effect which an intransignet [sic] attitude by Ceylon may have on the reception in the War Cabinet of proposal for declaration by His Majesty's Government as to full responsible government in internal affairs after the war. I should not expect in any case to find it easy to convince some of my colleagues that declaration is advisable on lines you and I have agreed, but if Ceylon Government insist upon refusing to compromise on arrangement of limited character for labour supply at this critical juncture on account of general suspicion of Indian immigration it will obviously add to doubts of my colleagues and they will not be impressed by fact that in Ceylon there is intensely bitter and suspicious feeling in this matter. On the contrary Ceylon statesmen of the future must of necessity take fully into account actualities of Ceylon's position and relations with India if Island's prosperity and ability to govern its own affairs are to be matters of reality. If India's present offer is to be rejected by Ministers then at least

---

[1] Caldecott's tel of 12 Mar stated that neither the CO nor the Government of India appeared to appreciate the 'intensely bitter and suspicious feeling' in Ceylon over the question of repatriation (see 151). Ceylon insisted on compulsory repatriation of the Indian workers in question at the end of the war; India was equally adamant on voluntary repatriation. Caldecott was emphatic that there was 'no possibility whatever of the Ministers accepting the Indian proposal, or if they did, of their continuing in office'. He also explained that Ministers and the State Council had launched a scheme for the recruitment of labour from rubber estates; Senanayake was said to be confident that the scheme would produce the maximum output. Civil labour battalions arriving from India would ease the problem by freeing Ceylonese labour (CO 54/982/6, no 83, Caldecott to Stanley, 12 Mar 1943).

there remains need for greatest care in method of communicating such a decision to Government of India with statesmanlike consideration for Indian susceptibilities and bearing in mind future assistance and facilities which Ceylon will in any case have to rely on continuing to obtain from India when normal conditions return, such as food and other supplies as well as market for copra.

I should like you to appreciate that I do not wish Ministers to be subjected to undue pressure such as might force their resignation but I do mean that they should reach their decision with their eyes wide open as far as you yourself can enlighten them in such ways as are open to you.

157   CO 54/982/6, no 89   21 Mar 1943
[Reforms]: inward unnumbered telegram (reply) from Sir A Caldecott to Mr Stanley

Your most secret and personal telegram of 16th March.[1]

Commander-in-Chief and I trust that any criticism by the War Cabinet of matters mentioned in your telegram may be tempered:—

(a) by consideration of difficulties of Ministers under the present constitution

(b) by appreciation of the inevitable shock to public opinion of rejection by India of the 1941 Agreed Conclusions as a basis even for post-war negotiations

(c) by the realization of the dilemma in regard to repatriation explained in (f) of my preceding telegram.[2]

Ministers are not in any sense a Cabinet, and have no Government majority to support them in the State Council. On the contrary, they are the creatures of Executive Committees, and the Executive Committees, creatures of the State Council. They thus inevitably incur criticism as agents rather than command support as leaders, and nothing short of radical amendment can remove this cardinal defect in the Constitution. My immediately preceding telegram has explained position vis-à-vis India, and we do not wish to conceal our joint opinion that the way in which they have handled our request was bound to cause reasonable disappointment and evoke natural feeling. Steps taken since December have reduced the need for immigrant tappers, and their request will receive review before reply to be sent to Indian telegram No. 1855 is determined. Grateful for earliest possible reply to question at the end of (f) in my telegram.

---

[1] See 156.

[2] Para (f) of Caldecott's unnumbered tel of 21 Mar read: 'We [Caldecott and Layton] feel it our duty to reiterate with emphasis, that after war some 50,000 Ceylonese now employed in or by Services must be thrown back upon the labour market, and unless any labourers specially recruited from India can be compulsorily repatriated, we do not ourselves see how the position can possibly be met. Would it be possible to assure the Ministers that failing eventual agreement between India and Ceylon as to any necessary measures of compulsory repatriation dictated by the question of war conditions, H.M. Government would be prepared to arbitrate? Ministers cannot possibly face the State Council unless they insure countrymen against unemployment attributable to immigration authorised with their consent' (CO 54/982/6, no 90).

In the event arbitration by HMG was never considered. Negotiations between India and Ceylon over compulsory repatriation (see 151, note 2) ended at the beginning of Apr 1943 as Ceylon launched its own local recruitment drive to make good the labour shortage (see 160).

158   CO 54/980/5/2, no 79   23 Mar 1943
[Reforms]: letter from G E Preston (Board of Trade) to C H Thornley[1]
on general safeguards for British goods under the proposed reforms

The President[2] is grateful to your Secretary of State for letting him see a copy of the memorandum[3] on the Ceylon Constitution which it is proposed to put before the War Cabinet.

The President considers that in the constitutional and political situation prevailing in Ceylon it will be out of the question to make any provision in the new Constitution for the continuance of Imperial Preference or for any specific treatment of United Kingdom goods. There remains, however, the question whether some general safeguard can be provided, such as is contained in the Royal Instructions to the Governor of Southern Rhodesia. These provide that the Governor shall not assent to certain classes of Bills without the King's instructions or unless such Bills contain clauses suspending their operation until His Majesty's pleasure has been signified. As the President understands the position in Southern Rhodesia, the classes of Bill covered by this provision include "any law of an extraordinary nature and importance whereby Our Prerogative or the rights and property of Our subjects not residing in the Colony or the trade and shipping of the United Kingdom and its dependencies may be prejudiced."

The President would be quite content that the Secretary of State's memorandum should go forward to the War Cabinet, on the understanding that the point mentioned above will be examined in the interdepartmental consultations mentioned in paragraph 13 of the memorandum.

---

[1] Private secretary to Stanley.   [2] Mr Hugh Dalton.   [3] See 161.

159   CO 54/980/5/2, no 78   24 Mar 1943
[Reforms]: letter from Mr Amery to Mr Stanley on responsible
government and the analogy between Ceylon and Burma

I have no comments on the form of your memorandum[1] about Ceylon of which you were good enough to send me a copy. I note that it is intended that the India and Burma Offices should be consulted later on the precise wording of the proposed declaration.

I should however like to say that I myself should much prefer to see the phrase "full responsible Government", which appears in the present draft, avoided. In connection with India, I am more and more driven to the conclusion that the communal differences have been much accentuated by the emphasis which has been laid in the past on "responsible self-government". In countries such as India, and I should have thought also Ceylon, where sharp communal divisions exist, responsible Government of the British type is, it seems to me, not feasible, and it is because we have led Indians to suppose that self-government and responsible Parliamentary Government are identical terms that the Muslims have been driven into the demand

---

[1] See 161.

for a separate Muslim State where a Muslim majority can prevail. Conditions in Ceylon may be a good deal different, but nevertheless I feel that it would be wise to substitute a more general phrase such as "full self-government under the Crown".

There is one other point—the case of Ceylon has some analogy with that of Burma. Within ten days at the latest I shall be circulating to the Cabinet a paper about our future policy in Burma. This will cover a very wide field, including material social and economic reconstruction, the direct rule which I think will be necessary during the reconstruction period, and also the immediate question of political warfare. But in my paper I shall propose that at some appropriate time, for example as soon as we have so effectively re-occupied Burma and restored order that military administration can give way to civil, we should issue a declaration of our policy. This would include an undertaking that after a period of direct rule lasting seven years, full self-government of a form congenial to Burman aspirations would be granted, not excluding control of foreign relations and defence though we should contemplate that provision for securing H.M.G.'s obligations for defence and important minorities would be laid down outside the constitution in a treaty between Burma and H.M.G. It is, of course, the case that Burma under the Act of 1935 enjoyed a wider degree of self-government than Ceylon now possesses and in the respect that under that Act Burma had control of her relations with other parts of the Empire (though not of her foreign relations) she had wider powers than those which you are now proposing for Ceylon after the war. It might I think be felt that we could not promise less to Ceylon after the war than we intend to promise to Burma and in any case it might be felt that Ceylon ought to be given at least the powers which Burma had in respect of relations with other parts of the Empire under the 1935 Act. It seems to me, therefore, that although my memorandum on Burma will have to cover ground not relevant to the case of Ceylon—questions arising out of re-conquest, reconstruction and the like due to the Japanese invasion—there might be some advantages in having the two cases considered at the same meeting. I do not, however, press this if you feel it urgently necessary to secure a decision on the Ceylon case.

160   CO 54/982/6, no 94   26 Mar 1943
[Rubber production]: inward unnumbered telegram from Sir A Caldecott to Mr Stanley on the dispute with India and the ministers' scheme for increasing rubber production

Commander-in-Chief and I interviewed the Board of Ministers yesterday and placed before them Indian telegram No.1,855 together with subsequent explanatory telegrams, and also your telegram No.271. As we expected, Ministers at first pressed for immediate and point blank rejection of the Indian offer.[1] They represented with considerable heat that they had with honesty and conviction voted with the rest of the State Council on the previous day in favour of the Motion introduced by private member on 10th February, stating that there was local labour available for maximum output of rubber, which had been fully debated in the light of full joint report by

---

[1] cf 151, note 2, 156, note 1 and 157, note 2.

Executive Committees of Labour, Industry, and Commerce and of Agriculture and Land. They fully recognised the essential duty of Ceylon to produce every possible ounce of rubber, but were as fully convinced of their ability to achieve this result with labour locally available. They very much hoped the circumstances would enable them to continue their co-operation with us as my Ministers, but such co-operation required on our part trust in their honest convictions and given undertakings. I explained at this point the constitutional position, and emphasised that if their assurance of securing sufficient labour for tapping were not fulfilled, the Governor would be constitutionally responsible for the rejection of the present Indian offer, and that my right to accept it *ex proprio motu* must be recognised, although my desire for continued Ministerial co-operation was not less than theirs. At this they again expressed the hope that no decision of mine would force them to resign. Discussion having thus taken the course which we had anticipated, C.-in-C. stated that proof of their pudding must lie in its eating, and that if by 1st June all tapping requirements had not *de facto* been met by local labour, the deficit would have to be imported from India on the only terms available. Ministers temporarily accepted this position but with the clear stipulation that their present acceptance would in no sense prejudice their freedom to resign office and make public protest if, in the event, the Indian offer has to be accepted even in part. It was finally agreed that I should draft for the agreement of the Board of Ministers at their regular meeting 29th March a polite temporary reply to India, which I have done as follows.

Begins. Your telegram No.1,855. Labour for intensified rubber production. State Council have accepted the joint report of the Executive Committees for Labour, Industry, Commerce and of Agriculture and Land, to the effect that maximum output can be achieved with labour locally available (? and) it has become necessary for me to postpone reply to the offer contained in your telegram under reply until the position can be reviewed in the light of results obtained from implementing the recommendations of the two Committees for provision of labour here. *Ends.*

161   CO 54/980/13, no 1, WP(43)129   27 Mar 1943

'Ceylon constitution': War Cabinet memorandum by Mr Stanley

I regret that I must again trouble my colleagues on the question of the Ceylon Constitution. I only do so because of recent telegrams from the Governor and from the Commander-in-Chief and of the wide repercussions which events in Ceylon may have upon the war effort of the United Nations. In order to make plain the present situation it is, I fear, necessary to [map] out something of the past history of this question.

2.   The present constitution of Ceylon is of the nature of a dyarchy. I need not trouble my colleagues with the full details of the very complicated scheme, but the facts relevant to the present problem are:—

(a) For the normal purpose of legislative and executive action the power is with a State Council, almost entirely elected on a system of universal suffrage, and a Board of Ministers comprising the elected Chairmen of the seven Executive Committees of the State Council, plus the three Officers of State (Chief Secretary, Legal Secretary, and Financial Secretary, who are permanent officials).

(b) Certain matters, such as external affairs, defence, public services, customs and finance, are reserved to the executive control of the Officers of State.

(c) The Governor retains full powers of certification and veto, extending both to executive as well as to legislative action, while additional provision is made for his assuming full control of the administration in the event of an emergency.

3. For some time before the war this constitution was admittedly not proving satisfactory, and recommendations for changes were under discussion in Ceylon. From the point of view of the present situation, the most important of the suggested changes was that the administrative duties hitherto reserved for the Officers of State should in future be allocated to the Ministers, except in regard to certain special subjects, over which the Governor would retain personal control. Moreover, the full powers of the Governor as set out in paragraph 2 (c) would remain without reduction. These proposals were debated at length in the Ceylon State Council, but, owing largely to minority difficulties, no basis of agreement was reached. Further examination of the problem was interrupted by the outbreak of war and, as it became increasingly clear that a settlement could not be satisfactorily carried out until after the war was over, the Governor was authorised to give Ministers an assurance that the position would be further examined and made the subject of further consultation by means of a Commission or Conference; that this could not be arranged under war conditions, but that the matter would be taken up with the least possible delay after the war.

4. In December of last year, owing to representations from the Governor that some further declaration was necessary if we were to retain the goodwill and co-operation of the Ceylonese Ministers, and if the whole-hearted participation of Ceylon in the war effort was to be continued, I approached the War Cabinet again. The War Cabinet then approved of a further statement to Ministers being made in the following terms:—

> "The re-examination of the reform of Ceylon's constitution after the war, to which His Majesty's Government stands pledged, will be directed towards the fullest possible development of self-governing institutions in Ceylon within the Commonwealth partnership, having regard both to the single interest of the Island and to the larger interest of the Commonwealth on which the Island's security and prosperity ultimately depend. In their approach to the question of revision of the constitution in that spirit and intention, there will be on the part of His Majesty's Government the fullest appreciation of the effort and resolution which Ceylon and her people have shown in defence of the Island and in the cause of the Commonwealth."

5. I have now had an opportunity of seeing the reactions of the Ministers in Ceylon to this declaration. Unfortunately, the effect upon them has been far less favourable than the Governor believed it would be, and I fear that as far as they are concerned it has completely failed in the desired effect. Their reply, to the effect that the statement was in far too indefinite and conditional terms to allay the growing concern in Ceylon, is included in Appendix I.[1] I have also received telegrams from the Governor and a joint telegram from the Governor and Commander-in-Chief

---

[1] See 148, tel no 71.

dealing fully with the position and making certain new proposals. These telegrams, together with my replies, are also set out in full in Appendix I.[2]

6. It will be seen from these telegrams that the Governor and Commander-in-Chief take a very serious view of what may happen if it is not possible, by some new declaration, to meet the desires and aspirations of the more moderate element in Ceylon. They expect immediate and progressive loss of co-operation and decrease of war effort, coupled with the deflection of the great bulk of now moderate opinion towards intransigent nationalism and the demand for the right of secession.

7. The Commander-in-Chief and the Governor, after pointing out these dangers, make proposals for a declaration which they feel, though it will not be acceptable to all should satisfy reasonable political opinion. I have set out in Appendix II the declaration which the War Cabinet approved in December side by side with the new declaration now proposed by the Governor and the Commander-in-Chief.[3]

8. A comparison of the two declarations shows that, while in the proposed declaration as in the authorised declaration, no hope is held out of any changes during the war, we should now be definitely committed to a far-reaching reform after the war. Instead of the aim of "the fullest possible development of self-governing institutions within the Commonwealth" we should have given a promise of "full responsibility for government under the Crown in all matters of internal civil administration." The only matters to be reserved would be external relations and defence, while, of course, the proposals do not include any right of secession. Thus, constitutionally, Ceylon, while not attaining full Dominion status, would be very much in the position now occupied by Southern Rhodesia.

9. There is, however, one overriding condition. The proposed constitution, when it has been worked out by a suitable Commission on [sic] Conference, and provided that His Majesty's Government are satisfied that it complies with the reservations in paragraph 8, must be approved by three-quarters of the Members of the State Council* (excluding Officers of State and the Speaker or other presiding member). The object of this condition is to ensure some safeguards for minority interests, as the Sinhalese (the majority community) cannot obtain the requisite majority, unless some at least, of the minority elements are in agreement with them.

10. I find the decision in these circumstances a very difficult one to make, but after much consideration I have come to the conclusion that I should recommend the War Cabinet to endorse the Governor's proposal for a fuller and more definite declaration. The arguments in favour of such a course are:—

(1) It is necessary to make such a declaration if we are to prevent the very serious deterioration in Ceylon's war effort which the Governor thinks is bound to result

---

* The present composition of the State Council is as follows:—

Sinhalese (including 8 Kandyans)	39 seats.
Ceylon Tamils	6 "
Indian Tamils	4 "
Europeans (including 3 Officers of State)	8 "
Muslims	3 "
Burghers	1 "
	61 "

---

[2] See 149, 150, 152, 153, 154.   [3] See 155, part II.

unless we go as far as this. I need not remind my colleagues of the vital importance of Ceylon, both as a strategical base and as the source of essential war materials, rubber in particular.

(2) Ceylon has up to now deserved extremely well of the Empire and its war effort, and the admittedly difficult constitution has been worked by Ministers with great goodwill and, perhaps, an unexpected degree of success. It would be a natural thing for them to compare the definite promises made to India, where, with all respect to India's war effort, the political element at least has been largely non-co-operative, with the indefinite hopes held out to Ceylon, where the elected Ministers have thrown themselves heart and souls into war production. This comparison may lead to the argument that more can be obtained from His Majesty's Government by making trouble than by methods of co-operation;

(3) The proposed declaration would be an encouragement to Sinhalese politicians to turn their minds to settlement with the minorities and to a realistic appreciation of their future relations with India; and

(4) Even under the declaration of December 1942, when we come after the war to a discussion of this question, we shall have to offer a great deal, if not all, of what is now contained in the Governor's proposed declaration. We shall, however, have lost the goodwill which we should gain by making the declaration now, and proposals which to-day, it is believed, will stabilise the situation, may by that time fall far short of the majority view.

11.   It is only fair, however, to put on the other side the very real difficulties which arise if the Governor's proposals are accepted. They are:—

(a) The only definite safeguard, for the various minorities lies in the requirement of approval by three-fourths of the State Council. I had feared that the discussion of constitutional reform would exacerbate the communal position and that we might risk losing the co-operation of the minorities in the war effort, but I have received the expressed assurance of the Commander-in-Chief and the Governor that they do not share this fear (see the Governor's telegram of the 17th February, paragraph 3).[4]

(b) A popular Government will assume for the first time complete financial responsibility just at a time when the post-war financial and economic problems of Ceylon may be most acute.

(c) There is no specific safeguard for British commercial interests in Ceylon. It is difficult to insert this in view of the fact that the promises made to India contain no such provision. Nor is there any definite safeguard for Indian commercial interests; but India would not be without bargaining power for this purpose.

12.   Nevertheless, I feel strongly that, even with all these difficulties, the balance of advantage lies in making a further declaration forthwith. In coming to this conclusion, I attach very great importance to the views expressed by the Governor and the Commander-in-Chief (1) that a declaration by His Majesty's Government in the terms now proposed will satisfy general political opinion in Ceylon, and (2) that if such a declaration is not made there will be a progressive failure of co-operation and a progressive tendency of moderate political opinion to become more extreme in its demands.

---

[4] See 153, part I.

13. I therefore recommend to my colleagues that general approval should be given to the declaration in the terms recommended by the Governor and set out in Appendix II, subject to (1) the examination of the actual wording by other Departments concerned, especially the Service Departments, India Office and the Board of Trade, in consultation with the Colonial Office, and (2) submission of the draft to the War Cabinet for final approval as soon as interdepartmental consultations are completed.[5]

---

[5] When Stanley's memo was considered by the War Cabinet on 1 Apr 1943, it was pointed out that the new declaration would not provide lasting safeguards for the interests of minorities. Concern was expressed that this might afford a dangerous precedent in further discussions of constitutional reform in India. It also seemed desirable that, if such a declaration were to be made, something should be said at the same time about the possibility of a commercial agreement to protect Indian and British commercial interests in Ceylon. Sir K Wood, chancellor of the Exchequer, was anxious that currency questions should be reserved to HMG and he suggested that there might be other points on which interested departments would want to see detailed amendments. Accordingly, the War Cabinet appointed a Cabinet Committee on the Ceylon Constitution to consider these issues. It was chaired by Sir J Anderson (lord president of the Council); other members were Stanley, Amery, Wood and Dalton (Board of Trade) (CO 54/980/13, no 2, WM 47(43)3). To assist the deliberations of the new Cabinet Committee, Stanley requested the governor's views on the reservation of currency, other categories of reserved subjects and the machinery by which the governor would deal with questions relating to defence and external affairs, enquiring in this latter respect whether it was still the intention to create a principal secretaryship to the governor as envisaged in paras 32–33 of Caldecott's despatch of 13 June 1938 (CO 54/980/5/2, no 88, Stanley to Caldecott, 31 Mar 1943).

162   CO 852/515/10   2 Apr 1943

[Rubber production]: minute by S Caine on a disagreement between Ceylon and the UK over the question of whether compensation or an increased price should be paid to rubber producers for slaughter tapping   [Extract]

. . . It has of course for some time been common ground that Ceylon ought to produce the maximum quantity possible of rubber, particularly during the current year which is the critical period before synthetic supplies become available in bulk. Some months ago the Ministry of Supply sent out a Mr. Fellowes to report on the position of rubber production in Ceylon and India and as the result of discussions he had with the authorities in Ceylon, the Ceylon Govt. submitted certain proposals for a further increase of production there. These proposals do not entirely commend themselves to the Ministry of Supply and they have suggested various alternatives. Unfortunately these alternatives have not proved acceptable to the Govt. of Ceylon and there appears to be no prospect of any compromise.

In order to understand the differences it is necessary to explain in the first place certain technical considerations and in the second the position as regards taxation. The principal technical consideration is that by an intensification of the tapping, that is by tapping the trees more frequently, it is possible to effect a substantial temporary increase in the rate of rubber production at the expense of a deterioration in the tree, and a falling off in subsequent production, or, if tapping is sufficiently intense, the ultimate destruction of the tree. For practical purposes intensified tapping may be dealt with in two stages, first what is known as the Double-three system which means making two cuts every three days instead of the usual one cut every other day, and second, the Double-two system which means two cuts every two days. The first involves some danger to the trees but if care is taken of them in other ways it should not cause permanent damage. The second is fairly certain to kill the trees within a year or two. On the technical side the Ceylon proposals aimed at a universal enforcement of the Double-three system and the application of the Double-two system to 20 per cent of each producer's acreage. In actual practice it is understood that a large majority of producers are already tapping on the Double-three system and the important new element introduced by the Ceylon proposals was the 20% "slaughter tapping". It was clear that producers would not follow a system which was bound to destroy a percentage of their plantations as well as jeopardise the remainder without some compensation and it is in fact on the terms of that compensation that the argument has taken place. It should however be interposed at this point that the Ministry of Supply would not themselves have urged the adoption of slaughter tapping at all and are still in two minds as to whether it is on balance desirable because, although it will mean more rubber now, it will mean less rubber in subsequent years. Their attitude has therefore been rather one of unwillingness to oppose the Ceylon proposal for fear of damping Ceylon's enthusiasm for rubber production, not one of enthusiastic support.

The taxation point is that in the case of concerns liable to U.K. taxation, that is approximately 40 to 45 per cent of the whole production, any additional receipts by way of extra price would merely add to the Excess Profits which are already being earned and would be wholly absorbed by the Ceylon and U.K. Excess Profit taxes which in combination take 100% of the excess profit. Concerns which are liable to Ceylon Taxation only are not affected in quite the same way as Ceylon E.P.T. is only 50 per cent.

The initial Ceylon proposal, which they have maintained with variations throughout, was for a straight addition to the price on all rubber produced, conditional on the compulsory enforcement of intensified tapping as already described. This proposal was originally put forward under the impression that it would be possible to exempt such additional price from E.P.T. and as this was not in fact possible the Departments concerned at this end put forward as an alternative the payment of compensation for actual replanting costs incurred in the replacement of trees destroyed by slaughter tapping.[1] Ceylon agreed that this method should be applied to the London concerns since otherwise they could receive no compensation at all, but contended that it would be neither practicable to apply it to the local concerns nor attractive to those concerns since what was wanted was immediate cash recompense and not a promise of future repayment of replanting costs. The Ministry of Supply then put forward a second alternative. They were in any case sceptical of the efficacy of an overall payment in actually increasing production and they therefore proposed to relate any additional payment to the actual excess over Ceylon's standard production (estimated at 100,000 tons). In order to leave the Ceylon Govt. a completely free hand as to how they would dispose of such additional payment, they proposed to pay the bonus to the Govt. and leave the internal distribution to them. Ceylon have however refused to accept this alternative and after further correspondence in which its exact character and the reasons for it had been more amply explained, they adhere to the request for a straight increase of price applicable to all

---

[1] Caine added in the margin: 'This would be a capital payment & not liable to tax.'

producers except the London companies who will perforce be dealt with on the compensation basis.

The last two telegrams indicate a very firm and possibly non-cooperative attitude on the part of the Ceylon Minister of Agriculture. The discussion has been brought sharply into the political arena by the adoption of a Motion in the State Council supporting the request for a straight increase of price. Before that, we had hoped to settle the matter on technical and commercial considerations, but it is now impossible to ignore the political aspects.

I fear that the above, complicated as it is, deals with only a few of the complexities of this subject. I will not attempt to cover them all but other factors which must be mentioned are that the Ceylon Minister is, as ever, very much concerned about the fortunes of the small peasant producers who are responsible for about 22% of Ceylon's rubber production; that in actual fact we are assured by Mr. Fellowes, and have every reason to believe, that these producers are already tapping as heavily as they possibly can and their production will not be increased by any rise in price; that we can probably in any case deal independently with the London Companies so that the only increase of production which is really in balance is that resulting from the slaughter tapping of Ceylon-owned plantations, amounting to perhaps to 5,000 tons per annum; and that on the other hand the Ministry of Supply are very apprehensive that a straight increase of price in Ceylon will have to be followed in Africa—British, French and Belgian, and is more likely to reduce than to increase production there. There is in addition the revenue interest of the Ceylon Gov. . . . We had feared also that there would be another political complication from the American side since if Ceylon production in fact falls short, the Americans might be critical of any refusal on H.M.G's part to agree to the terms asked by the Ceylon Govt. The Ministry of Production, however, believe that there is now a much better realisation of the unwisdom of simply offering high prices for everything on the American side and that they can deal with any criticisms of that nature.

As said at the commencement, the situation was discussed at a meeting attended by Mr. Ascoli (Rubber Controller), Mr. Peirson and Mr. Pyke, (Ministry of Supply), Mr. Morris and Miss Maclean (Min. of Production), Mr. Lee and Mr. Bromley (Trsy.), Sir Clifford Figg, Mr. Sidebotham, Mr. Carstairs,[2] Mr. Bull and myself. The general conclusion was that on the merits of the case no reason whatever was seen to change the views previously held and provided that Ceylon's present attitude did not mean that they would be unwilling even to cooperate in working the compensation scheme, the Ministry of Supply would prefer to confine themselves to an offer of compensation as indicated in para. 4 of No. 15. It was however recognised that account must be taken of the position if the Ceylon attitude meant that a refusal of their proposals in this matter would cause such ill feeling as to jeopardise their whole cooperation in the war effort and that it was also essential to find out whether in fact their non-acceptance would extend to a refusal to work the compensation scheme. It was felt therefore that the first stage should be to get a clear idea of the prospect on these two matters by sending a personal telegram to the Governor in reply to No. 135. I submit a draft accordingly. . . .[3]

---

[2] C Y Carstairs, assistant secretary, CO, head of Production Dept; secretary, Colonial Production Research Committee.
[3] Not printed.

163 CO 54/980/5/2, no 89					3 Apr 1943

[Reforms]: inward unnumbered telegram (reply) from Sir A Caldecott to Mr Stanley on reserved subjects

Your secret and personal telegram of 31st March.[1]

1. Commander-in-Chief and I consider that the safeguarding of currency will be met by the Governor's obligation to reserve all legislation concerning it *vide* next paragraph.

2. Provision regarding legislation on reserved subjects, *i.e.*, subjects in respect of which the Governor will retain full executive authority, should be incorporated in the new constitution and not be left solely for inclusion in future Royal Instructions. Following categories in Instruction 4 must be preserved:—

(4), (8), (9), (10), with the omission of the words "or public security" and further on, "or control of aerial navigation or aircraft."

(11) with the omission of the words "any extraordinary nature and" and of "or rights and property of our subjects not residing in the Island or trade and shipping of any part of our Dominions" *vide* remarks of the Duke of Devonshire in the House of Lords, July, 1942, ending "Guarantees and safeguards are incompatible with equal partnership."

(12) would need redrafting on the following lines: "Any Bill relating to docks, harbours, shipping, coastal and inland waters, buildings or land in such manner as to affect naval, military or aerial security, local or Imperial." Legislation under the omitted headings might of course evoke protest or counteraction of external relations. New constitution would need to arm the Governor with powers equivalent to those now contained in Article 22 of Order-in-Council in respect of his remaining reserved subjects, *e.g.*, in order to preserve friendly relations with an external protesting Government, it might become necessary for him to repeal or suspend legislation passed by the Legislature if the latter not prepared to do so itself.

3. Paragraph 32 and 33 of my despatch of 13th June, 1938. Anticipated that Principal Secretary of the Governor would be Chairman of the Public Services Commission. Under the present proposals this is doubtful, and the official designation of the Governor's right-hand man might await the drafting of the constitution. The essential point about him is that he will have no (repeat no) constitutional status whatever, and act only at the direction and on the responsibility of the Governor. As regards the presentation of motions, bills, etc., concerning the Governor's reserved subjects in the Legislature, this must be done by one of the Ministers after the Governor has consulted the Cabinet as envisaged in my despatch, and probably by the Chief Minister, but consideration of this point should await the drafting of the constitution. It is indeed important that the framework only of the new constitution should be definitely determined now, and that details of the design and procedure should be left for precise consideration and scrutiny by those entrusted with the preliminary and final drafting.

---

[1] See 161, note 5.

164   CO 54/980/13, no 5   10 Apr 1943

'Ceylon constitution': memorandum by Mr Stanley for the War Cabinet Committee on the Ceylon Constitution on reserved legislation, the safeguarding of minorities and British and Indian commercial interests

1. My colleagues on this Committee will remember that the statement regarding constitutional reform in Ceylon which was submitted to the War Cabinet for approval (Cabinet Paper WP(43)129)[1] was criticised on the grounds that (a) the new declaration contained insufficient safeguards for the interests of minorities, (b) the declaration ought to include some reference to a commercial agreement to safeguard Indian and British commercial interests, and (c) currency questions should be included amongst the subjects reserved to His Majesty's Government in the United Kingdom.[2]

2. In order to meet these criticisms I suggest the following alterations. If they prove acceptable to my colleagues, I would then consult the Governor as to the chances of their being accepted in Ceylon.

3. *Reserved legislation*
I feel that there would be considerable advantage in basing any proposals on a precedent, and I should suggest the adoption of the categories of reserved Bills contained in the Southern Rhodesia Royal Instructions of 1937. These include the following only as reserved:—

(1) Any law whereby any grant of land or money or other donation or gratuity may be made to the Governor;
(2) Any law affecting the currency of the Colony;
(3) Any law the provisions of which shall appear inconsistent with obligations imposed on Us by Treaty;
(4) Any law of an extraordinary nature and importance whereby Our prerogative or the rights and property of Our subjects not residing in the Colony or the trade and shipping of the United Kingdom and its Dependencies may be prejudiced;
(5) Any law containing provisions to which Our assent has been once refused, or which may have been disallowed by Us.

In addition in the case of Ceylon there would be two further general subjects reserved, viz: Defence and External Relations, which are referred to in the proposed draft statement. These would provide for the retention by His Majesty's Government of all control over

(a) the provision, construction, maintenance, security, staffing and manning of such Naval, Military and Air defences, equipment and establishments as His Majesty's Government may from time to time deem necessary for the security of the Commonwealth including that of the island, and
(b) Ceylon's relations with foreign countries and with other parts of the British Commonwealth of nations.

---

[1] See 161.   [2] See *ibid*, note 5.

4. *Safeguarding of minorities.*
It seems worth trying, whether we can avoid at this stage any attempt to frame detailed proposals, although I am not very hopeful as to acceptance in Ceylon. This course also has the advantage of following more closely the Indian precedent and thus avoiding complications in that quarter. I propose therefore the inclusion in the draft statement of a provision which would make the acceptance by His Majesty's Government of any proposals for a new constitution dependent upon His Majesty's Government being satisfied that the rights and interests of minorities are reasonably protected against discrimination.

5. *British and Indian commercial interests*
I propose the inclusion in the draft settlement of a provision for the negotiation of trade agreements by Ceylon with other interested members of the Commonwealth for the security of the latters' commercial interests in the Island.

6. I feel that the above proposals should fully meet the criticisms of the War Cabinet, and if my colleagues agree, I would refer them to the Governor for his report on the likelihood of their proving acceptable to Ceylon Ministers. If he feels they would have a reasonable chance of acceptance, we could then proceed with the detailed draft for resubmission to the War Cabinet. If, as I fear is more likely, he feels that they will prove unacceptable, I do not think I can carry the matter any further by this long-range telegraphic discussion. I should then propose that either the Governor, or, if he cannot leave, some one representing him should come back here for a detailed discussion, which might enable me to frame other proposals for the consideration of this Committee. Although that would entail considerable delay, it would in my view be essential, if any progress were to be made.

165   CO 54/980/13, no 6, GEN 3, 1st meeting   12 Apr 1943
'Ceylon constitution': minutes of War Cabinet Committee on Ceylon Constitution on Mr Stanley's memorandum

The Meeting had before them a Memorandum[1] by the Secretary of State for the Colonies in which he suggested certain alterations in order to meet criticisms which had been made of the proposed statement regarding constitutional reform in Ceylon which had been discussed by the War Cabinet on the 1st April, 1943, (W.M.(43) 47th Conclusions, Minute 3).[2]

The Secretary of State for the Colonies said that he felt that the alterations suggested in his memorandum should fully meet the criticisms of the War Cabinet. If his colleagues shared that view, he proposed to refer the proposed alterations to the Governor of Ceylon and to request his views regarding the likelihood of their proving acceptable to the Ceylon Ministers.

In the course of discussion, the following points were raised:—

(a) It was not proposed, in any negotiations with Ceylon Ministers, to refer to the precedent of Southern Rhodesia. If any such precedent were quoted, it would obviously be difficult in the future to resist demands for the extension to Ceylon of

---

[1] See 164.   [2] See 161, note 5.

any further concessions which it might prove possible to make in the case of Southern Rhodesia.

(b) Would not the Ceylon Ministers contend that the provision in regard to the safeguarding of minorities which it was now proposed to include in the draft statement was so vaguely worded as to afford a pretext for His Majesty's Government to reject almost any proposals for a new constitution?

It was the general view of the Meeting that, though the chances of Ceylon Ministers being prepared to accept this provision might be small, the suggestion was one which should be explored if only because of the limitations of the majority requirement as a means of safeguarding the rights and interests of minorities.

(c) The protection of the commercial interests of British subjects resident in Ceylon would be covered by the provision for the safeguarding of minorities suggested in paragraph 4 of the memorandum. The protection of the commercial interests of British subjects not resident in the Colony would be secured by the reservation referred to in paragraph 3(4) of the memorandum. In these circumstances, the proposal to include in the draft statement a provision for the negotiation of trade agreements by Ceylon with other interested members of the Commonwealth represented not so much a reservation required in order to ensure the protection of British commercial interests, as a derogation from the general reservation of External Relations (see paragraph 3(b) of the memorandum).

It was agreed that this should be made clear in any communication sent to the Governor of Ceylon. Some words should also be included to indicate that Ceylon might expect to receive benefits for such agreements as well as to confer them.

It was the general view of the Meeting that, subject to the points which had been raised in discussion, the alterations suggested in the memorandum by the Secretary of State for the Colonies should meet the criticisms of the War Cabinet.

In conclusion:

(1) The Secretary of State for the Colonies was invited to inform the Governor of Ceylon by telegraph of the alterations in the draft statement now proposed and to request his views on the likelihood of their proving acceptable to the Ceylon Ministers.

(2) The Secretary of State for the Colonies undertook to circulate to the Ministers concerned, for their concurrence, a draft of this telegram before its despatch.

166   CO 54/980/5/2, no 104   19 Apr 1943

[Reforms]: outward unnumbered telegram from Mr Stanley to Sir A Caldecott requesting clarification on the safeguards required to protect British and Indian commercial rights and minority interests

Your most secret and personal of 5th April. Constitution.

1. I am grateful for your endeavours to find formulae which would meet satisfactorily difficulties mentioned in my secret and personal telegram of 31st March[1] in manner least unpalatable to Ministers. I have carefully considered your

---

[1] See 161, note 5; also 163.

suggestions and I have had further consultation with those of my colleagues in the War Cabinet who are more particularly concerned.[2]

2. In certain respects your proposals in your telegram under reference would not have provided successful solution of those parts of the problem which offer special difficulty at this end viz:—

(1) safeguarding British and Indian commercial rights and,

(2) safeguarding interests of the several minority communities.

If therefore I now proceed to ask for your considered advice on certain conclusions which have been provisionally reached in my consultations here without detailing our difficulties in adopting your own suggestions I hope that you will not feel in the least that your advice has not been most valuable and helpful to me.

3. These conclusions are as follows:—

(a) categories of reserved Bills. These should be in effect the categories of Bills now reserved in Southern Rhodesia although no (repeat no) mention of Southern Rhodesia as a model for Ceylon would actually be included in the declaration. This would mean Bills of a nature now mentioned in Clause IV (i) Ceylon Royal Instructions Numbers (2), (4) (omitting reference to Bank Notes), (8), (11) and (17).

(b) Defence and External Affairs. These subjects would be matters of general reservation in the Constitutional instruments.

(c) Minorities. His Majesty's Government will require adequate safeguards for the rights and interests of the various minorities to be provided in any new constitution, and the proposed three-quarters majority in new paragraph 5 suggested in Part II of your telegram would not be regarded as adequate safeguard. It is most desirable to avoid in present circumstances any attempt to frame detailed proposals for this purpose, and therefore, we are in favour of inclusion in draft declaration of a provision in general terms only which would make the acceptance by His Majesty's Government of any proposals for new constitution dependent on His Majesty's Government being satisfied that the rights and interests of minorities are satisfactorily protected against discrimination.

(d) Commercial interests of United Kingdom, India and other members of the British Commonwealth. Your proposal for trade agreement between Ceylon and His Majesty's Government in which latter would negotiate with Ceylon on behalf of all members of Commonwealth would I am sure not only be unacceptable to India but also to Dominions, and I am quite satisfied that any negotiations for such an agreement would have to be conducted between all interested parties each of whom would be signatory. Accordingly I propose the inclusion in the draft declaration of a provision for the negotiation of trade agreements by Ceylon with other interested members of the Commonwealth for the security of the latter's commercial interests in the Island. It would naturally be appreciated in Ceylon that the Island might expect to receive benefits as well as incur obligations under such agreements. It would also need to be made clear that His Majesty's Government's general power to control the Island's external relations would not be deemed to be impaired by the negotiation of such agreements by Ceylon nor on

---

[2] See 165.

the other hand would it be deemed to imply the exercise of new powers of control by His Majesty's Government which would in future restrict Ceylon's present capacity to negotiate local and limited agreements with other countries e.g. postal agreements.

4. I have now to ask you for your candid personal advice on the likelihood of declaration modified in above respects being found acceptable to Ministers. If so I feel confident that I can obtain His Majesty's Government's approval, but I am equally confident that approval will not be forthcoming for early fresh declaration unless modified on these lines. If therefore you have to advise that these proposals would not repeat not have a reasonable chance of acceptance by Ministers my only course would be to ask that you yourself or Chief Secretary should come home for special consultation, and if your advice makes that course necessary I should like to know whether you would wish to come yourself or whether you would prefer to send the Chief Secretary.

5. I should like to assure you how clearly I appreciate the difficulty you must feel in assessing likely reaction of Ministers without possibility of consultation with them at this stage, but I know that I can rely upon you with your experience and your personal understanding of all aspects of the political situation to give me a balanced and carefully considered judgment on this difficult matter.

6. I have naturally assumed that you will discuss this matter with the Commander-in-Chief.

167 CO 852/515/10, no 155 23 Apr 1943
'Rubber from Ceylon': letter from F G Lee (Treasury) to S Caine explaining the chancellor's rejection of an increased price for Ceylon rubber

I am sorry that we have not been able to let you have an earlier decision on the price question which was discussed in your room on the 14th April.[1]

The papers have been submitted to the Chancellor together with an account of the various considerations which were urged at our discussion on the 14th April and at the earlier meetings which we have held on the subject. I am now asked to tell you that, while the Chancellor understands that the Colonial Office, the Ministry of Production and the Ministry of Supply consider that there is now no alternative but to give way to the demand of the Minister (in view of the importance of running no risk of a fall in Ceylon production) he is not able to agree that the Ceylon proposals should be accepted. I do not think that I need go into any detailed exposition of the reasons which have weighed with him in coming to this decision—they are those which we have formulated for ourselves on several occasions. Leaving aside what I may call the inflation argument and the consideration of repercussions on African rubber, the essence of the matter is that we have put forward a scheme which we consider fair and reasonable, that the Government of Ceylon has not examined that scheme on its merits but is virtually blackmailing us to accept an alternative course which would involve heavy additional payments by the Exchequer, with no guarantee

[1] cf 162.

whatever that such payments would be matched by any increase in rubber production. As I have said, the Chancellor's decision is that we must stand by our own scheme (which the Ceylon Government have agreed to operate if necessary) in the belief that if we take a firm line the risk that we may not get the full increased production from the large Ceylonese-owned estates—a risk which is by no means a certainty—will be outweighed by the powerful considerations on the other side.

I am sending copies of this letter to Morris and Peirson.[2]

---

[2] At the Ministries of Production and Supply respectively.

---

168 CO 54/980/5/2, no 106 24 Apr 1943
[Reforms]: inward unnumbered telegram (reply) in two parts from Sir A Caldecott to Mr Stanley, including a redraft of the proposed reforms declaration

Part I

1. I have discussed your most secret and personal telegram of the 19th April[1] with the C.-in-C., who concurs in the following reply. Part II of this telegram contains redraft of proposed declaration, amended and expanded to cover and implement fully all conclusions conveyed by your telegram, but in slightly different form from that contemplated by you. Reason for the slight difference is that the first reaction here to the declaration will be to compare it with the present Order-in-Council, Letters Patent and Royal Instructions as published in Ceylon Government Manual of Procedure, 1940. It is important, therefore, not to give our reservation of control over defence, external affairs, commercial interests, minority questions etc. greater prominence or emphasis than that given in the existing constitutional instruments. Instead, therefore, of limiting categories of reserved Bills to those now reserved in Southern Rhodesia, as proposed in your paragraph 3(a), I have included in paragraph 4 of Part II, additional categories based on items (9) (10) (12) (15) of Article 4(1) of the Ceylon Royal Instructions. Item (14) thereof is, of course, covered by (15), and now that we have extremely vocal Ceylon Indian National Congress, there is no occasion to provoke anti-Indian feeling by unnecessary repetition of (14). Results of these additions will be to leave our control over these matters exactly as it now is.

As regards your paragraph 3(b), I consider it advisable explicitly to retain the Governor's power of legislation, if necessary, on matters of defence and external affairs, and have so provided in paragraph 6, Part II.

Your paragraph 3(d). I cannot state too emphatically that, so long as His Majesty's Government reserves control of Ceylon's external affairs, Ceylon will look to His Majesty's Government for assistance, and if necessary, arbitration in negotiations with other parts of the Empire. It is essential that His Majesty's Government should acknowledge this obligation, and I have worded paragraph 5 of Part II accordingly.

2. Your paragraph 4. As you are aware, Ministers are neither always consistent individually, nor cohesive collectively, and it is impossible for me to advise, with any

---

[1] See 166.

certainty, what the reactions of each of them is likely to be. Successful Ceylon National Congress candidate at by-election to the State Council last week stated, in public speech after his election, that he attributed his success to Congress demand for complete independence, as opposed to constitutional reform. To this sentiment, I know Senanayake and a large body of moderate opinion to be at present opposed. Their view is that the only alternatives for Ceylon's future are:—

(a) absorption by India

(b) Internal Home Rule within the British Commonwealth of Nations, with His Majesty's Government prepared as Controller of her external relations, to arbitrate if need arises, between the conflicting claims of India and herself. If no promise as to (b) is given now, trend of all Ceylonese opinion will be towards throwing in their lot wholeheartedly with Indian Nationalists, and making the best terms possible with them. Commander-in-Chief and I have no doubt, whatever, that (b) and not (repeat not) (a) is in the interests of Imperial security *and as* proposed declaration goes further towards (b) than anything hitherto published I have no hesitation in advising that it should be made. As you are fully aware of my views and I of yours, I do not consider any useful object would be served by the Chief Secretary or myself coming home, whereas there are many reasons against it.

Part II

1. The postwar re-examination of the reform of Ceylon's constitution, to which His Majesty's Government stands pledged, will be directed towards the grant to Ceylon by the Order of His Majesty in Council of full responsibility under the Crown for internal administration and legislation subject to the following reservations.

2. H.M. Government will retain control over the provision, construction, maintenance, security, staffing and manning of such naval, military and air defences, equipment and establishments as H.M.G. may from time to time deem necessary for the security of the Commonwealth including that of the Island; the cost thereof being shared between the two Governments in agreed proportions.

3. Ceylon's relations with foreign countries and with other parts of the British Commonwealth of Nations will be subject to control and direction of H.M.G.

4. The Governor will not ratify or assent in the King's name to any measure dealing with the following subjects, without previously obtaining H.M. Instructions thereon:—

(1) any measure for grant of any land, money, gift or gratuity to the Governor;

(2) any measure affecting currency;

(3) any measure inconsistent with the obligations placed upon the Crown by treaty;

(4) any measure interfering with the control of H.M. Forces by sea, land or air;

(5) any measure relating to questions of defence or affecting naval military or air forces, Regular or Volunteers;

(6) any measure relating to docks, harbours, railways, shipping, coastal and inland waters, buildings or land in such manner as to affect naval, military or aerial security;

(7) any measure of importance whereby the Royal Prerogative or rights and property of His Majesty's subjects not residing in the Island, or trade and shipping

of any part of the Commonwealth may be prejudiced;

(8) any measure, the principle of which has evoked serious opposition by any racial, religious or other community, and which in the opinion of the Governor is likely to involve oppression or unfairness to any such community;

(9) any measure containing provisions to which Royal assent has been once refused or which have been disallowed by His Majesty.

5. The limitation imposed by Clause (7) of the preceding paragraph will not be deemed to prevent the Governor from assenting in the King's Name to any measure relating to, and conforming with, any agreement which may be entered into by Ceylon with any other part of the Commonwealth for security of external commercial interests within the Island. It is indeed the purpose of H.M.G. that such matters shall be settled by agreement, and H.M.G. will be pleased to assist in any negotiations.

6. The Governor will be vested with the necessary powers to enable him, in the event of default by the Legislature, to enact any direction of H.M.G. in regard to matters within the scope of paragraph 2 and 3 of this declaration.[2]

7. The framing of a constitution in accordance with the terms of this declaration will require such examination of detail and such precision of definition as cannot be brought to bear so long as the whole of the energies of the service and other Departments of H.M.G. must remain focussed on the successful prosecution of the war. H.M.G. will, however, once victory is achieved, proceed to examine by a suitable Commission or Conference such detailed proposals as the Ministers may in the meantime have been able to formulate in the way of a draft Order-in-Council, subject to the clear understanding that acceptance by H.M.G. of any proposals will depend:—

Firstly upon H.M.G. being satisfied that they are in full compliance with the preceding portions of this statement, and

Secondly, upon their subsequent approval by a three-quarters majority of all members of the State Council of Ceylon excluding officers of the State and the Speaker or other presiding officer.

8. In their consideration of this problem, H.M.G. have very fully appreciated and valued the contribution which Ceylon has made, and is making to the war effort of the British Commonwealth and United Nations, and the co-operation which under the Leadership of the Board of Ministers and State Council, has made this contribution effective.

---

[2] With the concurrence of Caldecott and Layton, paras 4–6 of this draft were revised by the CO (see 169 for the final version of the declaration). Stanley also raised the question of a reservation in respect of the public services but he did not anticipate that this would be necessary because they would be under the control of ministers through such machinery, eg a Public Services Commission, as they might devise. However, he did anticipate that the governor should require a special staff for matters in his reserved field and that such staff would have to be under the sole control of the governor and independent of ministers. Whether the cost of this establishment would be wholly a charge on Ceylon revenues would be a matter for consideration when the constitution was worked out in detail (CO 54/980/5/2, no 110, unnumbered tel, Stanley to Caldecott, 6 May 1943).

169   CO 54/980/13, no 8, WP(43)204   15 May 1943

'Ceylon constitution': War Cabinet memorandum by Mr Stanley.
Annex: amended reforms declaration

My colleagues will remember that when I brought this matter before them at the end of March (W.P. (43) 129), the War Cabinet invited a Committee under the Chairmanship of the Lord President of the Council to examine the draft Statement which it was proposed that His Majesty's Government should make on the question of Constitutional reform of Ceylon.[1]

2. My colleagues on this Cabinet Committee have now completed their examination of the draft Statement[2] and an amended form of the draft is annexed to this Memorandum which embodies alterations designed to meet the criticisms raised by the Cabinet and suggestions put forward by the Committee. The Governor of Ceylon has also expressed his concurrence in the draft.

3. Particular points which were the subject of special comment at our last meeting were:—

(a) The safeguarding of minority rights, and
(b) The protection of the commercial interests of British subjects not resident in Ceylon.

These matters are specifically referred to in paragraph 5 of the draft Statement as now amended under which any Bills in relation to them are to be reserved for the signification of His Majesty's Pleasure.

4. As regards the likelihood of a Statement in this form being acceptable to Ceylon Ministers, the Governor has reported that it is impossible for him to advise with any certainty what the reactions of individual Ministers are likely to be, though he is satisfied that there is a large body of moderate opinion which would be against any demand for complete independence as opposed to constitutional reform, and that, in its view, apart from absorption by India, the only other possibility for Ceylon's future is internal home rule within the British Commonwealth of Nations with His Majesty's Government prepared, as controller of her external relations, to arbitrate if need arises between the conflicting claims of India and herself. The Governor considers that if no promise as to internal home rule within the British Commonwealth of Nations is given now, the trend of all Ceylonese opinion will be towards throwing in their lot whole-heartedly with the Indian Nationalists, and of making the best terms possible with them. The Governor and the Commander-in-Chief have no hesitation in recommending that, as the proposed Statement goes further towards internal home rule within the British Commonwealth of Nations than anything hitherto published, it should be made.

5. The Board of Ministers in Ceylon have urged that a final reply to their request for reconsideration of the draft Statement approved by the War Cabinet in December last (W.P. (42) 564) should be made before the 25th May when the State Council reassembles and the question of constitutional reform will immediately be raised. The Governor has reported to me that notice of a motion demanding complete independence has already been tabled. The present Ministers who champion the

---

[1] See 161.   [2] See 164 & 165.

British connexion will be the subject of an attack by the Nationalist hot-heads unless the Leader of the State Council is in a position to make a satisfactory statement on this subject.

6. My colleagues on the Sub-Committee have unanimously approved of the amended Statement being submitted to the Cabinet with a view to its receiving the formal approval of His Majesty's Government, and I trust that this will now be forthcoming.

Annex to 169

In 1941 the following assurance was given to the Board of Ministers in Ceylon:—

"His Majesty's Government have had under further consideration the question of constitutional reform in Ceylon. The urgency and importance of the reform of the Constitution are fully recognised by His Majesty's Government, but before making decisions upon the present proposals for reform, concerning which there has been so little unanimity, but which are of such importance to the well-being of Ceylon, His Majesty's Government would desire that the position should be further examined and made the subject of further consultation by means of a Commission or Conference. This cannot be arranged under war conditions, but the matter will be taken up with the least possible delay after the war."

After further consideration, His Majesty's Government have decided that it is in the general interest to give greater precision to the foregoing statement with the object of removing any doubts regarding His Majesty's Government's intentions. Accordingly, His Majesty's Government have asked the Governor to convey to the Board of Ministers the following message:—

1. "The post-war re-examination of the reform of the Ceylon Constitution, to which His Majesty's Government stands pledged, will be directed towards the grant to Ceylon by Order of His Majesty in Council, of full responsible Government under the Crown in all matters of internal civil administration.

2. His Majesty's Government will retain control of the provision, construction, maintenance, security, staffing, manning and use of such defences, equipment, establishments and communications as His Majesty's Government may deem necessary for the Naval, Military and Air security of the Commonwealth, including that of the Island, the cost thereof being shared between the two Governments in agreed proportions.[3]

3. Ceylon's relations with foreign countries and with other parts of the British Commonwealth of Nations will be subject to the control and direction of His Majesty's Government.

4. The Governor will be vested with such powers as will enable him, if necessary, to enact any direction of His Majesty's Government in regard to matters within the

---

[3] Compare para 2 with the same para in Caldecott's draft (see 168, part II, para 2). The change was made at the request of the governor and Layton to enable HMG to insist, if necessary, upon roads and railways being kept up to the required military standards and upon possibly unremunerative sections of railways essential to defence (eg that to Trincomalee) not being abandoned (CO 54/908/5/2, no 114, unnumbered tel, Caldecott to Stanley, 8 May 1943).

scope of paragraphs 2 and 3 of this Declaration; and his assent to local measures upon these matters will be subject to reference to His Majesty's Government.

5. The present classes of reserved Bills in the Royal Instructions will be largely reduced under a new Constitution. Apart from measures affecting[4] Defence and External Relations it is intended that these shall be restricted to classes of Bills which—

(a) Relate to the Royal Prerogative, the rights and property of His Majesty's subjects not residing in the Island, and the trade and shipping of any part of the Commonwealth;
(b) Have evoked serious opposition by any racial or religious community and which in the Governor's opinion are likely to involve oppression or unfairness to any community;
(c) Relating to currency.

6. The limitations contained in the preceding paragraph will not be deemed to prevent the Governor from assenting in the King's name to any measure relating to, and conforming with, any trade agreements concluded with the approval of His Majesty's Government by Ceylon with other parts of the Commonwealth. It is the desire of His Majesty's Government that the Island's commercial relations should be settled by the conclusion of agreements, and His Majesty's Government will be pleased to assist in any negotiations with this object.

7. The framing of a Constitution in accordance with the terms of this Declaration will require such examination of detail and such precision of definition as cannot be brought to bear so long as the whole of the energies of the service and other Departments of His Majesty's Government must remain focussed on the successful prosecution of the war. His Majesty's Government will, however, once victory is achieved, proceed to examine by suitable Commission or Conference such detailed proposals as the Ministers may in the meantime have been able to formulate in the way of a complete constitutional scheme, subject to the clear understanding that acceptance by His Majesty's Government of any proposals will depend.

First, upon His Majesty's Government being satisfied that they are in full compliance with the preceding portions of the Statement; and

Secondly, upon their subsequent approval by three-quarters of all members of the State Council of Ceylon, excluding the officers of State and the Speaker or other presiding officer.

8. In their consideration of this problem His Majesty's Government have very fully appreciated and valued the contribution which Ceylon has made and is making to the war effort of the British Commonwealth and the United Nations, and the co-operation which, under the leadership of the Board of Ministers and the State Council, has made this contribution effective."[5]

---

[4] The CO draft included the word 'concerning' here. Caldecott and Layton requested that it be changed to 'affecting' in order to prevent any building, planting etc prejudicial to the safety or efficiency of ports and airfields (*ibid*).

[5] Stanley informed Caldecott on 21 May that Churchill had approved the statement and that an announcement would be made by the secretary of state in reply to a question in the House of Commons on 26 May (CO 54/980/5/3, no 140).

170   CO 54/980/5/3, no 154 A & B   8 June 1943

[Reforms]: inward telegram no 1054 in two parts from Sir A Caldecott to Mr Stanley transmitting the ministers' statement on the reforms declaration

[In view of the controversies that arose over the interpretation of the declaration of May 1943 (see 208 and 209), it is important to identify some of the preliminary stages in the evolution of the ministers' policy. Since there is little or no information on this in the official documents, it is necessary to turn to the Jennings manuscripts and, in particular, to his typescript 'Notes on the ministers' procedure, 1943–44'. The first stage, Jennings points out, was a preliminary memo circulated by Senanayake at a meeting of the Board of Ministers on 31 May 1943. This memo—drafted by Jennings—contained two points. First, that if the ministers were to prepare a scheme of responsible government which adhered to the limits set out in the May declaration, that scheme would be accepted by a commission or conference meeting immediately after the termination of hostilities. Secondly, the scheme would be implemented by an order-in-council if it were accepted by three-quarters of all members of the State Council other than the speaker and the officers of state. The memo proposed that the ministers prepare a draft constitution. Senanayake took no risks on this matter; he showed the memo to Drayton and it was also seen by Caldecott. Neither objected to this interpretation of the meaning of the declaration. Once the ministers agreed to undertake the task, it was decided that Senanayake should make a statement in that sense to the State Council. Jennings points out that there were three drafts of the statement, apart from the text that was ultimately approved by the Board of Ministers at their meeting of 7 June. The two points referred to above were incorporated in all these drafts and the final text. They also contained the following statement: 'It is important, too, that we should be able to draft our own Constitution and not be compelled to accept a Constitution thrust upon us by some commission sent from overseas.' The second draft was shown to Drayton who again said that he thought it quite fair. Drayton also saw the third draft which he amended himself to the point of producing his own version. The following extract from Jennings's 'Notes on the ministers' procedure, 1943–1944', clarifies the next stage in the evolution of the ministers' policy: '4. The Board of Ministers sat for eight hours on the 7th June 1943, and considered the draft statement at great length. They then adjourned for the production of clean copies. O.E.G[oonetileke] fetched me and told me that the C[hief] S[ecretary] had phoned to suggest that I should go through the draft. He tried to keep the drafting straight, but he thought that I should check it. Accordingly, I went through it with D.S. [Senanayake], and we agreed that the draft might stand. The Board met again the same evening, and approved the draft, which was read to the State Council the following day. . . .' The ministers' statement of 8 June is printed in *Reform of the Constitution* SP XVII, 1943, p 4.]

Part I

Your telegram No. 609.

Following is text of statement which Board of Ministers unanimously agreed should be made by Leader shortly after 2.p.m. when the State Council meets today:—

Statement begins.

The Board of Ministers have given careful consideration to declaration by His Majesty's Government on constitutional reform. It is in essence an undertaking that if the Board can produce a constitution which, in the opinion of a Commission or Conference, satisfies the conditions set out in paragraphs (2) to (6) thereof and if that constitution is subsequently accepted by three-quarters of all members of the State Council excluding officers of the State and the Speaker, His Majesty in Council will put that constitution into operation.

2.   The most important part of the declaration is that which undertakes to confer

full responsible Government in matters of internal civil administration. As we shall explain presently, we read it as going further than that, for it is obviously intended that even defence and external relations should be vested in the first instance in responsible ministers. Since our most urgent need, however, is to develop our own resources and determine our own way of life free from external control, it is to an unqualified undertaking for full responsible government in internal matters that emphasis must be laid. Among the consequences which would follow from that undertaking would be:—

Firstly, the abolition of officers of the State and transfer of their functions to responsible ministers;

Secondly, the acquisition of complete control over public services, the disappearance of present Public Services Commission and abolition of present powers of the Governor and the Secretary of State in respect of appointments, conditions of service etc;

Thirdly, the acquisition by the Legislature of full control over finance; and

Fourthly, the abolition of all special powers conferred on the Governor by the present Constitution.

It is important, too, that we should be able to draft our own constitution and not be compelled to accept a constitution thrust upon us by some commission sent from overseas.

3. All these would be substantial gains, and their (? there) would be no qualification to internal self-government except the Governor's power to reserve a Bill for the Royal Assent. The classes of measures in respect of which the Governor would be instructed to reserve would be reduced from 16 to 6, of which 2 would relate to defence and external affairs. Of the other 3, 2 would be of no great importance. One would deal with currency and we do not think that any government or legislature in Ceylon would wish to do anything to depreciate our currency. A second is designed for protection of racial or religious communities. It has not been necessary to use this provision in the past, and there is no reason to suppose that it will be necessary in the future. Nevertheless, it gives the various communities in the Island a protection of which we would not wish to deprive them, though we do not think that they will ever need it.

The third is of greater importance. It is not expressed in the declaration in formal language, but we assume that it would be inserted in the terms found in the Governor's present instructions, namely:

"Any Bill of any extraordinary nature and importance whereby our prerogative or rights and properties of our subjects not residing in the Island, or trading and shipping of any part of our Dominions or maybe prejudiced".

This provision would not be peculiar to Ceylon, for it has been in operation in all Dominions with responsible Government (?and still) is in some. In such territories it has acquired a definite and limited meaning which would have to be applied in Ceylon. Furthermore, if such a provision were inserted in instructions to the Governor of a self-governing Ceylon its force would be weak compared with its force in present instructions. It is applied at present on the advice of officers of the State by a Governor with power ample enough to put policy of British Government into operation. In a self-governing Ceylon the Governor would have no advisers save responsible ministers, and if he chose to exercise powers to the prejudice of Ceylon he would run the risk of being unable to find ministers prepared to work the constitution as he interpreted it. We think it unlikely that powers would be abused, but if it (?was) we feel sure that responsible ministers would know what action to take.

Part II

4. The restrictions in relation to defence and external affairs are in quite another category. We have already mentioned that the declaration does not assert that defence and external affairs would be withdrawn from the scope of self-government. These subjects would be transferred from the Chief Secretary to responsible ministers. In respect of certain closely defined matters of defence, however, the Governor would have an independent power of legislation in order to enact any direction from the British Government and he would also be instructed to reserve bills dealing with any of those matters. In respect of external affairs he would have a similar power of legislation and would be instructed to reserve bills other than those giving effect to Ceylon's trade agreements with other parts of the Commonwealth. We appreciate that Ceylon is not yet in a position to defend herself against aggressive powers. On the other hand, we do not believe that the Island can be defended without the assistance of her people. The declaration acknowledges the valuable contribution which Ceylon has made and is making to the war effort of the British Commonwealth and United Nations. There is no reason to suppose that it would fail to render a similar contribution if unfortunately similar circumstances should arise again. For this reason we do not think that special provisions relating to defence and external relations are necessary. We regret therefore that we are not to be regarded, as Canada and Australia are regarded, as potential allies in any just cause.

5. Imperial forces were stationed in the Dominions until they were fully prepared to take over the whole burden of their defence. Any Imperial force stationed in Ceylon would be for our protection as well as for protection of the Commonwealth as a whole. The Legislature would, however, determine what proportion of the cost should be borne by Ceylon. Unless the whole cost were to be met by Great Britain, therefore, the co-operation of the Legislature would be necessary. Nor does the declaration contemplate that external relations of the Island would be exclusively in the hands of Great Britain. The British Government would have the direction and control, but the initiative would rest with the Government of Ceylon. This would be true of trade agreements with other parts of the Commonwealth and, where any such agreements were concluded by the Government of Ceylon with other parts of the Commonwealth, with the approval of the British Government, the Governor would not be instructed to reserve the bills giving effect to them. Where it was convenient for Ceylon to be separately represented, as at New Delhi, there is nothing to prevent such a step being taken. It is essential to remember too that international agreements often relate to matters of internal civil administration, which are specifically left by the declaration to responsible ministers. In all matters of external relations, therefore, the responsible Government of Ceylon could make its influence felt and its wishes respected. The status of Ceylon would be quite different when a minister is responsible from what it is now, when external relations are vested in the Chief Secretary.

6. Even in respect of defence and external relations, therefore, the declaration marks a definite advance. It does not promise everything for which we have asked.

We do not like the qualifications which we have mentioned. We think, however, that the offer should be accepted in the belief on the one hand that qualifications are unnecessary, and on the other hand that they would decay from disuse as similar qualifications have decayed elsewhere. We also wish to point out that responsible Government, and that Government alone, will be entitled to speak for Ceylon in conferences of the British Commonwealth and Council of Nations.

7. We would add that every matter which is not defence or external affairs can only be regarded as a matter of internal civil administration, for example, determination of composition of the population of Ceylon, protective duties, trade and shipping subjects, only as regards trade and shipping, to reservations considered in paragraph 3 above.

8. The acceptance of a constitution satisfying these conditions is dependent upon its approval by three-quarters of all members of the State Council excluding officers of the State and the Speaker. This is a difficult condition but we believe that the State Council possesses the larger patriotism that transcends sectional differences. We propose therefore to draft a constitution in accordance with interpretation to declaration which we have given in the foregoing paragraphs. If we feel that we can commend it to the country, we shall, in due course, submit it to the State Council in the belief that it will obtain the necessary support. We shall do our best to secure the requisite majority, but not at the expense of the future welfare of Ceylon. We should like to make it plain however that if we fail we shall not stop there.

9. The declaration states that commission or conferences which will examine whether our draft constitution satisfies the declaration cannot meet until victory is achieved. We do not regard this condition as necessarily binding. The war may enter a phase in which consideration of these constitutional problems will become possible earlier. We therefore propose to make draft with all possible despatch. The undertaking will, however, give us an additional reason for hope that victory will not be long delayed.

10. We have given the declaration the interpretation that we think it is intended to bear and we propose to inform the Secretary of State that we are proceeding to frame a constitution in accordance with our interpretation.

Statement ends.
I telegraph this at Minister's request.

171 CO 54/980/5/3, no 161   18 June 1943
[Reforms]: inward unnumbered telegram from Sir A Caldecott to Mr Stanley on the response of the Board of Ministers to the secretary of state's message about their statement

Your secret and personal telegram of 11th June.
  Message contained in your telegram No. 648[1] was communicated to the Board of

---

[1] Tel 648 of 11 June from Stanley to Caldecott referred to the ministers' statement (see 170) and read: 'Please inform Board of Ministers that I have read their statement with great interest. They will not, I am sure, expect any detailed comments on it at this stage for the reason given in paragraph 7 of the Statement by H.M.G. [see 169]. But Ministers may rest assured that once victory is achieved, H.M.G. will be most

Ministers at their weekly meeting on 14th June. I have reason to anticipate that at their next meeting on 21st June Ministers will go back on paragraph 10 of their statement, contained in my telegram No. 1054,[2] and decide that failing acceptance by you of their own interpretation of the declaration by H.M. Government, they will not proceed further in the matter. However regrettable and disappointing this prospect may be, position must remain as stated in your secret and personal telegram of 9th June and I shall not feel myself able to advise any concession to what I consider entirely unreasonable attitude. Ceylon Daily News and affiliated newspapers are certain, however, to applaud it and the purpose of this telegram is to acquaint you with probable developments before any anticipatory mention of them appears in the Press.

ready to examine any scheme which they have formulated in accordance with the terms of H.M.G.'s Statement' (CO 54/980/5/3, no 160).
[2] See 170.

172   CO 54/982/6, no 117   29 June 1943

'Labour for rubber estates': inward unnumbered telegram from Sir A Caldecott to Mr Stanley expressing concern over the labour shortage. Minutes by S Caine and Sir C Figg[1]

Reference your secret and personal telegram of 7th June.
    Labour for rubber estates.
    Position continues to cause the C.-in-C. and myself grave anxiety, and was reviewed in the War Council yesterday. In spite of Resolution of the State Council reported by my telegram No. 627, no labour has yet been recruited by or through Ceylon Government, and any increases have been entirely due to the efforts of estate managements.[2] Figures adduced by the Minister of Agriculture and Lands in the War Council, indicated that over 6,000 tappers are still required, and we impressed upon him imperative necessity of making good this shortage at once. He and the Rubber Commissioner took over responsibility for the supply of labour only four weeks ago, and it is too early to pronounce on their effort which has been hitherto largely exploratory and statistical only, but the C.-in-C. made plain to the Minister that his pressure for increase of prices, vide my telegram No. 1190 could not (repeat not) of itself effect any increase of output on those very many estates which suffer from lack of labour. In any reply to that telegram, we suggest that this point might be made, and any increase of prices allowed to be contingent on the Government guaranteeing the necessary supply of labour for maximum production. Although shortage of 3,500 tons on our estimated output for the first six months may, to certain extent, be ascribed to the unusual amount of rain, Minister admitted in the War Council that unless there is early improvement in production, our output for 1943 will not exceed 105,000 whereas we have undertaken the minimum of 110,000. In conclusion, with reference to your secret and personal telegram of 24th June on the subject of the Rubber Commissioner's salary, we wish to assure you that there has never been any suspicion whatever of this officer withholding his maximum co-operation, but that on the contrary he has always worked all out.

[1] See 151, note 3.   [2] cf 156, note 1 and 160.

Minutes on 172

The official telegram No.1190 referred to reported the outcome of the offer of monetary compensation for slaughter-tapping and attempted to reopen the question of an over-all increase of price which had previously been rejected by H.M.G.[3] The actual figures of acceptances of the offer of compensation certainly appear disappointing although they were not in fact worse than we here had been prepared for. In that telegram the Ceylon Government also indicated that they saw little prospect of production in the next twelve months exceeding the figure of 110,000 tons which was the minimum asked for by H.M.G. Since, however, the decision had been taken on the basis that so long as that figure was attained we need not be seriously concerned, the new information did not present a very strong case for reopening the price issue. None the less, we understand that the Ministries of Production and Supply are still considering the matter, and we are still awaiting their views.

The further telegram now received admits what has always been the view held here that the real limiting factor is not price but labour. Unless some really considerable improvement can be made in the labour field, and it is difficult to see how that can be done unless Ceylon comes to terms with India, it may well be that production will in fact fall short of the 110,000 ton level; but whether any improvement can be achieved by making a concession on the price issue is more dubious and will similarly be a matter for discussion with the other Departments concerned.

In the meantime, pending such discussion, an interim acknowledgement of Sir Andrew Caldecott's telegram in the terms of Mr. Sidebotham's draft appears desirable.

S.C.
1.7.43

I agree. We have all along taken the view that labour was the crux of the matter in so far as the estates were concerned i.e. units that cannot be tapped by the owner and his family. It is true that the smallholder has recently been holding up his rubber – hoping, I think, for a higher price. If and when he is told there is going to be no increase he may decide to go ahead and take what he can get.

It is true, I am afraid, that the inevitably long delay in coming to a decision on this compensation question has given rise to the impression in Ceylon that the Ministry of Supply is no longer in urgent need of maximum production from Ceylon, and I did my best at a meeting of the Ceylon Association Council to-day to dispel this.

I am frankly not happy about the Governor's suggestion at "X" in 117. How can the Ceylon Government guarantee the necessary labour supply?

I am disturbed too at recent telegrams asking for further allocations of new planting from the I.R.R.C. It now appears that they estimate that 30,000 acres will be planted by the end of this year. I cannot believe that there has been surplus labour for this amount some of which could not have been used for tapping.

C.F.
1.7.43

---

[3] cf 162 and 167.

173   CO 54/980/5/3, no 175   6 July 1943

[Reforms]: inward telegram (reply) no 1280 from Sir A Caldecott to Mr Stanley transmitting a message from ministers expressing their dissatisfaction with HMG's reply to their statement on reform

Your telegram No. 648.[1]

Ministers have requested me to telegraph following message.

Begins. We are not satisfied with reply of H.M. Government to the statement made by us in State Council on 8th June, 1943,[2] on Reform Declaration by H.M. Government and duly conveyed to Secretary of State.

It will be recollected that in our reply to message of H.M. Government, conveyed to us by the Governor by letter dated 13th December, 1942, we stated "We regret that your reply is in far too indefinite and conditional terms to allay growing concern regarding our political status".[3]

It is recognised in the Declaration made by H.M.G. that it is in the general interest to give greater precision to the statement made in 1941 with the object of removing any doubts regarding H.M.G.'s intentions.

This Declaration itself, however, though in some respects more precise than previous statements, still in certain important and even vital matters, is, in our opinion, too indefinite in the general interests which the Secretary of State himself had in mind in making the Declaration.

We therefore made statement referred to above embodying our interpretation of certain Clauses of the Declaration, in order to give that precision which we considered necessary before proceeding to draft a Constitution as suggested in paragraph 7 of the Declaration.

We regret, however, that in reply of H.M.G. to our statement, there is no indication whatever that our interpretation is in accord with principles of the Declaration. Without such indication it will not be possible for us to undertake drafting of a Constitution in terms of the Declaration.

We would therefore request H.M.G. to state whether our interpretation falls within the Declaration. *Ends.*

---

[1] See 171, note 1.   [2] See 170.   [3] See 148, tel no 71.

174   CO 54/980/5/3, no 177   9 July 1943

[Reforms]: outward unnumbered telegram (reply) from Mr Stanley to Sir A Caldecott transmitting the secretary of state's response to the ministers' message

Your secret and personal telegram of 6th July.[1]

I am grateful to you for your estimate of importance to be attached to Ministers' change of front, and for your suggestions as to the reply to be made to the message from them contained in your telegram No. 1280 of the same date.

---

[1] See 173.

If you see no objection, I propose to reply in the following terms which may perhaps afford Ministers some assistance when the Motion referred to in your secret and personal telegram of 1st July is debated.

Begins. Please inform Ministers that I have learnt with regret that they are not satisfied with the reply which was given to their statement on the recent declaration by His Majesty's Government on post-war constitutional reform in Ceylon: that it is in view of the inability of His Majesty's Government in present wartime conditions to undertake the necessary detailed examination of proposals for constitutional reform, for the reasons explained in paragraph 7 of their declaration, that the declaration itself has had to be confined to a statement of broad principles. I feel sure that Ministers will appreciate that it would not have been possible for me to comply with their request without seeking from them further elucidation of their interpretation on a number of points, and to do so would have involved those detailed discussions which cannot be undertaken until after the war. In these circumstances it would clearly have been impossible for His Majesty's Government to express their definite acceptance of the interpretation of those various matters which Ministers' statement contained. Practical effect of such interpretation could only be seen in the detailed provisions of a new draft constitution, but Ministers may be assured that I have not found in their statement anything which must be regarded as essentially irreconcilable with the conditions contained in His Majesty's Government's statement.

Ministers have, I trust, realised that His Majesty's Government's declaration was made in all sincerity and with a very real desire to meet the wishes of the people of Ceylon within the framework which the declaration provides. I should wish Ministers to understand that even if they do not now feel themselves able to respond to the invitation to formulate a draft constitution the declaration stands in its entirety and the offer remains open. I should, however, deplore any delay in reaching a final settlement after the war which lack of preparatory work now would seem certain to involve, and I trust that on re-consideration Ministers may decide to adhere to the course which with such statesmanlike promptitude they proposed in their original statement to adopt. *Ends.*[2]

---

[2] Stanley's message was communicated to ministers on 11 July and they decided the following day (a) that the reply was sufficiently satisfactory for them to proceed with the draft of a new constitution, (b) that if further elucidation became necessary, they would seek information from HMG before proceeding with the draft, (c) that the leader of council would refer to the position in the course of his budget speech. Accordingly, an announcement was made in council on 15 July. Caldecott reported that public reception of the announcement had been good (CO 54/980/5/3, no 180, inward tel no 1340, Caldecott to Stanley, 17 July 1943).

175   CO 54/980/5/3, no 187   3 Sept 1943
[Reforms]: minute by W M Clyde[1] to J B Sidebotham on the drafting of the constitution

Here is the note which you suggested I should make:—

Senanayake, at my final meeting (1st August, 1943) with him in Ceylon—a lunch

---

[1] Adviser to the secretary of state for the colonies on wartime food supplies.

party attended also by Goonetilleke and Jennings—spoke of the Constitutional question and said:—"We shall get down to drafting the new Constitution as soon as the Budget debate is over. The debate usually lasts for about three weeks. I wish the Secretary of State to know that we shall get ahead with the drafting as quickly as we can. In fact, at the moment, Jennings is drawing up a first draft for us. Then, about December, we hope to come to London to discuss the matter—Goonetilleke, Jennings and myself."

These are his own words, as far as I can now recall them. Jennings, however, was not so confident as Senanayake that the Board of Ministers would reach agreement upon the terms of the proposed new Constitution in time for the visit to be made to London in December, 1943. Jennings says in his last letter to me "There is, as D.S." [Senanayake] "was careful to explain, a chance of our meeting again soon, though I think he was not making sufficient allowance for difficulties and disagreements on the Board."

176 WO 203/5174, COS(43)251   6 Sept 1943
[War]: report by the Defence of Bases Committee for the COS Committee on the importance of Ceylon for future operations in South-East Asia

At their Meeting on the 26th July, 1943 the Chiefs of Staff approved a telegram to the Commander-in-Chief, India, giving the revised scale of attack for Ceylon.

2. The Commander-in-Chief, Eastern Fleet, in his telegram No. 1116Z of 12th August stated that in his view an attack by Japanese carrier-borne aircraft on Ceylon ports is considered, once the Eastern Fleet is established in force in that area, to be more than a "remote possibility". The Commander-in-Chief, Ceylon, is also of the opinion that the scale of air attack has been underestimated.

3. We are inclined to agree with the above views and have accordingly amended the scale of attack in our revised defence plan.

4. We wish to emphasise the importance of Ceylon for future operations in South East Asia. So long as there is a threat from Japanese carrier-borne aircraft and aircraft based in the Andamans and Northern Sumatra, we consider that not only can no major reductions in the defences be recommended, but they should be maintained in excess of that required to meet the scale of air and sea attack at present assessed.

5. The scale of the Anti-aircraft guns now embodied in the plan agrees with the scale deemed necessary for the defence of vital points and airfields by the Commander-in-Chief, Ceylon, in the circumstances outlined in para. 4 above. These figures show a reduction of 24 H.A.A. and 16 L.A.A. guns against those embodied in the plan prepared in September, 1942.

6. Chiefs of Staff are now asked to approve revised Defence Plan at Annex.[1]

---

[1] Not printed.

177   CO 54/980/5/3, no 194   15 Nov 1943

[Reforms]: letter from Government of India, Department of Indians
Overseas, to India Office on the proposed post-war constitutional
reforms in Ceylon

I am directed to address you in regard to the proposed post-war constitutional
reforms in Ceylon and to say that the Government of India will be grateful for further
elucidation of the term "external relations" occurring in the statement[1] made by His
Majesty's Government on the proposal, as they are anxious to know whether it would
apply to India vis-à-vis Ceylon. I am also to request that His Majesty's Government
may kindly be moved to be good enough to accord to the Government of India the
fullest opportunity of examining the draft constitution and offering their comments
on it, so far as it affects the future of the Indian communities resident in the Island,
in such time as would allow full consideration of them by His Majesty's Government
before they take a final decision.[2]

---

[1] See 169, annex.

[2] In amplification of the point made in this letter, Mr Aney, representative of the Government of India in
Ceylon, informed Caldecott on 23 Dec 1943 that in drawing up a draft constitution, Ceylon ministers
should not assume that the joint report on Indo–Ceylon relations of Sept 1941 afforded any guidance for
determining the status, political or otherwise, of Indians in Ceylon. Caldecott conveyed this message to
the Board of Ministers (CO 54/986/5/1, no 1, despatch from Caldecott to Stanley, 12 Jan 1944).
   In Feb 1944, the Government of India repeated its request to be allowed the earliest opportunity to
comment on the reform proposals; it felt strongly that 'questions regarding the status of Indians in Ceylon
should be satisfactorily settled before the new constitution is introduced' (CO 54/986/5/1, no 14, R N
Gilchrist, India Office, to CO, 2 Mar 1944, enclosing tel from Government of India, 28 Feb).

178   WO 203/5832   29 Nov 1943

[SEAC]: minutes (item 91) of the 60th meeting of the Ceylon War
Council on the establishment of the supreme headquarters of SEAC at
Kandy

[In the preface to his edition of Mountbatten's personal diary for 1943–1946, Philip
Ziegler points out that the idea of appointing a supreme commander to take control of all
allied forces in South-East Asia had been mooted in May 1943. Mountbatten was far from
being the first choice. Churchill was at first not very enthusiastic when Amery suggested
Mountbatten's name but later he agreed. The secretariat of SEAC headquarters was
established first in New Delhi in Oct 1943. It was expected that the headquarters would
move to Kandy in Mar 1944; Mountbatten and his staff arrived in Kandy in mid-Apr 1944.
In his diary entry for 15 Apr 1944, Mountbatten noted: 'The set-up here [in Colombo] is
curious: the governor is definitely under the Commander-in-Chief's orders in all matters
pertaining to the defence of the Island, and operations generally. The Commander-in-
Chief is directly under my orders as Ceylon is part of the South-East Asia Command, so
presumably, the Governor is indirectly under my orders also' (P Ziegler, ed, *Personal
diary of Admiral the Lord Louis Mountbatten, supreme allied commander Southeast
Asia, 1943–1946* (London, 1988) p 99).]

His Excellency the Commander-in-Chief announced that Admiral Lord Louis
Mountbatten, the Supreme Allied Commander, South East Asia Command, had
decided to transfer his headquarters to Ceylon. The Kandy area had been chosen, and
the target date for the completion of the move was 15th March, 1944.

It was realised that the fact that this move is being made is bound to become generally known in time, but instructions have been given that for the present all correspondence in this connection is to be treated as secret, and no reference to the movements of the Supreme Commander or his headquarters will be permitted in the Press or in private correspondence.

His Excellency the Commander-in-Chief asked:—

(i)   the Civil Defence Commissioner to examine the A.R.P. measures in Kandy and the provision of food supplies for labour working in the scheme;
(ii) the Hon. Minister of Health to go into the question of sanitation in the areas to be occupied;
(iii) the Hon. Minister of Home Affairs to look into Police requirements; and
(iv) the Hon. Minister for local Administration to consider what steps could be taken to prevent the 'mushroom' growth of undesirable boutiques near camp sites.

His Excellency the Commander-in-Chief said that he would circulate to Ministers a sketch map of the areas to be used for this scheme. He had made it clear that there was to be no tree felling in the Botanical Gardens area at Peradeniya, and there would be no interference with public access to the flower gardens there.

A certain amount of inconvenience to the public could hardly be avoided, but in a war operation of this kind this would have to be accepted.

His Excellency the Governor said that the Board of Ministers would be glad to know that he had offered King's Pavilion, Kandy, to the Supreme Commander as his personal residence.

His Excellency the Commander-in-Chief went on to say that the move would entail no change in the present form of Government and administration in Ceylon, though they would have some additional Service authorities in the island to deal with. He had made it quite clear that there were no further sources of labour to be tapped in the island, and they would rely, for the extra labour required, on Indian labour battalions. He had also emphasised that most of the materials, apart from bricks and timber, would have to come from outside. He understood that the total personnel involved in the move (excluding labour units) was estimated at about 4,000, but thought it quite likely this would be increased in practice.

179   CO 54/980/8, no 38   1 Dec 1943
[Reforms]: resolutions passed by the Ceylon Indian Congress Committee at Hatton on 21 Nov 1943

1.   The Ceylon Indian Congress is strongly of opinion that, for a prosperous and happy Ceylon, it is of paramount importance that a system of equalised distribution of wealth be introduced in the economic and political structure of the country. To achieve this end, the C.I.C. considers a joint action by the progressive elements of all the communities in the island essential, making it possible for the development of political parties in the country, on the basis of political and economic issues. In the present state of the political development of Ceylon, the C.I.C. considers that such a development of political parties cannot be achieved unless the fears of the minorities are allayed and they are offered their due place in the body politic of the country.

During the period intervening between the formation of political parties and the present one, it is necessary that the principle of *Balanced Representation* between the minorities on the one hand, and the majority community on the other, be introduced in the forthcoming Reforms of the State Council, as a solution of the minority problem. The C.I.C. therefore hereby pledges itself to the principle of Balanced Representation in the State Council as a medium of achieving communal harmony for the purpose of paving the way for formation of political parties on economic issues, to achieve the goal of equalised distribution of wealth and socialised form of economy of the country.

2. The Ceylon Indian Congress is strongly of the opinion that any scheme of Reforms before it is presented to the Secretary of State for the Colonies, should be discussed in the country and by the State Council with particular reference to:—

(a) The Status of the country in the Reforms,
(b) The status of the Indians, and
(c) The solution of the Minorities's [sic] problem.

The Ceylon Indian Congress appeals to the Board of Ministers to get to their scheme the backing of the country and the State Council as a whole, and also that of the Indian community and the other minorities in the island. As deviation from this principle may prove injurious to the best interest of the country, the Ceylon Indian Congress hopes that the Board of Ministers will not violate the elementary principle of constitution-making for the country. The Ceylon Indian Congress appeals to the Secy. of States for Colonies, not to permit a disregard of the wishes of 10 lacs of Indians in the island and the other 10 lacs composing of other minorities by considering the scheme of the Board of Ministers before the same has been discussed in the country and opinion of the State Council obtained on the scheme, with particular reference, as outlined above, namely, that of the status of the country in the new Reforms, status of Indians and the solution of the problem of the minorities.

180   CO 952/514/14, no 414   24 Dec 1943

'Ceylon rubber prices': memorandum by C Y Carstairs[1] on the campaign for higher prices

After the loss of the Far East rubber producing territories, the most urgent action became necessary to increase production in the remaining sources of natural rubber. Of these, by far the most important is Ceylon, of which the production is of the order of 100,000 tons a year.

2. In order to underline the need for rubber, and to stimulate production, the price paid by the Ministry of Supply, who purchase the whole output, was raised from 11d per lb. to 1/2d, in spite of the fact that, at the time (i.e. early 1942) 11d represented an adequately remunerative price.

3. 1942 production did not come up to expectations, and costs of production rose sharply for a variety of reasons, including the increased cost of foodstuffs, supplies of all kinds, transport difficulties and severe competition for labour. The need for

---

[1] See 162, note 2.

rubber has not grown less, and it was suggested that, in order to bring forward maximum supplies during the period of greatest need (i.e. to about mid 1944), without excessively impairing production thereafter, arrangements should be made for slaughter tapping about 20% of trees, the remainder being tapped on the "double-three", the severest regime which the trees can stand without permanent injury.

4. As slaughter tapping involves of necessity the destruction of an asset which would otherwise continue to be productive, the Ceylon Government accepted a recommendation made by Mr. Fellowes, who visited Ceylon on behalf of the Ministry of Supply, that a deferred bonus of 15 cents per lb. should be paid over and above the current price of rubber, in order to afford some compensation. While it was agreed in London that some compensation was justifiable, the Ceylon proposal was held to be impracticable for fiscal reasons, since under E.P.T. it was not permissible to earmark reserves for replanting purposes. The scheme was accordingly modified to provide a replanting grant of £45 per acre to those producers who slaughter tapped 20% of their acreage within a specified period, while tapping the remainder on "double-three". This proposal met with a fair response from those producers (mainly the London-registered Companies) which are paying E.P.T. at 100%, but it did not prove attractive to the Ceylon-registered companies, which pay 50% E.P.T. only. The feeling therefore spread that H.M.G. had deliberately designed a scheme benefiting the U.K.-owned concerned producers only, and there resulted a renewed demand for a flat price increase, which was reinforced by a further rise in costs of production.

5. The Ceylon Government then (February 1943) proposed an overall increase of 5d per lb., except for those producers opting for the compensation scheme, but this was rejected by H.M.G. (March 1943), and the counter-suggestion made of a bonus for all tonnage in excess of 100,000, to be distributed at the discretion of the Ceylon Government. This in turn the Ceylon Government rejected and the campaign for a higher price continues. This demand has crystallised into a slogan of "rupee rubber", i.e. a price of 1/6d per lb. to the producer. This has been endorsed by a Resolution of the Ceylon State Council, supported by Europeans and Ceylonese alike. When various charges are added, this is equivalent to 1/7d f.o.b., or an increase of 5d per lb. Discussions have been proceeding with Mr. Saravanamuttu[2] on the basis of this proposal.

6. The pertinent considerations include as follows:—

(i) The 1944 "target" on the present basis is 110,000 tons. Mr. Saravanamuttu advises, however, that expectations have been so raised that if some concession is not granted, productive effort may suffer a set-back.

(ii) The advice of the Ceylon Government is that with the proposed price increase, production in 1944 may be raised by 10,000 to 15,000 tons: i.e. the difference between price increase and no price increase may be, not that between 110,000 tons and 120,000 *plus*, but between 100,000 tons and 120,000 tons *plus*.

(iii) The increase may be expected to come from (a) the smallholders and others, cultivating poor rubber, whose yields do not permit them at present price levels to pay current wages for tappers, and (b) the large Ceylon-owned estates, paying E.P.T. at 50%, who may be making a profit at present prices, but who will make

---

[2] Rubber commissioner, Ceylon.

extra efforts for a greater price. It is agreed that a price increase offers no additional incentive to the producers now paying 100% E.P.T.

(iv) That rubber is no longer so profitable as it was a year or so ago is shown by a marked decline in purchases of rubber estates, which for a time were changing hands freely at very high prices.

(v) The effect of often-repeated statements by U.S. authorities regarding the adequacy of supplies of synthetic rubber has been, in Ceylon as elsewhere, to spread the impression that an "all-out" effort is no longer necessary, especially one involving the destruction of capital assets by severe tapping. Mr. Saravanamuttu advises that mere announcements to the contrary are likely to be ineffective unless accompanied by some tangible evidence of a strong continuing demand, in the form of a price concession.

7. The proposal for a flat increase of 5d per lb. was considered inter-departmentally and rejected, on the ground that it would provide greatly excessive profits for a large part of the industry, even although in many cases 100% and in others 50% of the increase would return in E.P.T. Departments were however anxious to consider some means of meeting the needs of the marginal producers, and of providing an additional incentive to such others as would respond to it. The following alternatives were put forward:—

(a) a differential price scheme of paying a higher price to those producers in need of it.

(b) a bonus scheme linked to performance, whereby price would be adjusted quarterly in accordance with the amount by which the industry's production in the preceding quarter had exceeded an agreed "target" figure.

(c) a "rebate" scheme whereby the proposed flat price increase would be granted, but repaid 100% by those producers paying 100% E.P.T. and 50% by those paying 50% E.P.T.

8. (a) was rejected on administrative grounds, in that the numbers of small producers involved would be very large indeed, and the practical task of assessing and identifying their production, insuperable. (c) has also been rejected on various grounds of principle and expediency. There therefore remains to be considered (b), to the principle of which, as indicated in para. 5 above, the Ceylon Government is opposed. The reasons for this opposition are as follows:—

(i) the incentive will not apply to the individual producers, who may except to benefit by the exertions of his neighbours, or alternatively to lose through their apathy.

(ii) increased production can only come about through increased expenditure, and producers will be unwilling to undertake this expect in exchange for a spot increase in price, not a problematical subsequent bonus.

9. To these objections, which related to a scheme providing for the division of the bonus earned, if any, according to the efforts of each producer, there may be added in respect of the revised "quarterly" scheme, the danger that if in the first quarter production does not beat the datum figure, and the price does not therefore rise, the scheme will in all probability be killed as a means of increasing production, and the psychological reaction may be great.

181   CO 54/986/5/1, no 9, enclosure   9 Feb 1944

[Constitutional reform]: letter from Mr Senanayake to Sir A Caldecott
on the ministers' draft constitution

[On 2 Feb 1944 Senanayake sent Caldecott a letter enclosing a copy of the ministers' draft constitution, requesting that both should be sent to Stanley. Caldecott obliged in a despatch to the CO which included a copy of his letter of reply to Senanayake of 3 Feb. In this letter the governor explained that while he had undertaken only a 'cursory perusal' of the constitution (submitted in the form of a draft order-in council), he noted from Senanayake's letter that ministers contemplated a 'radical departure' from para 7 of HMG's declaration (see 169, annex) in that (a) ministers had not formulated a complete constitutional scheme and had left crucial questions regarding the form of legislature, franchise and representation to be considered otherwise than by a commission or conference 'required by the Declaration', and (b) that Senanayake's letter (specifically paras 2 and 3(1)) appeared to envisage the immediate consideration by HMG of the ministers' proposals without previous examination by the stipulated commission or conference and the introduction of a new constitution before the achievement of victory in the war (CO 54/986/5/1, no 8, Caldecott to Senanayake, 3 Feb 1944). Caldecott sent a despatch to London on 10 Feb 1944, enclosing a copy of Senanayake's reply to his letter which is reproduced here.]

I have consulted my colleagues on the terms of the second paragraph of Your Excellency's secret letter of the 3rd February, 1944, and we wish to submit to Your Excellency the following points for transmission to the Secretary of State for the Colonies for consideration by him at the same time as Your Excellency's letter under reference.

2. Regarding Your Excellency's comment in paragraph 2(a) of your letter, viz., that the Ministers have not framed a complete Constitutional Scheme, etc., we wish to make the following observations:—

(a) The first omission to which Your Excellency refers is that of "the form of the legislature." Presumably the reference is to Article 6 of the draft which empowers the Parliament of Ceylon to establish a Senate. We have already informed Your Excellency that we have decided upon a uni-cameral system. We consider, however, that the new Parliament should be able by ordinary legislation to establish a bi-cameral system if and when it so desires. In this connexion, it may be observed that the Legislative Assembly of Southern Rhodesia has been empowered to establish a bi-cameral system if it so desires.

(b) Your Excellency next refers to the absence of provisions relating to the franchise. In Canada, Australia, South Africa and Southern Rhodesia the existing election laws were maintained, but were made subject to alteration by the respective legislatures. We would have been glad to have followed these examples were it not that the present Elections Order-in-Council is in urgent need of alteration. That Order is defective not only in respect of the franchise but also in respect of election law generally. Regarding the former (viz., franchise), we wish to make it clear that we do not intend to propose any variation in adult franchise. Regarding the latter (viz., election law generally), a Select Committee of the State Council has already proposed numerous amendments (Sessional Paper XIV of 1938) and recent experience suggests that even more radical changes may be necessary. Further, the election law should be changeable by the Parliament of Ceylon in the same manner as in Canada, Australia, South Africa and Southern

Rhodesia and other parts of the British Commonwealth. For these reasons, we followed the example set by His Majesty's Government in 1931, and provided for a separate Elections Order-in-Council—*vide* Article 16(2) of the draft. We assume it to be our duty to prepare a new Elections Order-in-Council, and to bring the matter under early consideration.

(c) Your Excellency further refers to "representation." We have submitted a complete scheme on this subject, and have thus satisfied the terms of the Declaration. We must point out, however, that His Majesty's Government has required that the draft constitution be accepted by three-quarters of the members of the State Council. In paragraph (8) of our Statement,[1] we said that we would do our best to satisfy this difficult condition, but that if we failed we would not stop there. We have produced a scheme which will, we hope, enable the condition to be satisfied. We have also provided an alternative in case this part of our scheme is not agreed to by the requisite majority.

It will thus be seen that we have prepared a Constitutional Scheme as complete as is necessary for any purpose reasonably contemplated by the Declaration.

3. In view of the reference in Your Excellency's letter to the question of immediate consideration of our draft Constitution, we would like to set out our position at greater length:

(a) Your Excellency has already drawn attention in a published despatch (Sessional Paper XXVIII of 1938) to the inherent difficulties of working the present Constitution. The experience of another five years has not in any way diminished those difficulties.

(b) The difficulty of working the Constitution in time of peace has been enhanced in time of war. Subjects like food and price control, which were never contemplated by the Special Commissioners, have become of fundamental importance and have been fitted into the strait-jacket of the Constitution only with a great deal of friction and difficulty.

It is surprising that this Constitution has worked at all. The continuance of the present Constitution is not conducive either to the good government of the Island or to the full collaboration of the people of Ceylon in the war effort of the United Nations. It is essential both for Ceylon and for the war effort that the Constitution be changed as soon as possible.

4. It is no longer true, as it may have been in May, 1943, that the whole energies of the Departments of His Majesty's Government are "focussed on the successful prosecution of the war." His Majesty's Government and the Parliament of the United Kingdom are in fact spending much energy on the formulation of plans for Post-War Reconstruction. Such plans are as necessary in Ceylon as they are in the United kingdom, but under the present Constitution no authority has the necessary power for formulating them effectively. Nor is it possible for any such plans to be made in ignorance of the form of the Constitution under which they will be carried out.

5. For these reasons, the immediate consideration of our proposals is necessary. This may be done in whatever manner (as suggested in the Declaration or otherwise) His Majesty's Government may consider to be the best.

---

[1] See 170.

182   CO 54/986/5/1, no 6   15 Feb 1944

[Reforms]: inward telegram no 333 from Sir A Caldecott to Mr Stanley
transmitting a message of protest from G G Ponnambalam on behalf of
the minorities

Following submission is telegraphed at the request of Ponnamabalam, [sic] who
states that he has obtained signature thereto of all the minority members of the State
Council, except Mahadeva Razik and Pereira, of whom the last named has authorized
him to subscribe on his behalf.

Begins. On behalf of minority communities, representing more than one third of
the population of Ceylon, we beg leave to apprise you that neither His Majesty's
Government's declaration on the reforms of May, 1943, nor the Ministers' interpretations thereon, have been debated by the State Council.

The Ministers have refused to disclose in Council, or even in informal talks, their
draft proposals which we understand they are submitting for your approval. The
Ministers' procedure, therefore, prevents minority communities' view point regarding these proposals being disclosed to you.

Consideration by you of any proposals without reference to the opinion of the
minority communities would cause grave apprehension in view of vital difference of
opinion, particularly regarding:—

(a) Quantum of representation of different communities,
(b) Status of Indians and Europeans resident in Ceylon,
(c) The system of Executive Committees,
(d) The establishment of a second Chamber.

We therefore request you to withhold consideration of Ministers' proposals till
they are submitted to the State Council, to enable you to have full knowledge of the
opinion of all sections and interests before a Commission or Conference is
summoned.

The Ministers' procedure has aroused strong misgivings and resentment amongst
minority communities. *Ends*.[1]

---

[1] Stanley responded in tel 257 of 28 Feb to Caldecott: 'I should be grateful if, provided you see no
objection, you would inform Ponnambalam that his submission has been received: that as he is aware, the
acceptance by His Majesty's Government of any Constitutional scheme which Ceylon Ministers may
formulate is conditional on such a scheme being eventually adopted by three-quarters of all the Members
of the State Council: and that the discretion of Ministers as to the procedure which they may adopt in
framing a new draft Constitutional Scheme is not a matter with which I should consider it right to
interfere' (CO 54/986/5/1, no 7).

183   CO 54/986/5/1, no 10A   21 Feb 1944

[Reforms]: letter from Sir A Caldecott to G E J Gent on the ministers'
proposals for a new constitution. *Enclosure*: minute by Admiral
Drayton to Caldecott, 6 Feb 1944

In my personal letter of 8th February I wrote that I proposed to send in an early despatch my comments on the Ministers' proposals for a new constitution. On reconsideration however I feel that this would be a mistake, as sooner or later there is likely to be a demand for publication of official correspondence regarding the proposals and it is wise to avoid the contingency of having in such case to withhold anything. Moreover the invitation to put forward detailed proposals (paragraph 7 of the Declaration of His Majesty's Government) was extended to the Ministers alone and I should open myself to criticism if I butted in at this juncture, without waiting to be asked for it by the Secretary of State, with my own personal appraisement of their proposals. I have therefore decided to write this personal letter to you in order that you may be in a position to represent various aspects of the present position to the Secretary of State in connection with his consideration of the Ministers' communication.

2. As stated in my previous letter the Ministers have never once mentioned to me, much less discussed with me, the progress of their deliberations. They received, I have reason to believe, the constant co-operation of Dr. Ivor Jennings who, however great an authority on the British and other constitutions, naturally knows less about Ceylon politics than the Ministers themselves and is not a legal draughtsman. I understand also that the Ministers sought the views of the Officers of State but that these are not reflected in the draft scheme.

3. In tackling their task the Ministers, if not temporarily deaf and blind, must have known that there were three crucial points on which any successful scheme for constitutional reform must hinge.

(1) *Franchise.* During the Ministerial deliberations the Indian Government through their representative, Mr. Aney, stated that "in drawing up any draft constitution for Ceylon the Ministers should not proceed on the assumption that the Joint Report on Indo–Ceylon Relations of September, 1941, affords any guidance for determining the status political and otherwise, of Indians in Ceylon."[1] I reported this by my Confidential despatch of 12th January, 1944. In paragraph 2(b) of the enclosure to my Secret despatch of 10th February current Senanayake wrote "we wish to make it clear that we do not intend to propose any variation in adult franchise."[2] In subsequent conversation however he has told me that by this is meant only that the Ministers intend no departure from the principle of adult franchise but that they will insist on implementation of the Joint Report of 1941 in this regard!

(2) *Minority representation.* This question is at the bottom of nearly all political and communal disagreement in Ceylon. The Ministers had two courses open to them:—

(a) to put up their own reasoned solution without present reference to minority

---

[1] See 177, note 2.

[2] See 181. Caldecott queried this sentence in conversation with Senanayake on 11 Feb. He then wrote to Senanayake on 12 Feb, explaining that it had transpired during the conversation that the sentence was not intended to carry the meaning 'which appeared to me to attach to it'. In order to obviate any possibility of misunderstanding, the governor therefore requested amplification of the sentence in a further letter. Senanayake replied on 28 Feb: 'When we stated that we did not intend to propose any variation in adult franchise we were concerned solely with the franchise to persons possessing a domicile of origin. The other qualifications for the franchise referred to in Articles 7, 8 and 9 of the existing Elections Order-in-Council require our further consideration' (CO 54/986/5/1, no 19, despatch from Caldecott to Stanley, 29 Feb 1944, enclosures 1 & 2).

representatives, and to leave any discussion thereon to the Commission or Conference which will examine their proposals;

(b) to consult minority leaders now and to frame their proposals with reference to such consultation.

Having started off along course (a) the Ministers subsequently allowed themselves to be side-tracked into course (b), and then, having invited and granted a number of interviews (I have privately seen the Notes of one given to the European and Burgher representatives) and having promised others which did not eventuate, they headed back to course (a).

As a result they have got nowhere and have satisfied nobody. The Minority Members' Message contained in my telegram No.333[3] was the inevitable outcome of this shilly-shallying.

(3) *Form of legislature.* Although the Ministers have advocated a single chamber endued with power to create a second chamber one of them, Bandaranaike, in his paper "The Nation" has written consecutive leading articles on the need for a second chamber. In subsequent conversation Senanayake has indeed told me that he considers a second chamber essential to good government when the Governor's present restraining powers are removed. The reason he gave for not pressing the necessity was that he did not think a bicameral constitution would be approved by 75% of the State Council whereas the creation of a second chamber might be passed by a bare majority of one or two. The idea that the Ministers might educate and lead public opinion in this and other matters had not occurred to him. Nor apparently had he or the other Ministers realized that the creation of a second chamber might facilitate a solution of the Indian franchise impasse and of minority representation. This failure is extraordinary in the light of pointers that were given in the course of the interview granted to European and Burgher representatives. I can only infer that Dr. Ivor Jennings' known theoretical and doctrinaire preference for unicameral constitutions weighed more with them than practical local considerations.

4. I enclose with this letter copies of personal letters from Drayton and Nihill dealing seriatim with the Ministers' "Scheme", also a copy of a minute by the Commander in Chief, paragraph 4 of which requires slight correction.[4] Paragraph 39(b) of the Ministerial Scheme does *not* reproduce paragraph (2) of His Majesty's Government's Declaration. The insertion by the Ministers of the words "for such Forces, other than the Ceylon Defence Force and the Ceylon Royal Naval Volunteer Reserve" has completely altered and narrowed the scope of the reservation and cannot of course be accepted.

5. In an interview which he sought of me on 11th February Senanayake represented his own political position to me as follows:—

(i) Left wing politicians in the Island were out to bring about a period of non-cooperation and, in the matter of constitutional reform and world status, to throw Ceylon in with India;

(ii) he (Senanayake) had resigned from the Ceylon National Congress because of its decision to admit members of the Ceylon Communist Party (N.B. Not to be

---

[3] See 182.   [4] Only Drayton's minute to Caldecott is reproduced here.

confused with the proscribed Sama Samajists; the new party is Stalinist and allegedly pro-Allies);

(iii) if he was to be successful in arresting a leftist landslide there must be an early response by His Majesty's Government to the Ministers' constitutional scheme; even though (as he gathered from my letter acknowledging it)[5] I might not think that it met requirements.

6. I may here say that in my judgment Senanayake has recently undermined his position as Leader of the State Council to a very dangerous extent by weakness and instability. I am not thinking in this connection of his hysterial attack on myself in State Council—for which he has since atoned—but of his recurring failure to have things out with Bandaranaike. Here is an example of how he allows Bandaranaike to queer his pitch. As I reported some three years ago Bandaranaike has been flirting for a long time with the idea of a second chamber. At last the suggestion comes up for serious consideration with, I understand, Senanayake in support. Bandaranaike, determined that either he shall get sole credit for the idea or that it shall miscarry, suggests an impossible composition for the chamber, and Senanayake instead of standing up to him weakly drops the whole proposal; whereupon Bandaranaike promotes it with renewed enthusiasm in "The Nation"! Similarly in regard to Congress; Senanayake did not attend the meeting whereat the admission of Communists was approved; instead of fighting the issue he resigns post facto. Now he appeals for an early response from His Majesty's Government to a document in which, owing to his failure to captain the team, our Ministers have failed to suggest answers to the three cardinal questions in any scheme of democracy of who are to be represented? How are they to be represented? and On what are they to be represented?

7. The only form which, it appears to me, an early response to the Ministers' scheme can take is an immediate examination of the clauses of the draft Order-in-Council which refer to the reserved control of Ceylon's defence and external relations. They are clearly defective and unacceptable as they stand, and some headway will have been made if His Majesty's Government could have adequate clauses drafted now for incorporation in any constitution that may ultimately emerge.

8. Another form of response that might suggest itself is an earlier appointment than that promised of an investigatory Commission or Conference. The Ministers' scheme does not, however, provide the "something to bite on to" which I regard as essential to a speedy and successful outcome of any such Commission or Conference. There is, as I have stated many times before, no possibility of agreement by consent in this matter. A scheme has got to be prepared, examined by the Commission or Conference, accepted as a fair offer by His Majesty's Government and then put before the State Council for acceptance by a 75% majority. The scheme will have to be put before State Council to be swallowed whole or not at all. There can be no further arguing of particular points after the Commission or Conference has recommended a scheme and His Majesty's Government have offered it: the question must be yes or no; take it or leave it.

9. The question for immediate consideration therefore is:— Who, the Ministers

---

[5] See 181, note.

having left so many points unanswered or indeterminate, is to prepare an alternative scheme for examination by the promised Commission or Conference?

P.S. Since drafting this letter I have received from the Censor an intercept of a letter written by Jennings, of which I annex a copy.[6] This confirms my allusion to him in paragraphs 2 and 3(3).

Enclosure to 183

It is a pity that these proposals do not include the establishment of a Senate, because whatever is decided, the discussion of such proposals would at least demonstrate some of the functions and advantages of a Second Chamber.

2. The proposal that the establishment of a Senate should depend on the initiative of the State Council is likely to result in there not being a Senate, as it seems highly improbable that a State Council would voluntarily surrender some of its powers, when, broadly speaking, it will probably already regard those powers as inadequate.

3. There is nothing however in the Declaration by His Majesty's Government which prohibits the Board of Ministers from proposing a single-Chamber government, and there remain the two further stages of the examination of these proposals by a post-war Commission and their submission to the State Council, in which this policy *might* be changed.

4. As to the details of the proposals in relation to Defence, the definition of the reservation in paragraph 39 may give rise to considerable argument, but as it is the definition as laid down by His Majesty's Government in so many words in the Declaration, the Board of Ministers can hardly be criticised on this account. It will be for His Majesty's Government itself to take the initiative if it is felt on reconsideration that, for instance, the word "Communications" should be made more specific. I regard it as essential that it should be made clear once and for all that Communications include Railways, Ports, Air Ports, Land Telegraph, and W/T. Again, it has occurred to me that in the course of the discussion last year, His Majesty's Government stated that the word "Security" included such matters as the control of building in the vicinity of airfields.

On the point whether such matters are or are not reserved, the draft Order leaves the final decision to the Supreme Court of Ceylon. At least; this appears to be the intention of paragraph 41(3). This can not be accepted as the issue may well be one of Imperial importance from the point of view of defence.

5. The mention of "Shipping Services" in paragraph 40 seems unlikely to have any undesirable repercussions on Defence: in peace time such matters are dealt with on a commercial basis.

---

[6] Not printed.

184   CO 54/980/5/1, no 12   11 Mar 1944

[Reforms]: outward unnumbered telegram from Mr Stanley to Sir A Caldecott on the procedure for examining the ministers' scheme

Your secret despatches of 3rd and 10th February.[1]

Ceylon Constitution.

Question whether His Majesty's Government will be prepared to depart from decision that examination of any scheme prepared by Ministers for new Constitution would have to be deferred until victory is achieved is a matter which will require most careful consideration, and I am not in a position to express any opinion as to whether that decision can be varied or to commit His Majesty's Government in any way.

2.   But in the meantime I should be grateful for your personal advice by telegraph as to whether in the event of it being decided to proceed with the examination of the Ministers' scheme, this examination could best be carried out by (a) Commission or (b) Conference; and, whichever of these two procedures might be adopted, (c) where the examination should take place, and (d) how the examining body should be constituted.

3.   It would be very definitely understood that in the event of His Majesty's Government deciding to proceed with the appointment of a conference or commission they were not on that account in any way committed to accepting the Ministers' proposals as satisfying the first of the two conditions set out in paragraph 7 of His Majesty's Government's Declaration.[2]

4.   I have just received your secret telegram of 9th March, and note the action which you propose to take in paragraph 4 and your strong recommendation in paragraph 7 that, if at all possible, examination of scheme should be proceeded with.

5.   I will give fullest consideration to your suggestions but I am anxious that in conversations with Ministers you will take opportunity to make it clear that His Majesty's Government cannot be expected to take hasty decisions on matters of this kind.

---

[1] See 181, note.   [2] See 169, annex.

185   CO 54/986/5/1, no 21   17 Mar 1944

[Reforms]: inward telegram no 542 from Sir A Caldecott to Mr Stanley transmitting a message from the Board of Ministers requesting an early decision on the ministers' scheme

Your telegram No. 321.

Ministers have asked me to transmit the following message.

Begins. The Ministers note with gratification that you will give consideration to their request for immediate examination of the scheme submitted by them for a new constitution for Ceylon. While they fully realize that His Majesty's Government would not wish to take a hasty decision, they desire to submit that urgent local circumstances make early decision a vital necessity, in that, unless the life of the present State Council is extended by an Order-in-Council, it must be dissolved before the end of this year, so that a general election can take place early next year. While the Ministers have no doubt that, in the interest of the war effort, a general election at this time would be undesirable, a further extension of the life of the State Council is not likely to be acceptable to public opinion, unless the country were fully satisfied that plans for a new Constitution were under active consideration and that the next general election would be held under the new Constitution and within a reasonable time. The Ministers would be grateful if His Majesty's Government would, in view of these considerations, expedite their decision. *Ends.*

186   CO 54/980/5/1, no 22   18 Mar 1944
[Reforms]: inward unnumbered telegram (reply) from Sir A Caldecott to Mr Stanley recommending the appointment of a commission to examine the ministers' scheme

Your secret and personal telegram of 11th March.[1]

In conversation with the Ministers, 14th March, I impressed on them the points emphasised in your paragraphs 1, 3 and 5.

2. Before communicating to them the text of your telegram No. 321, I deleted therefrom the words "Board are accordingly," because the Board includes Officers of State, whereas the invitation to formulate Constitutional Scheme was, *vide* paragraph 7 of His Majesty's Government's Declaration, to the Ministers only.

3. Minister's reply is contained in my telegram No. 542.[2]

4. Your paragraph 2. Strongly advise Commission and not (repeat not) Conference, because the latter could only be productive if some measures of consent were reached, and this, as explained in my letter to Gent of 21st February, paragraph 8, cannot be anticipated.

5. Venue should certainly be Ceylon, or else complaint of inaccessibility would be made. From the Commissioners' own standpoint also, first-hand experience of local atmosphere important.

6. Strongly advise that the Ministers should be requested, well in advance of the arrival of the Commission, to supplement their scheme by definite proposals on the three crucial questions, mentioned in paragraph 2 (a) of enclosure (iii) to my despatch of 3rd February.[3]

7. Invite also attention to suggestion in paragraph 7 of my letter to Gent[4] in regard to reserving control of Defence and External Affairs.

8. Venture to suggest that the Commission should consist of three members only, of whom one should have experience in the Upper or both Houses of the British Parliament, one experience in the Lower House of a Dominion Parliament, and the third, British Treasury experience. Following names, though not perhaps of persons likely to be available, are indicative of the three types required—Soulbury, Bruce[5] and Leith Ross.[6] In my judgment, dons, or other constitutional theorists, must be studiously avoided. Essential also that none of the three should have had any previous association with Ceylon or other Colonial Administration, or with India.

---

[1] See 184.   [2] See 185.   [3] See 181, note.   [4] See 183.
[5] Stanley Bruce (1st Viscount Bruce of Melbourne cr 1947); prime minister of Australia, 1923–29; Australian high commissioner in London, 1933–1945; member of War Cabinet from 1942.
[6] Sir F Leith-Ross, deputy controller of finance, Treasury, 1925–1932; chief economic adviser to UK government, 1932–1946.

187   CO 54/986/5/1, no 25   31 Mar 1944

[Reforms]: outward unnumbered telegram (reply) from Mr Stanley to Sir A Caldecott explaining why HMG is not able to commit itself to the early appointment of a commission

Your secret and personal telegram of the 18th March.[1]

I have given most careful consideration to the question whether it is practicable for His Majesty's Government in present circumstances to take active steps to examine by a Commission or Conference the constitutional proposals which Ministers have formulated.

2. In their statement of the 8th June, 1943,[2] Ministers referred to the passage in His Majesty's Government's Declaration which made it clear that examination by Commission or Conference cannot be undertaken until victory is achieved. The Ministers contemplated however that the war might enter a phase in which His Majesty's Government might find it possible to proceed at an earlier date. I sincerely appreciate the energy and expedition with which they have formulated their scheme; and if I were able to take the view that the war is now entering a phase in which the Ministers' proposals could be fully examined by a Commission or Conference of the requisite calibre it would have been very welcome to me, as I fully appreciate the desirability of pressing on with this most important matter with the least possible delay.

3. The war is in fact entering on a momentous phase and I have regretfully come to the conclusion that with the best will in the world it is impracticable for His Majesty's Government at such a time to commit themselves to vary their undertaking by the earlier appointment of a Commission or Conference to examine the scheme in detail.

4. Nevertheless, I am prepared to undertake to re-examine the situation on the capitulation of Germany with the hope that His Majesty's Government may then find it practicable to go ahead. If this should prove to be the case I am confident that it would be their desire to do so. It will be understood that my undertaking is without any commitment as to His Majesty's Government's eventual decision. It is impossible at the present stage to estimate how long it may be before the actual re-examination can start. I hope however that in the interval Ministers will supplement their scheme by more complete proposals on the three crucial questions to which you refer in paragraph 6 of your secret and personal telegram under reference.

5. I appreciate that the conclusion in paragraph 3 above means that the matter of extending the life of the present State Council, or, alternatively, holding an election must now be decided, and I will consider this after receiving your reply to paragraph 7 of this telegram.

6. I should like you to know the reasons which have caused me to come to the conclusion mentioned above. The first is the impracticability of securing the services of thoroughly suitable personnel of the types you mention for a Commission in the present situation, but I hope that this stringency may be eased as soon as Germany surrenders. Secondly, it is impossible before victory is achieved, at least in Europe, for the hard pressed operational and planning staffs of the Services to formulate the

---

[1] See 186.   [2] See 170.

defence requirements of His Majesty's Government in Ceylon in the post-war situation, and unless the Commission or Conference can be given prior general guidance on that matter, which must be of the greatest importance to His Majesty's Government, it would be unable to do its work effectively.

7. I should like your advice as to (a) the method of communicating this decision to Ministers, having regard to the disappointment it must cause to them, and as to (b) probable political and other repercussions in Ceylon. Meanwhile I should like you to know that I am very sensible of the personal disappointment which you yourself will feel at this decision, especially since it is not now likely to be possible before the conclusion of your term of office as Governor to decide upon the final stages of constitutional reform to which you have devoted so much thought and sympathy, and on which your advice has been so consistently valuable to His Majesty's Government.

188   CO 54/986/7, no 14   4 Apr 1944
[Reforms]: letter from G G Ponnambalam to Sir A Caldecott forwarding a message for the secretary of state

A meeting of the Representatives of the Minority Communities in Council who desired you to send the last cablegram to the Secretary of State for the Colonies on the subject of Constitutional Reforms was held again to consider his reply.[1] They have asked me to request you to be good enough to forward the following reply:—

> "We have considered carefully your cablegram and are greatly disappointed with its text and tenor. We protest strongly against your appointing a Commission or Conference to consider only the Constitutional Scheme framed by Ministers all but one of whom belong to the Singhalese community. We feel this would be quite contrary to the spirit of your earlier declarations in which you stated that the position generally would be examined by a Commission or Conference. We constitute at least one quarter of the House and we claim the right of participation in or an opportunity of prior contribution to the deliberations of the Commission or Conference in the first instance."

We shall thank you to forward this by cable to the Secretary of State.[2]

---

[1] See 182, note 1.

[2] Caldecott replied to Ponnambalam in a letter on 6 Apr: 'I have the honour to acknowledge receipt of your letter dated the 4th April current in which you communicate the text of a telegraphic protest for transmission to the Secretary of State for the Colonies. Colonial Regulation 185 requires every such transmission to be accompanied by a report from the Governor, and before I can be in a position to make such a report in the present connection it is necessary that I should myself clearly comprehend what it is that is protested against and on what grounds. I have however been unable to find anything in the Secretary of State's message conveyed to you by my Secretary's letter of the 7th March at all inconsonant either in letter or in spirit with his earlier declarations, and have therefore to seek further elucidation from you before sending any telegram or despatch. I shall be grateful also to be informed why the word 'only' has been placed before the words "the constitutional scheme" in the second sentence of your draft telegram?' (CO 54/986/7, no 14).

189   CO 852/605/9, no 118, enclosure iv   4 Apr 1944

'The rubber position': memorandum by R L Buell on the strategic priority of rubber from Ceylon

[Buell was the American consul in Colombo. He presented his memo at an interview with Drayton in Apr 1944. W S Lockwood, the American representative on rubber at the US embassy in London who visited both India and Ceylon in the spring of 1944, was also present at the interview. Caldecott forwarded the memo to Stanley, together with a record of the interview and three other enclosures on the rubber situation, in his despatch of 18 Apr 1944 on the same file.]

1.   Natural rubber is the A-1 priority strategic material of which there is an insufficient supply to meet the requirements of the United Nations.

2.   An adequate supply of natural rubber is *vital* to *victory*.

3.   Despite *drastic* restrictions as to its use, consumption for *essential military* purposes exceeds *production*.

4.   Ceylon at present produces about 60% of *all* the natural rubber available to the United Nations.

5.   Supplies of natural rubber from other presently available sources *cannot* be materially increased during the war.

6.   Therefore, the production of natural rubber is the A-1 responsibility and the chief contribution of Ceylon towards victory.

7.   Although the high price of rubber will no doubt *stimulate* production, Ceylon faces the challenge of producing *every pound of rubber possible*. This is *not* being done today.

8.   The goal of maximum production can be achieved only with an abundant supply of good labour and contented labour.

9.   There is a serious shortage of labour to meet the requirements of the industries, food production campaign and military programs of Ceylon.

10.   Effort during the past year to recruit sufficient labour to meet such requirements have not solved the problem.

11.   Because of its essentiality to the war effort, the rubber industry should have priority over all other industries in its claim for labour, materials and transport.

12.   Food production, however essential, is for the duration of the war, secondary to rubber production since the United Nations can exchange food for rubber, but can obtain *sufficient* rubber *only from Ceylon*.

13.   Every measure is warranted to induce an adequate supply of competent labour to work on rubber estates, such as, (a) classifying rubber workers as essential, (b) supplying extra food rations, (c) providing such additional forms of compensation as may be deemed necessary.

14.   Even with the adoption of the foregoing necessary steps, however, the only solution to the problem of the labour shortage in Ceylon is *more labour*.

15.   To obtain more labour it is essential to remove restrictions on the immigration of labour for the duration of the emergency.

16.   The solution of this problem rests with the Governments of Ceylon and India and is *vital* to the military program of the United Nations.

190 CO 54/986/5/1, no 28   5 Apr 1944
[Reforms]: inward telegram no 48 from Admiral Layton to Mr Stanley urging the appointment of a commission

Your secret telegram[1] to the Governor has been shown to me. I feel that I must lose no time in expressing to you my deep concern regarding the effect on the war effort in Ceylon, and on the co-operation of the Ceylonese, of refusal to appoint a Commission. In my opinion, this would inevitably lead to a general election, which would hinge on secession to India or loyalty to the Empire and, in the prevailing political temperature, the former would start hot favourite.

2. At the moment we are setting up Headquarters, South East Asia Command, in Ceylon (a choice, I believe, strongly influenced by the more loyal atmosphere of Ceylon as compared with India) and we are making (? colossal corrupt group) preparations for onward offensive move. The success of this will be seriously jeopardised if we cannot count on the loyal co-operation of the Ceylon Government and people and I cannot say too strongly how much I should deplore any action which might undermine this.

3. With regard to paragraph 6 of your telegram, as the subject of defence (including communications) is to be reviewed anyway, I do not understand why it should be necessary now to formulate defence requirements of His Majesty's Government in Ceylon in post-war situation.

4. I fully appreciate the difficulty in finding three suitable men to form the Commission, but the danger we are faced with, at this vital moment of the war, demands, in my opinion, that this difficulty should be surmounted.

5. I further consider that possible risk to the security and success of their operations should be placed before the Chiefs of Staff Committee.

6. I hope you will forgive the straight speaking in this telegram, but I feel that nothing else would be justified.

---

[1] See 187.

191 CO 54/986/5/1, no 29   5 Apr 1944
[Reforms]: inward unnumbered telegram (reply) from Sir A Caldecott to Mr Stanley arguing that Ceylon might demand inclusion in a future independent India if a commission is not appointed

Your most secret and personal telegram of 31st March.[1]

My advice requested on two points in paragraph 7 is as follows:—

(a) Political exigencies will inevitably force Ministers to demand the publication forthwith of my secret despatches of the 3rd and 10th February with their enclosures,[2] your telegram No. 321, my telegram No. 542[3] and your reply thereto. Reply must therefore be worded suitably for such publication, and paragraphs 2 and 3 of your telegram appear to me to provide basis. Reference to the first reason given in your paragraph 6 should be avoided because difficulties of sending suitable

---

[1] See 187.   [2] See 181, note.   [3] See 185.

Commission for the short period necessary (which I of course fully appreciate) may not be generally understood here, in view of visits recently made by persons from the United Kingdom to Ceylon and other parts of the Empire. I am not sure that I appreciate the validity of the second reason given in your paragraph 6. Is it not constitutional powers in regard to defence and not defence requirements in the post-war situation which have to be formulated, and have not such powers been satisfactorily formulated in Acts like the Government of Burma Act, 1935? In regard to paragraph 4 I advise most strongly against the giving of any undertaking which does not commit His Majesty's Government. Ceylon public, being ignorant of constitutional niceties, regards you impersonally as the mouthpiece of His Majesty's Government vis-à-vis the Colonies. Any suggestion indeed of a Spenlow and Jorkins technique would at once arouse in the circumstances criticism and antipathy. Nor in my judgement will Ministers be in a position to fulfil the hope expressed by you in the last sentence of paragraph 4, not only because they are bound to be discredited in the public view, but also because publication of their present proposals will prevent addition thereto or variation thereof.

(b) I have no doubt that the political result of your reply will be a death blow to Senanayake's ideal of Ceylon as an internal self-governing unit of the British Commonwealth, and a general demand for inclusion in a new federal India, whose future right to secede has been explicitly conceded. In view of his past political history, *vide* paragraph 10 of my "Things Ceylonese" of the 20th August, 1940,[4] I anticipate that Bandaranaike will take a lead in this demand unless Senanayake should forestall him by a complete *volte face* and the enforced abandonment of his present ideal. Ceylon National Congress is already orientated towards India, and Mr. Aney, representative of the Government of India in Ceylon, takes every opportunity of emphasising in his public speeches Ceylon's cultural, economic, geographical, ethnical and historical unity with India. In short, the only course which could hold up political landslide towards demand for inclusion in a future independent India was complementary appointment of a Commission to examine Ministers' scheme, and now that this proves impossible there is nothing else to keep our already (?) dangerously fissiparous Ministry together or to obviate the necessity for general election, which may take place either next January after the passing of a vote on the Budget, and possibly gubernatorial reservation thereof, or almost (corrupt group) if Ministers desire to avoid the responsibility of another Budget. In this gloomy picture there is not even the consolation that present Ceylon relations will improve, because it is the shibboleth of native politicians on both sides of the Palk Straits that all differences are due to the present alien capitalist administrations, and could soon be settled between the emancipated peoples of both countries. Meanwhile the various Congresses will continue to stimulate rather than compose disagreement.

2. I most gratefully appreciate the kind regard for my personal feelings expressed in your paragraph 7, but I have tried throughout this correspondence to prevent any personal considerations weighing with me. Indeed my present admittedly sore disappointment is personal only in the sense that it is that of an Englishman who after 37 years in the Colonies believes whole-heartedly in the British Empire and deplores the prospects of its premier Colony being allowed to fall into the arms of a soon seceding India.

---

[4] See 64.

192   CO 852/605/9, no 100   **13 Apr 1944**

'Ceylon rubber situation': letter from R D Fennelly (Ministry of Production) to S Caine. *Enclosure*: memorandum by L S Thompson to P D Reed, 22 Mar 1944

[Lewis S Thompson and Philip D Reed were members of the American embassy in London. Reed was a US businessman who entered war work in 1941 with the Office of Production Management and its successor, the War Production Board, upon which he was chief of the Bureau of Industry Branches responsible for organising peacetime industries to war production. He was chief of the Mission for Economic Affairs in London (MEAL) between Oct 1943 and Dec 1944. The statement, 'Critical natural rubber situation', and table, 'Combined United Nations crude natural rubber situation', were attached to Thompson's memo.]

Philip Reed of M.E.A.L. recently handed the Minister of Production a memorandum on the Ceylon rubber situation, copy of which I enclose.

As you will see there is nothing in the memorandum that is new to us and the questions raised are those which were discussed in detail a year ago, between Ministers, without any definite conclusion being reached. I understand that the impasse between India and Ceylon over the additional labour was never broken, but that the amount of labour then required was obtained by a labour drive in Ceylon itself.

You will agree, I think, that before we could consider suggesting new negotiations between India and Ceylon, it would be necessary to be assured that additional labour at this juncture would result in a sufficiently big increase in the output of rubber to warrant the agitation which might be caused. I, myself, do not feel that anything like the 25,000 tons mentioned in Mr. Thompson's memorandum would be forthcoming and in this the Ministry of Supply agree. It would however perhaps be opportune, as it is now some time since this aspect of the Ceylon rubber situation was considered here, to make further enquiry as to whether the situation has changed at all.

If you have not got the information already would you consider the possibility of sending a telegram to the Governor, asking him whether in his view additional labour would at the present juncture result in a substantial increase in the rubber output and whether he could give any figure of what that increase might be. I realise this would have to be done tactfully.

I may say that this enquiry does not emanate from the Combined Raw Materials Board. So far as I can gather it was a more or less general enquiry from the American side and much of the detailed suggestion comes from Stanton.

Enclosure to 192

I understand you are lunching with Mr. Oliver Lyttelton[1] tomorrow and I thought you might wish to bring this matter to his attention.

Under date of March 15th, we received a cable from the Combined Raw Materials Board stating their acute concern over the labor situation for rubber production in

---

[1] Minister of production, 1942–1945.

Ceylon. Upon investigation with those most familiar with the rubber production situation in Ceylon, it was determined:—

1. That the price difficulties had been ironed out.
2. That with 20,000 additional rubber tapping laborers, an additional 25,000 tons of rubber per annum would be produced.
3. That the 20,000 rubber tapping laborers are available in Southern India.
4. That there is an impasse in importing these laborers, because the Indian Government refuses to send the laborers to Ceylon unless Ceylon will agree to allowing these laborers to remain in Ceylon after the war. That Ceylon is agreeable to the importation of 20,000 laborers, but insists on returning them to India after the war.
5. That there are two possible methods of breaking this deadlock and getting out this much needed additional 25,000 tons of rubber (25,000 tons is equal to better than 50% of the total annual production of the Western Hemisphere):—

(i) that the War Cabinet intervene in this matter to use its influence to break the deadlock between India and Ceylon
(ii) that the Armed Services induct 20,000 Indians with rubber tapping experience, place them in some type of uniform, and work out an arrangement for their use on the rubber estates of Ceylon, then demobilise them through the normal channels of troop demobilisation.

I would appreciate hearing from you your thoughts, after talking with Mr. Lyttelton, on this subject, as we must cable the Combined Raw Materials Board in the very near future.

CRITICAL NATURAL RUBBER STATION

1. Stocks of natural crude rubber, including liquid latex, in the United Nations (excluding the U.S.S.R.) totalled 555,000 long tons in January 1, 1943. By December 31, 1943, they had declined to approximately 220,000 long tons. Stocks of natural crude rubber in the United States during this 12-month period dropped from 423,000 tons to 139,000 tons. These and other figures mentioned below are reflected in the attached table.

2. In spite of the tremendous achievement in the construction and high volume operation of synthetic rubber plants in the United States during 1943, many types of large size aircraft, military, and essential commercial vehicle tyres still cannot be made exclusively from synthetic rubber but require the addition of substantial quantities of natural crude rubber. Crude rubber must still be used also in the manufacture of landing craft, self-sealing fuel cells and many other important war products.

3. It is estimated that such minimum essential use of natural crude rubber by the United Nations in 1944 will total 260,000 long tons. It is estimated that 174,000 tons of that amount will be consumed in the United States, 30,000 tons in Great Britain, 24,000 tons in Russia, 14,000 tons in Canada, 8,000 tons in Australia, and additional essential amounts totalling 10,000 tons in supplies to South Africa, Latin America, Spain, Sweden and other countries. India, Brazil, and Peru are either self-supporting or have an exportable surplus.

4. World production of natural crude rubber available to the United Nations is

estimated at 192,000 tons in 1944, including 110,000 tons from Ceylon and the exportable surplus from India, 30,000 from Latin America, including Mexican guayule, 16,000 from Liberia, 34,000 from other African sources and 2,000 from miscellaneous sources. Allowing for estimated allocations of 260,000 tons and production of only 192,000, the United Nations stocks by the end of 1944 would be reduced from 220,000 to approximately 152,000 long tons.

5.   The stock position outlook in the United States is even more critical. With the safe arrival of 50,000 tons of rubber from Ceylon in 1944, which represents a 30,000 ton increase over 1943 receipts from Ceylon, total imports cannot be expected to exceed 96,000 tons. Domestic consumption of 174,000 tons and re-exports to Canada and other countries of 13,000 tons would reduce our stocks during the year from 139,000 to 48,000 tons. The Branch Committee recommended that United States stocks should not fall below a danger line of 100,000 tons.

6.   In view of the number of grades comprising the balance, and of the hundreds of rubber manufacturers who have to consume it, and of the unavoidable delay in effecting deliveries, 48,000 is insufficient for uninterrupted production of finished goods, and would leave practically no stocks for use against 1945 requirements. The risk is obvious of reducing United States stocks to any such level. Therefore either the United States must drastically cut consumption in both essential military and vital transportation items or find ways and means to import more rubber.

Conclusion: There is no likelihood of substantially augmenting production from existing sources of supply. Therefore, as the year 1944 progresses, the shortage of crude rubber will have the effect of reducing military consumption and military programs. Therefore, the rapid completion of preparations now being made by the Washington and London Far Eastern Emergency Rubber Committees for the immediate procurement of rubber on reoccupation of presently enemy occupied Far Eastern territories is an essential first step toward providing for 1945 requirements.

This Committee believes the shortage of natural crude rubber must be considered as an important factor affecting strategic plans for the reoccupation of occupied areas.

COMBINED UNITED NATIONS CRUDE NATURAL RUBBER POSITION

			U.S. only
1. Estimated United Nations Stocks (exc. USSR) 31/12/42		555,000 long tons	423,000
2. Estimated United Nations Stocks (exc. USSR) 31/12/43		220,000 long tons	139,000
3. Estimated World Production available to United Nations during 1994:			
From: Ceylon and India	110,000		
Latin America	30,000		
Liberia	16,000		
Other Africa	34,000		
Miscellaneous	2,000	192,000	96,000
4. Estimated Total Available to United Nations during 1944		412,000	
5. Estimated Minimum Essential Consumption during 1944		260,000	187,000
6. Estimated United Nations stocks as of 31/12/44		152,000 long tons	48,000

193   CO 54/986/7, no 7   13 Apr 1944
'Reform of the Ceylon constitution': letter from the Ceylon Association, London to CO supporting the views of the minorities

I have the honour to inform you that we have been advised of the terms of the cable addressed to you by Minority Representatives of the State Council on the refusal of the Board of Ministers to disclose their draft proposals which, it is understood, they are about to submit to the Secretary of State for approval, reading as follows:—

> "On behalf of the Minority Communities representing more than one-third of the population of Ceylon we beg leave to apprise you that neither His Majesty's Government's declaration on Reforms of May 1943[1] nor the Ministers' interpretations thereon have been debated by the State Council.
>
> The Ministers have refused to disclose in Council or even in informed talks their draft proposals which we understand they are submitting for your approval. The Ministers' procedure therefore prevents minority communities' viewpoint regarding these proposals being disclosed to you.
>
> Consideration by you of any proposals without reference to opinion of minority communities would cause grave apprehension in view of vital differences of opinion particularly regarding:—
>
> (a) Quantum of representation of the different communities.
> (b) Status of Indians and Europeans resident in Ceylon.
> (c) The system of Executive Committees.
> (d) The establishment of a Second Chamber.
>
> We therefore request you to withhold consideration of the Ministers' proposals till they are submitted to State Council to enable you to have full knowledge of opinion of all sections and interests.
>
> The Ministers' procedure has aroused strong misgivings and resentment amongst minority communities."

We have noted that, in the declaration made by H.M. Government in May last, it is stated that measures relating to the rights of H.M. subjects not residing in the Island will be included in the class of reserved Bills and also that H.M. Government does not propose to enter into detailed discussions until victory has been achieved, but at the same time this Association wishes to support the request put forward by the Minority Representatives.

---

[1] See 169, annex.

194   CO 54/986/7, no 14   13 Apr 1944
[Reforms]: letter (reply) from G G Ponnambalam to Sir A Caldecott

I have the honour to acknowledge receipt of your letter dated the 6th April current in which you desired to elucidate further what it is that is protested against in our communication of the 4th instant.[1] I shall endeavour to assist you. You will recall

---

[1] See 188.

that in the last representation transmitted by you on our behalf to the Secretary of State we protested against the Ministers' procedure in that it prevented the opinion of the minority communities being disclosed to the Secretary of State and we requested him to withhold consideration of the Ministers' proposals till they are submitted to the State Council in order that he may have full knowledge of the opinion of all sections and interests in the country before a Commission or Conference was summoned.

The Secretary of State however, in his message which you communicated to us, does not reply to our request but asserts that "acceptance by His Majesty's Government of any constitutional scheme which the Ceylon Ministers may formulate is conditional on such a scheme being examined by a suitable Commission or Conference and being eventually accepted by three-quarters of all members of the State Council". The only interpretation that we have been able to place on this passage is that the Ministers' constitutional Scheme alone would be examined by a suitable Commission or Conference. This we feel would be clearly contrary to the spirit of his earlier declaration that "no substantial changes in the constitution could be introduced without further opportunity for examination of the conflicting views of the various interests concerned". There is nothing in his last message to us from which we could discern that the views of the minorities would also be heard and examined by the contemplated Commission or Conference. In these circumstances I would respectfully request your Excellency to forward our protest by cable at your earlier convenience to the Secretary of State.[2]

---

[2] Caldecott replied to Ponnambalam in a letter on 20 Apr: 'I have the honour to acknowledge the receipt of your letter dated the 13th April current. Despite its assistance I have been unable to discover anything in the Declaration of His Majesty's Government, or in the message from the Secretary of State for the Colonies conveyed to you by my Secretary's letter dated the 7th March, which would justify an inference that the promised examination by a suitable Commission or Conference of the Ministers' Constitutional Scheme will be without consideration of the position generally or without opportunity being afforded for examination of the conflicting views of the various interests concerned. I have therefore seen no justification for telegraphing the message contained in your letter of the 4th April but have transmitted it by the official Air Mail together with copies of the letters that have subsequently passed between us' (CO 54/986/7, no 14).

195 CO 54/986/5/1, no 33   13 Apr 1944
[Reforms]: outward unnumbered telegram (reply) from Mr Stanley to Sir A Caldecott requesting amplification of the governor's views before the War Cabinet is consulted over the appointment of a commission

I have now had opportunity of studying your own and Commander-in-Chief's top secret and personal telegrams of 5th April.[1] The whole question is clearly one on which it will be necessary for me to consult the War Cabinet but before doing so there are certain points on which I should be grateful for an amplification of your views.

2. You will appreciate that since their Declaration of May, 1943, His Majesty's Government have not abrogated in any subsequent correspondence the condition

---

[1] See 190 & 191.

that the examination of any constitutional scheme prepared by Ministers could not be undertaken until victory had been achieved. On the contrary, they have re-asserted it. It was only on such a condition that in May, 1943, His Majesty's Government were prepared to make the Declaration which they then made.

3. It is clear therefore that His Majesty's Government will need to be convinced that there are at present stage fresh reasons of overriding effect and importance requiring them to reconsider their condition. Such fresh reasons at this crucial stage will obviously be judged by their force in direct relation to our military purposes and capacity. Commander-in-Chief's telegram has shown special reasons of that character having Ceylon in view as base of South East Asia Command operations, and steps will be taken to place his view before the Chiefs of Staff. But I should also be grateful for your own appraisement of the possible repercussions of an announcement on the basis contemplated in most secret and personal telegram of the 31st March[2] on (1) the general internal security position in Ceylon, especially having regard to the present state of efficiency of the Ceylon Police Force, (2) on essential war production of vital commodities (rubber, tea, foodstuffs, etc.) in the Island and (3) nature and effect of Ceylonese non-co-operation which might result from political landslide apprehended in paragraph 1 (b) of your telegram. Would you expect for instance that loyalty of Ceylonese officers in general administration would come into question? I should like clearest estimate you can make which I can use if necessary to justify my recommending His Majesty's Government to advance from their previous decision.

4. I note from paragraph 7 of your secret telegram No. 490 that you consider it doubtful whether Ministers would not oppose a further extension of the life of the present Council, even if His Majesty's Government were to agree to the appointment of a Commission or Conference at the end of this or early next year, to examine their constitutional scheme.

I appreciate your difficulty in making any confident assessment of Ministers' probable attitude without being able to consult them, but if the doubt you express is well founded and a general election had to be held in any case, resulting in a landslide towards secession to India, what advantage would accrue if His Majesty's Government were to consider meeting Ministers' wishes by agreeing to the early appointment of a Commission or Conference? Would it not be open to criticism as a step which in those circumstances could be nothing more than a useless attempt at appeasement. I should be glad if you would consider this point also and furnish me with your advice.

Please show this telegram to the Commander-in-Chief.

---

[2] See 187.

196   CO 54/986/5/1, no 36   20 Apr 1944
[Reforms]: inward unnumbered telegram (reply) from Sir A Caldecott to Mr Stanley

Your secret and personal telegram of 13th April.[1]

Before replying to the three points in your paragraph 3 I will deal with points

---

[1] See 195.

raised in your paragraph 4. Doubt expressed paranthetically in paragraph 7 of my secret telegram No. 490 was subsequently allayed in the course of my conversation with the Ministers 4th March, reported in my secret and personal telegram of 18th March,[2] and by the terms of their message transmitted by my secret telegram No. 542.[3] Any statement promising the appointment of Commission this year should contain also statement that Article 19 of Ceylon State Council Order-in-Council of 1931 will be further amended by the substitution of 10 years for 9 years, and I do not contemplate that such statement if (repeat if) accompanied by such promise will meet with any wide or serious disagreement. My personal appraisement is that it would be generally welcomed whatever some few politicians might say or pretend to think.

2. Your paragraph 3 (1). Without any desire to be alarmist I cannot contemplate without the gravest apprehension the effect on internal security if, in addition to the present strain placed upon the police by:—

(a) The presence here of so many fighting forces and now of the S.E.A.C.
(b) Ensuring the safe working of ports and the guarding of so many vulnerable points.
(c) Policing so many war time controls and ration schemes, and
(d) Implementing whole body of Defence Regulations over and above the normal maintenance of law and order,

there should be superimposed the task of police supervision over general election. During the election campaign, consistency of His Majesty's Government (*vide* your paragraph 2) in stating that consideration of constitutional changes must await victory would be denounced from the hustings as British persistence in delaying reforms which are a necessary antecedent to the efficient future handling of problems of reconstruction which will demand immediate and wholetime attention as soon as hostilities cease. There is indeed no doubt whatever in my mind that political slogans would become increasingly anti-British as the election progressed, and that lasting political deterioration would ensue. Members of the State Council would, of course, find it politically necessary to stump the Island with similar slogans if the life of the present State Council were further prolonged without the simultaneous appointment of a Commission, and there would follow equally great deterioration of political morale and continuous burden upon the police.

3. Your paragraph 3 (2). The effect of a general election, or alternatively of a political campaign against its unconditional postponement, conducted in the circumstances indicated in my preceding paragraph would, without any doubt whatever, unsettle both the peasantry and estate employees, besides involving absences from work on polling day, and temporary dislocation of transport, and would result in increased labour unrest and diminution of output of rubber, tea, foodstuffs, etc. Further politicization of labour at the present juncture would be particularly dangerous and deplorable.

4. Your paragraph 3 (3). I do not fear disloyalty in the ranks of our permanent public services, but I do gravely fear the reduction in their operative efficiency and leadership which would follow the loss by them of co-operation on the part of the public, if the latter were permitted to become engulfed in a wave of nationalism and

---

[2] See 186.   [3] See 185.

anti-British propaganda that will be inevitable if a general election were held or refused while consideration of constitutional reform remains relegated to an undated future.

5. In conclusion, it will of course be realised how greatly a general election in England differs from one in Ceylon, where many constituencies are still in an Eatanswill category of development, and electors far more emotional than their British counterparts.

6. I have supplied the Commander-in-Chief with a copy of your telegram and of this reply in which he concurs.

197   CO 54/986/5/1, no 37   28 Apr 1944

[Reforms]: outward unnumbered telegram (reply) from Mr Stanley to Sir A Caldecott requesting a further appreciation

Your top secret and personal telegram of 20th April.[1] Ceylon constitution.

2. I have carefully reviewed the information and advice furnished in your own and in the Commander-in-Chief's recent telegrams on this matter and on the basis of those telegrams the following appear to me to be the adverse results, in effect, to be apprehended on defence grounds if His Majesty's Government do not agree to proceed with the examination of Ministers' scheme at an earlier stage:—

(a) Resignation of Ministers and general policy of non-co-operation adopted by Ceylonese political and other leaders and people which will have active anti-British nature and is likely to be successful in substantially interfering with war effort generally, internal security, and production of essential commodities.

(b) This deterioration would be likely to involve all sections of the community including police and other Government services, as well as essential labour at ports and on estates, and may be expected to be marked by general and prolonged civil disturbances.

(c) As Ceylon is to serve as the headquarters and operational base for operations planned on largest scale against Japan, such a situation in the Island would seriously jeopardize the success of these operations.

3. Please let me know whether you agree with the above estimate, and whether there are any further likely factors directly bearing upon the strategic situation which as stated in my top secret and personal telegram of 13th April[2] must at this crucial stage of the war be determining factors in His Majesty's Government's decision.

4. As explained in that telegram a decision by the War Cabinet will be necessary; but at this critical moment of the war when matters of greatly transcending importance are occupying the attention of His Majesty's Government it would be out of the question for me to bring up this matter for decision in present circumstances, and I must have all possible time and latitude to choose the appropriate moment at which to do so.

5. I appreciate that a decision must be taken sometime before end of year but you

---

[1] See 196.   [2] See 195.

and Commander-in-Chief will at the same time realize that His Majesty's Government may find it less difficult to take decisions according with your advice in respect of Ceylon if war operations in Europe in the meantime have made good progress.

I should like therefore to have your considered advice as to period for which decision can be deferred. Can situation be held until early autumn (say September) without risk of consequences developing which would interfere with operational efficiency of the Island? If not what is your estimate?

6. Please give Commander-in-Chief a copy of this telegram and consult with him. I want to be sure that I know your mind as clearly as possible. I assure you how conscious I am of great difficulty which you must feel in your personal judgment on these matters and how grateful I am for your readiness and ability to give me definite personal advice.

198   CO 54/986/5/1, no 39   5 May 1944
[Reforms]: inward unnumbered telegram (reply) from Sir A Caldecott to Mr Stanley

Your top secret and personal telegram of 28th April.[1]

I fully realize the difficulty of presenting in precis form appraisement of a complicated situation, but I fear that the summary set out in your paragraph 2 would afford grounds for two inferences:—

(1) that the attitude of Ceylon towards the war is one of mere indifference, or alternatively governed solely by self interest and
(2) that Ceylon is in reality undeserving of any further measures of self Government, neither of which inferences would be true to fact. Such inferences appear to me to arise from the omission of all reference to what I consider the nodal point of the present situation, i.e., the imminence and inevitability, unless extraneously prevented, of general election. This imminence has already begun though not yet gravely, to divert attention from the war effort to political manœuvres, and the position is bound to deteriorate progressively as the election looms nearer. Nor is there any doubt that the Ministers correctly represented to you in my telegram No. 542[2] that any further extension of the present State Council, so long as consideration of reform remains relegated to an undated future, would not be acceptable to public opinion. Unless therefore His Majesty's Government can promise to send Commission within the next eight months we are on the horns of the following dilemma; either we have

(a) dissolution in October and general election in January, at the latest, or
(b) enforced and unacceptable postponement of it by Order in Council,

and in either case the consequences summarized in paragraphs 2 and 3 of my telegram of 20th April,[3] which I cannot render more succinctly.

2. Your paragraph 2 omits also all reference to the drift towards India mentioned in paragraph (b) of my telegram of 5th April,[4] which would inevitably derive impetus

---

[1] See 197.   [2] See 185.   [3] See 196.   [4] See 191.

from general election, or from any postponement of it unaccompanied by simultaneous consideration of reforms.

3. On the points of details in your paragraph 2:—

(i) I do not contemplate resignation of the Ministers if His Majesty's Government refuses their request, but rather that the State Council will force me to dissolve it under Article 69 or Article 18.

(ii) I anticipate rapidly lessening co-operation rather than sudden total non-co-operation.

(iii) As already indicated in paragraph 4 of my telegram of 20th April I do not predict that political deterioration will directly affect the police or any other public service, but that their efficiency will be impaired by the absence of co-operation from the public.

(iv) I do not apprehend general or long civil disturbances which, if they should eventuate, would be far easier to deal with than rapid decrease and cessation of co-operation which I definitely foresee.

4. Your paragraph 5. While I might be able for a little while longer to induce the Ministers to remain patient, on the ground that the door has not been closed, on their request or reply given to my telegram No. 542, I cannot hope to keep the position stabilized for more than a few weeks because the Ministers must already be questioning their ability to present the 1944–1945 Budget in the State Council in early July with any hope of its being accepted if they prove unsuccessful in their request, and dissolution is due in October.[5]

5. General background is that the State Council is in its ninth year, but Ceylon, unlike the United Kingdom, has no real direct impact of the war, and does not possess a National Government, an obedient Government majority or a party system which can ensure that the public regards the war effort as not only paramount but exclusive.

6. Commander-in-Chief, to whom I gave copy of your telegram, desires me to add expression of his emphatic opinion that any further delay in announcement by His Majesty's Government that they will appoint Commission on reform this autumn and simultaneously postpone general election would be so prejudicial to the interests of the South Eastern Asia Command and the war efficiency of the Island generally, that reference to Chief of Staff should be immediate.

---

[5] On 6 May 1944, Caldecott transmitted to Stanley the following message from Senanayake: 'The Ministers desire to be informed whether His Majesty's Government has considered the constitutional scheme formulated by them, and what further measures His Majesty's Government propose to take in that connection. As the present State Council is due for dissolution not later than early next year, the public are also anxious to know reasonably early, the circumstances in which the next general election will be held.' Stanley replied to Caldecott in tel 583 on 15 May asking him inform Senanayake that the message had been received and that the views of HMG would be sent to the governor as soon as possible (CO 54/986/5/1, nos 41 and 46).

199   WO 203/5412   18 May 1944

'Constitutional reforms in Ceylon': minutes of a meeting of Advanced Headquarters, SEAC, at Queen's House, Colombo. *Appendices*: "A" and "B", notes by Sir A Caldecott and Admiral Layton

His Excellency the *Governor* began by explaining the constitutional position, regarding which he circulated a short appreciation which is attached as Appendix "A". He summarised the position by stating that in view of a request from his Ministers for immediate consideration of their constitutional proposals he had asked His Majesty's Government to agree before the Budget Session in July to appoint at a date before the end of 1944, commissioners to consider them. If this request was not accepted it would be necessary either to face a General Election some time in the Autumn or New Year with consequent dislocation of War Effort, labour and public services, and a possible permanent embittering of relations; or, failing this, to extend once more the life of the State Council by an Order in Council which, without the appointment of a Commission, would precipitate grave political discontent, of which the attendant consequences would be similar to those of an election.

His Excellency the *Commander-in-Chief* [1] read a paper which he had prepared setting out his views, which is attached as Appendix "B". In this, he outlines the reaction affecting the War Effort which he considered likely if it were decided not to accept the Ministers' request for the appointment of a Commission. He particularly emphasised the effect on labour, and the possibilities of disturbances and riots which would lead to a demand for troops.

The *Governor* explained briefly the history of his communication with the Secretary of State, and the *Commander-in-Chief* explained that he had requested the Colonial Secretary to place the matter before the War Cabinet and the Chiefs of Staff in order to link the question with its effect on the War Effort. It was no doubt as a result of this that the *Supreme Allied Commander* had been asked to express his views as to the extent to which non-co-operation by the bulk of the local population and disturbances might affect military operations in his Command.

The *Supreme Allied Commander* [2] pointed out that the political aspects were much wider than those merely affecting *Ceylon*. The attitude of His Majesty's Government had so far been that they could not give their attention to the detailed working out of constitutional reforms in *India*, *Burma*, *Malaya* or *Ceylon* until victory was achieved. Any consideration of the claims of *Ceylon* at this stage would affect by implication these other countries as well.

The *Governor* pointed out that in the case of *Ceylon* the proposals were much less far reaching than those put forward by *India* and *Burma*. Defence, and external affairs would be reserved subjects and remain in British hands, while bills affecting currency, minorities and the property of non-residents would be reserved bills. Further, the announcement now that Commissioners would be appointed before the end of the year would be sufficient. From the date of their appointment the Commissioners might take eight or nine months to frame their proposals which would then require consideration by H.M. Government and the Ministers and ultimate submission to the State Council, and the probability therefore was that the

---

[1] Admiral Layton.   [2] Admiral Mountbatten.

war with *Germany* would be over, and the war with *Japan* might be hoped to be nearing its end, before proposals would require any detailed consideration by His Majesty's Government.

The *Supreme Allied Commander* said that he had not appreciated these points, which he thought should be made clear to the Chiefs of Staff. He went on to say that if the need for troops arose, British troops in South East Asia were most unlikely to be available, as there was a grave shortage of them. He asked whether Indian or African troops could be used.

The *Governor* and the *Commander-in-Chief* pointed out that the use of Indian troops to deal with riots in 1915 had caused much political ill-feeling and was still remembered with bitterness. The same consideration would apply in a greater degree to the use of African troops, whose relations with the native population were in any case not altogether satisfactory.

Lieut-General Sir Henry Pownall[3] asked whether there was any possibility that the political feeling which would result from the refusal to accede to the Ministers' request would be confined to the politically minded classes and would not spread to the labour. The *Governor* was definitely of the opinion that both the dislocation connection with the election and any subsequent political non-co-operation would affect the labour. The first act of election agents and political agitators would be to address large bodies of men collected together in the form of organised labour. They would, he considered, go first to rubber and tea plantations, docks, factories, and the labour collected for airfields and other large works.

The *Supreme Allied Commander* agreed that it was essential that the dislocation consequent upon elections should be postponed if possible until victory was attained, and undertook to despatch a signal to the Chiefs of Staff supporting the request for the appointment of a Commission. He suggested that the signal should, in the first place, stress the limited nature of the request now made by the Ministers, and should go on to point out the unfortunate results which refusal of the request was likely to have on:—

(a) the rubber industry.
(b) the movement of coal, and consequently communications.
(c) dock labour and therefore the port of *Colombo* and *Trincomalee* as a fleet base.
(d) the tea industry.

He considered that the signal should state that if disturbances were caused, there were no British troops in South East Asia available to deal with them, and that the Governor was not prepared to accept the use of Indian or African troops for this purpose.

Mr. Keswick[4] pointed out that disturbances on a wide scale, or even widespread political disaffection, would have a most adverse effect on American opinion, which was at the present stage of the utmost importance; while a gesture of conciliation would have a correspondingly good effect. Similarly, disaffection in *Ceylon* would have a very adverse effect on our propaganda in *Burma* and *Malaya*, and to some extent *Sumatra* while a conciliatory move would assist in combatting Japanese propaganda regarding the freeing of these areas by S.E.A.C.

---

[3] Chief of staff, SEAC.   [4] Acting political adviser, SEAC.

Lieut-General Sir Henry Pownall pointed out that the request by the Ministers at present was moderate, and that if it was refused, it was unlikely that, at a later date, public opinion would be content with so little.

Major-General Harrison[5] explained that the minority of the labour employed on works projects was uniformed or imported. If trouble occurred among *Ceylon* labour before the end of 1944, a number of projects would be affected. By 1945, however, it should be possible to complete works projects remaining with uniformed labour, and although delay would be caused, it would be much less. It was pointed out that imported labour also would be affected if a breakdown in communications caused any difficulties in food supply.

The *Supreme Allied Commander* directed Major-General *Harrison* to prepare an estimate of the delay in work which would be caused by labour trouble, recognising that such an estimate must vary widely within limits according to the date of the trouble.

The *Governor* said that he did not consider that the trouble would spread to the public services, though it might cause a reduction in effort and a general loss of efficiency.

The *Supreme Allied Commander* directed his staff to draft a signal to the Chiefs of Staff which would be shown to His Excellency the *Governor* and to the *Commander-in-Chief* before despatch; and a brief for *Sir Henry Pownall* in case he had to discuss this subject in *London*.

Appendix "A" to 199: 'Short appreciation of position': note by Sir A Caldecott, 18 May 1944

1. Under Article 19 of the Ceylon (States Council) Order-in-Council, 1931, the term of a State Council expires not later than five years from the last general election. Under this Article a general election was due in January, 1941.

2. By Order-in-Council, 1940 the term was extended to seven years; by Order-in-Council, 1942, the term was extended to nine years.

3. The Council is now in its ninth year and unless a further extension is enacted by Order-in-Council there must be a general election in January, 1945.

4. The 1940 and 1942 extensions were recommended by me in the knowledge that they would be acceptable to the Ministers, to the State Council and to the public of Ceylon. If they had not been acceptable I should before now have been forced to dissolve the Council under Article 18 (for obstruction, or non-cooperation, and it must be remembered that in Ceylon the State Council constitutes the executive as well as the legislative authority) or under Article 69 (for refusing to find necessary funds).

5. A further extension of the life of the State Council will be acceptable to the Ministers only if their constitutional scheme is examined in the immediate future. If there is no promise of such examination the Ministers, even if they wanted to remain in office, would have no support from the public and would incur intense opposition from the Press. They would be forced to request dissolution and I to grant it under Article 18.

---

[5] Engineer-in-chief, SEAC.

6. Unless therefore the term of State Council is extended further by an Order-in-Council accompanied by an announcement of an early Commission to examine the Ministers' constitutional scheme we must have a general election in January at the latest; and my own anticipation is that one will be forced earlier, probably next month before introduction of the budget in July. If a budget were passed, with a general election immediately ahead in January, I foresee a vote-catching irresponsible financial programme and a consequent necessity for gubernatorial reservation of the Supply Bill. The result of this on Ceylon politics at the threshold of a general election could only be disastrous.

7. A general election in England takes a month or so. Local conditions (availability of police, transport, etc.) renders it impossible in Ceylon to accomplish it under three months. The superimposition of three months electioneering turmoil on top of our present problems of labour, crime and transport cannot be reconciled with security or even moderate efficiency in the present vital stage of South East Asian hostilities.

8. There are no political parties in Ceylon to keep candidates for election under the restraint of policy or programme. The nearest approach to parties are the Ceylon National Congress (who recently ignored the Governor and sent a demand for complete independence direct to the Prime Minister and others) and the Sinhala Maha Sabha, which was first in the field some years ago with the demand for absolute independence.

9. General public opinion in the Island is not at present behind the Congress or the Sabha in the demand for independence. It would be found to be in support of the Ministers in their acceptance of partnership in the British Commonwealth on the terms laid down in His Majesty's Government's recent declaration.

10. At a general election however His Majesty's Government's declaration would be represented as mere procrastinative bluff in the light of their reluctance to give immediate consideration to the Ministers' constitutional scheme, and the electoral slogans will be anti-British and secessionistic. The effect of such a release of poison gas from the hustings up and down the Island on the morale of labour and peasantry cannot be over-rated.

11. The Ceylon Indian Congress has recently been flirting violently with the Ceylon National Congress, and secessionism from Britain will be largely associated in the speeches of many candidates, with an Indo-Ceylon Anschluss and Gandhi-ism.

12. If there are those who consider that the holding of a general election with the inevitably concomitant

(a) dislocation of transport;
(b) interference with hours and days of labour on military works, estates, public works, factories and food production;
(c) political stunting and distraction of attention from the war effort;
(d) diversion of police activities from the detection and prevention of crime to the supervision of elections; and
(e) fanning of discontent among all classes

can be reconciled with the selection of Kandy as Headquarters of the South East Asia Command or with Ceylon's pivotal position as a base for hostilities further East, I am definitely not one of them. The Ceylonese, although like other tropical Orientals they require continuous prodding into action, have been far from non-cooperative. They know that when I was appointed Governor in 1937 I was commissioned to report on constitutional reform and that I did so in June 1938. They have read the report (Sessional Paper XXVIII of 1938) in which I roundly condemned the present constitution as utterly inefficient, and they feel that something must be done about replacing it before they are faced with all the problems and work of post-war reconstruction. Taking either a short or a long view from a military or civil standpoint I think that it would be a great blunder to give these people ground for non co-operation because of the (admitted) difficulty of finding three Commissioners to come out here during the next seven or eight months.

Appendix "B" to 199: note by Admiral Layton [nd]

The following are the reaction [sic] affecting the war effort which I consider likely in the event of an unfavourable decision on the Ministers' request for the early appointment of a Commission on Constitutional Reform.

2. It will be necessary for the Ministers at once to turn their attention mainly to their own political future, and in their own interest to divert the attention of the public to this. This is bound to react unfavourably on the administration of the Ministers' departments, which, even in normal times, requires constant drive and supervision to maintain efficiency.

The occasion is bound to be one in which political division will impair the already feeble cohesion of the Ministers as a Government. They will inevitably themselves be more impatient of the demands and restrictions occasioned by the War.

They will have to find some slogan which will go down with the uneducated populace, and there is little doubt that the suggestion that Ceylon should throw in her lot with India would in the circumstances command a good deal of public support. Any opposition to this policy would involve the resuscitation of many bitter political controversies between Ceylon and India and certainly hinder co-operation between the two countries on the War Effort.

To sum up, on the Ministerial level we must expect a general tendency to lose interest in the War and pay little attention to its needs. The attitude would probably be that the Allies are bound to win the war, and that there is no need for the Ceylonese to do anything but look to their own interests and achieve what they can of their aims and aspirations in spite of British obstruction and delay.

In their public speeches the Ministers would hardly be able to avoid attacking H.M. Government as being false to the principles of the United Nations in suppressing Ceylonese aspirations to freedom.

3. This change in the Ministerial attitude is bound to be reflected in the departments under their control. There will be inevitably a tendency to revive the importance of things concerning Ceylon only, as opposed to those connected with the War. There will be an increasing tendency to treat European heads of departments and other officials as being here on sufferance, and to be replaced by Ceylonese as soon as may be.

4. The State Council is, as a body, practically unanimous that the proposals of H.M. Government hitherto have been inadequate and ungenerous. As far back as March, 1942, the Council passed a resolution demanding Dominion Status and the Ministers in expressing their deep disappointment and dissatisfaction at the reply of H.M. Government certainly did so with the full approval of the Council. There exists

a considerable body of members who think that the Ministers have not insisted nearly strongly enough on their demands. If the latest request of the Ministers is refused, there is little doubt that this body of opinion in the State Council will vent itself in some extremely inflammatory speeches in the Council and that, if the Ministers do succeed in working out a united policy to put to the country at an election there will be opposition to it from a more extremely nationalist angle, designed to sever the British connection at all costs and as soon as possible.

5. Our main needs for war purposes from Ceylon are:—

A. Efficient public services, e.g.,
Road and Rail Transport;
Ports and Harbours;
Posts and Telegraphs;
Police.
B. A contented and efficient labour force for employment on Service Works.
C. Maximum output of certain important products such as rubber, tea, copra and timber.
D. Harmonious relations between the populace and the various units of British and Allied Forces.

The maintenance of each of these four things is in any case a task of some difficulty and magnitude. It is indisputable that that task must be gravely hampered by an atmosphere in which the people are told by their own leaders that their natural aspirations are being thwarted by the same extraneous government which is constantly urging them to accept further restriction and hardship and make greater efforts in the name of the War Effort.

As regards labour in particular, there have been increasing signs recently of restlessness and attempts to exploit the situation by strike action. The main reason for this is the feeling that now is the time, while the demand for labour so greatly exceeds the supply, to bring pressure to bear to achieve better conditions.

The labour leaders also feel that now is the time to acquire influence and prestige amongst the workers. The introduction of a specific cause of political discontent is bound to be seized on by such leaders and to lead to more and more agitation.

It is in this direction that outbreaks of violence are most to be feared. These are more likely to arise from our efforts to break strikes which might hamper the War Effort than from any other cause. A large-scale strike in the harbour area at Colombo, and efforts to break it in a time of extreme political tension might well lead to serious riots, which would in our present situation be disastrous.

Relations between troops and populace in Ceylon have on the whole been good up to date, but they have required constant watching. Small incidents which subside quickly in normal times would equally quickly be exaggerated and spread in a political atmosphere which would encourage the exploitation of anti-British feelings by politicians.

7 [sic]. I do not anticipate any disloyalty or specific refusal of co-operation on the part of the Police, nor indeed on the part of any of the Public Services. What is to be expected is rather a loss of goodwill and enthusiasm on the part of the populace in general. This would be such as would, in my opinion, make the already cumbersome and dilatory procedure of administration through the executive committees an impossible hindrance to the achievement of the maximum War Effort.

8. I would finally draw attention to the almost complete absence of British (U.K.) military forces from the Island, particularly infantry. If we were faced with internal unrest, the security of the base will demand a substantial allotment of these troops, as we must have a really reliable body of men who are available instantly to put down trouble without prejudice to any other operations.

200 WO 203/5412   22 May 1944

[Reforms]: inward telegram no SAC 2636 from Admiral Mountbatten to Chiefs of Staff assessing the probable impact on the activities of SEAC if an election is held in Ceylon

Your 2544 of 15 May.

1. I have had a discussion[1] with *Admiral Layton* and the Governor, from which the following factors affecting the general position have emerged:—

(a) His Majesty's Government in 1943 definitely promised constitutional reforms aiming at responsible government under the Crown in all matters of internal civil administration. H.M.G. to retain control of defence and external affairs.

(b) At the same time they stated that they cannot give proposals to achieve (a) above the necessary attention until victory is achieved.

(c) The Ministers of Ceylon have now asked that their proposals should be examined immediately.

(d) The Governor considers that if announcement of an early commission to consider this is not received before the next Budget Session in July, the Ministers may ask for a dissolution which would involve a General Election in the Autumn. In any case unless a special Order in Council is passed a dissolution in October and General Election in January are inevitable.

(e) The Governor and *Admiral Layton* consider that a General Election would involve serious dislocation of the life of the colony during the three months of the election activities and considerable political ill-feeling thereafter, the consequences of which are set out in my para. 2 below.

(f) The Governor and *Admiral Layton* considers that the life of the State Council could safely be prolonged and a General Election postponed by order in council for a further period of two years, if, but only if, announcement were made now that a commission would be appointed before the end of the year. They point out that report of the commission would not be ready for some eight or nine months and that any scheme based on it would have to go before the State Council. Attention of H.M.G. is not therefore likely to be required until a period when it is to be hoped that victory will have been achieved at least against *Germany*.

2. Consequences of dislocation at time of election and of subsequent political ill-feeling.

Immediate general strike and general declaration of non-cooperation are not anticipated. What is believed probable is a rapid decrease and cessation of c-operation [sic] with following results:—

---

[1] See 199.

(a) Adverse affect on labour, affecting:—

    (i) Production and export of rubber, to a serious extent.

    (ii) Movement of coal, and therefore communications.

    (iii) Operation of ports and particularly *Trincomalee* as a fleet base.

    (iv) Construction of Naval installations and airfields for Fleet Air Arm and R.A.F.

    (v) Production and export of tea for H.M.G.

(b) Breakdown of communications might lead to local shortages of food, which, coupled with excitement of inter-communal feeling caused by electioneering, would increase probability of riots. Strikes (though not an immediate general strike) would also be probable. For political reasons, Governor insists that use of Indian or African troops to restore order is unacceptable, and British troops essential. As you are aware, shortage of British troops in my command is already acute and is affecting all my plans. They could only be found for Ceylon at the expense of current operations. The knowledge that we were even contemplating such a possibility would immediately cause deterioration in American relations (see (c) below).

(c) Deterioration in political position in Ceylon would have adverse effect on American opinion. Any conciliatory step would be correspondingly valuable vis-à-vis Americans.

(d) Japanese propaganda is at present playing up grant of freedom to occupied territories. My task in *Burma, Malaya*, and to a lesser extent, *Sumatra*, would be made more difficult by fact of strained relations in Ceylon, while appointment of a commission to examine Ministers' proposals would be of positive assistance.

(e) Although it is not expected that actual disaffection will occur among the uniformed services, e.g., police, semi-military labour, etc, a loss of efficiency and keenness is to be expected.

3. Based on the above summary of position as interpreted by Governor and Commander-in-Chief, I estimate the effect on military operations in my command as follows:—

(a) Slowing up of preparations to receive the Fleet and particularly the Fleet Air Arm. Completion of current projects would be delayed by an indeterminate period not less than six months.

(b) In event of strikes, which would be probable, existing military labour would be insufficient to clear ports or maintain communications. Although it is not proposed to mount operations from Ceylon, resulting paralysis might mean that the Fleet would have to be based elsewhere, with consequent increased difficulties in the assembly and sailing of convoys.

(c) Situation which might involve use of British troops in Ceylon would affect current operations seriously and accentuate (d) below.

(d) Deterioration of relations with Americans.

(e) Considerable increase in difficulties of propaganda warfare.

4. Outside my Command, it appears to me that the major military consequences would be reduction in the export of essentials such as rubber, tea and copra, of which

undoubtedly rubber is the most important in view of the known serious shortage of crude rubber.[2]

---

[2] This tel was shown to Churchill who minuted: 'It would be a great folly to have an election in Ceylon in the next few years. They are making heaps of money out of us at the present time, and the whole area must be regarded as a war zone' (PREM 4/50/16, Churchill to General Ismay for COS Committee, 25 May 1944).

201   CO 54/986/7, no 18   5 June 1944
[Reforms]: inward telegram no 1033 from Sir A Caldecott to Mr Stanley transmitting a message from G G Ponnambalam urging the appointment of a commission and the undesirability of an election

My despatch No. 96.

Following submission is telegraphed to you at the request of Ponnambalam on behalf of Members of the Minority Community in the State Council. *Begins*.

1. The Representatives of the Minority Community on the State Council of Ceylon are strongly of opinion that a Commission or Conference should be appointed as early as possible within the next twelve months to examine the constitutional proposals of the Ministers, as well as the criticisms of the Minority [sic] thereon, including their alternative proposals.

2. The Representatives of the Minority Community in the State Council strongly urge the undesirability of holding another General Election under the present Constitution for the following reasons:—

(a) The circumstances mentioned by the S. of S. in his despatch published on 14th June, 1940 for postponing General Election namely:

(i) The general dissatisfaction with the present Constitution.
(ii) The necessity for arriving at decision regarding franchise and delimitation of constituencies remain unaltered.

(b) The circumstances mentioned by the S. of S. in his despatch of 10th February, 1942, with regard to the necessity for not distracting the people and the Government of Ceylon from a total war effort remain unaltered if not aggravated.

(c) The reduction in the present proportion of Minority Members to those of the Major Community, which is possible in a new Council elected under the present Constitution may have a fatal bearing on the issue of the Constitutional Reform, which is to be ultimately decided by a three-quarter majority of the Council.

(d) Constitutional reform is likely to be delayed in the event of a General Election, due to possible changes in the personnel of the Board of Ministers.

(e) From the point of view of the Minority Community it is of the utmost importance that amendment of the present Constitution, which has already operated to their detriment, should precede a General Election. *Ends*.

202   CAB 66/50, WP(44)299   7 June 1944

'Ceylon constitution': War Cabinet memorandum by Mr Stanley recommending the appointment of a commission

1. I am sorry that at this particular time I should have to trouble my colleagues with this matter, but owing to its operational implications I feel that only the War Cabinet can take the decision.

2. A year ago a Declaration was made, with the approval of the War Cabinet, of the intentions of His Majesty's Government regarding Constitutional reform in Ceylon (W.P. (43) 204). I attach the Declaration as Annexure I[1] to this memorandum, but the point of importance in relation to the present difficulty is that while the Ministers were invited forthwith to formulate proposals for a new Constitution, it was specifically stated that the examination of these proposals by His Majesty's Government could not be undertaken until after victory had been achieved.

3. The Ceylon Ministers immediately set themselves to the task of formulating their proposals, and have now submitted them to me with an urgent request that the further examination of their proposals should not be delayed until the end of the war but should be undertaken now. By that they mean that a Commission from this country should be sent to Ceylon not later than the end of the year and that His Majesty's Government should give an assurance now that this will be done. They point out the increasing difficulties of working the present admittedly unsatisfactory form of Constitution in war conditions and the great difficulty of undertaking the necessary post-war planning in ignorance of the likely form of the Constitution under which the plans will have to be carried out.

4. There is, unfortunately, a political complication which makes it impossible to ignore this demand. The life of the present State Council has already been extended for a period of four years beyond its statutory limit. This extension has been secured by an annual amendment of the Order in Council with the consent of Ministers in order to avoid a General Election in the Island in war conditions. Unless a further extension is arranged, the dissolution of the Council will be necessary this autumn, and a General Election will follow in January next. I am advised by the Governor most specifically that the Ministers will not consent to a further extension unless they can be assured that progress will be made with the examination of their Constitutional proposals.

5. Even if, in our desire to avoid the obvious evil results of a General Election, the life of the State Council were to be extended by an amendment of the Order in Council, without the consent and indeed in opposition to the wishes of the Ministers, and we were prepared to face the probability of their consequent non-co-operation, it is doubtful whether we should secure our object. Under the present Constitution a defeat of Ministers in the State Council on a major issue requires a dissolution and consequent elections within three months. It would be an easy matter for the State Council to reject the Budget in July and thereby force an election. It appears, therefore, that His Majesty's Government must either accept the Ministers' demand and proceed with the examination or face a General Election within the next few months.

[1] See 169.

6. From the purely Colonial Office point of view, the choice between these two courses is not easy to make. Against the decision to proceed with the examination are the following arguments:—

(a) we deliberately stipulated in our Declaration last year that we could not go ahead with the Constitutional question until we had won the war, and to vary that decision now would have the appearance of weakness and of giving way to the Ministers' clamour;

(b) there may be a real practical difficulty in finding men of sufficient calibre to undertake the work of this Commission during the coming winter;

(c) the mere presence of the Commission and the necessity for various minority interests to state their claims will lead to political excitement in Ceylon, even though that may be of a much less damaging character than would be caused by a Ministerial crisis or a General Election.

In favour of accepting the proposals are the arguments that:—

(a) the present Constitution is admittedly an awkward and difficult one, and the Ministers are right in claiming credit for the fair measure of success with which they have worked it in war conditions;

(b) we have consistently pursued a course designed to avoid political excitement in Ceylon during the war. The necessity of this is even more obvious in the coming months. Insistence on the letter of our Declaration last year would quite clearly, in the opinion of those qualified to advise, land us in the most acute difficulties with the Ministers and the State Council.

7. I confess that if I had to reach a conclusion on purely political considerations I should find the issue difficult to decide, but the determining factors obviously must be the position of Ceylon as an essential operational base in the coming months in the Far East, and the effect a political crisis might therefore have upon future operations.

8. I accordingly put the whole position to the Chiefs of Staff for their advice on that aspect. They have obtained the considered advice of the Supreme Allied Commander, South-East Asia Command, in the telegram attached as Annexure II.[2] They endorse his view, which is emphatically in favour of accepting the Ministers' demands.

9. Moreover in view of the present urgency of rubber supplies, in which respect Ceylon is by far the most considerable source for natural rubber, I have been assured by the Minister of Production that a very serious view must be taken of any diminution of these supplies. Paragraph 2 (a) (i) of the Supreme Allied Commander's telegram refers particularly to that risk.

10. I accordingly have no hesitation in recommending to my colleagues that His Majesty's Government should take the decision now that a Commission should be appointed to proceed with the examination of the Ministers' Constitutional proposals, and should visit Ceylon for this purpose about the end of this year, and that the life of the present State Council should be prolonged by the necessary amendment of

---

[2] See 200.

the Order in Council for a further term of two years as recommended by the Governor and Admiral Layton.[3]

---

[3] The Army Council Secretariat prepared a brief for Sir J Grigg (secretary of state for war) on Stanley's memo. The brief outlined the political situation and the views thereon of Mountbatten. It explained that the COS had endorsed the recommendation that a commission should be appointed before the end of the year. The General Staff had nothing to add but the quarter-master general had observed that, from the administrative aspect, 'any dislocation in Ceylon would be a serious embarrassment entailing commitments which would be hard to meet. Uniformed labour would have to be imported for the work required by the Navy and Royal Air Force; British troops would be required for internal security. Both these commitments would involve administrative overheads to maintain them apart from camp construction. Moreover, the production and export of rubber is essential for our general military needs which would affect the construction and working of the India base'. The brief concluded that the secretary of state for war should support the recommendation for the appointment of a commission (WO 32/10099, ACS/B/931, 12 June 1944).

Subject to the understanding that the appointment of a commission did not entail for HMG any further commitment than that contained in the 1943 declaration, the War Cabinet approved the recommendations in para 10 of Stanley's memo on 13 June 1944. In discussion, Amery urged that the announcement of the appointment of a commission should include a statement that facilities would be accorded to the Indian and other minorities in Ceylon to express their point of view before the commission (CO 54/986/10, no 14, WM 77(44)4).

203   CO 54/986/5/1, no 52   14 June 1944

[Reforms]: outward unnumbered telegram from Mr Stanley to Sir A Caldecott on the appointment of a commission

My secret telegram No. 583.[1]

His Majesty's Government have decided to accede to Ministers' request for the appointment of a Commission, which will, it is hoped, visit Ceylon at the end of the year, to examine their constitutional scheme. This step does not, of course, involve any modification of the conditions set forth in the Declaration by His Majesty's Government in May, 1943, as to eventual approval by His Majesty's Government of any new constitution.

2. This decision will be embodied in a fresh Declaration by His Majesty's Government, but I shall naturally want time to consult you as to precise wording. The Declaration would at the same time, state that with the object already declared of avoiding a general election in Ceylon during the war and consequent dislocation of Ceylon's war effort, the Ceylon (State Council) Order in Council would be amended to prolong the life of the existing constitution for further period of two years. This is as contemplated in discussions between Supreme Allied Commander S.E.A.C., Admiral Layton and yourself.

3. I am anxious to relieve Ministers' anxieties with the least possible delay in anticipation of formal statement which will be made as early as is practicable, and should be grateful, provided that you have no objection to this course, if you would in confidence now communicate to Senanayake for the personal information of himself and his ministerial colleagues His Majesty's Government's decision to proceed with the appointment of the Commission and to extend the life of the existing State Council for a further period of two years for the reasons stated above.

4. Please show this telegram to Admiral Layton.

---

[1] See 198, note 5.

204 CO 54/986/5/1, no 53   18 June 1944

[Reforms]: inward unnumbered telegram from Sir A Caldecott to Mr Stanley on the appointment of a commission and Mr Senanayake's reaction

Most grateful for your secret and personal telegram of 14th June[1] which reached me 16th June marked "without priority" on which date, having communicated its sense orally to Senanayake, I confirmed my conversation by secret and personal letter[2] which he could show to his colleagues. In both my oral and written communications, I amended first sentence of your telegram to read "His Majesty's Government have decided to accede to Ministers' request for immediate examination of their constitutional scheme by appointment of a Commission which, will it is hoped, visit Ceylon at the end of the year." This amendment was necessary because (vide paragraph 2 (b) of enclosure No. 3 to my secret despatch of 3rd February forwarding their scheme) the Ministers did not (repeat not) request appointment of Commission but, on the contrary, hoped to avoid one. I also substituted the word "Council" for "Constitution" in penultimate sentence of your paragraph 2. On hearing the news, Senanayake smiling said "that should make things easier for us" and I have no doubt that if the Declaration by His Majesty's Government can be expedited, things will at once become easier for everybody. Grateful therefore if drafting of Declaration may receive easiest (?earliest) possible attention of His Majesty's Government. I suggest that it need not be long but should be confined to statement on the lines of your telegram.

---

[1] See 203.

[2] Dated 16 June 1944, the final sentence of Caldecott's letter to Senanayake read: 'I shall be grateful if you will be so good as to impress upon your colleagues the personal and secret nature of this anticipatory communication pending issue of the formal statement by His Majesty's Government' (WO 203/5412).

205 CO 54/986/5/1, no 54   19 June 1944

[Reforms]: outward unnumbered telegram from Mr Stanley to Sir A Caldecott transmitting a draft declaration announcing the appointment of a commission

My secret and personal telegram 14th June.[1] Following is provisional draft of fresh Declaration by His Majesty's Government on which I should be grateful for observations of yourself and Commander-in-Chief.

Begins. In their Declaration of 1943 on the subject of the reform of the Ceylon constitution, His Majesty's Government invited the Ceylon Ministers to submit proposals for a new constitution, and promised that once victory was achieved such detailed proposals as the Ministers might in the meantime have been able to formulate in the way of a complete constitutional scheme would be examined by a Commission or Conference. Ministers have now submitted their draft scheme with an urgent request that arrangements may be made for its examination at an earlier date than that contemplated in the Declaration.

---

[1] See 203.

His Majesty's Government, have accordingly decided to appoint a Commission to examine the Ministers' proposals, which would visit Ceylon for this purpose towards the end of the present year. The adoption of this course does not entail in other respects any modification of the Declaration by His Majesty's Government in regard to the eventual approval by His Majesty's Government of any new constitution. It is the intention of His Majesty's Government that the appointment of the Commission should provide full opportunity for consultation to take place with the various interests, including the minority communities, concerned with the subject of constitutional reform in Ceylon and with the proposals which Ministers have formulated.

Further, in accordance with the object already declared of avoiding a general election in Ceylon during the war, with consequent dislocation of Ceylon's war effort, the Ceylon (State Council) Order in Council, 1931, will be amended so as to prolong the life of the existing State Council for a further period of two years. *Ends.*[2]

---

[2] Stanley made this announcement in the House of Commons on 5 July 1944.

---

206   CO 54/986/5/1, no 63   27 June 1944
[Reforms]: inward unnumbered telegram from Sir A Caldecott to Mr Stanley reporting a press leak about the appointment of a commission

Since replying to your secret and personal telegram of 24th June I have seen *Ceylon Daily News* this morning wherein article by its political correspondent carries the following three headlines:—

(i)   Reforms despatch from Whitehall.
(ii) Two years more for the present Council.
(iii) One-man Commission coming out.

Article begins as follows:—

> "Two Ministers and a State Councillor speaking at the annual sessions of the Sinhala Maha Sabha last Saturday gave important information regarding the contents of a despatch recently received from Whitehall which had so far been kept secret." Article proceeds to quote the speech of the President Bandaranaike which contains nothing of the nature alleged. It then continued as follows: "That Kannangara, Minister for Education, revealed that an intimation had been received from Whitehall and all he could say was that there was no need to regret the extension of the present State Council." Speech of *Jayasuriya* M.S.C. is next reported, but contains nothing of the nature alleged. Political correspondent concludes by paragraph which contains the following statements and comments: "leaders of Sabha dropped other hints to some of their more trustworthy followers from outside, and from enquiries made in these circles I have been able to learn that the Secretary of State's despatch contains two important decisions (described as in headlines (i) and (ii) above). Public will understand why leaders of Sabha were so eager to be

---

[1] See 204, note 2.

the first with the news and perhaps take all the credit for it when the despatch is actually announced."

2. On reading the above I instructed the Chief Secretary to apprise the Information Officer that any statements that may have been recently made here by any person concerning constitutional reform have been entirely without authorization, and that I have nothing to communicate on this subject. I also summoned Senanayake and told him that I must have explanation from him and his colleagues as to disclosure of communication confided to them under absolute secrecy.[1]

3. Later this morning Senanayake brought Bandaranaike and Kannangara to interview me, both of them indignant at what they represented as slander by the *Ceylon Daily News* in regard to which they intend to take legal opinion. Former showed me manuscript of his Presidential address which contained no disclosure, and latter reported that the following question had been put to him while taking the chair at the afternoon session in the absence of the former: "Is the Chairman, being a Minister, in a position to explain the present position to us?"—to which he replied "as regards the present situation there is no need to despair, but as regards what is contained in the despatch from the Secretary of State for the Colonies I am not at liberty to disclose anything." I have impressed upon him that such a reply lent itself to the inference that some despatch on the subject has been received, but knowing his integrity I do not doubt that the *Daily News*, which is very hostile to Maha Sabha, took advantage of such inference to father upon the two Sabha Ministers information which they had obtained from other sources. I have reason strongly to suspect the Minister for Health, George Silva, as the main source, but the Chief Secretary informs me that he understands Oldfield and Ponnambalam to have mentioned receipt of private advices from London indicating early Commission.

4. There is no further action which I can take, except to await information as to what legal advice is given to Bandaranaike, but Senanayake asks me to express his extreme regret that so discreditable a development should have occurred.

207 CO 54/986/5/1, no 69   9 July 1944
[Reforms]: inward unnumbered telegram from Sir A Caldecott to Mr Stanley transmitting a resolution of the Working Committee of the Ceylon National Congress rejecting the declaration announcing the appointment of a commission

See my immediately preceding secret and personal telegram.[1]

Whereas the original Declaration by His Majesty's Government on constitutional reform, read out in the State Council on 26th May, 1943, was declared by the Secretary of State for the Colonies, and understood by the Board of Ministers and the people of this country, to mean that, if the Board of Ministers could produce a constitution which, in the opinion of a Commission or Conference, satisfies the conditions in paragraphs 2 to 6 thereof, and that constitution is subsequently accepted by threequarters of all the Members of the State Council, excluding the

---

[1] Not printed; the tel in question referred to a meeting of the Working Committee of the Ceylon National Congress on 8 July which approved the above declaration.

Officers of State and the Speaker, His Majesty in Council will put that constitution into operation and, whereas the latest Declaration of His Majesty's Government, made on 5th July, 1944, is a gross violation of that undertaking in that a Commission is to be sent out to explore the whole subject of constitutional reforms in Ceylon, this Congress fears that this is an attempt to take away from the people of Ceylon the undoubted right that they have to draft their own constitution and to impose upon them a slave constitution drafted by the foreign ruler, and calls upon the country and the State Council.

(a) To reject the Declaration made by His Majesty's Government on 26th May, 1943, and subsequent Declarations.

(b) To boycott such Commission or Conference.

(c) To make a united demand for the immediate recognition of Ceylon's right to independence and for a free constitution.

This Congress authorizes the Working Committee to summon a special session of the Congress to take all steps necessary to implement this resolution. This Congress demands the immediate dissolution of the State Council and the holding of a general election on the issue of complete independence.

208   CO 54/986/5/1, no 72   11 July 1944

[Reforms]: inward telegram no 1274 from Sir A Caldecott to Mr Stanley transmitting a message from ministers contesting the terms of reference for the commission

Constitutional reform. Following communication, marked by them secret, is telegraphed to you at the request of Ministers. I will send you my report thereon after due consideration and in the light of anything that may be said on the subject in the State Council this week. *Message begins:*—

Your Excellency.

The Ministers have given careful consideration to statement on constitutional reform[1] made by the Secretary of State in the House of Commons on the 5th July, 1944. While they would have welcomed decision to consider their draft scheme at an early date, they regret to find that the statement of 5th July contains, in their opinion, a fundamental departure from the Declaration of 1943, which authorized them to submit detailed proposals in the way of a complete constitutional scheme subject to conditions set out in paragraphs (2) to (6) of the Declaration.

2. Ministers' interpretation of their mandate—an interpretation on which alone they were prepared to act—was made plain in statement made by the Leader of the State Council on 8th June, 1943.[2] In paragraph 1 it was asserted that the Declaration was "in essence an undertaking that if the Board can produce a constitution which, in the opinion of a Commission or Conference, satisfies the conditions set out in paragraphs (2) to (6) thereof, and if that constitution is subsequently accepted by threequarters of all the members of the State Council, excluding Officers of the State and the Speaker, His Majesty in Council will put that constitution into operation." In

---

[1] See 205.   [2] See 170.

their message dated 6th July, 1943, which was telegraphed to the Secretary of State, the Ministers stated "We regret, however, that in reply of His Majesty's Government to our statement there is no indication whatever that our interpretation is in accordance with the principles of the Declaration. Without such indication it will not be possible for us to undertake the drafting of a constitution in the terms of the Declaration. We would, therefore, request His Majesty's Government to state whether our interpretation falls within the Declaration."[3] The Secretary of State in his reply communicated by Your Excellency's letter of 11th July, 1943, stated "the Ministers may rest assured that I have not found in their statement anything which must be regarded as essentially irreconcilable with the conditions contained in His Majesty's Government's statement."[4]

3. Having received this assurance, the Ministers felt justified in assuming that, instead of a constitution being framed for this country by His Majesty's Government, the Ministers in their capacity as representatives of the people of this country, were to frame a constitution which His Majesty's government undertook to accept subject only to two conditions:—

(a) that His Majesty's Government should be satisfied that it was in full compliance with paragraphs (2) to (6) of the Declaration, and

(b) that it was subsequently approved by threequarters of all the members of the State Council of Ceylon excluding Officers of the State and the Speaker or other presiding officer.

Compliance with the first condition was obviously intended to satisfy His Majesty's Government that restrictions contemplated by them in their Declaration were satisfactorily provided for; compliance with the second condition was as obviously intended to satisfy His Majesty's Government that there was sufficient support in the country for Ministers' proposals to justify their acceptance. It should further be noted that in reply to representations by Mr. G. G. Ponnambalam, M.S.C., on behalf of some of the minority members of the State Council, the Secretary of State merely repeated the substance of paragraph (7) of the Declaration: "as he is aware acceptance by His Majesty's Government of any constitutional scheme which Ceylon Ministers may formulate is conditional on such a scheme being examined by suitable Commission or Conference and being eventually accepted by threequarters of all the members of the State Council: and that discretion of Ministers as to procedure which they may adopt in framing a new draft constitutional scheme is not matter with which I should consider it right to interfere."[5]

In reply to representations from Ceylon Congress, Secretary of State did not even mention "Commission or Conference": "it will be appreciated that one of the conditions of acceptance by His Majesty's Government of a new constitutional scheme which may be formulated by Ceylon Ministers, is that scheme should eventually be accepted by threequarters of all the Members of the State Council and that I am not prepared to interfere with discretion of Ministers as to when and in what manner they should formulate a scheme with this object."

These representations arose because the leader of the State Council, in answer to question in the Council on 16th November, 1943 stated that "a finished product" (i.e. the scheme as approved by His Majesty's Government) and not "an unfinished

---

[3] See 173.   [4] See 174.   [5] See 182.

product" (or draft scheme) would come before the Council in due course (Ceylon Hansard 1943, Page 2455). It is thus clear that the Secretary of State approved Ministers' interpretation of the Declaration and that he considered any protection which minority members needed was to be found in requirement that "the finished product" required the approval of threequarters of all the members of the State Council.

4. In statement of 5th July, 1944, however, His Majesty's Government stated that Commission proposed to be appointed for the purpose of examining Ministers' proposals is to be provided with "full opportunities for consultations to take place with various interests, including minority communities concerned with the subject of constitutional reform in Ceylon and with the proposals which Ministers have formulated." This clearly means that function of the Commission is not to be limited to determining whether Ministers' draft conforms with paragraphs (2) to (6) of Declaration of 1943. For such a purpose, consultations with "various interests" would not be necessary. Consultations would be of use only if the whole problem was to be considered afresh and the constitutional requirements of Ceylon were to be determined not by Ministers and at least threequarters of the State Council, but by a Commission appointed by the Secretary of State. The undertaking to put into operation any scheme framed by the Ministers which:—

(a) satisfied His Majesty's Government that it was in full compliance with paragraphs (2) to (6) of the Declaration of 1943, and
(b) was subsequently approved by threequarters of all the Members of the State Council excluding the Officers of the State and the Speaker or other presiding officer, has been withdrawn.

5. This fundamental alteration the Ministers are unable to accept. It has been made, too, without any consultation with, or even notice to the Ministers. It was not even mentioned in the personal letter which Your Excellency sent to the Leader of the State Council on 16th June, 1944. Had we been informed that this Commission was not only to examine whether the constitutional scheme of the Ministers satisfied paragraphs (2) to (6) of the Declaration but also to consider all the Ministers' proposals in consultation with "various interests" the Ministers would immediately have protested. We were not so informed until the morning of 5th July and Your Excellency then stated that it was too late for representations to be made to the Secretary of State. His Majesty's Government has not only broken what we understood to be an undertaking, but has done it in such a manner that we have been given no opportunity of questioning it.

6. In the circumstances the Ministers have no alternative but to decline to take any part in the deliberations of the proposed Commission. They are prepared to stand by the Declaration of 1943, to discuss with the Commission whether their scheme satisfied paragraphs (2) to (6) of that Declaration, and, on His Majesty's Government being satisfied on this point, to submit the scheme to the State Council.

7. We should be grateful if Your Excellency would telegraph this memorandum to the Secretary of State.[6]

---

[6] The Board of Ministers were distressed at what they regarded as a clear change of policy. Until the first weeks of Jan 1944 they had not been given any indication that their interpretation of the meaning of the declaration of May 1943 was unacceptable, either to Caldecott and the officers of state or to the secretary of

(Signed) D. S. Senanayake,
Vice-Chairman,
Board of Ministers and Leader of the State Council.

Colombo, 11th July, 1944.

Message ends, and is followed by copy of following letter addressed by Mahadeva to Senanayake:

> "While I am in agreement with interpretation placed on the Declaration by Ministers, I am still of the opinion that the question of representations, on which alone I was not able to agree with my colleagues, should be referred to a Royal Commission, and that we should abide by its decision."

---

state and his officials. As Senanayake's constitutional adviser and the person responsible for the general principles of the ministers' draft constitution, Jennings was equally upset. In para 5 of his typescript 'Notes on the Ministers' procedure, 1943–44', he explained: 'It seems to me that the documents [see 170, note] cannot be interpreted in any way other than that the ministers assumed that the commission or conference would examine their draft constitution and that draft constitution only. These documents were seen by the Officers of State and the Governor. The Chief Secretary was consulted about both documents before they were circulated, and had one of them amended. The Ministers' statement was considered in the Board of Ministers while the C[hief] S[ecretary] was presiding and the other Officers of State were present. The C[hief] S[ecretary] himself tried to keep the drafting straight. If the Officers of State considered the ministers were misunderstanding the whole procedure, they should surely have said so. More than that, considering the part taken by the C[hief] S[ecretary] in drafting of the statement, he *would* surely have said so. I can therefore draw only one conclusion, that the Governor and the Officers of State considered that the ministers had correctly understood what they were being asked to do, and that at this stage there was no idea, at least in Ceylon, that a commission would be sent out to examine not merely the ministers' scheme, but the proposals of "various interests" including minorities. If this is so, either the local representatives of HMG were themselves misinterpreting the intentions of the Secretary of State, or the policy was subsequently changed and the Secretary of State has gone back upon his undertakings.'

---

209   CO 54/986/5/2, no 93   July 1944

[Reforms]: memorandum by Sir A Caldecott explaining his own position in regard to the ministerial protest against HMG's declaration of 5 July 1944

1. In paragraph 39 of my Reforms Despatch of 1938 (Sessional Paper XXVIII—1938) I expressed no opinion as to whether a Commission should be sent out as a result of my report or not. I had on file representations which I had invited from all communities and I suggested that, if a Commission came, it should work and find on these. Needless to say I contemplated that, if a Commission were to be sent, it would arrive in 1938 or 1939. I did not suggest that representations made to me in 1938 should be taken to be of permanent sufficiency, any more than I now feel myself bound to my recommendations of 1938 as indicating the maximum of constitutional reform that could be justified today. The representations then made to me, as well as my recommendations, are over six years old, and neither could sensibly or reasonably be taken by anybody as final.

2. The Ministers' view that the representations and recommendations made in

---

1938 formed a sufficient basis for determination of constitutional reform in 1941 was put forward by them on 1st October, 1941, vide Document No.6A in Sessional Paper XIII—1943.[3] Document 9 therein explained His Majesty's Government's inability to accept this Ministerial view; they "had reluctantly reached their conclusion that in the face of wide measures of local disagreement no substantial changes in the existing constitution could be introduced without further opportunity for examination of the conflicting views of the various interests concerned, which is impracticable in war conditions but will be taken in hand as soon as peace is won".[4] The wording of the similar passages in the public statement that followed (Document No.10A) ran as follows:—"Before taking decisions upon the present proposals for reform, concerning which there has been so little unanimity, but which are of such importance to the well-being of Ceylon, His Majesty's Government would desire that the position should be further examined and made the subject of further consultation by means of a Commission or Conference. This cannot be arranged under war conditions, but the matter will be taken up with the least possible delay after the war". The dissatisfaction of the Ministers with the attitude of His Majesty's Government and a repetition of their view that there was no need for any further consultation by means of a Commission or Conference is contained in Document No.11 and the Secretary of State's acknowledgement of the receipt of their communication is in Document No.13.[5]

3. The declaration by His Majesty's Government of 26th May, 1943, began by citing the 1941 assurance quoted in the preceding paragraph and went on to convey a message to give greater precision to it. In paragraph (7) of this message it was stated as follows:—

"His Majesty's Government will however, once victory is achieved, proceed to the examination by a suitable Commission or Conference of such detailed proposals as the Ministers may in the meantime have been able to formulate in the way of a complete constitutional scheme; subject to the clear understanding that the acceptance by His Majesty's Government of any proposals will depend, firstly, upon His Majesty's Government being satisfied that they are in full compliance with the preceding portion of this statement and, secondly, upon their subsequent approval by three quarters of all the members of State Council excluding the Officers of State and the Speaker or other presiding Officer".[6]

I understand the present claim of the Ministers to be that this portion of the Message could only be construed as limiting the function of any Commission or Conference appointed to examine the complete constitutional scheme which they were invited to put forward to ascertaining whether it satisfied or not the stipulations contained in paragraphs (2) to (6) of the Message: that is to say that it abrogated the original purpose of a Commission or Conference as explained in the documents quoted in my paragraph 2 supra, i.e. examination of the conflicting views of the various interests concerned in view of the little unanmity there had been on my 1938 proposals.

4. The possibility of such a limitative interpretation seems to me clearly precluded on two grounds (1) nobody would think of appointing a Commission or Conference to examine and report upon points that require scrutiny and answer by

---

[3] See 107.   [4] See 109.   [5] See 111, 112.   [6] See 169, annex.

constitutional lawyers and draughtsmen (2) a Message issued for the explicit purpose of giving precision to a former statement cannot be rightly interpreted as abrogating a clear and pivotal provision in such statement.

5. The Ministers however, I understand, maintain that the Secretary of State has actually approved such a limitative and abrogative interpretation because it was precisely this interpretation that was set out in the first paragraph of their Statement of June 8th, 1943[7] (Sessional Paper XVII/1943) wherein he had not found "anything that must be regarded as essentially irreconcilable with the conditions contained in His Majesty's Government's Statement."[8] The Secretary of State's telegram from which this is a quotation is printed on page 6 of Sessional Paper XVII–1943. The first part of it explained why His Majesty's Government had been unable to express definite acceptance of the Ministers' interpretation of various matters in their Statement. The reason was that they could not do so without seeking further elucidation, a process which would have involved detailed discussions that could not be undertaken until after the war. What the Secretary of State expressed was not an acceptance of any of the Ministers' interpretations but an assurance that he had found nothing in them irreconcilable with the conditions contained in the Statement of His Majesty's Government. A clear road indeed stood open towards a conciliation of the first paragraph of the Ministers' statement with the purpose of His Majesty's Government that there should be 'further opportunity for examination of the conflicting views of the various interests concerned'. The Ministers could (as I and probably many others anticipated that they would) have consulted with representatives of the various interests and have supplemented their scheme with a record of the representations made and of their conclusions thereon. The whole position would then have been before His Majesty's Government (the views of the various interests having been invited and recorded) and the Commission or Conference would after perusal of the records have needed only final consultation with the Ministers on any points requiring elucidation or discussion.

6. The event however was otherwise. On the 2nd February, 1944, I received together with the Ministers' scheme a letter from the Vice Chairman of the Board of Ministers, in which no mention was made of any consultation with the various interests concerned but in which it was stated

(A) that the Ministers bore in mind the possibility of a modification or alteration by the State Council of their recommendation in regard to (i) the question of a unicameral or bicameral form of government (ii) Representation (that is to say it was not a scheme that was to be put before State Council for acceptance or rejection, but with opportunities for alteration);
(B) that the Minister for Home Affairs (the only Minister belonging to a Minority Community) was not in agreement for the proposals in regard to Representation and that he considered that "the entirety of this question, which is a matter of considerable controversy, should be settled by a Royal Commission."

6. In acknowledging the Vice-Chairman's letter and the accompanying Scheme I pointed out:—

(a) that the Scheme was not a "complete constitutional scheme" as contemplated

---

[7] See 170.   [8] See 174.

by paragraph (7) of the Message in His Majesty's Government's declaration of 26th May, 1943, because such crucial questions as the form of legislature, franchise and representation were left for consideration "otherwise than by the Commission or Conference required by the Declaration";

(b) that two passages in the letter "appeared to envisage the immediate consideration of His Majesty's Government of the Ministers' proposals without previous examination by the stipulated Commission or Conference".[9]

7.   In reply to (a) the Vice-Chairman on February 9th submitted certain points as explanatory of the omissions for transmission to the Secretary of State for consideration. These were duly forwarded. Incidentally the draft of a new Elections Order in Council therein foreshadowed has not yet been submitted. In regard to (b) the Vice-Chairman ended his letter with the following paragraph:—

"For these reasons the immediate consideration of our proposals is necessary. This may be done in whatever manner (as suggested in the Declaration or otherwise) His Majesty's Government may consider the best."

There is no suggestion here that consideration of the form of legislature, franchise and representation (none of them matters impinging on paragraphs (2) to (6) in the statement of His Majesty's Government) were to be considered only in relation to those paragraphs!

8.   On 15th February, 1944, I sent a telegram to the Secretary of State containing a submission from Mr. Ponnambalam on behalf of all except two minority members of State Council. It complained that the Ministers had refused to disclose their proposals and thus prevented the minority communities view-point being represented. It ended by asking the Secretary of State to withhold consideration of the Ministerial proposals till they were submitted to State Council, in order that he might have a full knowledge of the opinions of all sections and interests before a Commission or Conference is summoned. The Secretary of State on the 7th March replied that the acceptance by His Majesty's Government of any constitutional scheme which the Ceylon Ministers might formulate was conditional on such a scheme being examined by a suitable Commission or Conference and being eventually accepted by three quarters of all members of State Council; and that the discretion of the Ministers as to the procedure which they might adopt in framing a new draft constitutional scheme was not a matter in which he (the Secretary of State) should consider it right to interfere.[11]

9.   On the 14th March I conferred with the Ministers in connection with a personal telegram which I had received from the Secretary of State.[12] The Secretary of State intimated that "if His Majesty's Government were to see their way to proceeding with the appointment of a Commission or Conference before achievement of victory they were not on that account in any way committed to accepting the Ministers' proposals as satisfying the first of the two conditions set out in paragraph 7 of His Majesty's Government's Declaration" "(i.e. that the proposals must be in full compliance with the stipulation in paragraphs (2) to (6))." I pointed out to the Ministers that this meant that any Commission or Conference would concern itself only with examination of the local provisions of their scheme in or after consultation

---

[9] See 181, note.   [10] See 181.   [11] See 182, note 1.   [12] See 184, 185.

with the various interests concerned and that the scheme's compliance with stipulations (2) to (6) would need independent examination by His Majesty's Government's legal advisers and draughtsmen. I state that this was quite clear also from the reply given to Mr. Ponnambalam which could only mean that the minorities need not be apprehensive because the contents of the Ministers' scheme would be examined by a Conference or Commission which would ascertain their views, and that any constitution that might emerge from His Majesty's Government's consideration of the Commission's or Conference's report would still require acceptance by 75% of the State Council. It transpired that the Ministers had not all of them yet seen Mr. Ponnambalam's message, which I had transmitted in an open telegram, and that none of them had seen the Secretary of State's reply as it had arrived only a week ago. I attached a copy of both therefore to my personal letter to Mr. Senanayake of 15th March in which I confirmed the communications which I had made at the conference on the Secretary of State's authority.

10. I consider that if Mr. Senanayake or any of his colleagues attached the different, and to my mind untenable, interpretation to these telegrams which he has now put forward in paragraph 3 of the Ministers' present protest to the Secretary of State I had the right to expect that I should be informed of the fact. I was not.

11. On 22nd April I addressed to the Secretary of State my open despatch No. 96 in which I wrote "the main purpose of a Commission or Conference to examine the Ministers' constitutional proposals will obviously be to invite and investigate criticisms thereof". This despatch was circulated to the Board of Ministers on the 2nd May. I received no comment on it from any of the Ministers, but it is now stated in paragraph 3 of their present protest that the equivalent passage in the recent announcement of the Secretary of State was "without consultation with or even notice to the Ministers". A sufficient reason for not mentioning the passage in my personal letter to Mr. Senanayake of 16th June 1944, (not incidentally as stated in the present protest, addressed to him as Leader of the State Council because its contents were for communication to the Ministers only, though their substance came somehow to be communicated to the Press)[13] was that the announcement had not yet (as I pointed out in the letter) been drafted; but I may add that if I had been in a position to foresee the inclusion of the passage I should not have thought of mentioning it in my letter because the position lay as described in my two preceding paragraphs.

12. My first apprisal of the fact that the Ministers would object to the Commission's consulting with the various interests concerned was when Mr. Senanayake made and explained his verbal request to me (at 10.15 a.m. on 5th July) that the announcement should be stopped—a request which I said it was too late to consider. The preceding paragraphs of this memorandum will have indicated the measure of surprise and astonishment with which I have listened to his request, and to the reason for it.

---

[13] See 204, 206.

210   CO 54/986/5/2, no 84   20 July 1944

[Reforms]: inward unnumbered telegram in five parts from Sir A Caldecott to Mr Stanley transmitting a draft reply to the ministerial protest

[Having set out his own position in a separate memo (see 209), Caldecott drafted the following reply to ministers which was to be issued by the secretary of state.]

My immediately preceding secret and personal telegram of 20th July.

First of five parts of draft reply referred to.

Begins.   1.   I have read with much care the Ministers' message to me telegraphed by the Governor on 11th July, 1944. It is a great disappointment to me that the misunderstanding which underlies their present representation should ever have arisen and, in this reply to their message, I will, therefore, clearly state the position as I see it.

2.   For this purpose, it is necessary for me to go back to Document No. 6A in Ceylon Session Paper XIII—1943, wherein the Ministers put forward their views that the appointment of a Commission or the holding of a Conference for a further investigation of the question of constitutional reform (the need for which I had stated in the message reproduced in Document No. 5) was unnecessary and undesirable, in view of the Governor's consultation with all sections of opinion in 1938, and of the careful consideration given to his recommendations by the State Council in 1939.

3.   Document No. 9 informed the Ministers in reply that His Majesty's Government had reluctantly reached the conclusion that, in the face of wide measure of local disagreement, no substantial change in the existing constitution could be introduced without further opportunity for the examination of the conflicting views of the various interests concerned.

4.   The statement of His Majesty's Government communicated to the State Council on 26th October, 1942, (Document No. 10A) declared that, before taking decision upon the present proposals for reform, concerning which there had been so little unanimity, but which were of such importance to the well-being of Ceylon, His Majesty's Government would desire that the position should be further examined by means of a Commission or Conference.

5.   This statement was cited word for word at the beginning of the Declaration by His Majesty's Government dated 26th March, 1943, printed as Section (1) of Ceylon Session Paper XVII—1943. The remainder of the Declaration was for the explicit purpose of "giving greater precision to the foregoing statement, with the object of removing any doubt regarding His Majesty's Government's intentions."

Part 2

6.   It never for a moment occurred to me that a Declaration made for the explicit purpose of giving precision to a previous statement could, much less would, be interpreted in any responsible quarter as abrogating a cardinal point of the previous statement. I have explained (paragraph (3) Session Paper XVII—1943) that war time conditions precluded a detailed examination of the Ministers' statement of 8th June, 1943 (paragraph (2)), but I may say that even if such examination had been possible,

I could not for the above reason have construed paragraph 1 of that statement as aiming at depriving His Majesty's Government of all means of having before them the up to date views of the various interests concerned on any Ministerial proposals, before submission to the State Council of a complete constitutional scheme.

7.   There was no indication in the Ministers' statement of 8th June, 1943, of the claims now put forward in paragraph 3 of their present communication, that they have been entrusted with the framing of a constitution "as Representatives of the people of Ceylon." This representative capacity does not pertain to them and the invitation to formulate a scheme was extended to them as Ministers under the present constitution.

8.   My assurance (paragraph 5 Session Paper XVII—1943) that I had not found in the Ministers' statement of 8th June, 1943, anything which must be regarded as essentially irreconcilable with the conditions contained in His Majesty's Government's statement of 26th May, 1943, was one from which I have nothing to retract. It was open to the Ministers to implement the purpose of His Majesty's Government, (made known to them by documents 9 and 10A in Session Paper XIII—1943 and by the first paragraph of His Majesty's Government's Declaration of 26th May, 1943), by consulting all interests concerned and transmitting record of such consultations at the same time as their constitutional scheme for review by Examinatory Commission or Conference. This of course, would have avoided original and independent consultations with the various interests by the Commission or the Conference.

Part 3

9.   It is now necessary for me to refer to the actual events. On the 3rd February, 1944 the Governor sent to me the Ministers' printed scheme together with copy of a forwarding letter from the Vice-Chairman of the Board of Ministers in which he explained

(a) That the Ministers had in mind the possibility of the State Council modifying or altering their recommendations in regard to the form of legislature and representation (i.e., their scheme in regard to the two cardinal points was not one for acceptance or alternatively for rejection by the State Council but one for possible modification by it) and

(b) That the Minister for Home Affairs was not in agreement with the proposal regarding representation, the entirety of which question was a matter of considerable controversy and should, in his opinion, be settled by a Royal Commission.

10.   The Governor also sent me a copy of the letter whereby he had acknowledged receipt of Ministers' scheme and of the Vice-Chairman's forwarding letter. In his acknowledgement the Governor pointed out:—

(a) That the scheme was not a "complete constitutional scheme" as contemplated by paragraph (7) of the message in His Majesty's Government's Declaration of 26th May, 1943, because such crucial questions as the form of legislature, franchise and representation were left for consideration "otherwise than by the Commission or Conference required by the Declaration."

(b) That two passages in the letter "appeared to envisage the immediate (immediate) consideration of His Majesty's Government of the Ministers' proposal without previous examination by the stipulated Commission or Conference."

11. On the 10th February, the Governor sent me a copy of the Vice-Chairman's reply to his letter. In it the Vice-Chairman in regard to (a) tendered the reason for regarding the scheme "as complete as is necessary for any purpose reasonably contemplated by the Declaration," and in regard to (b) ended his letter with this paragraph:—

> "For these reasons immediate consideration of our proposal is necessary. This may be done in whatever manner (as suggested in the Declaration or otherwise) His Majesty's Government may consider best."

I must frankly confess my inability to reconcile this statement with the Ministers' present protest.

Part 4

12. In paragraph 3 of the latter, the Ministers note the omission of any reference to a Commission or Conference in a reply given by me to certain representations by the Ceylon Indian Congress. The inference which the Ministers apparently wish to be drawn from this omission is directly negatived by the answer, which I sent on the same date, to a representation relating to the eligibility of ex-convicts to sit in the Legislature under any new constitution. I replied that, as Mr. X "is no doubt aware from the statement made by His Majesty's Government at the end of last May, it is their intention that detailed proposals under any new scheme for constitution reform formulated by the Ministers should, in due course, be examined by a suitable Commission or Conference, and that I cannot anticipate such examination." I am informed by the Governor that my despatch directing this reply to Mr. X was circulated to the Board of Ministers, simultaneously with my despatch directing the reply to the Ceylon Indian Congress. The date of circulation was 1st February, 1944, and I do not see justification for a citation of the latter without the former. They were indeed immediately consecutive despatches.

13. In their paragraph 3, the Ministers also attach to a reply, sent to me to representations by Mr. Ponnambalam, a meaning contrary to what I consider its clear import. The Governor, moreover, informs me that, at a Conference with the Ministers on 14th March, he explained to them that my telegram could only mean that the minority need not be apprehensive because the contents of the Ministers' scheme would be examined by a Commission or Conference, which would ascertain their views, and that any Constitution that might emerge from His Majesty's Government's consideration of the Commission's or Conference's report would still require acceptance by 75 per cent. of the State Council. He sent copies of telegrams relating to Mr. Ponnambalam's representations and to my reply to the Vice-Chairman next day. Telegrams were also circulated to Members in the ordinary course.

13. On 22nd April, the Governor addressed to me an open despatch in which he wrote as follows:—

> "The main purpose of a Commission or Conference to examine the Ministers' Constitutional proposals will obviously be to invite and investigate criticism thereof."

The enclosures to this despatch related to the further representations made by Mr.

Ponnambalam. A copy of the despatch and its enclosures was circulated to the Board of Ministers on 2nd May.

Part 5
15. I am unable to reconcile the facts given in the two preceding paragraphs with representations in paragraph 5 of the Ministers' present message. When the Governor wrote his letter of 16th June to the Honourable Mr. D. S. Senanayake (not incidentally to the leader of the State Council), he was not aware of the form which His Majesty's Government's coming Declaration would take. The letter in fact explained this. If, however, he had been in a position to know that it would contain a reference to the consultation by the Commission with various interests including the Minority Community, I do not suppose that it would have occurred to him to apprise the Ministers again of what he had already told them. He has indeed reported to me that the representations, made to him orally by the Vice-Chairman on the morning of 5th July, caused him the greatest astonishment and surprise.

16. In conclusion, I greatly regret the Ministers' decision not to take any part in the deliberation of the Commission, except to discuss with it whether their scheme satisfies paragraphs (2) to (6) of His Majesty's Government's Declaration of 26th May, 1943. As the Governor explained to the Ministers by my direction on 14th March (and confirmed by letter to the Vice-Chairman the following day), the possible event (since fulfilled) of His Majesty's Government proceeding with a Commission or Conference, before the achievement of victory, would not mean that they would on that account be "in any way committed to accepting the Ministers' proposals as satisfying the first of the two conditions set out in paragraph 7 of His Majesty's Government's Declaration" (i.e., the requirements of paragraphs (2) to (6)). Any discussion, therefore, in regard to the subject mentioned in those paragraphs, that may take place between the Commission and the Ministers, will in no degree prejudice the ultimate decision of His Majesty's Government in relation to them.

17. In the vital interest of Ceylon's welfare, I earnestly invite a reconsideration of the Ministers' decision in order that the Commission may, in the execution of its onerous task, enjoy the fullest possible local co-operation. *Ends.*

211 CO 54/986/5/2, no 87   21 July 1944
[Reforms]: inward unnumbered telegram from Sir A Caldecott to Mr Stanley transmitting an extract from Mr Senanayake's budget speech to the State Council

My secret and personal telegram of 21st July.

I do not think I have given members of this House an opportunity of seeing how essential freedom in our trusteeship is if we are to make any effective progress in improving life in Ceylon. I do not think members realise how strong is the stranglehold of the Colonial Office when it comes to a question between the interests of the people of Ceylon and the preserves of vested interests. In this connection it would be better to get accustomed to a new term which recent correspondence on the reforms has introduced. The new description of vested interests is various interests rather an effective disguise. I have referred to the present position in regard to the Crown Lands Bill. This Bill was introduced in this House on 29th May, 1940. Its second reading was passed on 27th June, 1940. The committee stage of the Bill took nearly thirty months. Vested interests now termed various interests intervened at this stage. The Bill passed its third reading on 2nd December, 1942. His Excellency the Governor reserved his assent to the Bill but recommended to the Secretary of State that the Ordinance be tendered for his Majesty's assent. Vested interests rather than various interests now turned their attention to London. Sections of the Bill affecting those interests are still under discussion between the Colonial Office and the Government of Ceylon. In the meantime the whole land policy of Ceylon has to be implemented by means of circulars. Sir, isn't this a remarkable instance of how powerful are the voices of monied groups in the Chambers of our Rulers in London. A Commission of Inquiry. There is yet another outstanding example of similar treatment by the Colonial Office. Since 1935 the Board of Ministers have been trying to get the rate of interest reduced from 8 per cent. to 6 per cent. on the balance of the Widows' and Orphans' Pension Fund. We do not want this money we are forced to keep it and to pay 8 per cent. The reduction of this rate of interest was one of the Budget adjustments of several years ago. The Fund is bursting its bounds and pensions have been doubled and trebled. The investment return on this Fund is barely 3 per cent. but we have to find from general revenue an additional 5 per cent. on a sum of over Rs. 12,000,000. I was informed few days ago by the Financial Secretary that the Secretary of State has at last given way and that the details will be available to the Ministers on Monday next. Empire propagandists often describe the present constitution of Ceylon as a great experiment in freedom that is freedom of a type. I do hope that a Secretary of State for the Colonies does find the time at least to read the Budget proceedings of a not too unimportant part of the Colonial Empire. In that expectation may I suggest that one of the earliest responsibilities not only of himself but also of the Cabinet and of the House of Commons is to set up a Commission of Inquiry to investigate into the working methods of the Colonial Office. I submit that in this brave new world which is said to be round the corner so far as places like Ceylon go the blood that is being shed on the fields of Normandy and on the plains of Imphal would have been shed in vain unless the whole of the Colonial Office procedure is altered and reorganised. One indispensable requirement is the building of impenetrable walls through which vested interests cannot poison the mind of a Secretary of State against the people whom he has to protect. Another requirement is an accurate knowledge and proper understanding of the needs of the people. A knowledge and understanding which cannot be acquired only from the reports of those who know neither our language nor our customs, nor our people. Constitutional reforms. In introducing the Budget last year I informed the House that the Ministers would apply themselves at once to the very great responsibility and privilege of formulating a new constitution in accordance with the Ministers' statement on His Majesty's Government's Declaration of 1943. I added to quote my words the war is already entering a phase which gives us every reason to hope that the examination of this draft constitution could be proceeded with before the hour of final victory. Sir, in accordance with this settled procedure a draft constitutional scheme was submitted to the Secretary of State through His Excellency the Governor on 2nd February, 1944. As I had indicated to the House twelve months ago the Ministers asked for an immediate examination of their draft scheme. I was informed on the 16th of last month by His Excellency the Governor that the Secretary of State had agreed to the Ministers' request for an immediate examination of their proposals. In a statement issued by His Majesty's Government on the 5th of this month there appeared, however, a fundamental alteration of the 1943 Declaration which the Ministers were unable to accept. This alteration was made without any consultation with or even notice to the Ministers. The Ministers have therefore informed the Secretary of State that in the circumstances they have no alternative but to decline to take any part in the deliberations of the proposed Commission. The Ministers have asked permission to table in this House their communication dealing with this matter. The House will soon be aware of the full story. Once again our hopes have been rudely shattered. One would have thought that after Malaya, Burma, and India our Colonial Administration and its advisers would have learnt their lessons. No, sir, we are seeing again the same old stock in trade of half truths, excuses and broken pledges. The plan of campaign is still the same divide and rule. The whole proceeding would have been humorous were it not so dangerous. We have seen in the last few weeks how the witches cauldron has been heated and stirred up. I can see the chief actors quite clearly. I only propose to tell them this much now you are playing with explosives. Deepening gloom. Through this year Members of this House have shown their confidence in the Ministers in their acceptance of His Majesty's Government's Declaration and the procedure followed in drafting a constitution. The document when tabled by me will show clearly the Ministers present attitude and the reasons therefor. Sir, nobody regrets more than I the deepening gloom of all this. But I am not without hope. There are many in this House like myself who have had a long and close connection with the technique of Colonial administration. Sir, it is often for us a long and weary road. Life is a moving curve of flattery, optimism, misrepresenta- tion thinly veiled intimidation and pessimism. It is a great school of experience however. You get tough. After some time you do not get easily disheartened. Sir, the American Vice-President Wallace said recently that the coloured peoples of Asia were on the march. He said that America must ensure a free Asia with even erring Japan having her proper place in it. Sir, Ceylon is a blessed country. I cannot believe that whilst the rest of Asia, including Japan, is free, Ceylon's reward is to be national disunity, bondage and serfdom. No, sir, some day we shall get our due if not at the bar of English public opinion then at the bar of world opinion. Ceylon too will march on with the rest of Asia.

212   CO 54/986/5/2, no 90   25 July 1944
[Reforms]: outward unnumbered telegram (reply) from Mr Stanley to Sir A Caldecott on the proposed reply to ministers

Your secret and personal telegrams of 20th July.

I am glad to learn that you do not anticipate that Ministers are likely to publish their message without waiting my reply, but I am very grateful for the detailed draft reply to Ministers which you have sent me.[1]

2.   But on a close study of all the papers available to me here, I must let you know that I am not entirely satisfied that I have in fact a complete answer to Ministers'

---

[1] See 210.

protests. The protest is, as I understand it from paragraph 4 of your telegram No. 1274[2] in particular, not (repeat not) that a Commission is to be appointed to examine Ministers' proposals, but that Commission is to consult with "various interests including minority communities" over the whole field of the Ministers' scheme, whereas under terms of His Majesty's 1943 Declaration the field of examination by means of a Commission was expressly limited, and separate provision was made for minorities to be safeguarded by the requirement that acceptance of any constitutional scheme by His Majesty's Government would depend on the approving vote of three-quarters of the State Council.

3. It is my intention to wait your fast Air Mail despatch before deciding upon terms of reply to Ministers' message, and I shall particularly search in it for full exposition of facts on which I can rely to dispose of the apparent and important discrepancy which Ministers claim to see between His Majesty's Government's 1943 Declaration and His Majesty's Government's Statement of 5th July, 1944.

4. This is obviously a matter of importance since, if Ministers are right, it seems that within the terms of the 1943 Declaration locus of Commission in respect of consultation with various interests including minorities in Ceylon will have to be confined to reporting to His Majesty's Government as to:—

(i) whether the Ministers' scheme satisfactorily provides for His Majesty's Government's requirements under paragraph 5 of the 1943 Declaration, and
(ii) whether the Ministers' proposals are sufficiently formulated as a complete constitutional scheme, so that His Majesty's Government may be satisfied that condition of subsequent approval by three-quarters of the State Council will be based upon full understanding of whole scheme of reform to be finally adopted.

5. With reference to my telegram No. 852, Amending Order in Council is now prepared, and unless I hear from you to the contrary, it will be submitted to His Majesty in Council at a very early date.

---

[2] See 208.

213   CO 54/986/5/2, no 93A   27 July 1944
[Reforms]: inward unnumbered telegram (reply) from Sir A Caldecott to Mr Stanley on the proposed reply to ministers

Your secret and personal telegram of 25th July.[1] I am greatly disturbed by the terms of your paragraphs 2, 3 and 4 which seem to me to forbode disaster. Ministers' case is not (repeat not) that recent Declaration by His Majesty's Government is contradictory to 1943 Declaration but that it is contradictory to paragraph (1) of their interpretation thereof in their statement of 8th June, 1943 and that message authorized by your telegram No. 791 printed as document (5) in session paper 17 of 1943 was an unconditional acceptance by you of that interpretation.

2. As I have pointed out in my despatch of 13th July and my secret and personal telegram 20th July (corrupt group) such an acceptance would have abrogated

---

[1] See 212.

essential element of preamble to His Majesty's Government's Declaration which was reiteration of assurance given in 1941.

3. You will remember that by my secret and personal telegram of 6th July, 1943 I drafted a reply to the Ministers' interpretation which declined any degree of acceptance and if I had thought for a moment that your own reply to document (5) was meant as, or could be reasonably represented to be, such an unconditional acceptance of Ministers' interpretation as to rob minorities of assurance given in 1941 Declaration that they would be consulted in formative stage of any new constitution, I would have advised most strongly against making that reply. You stated therein, however, that practical effect of their interpretation could only be seen in detailed provisions of a new draft constitution and you only accorded a negative of essential irreconcilability.

4. The only way of reconciling Ministers' interpretation with your reply was for them to consult minorities and report their views to you when forwarding their proposals. This they have omitted to do and it is clear enough now that the Ministers intended paragraph 1 of their interpretation as a ramp for excluding minority consultation from formative stage of their scheme and are now representing your reply as acquiescence by you therein.

5. It will of course be realized that I cannot serve my remaining weeks here with honour or indeed retire with honour unless the Ministers, State Council, and the public are made aware of my own position as set out in my despatch and in my suggestions for a reply to the Ministers' protest. If, as now seems indicated in your telegram, a different view from mine is taken by you, an explanation of my position will still be necessary. On a review of all papers I have been unable to trace any divergence between our views and have always understood the intention of His Majesty's Government to be as expressed so clearly in paragraph 2 of your despatch No. 19, which was in my hands when I commented on the Ministers' proposals *vide* paragraphs 10 and 11 of my suggestions for reply to the Ministers' protest.

6. Reference your paragraph 5, amending Order-in-Council should not (repeat not) be proceeded with before reply to Ministers' protest is made public and accompanied by unequivocal statement that Commission is coming. Senanayake's Budget outburst illustrates what would be and would in any case have been declaimed from every election platform all over the island in the event of general election this year or next and I cannot reconcile such prospect with the interest of South East Asia Command or war effort generally.

7. With reference to your secret and personal telegram (1) of 25th July, Senanayake did not get your communication until the morning after his Budget speech.[2] In his recent mood, speech would undoubtedly have been even worse if he had received it before. He is now on tour and I have no opportunity of talking to him on this subject but in any case I do not advise any approach by me until your reply to Ministers' protest has been settled.

8. In conclusion notice of the following motion has been given in State Council by private member Javasuriya [sic][3] who is usually the mouthpiece of Bandaranaike.

Begins. That this Council is of opinion that Ministers should immediately prepare a draft constitution for Ceylon in consultation with any sections of people of this country that may be necessary and without reference to the 1943 Declaration of the

---

[2] See 211.

[3] This was A P Jayasuriya.

British Government and bring it before the State Council for consideration. *Ends.*

This does not portend any demand for early dissolution even if State Council should not like whatever reply is sent to ministerial protests. Motion is indeed interesting as reflecting necessity for consultation with sections of people before any scheme is launched.

214   CO 54/986/5/2, no 96   29 July 1944
[Reforms]: inward unnumbered telegram from Sir A Caldecott to Mr Stanley on the reply to ministers and the functions of a commission

Reforms.

Assume that you have now received my secret despatch of 13th July of which duplicate went by airmail on 17th July. May I suggest that, if possible, reply be sent to the Ministers' protest before the State Council meets 8th August.

2. Whatever form reply may take I think it should conclude with a summary of Commission's functions bringing out the following points:—

(a) Commission advises His Majesty's Government, who are free to accept or reject the advice tendered: it is in no sense a tribunal making award which binds anyone,

(b) Its main purpose is to invite and investigate criticism of the Ministers' proposals, and is to advise His Majesty's Government thereon: it is not to examine and investigate the problem of constitutional reform *de novo*,

(c) If the Ministers' proposals had constituted a complete and detailed scheme, the work of the Commission would have been reduced to the minimum, and would have held out prospect of greatest and most speedy measure of success, and there is still time for the Ministers to remedy this defect. If they do not do so the Commission will, in some degree, be compelled to go outside (b).

3. Such a summary would take the place of paragraph 16 of the draft reply submitted by my telegram of 20th July[1] and would form suitable preface to appeal for reconsideration suggested by paragraph 17.

---

[1] See 210.

215   CO 54/986/5/2, no 104   [6 Aug 1944]
[Reforms]: text of Mr Stanley's reply to ministers

I have studied the Ministers' message as telegraphed by the Governor on July 11th.[1] I would invite the Ministers' attention to the correspondence published in Sessional Papers XIII and XVII of 1943. In particular I would refer to numbers 5, 6(a) and 9 of the first Sessional Paper above referred to and to the Declaration made by His Majesty's Government in 1941 that "before taking decisions upon present proposals for Reforms concerning which there has been so little unanimity, but which are of such importance to the well being of Ceylon, His Majesty's Government would desire

---

[1] See 208 (for subsequent cross references, see 209).

that the position should be further examined and made the subject of further consultation by means of a Commission or Conference."

2. That Declaration was specifically repeated in the Declaration made by His Majesty's Government in May 1943 which was expressly designed to give greater precision to the 1941 Statement "with the object of removing any doubts regarding His Majesty's Government's intentions". The Ministers cannot justifiably claim that a Declaration made for such a clearly stated purpose could abrogate a cardinal point of the previous Statement.

3. I am unable to accept the argument contained in paragraph 2 of the Ministers' message for reasons that will be apparent to any one who reads the whole of Document No.5 in Sessional Paper XVII of 1943 and in particular the second, third and fourth sentences thereof.

4. It is now necessary for me to refer to actual events. On the 3rd February, 1944, the Governor sent to me the Ministers' printed scheme together with the copy of a forwarding letter from the Vice Chairman of the Board of Ministers in which he explained (a) that the Ministers had in mind the possibility of the State Council modifying or altering their recommendations in regard to the form of the legislature and representation (i.e. their scheme in regard to two cardinal points was not one for acceptance or alternatively for rejection by the State Council but one for possible modification by it) and (b) that the Minister for Home Affairs was not in agreement with the proposals regarding representation, the entirety of which question was a matter of considerable controversy and should in his opinion be settled by a Royal Commission.

5. The Governor also sent me a copy of the letter whereby he had acknowledged receipt of the Ministers' Scheme and of the Vice Chairman's forwarding letter. In his acknowledgement the Governor pointed out:—

(a) that the Scheme was not a "complete constitutional scheme" as contemplated by paragraph (7) of the Message in His Majesty's Government's Declaration of 26th May, 1943, because such crucial questions as the form of legislature, franchise and representation were left for consideration "otherwise than by the Commission or Conference required by the Declaration".

(b) that two passages in the letter "appeared to envisage the immediate consideration by His Majesty's Government of the Ministers' proposals without previous examination by the stipulated Commission or Conference".

6. On the 10th February the Governor sent me a copy of the Vice Chairman's reply to his letter. In it the Vice Chairman in regard to (a) tendered reasons for regarding the Scheme "as complete as is necessary for any purpose reasonably contemplated by the Declaration", and in regard to (b) ended his letter with this paragraph:—

"For these reasons the immediate consideration of our proposals is necessary. This may be done in whatever manner (as suggested in the Declaration or otherwise) His Majesty's Government may consider to be best."

I must frankly confess my inability to reconcile this statement with the Ministers' present message.

7. In paragraph 3 of the latter the Ministers note the omission of any reference to a Commission or Conference in a reply given by me to certain representations by the

Ceylon Indian Congress. The inference which the Ministers apparently wish to be drawn from this omission is directly negatived by the answer which I sent on the same date to a representation relating to the eligibility of ex-convicts to sit in the legislature under any new Constitution. I replied that, as Mr. X "is no doubt aware from the statement made by His Majesty's Government at the end of last May, it is their intention that the detailed proposals under any new Scheme for Constitutional reform formulated by Ministers should in due course be examined by a suitable Commission or Conference, and that I cannot anticipate such examination". I am informed by the Governor that my despatch directing this reply to Mr. X was circulated to the Board of Ministers simultaneously with my despatch directing the reply to the Ceylon Indian Congress. The date of circulation was 1st February, 1944, and I do not see the justification for a citation of the latter without the former. They were indeed immediately consecutive despatches.

8. In their paragraph 3 the Ministers also attach to a reply sent by me to representations by Mr. Ponnambalam a meaning contrary to what I consider its clear import. The Governor moreover informs me that at a Conference with the Ministers on 14th March he read to the Ministers both Mr. Ponnambalam's telegram and my reply, explaining that they could only mean that the minorities need not be apprehensive because the contents of the Ministers' Scheme would be examined by a Commission or Conference which would ascertain their views and that any Constitution that might emerge from His Majesty's Government's consideration of the Commission's or Conference's Report would still require acceptance by 75% of the State Council. He sent copies of the telegrams relating to Mr. Ponnambalam's representations and to my reply to the Vice Chairman next day. The telegrams were also circulated to the Ministers in the ordinary course.

9. On the 22nd April the Governor addressed to me an open despatch in which he wrote as follows:—

> "the main purpose of a Commission or Conference to examine the Ministers' constitutional proposals will obviously be to invite and investigate criticisms thereof".

The enclosures to this despatch related to further representations by Mr. Ponnambalam. A copy of the despatch and its enclosures was circulated to the Board of Ministers on the 2nd May.

10. If the Ministers did not accept that interpretation of the Commission's functions or found any divergence between it and the 1943 Declaration by His Majesty's Government I should have expected them to bring the matter to the immediate notice of His Majesty's Government. On the contrary they made no such intimation to me until their present message. I cannot too strongly emphasize that at no time has His Majesty's Government contemplated nor indeed would His Majesty's Government contemplate taking decisions on matters of such constitutional importance as those now under consideration without a full knowledge of the opinion of the various interests concerned.

11. In conclusion the purpose of His Majesty's Government is that the Commission should advise them on the Ministers' proposals and not that it should examine and investigate the problem of Constitutional reforms de novo. For the proper fulfilment of this function it is necessary that the Commission should be in a position to study all aspects of the Ministers' proposals and to elicit further information from

them on any part of the proposals which may appear insufficiently complete and detailed. The examination of the Ministers' Scheme will include examination of any criticisms of it by various interests in the Island which are concerned. The Commission will then tender its advice to His Majesty's Government and, in the light of such advice and of all other relevant factors, His Majesty's Government will then reach their conclusions. The Ministers have indeed made a special and valuable contribution in that, despite the stress and pre-occupations of war time, they have succeeded in formulating a scheme for constitutional reform as they were invited to do. I feel that I can fairly ask the Ministers to give their attitude towards the work of Commission further consideration.

12.   In acceding to the Ministers' request that their message be published I also authorise the publication of this reply. I consider also that the need for a full and proper understanding of the position requires the publication of all the correspondence referred to in the Ministers' message and in this reply and I trust that they will concur in this course.

216   CO 54/986/5/2, no 113   18 Aug 1944
[Reforms]: inward unnumbered telegram from Sir A Caldecott to Mr Stanley transmitting the text of a letter from ministers contesting the secretary of state's reply

Reform. I have received, this morning, the following letter from Ministers, accompanied by the request that it be immediately telegraphed to you. My comments will follow when I have had time for careful consideration of it.

Letter begins. The Ministers have studied with care the reply of the Secretary of State enclosed with Your Excellency's letter S.1/11 of the 6th August, 1944.[1] They regret to find that the Secretary of State for the Colonies's interpretation of Declaration of 1943 is quite inconsistent with the basis on which they undertook to prepare a draft constitution. They gave to the Declaration of 1943 what still appears to them to be the only reasonable meaning. That meaning they expressed in statement made by the Leader of the State Council on the 8th June, 1943. "It (the Declaration of 1943) is, in essence, an undertaking that if the Board can produce a constitution which, in the opinion of a Commission or a Conference, satisfies the conditions set out in paragraphs (2) to (6) thereof, and if that constitution is subsequently accepted by three-quarters of all members of the State Council excluding officers of the State and the Speaker, His Majesty in Council will put that constitution into operation." That statement was agreed upon at a meeting of the Board of Ministers over which the Chief Secretary presided and at which other officers of State were present. Though officers of State took an active part in discussion of (draft) statement, no suggestion was made by them that any other interpretation was possible than that given by Ministers on the question of the precise procedure intended to be followed in dealing with constitutional proposals formulated by Ministers. Before, however, undertaking to draft a constitution in

---

[1] See 215.

terms of the Declaration of 1943, the Ministers expressly enquired of the Secretary of State whether interpretation placed on the Declaration by them in their statement of 8th June, 1943, was in accord with the principles of that Declaration and the Secretary of State assured them that he had not found in their statement anything that must be regarded as essentially irreconcilable with conditions contained in the Declaration. The Ministers have, all along, acted on that interpretation and they did not at any stage either contemplate or indicate in any manner even a modification of that interpretation. In fact, in November, 1943, the Leader of the State Council (Vice Chairman of the Board of Ministers) made it clear in replying to a question asked him in the State Council, that procedure being followed was that indicated in their statement of the 8th June, 1943.

2. It would now transpire that, even on preliminary question of procedure, the Secretary of State disagrees fundamentally from views of Ministers as clearly expressed in their statement of the 8th June, 1943. The Ministers would have expected that the Secretary of State, as soon as he realised that there was a divergence of opinion on such an important matter, would at least have brought it directly to the notice of the Ministers who would then have been in a position to make representations on it before any definite action was taken by the Secretary of State contrary to the Ministers' interpretation. It is, perhaps, significant that the Secretary of State does not in his last reply refer to the Ministers' interpretation of the declaration of 1943, which interpretation was further emphasized in their message of 11th July, 1944.

3. The Ministers wish again to make their position perfectly clear. In their statement of 8th June, 1943, they stated that Declaration of 1943 did not promise everything for which they have asked and that they did not like the qualification(s) in it. They were, nevertheless, prepared to accept the offer in the Declaration if the Secretary of State agreed that their interpretation of it was in accord with the principles of that Declaration. One of the chief points in that interpretation and one chief reason that led them to that decision was the recognition by His Majesty's Government that this country should not be invited merely to accept a constitution framed by His Majesty's Government, but that ministers, on behalf of the people, should prepare a constitutional scheme. His Majesty's Government was only concerned with the constitution in so far as it embodied provisions referred to in paragraphs (2) to (6) of the Declaration of 1943. The difficult and unusual requirement that the Ministers' scheme should subsequently obtain the approval of three-quarters of the members of the State Council could only mean that, having entrusted to the Ministers the task of preparing a constitution, His Majesty's Government considered the requirement as sufficient proof that the Ministers' scheme was generally acceptable to the country.

4. The decision of His Majesty's Government to appoint a commission to carry out investigations with terms of reference now proposed radically changes the situation. It is quite possible that the constitution to be placed before the State Council will not be the Ministers' proposals (subject only to the Secretary of State being satisfied that paragraphs (2) to (6) of the Declaration have been complied with) but an entirely different scheme. In other words, it will not be a constitution prepared by the Ministers but a constitution acceptable to His Majesty's Government, not only with reference to provisions in paragraphs (2) to (6) of the Declaration, but with reference to every detail of it.

5. As the basis on which the Ministers agreed to frame, and did frame, their constitutional scheme has now been radically changed by the Secretary of State, the Ministers are obliged to withdraw their scheme, which they do with regret.

6. The Ministers desire at the same time that this letter and the documents referred to in Your Excellency's letter of 6th August, 1944, but excluding the constitutional scheme forwarded with their letter of 2nd February, 1944 should be published as a Sessional Paper. Letter follows. *Ends.*

217 CO 54/986/5/2, no 117   19 Aug 1944

[Reforms]: inward unnumbered telegram from Sir A Caldecott to Mr Stanley transmitting the draft of a reply to the ministers' letter

Reforms.

I think it will be most convenient to tender my comments on the Ministers' latest message in the form of the following draft reply for your consideration.

Draft Begins. 1. I have read the Ministers' communication of 16th August[1] with the same careful attention that I gave to their previous message of 11th July.

2. With regard to its first paragraph, I have already given the reasons for my inability to accept the Ministers' interpretation of the Declaration of 1943 in any sense abrogative of the essential purpose of that Declaration, which was to give greater precision to the previous Declaration of 1941.

3. I again invite reference to the second, third and fourth sentences of Document 5 in Session Paper XVII of 1943. There might have emerged nothing irreconcilable between the Ministers' interpretation and the purpose of the Declarations of 1941 and 1943, if the Ministers had obtained and recorded the views of all interests concerned and appended them to their scheme.

4. With reference to paragraph 2, the Governor by his letter of 3rd February, 1944, drew immediate attention to two points on which the Ministers appeared to contemplate a radical departure from the procedure stipulated by the Declaration of 1943. I felt it superfluous to endorse the Governor's views after reading the passage in the Vice-Chairman's answer quoted in paragraph 6 of my reply to the Ministers' message of 11th July.

5. In regard to paragraph 3, the invitation extended to the Ministers in paragraph 7 of the 1943 Declaration was addressed to them only in their capacity under the existing constitution. The fact that they have been unable to tender a unanimous recommendation on so basic a matter as the representation illustrates the degree to which a reference to them as possessing a "capacity as representatives of the people" would have been unjustified. It also clearly confirms the necessity for the Commission or Conference required by the 1941 and 1943 Declarations.

6. I note with regret that the scheme put forward by the Ministers is now withdrawn by them and that, at their request, it will not be published before the arrival of the Commission. I cannot, however, keep the Commission in ignorance of the contents of the scheme, but will inform them that it no longer possesses ministerial authority or support of the draft. *Ends.*

---

[1] See 216 where the date is recorded as 18 Aug.

I have not thought it necessary or desirable to refer to the insinuation that Officers of State were privy to the Ministers' interpretation of the 1943 Declaration. As you are aware, Officers of State have no vote in the Board and the question of agreement or disagreement was never put to them nor could they have answered if it had been without prior reference through me to you.

I will proceed with the preparation of Session Paper, which will, of course, include the Ministers' latest message and whatever reply you may decide to send.

218   CO 54/986/5/2, no 119   23 Aug 1944

[Reforms]: outward unnumbered telegram (reply) from Mr Stanley to Sir A Caldecott on the proposed reply to ministers

Thank you for your telegram secret and personal (2) of 19th August.[1]

2. I note with regret that Ministers now withdraw their scheme, but in view of the decision taken and announced by His Majesty's Government on the strength of the communication to me of the scheme by Ministers, I could not agree that proposed publication of messages and other relevant documents could exclude text of scheme. It seems to me indeed to be necessary to include that document in order that His Majesty's Government's concern to consult all interests affected may be appreciated by public. It would of course be made clear that Ministers no longer wish to sponsor that scheme.

3. As regards question of reply to Ministers' message of 18th August, I accept your advice if you feel that it is desirable for me to send some further reasoned reply but in that case I should prefer to delete paragraph 5 from your draft as it seems to me perhaps unnecessarily provocative. Final paragraph also will need reconsideration in light of paragraph 4 of this telegram in respect of Commission.

4. Keeping our main immediate purpose always in view, viz., to avoid at this juncture serious political trouble in Ceylon detrimental to military operations in the Far East, it is important to study means of helping Ministers to extricate themselves from their present position without of course yielding any major point in our own case. I should much like to know what plan they have in mind now that they have thrown overboard their scheme and presumably with it their request for its examination by His Majesty's Government. It remains the view of His Majesty's Government that the framing of proposals for constitutional reform should properly be the task of statesmanship in Ceylon and our aim should be to restore effort in that direction.

5. Important immediate question is whether in present situation we are to proceed with appointment of Commission to visit Ceylon this winter. You and Commander-in-Chief consider it important that the Commission should proceed as planned. But purpose of Commission as stated in His Majesty's Government's Declarations in 1943 and July 1944 was examination of scheme formulated by Ministers. Without prejudice to eventual decision as to Commission I should like to have your views as to what would be function of Commission if Ministers continue to disown their scheme, and whether our main purpose mentioned above would be likely to be damaged if Commission had non-co-operative reception in Ceylon.

---

[1] See 217.

6. There remains also need for early decision regarding deferment of general elections—see paragraph 6 of your secret and personal telegram of 27th July,[2] and your secret and personal telegram of 21st August.

7. In view of above considerations I should now like to have considered advice of yourself and Commander-in-Chief with appreciation of political situation which may be expected to develop as affecting our main present purpose in the Island.

---

[2] See 213.

---

219 CO 54/986/5/2, no 121   26 Aug 1944

[Reforms]: inward unnumbered telegram (reply) from Sir A Caldecott to Mr Stanley on the proposed reply to ministers

Reforms. Your secret and personal (1) telegram of 23rd August,[1] paragraphs 4 and 5. Political position and outlook may be shortly but adequately summarized as follows:—

(i) Ministers as usual lack unity and cohesion, and there is little prospect of further constructive effort by them jointly or on their own initiative.

(ii) On the other hand anticipation of Commission has given rise to growing demand for inter-sectional consultations in the hope of evolving some agreed suggestions to place before it. In such consultations Ministers may individually if not collectively take part.

(iii) If the Commission were now cancelled or postponed all sections including Ministers would proclaim it as breach of undertaking, and the whole Island become disaffected with disastrous effect on the war effort.

2. Your paragraph 2, Ministers will sooner or later be forced into publication of their scheme by public opinion, and in our judgment it would be unwise to make publication of rest of correspondence conditional on its inclusion. We recommend however, substitution of the following for paragraph 6 of draft reply submitted by my telegram of the 19th August.[2]

Begins. I note with regret that the scheme put forward by Ministers is now withdrawn by them. I cannot however consistently with recent statements of His Majesty's Government withhold it from the Commission, nor preclude the Commission from consulting various interests regarding it, although it will be made clear it no longer has Ministerial endorsement. Its exclusion from correspondence which Ministers are agreed to publish causes me great disappointment because, as stated in my reply to Minister's message of 11th July, I regard its formulation as having been a special and valuable contribution by them, which could be made the base of pregnant consultations between various interests in anticipation of the Commission's arrival. *Ends.*

3. Your paragraph 3.

If no reference at all is made to claim by the Ministers to represent the people of Ceylon, they will regard this claim as admitted. We recommend therefore substitution of the following paragraph for paragraph 5 in my previous telegram.

---

[1] See 218.   [2] See 217.

Begins. With reference to paragraph 3, the invitation extended to Ministers in paragraph 7 of 1943 Declaration was addressed to them in their capacity within the present constitution, whereunder only the State Council can be said to represent the people. Whatever the degree or nature of the Ministers' representative capacity, the opinion of the only members of a minority of the community among them, that the entire question of representation requires settlement by a Royal Commission, could not have been justifiably ignored. *Ends.*

4. We strongly urge that reply suggested in my secret and personal (2) telegram of 19th August with the above two amendments should be given at the earliest possible date, and that sessional paper be issued immediately thereafter containing documents listed in my secret and personal (1) telegram of 19th August minus Ministers' scheme (omission of which will be explained by footnote referring to paragraph 6 of their message of 18th August) plus that message and your reply thereto.

5. We also recommend that as proposed in paragraph 6 of my telegram of 27th July[3] amending Order in Council to proposed elections be enacted as soon as sessional paper mentioned in previous paragraph has issued.

6. Above paragraphs contain joint recommendations of Commander-in-Chief and myself. As the Chief Secretary is in continuous contact with the Ministers and the State Council, I asked him for independent report in regard to the points raised in paragraphs 4 and 5 of your telegram. His report, which corroborates our own summary, follows in my immediately following telegram.[4]

---

[3] See 213.   [4] Not printed.

---

220   CO 54/986/5/2, no 123   28 Aug 1944
[Reforms]: outward telegram (reply) from Mr Stanley to Sir A Caldecott on the proposed reply to ministers

Very much obliged for your two secret and personal telegrams of 26th August.[1]

1. I of course accept advice of Commander-in-Chief and yourself that I should send reply in sufficient detail to Ministers' message and I have carefully reconsidered your suggested draft as now revised. Terms of reply which I should prefer to send to them, unless Commander-in-Chief and yourself see any strong objection, are not identical with your draft as you will see from my immediately following secret telegram No. 1035. The chief points of difference are:—

(a) Omission of second sentence in your paragraph 3.
(b) Redraft of paragraph 5. On latter point I feel that your draft may be open to misrepresentation as effort on my part to cause jealousy between Board of Ministers and State Council and also exacerbate difference between Mahadeva and rest of Ministers.

2. I fully appreciate your valuable advice about Commission and I agree that we should maintain our purpose in this respect. I hope to be able shortly to telegraph about its composition, and, in the meantime, I should be glad to receive your views

---

[1] See 219.

as to suitable terms of reference. Lord Soulbury has already consented to act as Chairman.

3. I agree to publication of Sessional Paper as proposed in paragraph 4 of your secret and personal telegram (1) of 26th August.

4. I also agree that amending Order in Council to postpone elections should be submitted for His Majesty's approval as soon after publication of Sessional Paper as possible.

5. I note particularly in Chief Secretary's report that there has been influential demand made by speakers in State Council in favour of formulation of agreed constitutional scheme in anticipation of Commission's arrival, and I hope that Ministers may give early and favourable consideration to this course.

221 CO 54/986/5/2, no 124   [28 Aug 1944]
[Reforms]: final text of Mr Stanley's reply to ministers

I have read the Ministers' communication of August 18th[1] with the same careful attention that I gave to their prevous message of July 11th.

2. With regard to its first paragraph I have already given reasons for my inability to accept the Ministers' interpretation of the Declaration of 1943 in any sense abrogative of the essential purpose of that Declaration which was to give greater precision to the previous Declaration of 1941.

3. With reference to paragraph 2 the Governor in his letter of February 3rd 1944 to the Vice-Chairman of the Board of Ministers drew immediate attention to two points on which the Ministers appeared to contemplate a radical departure from the procedure stipulated by the Declaration of 1943. I felt it superfluous to endorse the Governor's view after reading that passage in the Vice-Chairman's answer quoted in paragraph 6 of my reply to the Ministers message of July 11th.

4. With reference to paragraph 3 the invitation extended to the Ministers in paragraph 7 of the 1943 Declaration was addressed to them in their capacity within the present constitution, and it is fair for me to point out that on the important question of representation the Minister for Home Affairs recorded his dissent from the Ministers' Scheme.

5. I note with regret that the Scheme put forward by the Ministers is now withdrawn by them. I cannot however consistently with the recent statement of His Majesty's Government withhold it from the Commission nor preclude the Commission from consulting various interests regarding it, although it will be made clear that it no longer has Ministerial endorsement. Its exclusion from the correspondence which the Ministers are agreed to publish causes me great disappointment because, as stated in my reply to Ministers' message of July 11th, I regard its formulation as having been a special and valuable contribution by them which could be made the basis of fruitful consultations between various interests in anticipation of the Commission's arrival.

---

[1] See 216.

222   WO 203/5412   30 Aug 1944

[Reforms]: letter from Admiral Layton to Admiral Mountbatten on the appointment of the Soulbury Commission

In continuance of my letter of 27th July on the subject of the Constitutional Reform question in Ceylon, I am now sending for your information a copy of

1. Secretary of State's reply to the Ministers' message of 11th July 1944.[1]
2. A further message from the Ministers dated 18th August 1944.[2]
3. The Secretary of State's further reply to 2.[3]

These three documents will be published later this week together with all the other papers, except the Ministers' draft scheme. The replies of the Secretary of State were drafted in consultation with the Governor and myself. I also enclose for your personal information a copy of a telegram giving a report by the Chief Secretary on the political situation;[4] this is of course 'Secret' and will remain so. The references are to a message from the Secretary of State which you have not seen, but they do not affect the general sense at all.

We have since been assured that the Commission will definitely come out, and that Lord Soulbury will be its Chairman. It seems unlikely that the Ministers can maintain their proposal to boycott it, in face of the general interest displayed by everyone else, and you will see from the Chief Secretary's report that Senanayake's attitude has not commanded any support in the Budget Debate.

The Commission will presumably have to start by studying the Ministers' scheme, which accordingly will have to be published some time between now and then. It is a very faulty and incomplete document (which is possibly why the Ministers have hurriedly abandoned it as soon as it looked like seeing the light of day), but it is the only one in the field unless the State Council manage to produce another.

Our general expectation therefore is that the Commission will successfully absorb the political energies of the country and thus avoid the necessity for a general election.

---

[1] See 215.   [2] See 216.   [3] See 221.   [4] Not printed.

223   CO 54/986/7, no 35   1 Sept 1944

[Tamils]: letter from S Ponniah to Mr Stanley emphasising the differences between 'Tamil Ceylon and the rest of Ceylon'

With reference to the future political reforms to be granted to Ceylon, I beg to state that the Tamil speaking part of Ceylon (re: comparison of other minor communities with the Tamils) is a well defined territory where Tamil only is spoken. Besides, it had its own history, civilization, politics and Kingdom for roughly about 1,500 years or perhaps more. It had been and is different from the rest of all Ceylon by history, race, language, creed, culture, customs and manners, politics, civilization and the ideals of life.

---

[1] Ponniah was a Tamil doctor from South Arcot in southern India.

Tamil Ceylon is a unit by itself. If Tamil Ceylon with Jaffna as centre is created a separate political unit by the World Protecting British Nation, the story will be different. Jaffna will play the part of a bond of union between Mother India and Daughter Lanka (Ceylon) and of a buffer political unit medium between these two countries for the happy betterment of their mutual feelings and their economic, political and cultural progress. The best of understanding has still to be reached between these two countries and it is essential and vital that it should be reached soon as attested by war time troubles.

Some politicians will try to plaster over the differences between Tamil Ceylon and the rest of Ceylon but it is extremely difficult to make the two ends meet. The promises of these politicians are with selfish motives, short-lived and ideologic. They are ambitious and power-loving; they want to satisfy their feelings of supremacy and to bring all Ceylon under one umbrella. If the ideas and ideals of these politicians are carried through, the Tamil people of Ceylon will be reduced to the position of ryots and serfs. Almost all the coveted high posts will be occupied by the major community as was the beginning [sic] seen during the past decade or two. All the public money will be spent to better their own lands and people. The Tamils will suffer economically and they will deteriorate and degenerate mentally and morally. The Tamil language and culture will slowly disappear, the beginning of which is seen in the Ceylon University. Whereas in India they are Tamilising sciences and are beginning to teach Mathematics and Sciences in Tamil in the schools and colleges. Incidentally I may add a Jaffna University has to come into being sooner or later.

During the present war myself and a good part of the Tamil people who share my views had our mouths shut loyally. That being so, I beg to request your honour to give us a period of two years after the signing of peace and grant Ceylon's fate deciding reforms after that period. To grant reforms on war time political activity is not fair. It is not fair to base these all important reforms on the recommendations of a Commission that comes in a hurry from a distant part of the globe perhaps as first visitors to the island. To base reforms on memorials, deputations, audiences with the highest authorities in Ceylon and London and by other general methods, is more reliable and fair.

I request your honour not to commit us irretrievably into the hands of any community by hurried measures. I may add that the difference between Tamil Ceylon and the rest of Ceylon is greater than that between Spain and Portugal or Norway and Sweden or Holland and Belgium or Equdor [sic] and Brazil or Ulster and the rest of Ireland.

224   CO 54/986/5/3, no 131   1 Sept 1944

[Reforms]: inward telegram from Sir A Caldecott to Mr Stanley on the terms of reference for the Soulbury Commission

Your secret and personal telegram of 28th August.[1] Paragraph 2.

Recommend that terms of reference should:—

(a) enable the Commission to examine not only Ministers' recently withdrawn

---

[1] See 220.

proposals, but also any agreed scheme which may evolve between now and their arrival,

(b) preclude examination of any scheme which is not designed to implement His Majesty's Government's Declaration of 28th May, 1943,

(c) entitle the Commission to fill in gaps in any proposals submitted to them, as it is unlikely that any local scheme will be found comprehensive or sufficiently detailed. Wording on the following lines would appear to meet this threefold requirement.

Begins. To visit Ceylon in order to examine and invite criticism of any proposals for reform in the Island which have the object of giving effect to the Declaration of His Majesty's Government on that subject dated 26th May, 1943, and to advise on all measures necessary to obtain (? attain intended) that object.[2] *Ends.*

---

[2] Stanley replied on 4 Sept: 'I agree generally with (a), (b) and (c) but as Ministers' present decision is to disown their scheme I think terms should also enable Commission to consider any other schemes in pursuance of His Majesty's Government's 1943 Declaration which may be available for their consideration.

2. I also feel that I should adhere to the assurance in His Majesty's Government's 1944 Statement that Commission's visit should provide full opportunity for consultation with various interests concerned including minorities. I have therefore redrafted suggested terms of reference as follows and should be glad to know whether you and Commander-in-Chief concur.

Begins. (1) To examine any proposals for constitutional reform in Ceylon made in pursuance of His Majesty's Government's Declaration of the 26th May, 1943;

(2) To visit Ceylon in order to consult with the Governor, the Board of Ministers and representatives of the various interests in the Island (including the minority communities) concerned with the subject of constitutional reform, with a view to making a Report to His Majesty's Government on all measures necessary to attain the object stated in their Declaration of the 26th May, 1943. *Ends.*

3. Neither above terms of reference nor those suggested by yourself contain specific provisions for consultation with Commander-in-Chief or other Service authorities in Ceylon. Do you and Commander-in-Chief consider such provision to be necessary? If so please suggest suitable additional words' (CO 54/986/5/3, no 132).

---

225   CO 54/986/5/3, no 136   8 Sept 1944

[Reforms]: inward unnumbered telegram (reply) from Sir A Caldecott to Mr Stanley on the terms of reference for the Soulbury Commission

Your secret and personal telegram of the 4th September.[1]

As regards paragraph (1) of your alternative draft it would seem that only the Ministers' scheme could with literal accuracy be said to be "in pursuance of" His Majesty's Government's Declaration, and that was why our draft provided for the examination of any proposals which have the object of giving effect to the Declaration of His Majesty's Government. As regards paragraph (2) mention of Governor and Board of Ministers would appear unnecessary, while mention of the latter would enable Congress politicians to force the Ministers into announcement of a boycott, thus entailing subsequent amendment of the terms of the Commission.

For the above reasons the Commander-in-Chief and I advise the adoption of the draft submitted by my previous telegram (which was designed to meet important

---

[1] See 224, note 2.

point mentioned in your telegram), but with the substitution of the following for the last 18 words thereof.

Begins. dated 26th May, 1943, and, after consultation with various interests in the island, including minor communities concerned with the subject of constitutional reform, to advise on all measures necessary to attain that object. *Ends.*

This substitute passage will emphasize the essential consultative function of the Commission, while mention of invitation of criticism, which is essential antecedent to consultation, will remain as at the beginning of my draft. We do not think the terms of reference should contain reference to Commander-in-Chief or other Service authorities.

Grateful if terms might be referred to us in final draft before receiving your approval.

226 CO 54/986/5/3, no 138   12 Sept 1944
[Reforms]: inward unnumbered telegram from Sir A Caldecott to Mr Stanley on ministerial intentions to table their constitutional scheme in the State Council

I have just received letter from Senanayake stating that Ministers will table in the State Council to-day their constitutional scheme, together with a long explanatory memorandum dated 11th September. This action of theirs is in my judgment to be welcomed, though they might have given me longer notice.

2.   Political events since I came to Nuwara Eliya a week ago have moved rapidly, and with some promise of tangible results. On 7th September Bandaranaike gave a dinner to members of the State Council, at which 44 members were present, who afterwards formed themselves into a conference for the purpose of drawing up united demand for political reform. Senanayake and Kotalawala were not present. After discussion they set up Committee of 26 members to frame a constitutional scheme. Committee comprises 5 Ministers excluding the two just mentioned, 6 Lowland Sinhalese, 3 Kandyans, 4 Ceylon Tamils, 3 Muslims, 2 Indian Tamils, 2 unofficial British, 1 Burgher. The conference instructed this Committee to proceed without delay and to report to the conference by the end of this month. Committee agreed to have its first meeting this evening, 12th September. I am indebted to the Chief Secretary for all the information contained in this paragraph, as no communication on the subject has been addressed to me by Bandaranaike or anybody else.

3.   It is too early to assess the probable results of this movement, but so far there seems no prospect of the Commission being opposed, much less boycotted. Senanayake has clearly lost ground to Bandaranaike, and has recently shown neither restraint nor leadership.

227   CO 54/986/5/3, no 151   18 Sept 1944

[Reforms]: outward unnumbered telegram from Mr Stanley to Sir A Caldecott on the terms of reference for the Soulbury Commission

Your secret and personal telegram of 15th September.

I appreciate the special advantages of an announcement of the kind mentioned in paragraph 2. of your telegram. As, however, I have not yet been able to complete membership of Commission apart from Lord Soulbury as Chairman, announcement I could make at this moment would be on the following lines.

Begins. His Majesty's Government have already announced their decision to send a Commission to visit Ceylon towards the end of the year for consultation on the question of constitutional reform. Lord Soulbury has accepted my invitation to be Chairman of the Commission whose terms of reference will be as follows (terms as now agreed with you will then be quoted). It is expected that the membership of the Commission will be completed and announced shortly. *Ends.*

Please telegraph with the least possible delay whether you have any amendment[1] to suggest to the above announcement which I hope to release for publication in the morning papers of Thursday, 21st September.[2]

---

[1] Caldecott in a tel of 19 Sept had 'only one small amendment to suggest in the proposed announcement, i.e. towards the end of the first sentence, instead of "for consultation on question of" substitute "in connection with". Reason for proposed amendment is that the purpose of the commission is set out in the terms of reference, and it might prove impolitic to emphasize its consultative as distinct from its examinational functions' (CO 54/986/5/3, no 152).

[2] The press announcement of 20 Sept 1944 on the appointment of the commission read as follows:—
  'His Majesty's Government have already announced their decision to send a Commission to visit Ceylon towards the end of the year in connexion with constitutinal reform. Lord Soulbury has accepted the invitation to be Chairman of the Commission whose terms of reference will be as follows:—
    "To visit Ceylon in order to examine and discuss any proposals for constitutional reform in the Island which have the object of giving effect to the Declaration of His Majesty's Government on that subject dated 26th May, 1943; and, after consultation with various interests in the Island, including minority communities, concerned with the subject of constitutional reform, to advise His Majesty's Government on all measures necessary to attain that object".
  It is expected that the membership of the Commission will be completed and announced shortly.'

228   CO 554/986/7, no 28   21 Sept 1944

[Kandyan treaty rights]: minutes by Trafford Smith and J B Sidebotham

[These minutes were written in response to a tel sent on 17 Sept 1944 by T B Panabokke, president of the Kandyan National Assembly, to Mr Stanley which read: 'The Kandyan National Assembly representing three fifths Ceylon and two million people submits Kandyan rights in treaty of 1815 is [sic] part of Ceylon laws. Reform proposals of ministers and of minorities violate treaty rights of Kandyan nation. Request terms of reference of commission on Ceylon constitution include rights guaranteed by His Majesty. Memorial follows.']

The Kandyan Convention of the 2nd March, 1815, will be found at Appendix V of the Donoughmore Report (my copy herewith which I should like back in due course).

This Kandyan question will probably come before the Commission in Ceylon, and we are likely to hear a good deal more of it before the new Constitution is produced. If I read it correctly, the present telegram requests that the Commission's terms of reference should include the rights guaranteed by the Convention of 1815. How this is to be achieved is not immediately obvious, and perhaps the Kandyan National Assembly are really asking that the Convention rights should be respected in the new Constitution. At all events, the action required now appears to be to telegraph the text of (28) to the Governor and ask him, if he sees no objection, to inform the President of the Assembly that the Secretary of State has received his telegram, and to draw his attention to the terms of reference of the Commission which have now been announced in Ceylon. ? So proceed, pending the arrival of the promised memorial.

T.S.
21.9.44

The Kandyan claim is dealt with at length in Chapter VI of the Donoughmore Report. The conclusion reached on page 106 of that report that "the solid fact remains that for almost 100 years, or three-quarters of the whole period of British rule in Ceylon, the Kandyan Provinces have been merged for all administrative purposes with the remainder of the Island" and that "the time has long since passed when an experiment of granting to each of the three largest communities a separate Government for the area principally occupied by them could have been attempted without the certainty of inflicting hardship on one or all of them" is as sound to-day as when it was written in 1928.

I should take action on the lines proposed by Mr. Trafford Smith, but by fast air mail, and note this telegram for communication to the Commission, together with the memorial when it is received.

J.B.S.
21.9.44

229   CO 852/605/11, no 213   13 Oct 1944

'Ceylon rubber': outward telegram from Mr Lyttelton[1] to Sir C Hambro[2] (Washington) explaining why there is little or no prospect of obtaining additional labour for Ceylon rubber plantations

Would you please pass following message to Batt.[3] *Begins.* "Am sorry to say that there seems to be little or no prospect of obtaining additional labour for the Ceylon rubber plantations. Ministers concerned here have given considerable thought to the problem and explored various ways of overcoming the political differences between Ceylon and India which are involved in any transfer of labour. It is now clear that these cannot be resolved at present and that any attempt to force the issue might have results quite the opposite of those intended.

---

[1] Minister of production, member of War Cabinet, 1942–1945; later secretary of state for colonies, 1951–1954.

[2] UK member, Combined Raw Materials Board and head of British Raw Materials Mission, Washington, 1944–1945.

[3] US member, Combined Raw Materials Board.

2. I am sure you will agree that Ceylon has done a fine job during the war in achieving a considerable rise in rubber output of the island at the expense I fear of future productivity through slaughter tapping. The pressure to increase food production has in itself affected the amount of labour available for rubber as have the intensive efforts made to turn the island into a base for Far East operations. Quite apart from the political and other practical reasons which weigh against effective pressure being directed to induce the Government of India to moderate their attitude, I should not like to be a party to any step which might affect Ceylon's co-operation in the war and I hope you will agree that we are right in the circumstances in not forcing this issue with either India or Ceylon." *Ends.*

230   CO 54/988/2, no 4   27 Oct 1944

[Indo–Ceylon relations]: inward telegram no 2014 from Sir R Drayton to Mr Stanley on the response of the Board of Ministers to a representation from the Government of India concerning the rights and status of Indians in Ceylon

[On 2 Sept Aney informed Caldecott that the GOI was ready to enter negotiations with the Ceylon government for a settlement of the general question of the rights and status of Indians in Ceylon. The GOI believed that a settlement was 'eminently desirable at the present time' when constitutional reform in Ceylon was under discussion. It was hoped that this declaration would serve 'to remove the apprehension which seems to prevail in some quarters in Ceylon that the Government of India want such negotiation to take place at the end of the war and not before' (CO 54/988/2, no 5). Stanley requested information about the reaction of the Board of Ministers, in response to which Drayton (officer administering the government in the interval between the end of Caldecott's governorship and the arrival of Sir H Moore), sent this reply.]

Your secret telegram No. 1320.

Board's views may be summarized as follows:—

(a) They regard general question of rights and status of Indians in Ceylon as substantially a different matter from particular problem of constitutional reform which is the subject of enquiry by Commission. Former question is, in their view, proper subject for negotiation between the Governments concerned and, while Commission will have to concern itself with problems of franchise and representation as affecting Indians among others in Ceylon, they should not concern themselves with the many other matters that fall into category of rights and status of Indians in Ceylon. They do not, therefore, regard Royal Commission's task as necessitating a resumption of negotiations on the general question.

(b) They do not want case for Indian community in Ceylon to be presented or openly sponsored before Commission by Government of India.

(c) They do not think any agreed basis exists today for resumption of negotiations and, unless such a basis were found before negotiations were resumed, they would be bound to fail.

(d) They do not want to appear hostile to resumption of negotiations as soon as a favourable opportunity occurs and Government of India is, therefore, being asked for their views as to a possible basis for resuming negotiations.

2. Reply to Aney's letter will follow the lines of (a) and (b) above. Text will be sent by air mail very shortly.

3. I agree with opinions expressed in Sir A. Caldecott's secret despatch of 5th October, with which Ministers' views are not in conflict.

231 CO 54/986/5/3, no 171   11 Nov 1944
[Reforms]: inward unnumbered telegram from Sir R Drayton to Mr Stanley on the appointment of a new reforms committee

Caldecott's secret and personal telegram of 15th September.

It is announced in the local Press that the Reforms Committee referred to has dissolved without reaching agreement on any point.

2. It is also stated that, after most of the minority Members had withdrawn, another Committee was formed at the suggestion of Bandaranaike, who, according to the *Times*, said that he was now frankly not prepared to stand by the Declaration of the Secretary of State and that he was for a free Ceylon and that it was on that footing that he suggested that a constitution should be drafted. He proposed that it should be referred to the State Council, if possible before the arrival of the Reforms Commission, or at any rate before its departure.

3. Papers differ as to the proposed constitution of the new Committee, but I understand on good authority that, in addition to four Ministers namely Bandaranaike, Kannangara, Corea, and George De Silva, the Members for Panadure [sic], Dumbara, Galagedara, Galle, and Colombo Central were also chosen. Last named is the only minority Member proposed. It is not known how many have accepted. Corea and De Silva were not present when the Committee was proposed.

4. No reporters were present when any of the proceedings described above took place and I have not received any official report on the matter.

5. It is impossible to conjecture at present whether the proposed Committee will come into being or be active if it does. On the other hand, it must be admitted that:—

(a) The attitude imputed to Bandaranaike is consistently that which he expressed in the Board of Ministers when the Committee was being discussed last year.
(b) There is no real agreement between Bandaranaike and Senanayake on the question of reform.
(c) If the four Ministers do serve on the Committee, it will have the appearance of leaving Senanayake in a minority which consists of Conservative capitalist, as opposed to more advanced, non-capitalist, elements in the Board.

6. The meeting of the State Council next week may result in Senanayake being compelled to reveal his attitude towards the proposed Committee. I will inform you of any further developments as soon as I have any authentic news.

232   CO 54/986/5/3, no 203   19 Dec 1944

[Reforms]: inward unnumbered telegram from Sir H Moore to Mr
Stanley conveying Mr Senanayake's views on the procedure for the
Soulbury Commission

Reference my secret and personal of to-day's date. I have had full discussions with
Senanayake and the Chief Secretary, as to the procedure to be adopted on the arrival
of the Commission, and he expressed general agreement with (a) and (b) of my
telegram No. 2343, and draft communique is being prepared on these lines for the
approval of Lord Soulbury, on arrival.

I also conveyed to him, in confidence, substance of statement referred to in your
secret and personal telegram of the 30th November, but he strongly deprecated any
reference being made to the three-quarter majority proviso in any public announcement to be made by Lord Soulbury on first arrival, as being likely not only to create
lack of confidence in His Majesty's Government's honesty of purpose in appointing
the Commission, but also to make his own position more difficult in co-operating
with the Commission, as he intends to do. His contention is that the three-quarter
proviso could reasonably be insisted upon for a locally devised scheme, but since any
recommendations of the Commission, even if based on the Minister's published
scheme, will now result in a Commission made, and not a Ceylon made, constitution, the Secretary of State should be free to approve of it provided that he and the
Commission are satisfied that minority interests are adequately safeguarded whether
or not it obtains a three-quarter majority on presentation to the State Council.

I therefore propose to advise Lord Soulbury to avoid all reference to this in the first
announcement, but since the Commission may be challenged on the point later, I
should be glad for guidance as to the reply I should give to Sananayake's [sic]
personal representations. His view appears to be that any constitution which the
Commission is likely to recommend will fail to obtain three-quarters majority, but
that if there is a substantial majority including minority opinion, in favour of it in
the State Council, the Secretary of State should be free to adopt it. The Chief
Secretary, who concurs in the above, points out that the fact, however, cannot be
overlooked that it has been publicly represented that in the interests of minorities,
both safeguards of examination by the Commission and of a three-quarters majority
were provided in regard to the Minister's scheme.

233   CO 54/988/2, no 15   13 Jan 1945

[Indo–Ceylon relations]: despatch from Sir H Moore to Mr Stanley on
the re-opening of negotiations. *Enclosures* 1 and 2

I have the honour to refer to Sir Robert Drayton's secret despatch of 31st October,
1944, enclosing correspondence with the Government of India relating to the
re-opening of negotiations regarding the rights and status of Indians in Ceylon.

2. I enclose a copy of a further message from the Government of India which was
received by me at the hands of Mr. Aney, their Representative in Ceylon, on 19th
December, 1944.

3. The Board of Ministers considered the message and concurred in the reply dated 11th January a copy of which is enclosed.

Enclosure 1 to 233: letter from M S Aney to Sir H Moore, 19 Dec 1944

I have been asked by the Government of India to communicate to the Government of Ceylon the following reply to the Chief Secretary's letters No. CF. 68/44 dated 21st October, 1944, and 27th October, 1944:—

> "The Government of India thank the Government of Ceylon for their letters dated 21st and 27th October. They have noted the views of the Government of Ceylon. They feel that while in theory it may be possible to distinguish between questions of constitutional reform and other questions it is virtually impossible to maintain this distinction in practice.
>
> 2. They would however like to add that the appointment of the Royal Commission on constitutional reforms was not the only reason for suggesting the reopening of negotiations. The Government of India had had reports of statements made by Ceylon Ministers that they would welcome such negotiations but that they thought that the Government of India wanted the Indian question to be left over until the war was won. These statements of Ceylon Ministers were the immediate occasion for the Government of India to intimate their readiness to resume negotiations as they were anxious to dispel any misapprehension that might have been caused by the Ministers' statements. The Government of India will be able to indicate their views as to basis for negotiations after the Government of Ceylon have signified their willingness to resume negotiations."

Enclosure 2 to 233: letter from Sir R Drayton to M S Aney, 11 Jan 1945

I have the honour to refer to the communication of the Government of India regarding the resumption of negotiations between the two Governments, dated the 19th December, 1944, which was handed to His Excellency the Governor by Mr. Aney, the Representative of the Government of India in Ceylon, on the same date.

2. The Board of Ministers note that the Government of India do not think that the resumption of negotiations must be left over until after war is won.

3. What appears, however, to the Board to be of first importance is that, before negotiations are resumed, there should be, as was the case when negotiations were resumed in 1941, an agreed basis for such resumption. This basis would normally have been specifically the Joint Report of 1941: that Report is still a basis acceptable to the Government of Ceylon but the Government of India have indicated that they do not envisage it as being a basis of resumed negotiations. The Government of Ceylon trust that the Government of India will find it possible to reconsider their attitude on the point and accept the agreed conclusions of the Joint Report of 1941 as being the basis for the resumption of negotiations. If, however, the Government of India find it impossible to adopt this attitude, the Government of Ceylon have no doubt that the Government of India will realize that no other basis for the resumption of negotiations could be considered by the Government of Ceylon if that

basis rejected in advance any of the agreed conclusions contained in the Joint Report of 1941. The Government of India will readily appreciate that any agreed basis must not preclude the possibility of resumed negotiations resulting in an agreement over the whole field which is at least as acceptable to Ceylon as the agreement contained in that Report. If an agreed basis for the resumption of negotiations can be found, the Government of India may rest assured that the Government of Ceylon would be ready to resume negotiations at a date most convenient to both Governments. It was with this object in mind that the request which is contained in paragraph 3 of the Acting Chief Secretary's letter dated 21st October, 1944, was made and the Board desire me to repeat that request.

234   CO 54/988/2, no 16, enclosure   14 Jan 1945
[Indo–Ceylon relations]: letter from Sir H Moore to Lord Wavell on the re-opening of negotiations

> [In a covering letter of the same date to Gent at the CO, Moore explained that he had sent this letter to Wavell 'in the hope, I fear a vain one, that he may be able to get the Government of India to suggest a formula for the resumption of negotiations which the Ceylon Ministers can reasonably be expected to accept'. He added; 'At the present time Aney has shown no sign of being willing as a war-time measure to consider examining the labour problem as distinct from the general franchise and constitutional issues involved' (CO 54/988/2, no 16).]

With reference to my letter of the 8th of December, Mr. Aney called on me shortly after I wrote to you to present to me officially the Government of India's reply to my Chief Secretary's letters of the 21st and 27th of October, 1944.

For convenience of reference I enclose a copy of that communication together with a copy of the Chief Secretary's reply thereto of the 11th January, 1945.[1] You will no doubt be informed of this correspondence through the usual official channels.

As I wrote to you earlier my immediate concern is lest the continuation of the present state of affairs should have an adverse effect on Ceylon's war effort particularly in respect of rubber output owing to labour difficulties. The object of this letter therefore is to say that although the reply of the Ceylon Ministers may from India's point of view not appear to carry us much further my personal belief is that among the majority of them at any rate there is a genuine desire to resume negotiations if a basis can be found which contains some promise of success. I trust therefore that the Government of India will read the Ministers' reply in that light and may feel able to suggest a basis for the resumption of negotiations which will enable the Ceylon Ministers to feel that they are free to exercise an unfettered judgment as negotiations proceed.

---

[1] See 233, enclosure 2.

235   CO 54/986/6/1, no 24   23 Mar 1945

[Reforms]: inward unnumbered telegram from Sir H Moore to Mr Stanley on the timetable for the Soulbury Commission

Following is tentative timetable to which Lord Soulbury is working.

I   Third week in June. Report (possibly not in the final form) to be addressed to you.

II   Copy to be sent simultaneously to me for my personal observations.

III   Before the last week in July, my observations and those of your Advisers to be in your hands.

IV   Last week in July, Senanayake to be invited by you, in his capacity as Vice Chairman of the Board of Ministers and Leader of the House, for personal consultations on the draft Recommendations.

V   Report to be published as soon as possible thereafter with a view to submission to the State Council in September.

From the local point of view, it is of the first importance, if Senanayake's general agreement is secured in London, that the Report should be brought before the State Council with the least possible delay. I do not, of course, know whether the date of the United Kingdom General Election has yet been fixed and, if so, whether it need affect the proposed timetable, but I should be grateful for the earliest possible expression of your views. Nihill has applied for leave and should go at once so as to be back in the autumn, or earlier if necessary. He would then be available for consultations in London in May, which Lord Soulbury would welcome.

Soulbury and Drayton concur in the above.

236   CO 54/986/16/1, no 4   11 Apr 1945

[Reforms]: despatch from Sir H Moore to Mr Stanley on the debate in the State Council on the Free Lanka Bill

[Informing Stanley in Dec 1944 that this bill (also referred to as the Dominion Status or Sri Lanka Bill) had been prepared by Bandaranaike and gazetted over his signature, Moore explained: 'As far as I can gather, Senanayake thinks that Bandaranaike is making a mistake and does not propose to stop him. I have reason to believe that Senanayake intends to co-operate fully with the [Soulbury] Commission and do not think that Bandaranaike's Bill need be taken very seriously' (CO 54/986/5/3, no 200, Moore tel to Stanley, 19 Dec 1944). Senanayake was said by Moore to regard the subsequent debate on the bill as 'rather a joke' (CO 986/6/1, no 10, tel, 10 Feb 1945) and when the debate ended the governor sent the following summary of the result on 23 Mar: 'Dominion Status Bill passed third reading by forty to seven, with one declining to vote. Chief Secretary Reports as follows:—Amendments made unimportant. Majority falls short of three fourths by two. It comprised three Ceylon Moors, two Ceylon Tamils and one Indian Tamil supported by Senanayake voted for the Bill. Mahadeva declined to vote. Minority comprised three Europeans, one Burgher, two Indians and one Ceylon Tamil. Ponnambalam and Aluwihare disliked many of its provisions, but did not wish to be represented as opposed to claims included in the Dominion status. Notable feature, however, is the support to the Bill given by the three Ceylon Moors. Some secret accord with Bandaranaike may safely be presumed' (*ibid*, no 23).]

I have the honour to refer to my despatch No. 106 of even date by which I transmitted to you for the signification of His Majesty's pleasure an Ordinance to provide for a new Constitution for Ceylon.

2. I enclose a memorandum by the Chief Secretary[1] on the debates in the State Council on this Bill. The Memorandum provides a most valuable commentary on the passage of the Bill through the Council, and I find myself in general agreement with the views expressed therein. In addition I propose in this despatch to summarise the events which led up to the introduction of the Bill and to give you my views generally as to its political significance.

3. As appears from paragraphs 2 and 5 of Secret and Personal telegram of November 11th, 1944,[2] addressed to you by the Officer Administering the Government, it was in that month that the Minister for Local Administration gave the first real indication of his intention to repudiate the Declaration of 1943 and to embark upon a political strategy with which he knew the Leader of the State Council strongly disagreed.

4. The motion requesting the Ministers to introduce a Dominion Status Bill into the State Council, although moved by a private member, was admittedly inspired by the Minister for Local Administration and moved at his instigation. The debate on this motion was noteworthy for the fact that the Minister for Local Administration repudiated the suggestion that the introduction of the Bill would imply a boycott of the Soulbury Commission (see paragraph 3 of the Secret and Personal telegram of November 24th addressed to you by the Officer Administering the Government). As appears from paragraph 8 below the Minister's attitude on this point changed as the Bill progressed and its passage through the Council seemed more assured. You will recollect that the Leader of the State Council, the Minister for Home Affairs and the Minister for Communications and Works refrained from voting on this motion which was passed on November 24th 1944.

5. The following extract from the Minutes of the meeting of the Board of Ministers held on December 18th 1944 reveals the attitude of the Leader of the State Council and the other Ministers to the Bill:—

> "The Financial Secretary referred to the draft Ceylon Constitutional (Dominion Status) Bill in the name of the Minister for Local Administration. It had been forwarded to the Government Printer by the Secretary to the Board with a note that the Minister for Local Administration had desired that it should be published in a Gazette Extraordinary. He stated that it appeared doubtful whether it was correct for a Minister to introduce a Bill dealing with a subject which was not allocated to his Executive Committee under the Constitution and he would like the Board to examine that aspect of the question.
>
> The Vice Chairman (Leader of the State Council) stated that the Bill was being introduced in accordance with the wishes of the State Council and that it was being sponsored by the Minister for Local Administration on behalf of a majority of the Ministers. He added that although he was in favour of a Dominion Status Constitution for Ceylon he was nevertheless prepared to accept the constitution prepared by the Ministers in accordance with the Secretary of State's Declaration of May 1943. He was therefore of the view that the present time was not an opportune moment to introduce the Bill in

---

[1] Not printed.   [2] See 231.

regard to which he desired to retain his freedom of action. He therefore preferred that the Bill, which a majority of the Ministers wanted introduced now, should be introduced by a Minister who was keen on its immediate introduction.

The Minister of Health was of the view that the decision of the State Council on a matter of this importance should be implemented by the Board, and that the Bill should be introduced by the Leader of the State Council himself. The Chairman however pointed out that the Officers of State could not be associated with a Bill which they had not seen.

After discussion the Ministers agreed to the introduction of the Bill by the Minister for Local Administration."

6. The point made by the Financial Secretary in the Board of Minutes which is referred to in the opening sentence of the extract of the minutes set out in the previous paragraph had first been raised by him with me. The Financial Secretary had asked for my direction in the matter, but I felt that it would not be wise for me to intervene and it was on my suggestion that the Financial Secretary raised the matter in the Board of Ministers.

Subsequently, in the debate on the Bill, the point whether the Bill had been properly introduced was taken and the Speaker held that it had.

7. The mover's speech on the first reading was noteworthy for two points:—

(a) he made it quite clear that he regarded the Bill as having the dual object of embarrassing the Secretary of State when he came to consider the recommendations of the Soulbury Commission and of being a lever by which greater concessions might be obtained;

(b) he indicated a mild opposition to a Second Chamber (vide paragraph (e) of my Secret and Personal telegram of January 19th), an attitude which, I am informed, was inconsistent with the attitude that he adopted when conferring with the minorities in 1943 but was probably inspired by his knowledge of the fact that the Leader of the State Council then favoured a Second Chamber.

8. In the second reading the mover joined in the general condemnation of the Second Chamber as soon as he realised that there was almost unanimous opposition to such a Chamber but it may well be that he regards the rejection of the conception of a Second Chamber solely as a strong bargaining counter.

In the same debate the mover notwithstanding his attitude to the Soulbury Commission in November, 1944 (see paragraph 4 above) declared that it was wholly inconsistent for any member of the State Council to appear before the Commission.

9. The mover of the Bill may be said to have started slowly and finished strongly: as appears from this despatch he did not scruple to change his attitude as he felt his strength.

The support given by the Ceylon Moslems to the third reading and the fact that the Leader of the State Council voted for the third reading cannot be ignored and it must be admitted that he has temporarily weakened the Leader's position.

The latter's task in getting the country to accept a new constitution which is based on the 1943 Declaration has been made more difficult by the passage of this Bill and, if the Leader were to fail in this task, the Minister for Local Administration will have strengthened his position to succeed him and negotiate for higher stakes.

10. While the above is, I believe, a fair appreciation of the political effect which the passage of this Bill has had on the relative position of the Leader of the State Council and the Minister for Local Administration in the State Council, it would in my view be a mistake to suppose that much importance has been attached to its passing by the country as a whole. The facts are that its staging contemporaneously with the sittings of the Soulbury Commission was generally regarded as a piece of political play-acting which should not be taken very seriously. Public interest throughout was chiefly centered on the proceedings of the Commission, and the debates on the Bill itself suffered from an atmosphere of unreality which was reflected not only in the light-hearted manner in which clauses of major importance were disposed of, but also by the poor attendance of members themselves. Had any of them seriously believed that there was any likelihood of a Bill of such great importance receiving the Royal Assent, it would not have secured a passage through a depleted house in a matter of 16 days.

237 CO 54/986/6/1, no 30   18 Apr 1945
[Reforms]: CO record of a discussion with members of the Soulbury Commission

The *Duke of Devonshire* welcomed Lord Soulbury and his colleagues on their return from Ceylon and said that from all reports so far received their visit to the island seemed to have been a great success. He explained the Secretary of State's inability to welcome the Commission personally in view of his illness.

Lord Soulbury said that he assumed that it was the view of the Colonial Office that the new Constitution should be one which was acceptable to the interests concerned in Ceylon, especially to the present Government and State Council, rather than that it should be imposed by H.M.G. All the discussions he had had with Mr. Senanayake and others showed that time was the important factor, especially as the former was not in robust health. Mr. Senanayake had undertaken to do his best to carry the new Constitution through the State Council, assuming its provisions were reasonably satisfactory to him, and discussions with him had given no grounds for doubting that the recommendation the Commission at present had in mind would, with the exception of one or two difficult questions, be acceptable.

Lord Soulbury therefore proposed that the Commission and the Colonial Office should endeavour to follow a timetable, of which a copy is attached. (See also 24 and 25 on this file.) Notwithstanding the Secretary of State's telegram at 25, Lord Soulbury pressed that every effort should be made to adhere to this timetable, which he had discussed with Mr. Senanayake, especially in regard to the latter's proposed visit to England at the end of July.

The difficulties surrounding this visit, at a stage when the Secretary of State could hardly have had time to consult the Cabinet and be in a position to give a clear indication of H.M.G.'s intentions, were discussed at length; it was finally considered that since Mr. Senanayake knew of the proposed arrangements, it would probably be necessary to issue an invitation in any case, though this would have to be on a purely informal basis and with a clear understanding that the Secretary of State could not be in a position to give any promises or enter into any commitments as to the future Constitution.

It was pointed out that the Tamil Minority leader, Mr. G.G. Ponnambalam, would inevitably ask for facilities to fly to this country and interview the Secretary of State. The general opinion was that the Secretary of State could hardly refuse to see him.

The question of discussion of the Defence reservations in the new Constitution with the Service Departments was briefly raised. It was decided that the Commission should send a letter to those concerned, setting out the present position and suggesting that a meeting should be held at 3 p.m. on 11th May at the Colonial Office to discuss whatever points the Service Departments might have to raise.

It was also arranged that the Secretary of State should see the Commission during the morning of 11th May and that, if necessary, a further session should be held on that date with Mr. Norman Young of the Treasury on the subject of currency.

238   CO 54/986/6/1, no 31   24 Apr 1945
[Reforms]: inward unnumbered telegram from Sir H Moore to Sir G Gater on the question of inviting Mr Senanayake to London

I do not know whether the Secretary of State has had opportunity of discussing with Lord Soulbury paragraph IV of the tentative programme outlined in my secret and personal telegram of 23rd March.[1]

With the appointment of Goonetilleke as Financial Secretary, which has been well received, I have been considering the possibility of Drayton taking some leave, in which event there would probably be no local objections now to Collins acting.

There has been no (repeat no) official suggestion that the Secretary of State would invite Senanayake home for discussions at some appropriate stage, but I have no doubt that person named expects it. In order to assist me in deciding when Drayton could best be spared, I would be grateful for any further information you can give me as to procedure, and whether the Secretary of State would prefer Drayton and Senanayake to be home at the same time. I am inclined to think that Senanayake would welcome some such arrangement, though I have naturally not discussed it with him, but I could sound Goonetilleke on the point if you could indicate a general line by next Saturday.

---

[1] See 235.

239   ADM 116/5546   25 Apr 1945
[Reforms]: letter from Trafford Smith to A P Shaw (Admiralty) on consultation with the service departments on defence issues

May I refer to C.O.S. (44)996(0) of 28th November, 1944, dealing with the effect of the political situation in Ceylon on operations? You will see from that Paper and the Chiefs of Staffs Committee's decision that it was agreed that there was no need for the Chiefs of Staff to see the Commission on Constitutional Reform before their departure.

The Commission has now returned to this country and Lord Soulbury, the Chairman, has asked me to approach the Service Departments in order to arrange a meeting at which any questions they may wish to raise in connection with the reservation of Defence under the new Constitution can be discussed before the Commission finally formulates its recommendations. For convenience of reference, I enclose a copy of the Declaration of His Majesty's Government dated 26th May, 1943,[1] referred to in the Commission's terms of reference which are set out in the Chiefs of Staff paper under reference.

As will be obvious from these terms of reference, the Commission's Report will be primarily concerned with political issues affecting the new Constitution, and, insofar as they have at present considered the Defence question, the Commissioners feel inclined to confine themselves to a recommendation in general terms relating to the disposition of the portfolios of Defence and Foreign Affairs under a new Constitution and to some recommendation as to the channels of communication between the Ceylon Government and His Majesty's Government in these matters.

The Service Departments would no doubt have views on this latter question and also on various other issues which arise, such as the extent to which Emergency powers of control over, for example, communications and harbours in Ceylon should be reserved as a necessary attribute of Defence notwithstanding the fact that these departments fall within the province of a Ceylon Minister and would ordinarily be regarded as "Internal Affairs".

Lord Soulbury proposes to have a meeting for the purpose of a general exchange of views on these and other relevant questions, and has asked me to suggest 3 o'clock on the afternoon of Friday, 11th May, in the Colonial Office Conference Room (Downing Street Building) as the Commission (which is at present working in Cardiff) will be in London on that date. I shall be glad if you will let me know whether a representative of the Admiralty will be able to attend. I am writing similarly to Nangle at the War Office and Dickson at the Air Ministry.

---

[1] See 169, annex.

Index of Main Subjects and Persons

This is not a comprehensive index, but a simplified and straightforward index to document numbers, together with page references to the Introduction in part I, the latter being given at the beginning of the entry in lower-case roman numerals. It is designed to be used in conjunction with the summary lists and chapter headings of the preliminary pages to both parts of the volume. A preceding asterisk indicates inclusion in the Biographical Notes at the end of part II. Where necessary (e.g., in particularly long documents), and, if possible, paragraph numbers are given inside round brackets. The following abbreviations are used:

    N – editor's link note (before main text of document)

    n – footnote

Documents are divided between the two volume parts as follows:

    nos   1–239   part I

    nos 240–446   part II